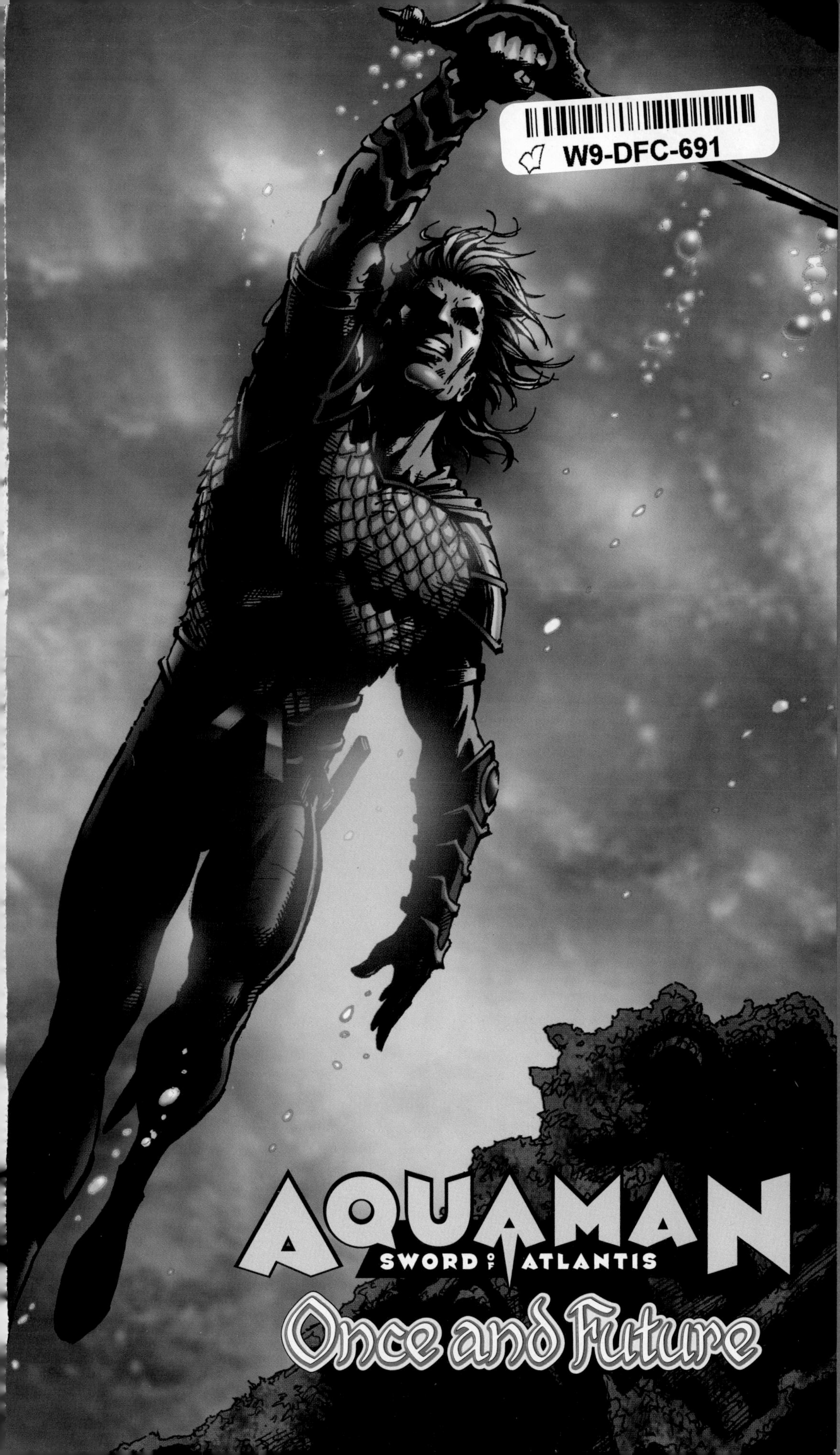
AQUAMAN
SWORD OF ATLANTIS
Once and Future

Dan DiDio
Senior VP-Executive Editor
Joey Cavalieri
Editor-original series
Michael Wright
Associate Editor-original series
Bob Harras
Group Editor-collected edition
Robbin Brosterman
Senior Art Director
Paul Levitz
President & Publisher
Georg Brewer
VP-Design & DC Direct Creative
Richard Bruning
Senior VP-Creative Director
Patrick Caldon
Executive VP-Finance & Operations
Chris Caramalis
VP-Finance
John Cunningham
VP-Marketing
Terri Cunningham
VP-Managing Editor
Stephanie Fierman
Senior VP-Sales & Marketing
Alison Gill
VP-Manufacturing
Hank Kanalz
VP-General Manager, WildStorm
Lillian Laserson
Senior VP & General Counsel
Jim Lee
Editorial Director-WildStorm
Paula Lowitt
Senior VP-Business & Legal Affairs
David McKillips
VP-Advertising & Custom Publishing
John Nee
VP-Business Development
Gregory Noveck
Senior VP-Creative Affairs
Cheryl Rubin
Senior VP-Brand Management
Jeff Trojan
VP-Business Development, DC Direct
Bob Wayne
VP-Sales

AQUAMAN: SWORD OF ATLANTIS
ONCE AND FUTURE

Following the world-shattering events known as the
Infinite Crisis, the stories of the DC Universe catapulted
ahead one year where the World's Greatest Super-Heroes
continue their adventures in new settings and situations!

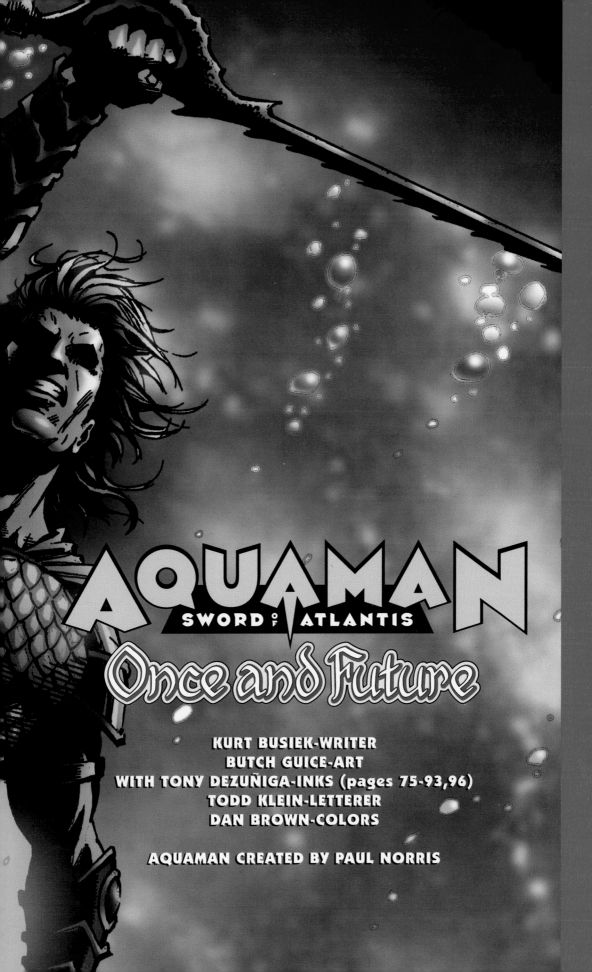

AQUAMAN
SWORD OF ATLANTIS
Once and Future

KURT BUSIEK-WRITER
BUTCH GUICE-ART
WITH TONY DEZUÑIGA-INKS (pages 75-93,96)
TODD KLEIN-LETTERER
DAN BROWN-COLORS

AQUAMAN CREATED BY PAUL NORRIS

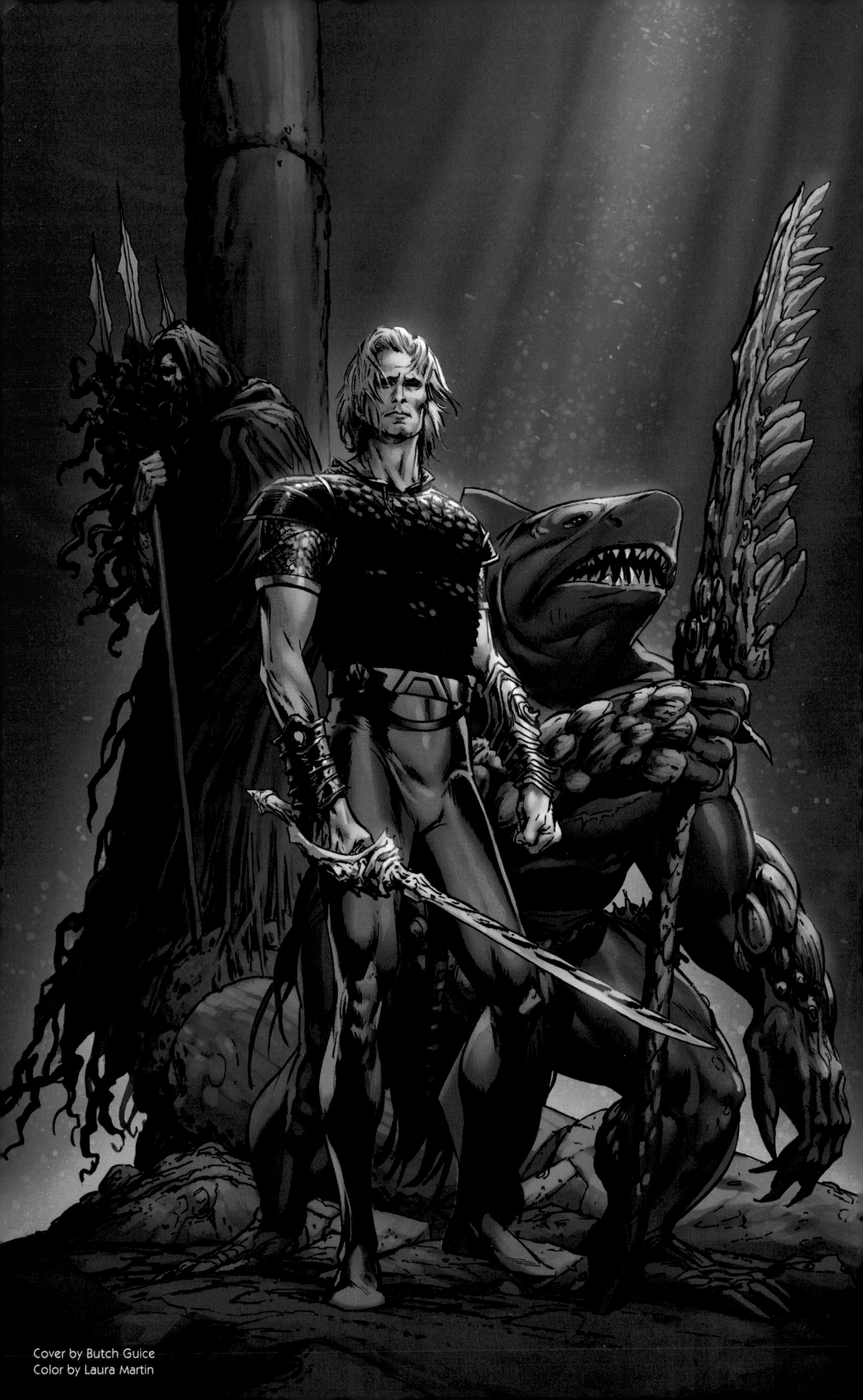

Cover by Butch Guice
Color by Laura Martin

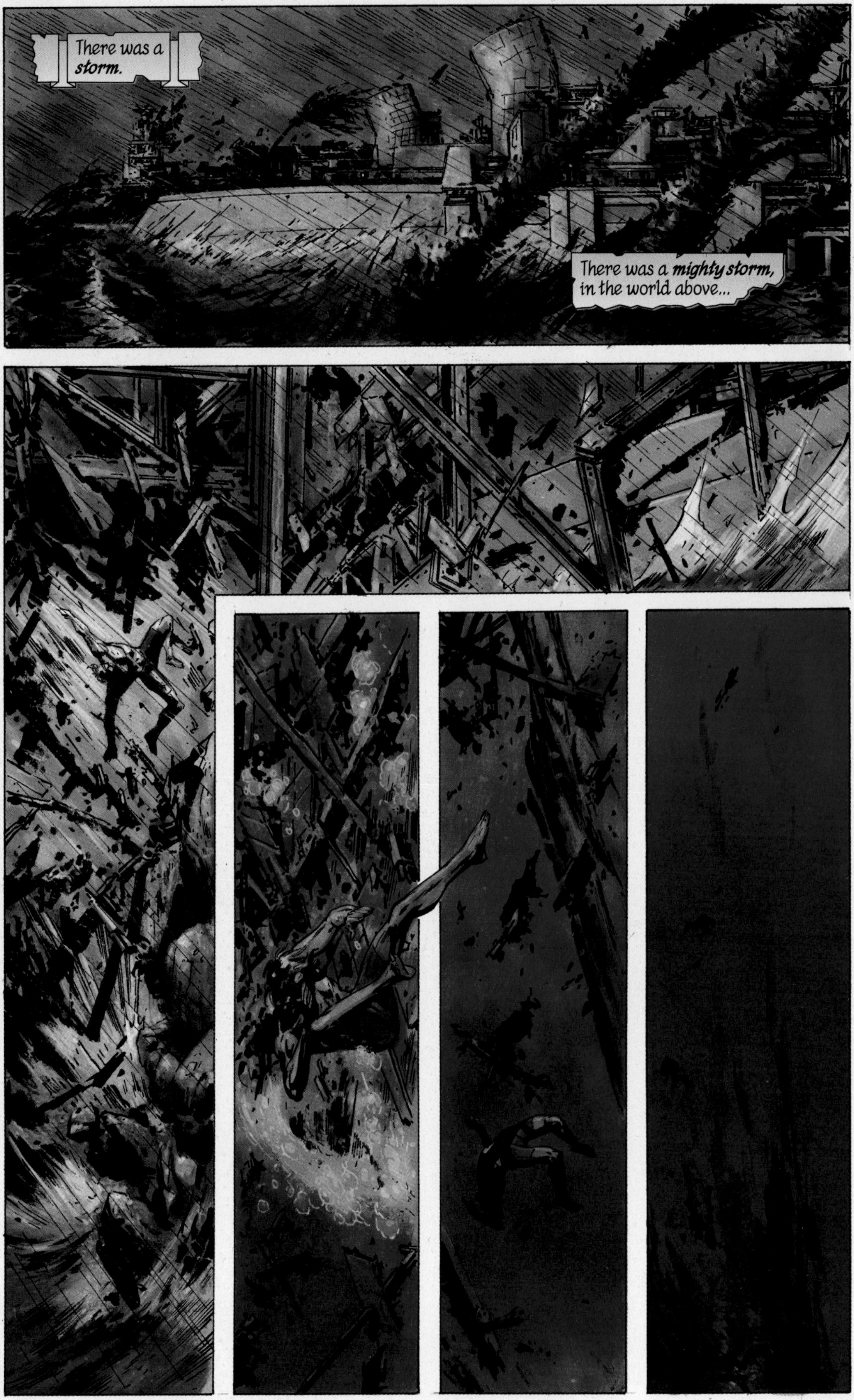
There was a *storm.*
There was a ***mighty storm,*** in the world above...

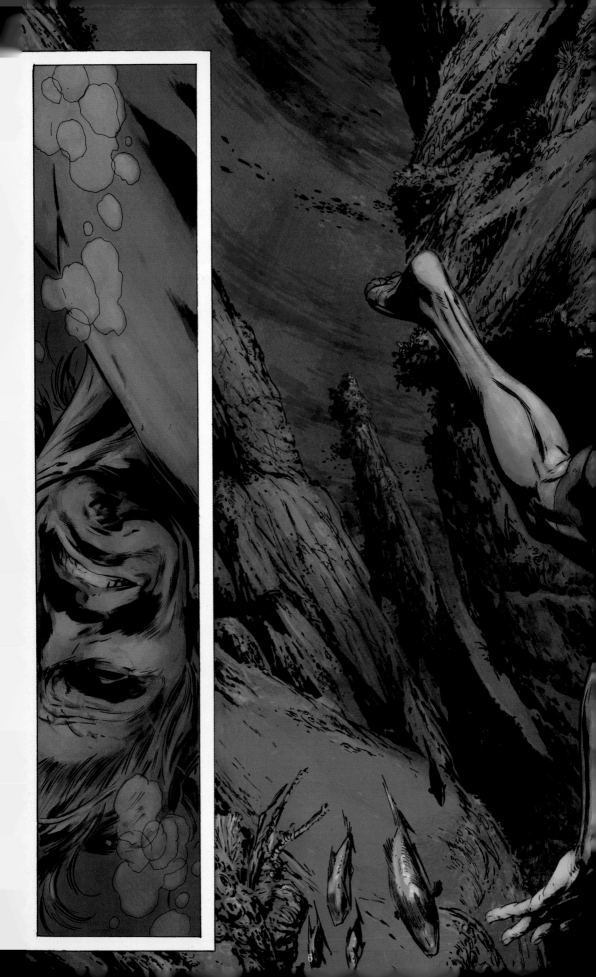

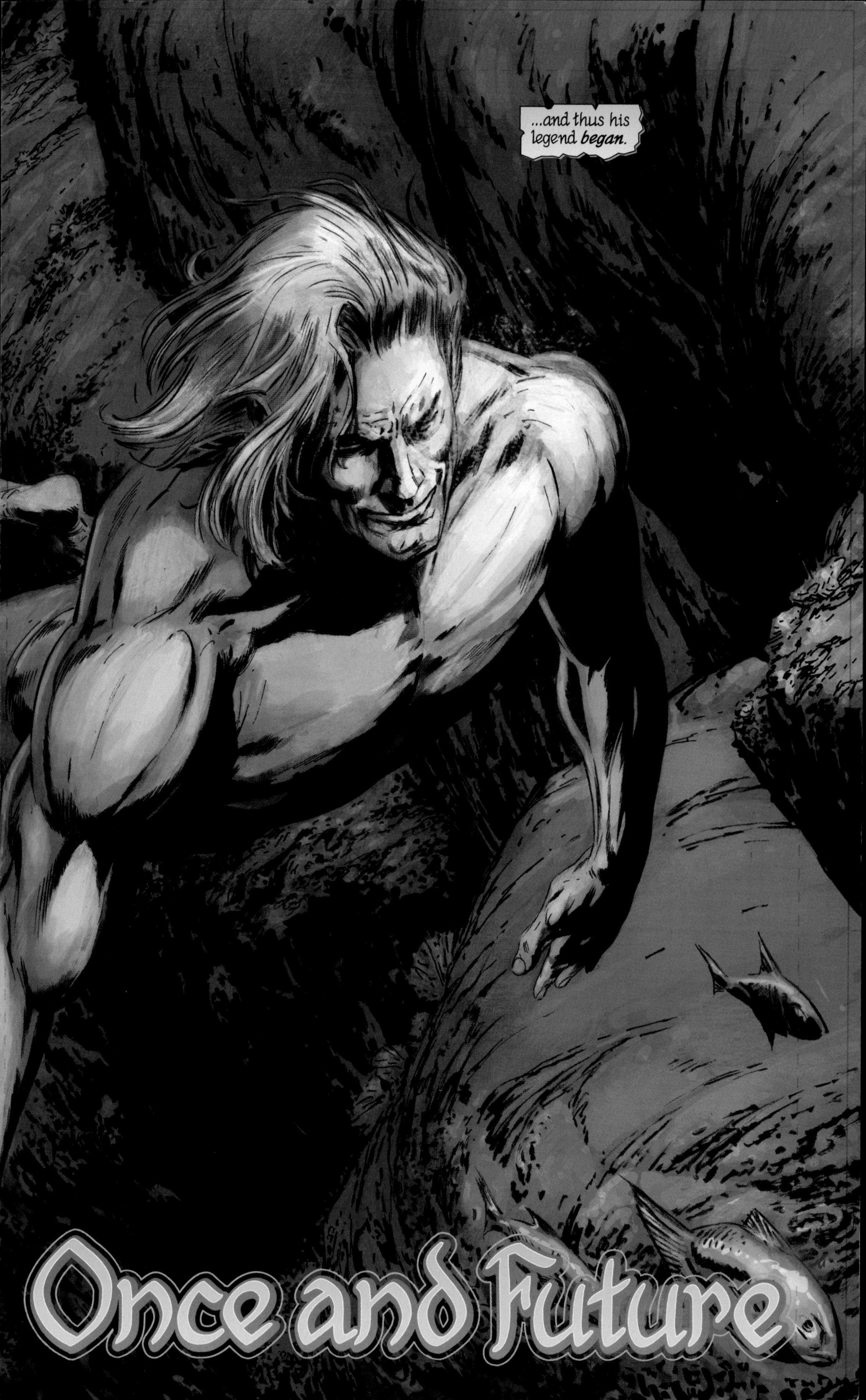
...and thus his legend *began*.
Once and Future

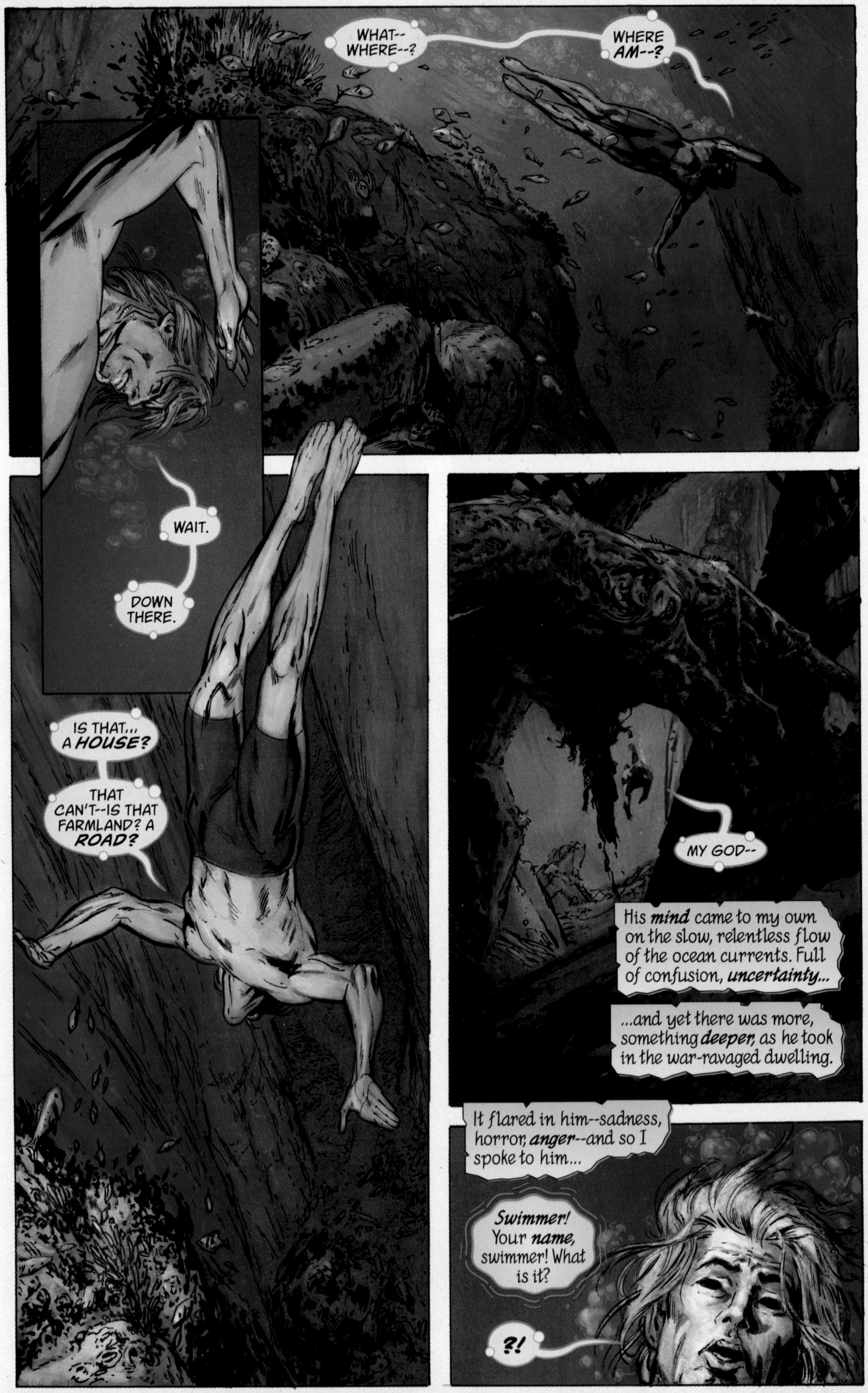
WHAT--
WHERE--?
WHERE AM--?
WAIT.
DOWN THERE.
IS THAT... A HOUSE?
THAT CAN'T--IS THAT FARMLAND? A ROAD?
MY GOD--
His mind came to my own on the slow, relentless flow of the ocean currents. Full of confusion, uncertainty...
...and yet there was more, something deeper, as he took in the war-ravaged dwelling.
It flared in him--sadness, horror, anger--and so I spoke to him...
Swimmer! Your name, swimmer! What is it?
?!

MY NAME'S *ARTHUR.* ARTHUR CURRY. BUT--

Curry! Then you *are* he!

You are *needed,* Arthur Curry--and *swiftly!*

WAIT-- WHO ARE--

There is no *time!* The need is *urgent!*

Go! Go! I will *guide* you!

But go *now!*

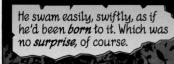He swam easily, swiftly, as if he'd been *born* to it. Which was no *surprise,* of course.

The *Carassian hills* were barely two leagues off, and when he reached them...

WHAT IN...?

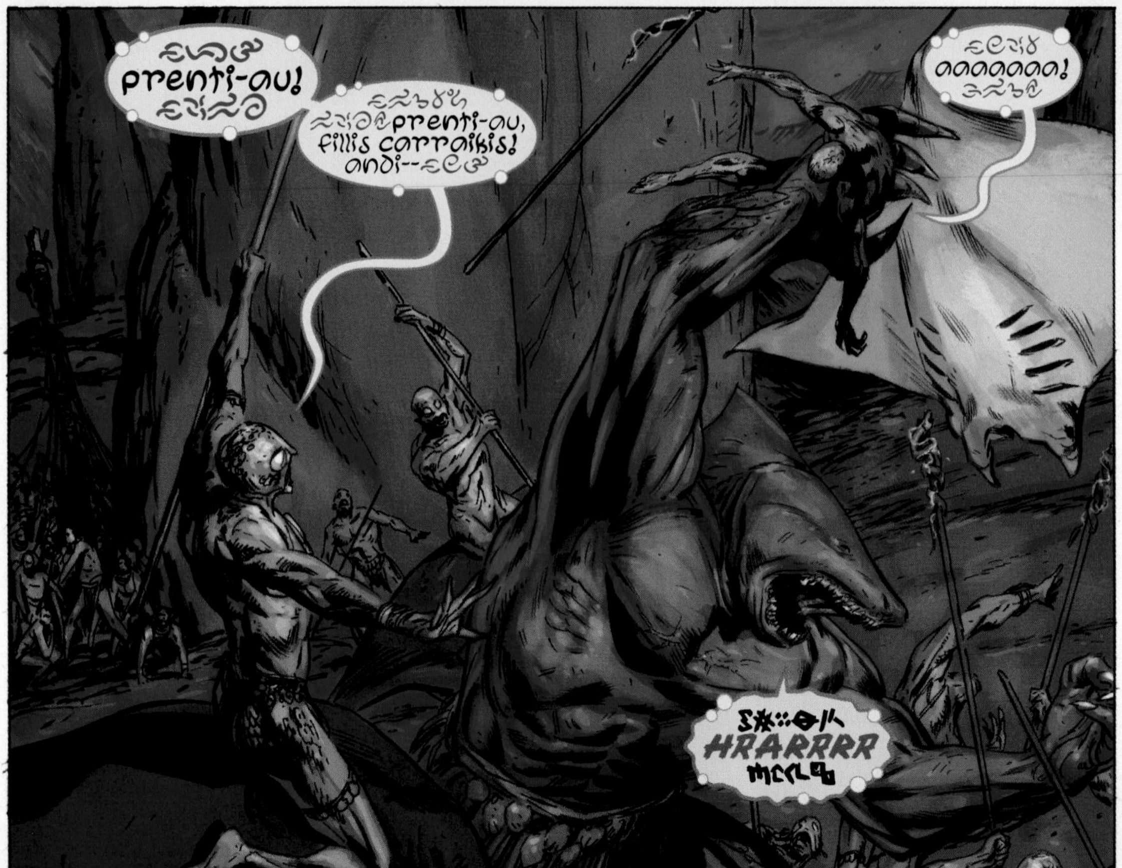
prenti-au!
prenti-au, fillis carraikis! andi--
aaaaaaa!
HRARRRR
nnh

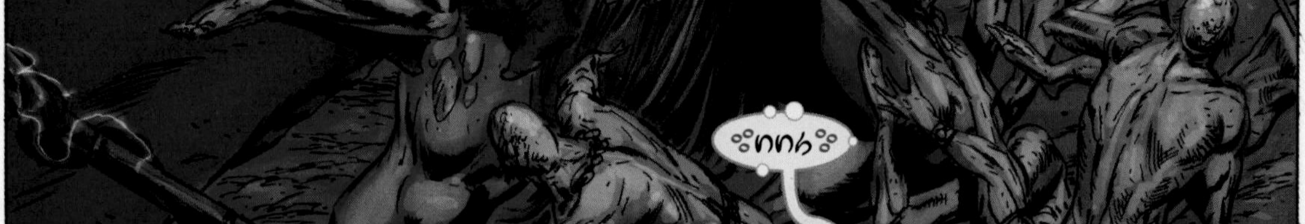
Quickly! Your aid is needed!
WHAT, AGAINST THAT MONSTER?!
No! He is Nanaue, the King Shark! You must save him! The future of the oceanscape depends on it!
WHAT?

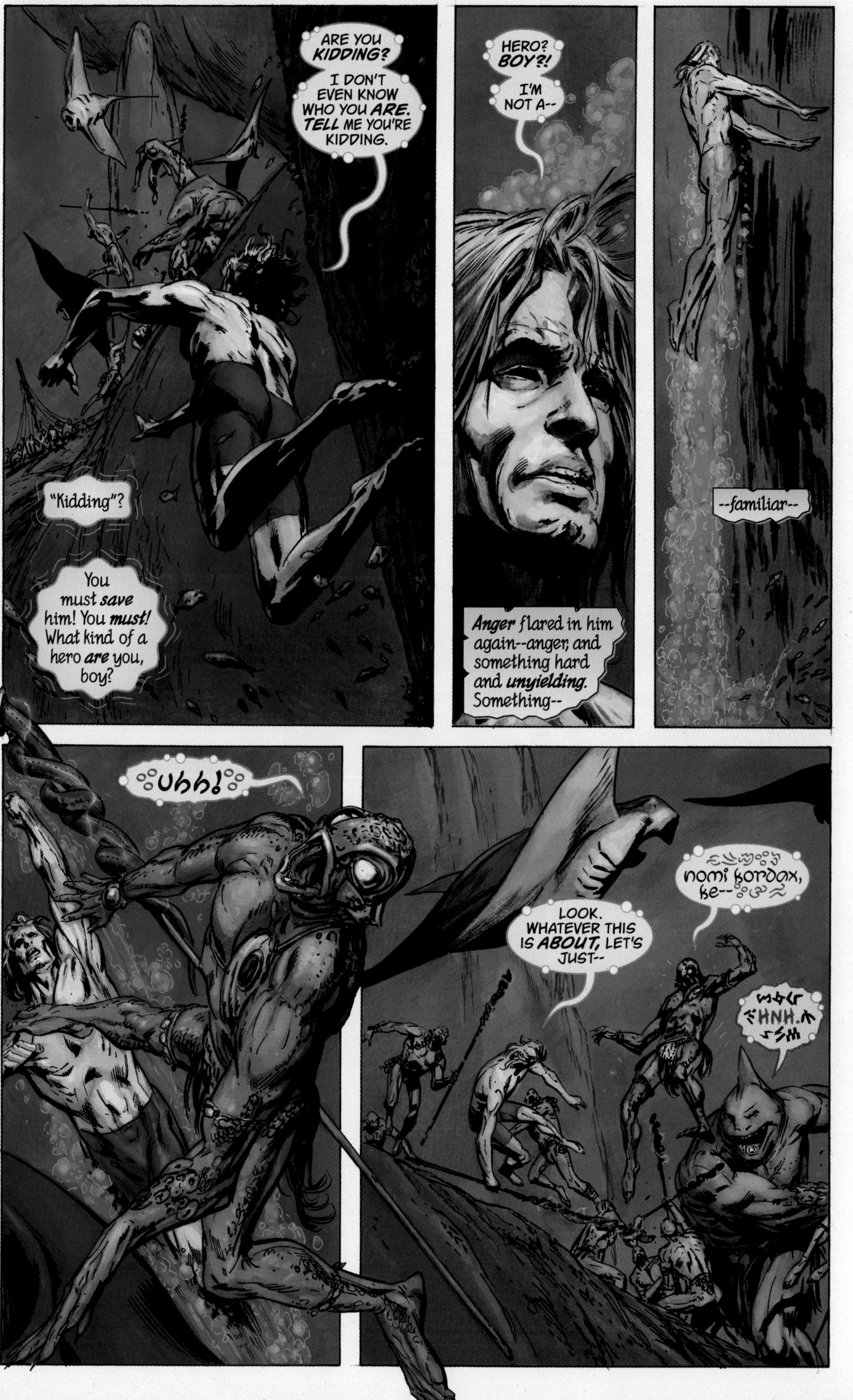
ARE YOU KIDDING?
I DON'T EVEN KNOW WHO YOU ARE. TELL ME YOU'RE KIDDING.
"Kidding"?
You must save him! You must! What kind of a hero are you, boy?
HERO? BOY?!
I'M NOT A--
Anger flared in him again--anger, and something hard and unyielding. Something--
--familiar--
Uhh!
nomi kordax, ke--
LOOK. WHATEVER THIS IS ABOUT, LET'S JUST--

ke--?

The intrusion was little more than a momentary *distraction*--

--but Nanaue saw his chance and *seized* it, striking as hard and ruthlessly as his implacable brethren.

DUUKH!!

OH, *GREAT.* I DON'T SUPPOSE YOU EVEN CON-SIDERED RUNNING AWAY? IT'D BE EASIER THAN--

MALEMA-O! LAKU HÁMAKI--

IAHT!!

IAHT!!

MIDANKA!

MIDANKA--

YEAH, YEAH, MIDANKA *MIDANKA.* I'D WRITE IT DOWN, BUT I LOST MY PEN. YOU WANT A *NNH* PIECE OF ME, GUYS?

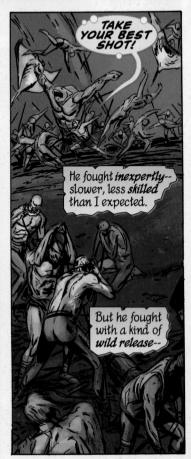

TAKE YOUR BEST SHOT!

He fought *inexpertly--* slower, less *skilled* than I expected.

But he fought with a kind of *wild release--*

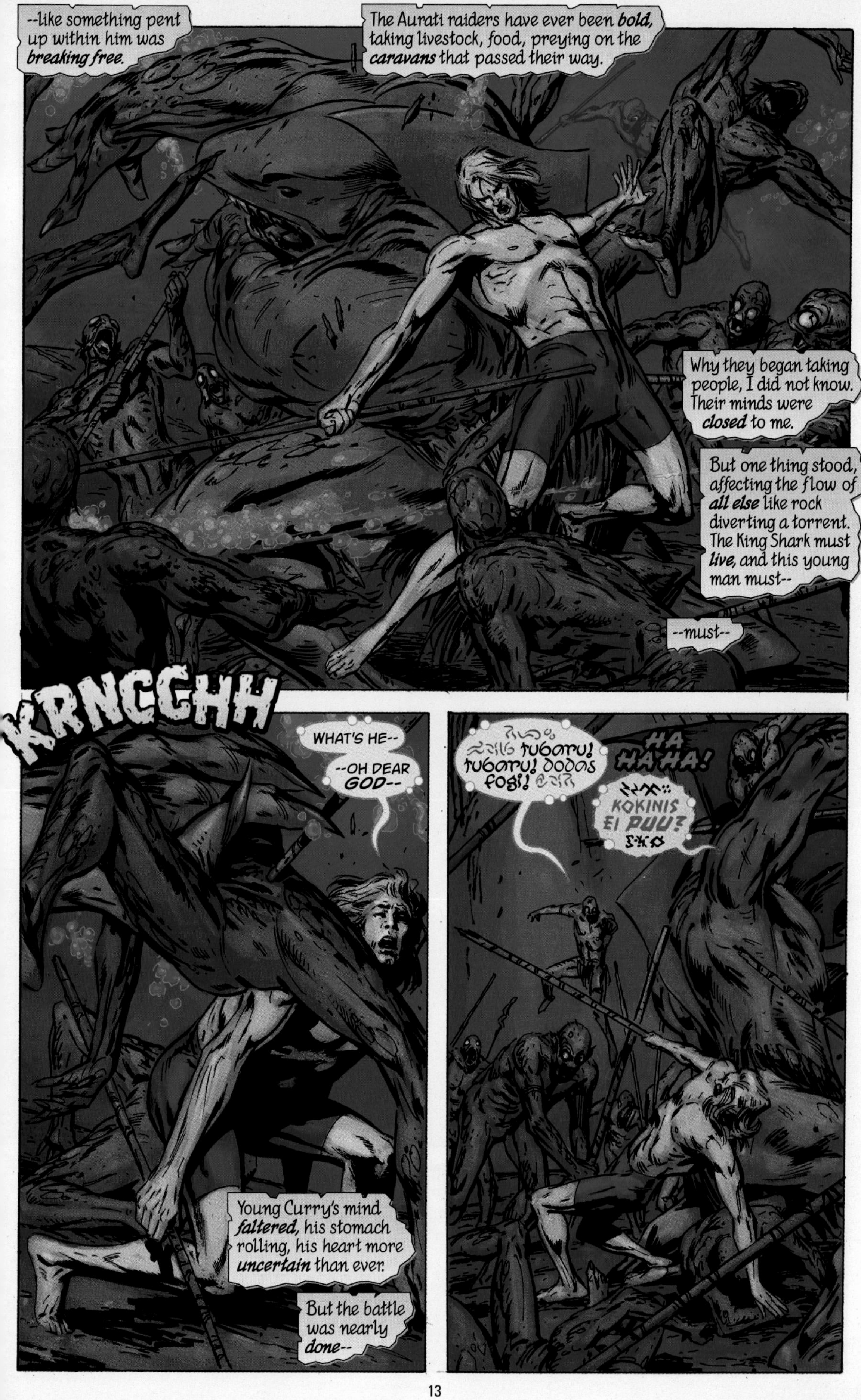
--like something pent up within him was breaking free.
The Aurati raiders have ever been bold, taking livestock, food, preying on the caravans that passed their way.
Why they began taking people, I did not know. Their minds were closed to me.
But one thing stood, affecting the flow of all else like rock diverting a torrent. The King Shark must live, and this young man must--
--must--
KRNCGHH
WHAT'S HE--
--OH DEAR GOD--
Young Curry's mind faltered, his stomach rolling, his heart more uncertain than ever.
But the battle was nearly done--
tubaru! tubaru! dodas fogi!
HA HA HA!
KOKINIS EI PUU?

--for the King Shark had called his *brethren.*

ɛ̃Ɛ̃Ɔ koɪɔɔx íɔíxu...

SHARKS!

ALL THIS *BLOOD!* THEY'RE-- THEY'LL--

ʊⁿɛⁿ ʊKI *WALAO,* YOU LITTLE *FOOL--*

--AND *MOVE!*

I BRING COUSINS, BUT... WHEN *BLOOD- MADNESS* ON THEM...

...NO ONE... *CONTROL* THEM...

They were free. And *allies,* at least for the moment.

OKAY, SPOOKY HEAD- VOICE. I SAVED YOUR *SHARK- GUY.* WHAT *NOW?*

HUH?

Bring him *with* you. Follow the course I am showing you now. It will *lead* you...

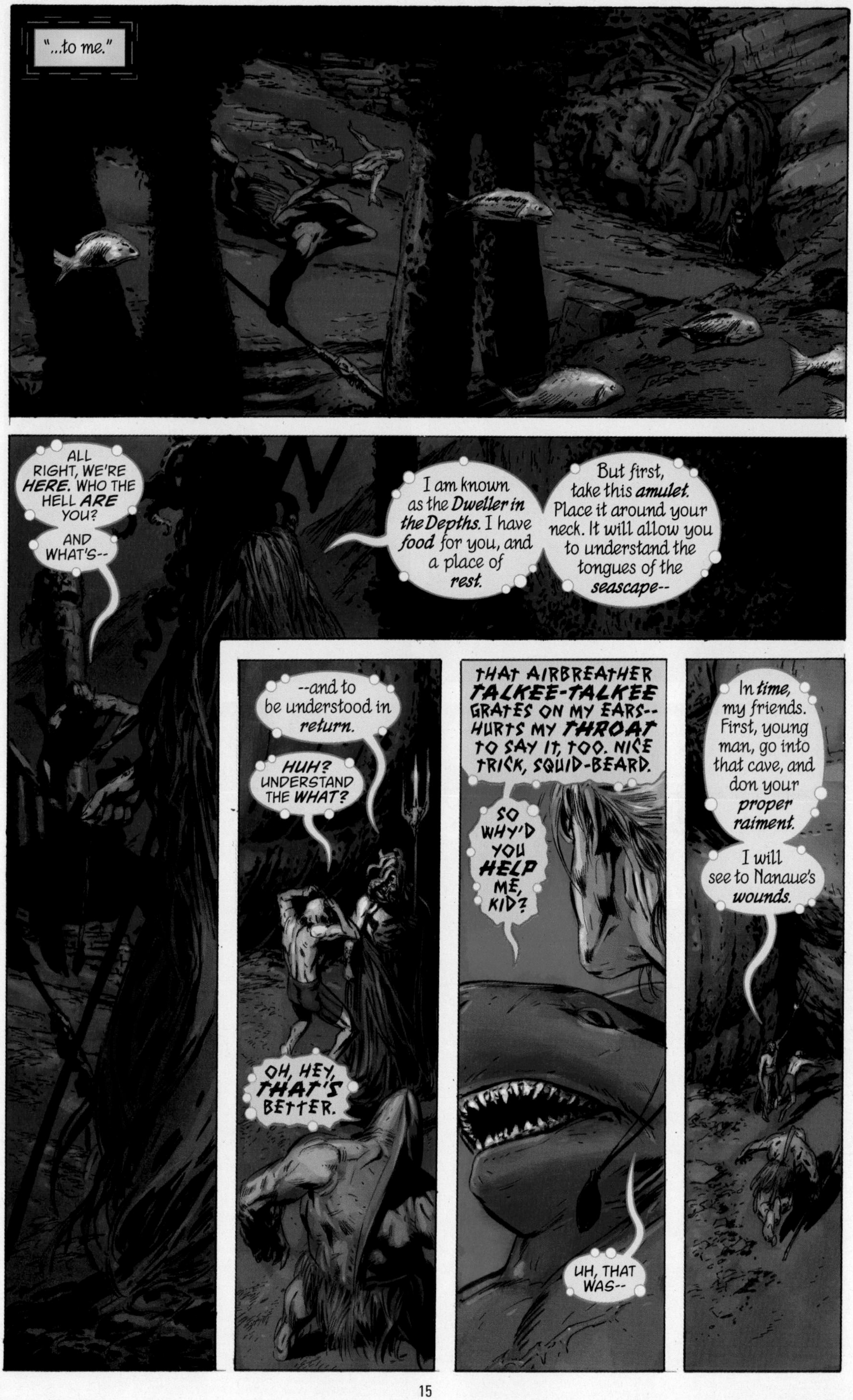
"...to me."
ALL RIGHT, WE'RE HERE. WHO THE HELL ARE YOU?
AND WHAT'S--
I am known as the Dweller in the Depths. I have food for you, and a place of rest.
But first, take this amulet. Place it around your neck. It will allow you to understand the tongues of the seascape--
--and to be understood in return.
HUH? UNDERSTAND THE WHAT?
OH, HEY, THAT'S BETTER.
THAT AIRBREATHER TALKEE-TALKEE GRATES ON MY EARS-- HURTS MY THROAT TO SAY IT, TOO. NICE TRICK, SQUID-BEARD.
SO WHY'D YOU HELP ME, KID?
UH, THAT WAS--
In time, my friends. First, young man, go into that cave, and don your proper raiment.
I will see to Nanaue's wounds.

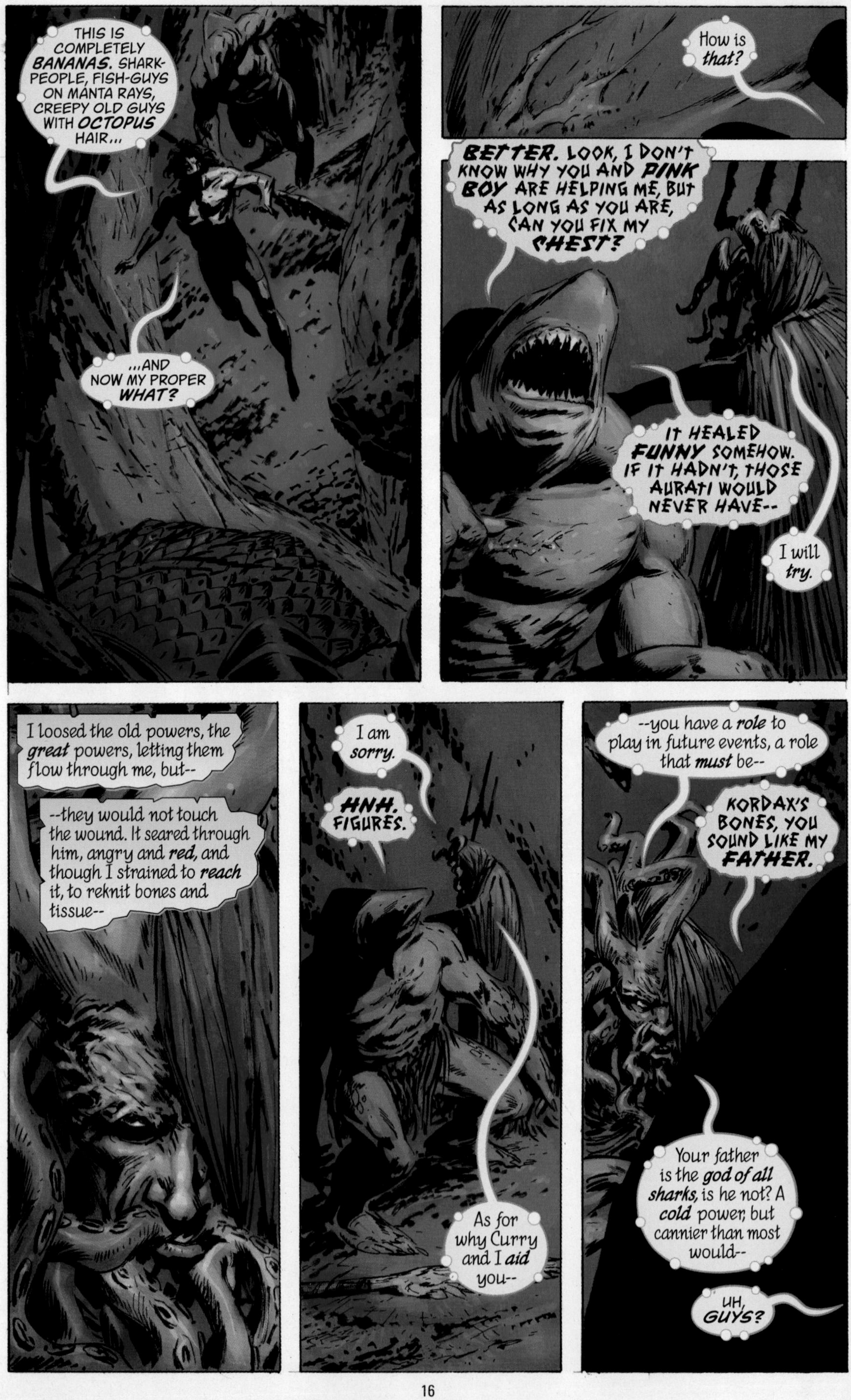
THIS IS COMPLETELY BANANAS. SHARK-PEOPLE, FISH-GUYS ON MANTA RAYS, CREEPY OLD GUYS WITH OCTOPUS HAIR...
...AND NOW MY PROPER WHAT?
How is that?
BETTER. LOOK, I DON'T KNOW WHY YOU AND PINK BOY ARE HELPING ME, BUT AS LONG AS YOU ARE, CAN YOU FIX MY CHEST?
IT HEALED FUNNY SOMEHOW. IF IT HADN'T, THOSE AURATI WOULD NEVER HAVE--
I will try.
I loosed the old powers, the great powers, letting them flow through me, but--
--they would not touch the wound. It seared through him, angry and red, and though I strained to reach it, to reknit bones and tissue--
I am sorry.
HNH. FIGURES.
As for why Curry and I aid you--
--you have a role to play in future events, a role that must be--
KORDAX'S BONES, YOU SOUND LIKE MY FATHER.
Your father is the god of all sharks, is he not? A cold power, but cannier than most would--
UH, GUYS?

SOMEONE'S **REALLY** GOT TO TELL ME WHAT'S GOING ON HERE...
AQUAMAN?!
WHAT IN THE **BLOODY** DEEP...?

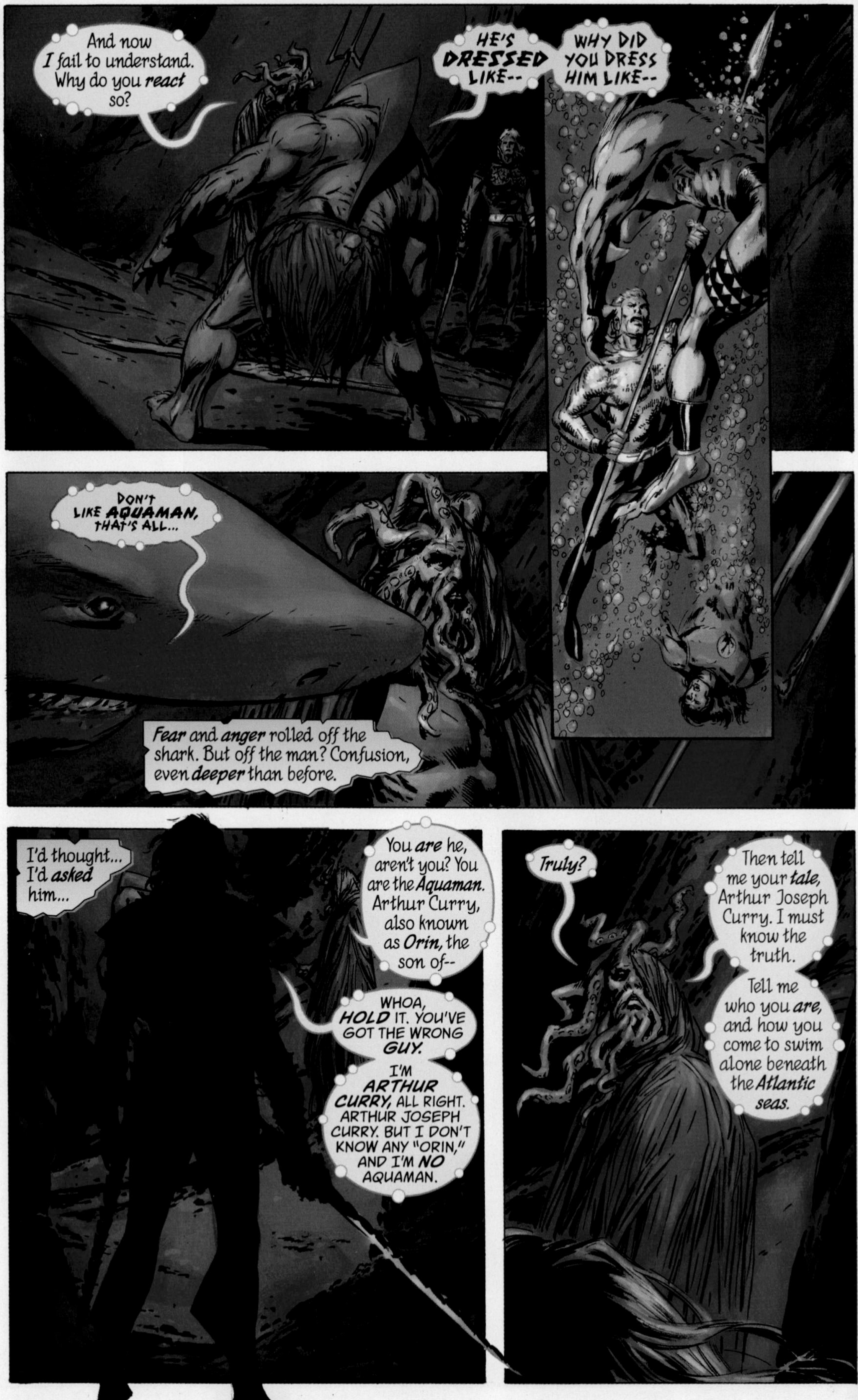

And now I fail to understand. Why do you react so?
HE'S DRESSED LIKE--
WHY DID YOU DRESS HIM LIKE--
DON'T LIKE AQUAMAN, THAT'S ALL...
Fear and anger rolled off the shark. But off the man? Confusion, even deeper than before.
I'd thought... I'd asked him...
You are he, aren't you? You are the Aquaman. Arthur Curry, also known as Orin, the son of--
WHOA, HOLD IT. YOU'VE GOT THE WRONG GUY.
I'M ARTHUR CURRY, ALL RIGHT. ARTHUR JOSEPH CURRY. BUT I DON'T KNOW ANY "ORIN," AND I'M NO AQUAMAN.
Truly?
Then tell me your tale, Arthur Joseph Curry. I must know the truth.
Tell me who you are, and how you come to swim alone beneath the Atlantic seas.

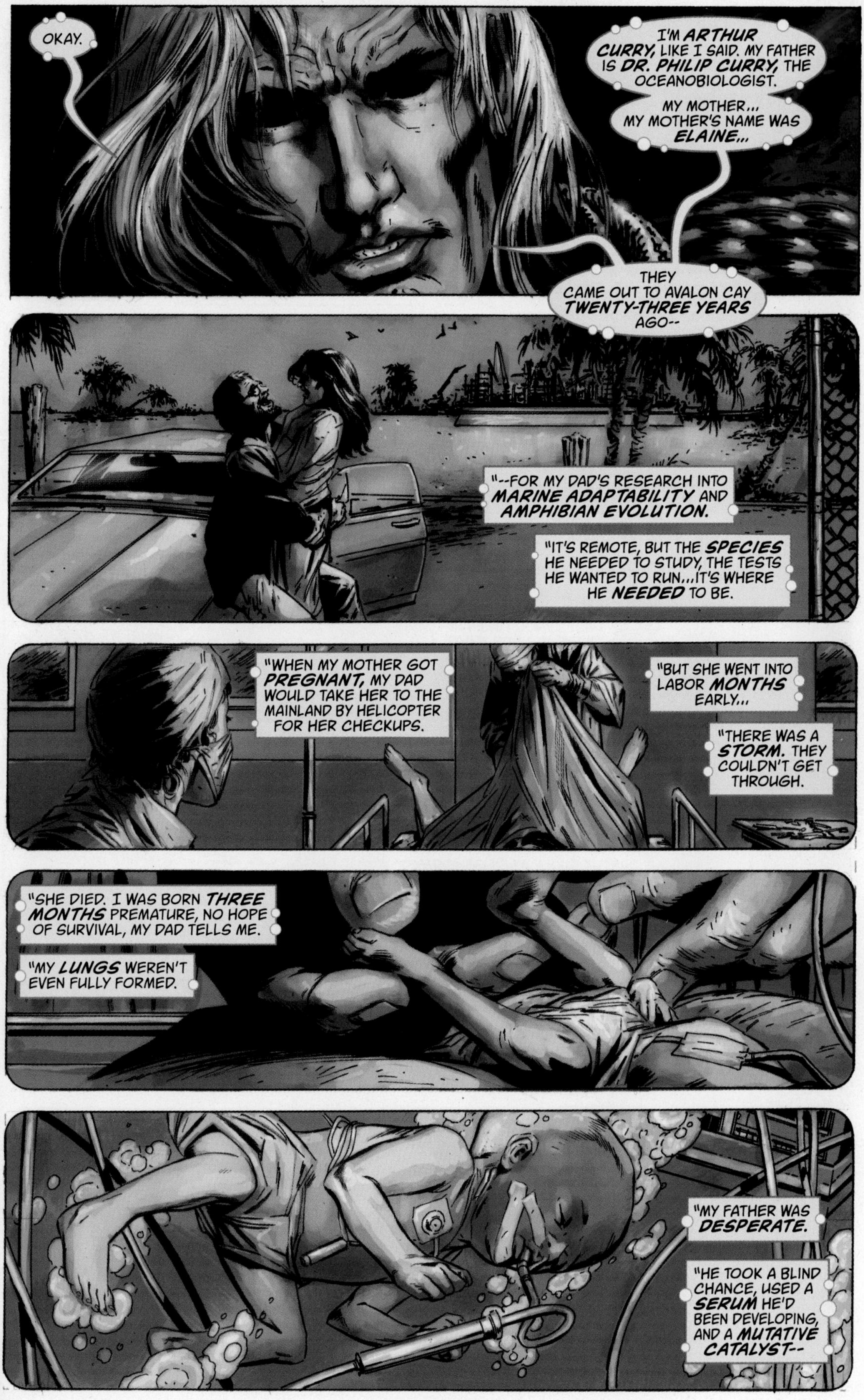
OKAY.
I'M ARTHUR CURRY, LIKE I SAID. MY FATHER IS DR. PHILIP CURRY, THE OCEANOBIOLOGIST.
MY MOTHER... MY MOTHER'S NAME WAS ELAINE...
THEY CAME OUT TO AVALON CAY TWENTY-THREE YEARS AGO--
"--FOR MY DAD'S RESEARCH INTO MARINE ADAPTABILITY AND AMPHIBIAN EVOLUTION.
"IT'S REMOTE, BUT THE SPECIES HE NEEDED TO STUDY, THE TESTS HE WANTED TO RUN...IT'S WHERE HE NEEDED TO BE.
"WHEN MY MOTHER GOT PREGNANT, MY DAD WOULD TAKE HER TO THE MAINLAND BY HELICOPTER FOR HER CHECKUPS.
"BUT SHE WENT INTO LABOR MONTHS EARLY...
"THERE WAS A STORM. THEY COULDN'T GET THROUGH.
"SHE DIED. I WAS BORN THREE MONTHS PREMATURE, NO HOPE OF SURVIVAL, MY DAD TELLS ME.
"MY LUNGS WEREN'T EVEN FULLY FORMED.
"MY FATHER WAS DESPERATE.
"HE TOOK A BLIND CHANCE, USED A SERUM HE'D BEEN DEVELOPING, AND A MUTATIVE CATALYST--

"I *LIVED*."

"I GREW *GILLS*. MY SKIN, MY CIRCULATORY SYSTEM, MY MUSCLES--THEY ALL CHANGED, ALL *ADAPTED*."

"SINCE THEN, I'VE LIVED IN THE MAIN TANK AT THE *CURRY-JONAS OCEANOGRAPHIC CENTER* AT AVALON CAY. EXCEPT FOR A FEW SUPERVISED EXCURSIONS INTO THE *OCEAN*."

"MY FATHER DIVIDES HIS TIME BETWEEN *CONVENTIONAL RESEARCH* AND TRYING TO *CURE* ME..."

DIDJA *SEE*, DAD? I MUSTA BEEN UP IN THE AIR FOR *FIVE MINUTES*!

GOOD WORK, ART. *GREAT* WORK. I'LL JUST HAVE GEIST RERUN A SET OF *CHEM-LEVELS*, AND WE'LL SEE WHAT WE *SEE*, HM?

"...WORKING ON STRENGTHENING MY *LUNGS*, ISOLATING HOW THE SERUM *ALTERED* ME."

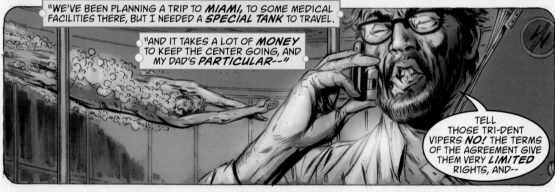

"WE'VE BEEN PLANNING A TRIP TO *MIAMI*, TO SOME MEDICAL FACILITIES THERE, BUT I NEEDED A *SPECIAL TANK* TO TRAVEL."

"AND IT TAKES A LOT OF *MONEY* TO KEEP THE CENTER GOING, AND MY DAD'S *PARTICULAR*--"

TELL THOSE TRI-DENT VIPERS *NO!* THE TERMS OF THE AGREEMENT GIVE THEM VERY *LIMITED* RIGHTS, AND--

"BUT I'VE SEEN MIAMI ON *TELEVISION*."

"*MOST* OF WHAT I'VE SEEN, I GUESS, I'VE SEEN ON TELEVISION."

BUT LAST NIGHT, THERE WAS-- THERE WAS A *STORM*--

I'VE GOT TO GET *BACK* THERE. IF IT WAS *BAD ENOUGH* TO RUPTURE THE TANK, SEND ME INTO THE SEA--

I'VE GOT TO SEE IF EVERYONE'S *ALL RIGHT.*

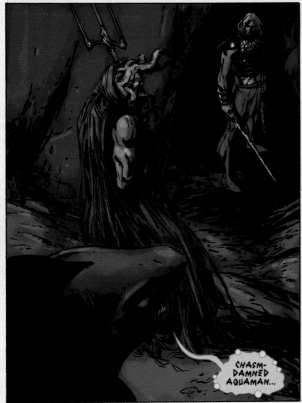

CHASM-DAMNED AQUAMAN...

WHAT?

Is it *possible?* You *are* barely more than a boy...

A storm at his *birth,* a storm at his *release.* Can you truly not *know* yourself? Can none of it have *happened* yet?

Did I-- have I seen the *future?*

I'M *REALLY TIRED* OF THIS *"BOY"* STUFF. WILL YOU *STOP BABBLING* AND *TELL ME WHAT YOU'RE TALKING ABOUT?!*

Have a *care,* lad. I will be treated with *respect.*

I know a tale *like* yours--a human scientist, his son--I thought it was from *long, long ago.* I must have been mistaken.

And little of it was *true.*

21

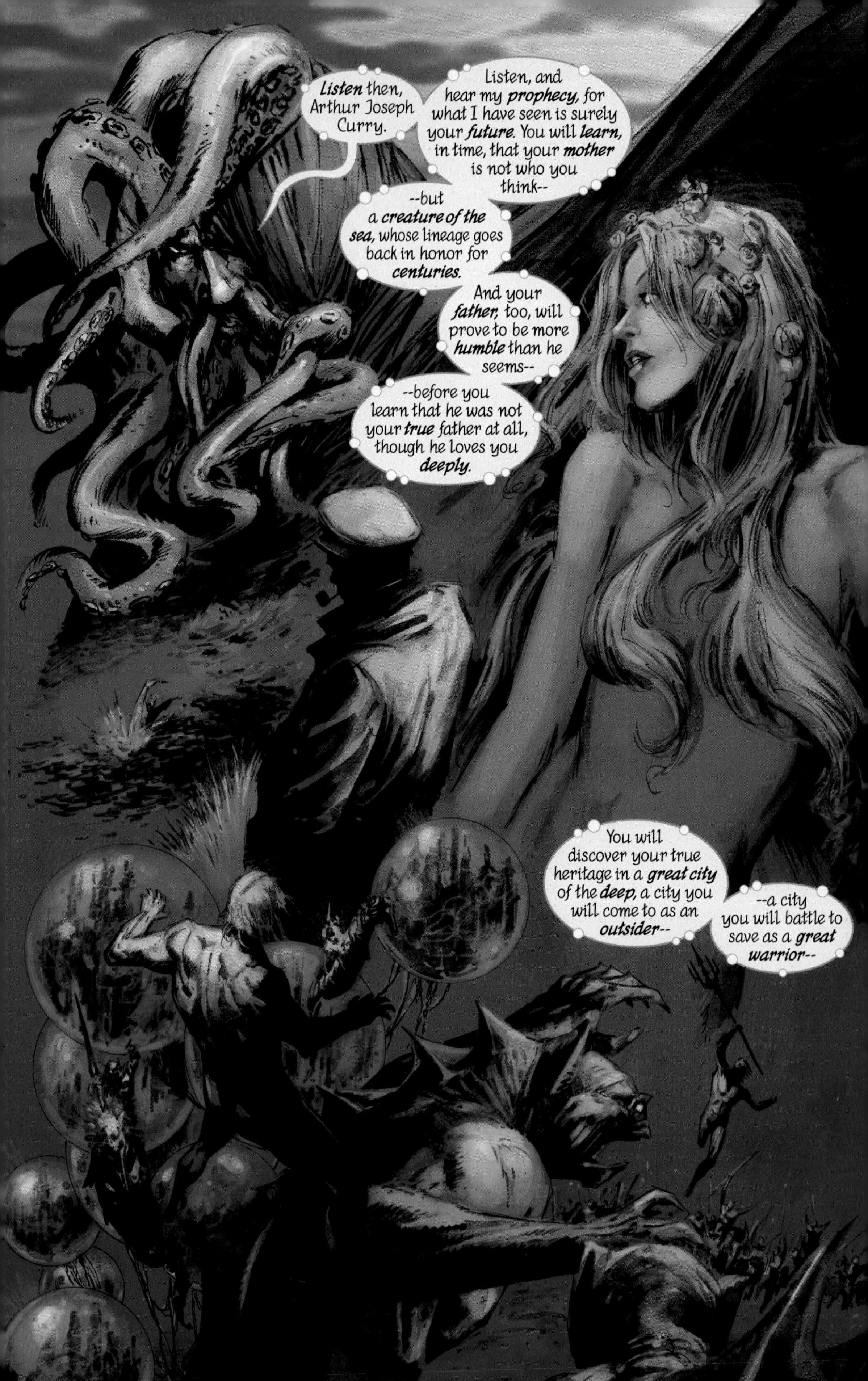
Listen then, Arthur Joseph Curry.
Listen, and hear my prophecy, for what I have seen is surely your future. You will learn, in time, that your mother is not who you think--
--but a creature of the sea, whose lineage goes back in honor for centuries.
And your father, too, will prove to be more humble than he seems--
--before you learn that he was not your true father at all, though he loves you deeply.
You will discover your true heritage in a great city of the deep, a city you will come to as an outsider--
--a city you will battle to save as a great warrior--

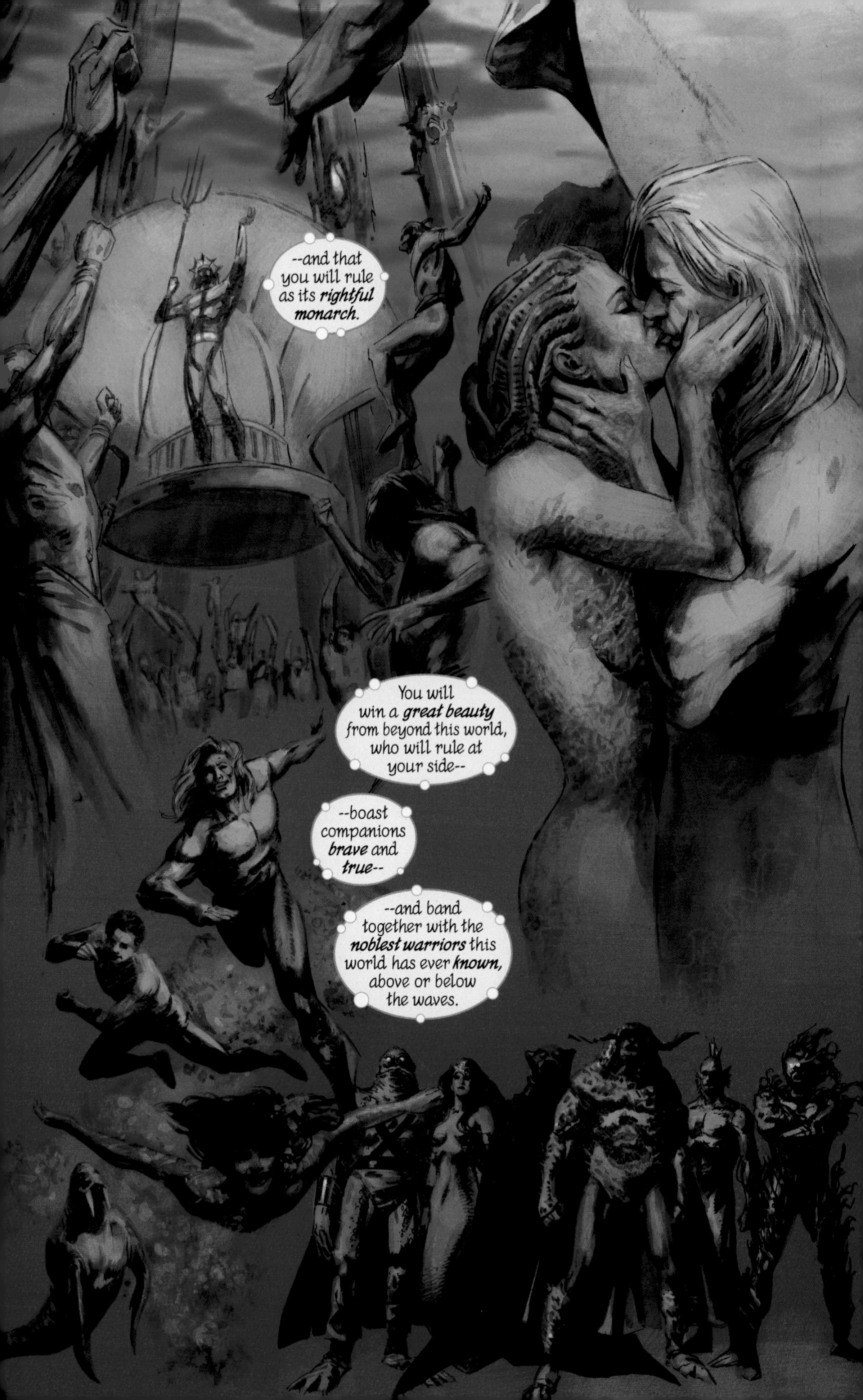
--and that you will rule as its *rightful monarch*.
You will win a *great beauty* from beyond this world, who will rule at your side--
--boast companions *brave* and *true*--
--and band together with the *noblest warriors* this world has ever *known,* above or below the waves.

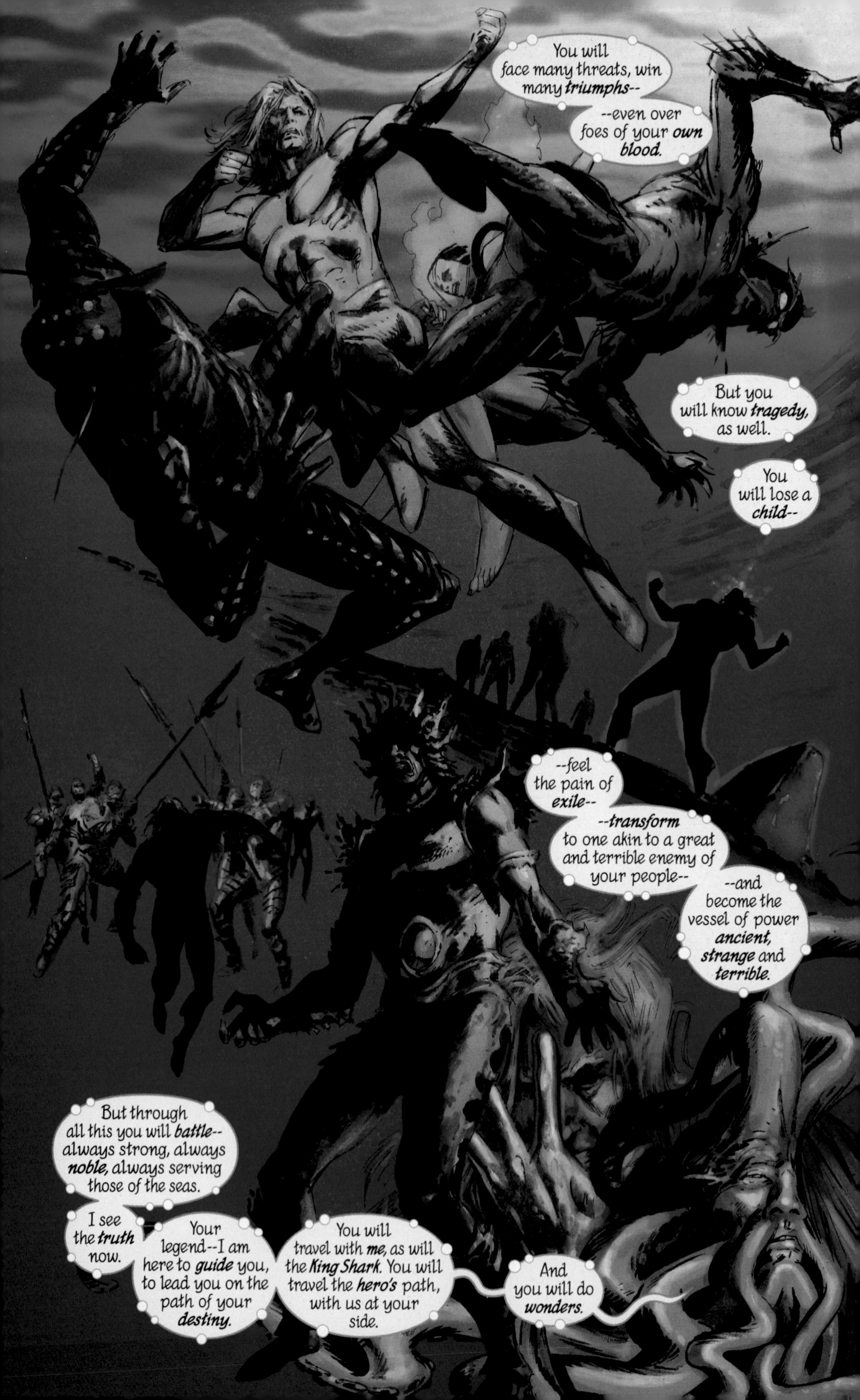
You will face many threats, win many *triumphs*--
--even over foes of your *own blood*.
But you will know *tragedy*, as well.
You will lose a *child*--
--feel the pain of *exile*--
--*transform* to one akin to a great and terrible enemy of your people--
--and become the vessel of power *ancient*, *strange* and *terrible*.
But through all this you will *battle*--always strong, always *noble*, always serving those of the seas.
I see the *truth* now.
Your legend--I am here to *guide* you, to lead you on the path of your *destiny*.
You will travel with *me*, as will the *King Shark*. You will travel the *hero's* path, with us at your side.
And you will do *wonders*.

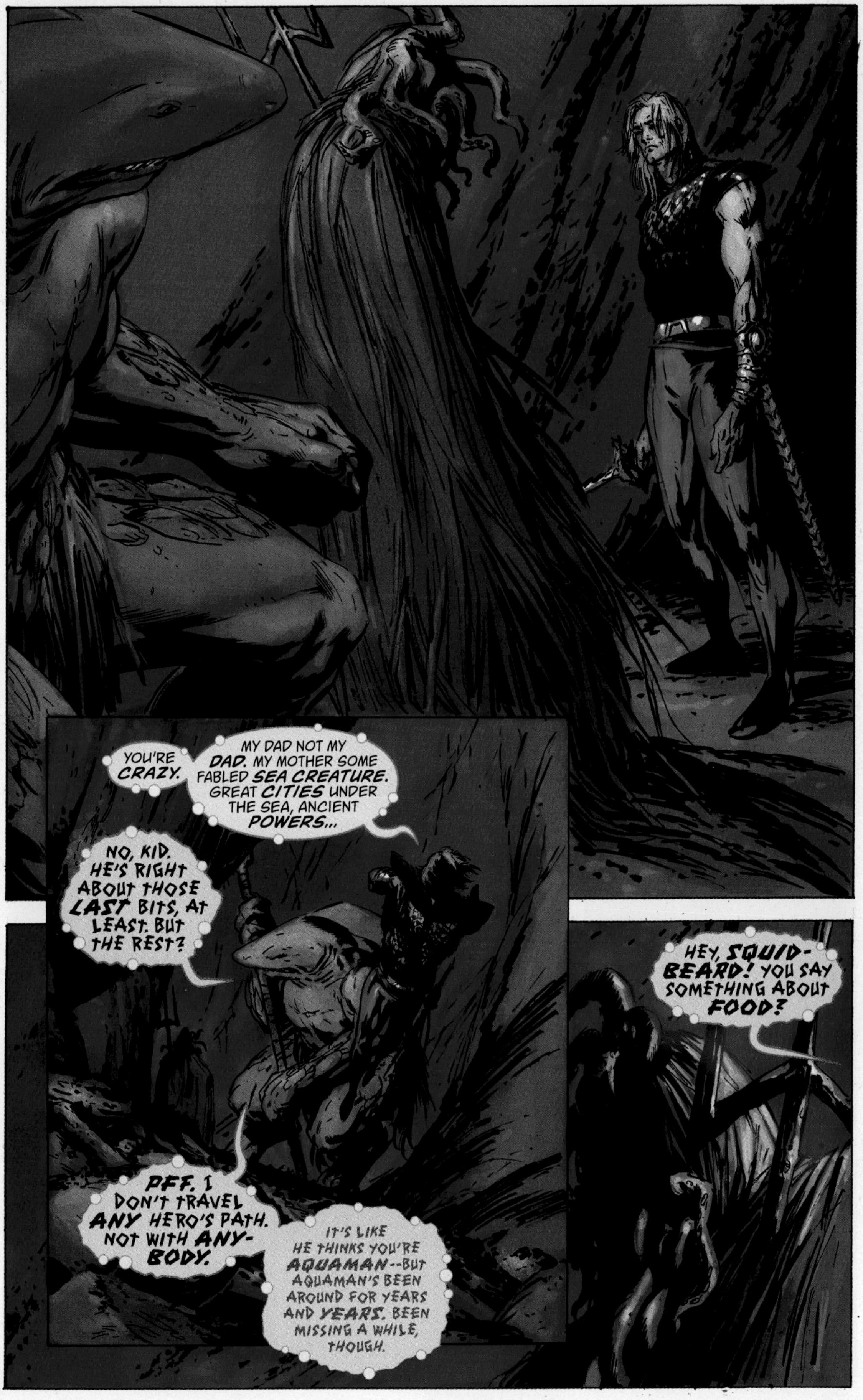
YOU'RE CRAZY.
MY DAD NOT MY DAD. MY MOTHER SOME FABLED SEA CREATURE. GREAT CITIES UNDER THE SEA, ANCIENT POWERS...
NO, KID. HE'S RIGHT ABOUT THOSE LAST BITS, AT LEAST. BUT THE REST?
PFF. I DON'T TRAVEL ANY HERO'S PATH. NOT WITH ANY-BODY.
IT'S LIKE HE THINKS YOU'RE AQUAMAN--BUT AQUAMAN'S BEEN AROUND FOR YEARS AND YEARS. BEEN MISSING A WHILE, THOUGH.
HEY, SQUID-BEARD! YOU SAY SOMETHING ABOUT FOOD?

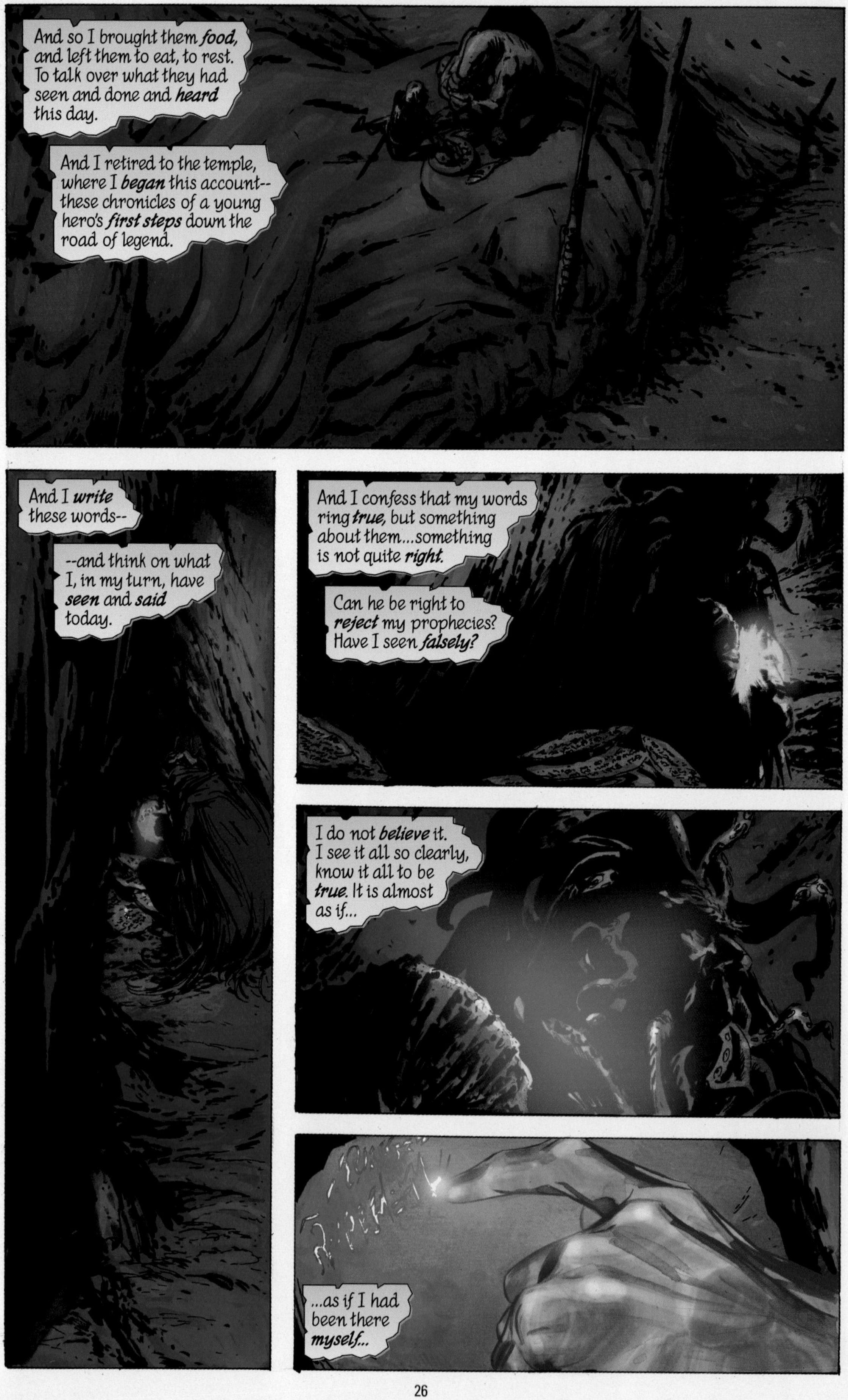
And so I brought them *food*, and left them to eat, to rest. To talk over what they had seen and done and *heard* this day.
And I retired to the temple, where I *began* this account--these chronicles of a young hero's *first steps* down the road of legend.
And I *write* these words--
--and think on what I, in my turn, have *seen* and *said* today.
And I confess that my words ring *true*, but something about them...something is not quite *right*.
Can he be right to *reject* my prophecies? Have I seen *falsely*?
I do not *believe* it. I see it all so clearly, know it all to be *true*. It is almost as if...
...as if I had been there *myself*...

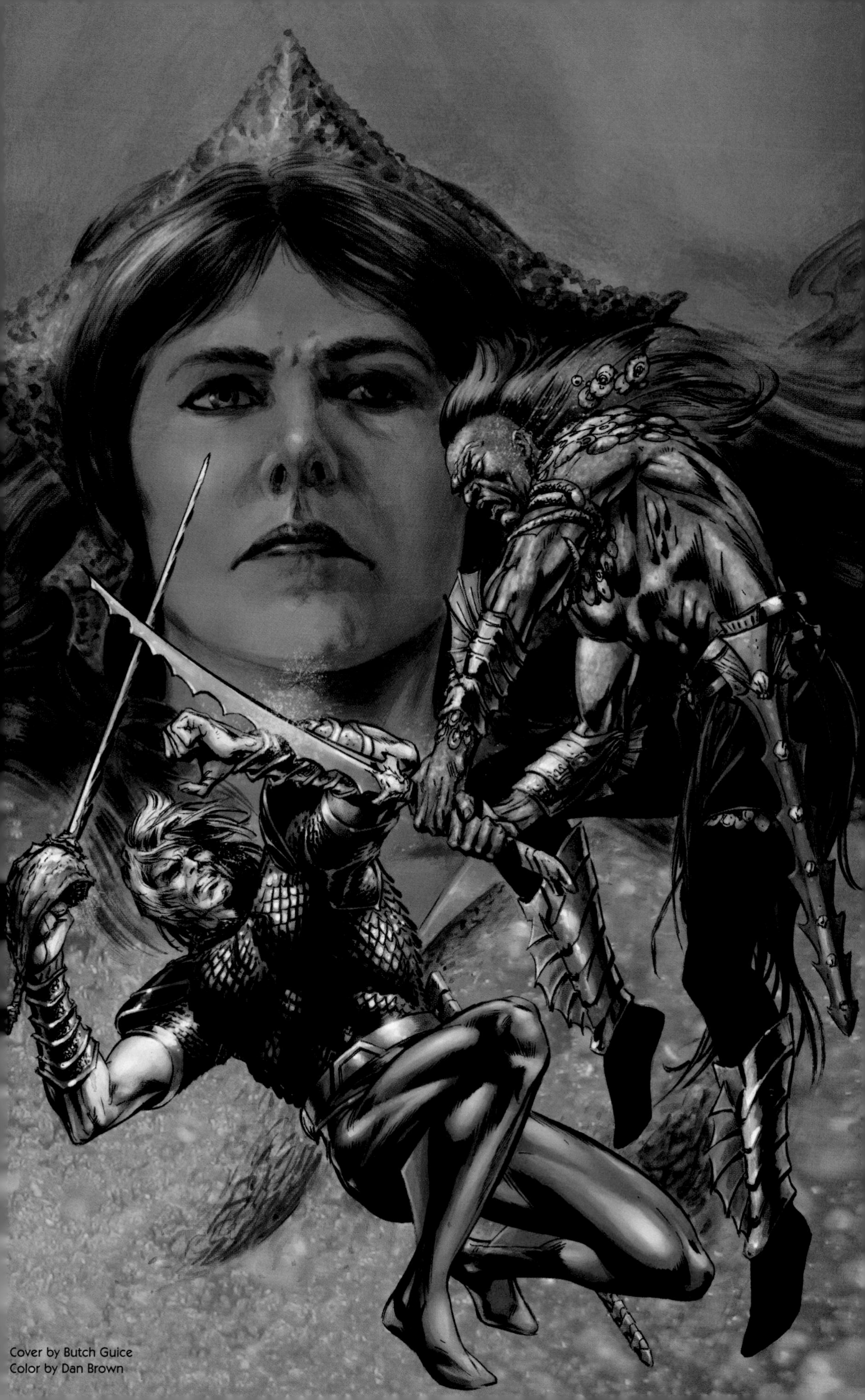

Cover by Butch Guice
Color by Dan Brown

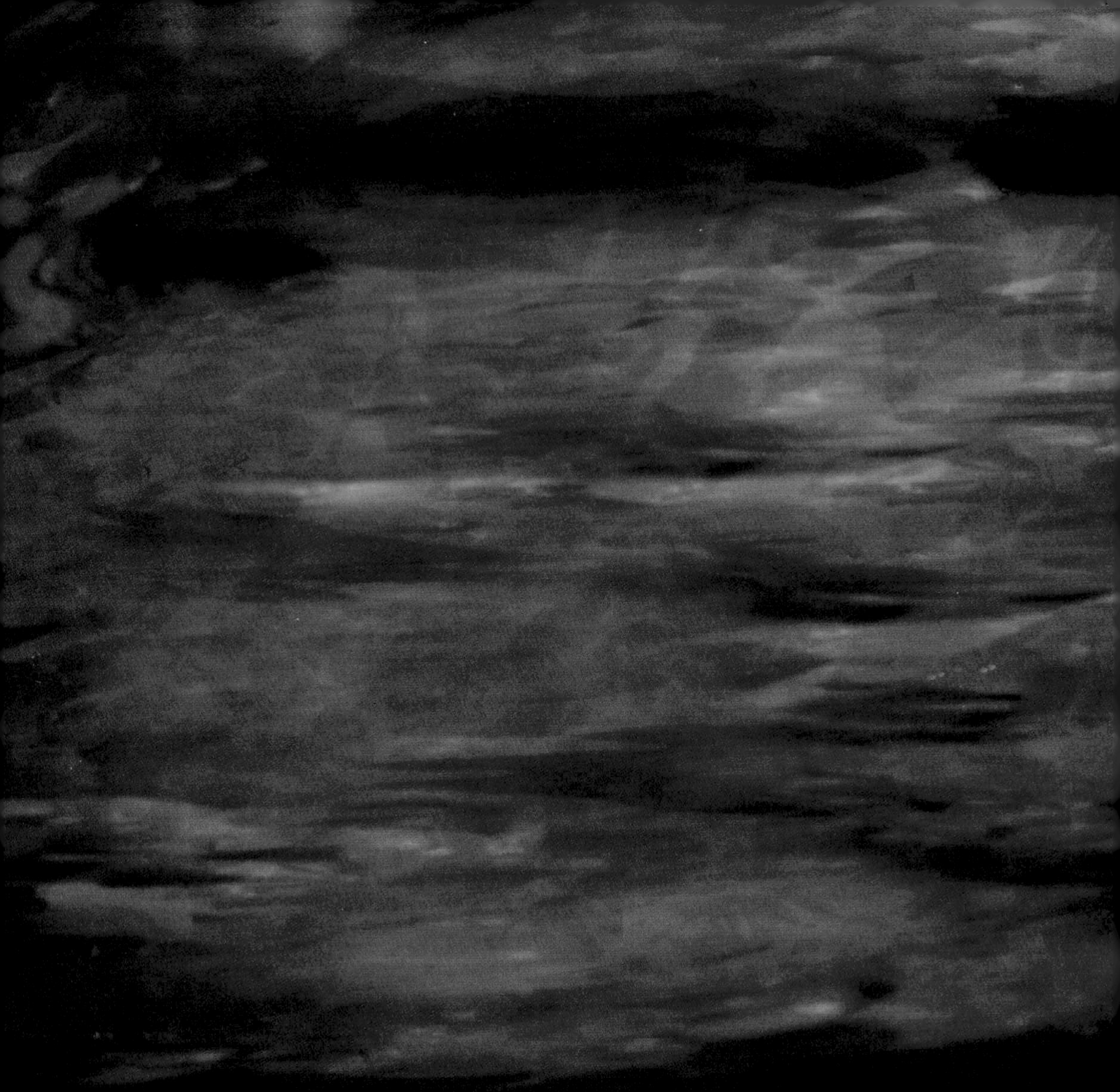

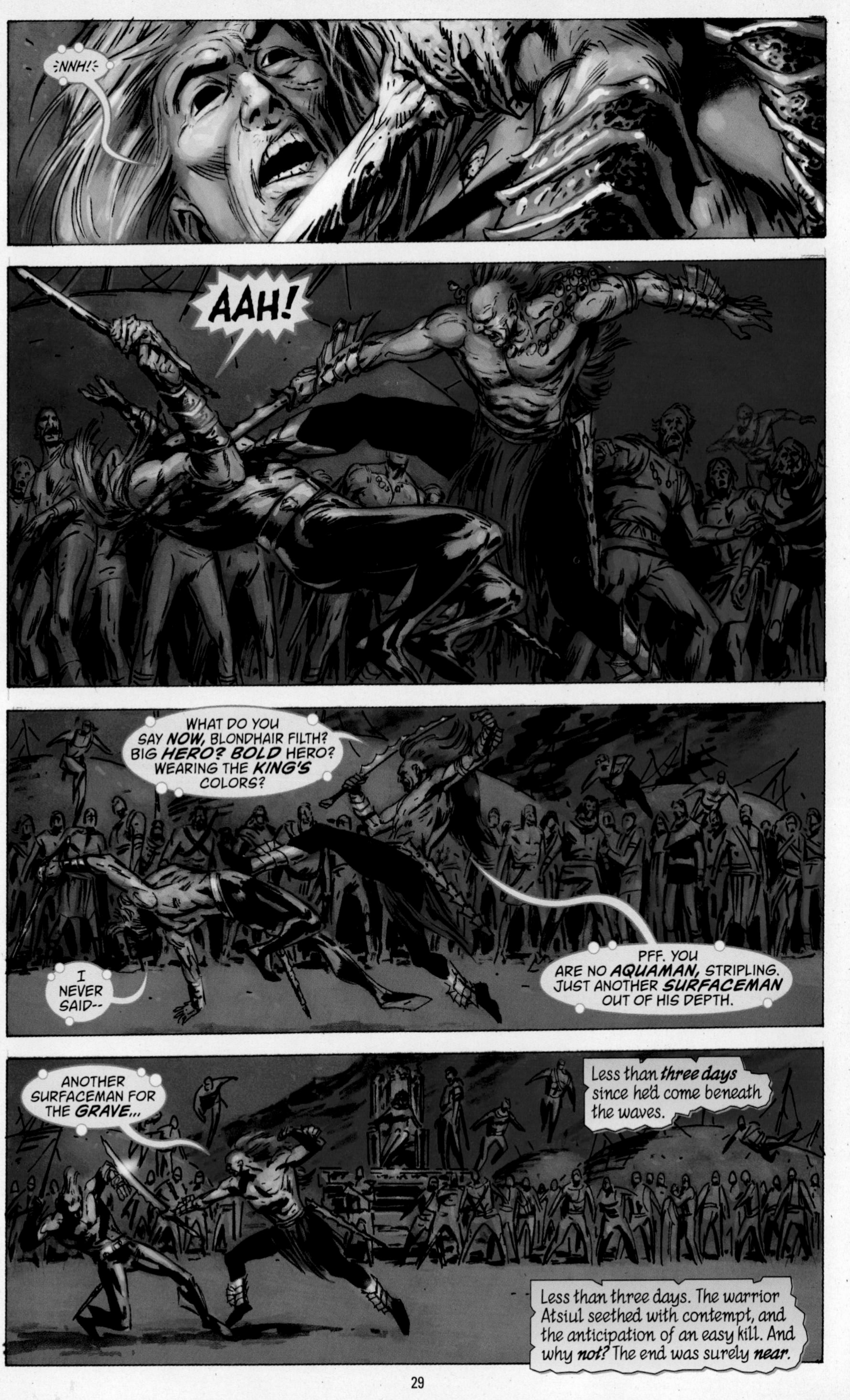
NNH!
AAH!
WHAT DO YOU SAY NOW, BLONDHAIR FILTH? BIG HERO? BOLD HERO? WEARING THE KING'S COLORS?
I NEVER SAID--
PFF. YOU ARE NO AQUAMAN, STRIPLING. JUST ANOTHER SURFACEMAN OUT OF HIS DEPTH.
ANOTHER SURFACEMAN FOR THE GRAVE...
Less than three days since he'd come beneath the waves.
Less than three days. The warrior Atsiul seethed with contempt, and the anticipation of an easy kill. And why not? The end was surely near.

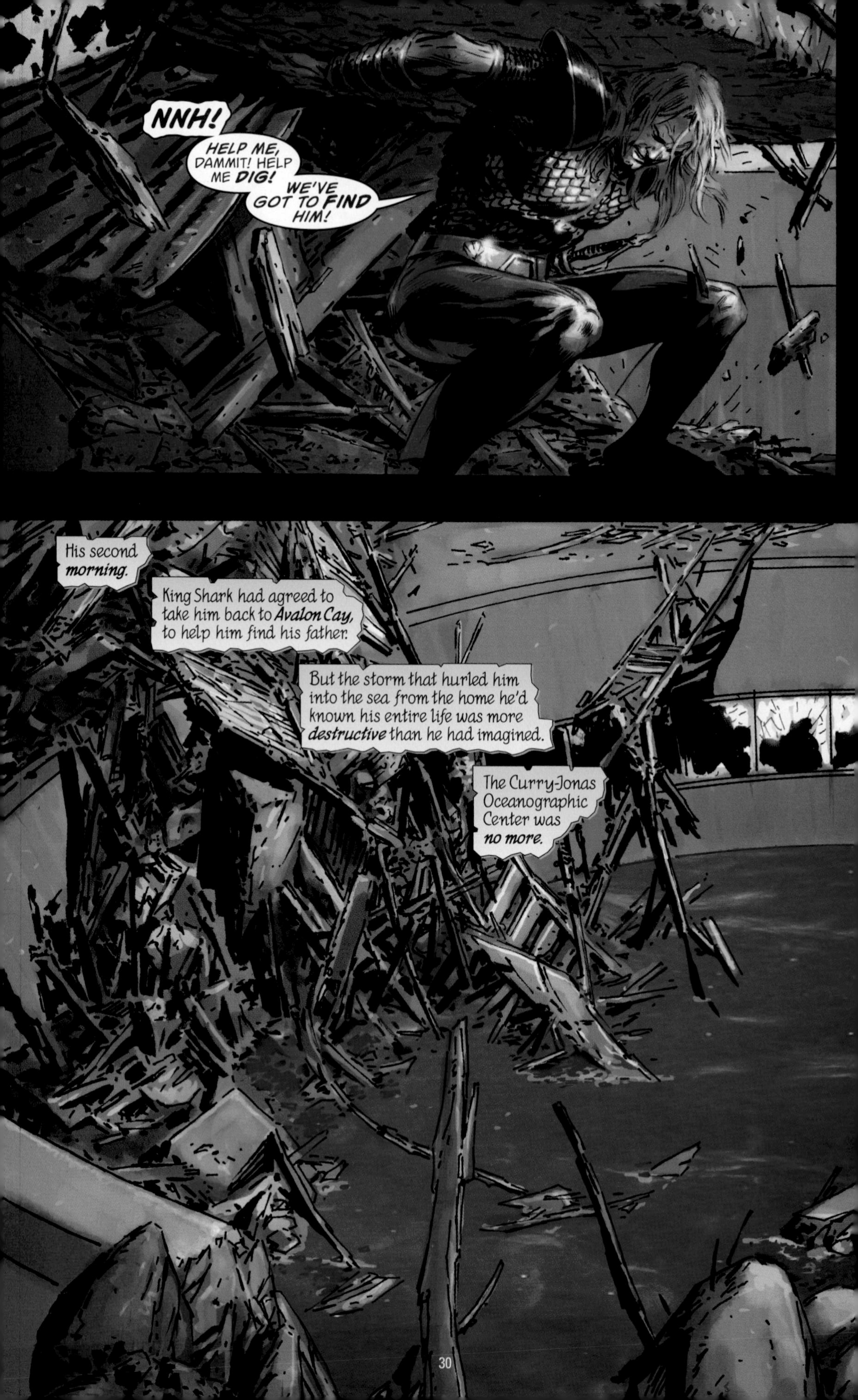
NNH!
HELP ME, DAMMIT! HELP ME DIG!
WE'VE GOT TO FIND HIM!
His second morning.
King Shark had agreed to take him back to Avalon Cay, to help him find his father.
But the storm that hurled him into the sea from the home he'd known his entire life was more destructive than he had imagined.
The Curry-Jonas Oceanographic Center was no more.

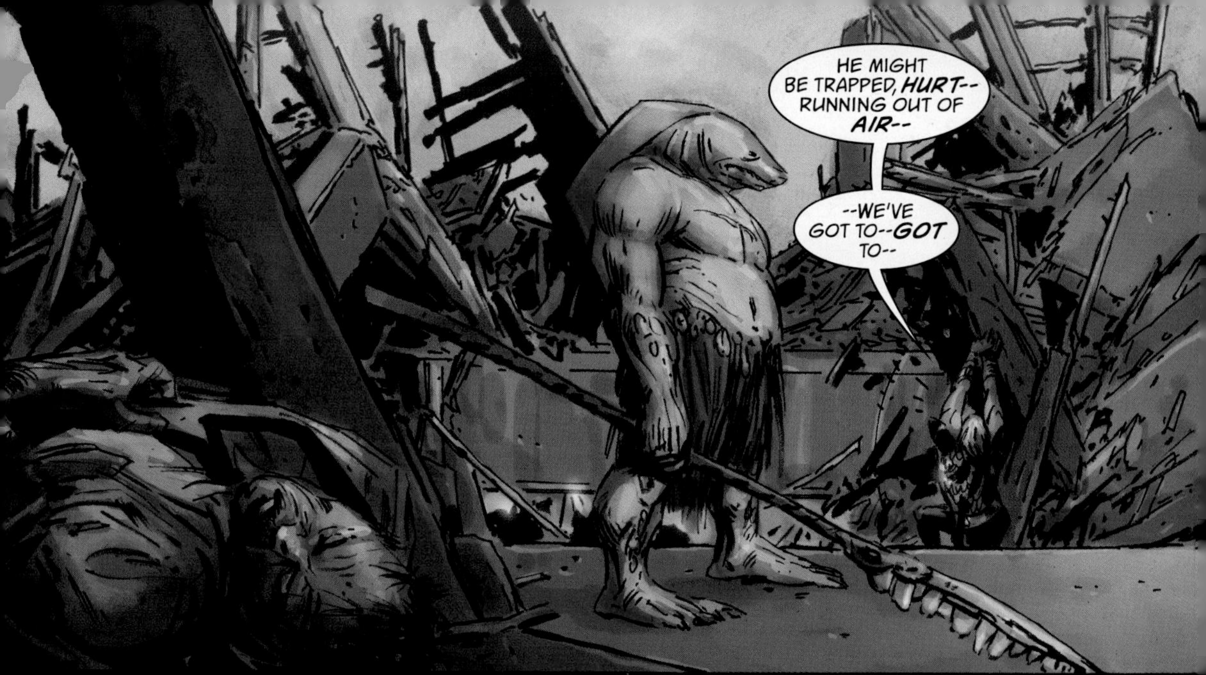
HE MIGHT BE TRAPPED, HURT-- RUNNING OUT OF AIR--
--WE'VE GOT TO--GOT TO--

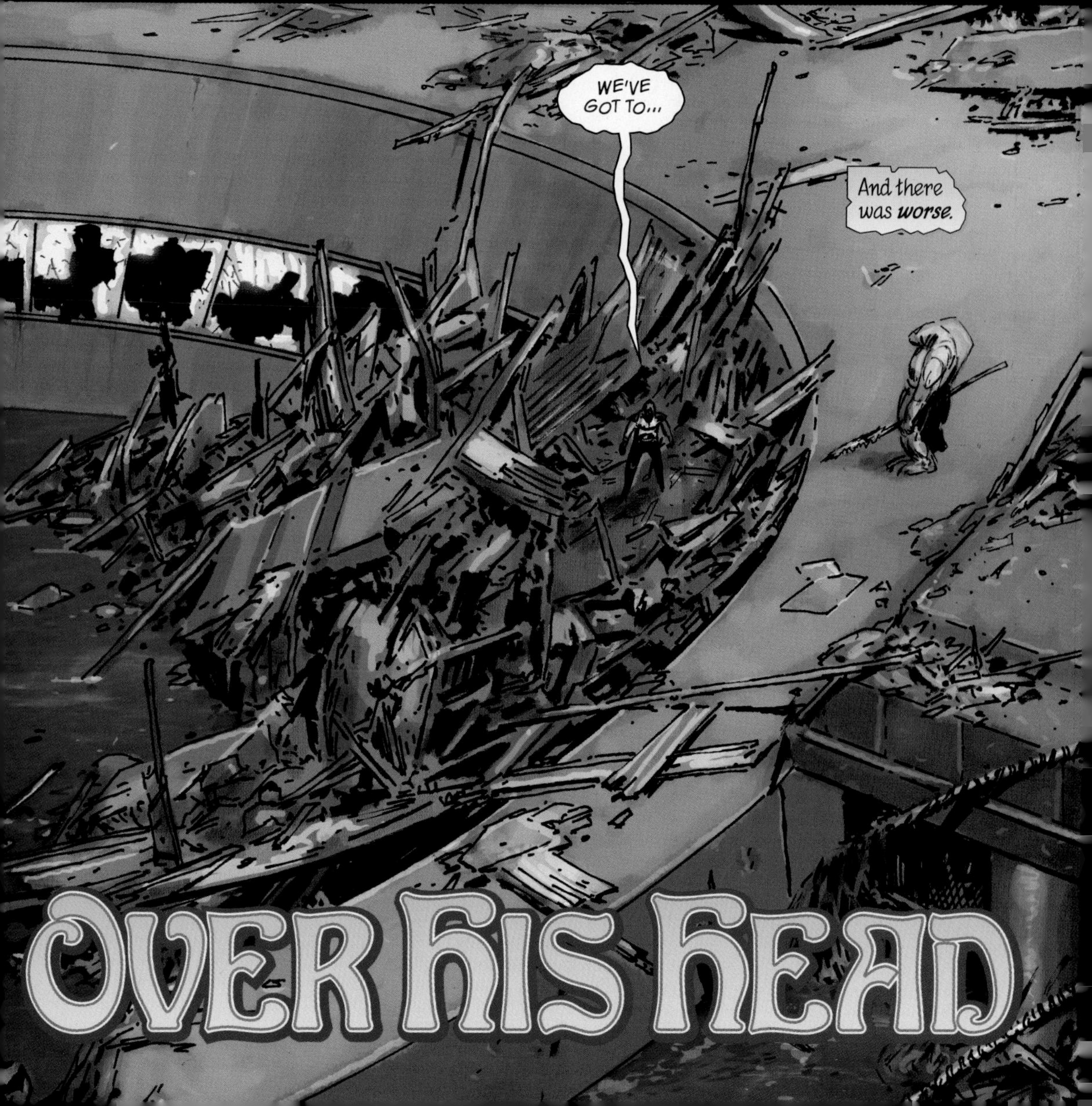
WE'VE GOT TO...
And there was worse.
OVER HIS HEAD

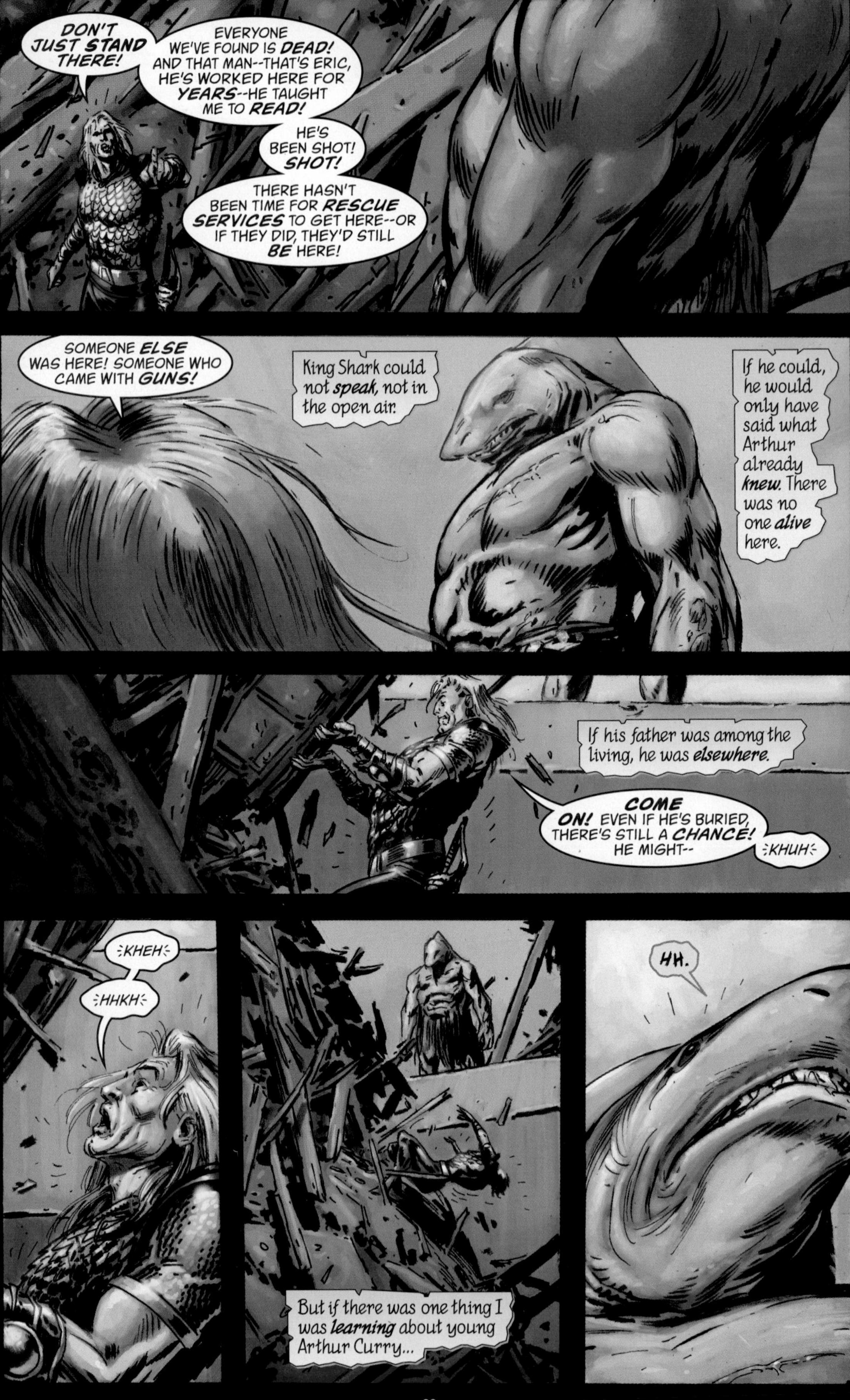

DON'T JUST STAND THERE!
EVERYONE WE'VE FOUND IS DEAD! AND THAT MAN--THAT'S ERIC, HE'S WORKED HERE FOR YEARS--HE TAUGHT ME TO READ!
HE'S BEEN SHOT! SHOT!
THERE HASN'T BEEN TIME FOR RESCUE SERVICES TO GET HERE--OR IF THEY DID, THEY'D STILL BE HERE!
SOMEONE ELSE WAS HERE! SOMEONE WHO CAME WITH GUNS!
King Shark could not speak, not in the open air.
If he could, he would only have said what Arthur already knew. There was no one alive here.
If his father was among the living, he was elsewhere.
COME ON! EVEN IF HE'S BURIED, THERE'S STILL A CHANCE! HE MIGHT--
KHUH
KHEH
HHKH
But if there was one thing I was learning about young Arthur Curry...
HH.

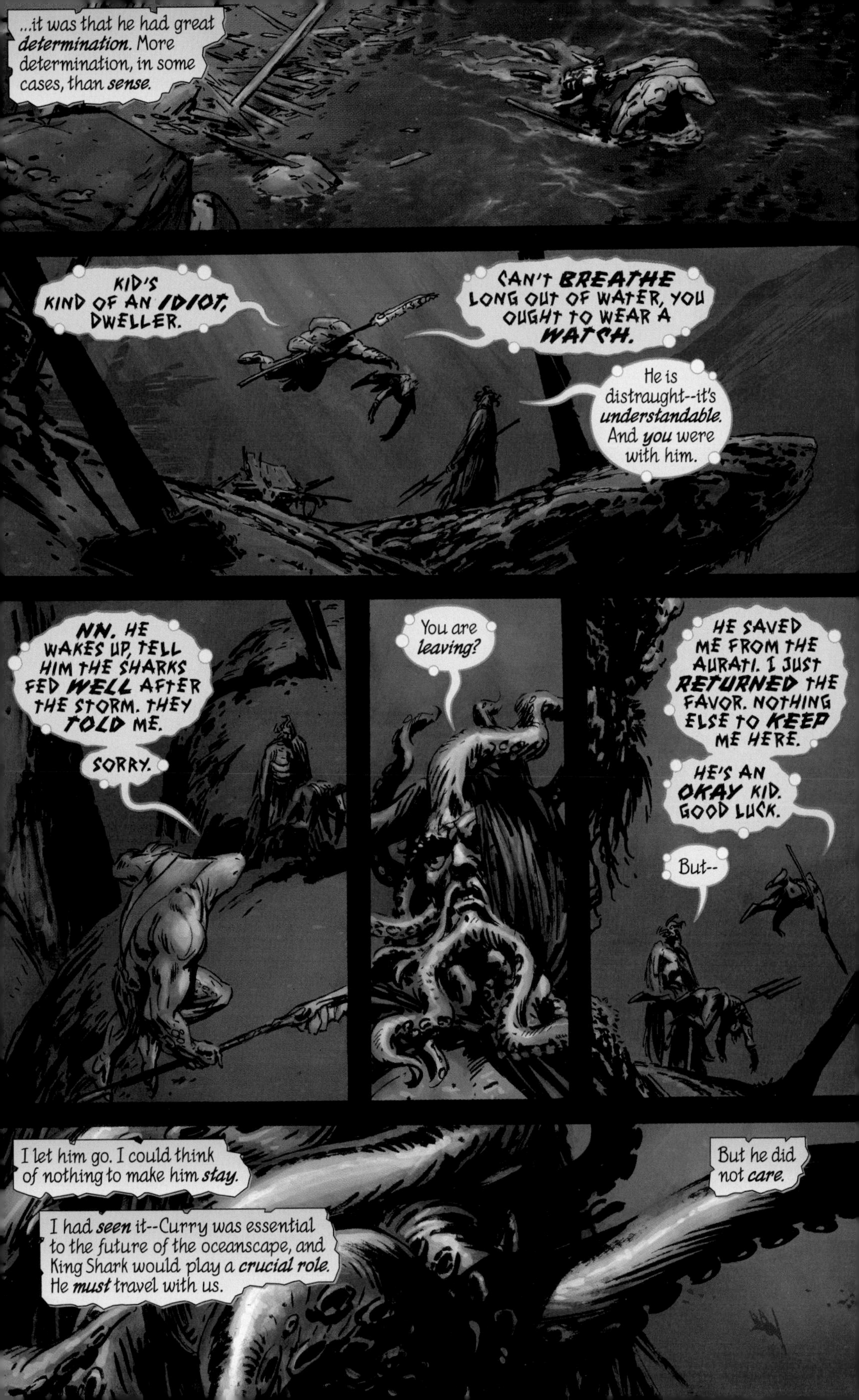

...it was that he had great determination. More determination, in some cases, than sense.
KID'S KIND OF AN IDIOT, DWELLER.
CAN'T BREATHE LONG OUT OF WATER, YOU OUGHT TO WEAR A WATCH.
He is distraught--it's understandable. And you were with him.
NN. HE WAKES UP, TELL HIM THE SHARKS FED WELL AFTER THE STORM. THEY TOLD ME.
SORRY.
You are leaving?
HE SAVED ME FROM THE AURATI. I JUST RETURNED THE FAVOR. NOTHING ELSE TO KEEP ME HERE.
HE'S AN OKAY KID. GOOD LUCK.
But--
I let him go. I could think of nothing to make him stay.
But he did not care.
I had seen it--Curry was essential to the future of the oceanscape, and King Shark would play a crucial role. He must travel with us.

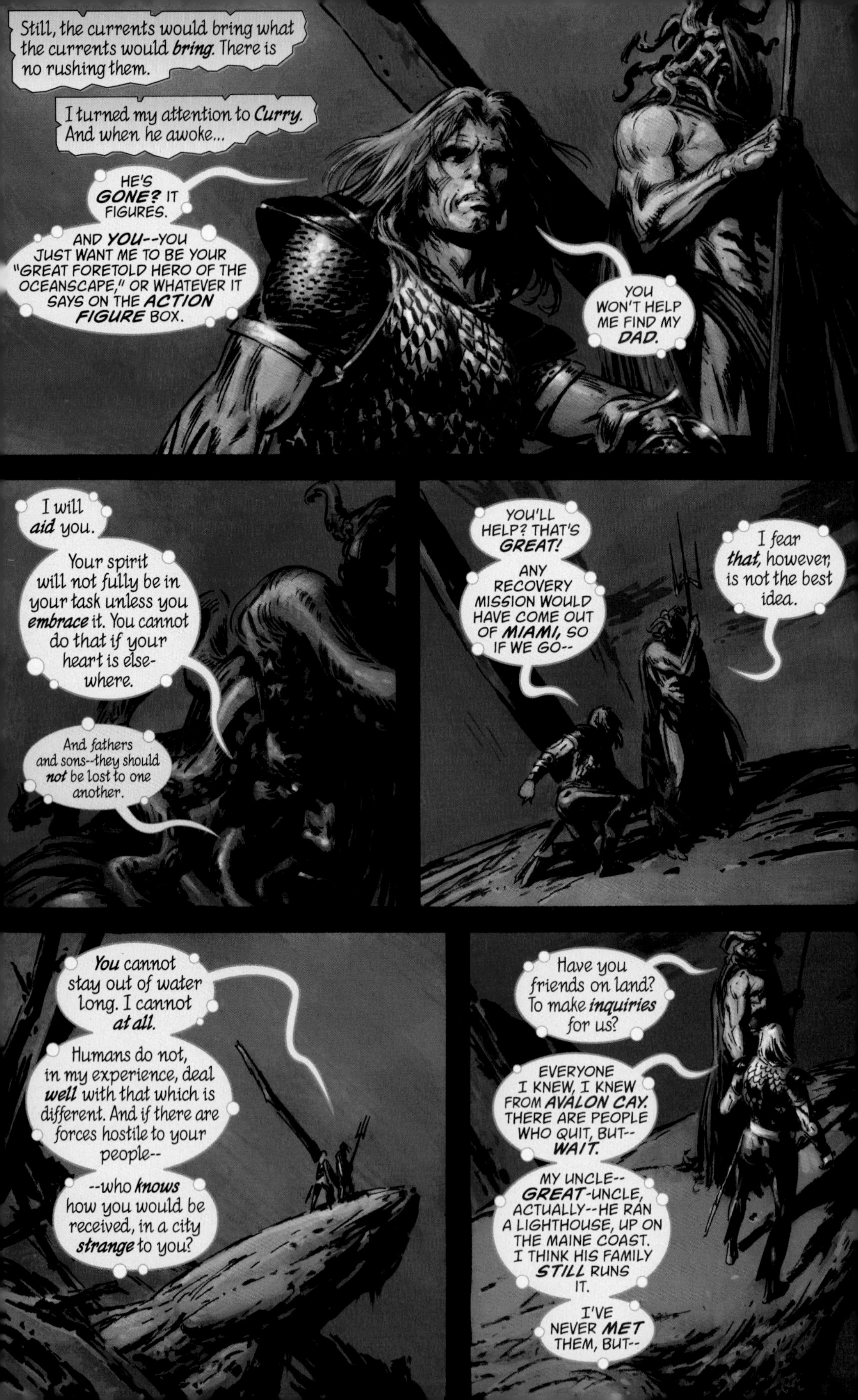
Still, the currents would bring what the currents would *bring*. There is no rushing them.
I turned my attention to *Curry*. And when he awoke...
HE'S *GONE?* IT FIGURES.
AND *YOU*--YOU JUST WANT ME TO BE YOUR "GREAT FORETOLD HERO OF THE OCEANSCAPE," OR WHATEVER IT SAYS ON THE *ACTION FIGURE* BOX.
YOU WON'T HELP ME FIND MY *DAD*.
I will *aid* you.
Your spirit will not fully be in your task unless you *embrace* it. You cannot do that if your heart is else-where.
And fathers and sons--they should *not* be lost to one another.
YOU'LL HELP? THAT'S *GREAT!*
ANY RECOVERY MISSION WOULD HAVE COME OUT OF *MIAMI*, SO IF WE GO--
I fear *that*, however, is not the best idea.
You cannot stay out of water long. I cannot *at all*.
Humans do not, in my experience, deal *well* with that which is different. And if there are forces hostile to your people--
--who *knows* how you would be received, in a city *strange* to you?
Have you friends on land? To make *inquiries* for us?
EVERYONE I KNEW, I KNEW FROM *AVALON CAY*. THERE ARE PEOPLE WHO QUIT, BUT-- *WAIT*.
MY UNCLE-- *GREAT*-UNCLE, ACTUALLY--HE RAN A LIGHTHOUSE, UP ON THE MAINE COAST. I THINK HIS FAMILY *STILL* RUNS IT.
I'VE NEVER *MET* THEM, BUT--

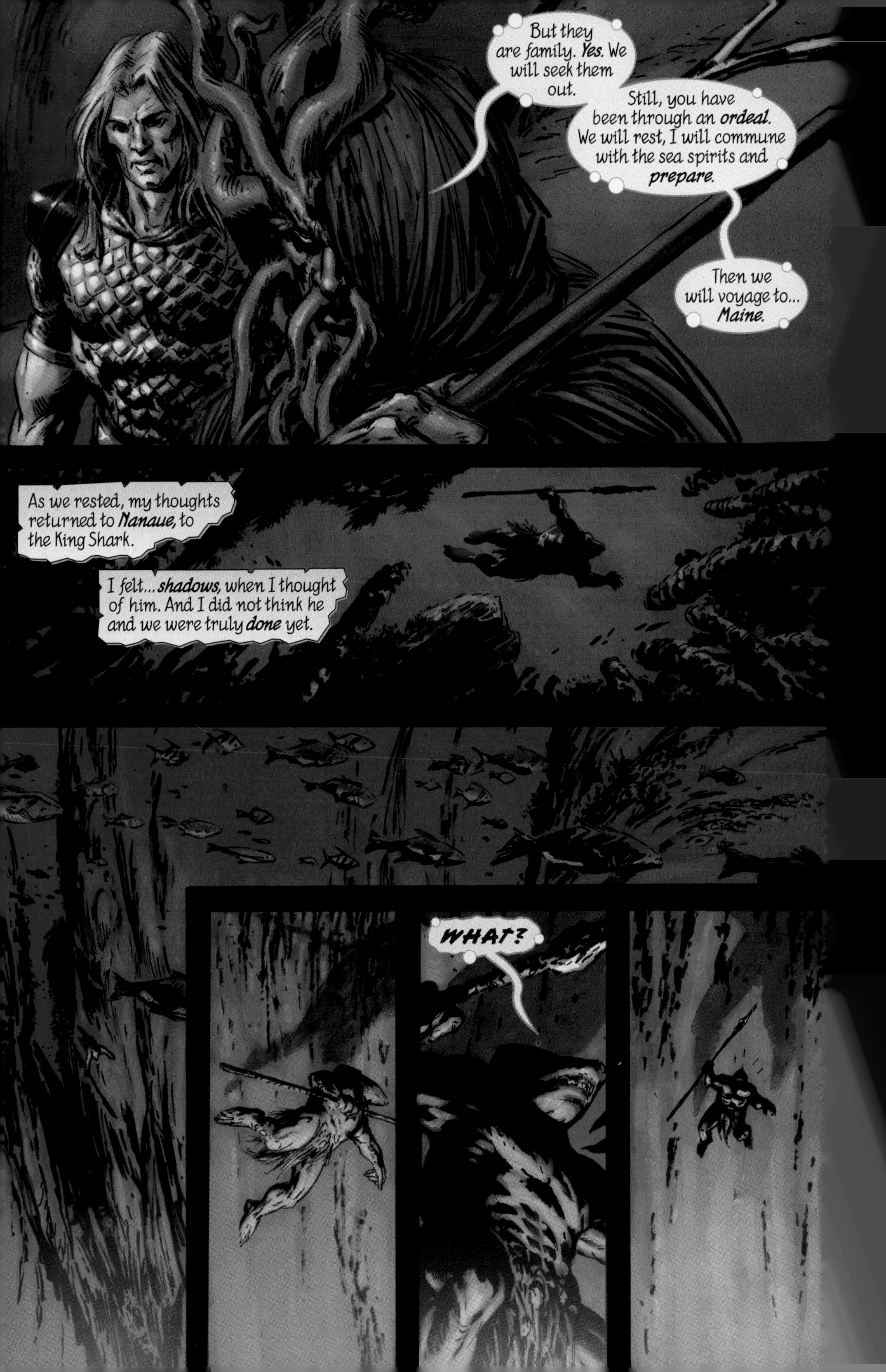

But they are family. *Yes.* We will seek them out.
Still, you have been through an *ordeal.* We will rest, I will commune with the sea spirits and *prepare.*
Then we will voyage to... *Maine.*
As we rested, my thoughts returned to *Nanaue,* to the King Shark.
I felt... *shadows,* when I thought of him. And I did not think he and we were truly *done* yet.
WHAT?

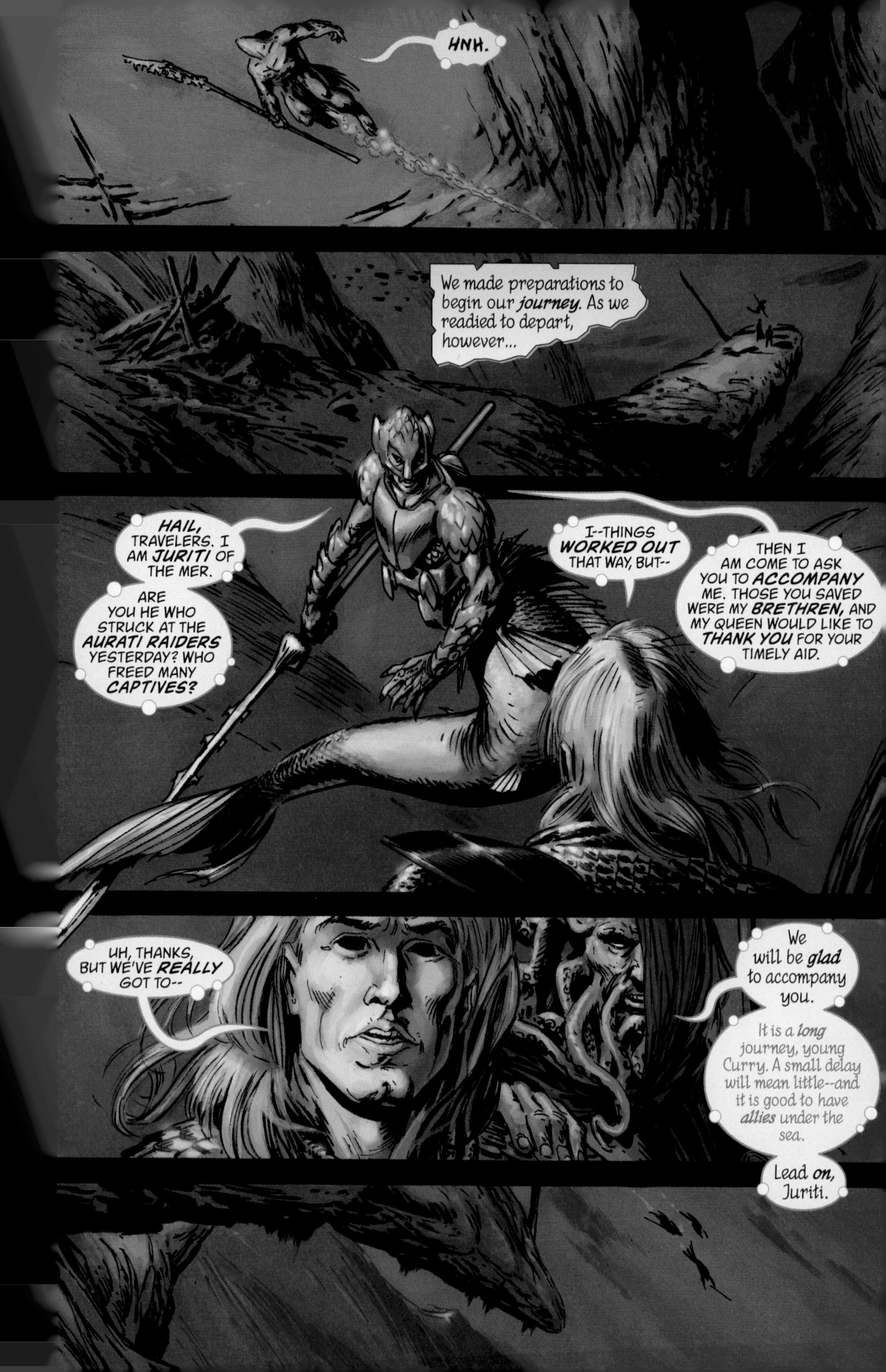
HNH.
We made preparations to begin our journey. As we readied to depart, however...
HAIL, TRAVELERS. I AM JURITI OF THE MER.
ARE YOU HE WHO STRUCK AT THE AURATI RAIDERS YESTERDAY? WHO FREED MANY CAPTIVES?
I--THINGS WORKED OUT THAT WAY, BUT--
THEN I AM COME TO ASK YOU TO ACCOMPANY ME. THOSE YOU SAVED WERE MY BRETHREN, AND MY QUEEN WOULD LIKE TO THANK YOU FOR YOUR TIMELY AID.
UH, THANKS, BUT WE'VE REALLY GOT TO--
We will be glad to accompany you.
It is a long journey, young Curry. A small delay will mean little--and it is good to have allies under the sea.
Lead on, Juriti.

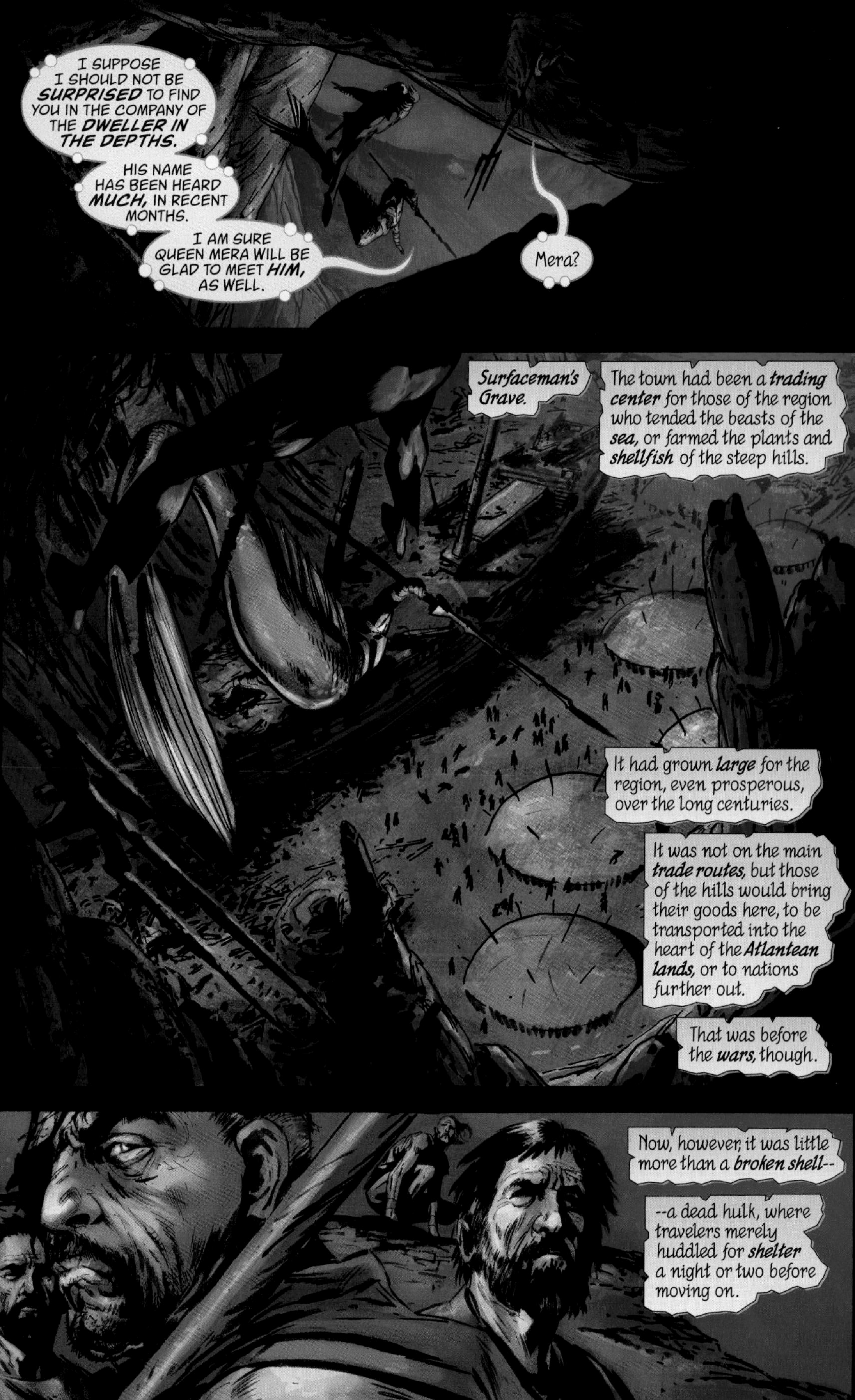
I SUPPOSE I SHOULD NOT BE SURPRISED TO FIND YOU IN THE COMPANY OF THE DWELLER IN THE DEPTHS.
HIS NAME HAS BEEN HEARD MUCH, IN RECENT MONTHS.
I AM SURE QUEEN MERA WILL BE GLAD TO MEET HIM, AS WELL.
Mera?
Surfaceman's Grave.
The town had been a trading center for those of the region who tended the beasts of the sea, or farmed the plants and shellfish of the steep hills.
It had grown large for the region, even prosperous, over the long centuries.
It was not on the main trade routes, but those of the hills would bring their goods here, to be transported into the heart of the Atlantean lands, or to nations further out.
That was before the wars, though.
Now, however, it was little more than a broken shell--
--a dead hulk, where travelers merely huddled for shelter a night or two before moving on.

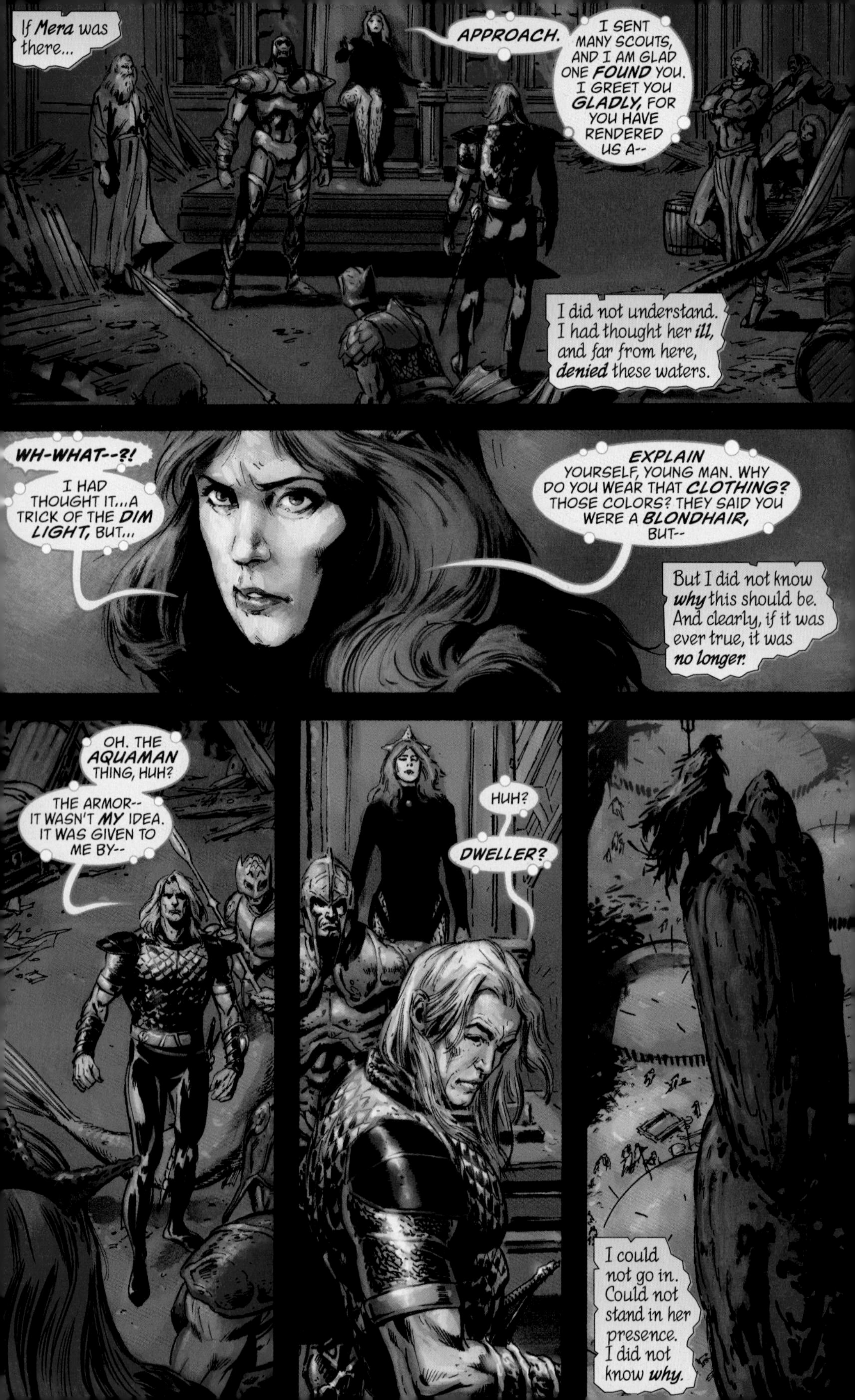
If Mera was there...
APPROACH.
I SENT MANY SCOUTS, AND I AM GLAD ONE FOUND YOU. I GREET YOU GLADLY, FOR YOU HAVE RENDERED US A--
I did not understand. I had thought her ill, and far from here, denied these waters.
WH-WHAT--?!
I HAD THOUGHT IT...A TRICK OF THE DIM LIGHT, BUT...
EXPLAIN YOURSELF, YOUNG MAN. WHY DO YOU WEAR THAT CLOTHING? THOSE COLORS? THEY SAID YOU WERE A BLONDHAIR, BUT--
But I did not know why this should be. And clearly, if it was ever true, it was no longer.
OH. THE AQUAMAN THING, HUH?
THE ARMOR-- IT WASN'T MY IDEA. IT WAS GIVEN TO ME BY--
HUH?
DWELLER?
I could not go in. Could not stand in her presence. I did not know why.

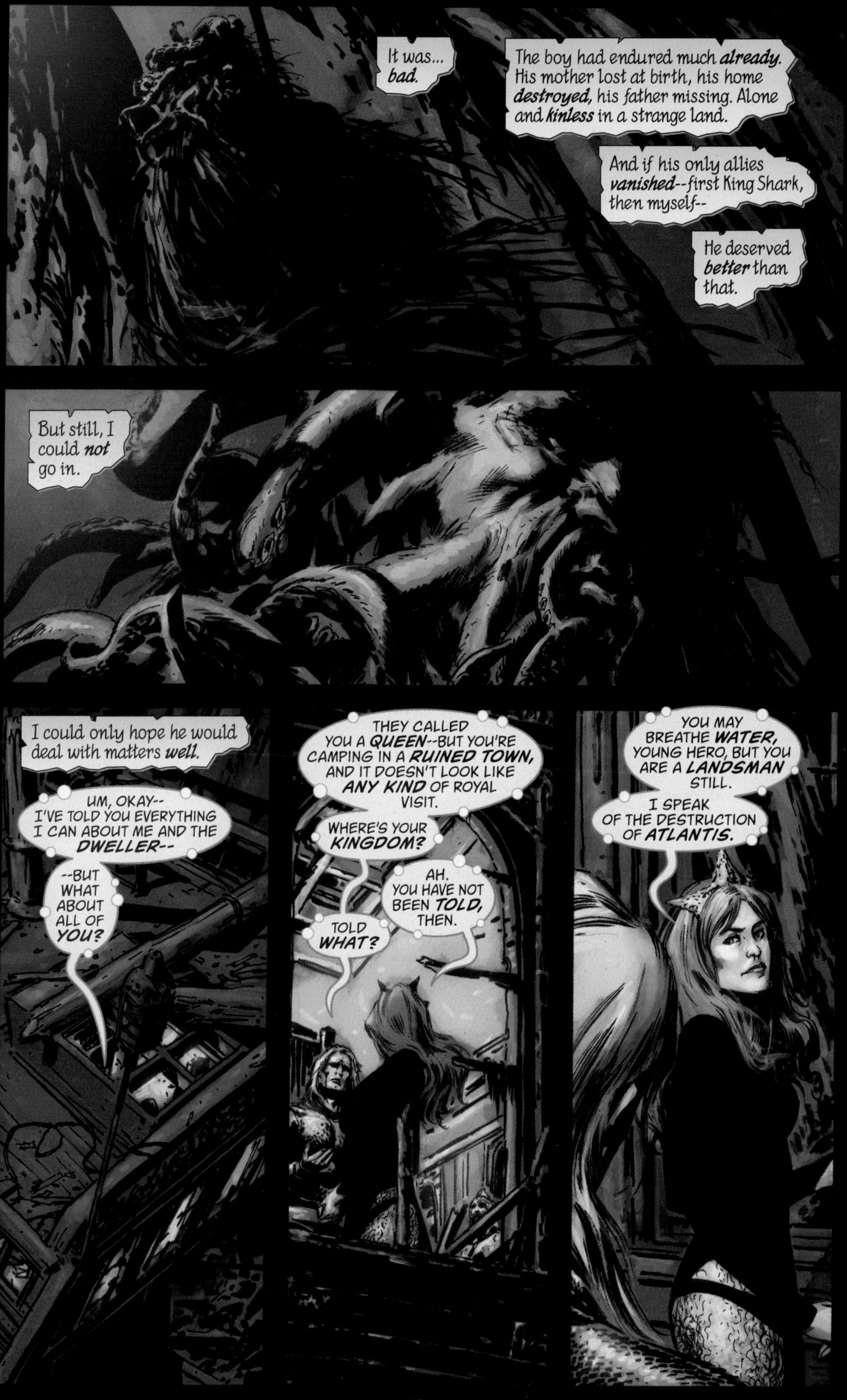
It was... bad.
The boy had endured much already. His mother lost at birth, his home destroyed, his father missing. Alone and kinless in a strange land.
And if his only allies vanished--first King Shark, then myself--
He deserved better than that.
But still, I could not go in.
I could only hope he would deal with matters well.
UM, OKAY-- I'VE TOLD YOU EVERYTHING I CAN ABOUT ME AND THE DWELLER--
--BUT WHAT ABOUT ALL OF YOU?
THEY CALLED YOU A QUEEN--BUT YOU'RE CAMPING IN A RUINED TOWN, AND IT DOESN'T LOOK LIKE ANY KIND OF ROYAL VISIT.
WHERE'S YOUR KINGDOM?
AH. YOU HAVE NOT BEEN TOLD, THEN.
TOLD WHAT?
YOU MAY BREATHE WATER, YOUNG HERO, BUT YOU ARE A LANDSMAN STILL.
I SPEAK OF THE DESTRUCTION OF ATLANTIS.

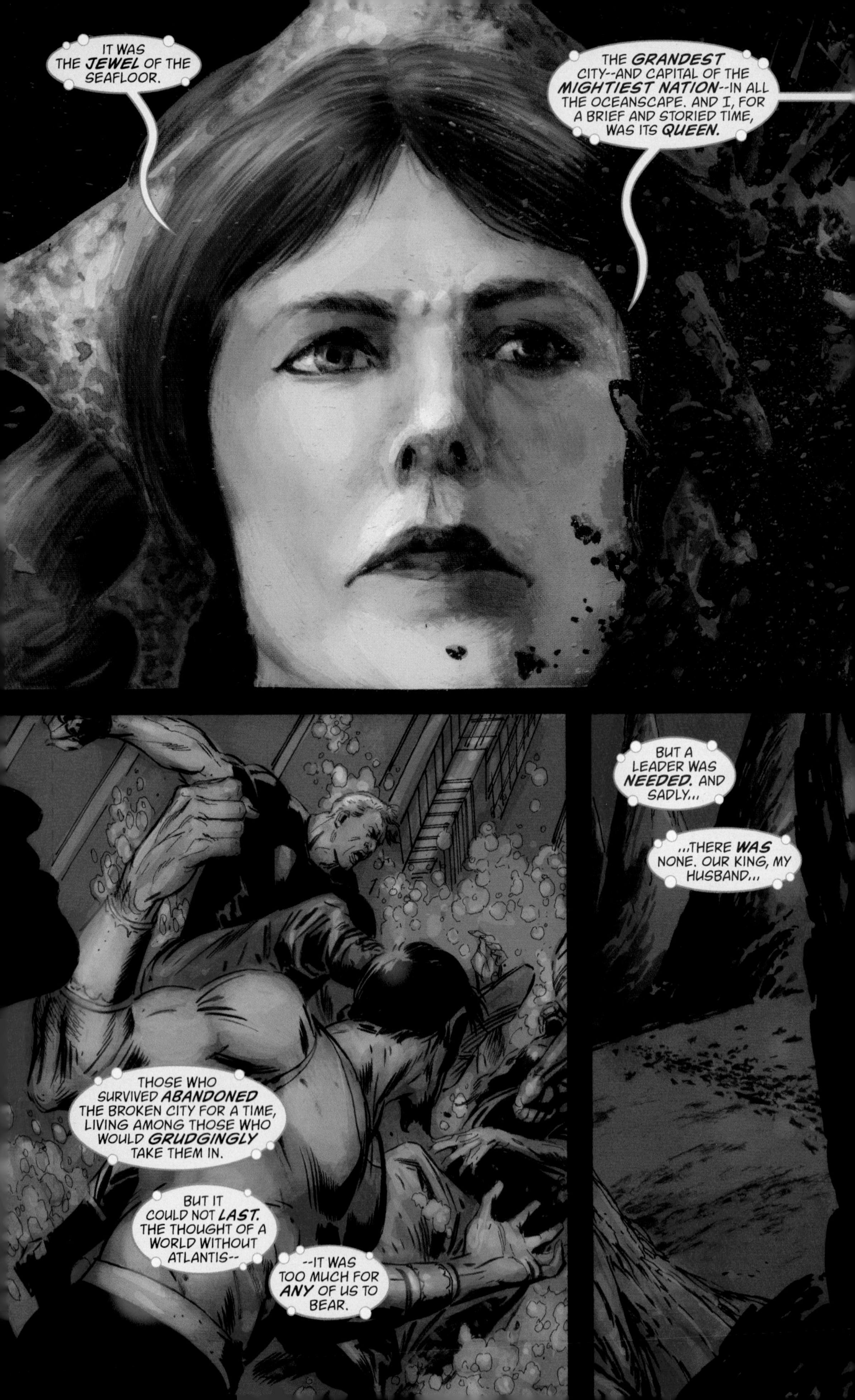
IT WAS THE JEWEL OF THE SEAFLOOR.
THE GRANDEST CITY--AND CAPITAL OF THE MIGHTIEST NATION--IN ALL THE OCEANSCAPE. AND I, FOR A BRIEF AND STORIED TIME, WAS ITS QUEEN.
THOSE WHO SURVIVED ABANDONED THE BROKEN CITY FOR A TIME, LIVING AMONG THOSE WHO WOULD GRUDGINGLY TAKE THEM IN.
BUT IT COULD NOT LAST. THE THOUGHT OF A WORLD WITHOUT ATLANTIS--
--IT WAS TOO MUCH FOR ANY OF US TO BEAR.
BUT A LEADER WAS NEEDED. AND SADLY...
...THERE WAS NONE. OUR KING, MY HUSBAND...

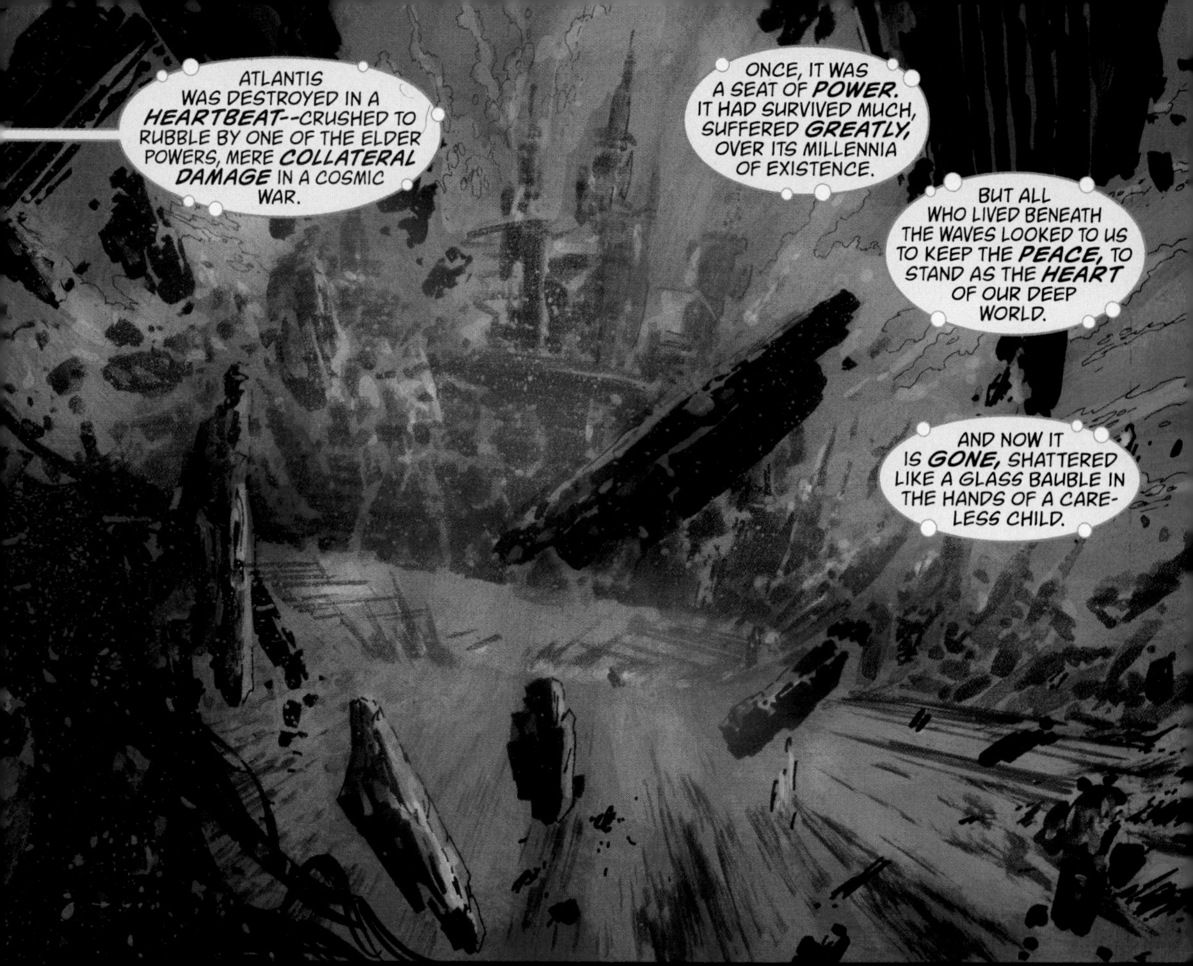
ATLANTIS WAS DESTROYED IN A HEARTBEAT--CRUSHED TO RUBBLE BY ONE OF THE ELDER POWERS, MERE COLLATERAL DAMAGE IN A COSMIC WAR.
ONCE, IT WAS A SEAT OF POWER. IT HAD SURVIVED MUCH, SUFFERED GREATLY, OVER ITS MILLENNIA OF EXISTENCE.
BUT ALL WHO LIVED BENEATH THE WAVES LOOKED TO US TO KEEP THE PEACE, TO STAND AS THE HEART OF OUR DEEP WORLD.
AND NOW IT IS GONE, SHATTERED LIKE A GLASS BAUBLE IN THE HANDS OF A CARELESS CHILD.
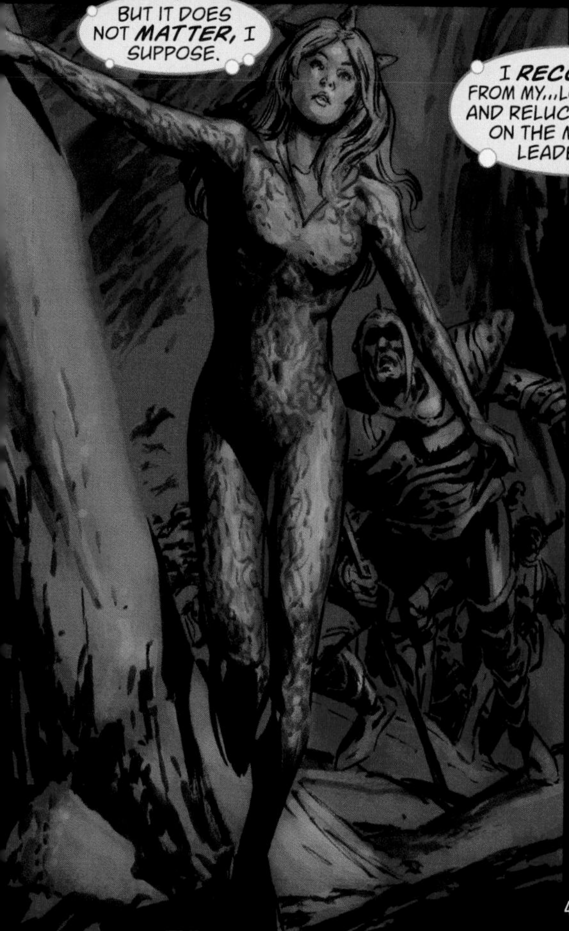
BUT IT DOES NOT MATTER, I SUPPOSE.
I RECOVERED FROM MY...LONG ILLNESS, AND RELUCTANTLY TOOK ON THE MANTLE OF LEADERSHIP.
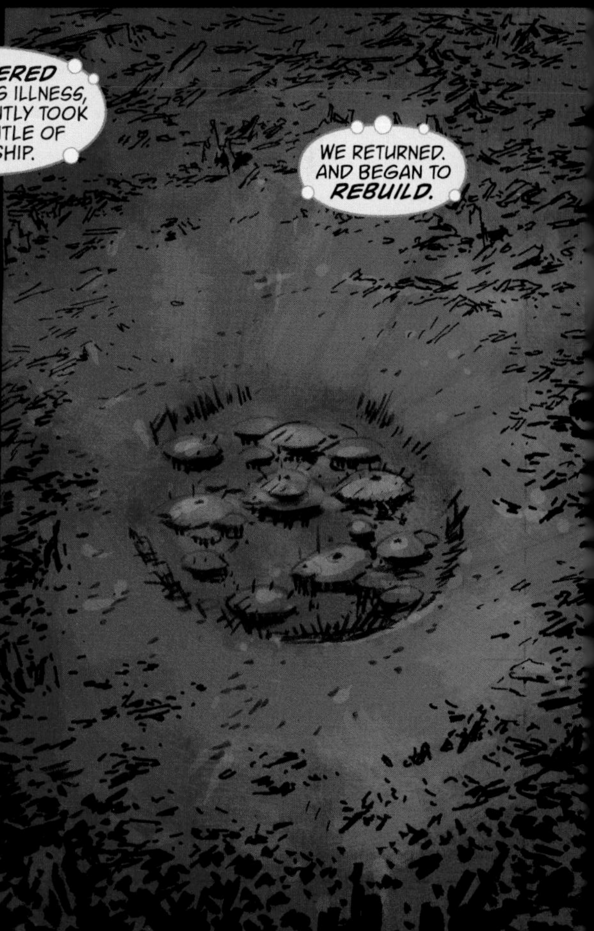
WE RETURNED. AND BEGAN TO REBUILD.

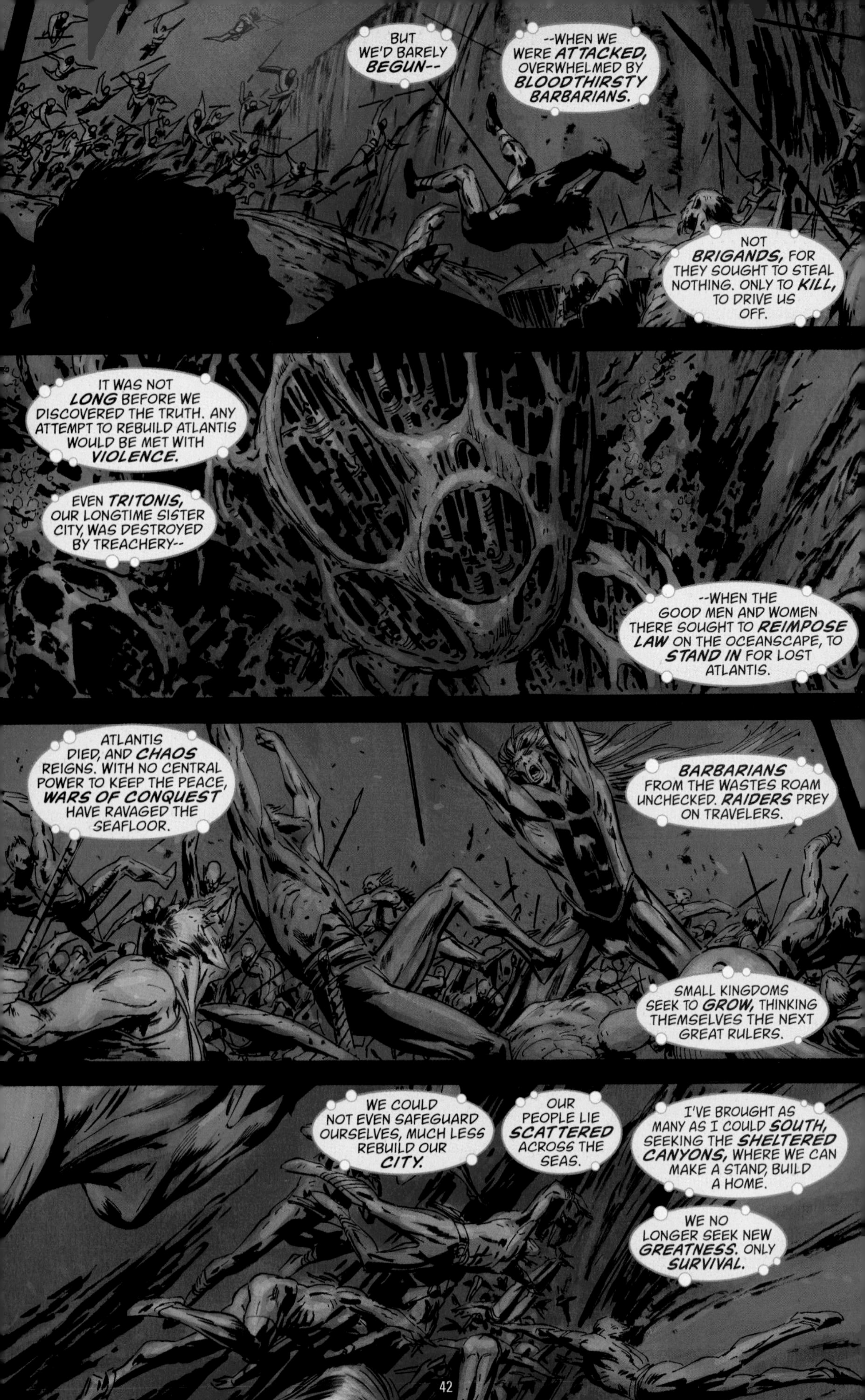
BUT WE'D BARELY BEGUN--
--WHEN WE WERE ATTACKED, OVERWHELMED BY BLOODTHIRSTY BARBARIANS.
NOT BRIGANDS, FOR THEY SOUGHT TO STEAL NOTHING. ONLY TO KILL, TO DRIVE US OFF.
IT WAS NOT LONG BEFORE WE DISCOVERED THE TRUTH. ANY ATTEMPT TO REBUILD ATLANTIS WOULD BE MET WITH VIOLENCE.
EVEN TRITONIS, OUR LONGTIME SISTER CITY, WAS DESTROYED BY TREACHERY--
--WHEN THE GOOD MEN AND WOMEN THERE SOUGHT TO REIMPOSE LAW ON THE OCEANSCAPE, TO STAND IN FOR LOST ATLANTIS.
ATLANTIS DIED, AND CHAOS REIGNS. WITH NO CENTRAL POWER TO KEEP THE PEACE, WARS OF CONQUEST HAVE RAVAGED THE SEAFLOOR.
BARBARIANS FROM THE WASTES ROAM UNCHECKED. RAIDERS PREY ON TRAVELERS.
SMALL KINGDOMS SEEK TO GROW, THINKING THEMSELVES THE NEXT GREAT RULERS.
WE COULD NOT EVEN SAFEGUARD OURSELVES, MUCH LESS REBUILD OUR CITY.
OUR PEOPLE LIE SCATTERED ACROSS THE SEAS.
I'VE BROUGHT AS MANY AS I COULD SOUTH, SEEKING THE SHELTERED CANYONS, WHERE WE CAN MAKE A STAND, BUILD A HOME.
WE NO LONGER SEEK NEW GREATNESS. ONLY SURVIVAL.

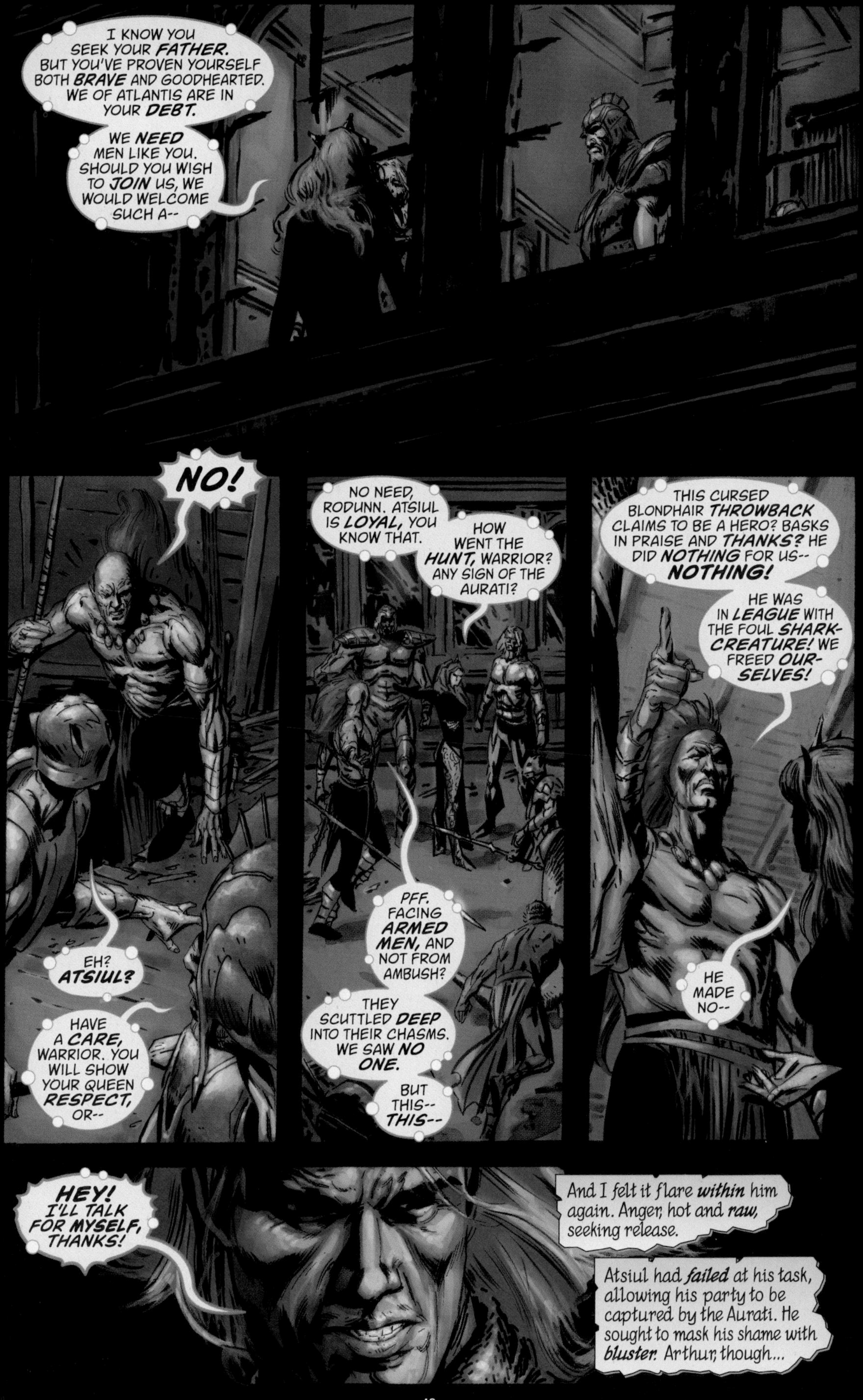
I KNOW YOU SEEK YOUR FATHER. BUT YOU'VE PROVEN YOURSELF BOTH BRAVE AND GOODHEARTED. WE OF ATLANTIS ARE IN YOUR DEBT.
WE NEED MEN LIKE YOU. SHOULD YOU WISH TO JOIN US, WE WOULD WELCOME SUCH A--
NO!
EH? ATSIUL?
HAVE A CARE, WARRIOR. YOU WILL SHOW YOUR QUEEN RESPECT, OR--
NO NEED, RODUNN. ATSIUL IS LOYAL, YOU KNOW THAT.
HOW WENT THE HUNT, WARRIOR? ANY SIGN OF THE AURATI?
PFF. FACING ARMED MEN, AND NOT FROM AMBUSH?
THEY SCUTTLED DEEP INTO THEIR CHASMS. WE SAW NO ONE.
BUT THIS-- THIS--
THIS CURSED BLONDHAIR THROWBACK CLAIMS TO BE A HERO? BASKS IN PRAISE AND THANKS? HE DID NOTHING FOR US-- NOTHING!
HE WAS IN LEAGUE WITH THE FOUL SHARK-CREATURE! WE FREED OURSELVES!
HE MADE NO--
HEY! I'LL TALK FOR MYSELF, THANKS!
And I felt it flare within him again. Anger, hot and raw, seeking release.
Atsiul had failed at his task, allowing his party to be captured by the Aurati. He sought to mask his shame with bluster. Arthur, though...

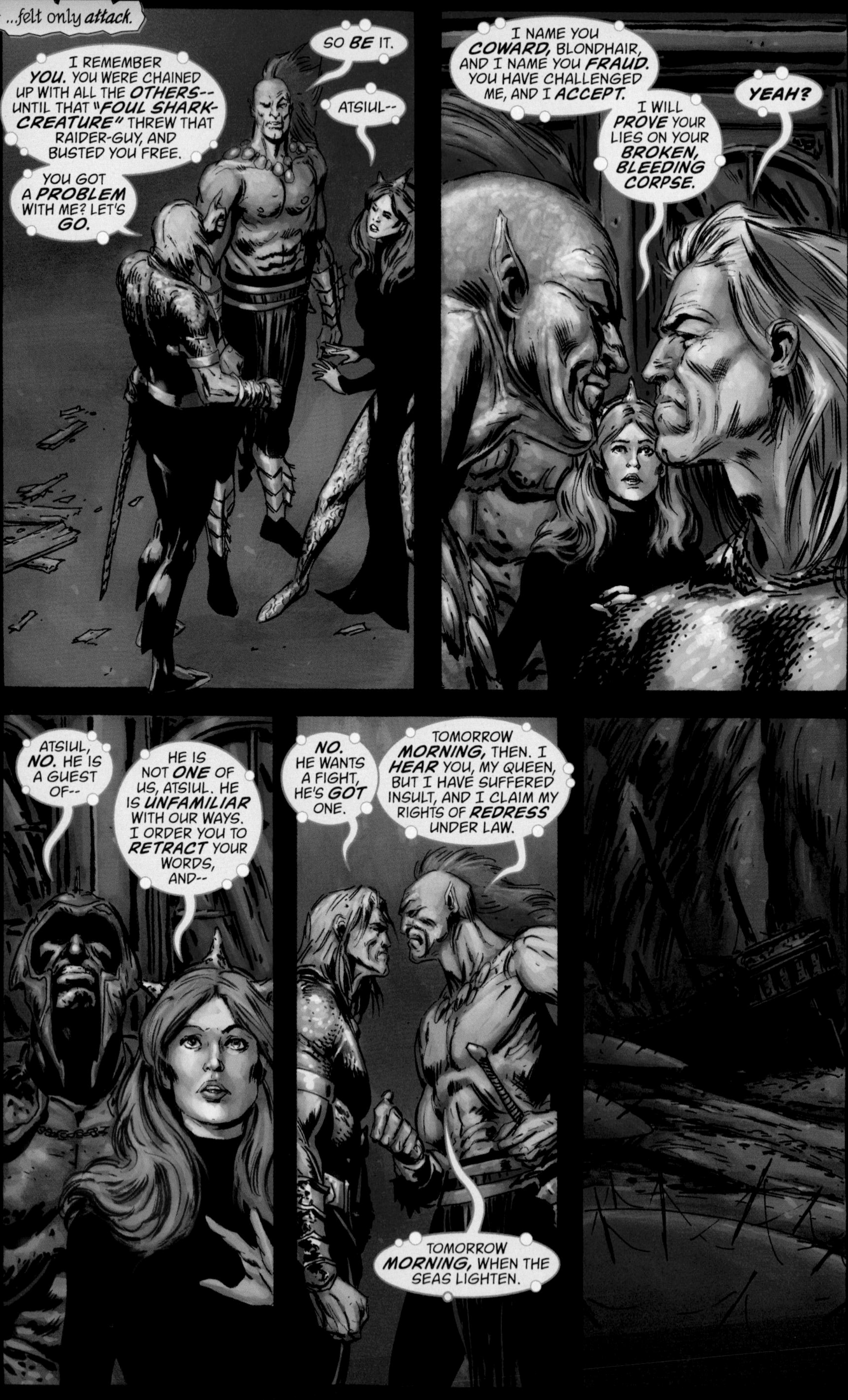
...felt only attack.
I REMEMBER YOU. YOU WERE CHAINED UP WITH ALL THE OTHERS-- UNTIL THAT "FOUL SHARK-CREATURE" THREW THAT RAIDER-GUY, AND BUSTED YOU FREE.
YOU GOT A PROBLEM WITH ME? LET'S GO.
SO BE IT.
ATSIUL--
I NAME YOU COWARD, BLONDHAIR, AND I NAME YOU FRAUD. YOU HAVE CHALLENGED ME, AND I ACCEPT.
I WILL PROVE YOUR LIES ON YOUR BROKEN, BLEEDING CORPSE.
YEAH?
ATSIUL, NO. HE IS A GUEST OF--
HE IS NOT ONE OF US, ATSIUL. HE IS UNFAMILIAR WITH OUR WAYS. I ORDER YOU TO RETRACT YOUR WORDS, AND--
NO. HE WANTS A FIGHT, HE'S GOT ONE.
TOMORROW MORNING, THEN. I HEAR YOU, MY QUEEN, BUT I HAVE SUFFERED INSULT, AND I CLAIM MY RIGHTS OF REDRESS UNDER LAW.
TOMORROW MORNING, WHEN THE SEAS LIGHTEN.

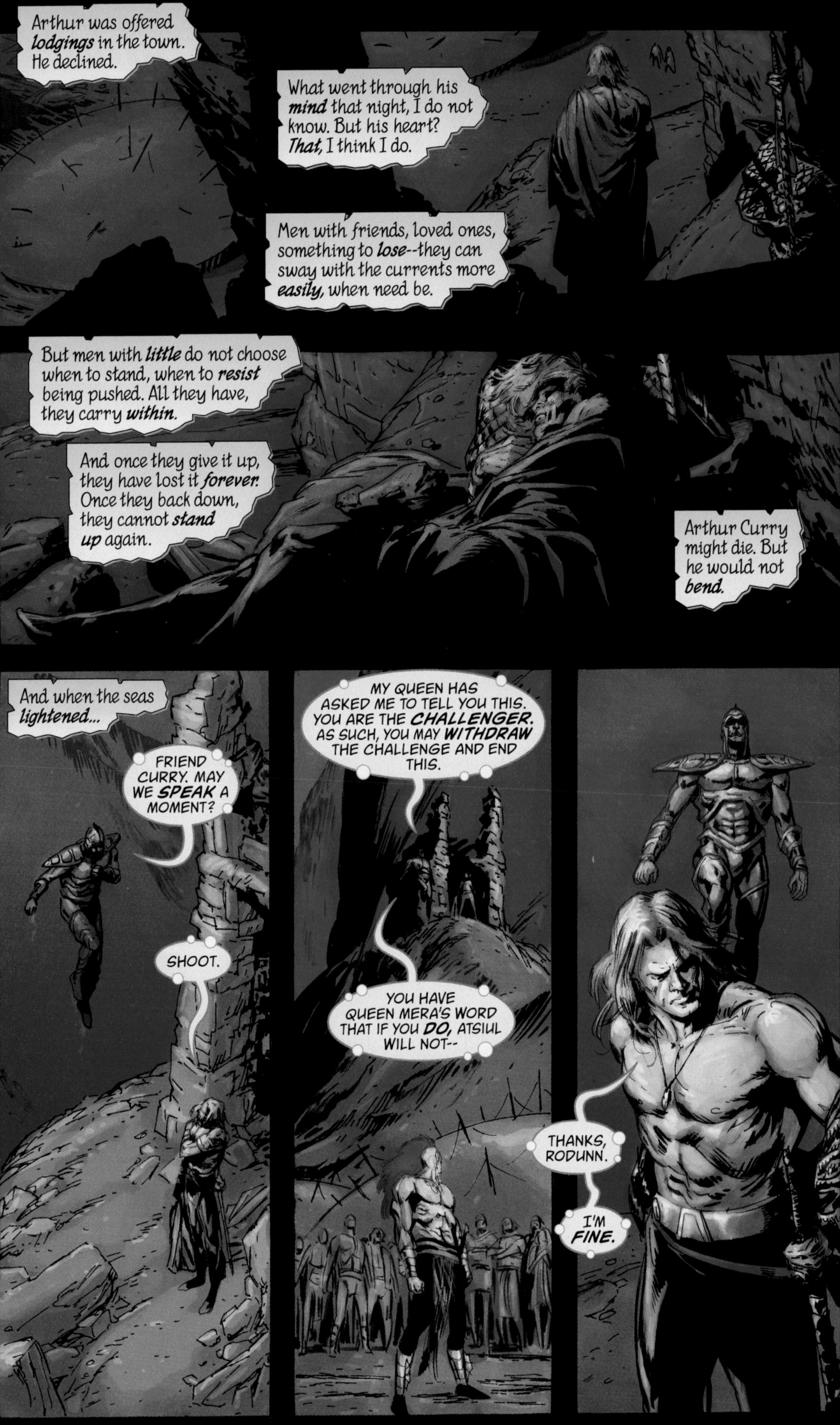
Arthur was offered lodgings in the town. He declined.
What went through his mind that night, I do not know. But his heart? That, I think I do.
Men with friends, loved ones, something to lose--they can sway with the currents more easily, when need be.
But men with little do not choose when to stand, when to resist being pushed. All they have, they carry within.
And once they give it up, they have lost it forever. Once they back down, they cannot stand up again.
Arthur Curry might die. But he would not bend.
And when the seas lightened...
FRIEND CURRY. MAY WE SPEAK A MOMENT?
SHOOT.
MY QUEEN HAS ASKED ME TO TELL YOU THIS. YOU ARE THE CHALLENGER. AS SUCH, YOU MAY WITHDRAW THE CHALLENGE AND END THIS.
YOU HAVE QUEEN MERA'S WORD THAT IF YOU DO, ATSIUL WILL NOT--
THANKS, RODUNN.
I'M FINE.

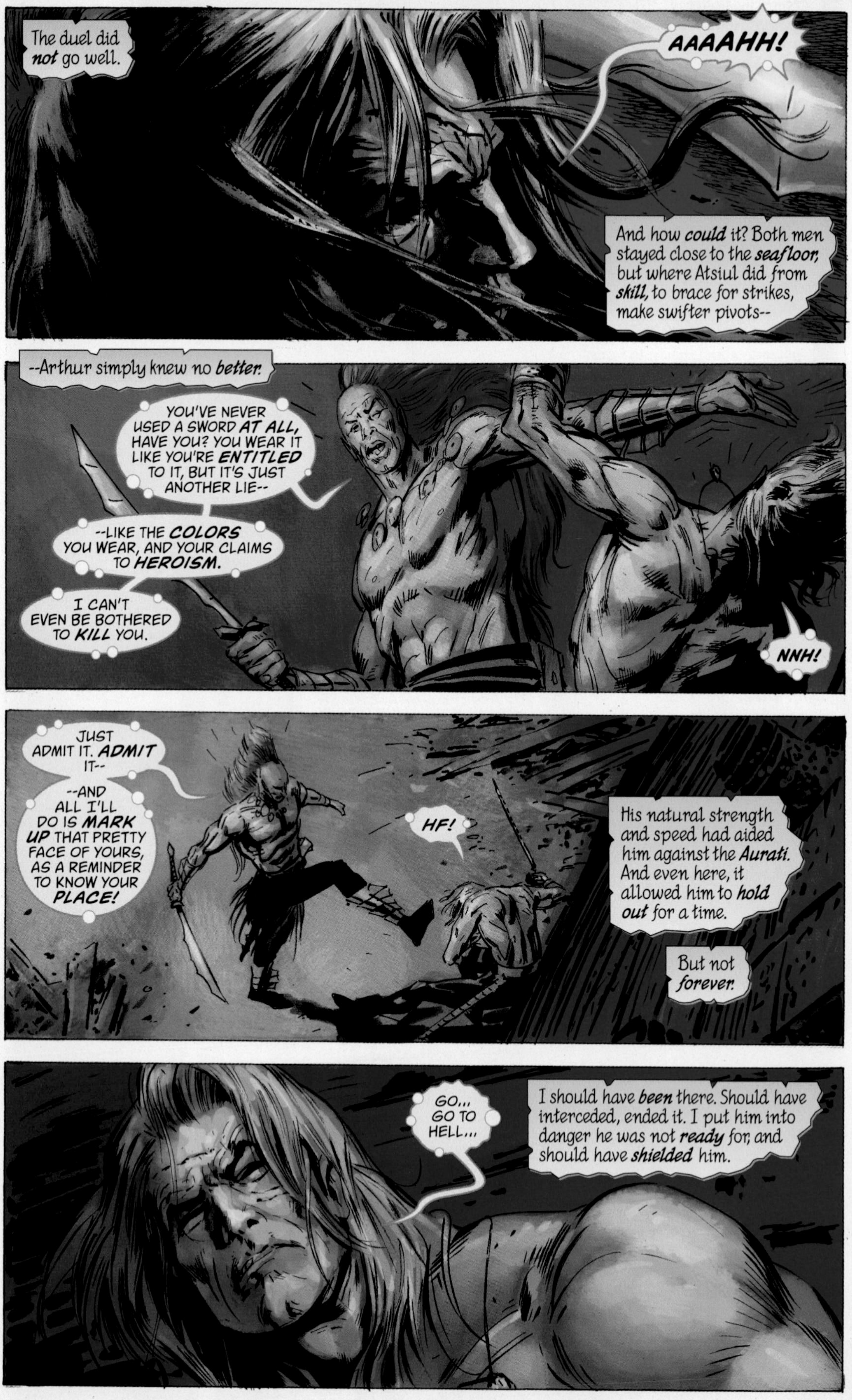
The duel did not go well.
AAAAHH!
And how could it? Both men stayed close to the seafloor, but where Atsiul did from skill, to brace for strikes, make swifter pivots--
--Arthur simply knew no better.
YOU'VE NEVER USED A SWORD AT ALL, HAVE YOU? YOU WEAR IT LIKE YOU'RE ENTITLED TO IT, BUT IT'S JUST ANOTHER LIE--
--LIKE THE COLORS YOU WEAR, AND YOUR CLAIMS TO HEROISM.
I CAN'T EVEN BE BOTHERED TO KILL YOU.
NNH!
JUST ADMIT IT. ADMIT IT--
--AND ALL I'LL DO IS MARK UP THAT PRETTY FACE OF YOURS, AS A REMINDER TO KNOW YOUR PLACE!
HF!
His natural strength and speed had aided him against the Aurati. And even here, it allowed him to hold out for a time.
But not forever.
GO... GO TO HELL...
I should have been there. Should have interceded, ended it. I put him into danger he was not ready for, and should have shielded him.

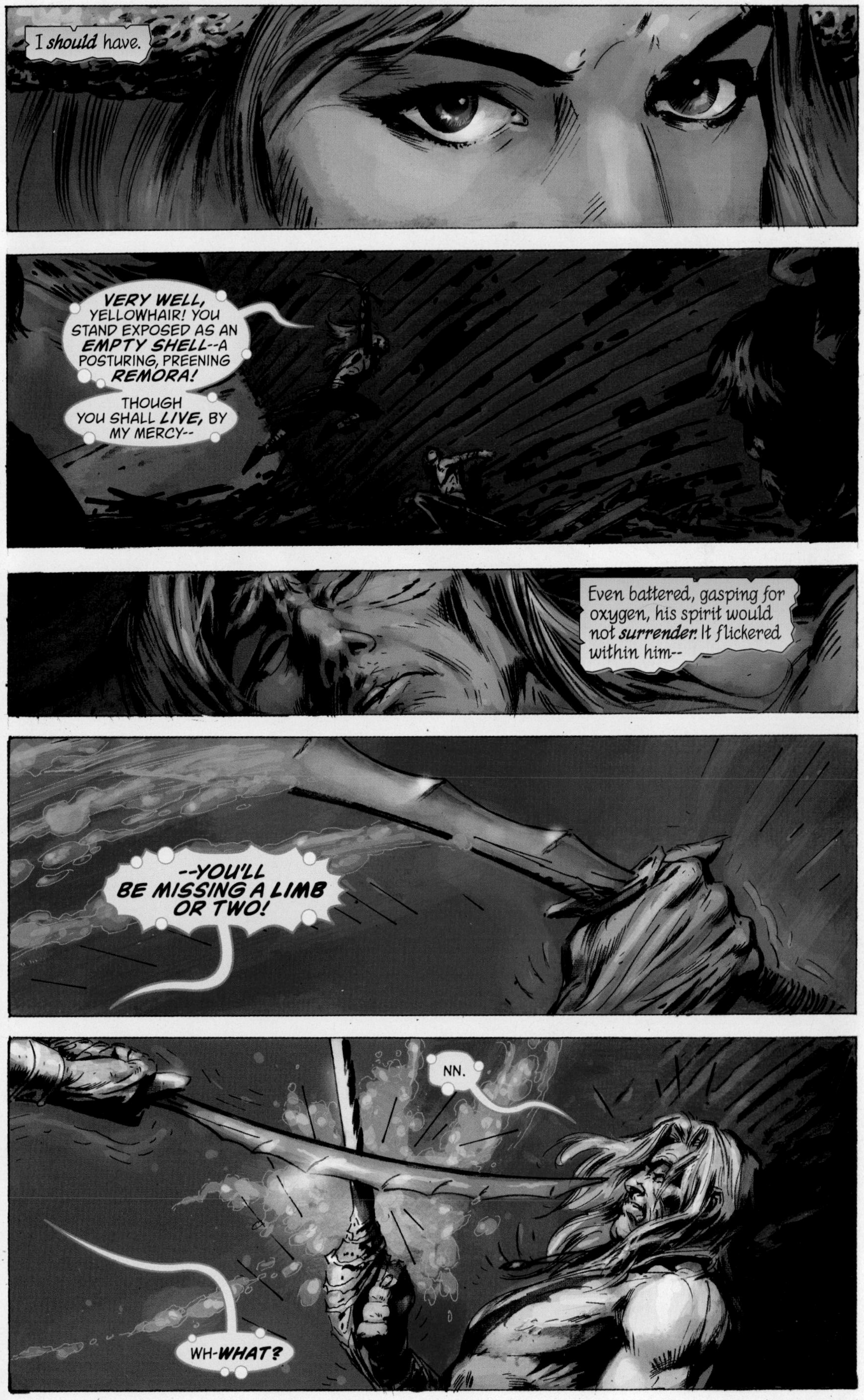
I should have.
VERY WELL, YELLOWHAIR! YOU STAND EXPOSED AS AN EMPTY SHELL--A POSTURING, PREENING REMORA!
THOUGH YOU SHALL LIVE, BY MY MERCY--
Even battered, gasping for oxygen, his spirit would not surrender. It flickered within him--
--YOU'LL BE MISSING A LIMB OR TWO!
NN.
WH-WHAT?

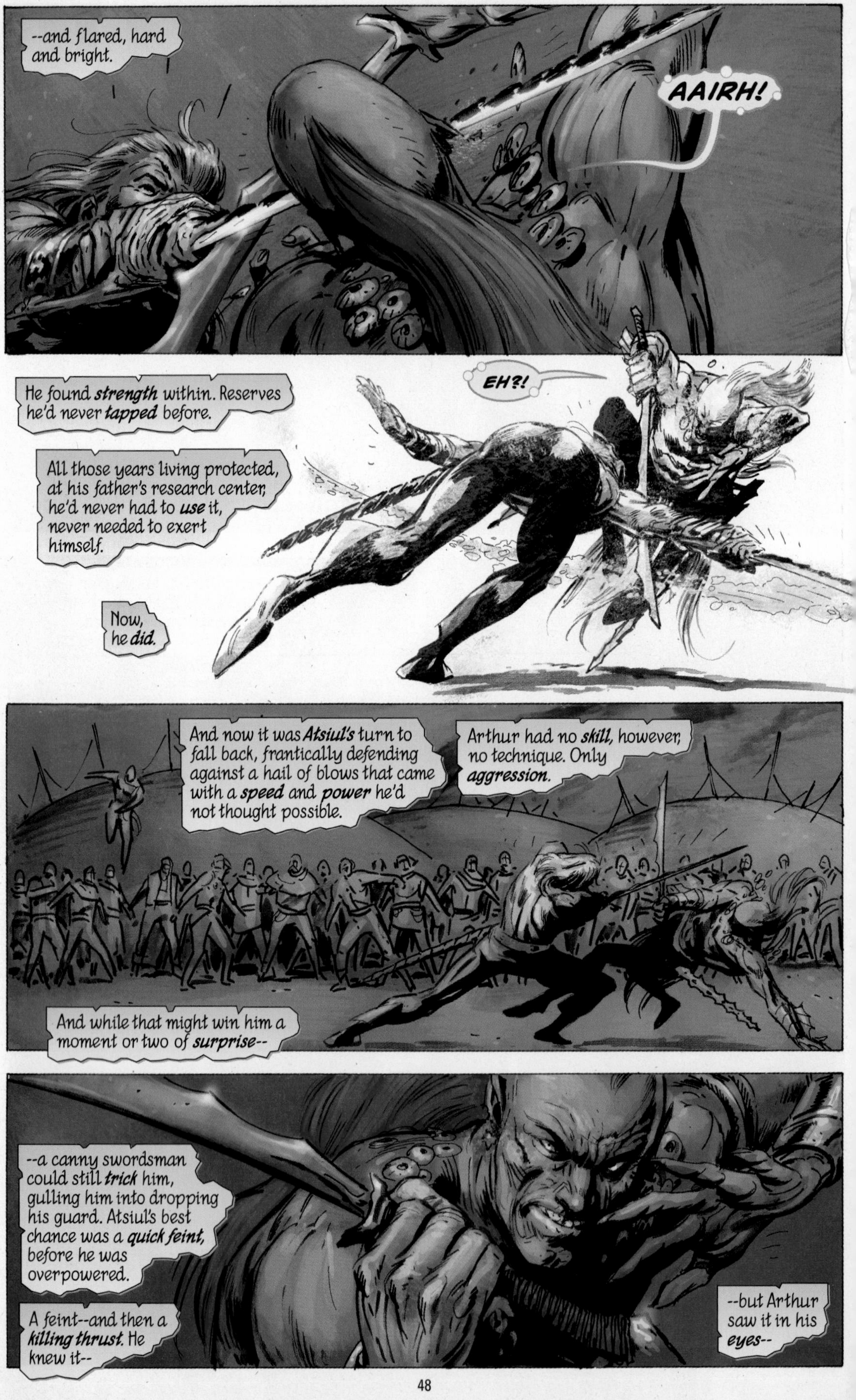
--and flared, hard and bright.
AAIRH!
He found strength within. Reserves he'd never tapped before.
EH?!
All those years living protected, at his father's research center, he'd never had to use it, never needed to exert himself.
Now, he did.
And now it was Atsiul's turn to fall back, frantically defending against a hail of blows that came with a speed and power he'd not thought possible.
Arthur had no skill, however, no technique. Only aggression.
And while that might win him a moment or two of surprise--
--a canny swordsman could still trick him, gulling him into dropping his guard. Atsiul's best chance was a quick feint, before he was overpowered.
A feint--and then a killing thrust. He knew it--
--but Arthur saw it in his eyes--

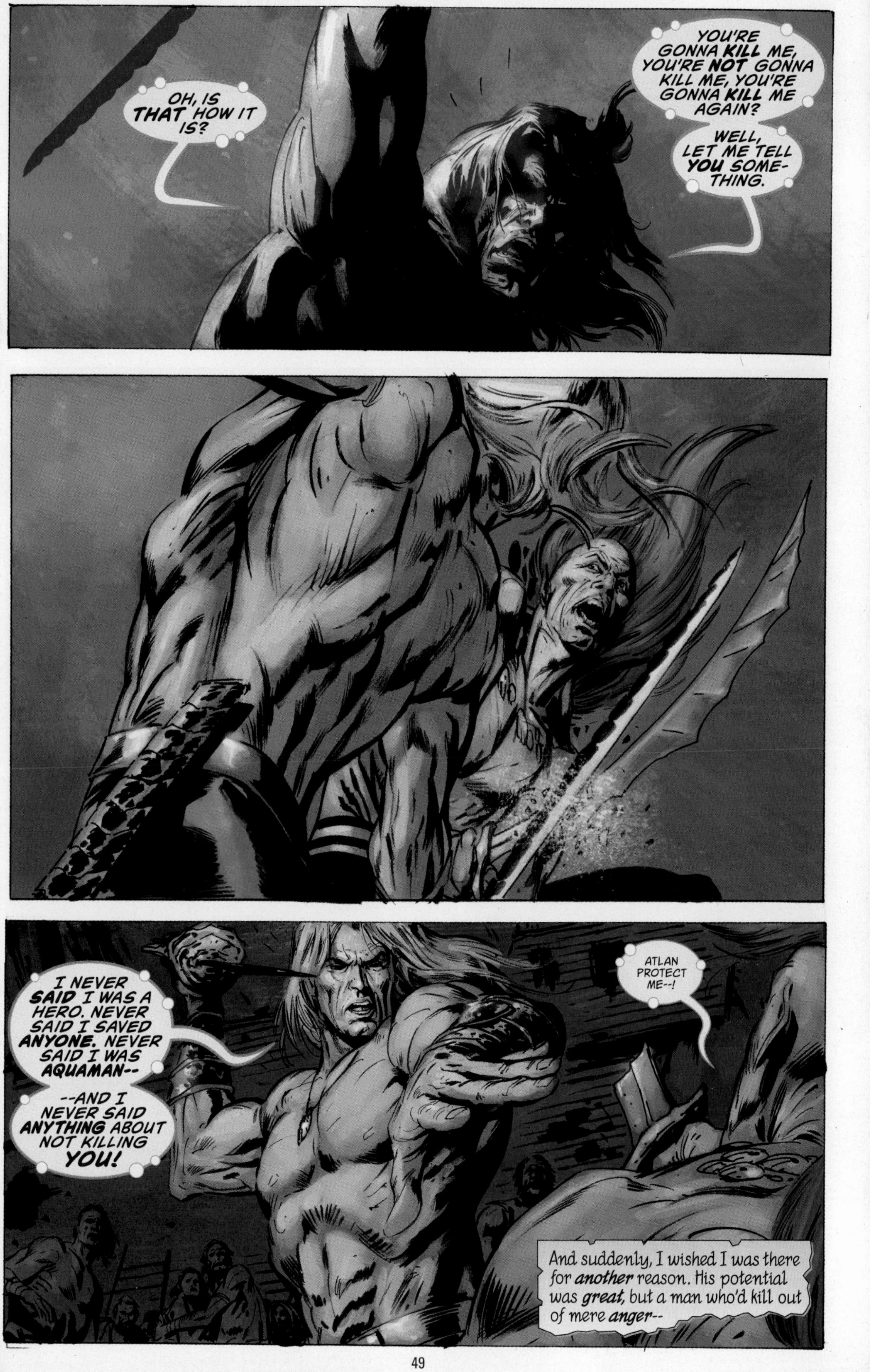
OH, IS THAT HOW IT IS?
YOU'RE GONNA KILL ME, YOU'RE NOT GONNA KILL ME, YOU'RE GONNA KILL ME AGAIN?
WELL, LET ME TELL YOU SOMETHING.
I NEVER SAID I WAS A HERO. NEVER SAID I SAVED ANYONE. NEVER SAID I WAS AQUAMAN--
--AND I NEVER SAID ANYTHING ABOUT NOT KILLING YOU!
ATLAN PROTECT ME--!
And suddenly, I wished I was there for another reason. His potential was great, but a man who'd kill out of mere anger--

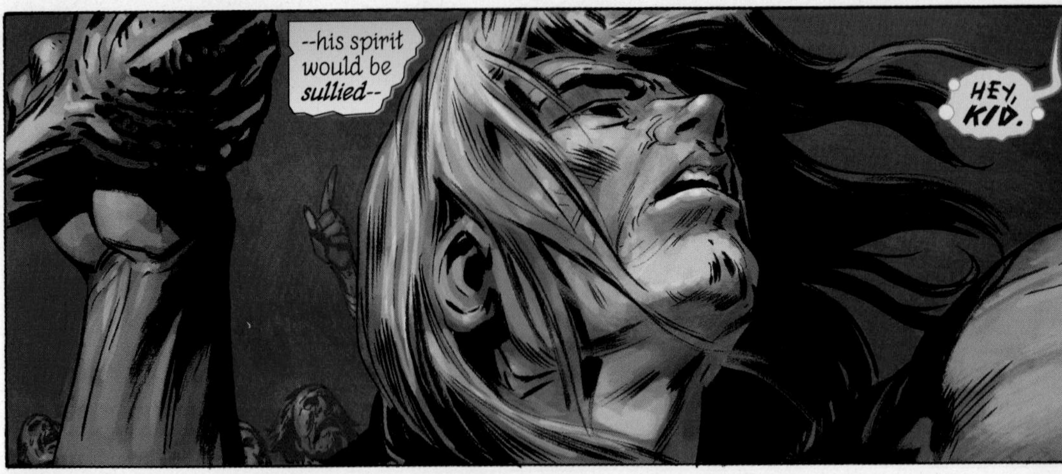
--his spirit would be *sullied*--
HEY, **KID.**

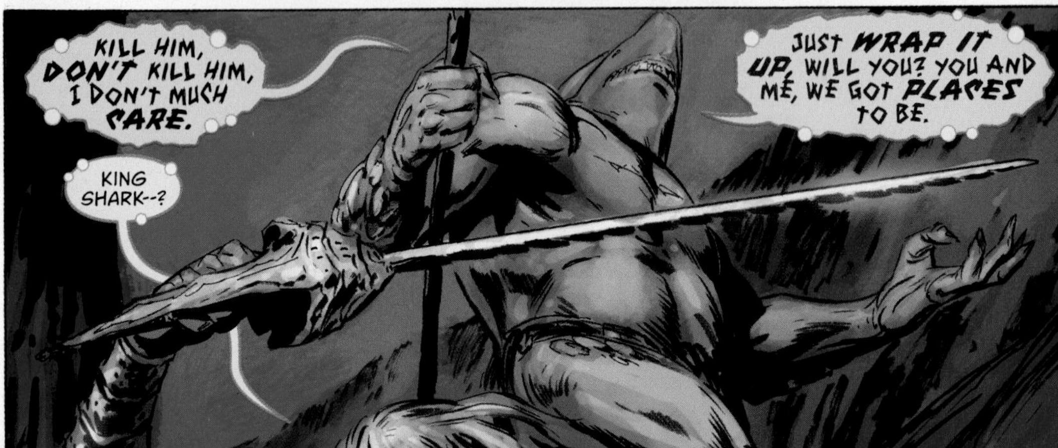
KILL HIM, **DON'T** KILL HIM, I DON'T MUCH **CARE.**
JUST **WRAP IT UP,** WILL YOU? YOU AND ME, WE GOT **PLACES** TO BE.
KING SHARK--?

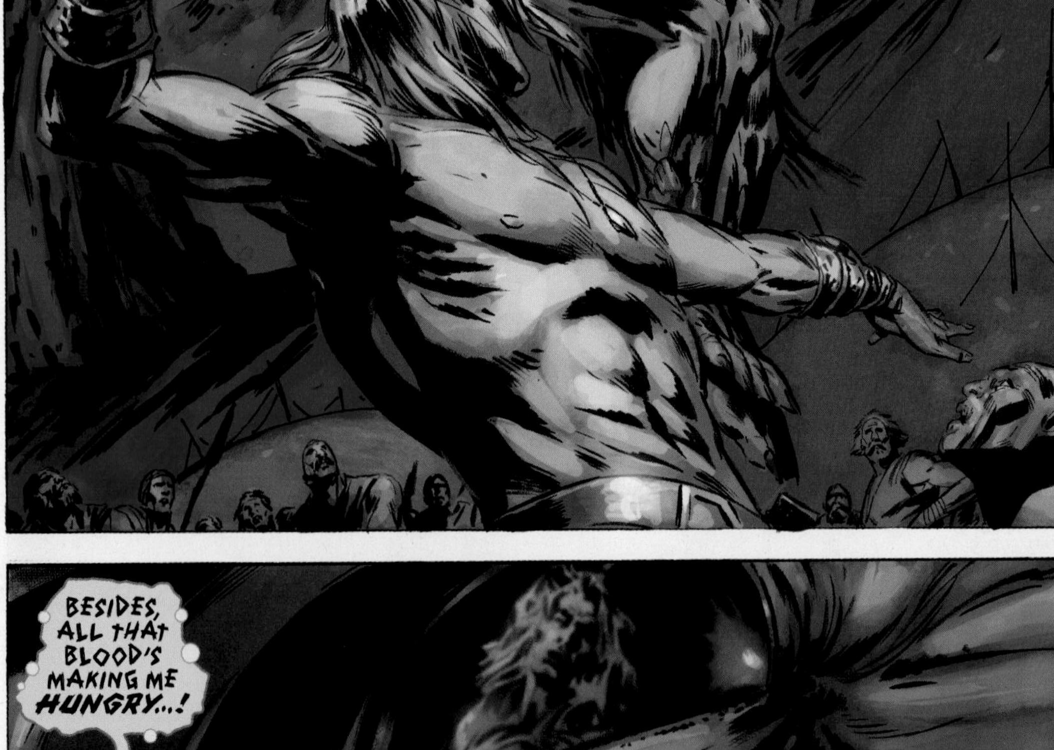
BESIDES, ALL THAT BLOOD'S MAKING ME **HUNGRY...!**

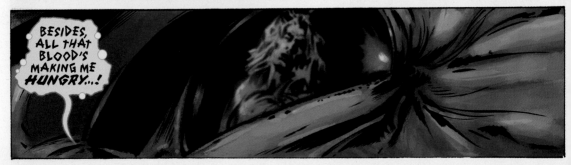

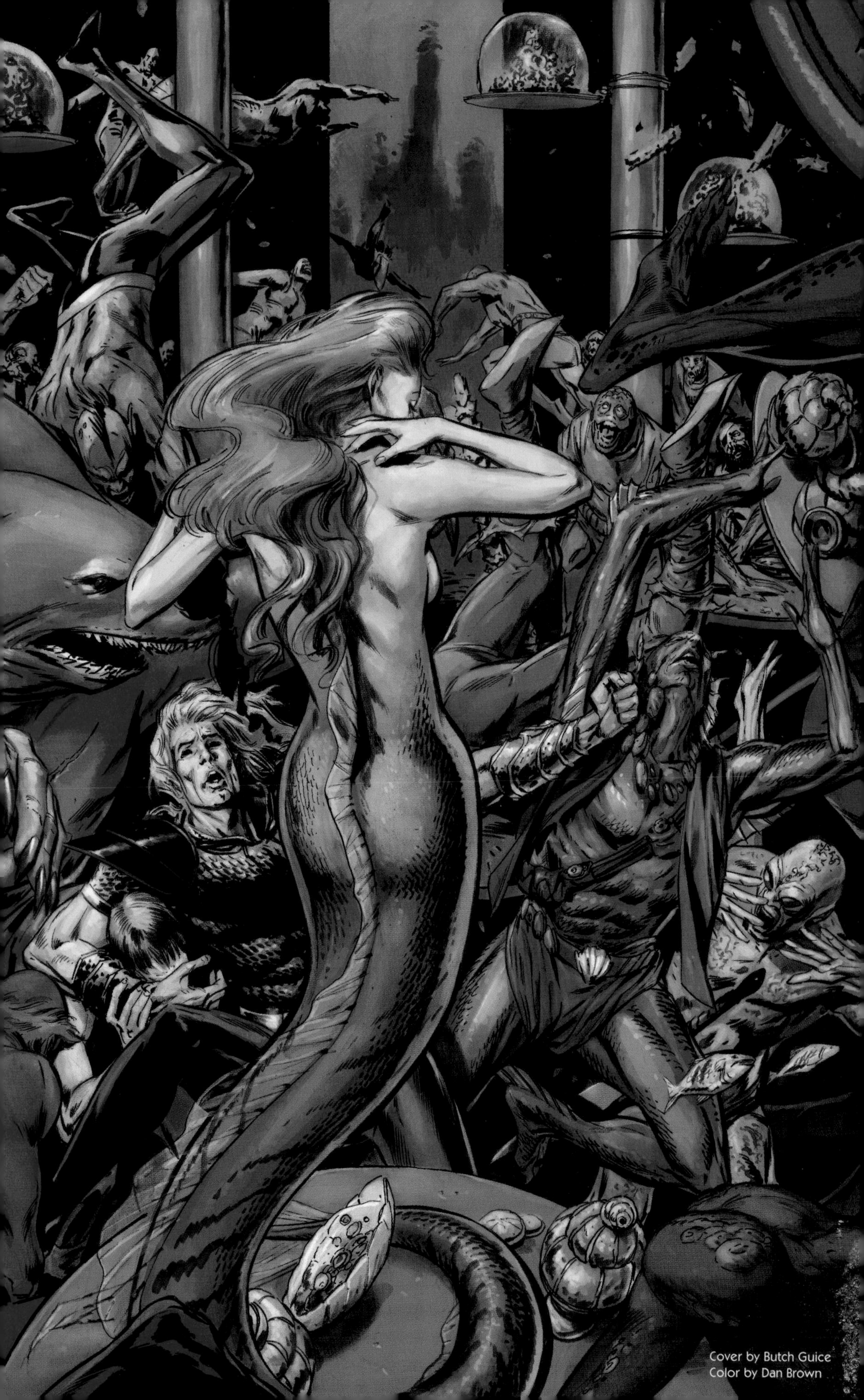
Cover by Butch Guice
Color by Dan Brown

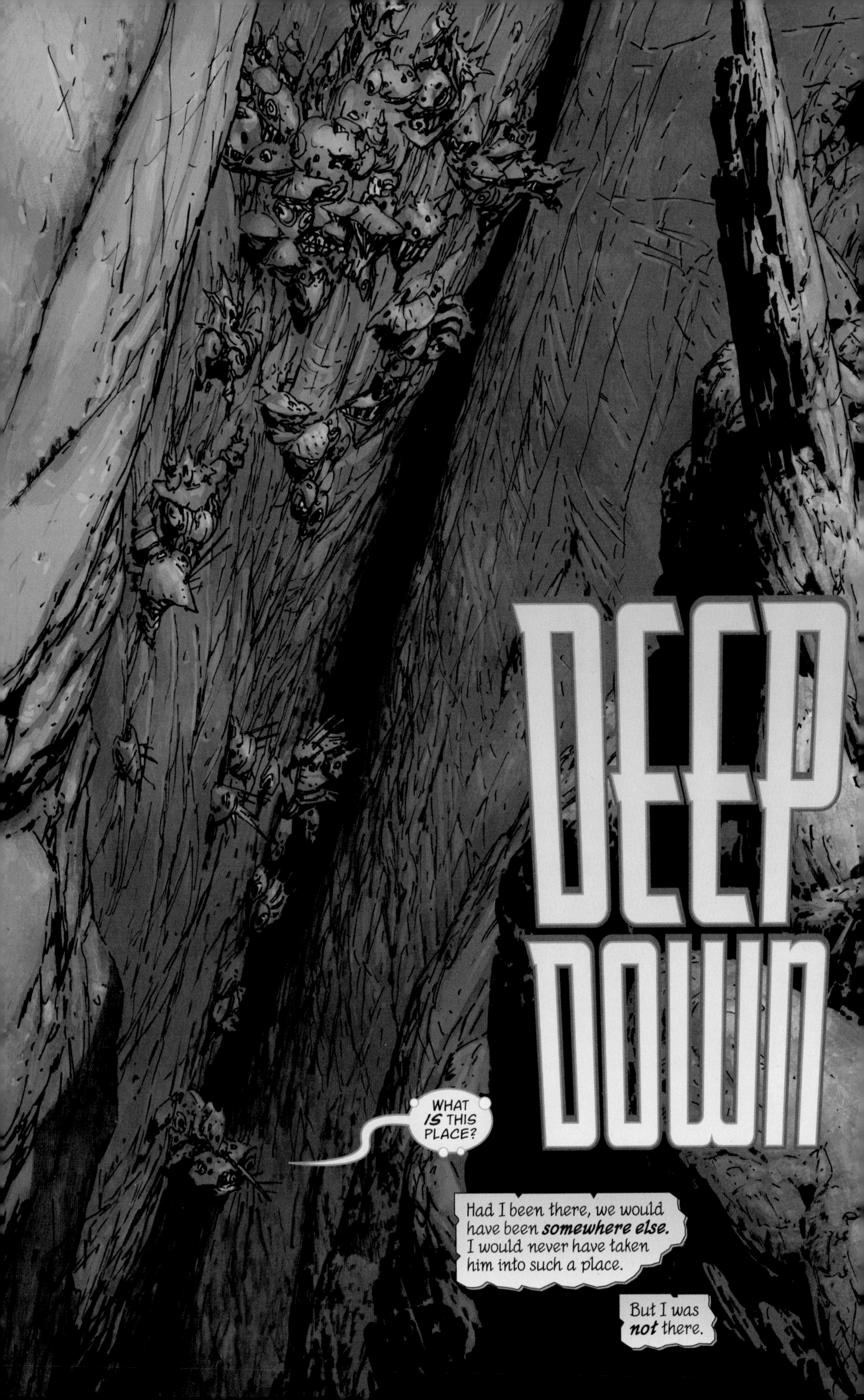
DEEP DOWN
WHAT IS THIS PLACE?
Had I been there, we would have been somewhere else. I would never have taken him into such a place.
But I was not there.

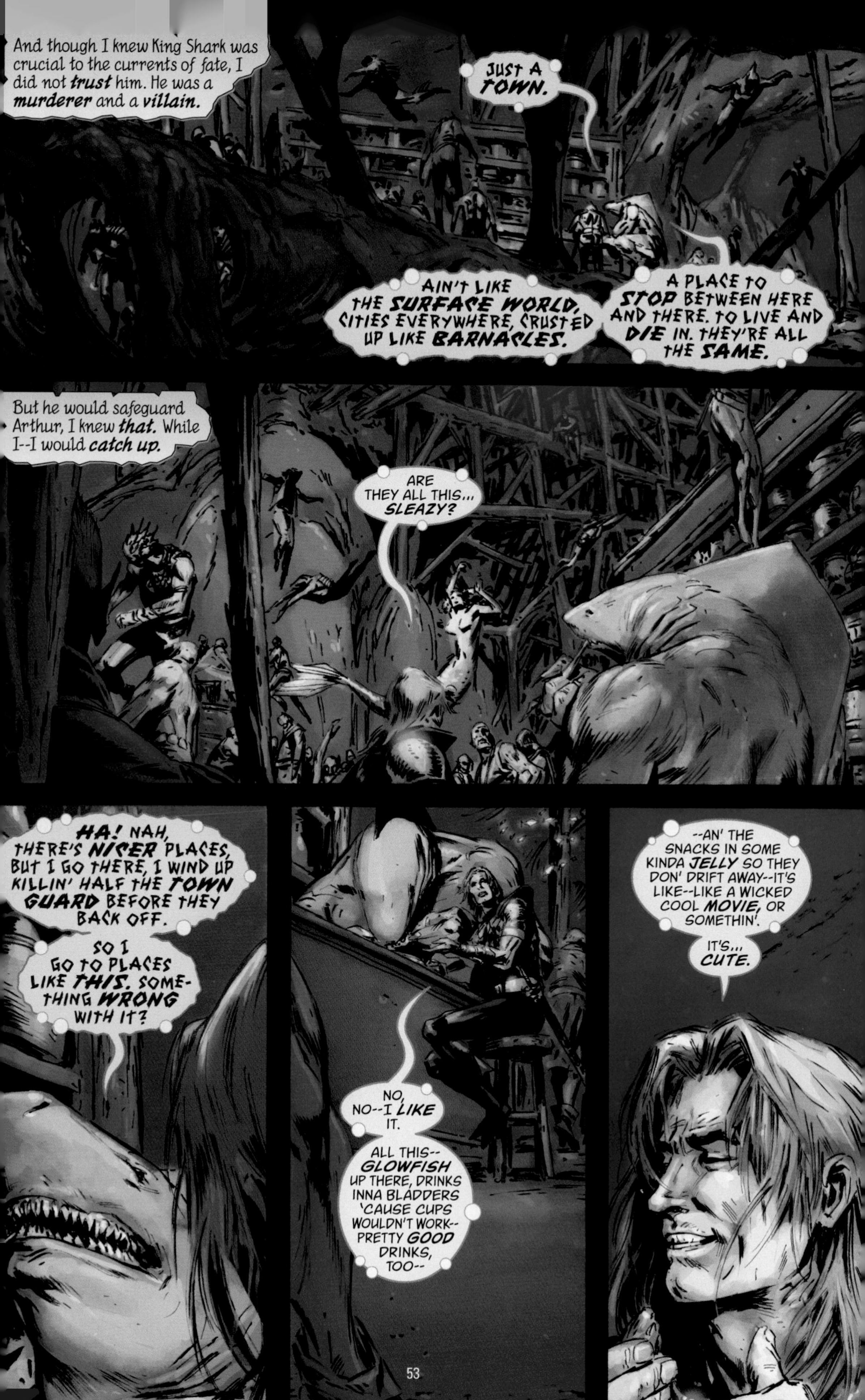
And though I knew King Shark was crucial to the currents of fate, I did not trust him. He was a murderer and a villain.
JUST A TOWN.
AIN'T LIKE THE SURFACE WORLD, CITIES EVERYWHERE, CRUSTED UP LIKE BARNACLES.
A PLACE TO STOP BETWEEN HERE AND THERE. TO LIVE AND DIE IN. THEY'RE ALL THE SAME.
But he would safeguard Arthur, I knew that. While I--I would catch up.
ARE THEY ALL THIS... SLEAZY?
HA! NAH, THERE'S NICER PLACES, BUT I GO THERE, I WIND UP KILLIN' HALF THE TOWN GUARD BEFORE THEY BACK OFF.
SO I GO TO PLACES LIKE THIS. SOMETHING WRONG WITH IT?
NO, NO--I LIKE IT.
ALL THIS--GLOWFISH UP THERE, DRINKS INNA BLADDERS 'CAUSE CUPS WOULDN'T WORK--PRETTY GOOD DRINKS, TOO--
--AN' THE SNACKS IN SOME KINDA JELLY SO THEY DON' DRIFT AWAY--IT'S LIKE--LIKE A WICKED COOL MOVIE, OR SOMETHIN'.
IT'S... CUTE.

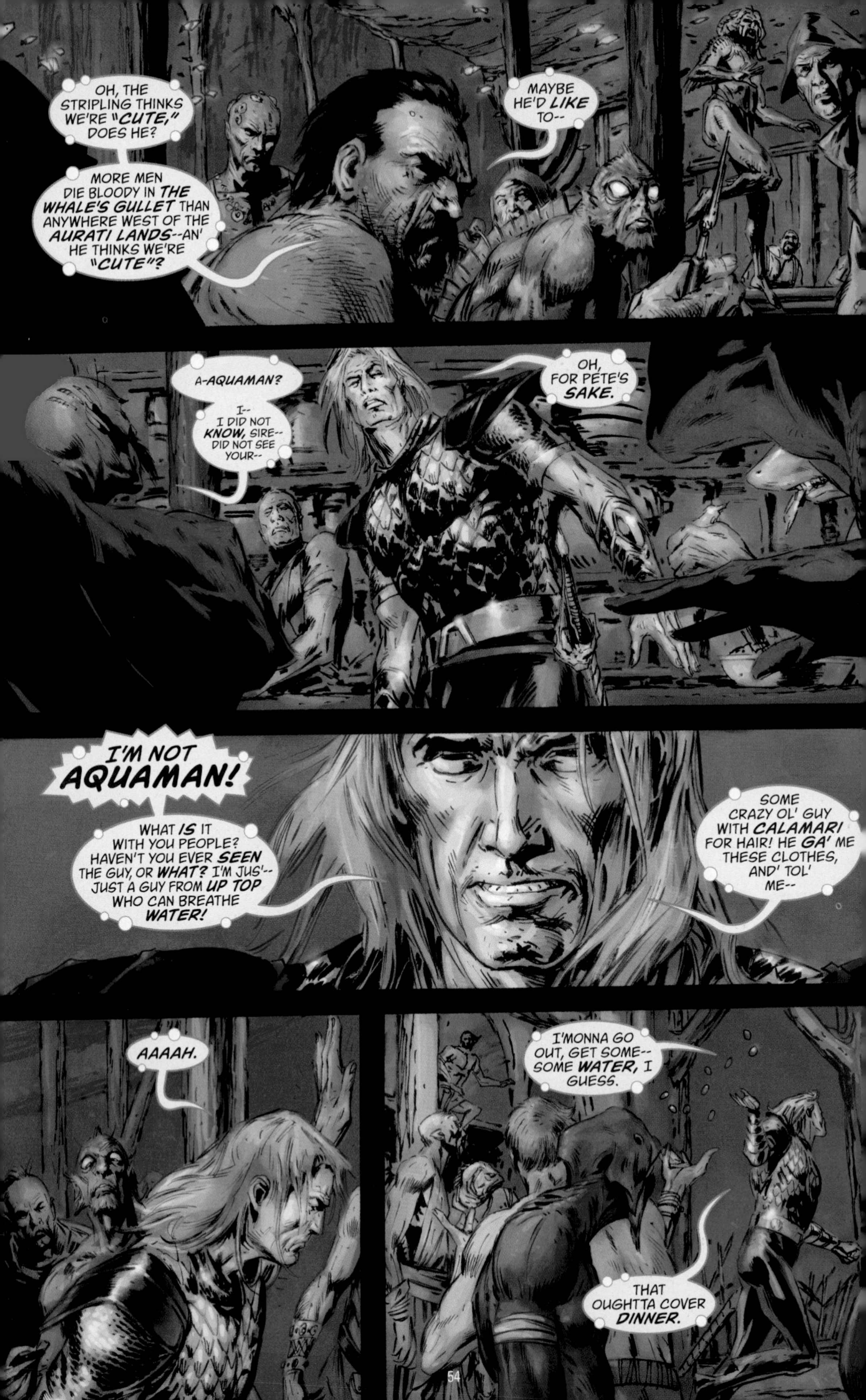

OH, THE STRIPLING THINKS WE'RE "CUTE," DOES HE?
MORE MEN DIE BLOODY IN THE WHALE'S GULLET THAN ANYWHERE WEST OF THE AURATI LANDS--AN' HE THINKS WE'RE "CUTE"?
MAYBE HE'D LIKE TO--
A-AQUAMAN?
I-- I DID NOT KNOW, SIRE-- DID NOT SEE YOUR--
OH, FOR PETE'S SAKE.
I'M NOT AQUAMAN!
WHAT IS IT WITH YOU PEOPLE? HAVEN'T YOU EVER SEEN THE GUY, OR WHAT? I'M JUS'-- JUST A GUY FROM UP TOP WHO CAN BREATHE WATER!
SOME CRAZY OL' GUY WITH CALAMARI FOR HAIR! HE GA' ME THESE CLOTHES, AND' TOL' ME--
AAAAH.
I'MONNA GO OUT, GET SOME-- SOME WATER, I GUESS.
THAT OUGHTTA COVER DINNER.

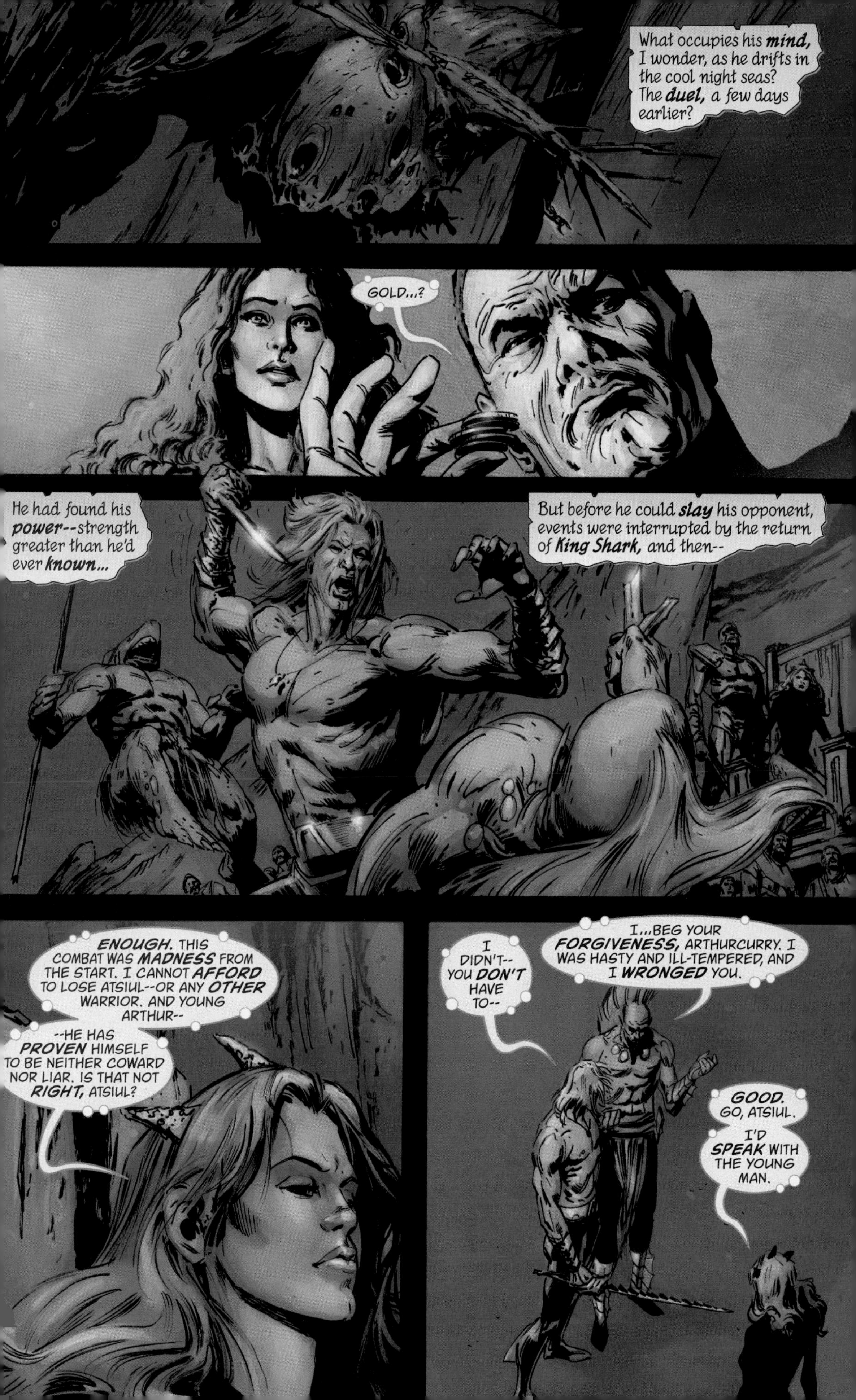
What occupies his mind, I wonder, as he drifts in the cool night seas? The duel, a few days earlier?
GOLD...?
He had found his power--strength greater than he'd ever known...
But before he could slay his opponent, events were interrupted by the return of King Shark, and then--
ENOUGH. THIS COMBAT WAS MADNESS FROM THE START. I CANNOT AFFORD TO LOSE ATSIUL--OR ANY OTHER WARRIOR. AND YOUNG ARTHUR--
--HE HAS PROVEN HIMSELF TO BE NEITHER COWARD NOR LIAR. IS THAT NOT RIGHT, ATSIUL?
I...BEG YOUR FORGIVENESS, ARTHURCURRY. I WAS HASTY AND ILL-TEMPERED, AND I WRONGED YOU.
I DIDN'T--YOU DON'T HAVE TO--
GOOD. GO, ATSIUL.
I'D SPEAK WITH THE YOUNG MAN.

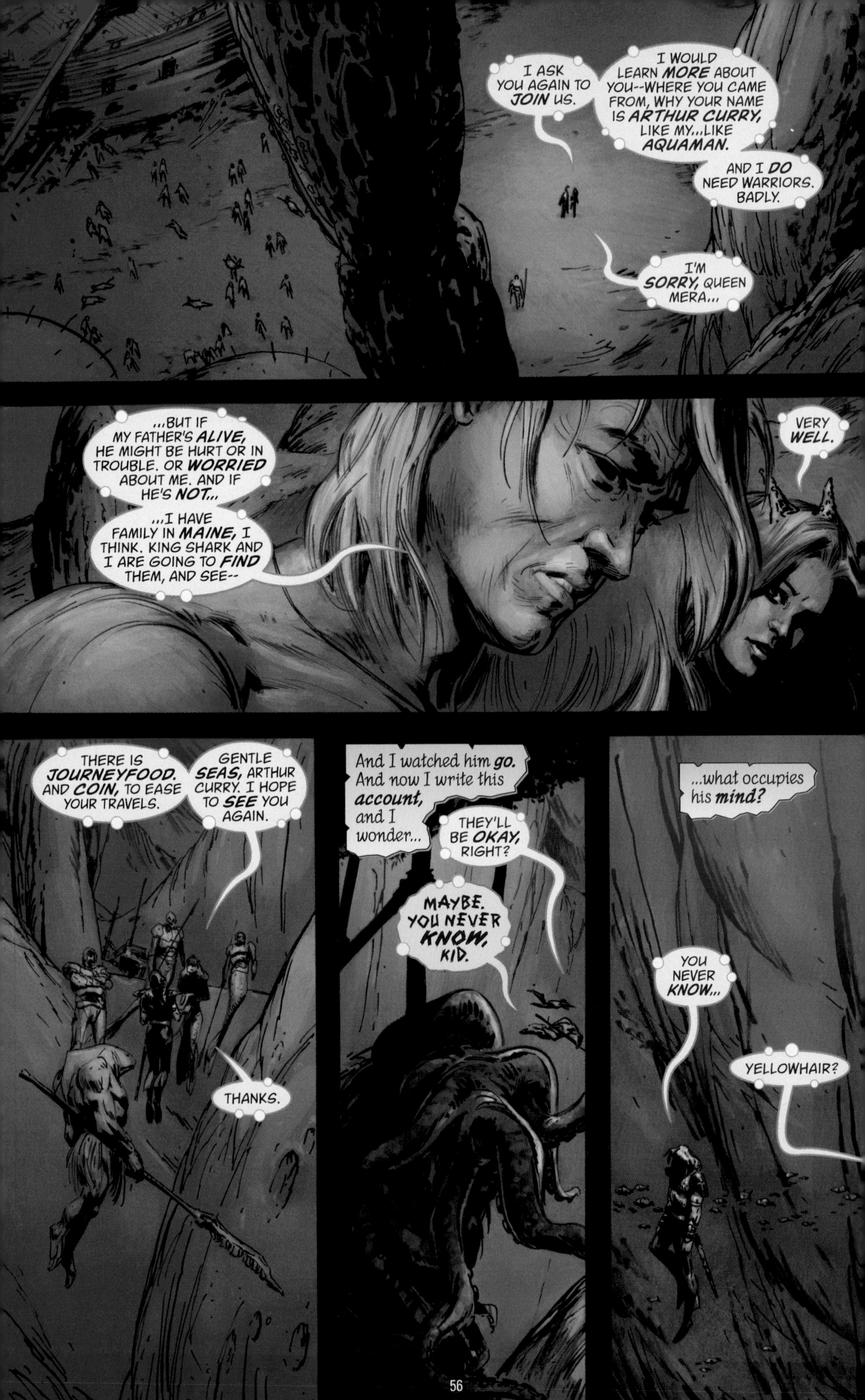
I ASK YOU AGAIN TO JOIN US.
I WOULD LEARN MORE ABOUT YOU--WHERE YOU CAME FROM, WHY YOUR NAME IS ARTHUR CURRY, LIKE MY...LIKE AQUAMAN.
AND I DO NEED WARRIORS. BADLY.
I'M SORRY, QUEEN MERA...
...BUT IF MY FATHER'S ALIVE, HE MIGHT BE HURT OR IN TROUBLE. OR WORRIED ABOUT ME. AND IF HE'S NOT...
...I HAVE FAMILY IN MAINE, I THINK. KING SHARK AND I ARE GOING TO FIND THEM, AND SEE--
VERY WELL.
THERE IS JOURNEYFOOD. AND COIN, TO EASE YOUR TRAVELS.
GENTLE SEAS, ARTHUR CURRY. I HOPE TO SEE YOU AGAIN.
THANKS.
And I watched him go. And now I write this account, and I wonder...
THEY'LL BE OKAY, RIGHT?
MAYBE. YOU NEVER KNOW, KID.
...what occupies his mind?
YOU NEVER KNOW...
YELLOWHAIR?

IT IS ME. *TEJAIA.* DID YOU... DID YOU *LIKE* MY DANCE?

UH, YES, I--

--*LIKED* IT?

I LIKE *YOU.* YOU ARE SO *LEAN,* SO HANDSOME. SO *DIFFERENT.*

I, OH... UH.

IT'S *YOU.*

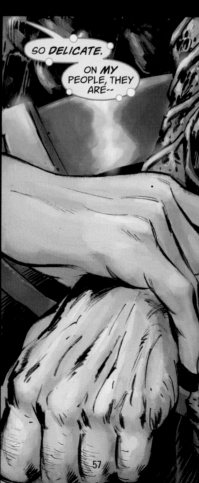

YOUR EYES, *DARK* AND *DEEP* AS A BARRACUDA'S. YOUR HAIR, YOUR *GILLS*--

MAY I?

UM, SURE--

SO *DELICATE.* ON *MY* PEOPLE, THEY ARE--

--*DOWN HERE.*

HNN.

57

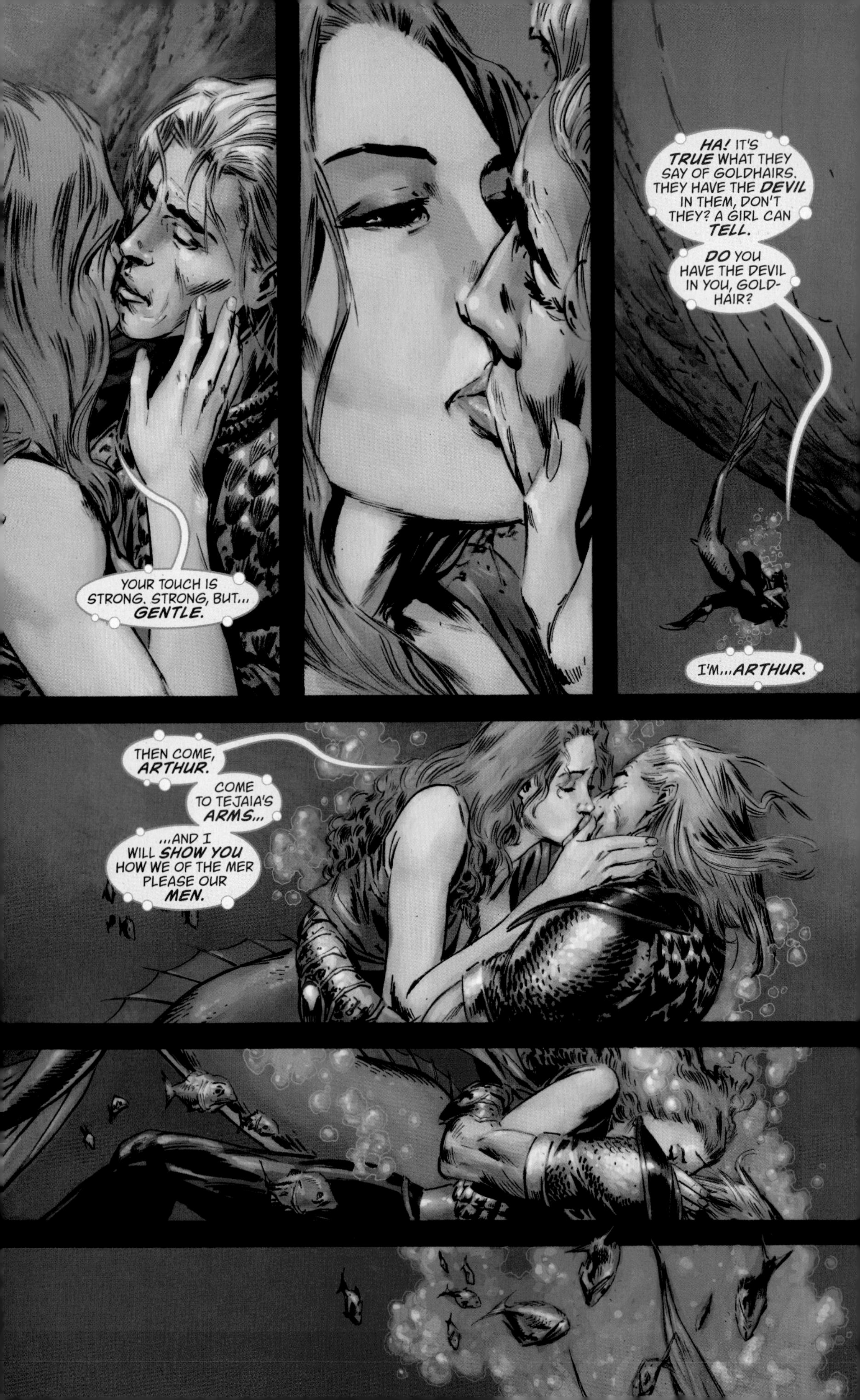
YOUR TOUCH IS STRONG. STRONG, BUT... GENTLE.
HA! IT'S TRUE WHAT THEY SAY OF GOLDHAIRS. THEY HAVE THE DEVIL IN THEM, DON'T THEY? A GIRL CAN TELL.
DO YOU HAVE THE DEVIL IN YOU, GOLD-HAIR?
I'M...ARTHUR.
THEN COME, ARTHUR.
COME TO TEJAIA'S ARMS...
...AND I WILL SHOW YOU HOW WE OF THE MER PLEASE OUR MEN.

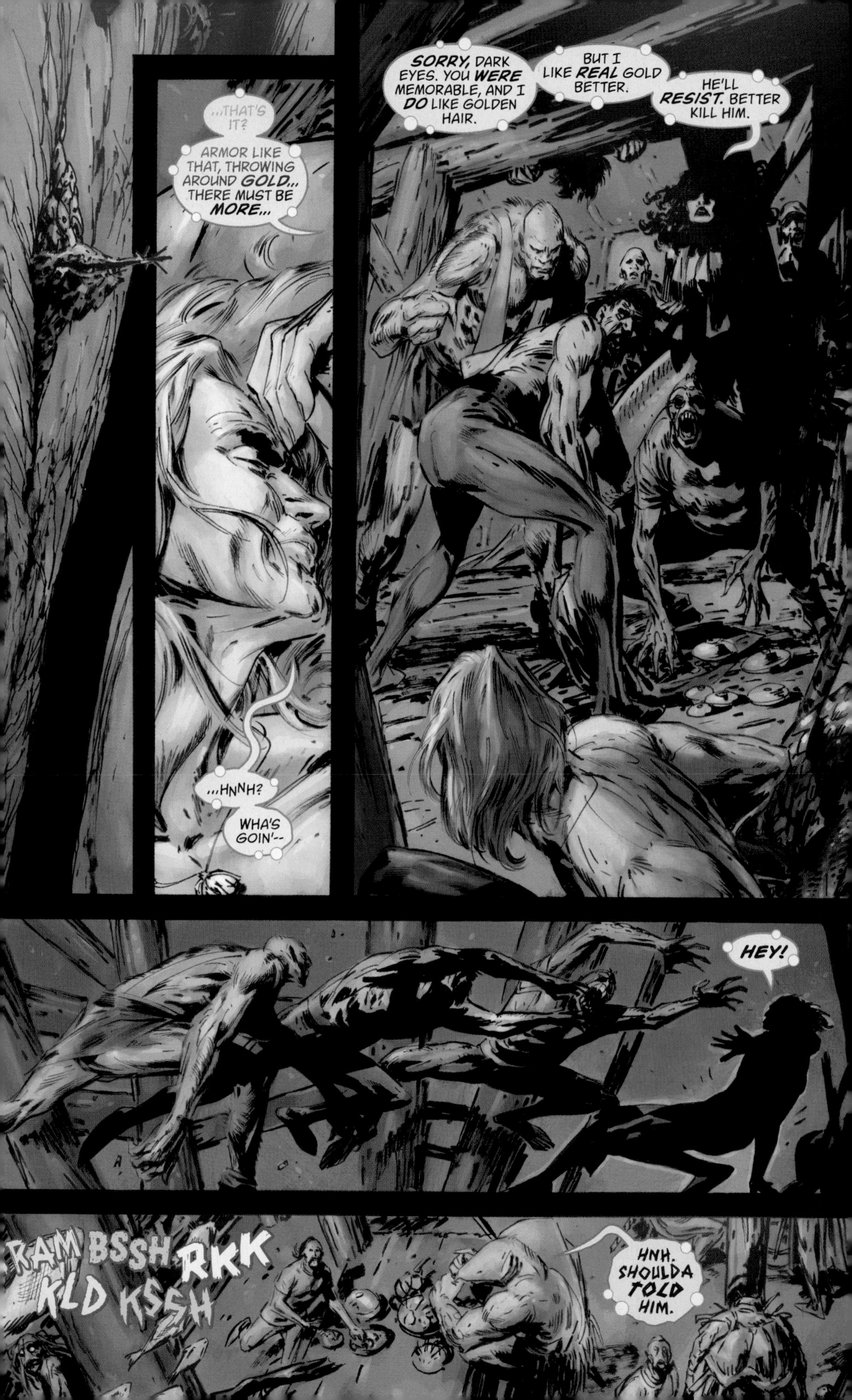
...THAT'S IT?
ARMOR LIKE THAT, THROWING AROUND GOLD... THERE MUST BE MORE...
...HNNH?
WHA'S GOIN'--
SORRY, DARK EYES. YOU WERE MEMORABLE, AND I DO LIKE GOLDEN HAIR.
BUT I LIKE REAL GOLD BETTER.
HE'LL RESIST. BETTER KILL HIM.
HEY!
RAM BSSH RKK KLD KSSH
HNH. SHOULDA TOLD HIM.

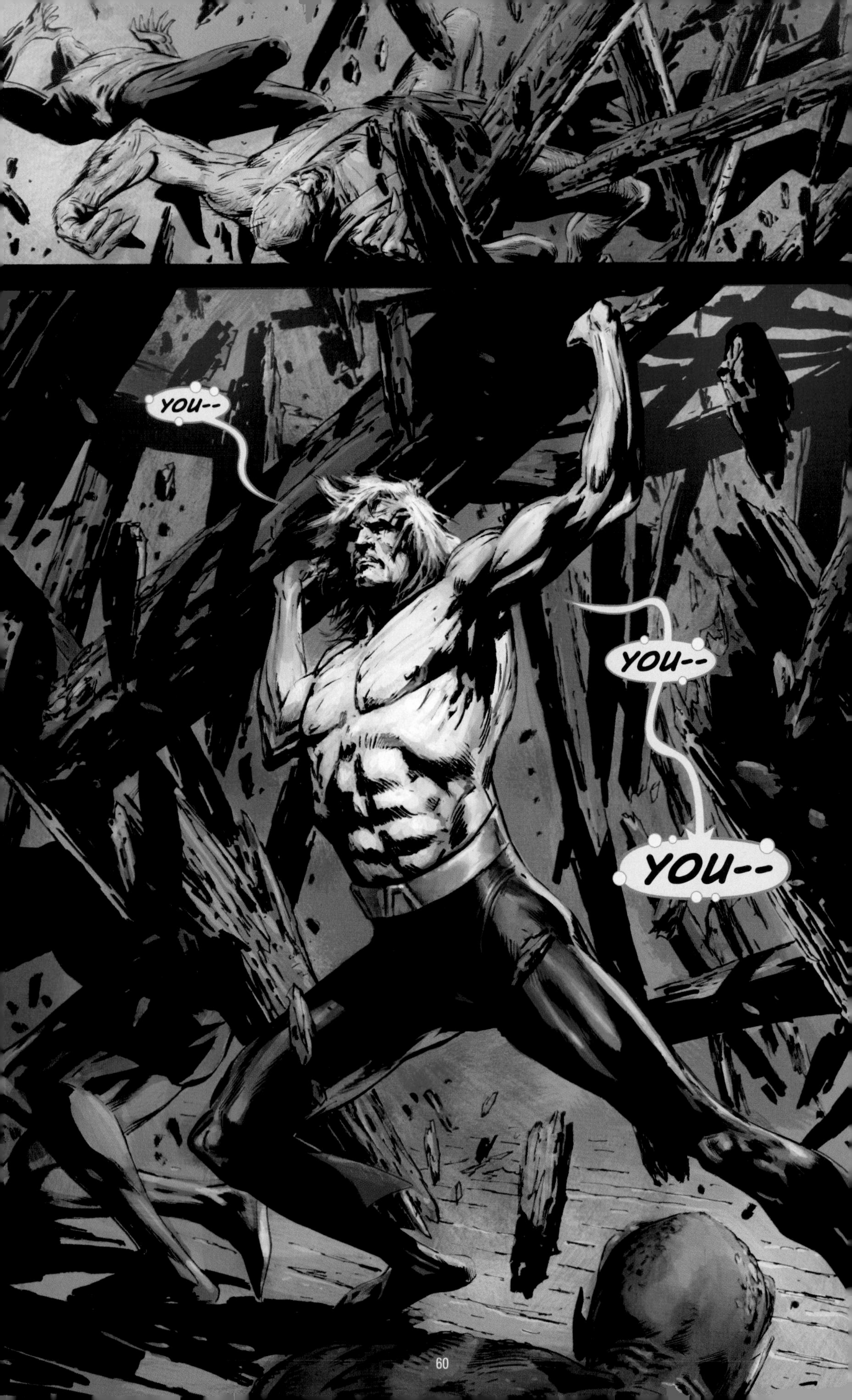
YOU--
YOU--
YOU--

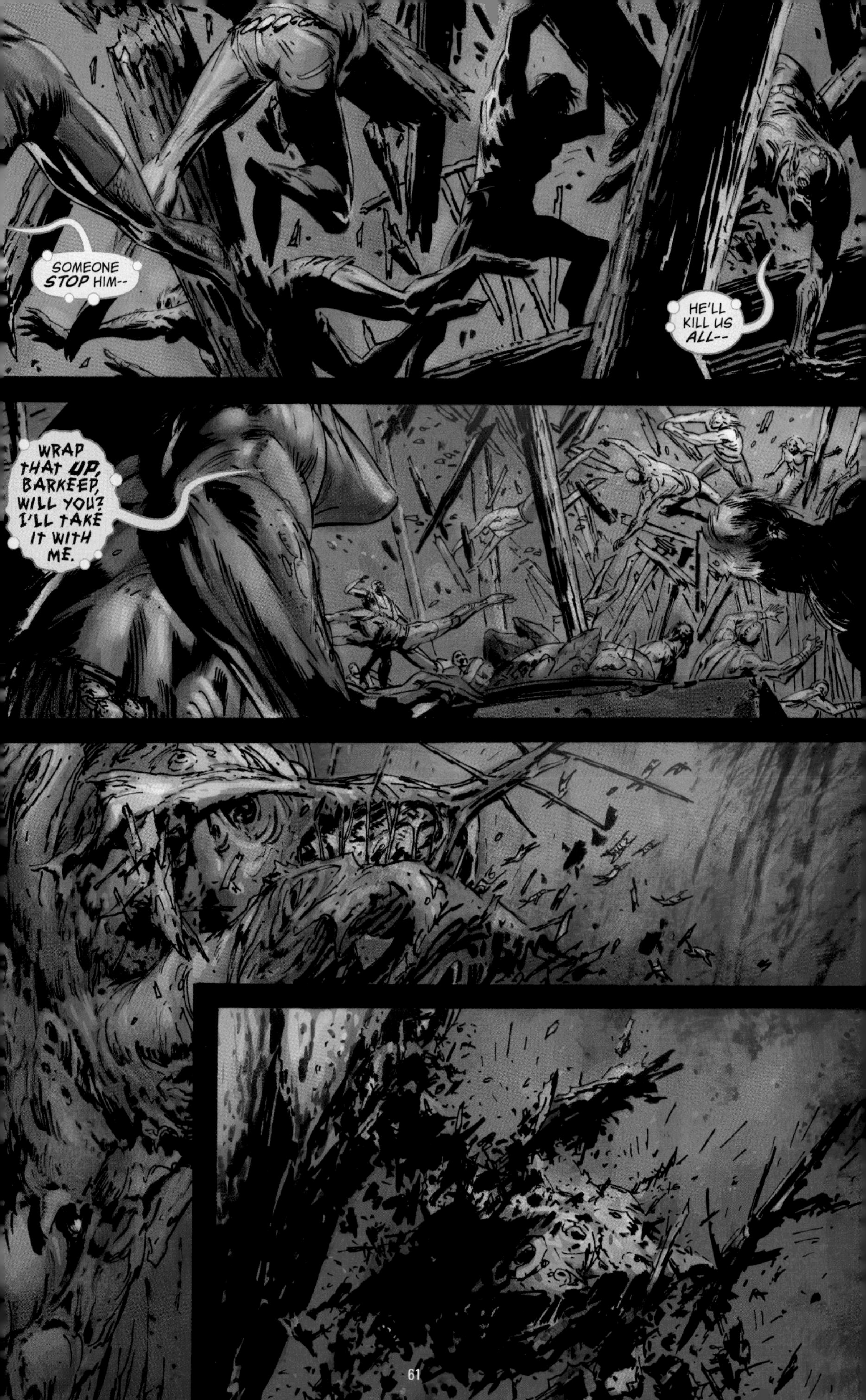
SOMEONE STOP HIM--
HE'LL KILL US ALL--
WRAP THAT UP, BARKEEP, WILL YOU? I'LL TAKE IT WITH ME.

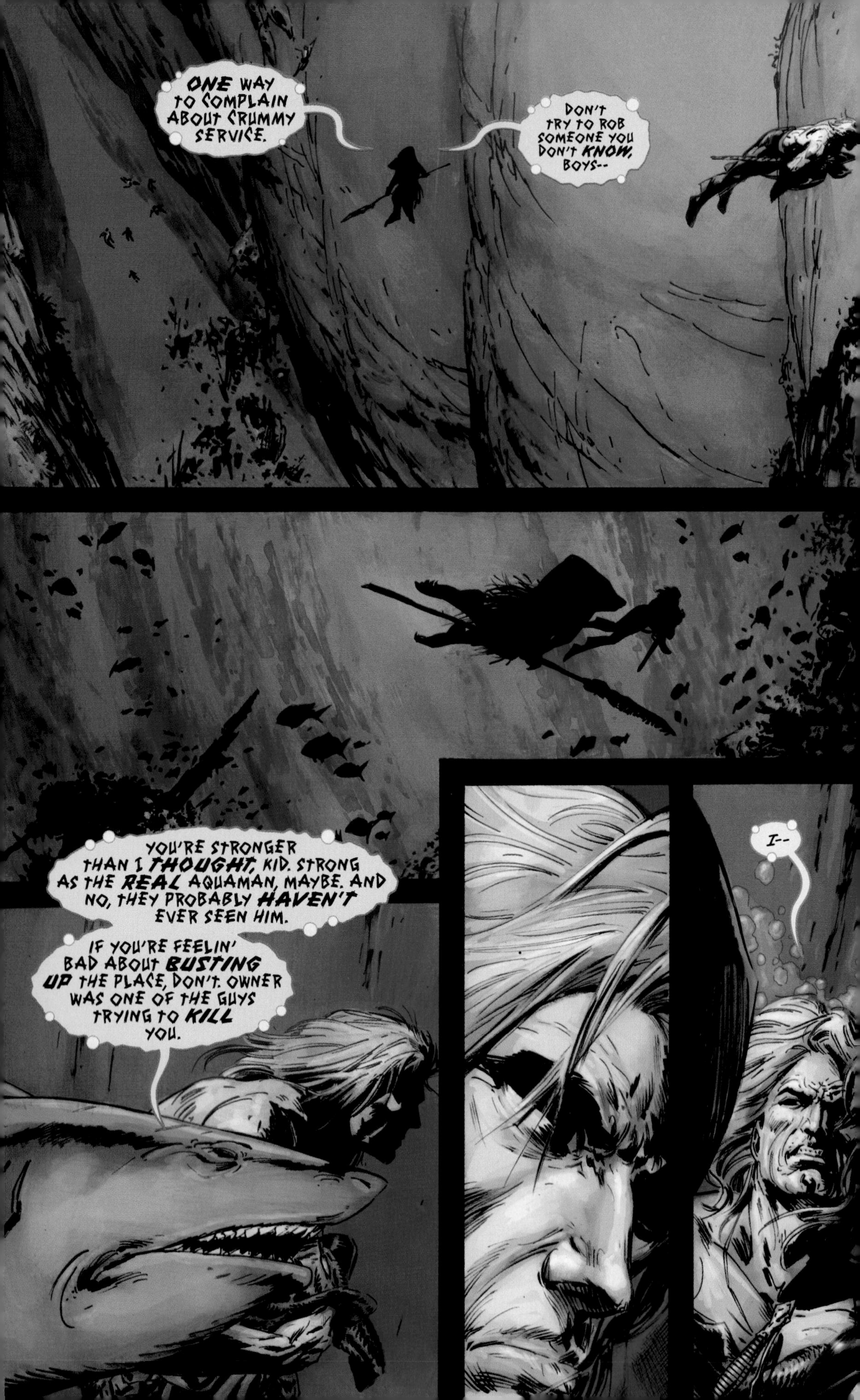
ONE WAY TO COMPLAIN ABOUT CRUMMY SERVICE.
DON'T TRY TO ROB SOMEONE YOU DON'T KNOW, BOYS--
YOU'RE STRONGER THAN I THOUGHT, KID. STRONG AS THE REAL AQUAMAN, MAYBE. AND NO, THEY PROBABLY HAVEN'T EVER SEEN HIM.
IF YOU'RE FEELIN' BAD ABOUT BUSTING UP THE PLACE, DON'T. OWNER WAS ONE OF THE GUYS TRYING TO KILL YOU.
I--

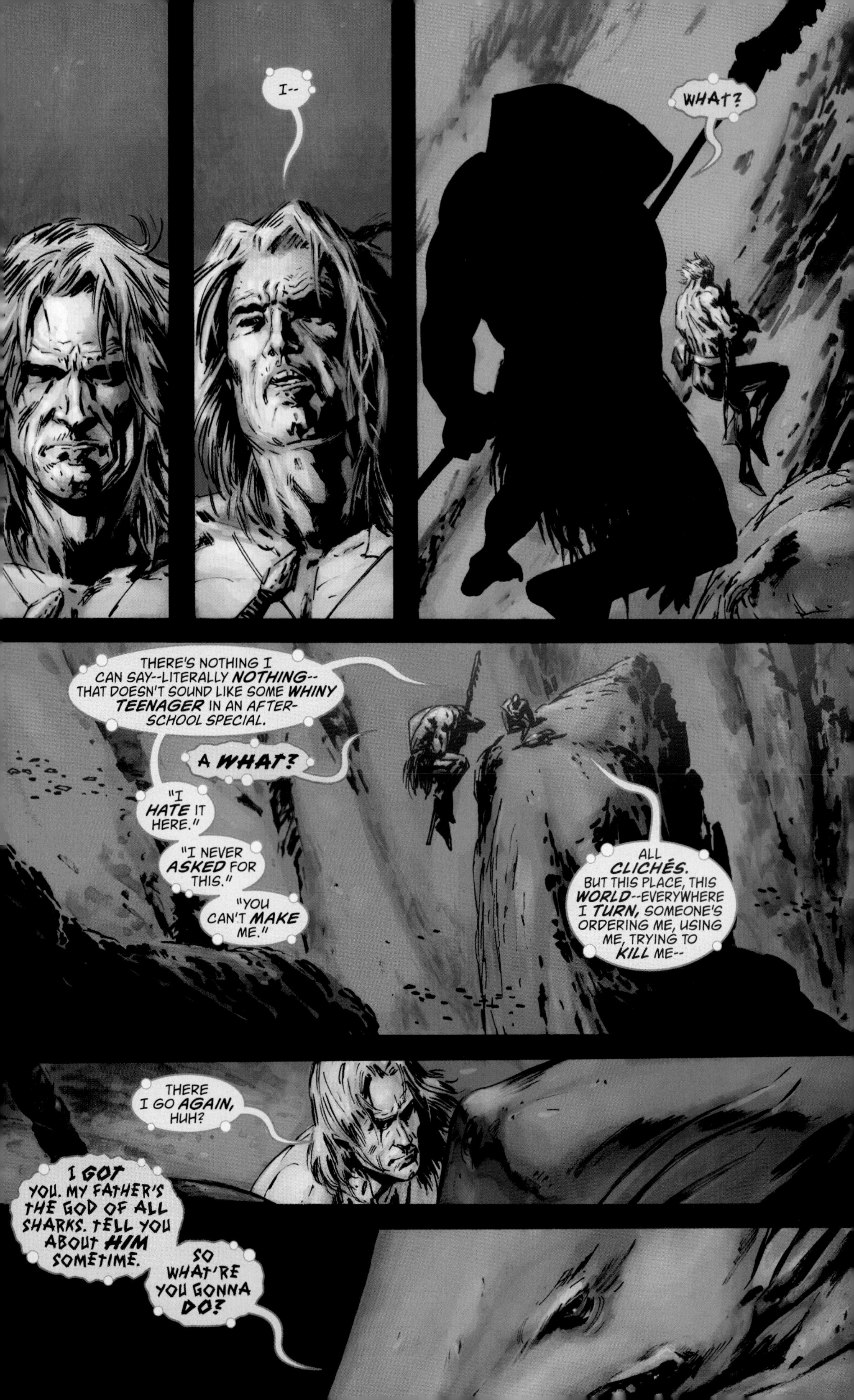
I--
WHAT?
THERE'S NOTHING I CAN SAY--LITERALLY NOTHING--THAT DOESN'T SOUND LIKE SOME WHINY TEENAGER IN AN AFTER-SCHOOL SPECIAL.
A WHAT?
"I HATE IT HERE."
"I NEVER ASKED FOR THIS."
"YOU CAN'T MAKE ME."
ALL CLICHÉS. BUT THIS PLACE, THIS WORLD--EVERYWHERE I TURN, SOMEONE'S ORDERING ME, USING ME, TRYING TO KILL ME--
THERE I GO AGAIN, HUH?
I GOT YOU. MY FATHER'S THE GOD OF ALL SHARKS. TELL YOU ABOUT HIM SOMETIME.
SO WHAT'RE YOU GONNA DO?

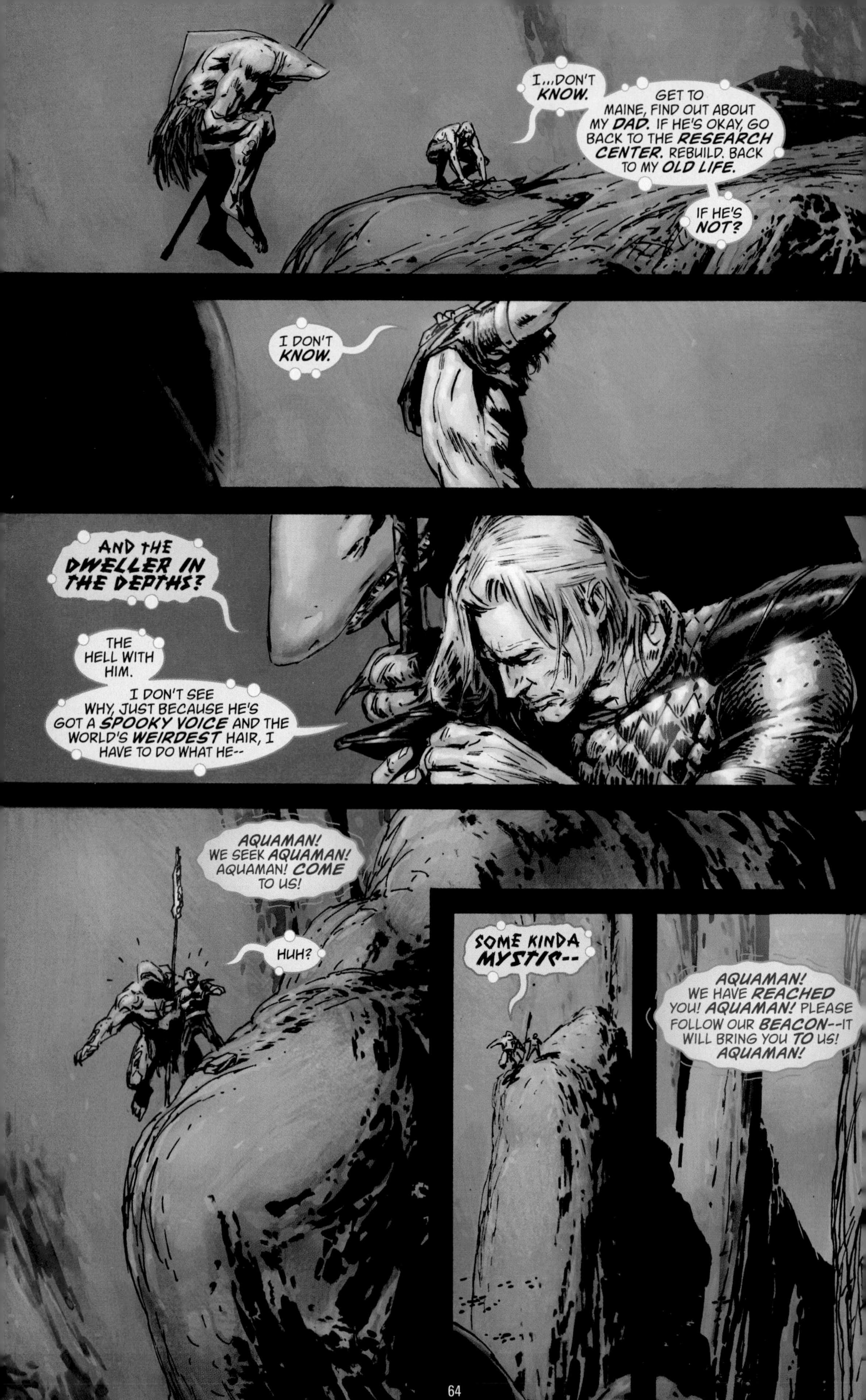

I...DON'T KNOW.
GET TO MAINE, FIND OUT ABOUT MY DAD. IF HE'S OKAY, GO BACK TO THE RESEARCH CENTER. REBUILD. BACK TO MY OLD LIFE.
IF HE'S NOT?
I DON'T KNOW.
AND THE DWELLER IN THE DEPTHS?
THE HELL WITH HIM.
I DON'T SEE WHY, JUST BECAUSE HE'S GOT A SPOOKY VOICE AND THE WORLD'S WEIRDEST HAIR, I HAVE TO DO WHAT HE--
AQUAMAN! WE SEEK AQUAMAN! AQUAMAN! COME TO US!
HUH?
SOME KINDA MYSTIC--
AQUAMAN! WE HAVE REACHED YOU! AQUAMAN! PLEASE FOLLOW OUR BEACON--IT WILL BRING YOU TO US! AQUAMAN!

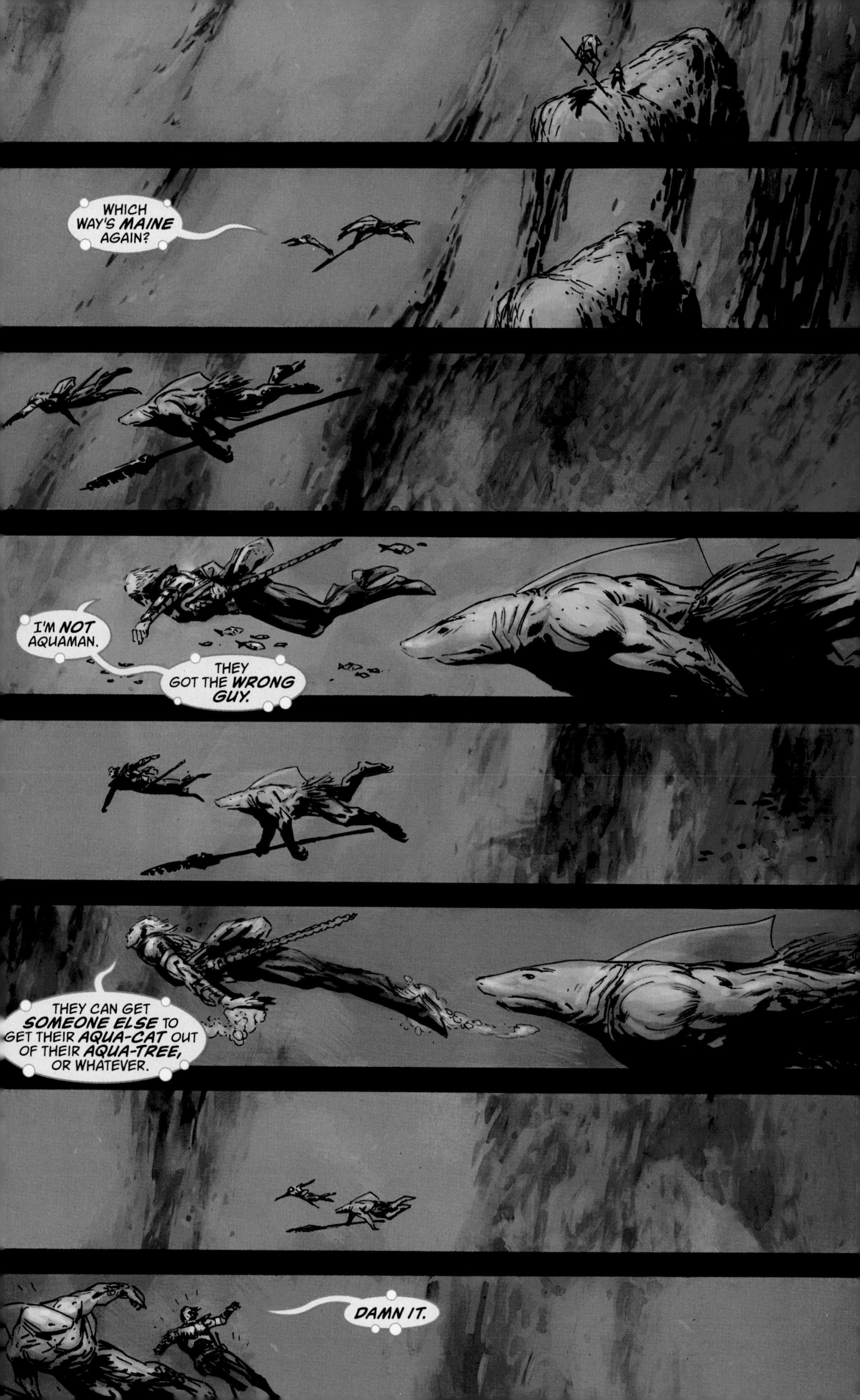
WHICH WAY'S MAINE AGAIN?
I'M NOT AQUAMAN.
THEY GOT THE WRONG GUY.
THEY CAN GET SOMEONE ELSE TO GET THEIR AQUA-CAT OUT OF THEIR AQUA-TREE, OR WHATEVER.
DAMN IT.

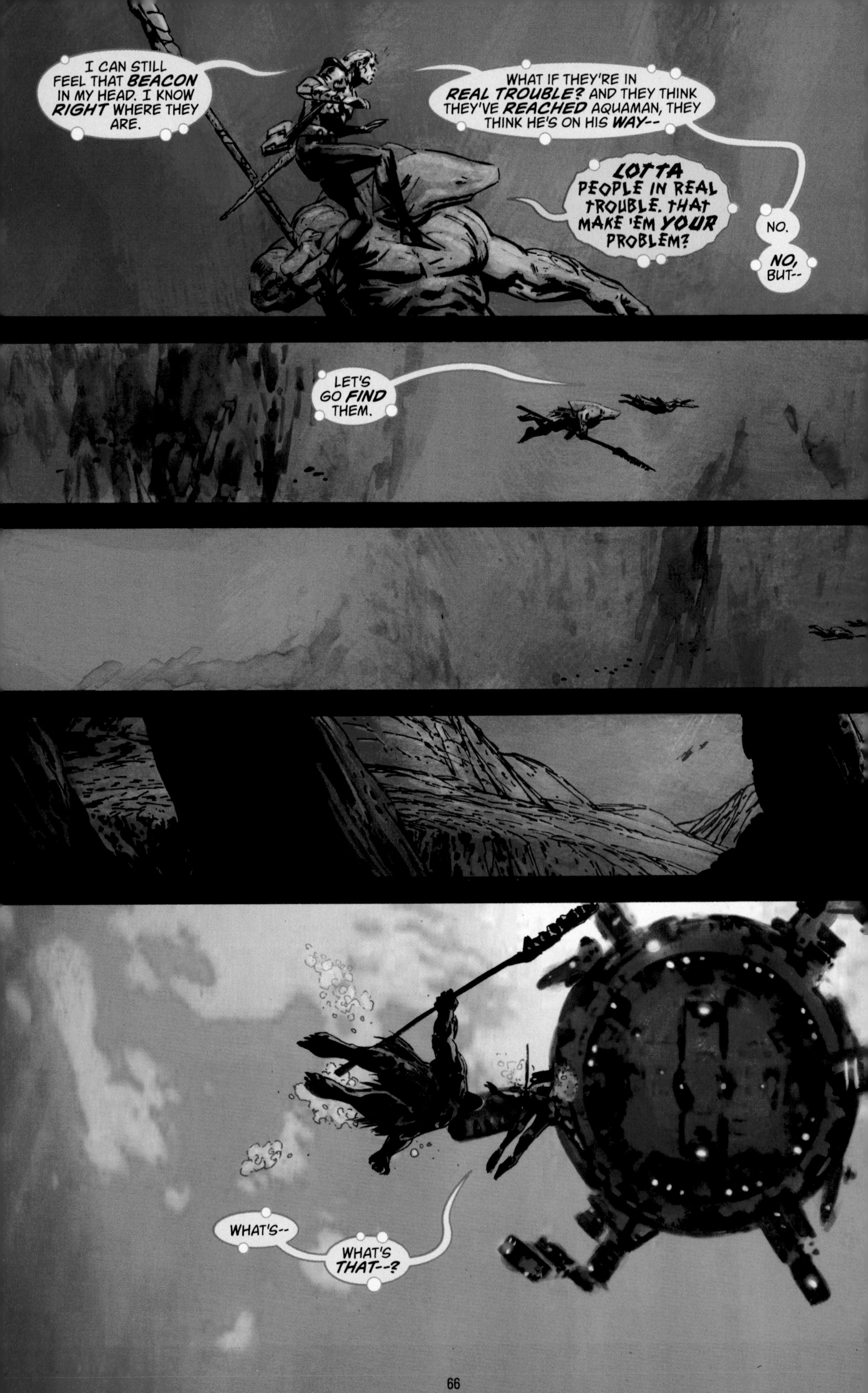
I CAN STILL FEEL THAT BEACON IN MY HEAD. I KNOW RIGHT WHERE THEY ARE.
WHAT IF THEY'RE IN REAL TROUBLE? AND THEY THINK THEY'VE REACHED AQUAMAN, THEY THINK HE'S ON HIS WAY--
LOTTA PEOPLE IN REAL TROUBLE. THAT MAKE 'EM YOUR PROBLEM?
NO.
NO, BUT--
LET'S GO FIND THEM.
WHAT'S--
WHAT'S THAT--?

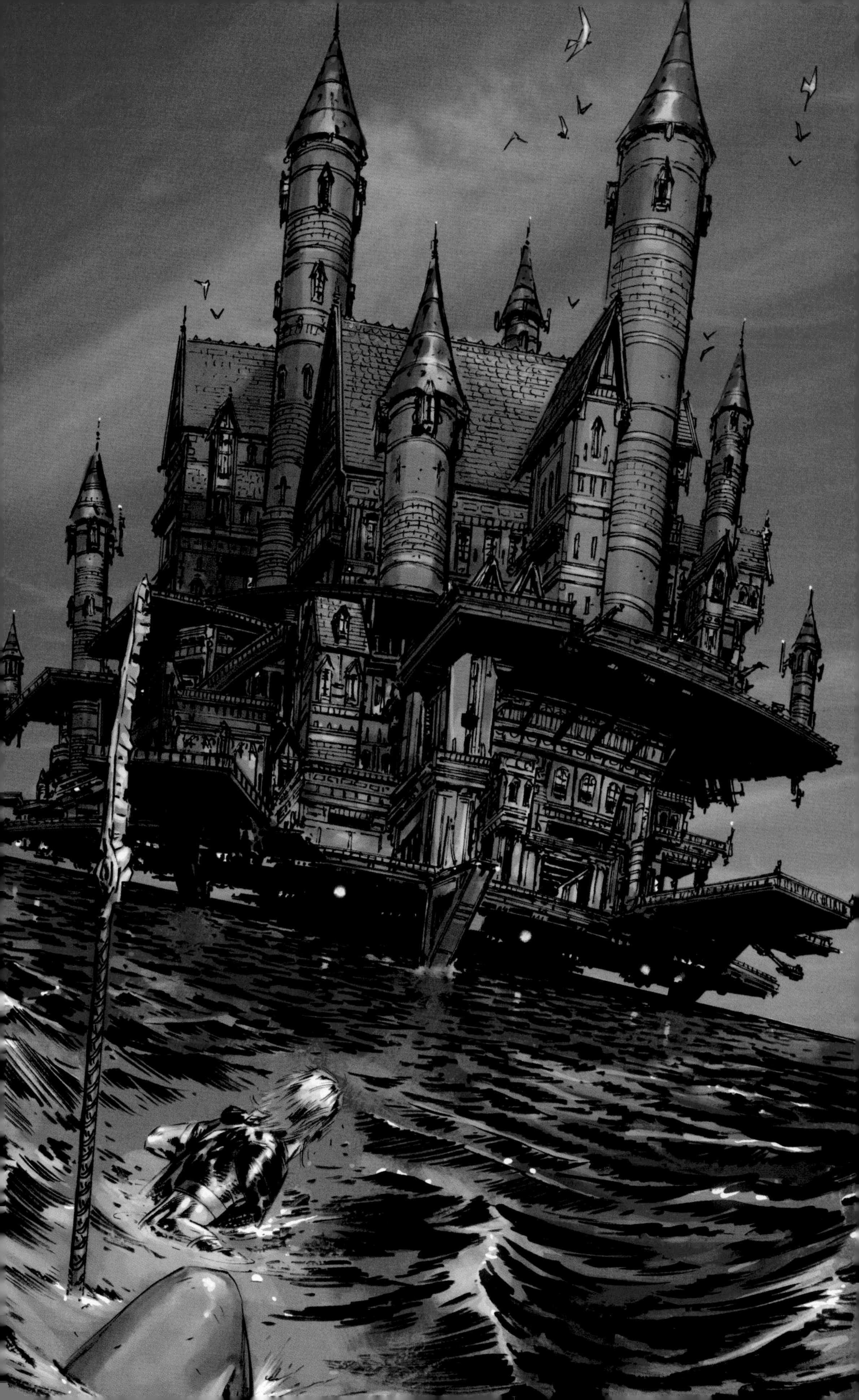

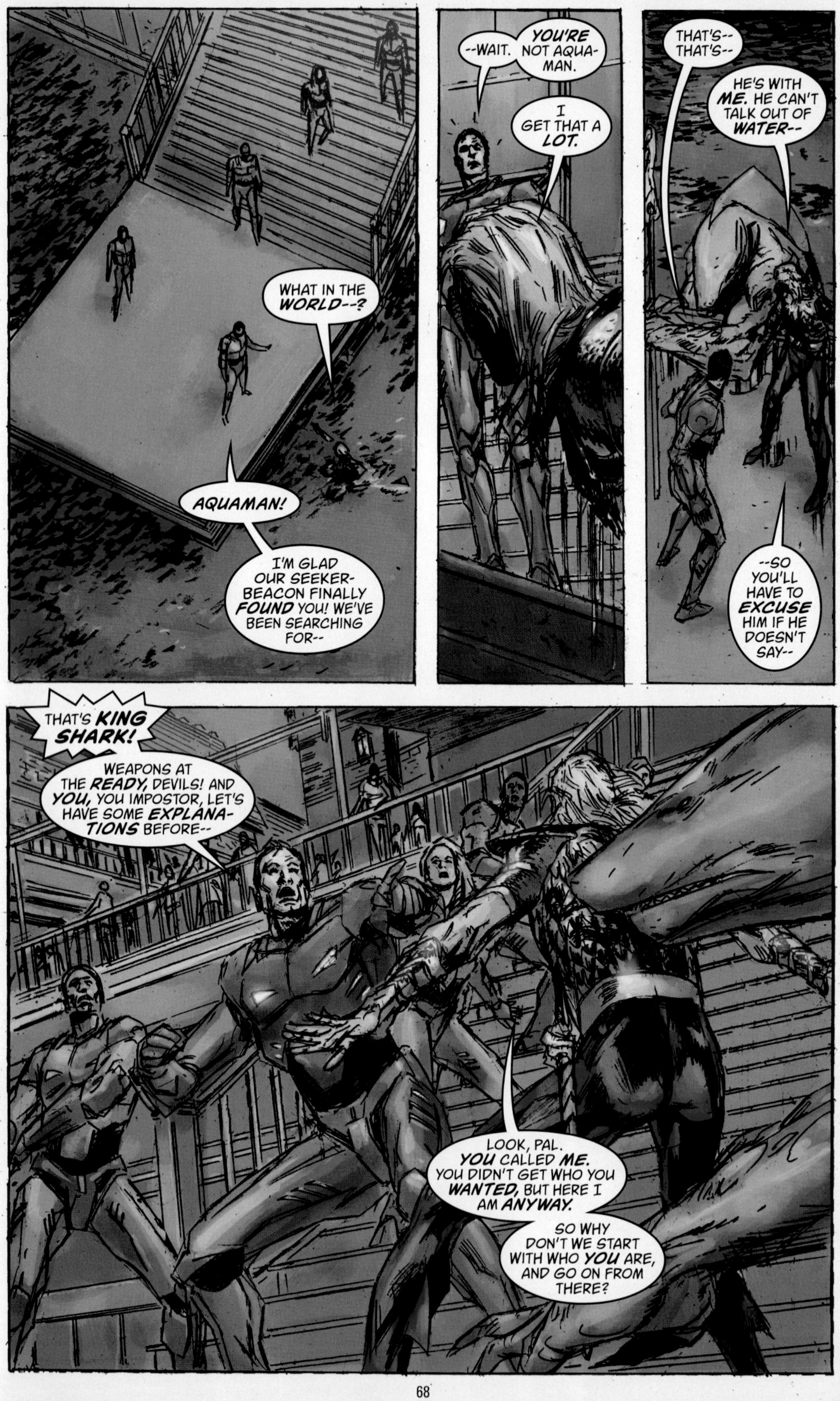
WHAT IN THE WORLD--?
AQUAMAN!
I'M GLAD OUR SEEKER-BEACON FINALLY FOUND YOU! WE'VE BEEN SEARCHING FOR--
--WAIT.
YOU'RE NOT AQUA-MAN.
I GET THAT A LOT.
THAT'S-- THAT'S--
HE'S WITH ME. HE CAN'T TALK OUT OF WATER--
--SO YOU'LL HAVE TO EXCUSE HIM IF HE DOESN'T SAY--
THAT'S KING SHARK!
WEAPONS AT THE READY, DEVILS! AND YOU, YOU IMPOSTOR, LET'S HAVE SOME EXPLANA-TIONS BEFORE--
LOOK, PAL. YOU CALLED ME. YOU DIDN'T GET WHO YOU WANTED, BUT HERE I AM ANYWAY.
SO WHY DON'T WE START WITH WHO YOU ARE, AND GO ON FROM THERE?

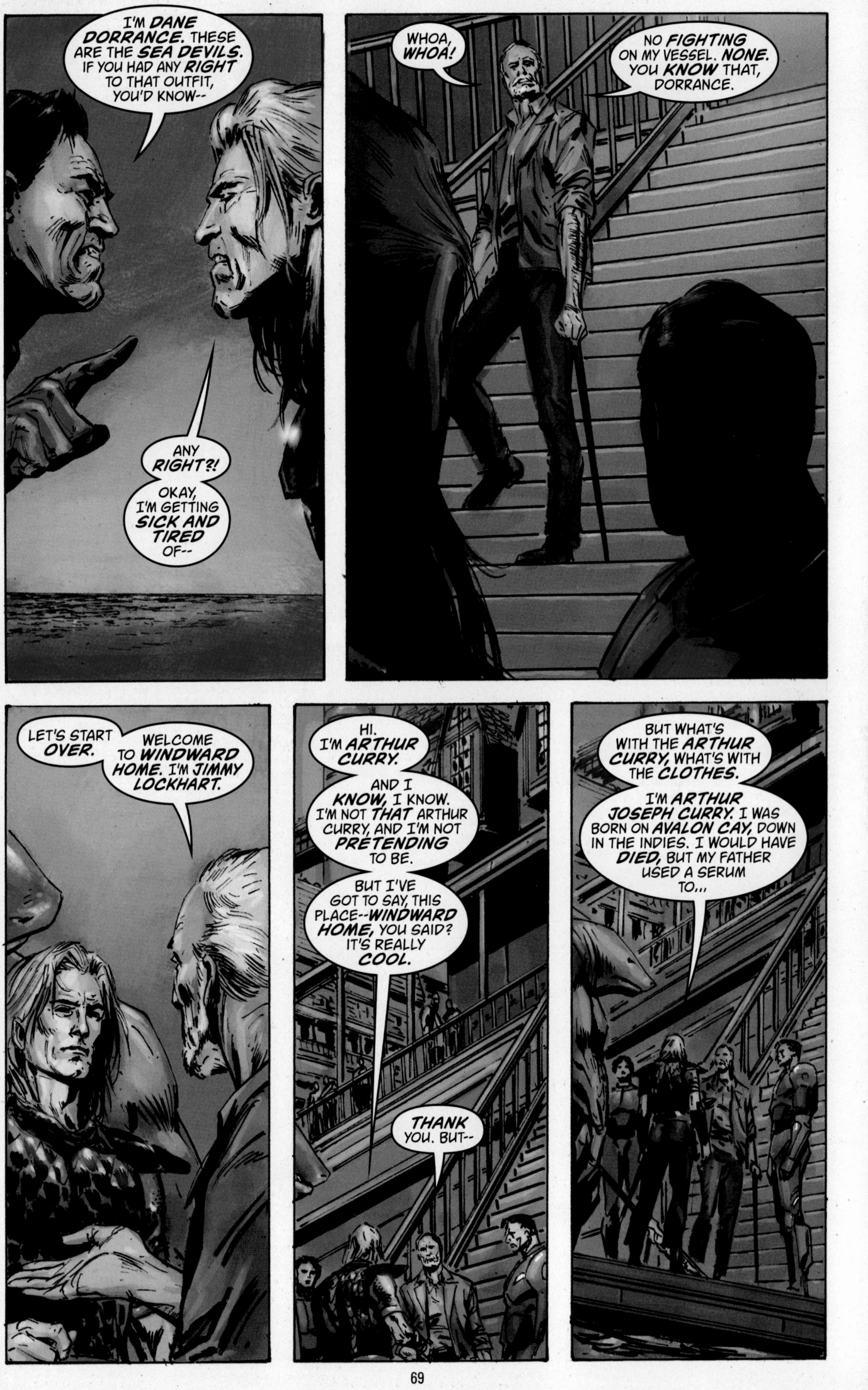
I'M DANE DORRANCE. THESE ARE THE SEA DEVILS. IF YOU HAD ANY RIGHT TO THAT OUTFIT, YOU'D KNOW--
ANY RIGHT?!
OKAY, I'M GETTING SICK AND TIRED OF--
WHOA, WHOA!
NO FIGHTING ON MY VESSEL. NONE. YOU KNOW THAT, DORRANCE.
LET'S START OVER.
WELCOME TO WINDWARD HOME. I'M JIMMY LOCKHART.
HI. I'M ARTHUR CURRY.
AND I KNOW, I KNOW. I'M NOT THAT ARTHUR CURRY, AND I'M NOT PRETENDING TO BE.
BUT I'VE GOT TO SAY, THIS PLACE--WINDWARD HOME, YOU SAID? IT'S REALLY COOL.
THANK YOU. BUT--
BUT WHAT'S WITH THE ARTHUR CURRY, WHAT'S WITH THE CLOTHES.
I'M ARTHUR JOSEPH CURRY. I WAS BORN ON AVALON CAY, DOWN IN THE INDIES. I WOULD HAVE DIED, BUT MY FATHER USED A SERUM TO...

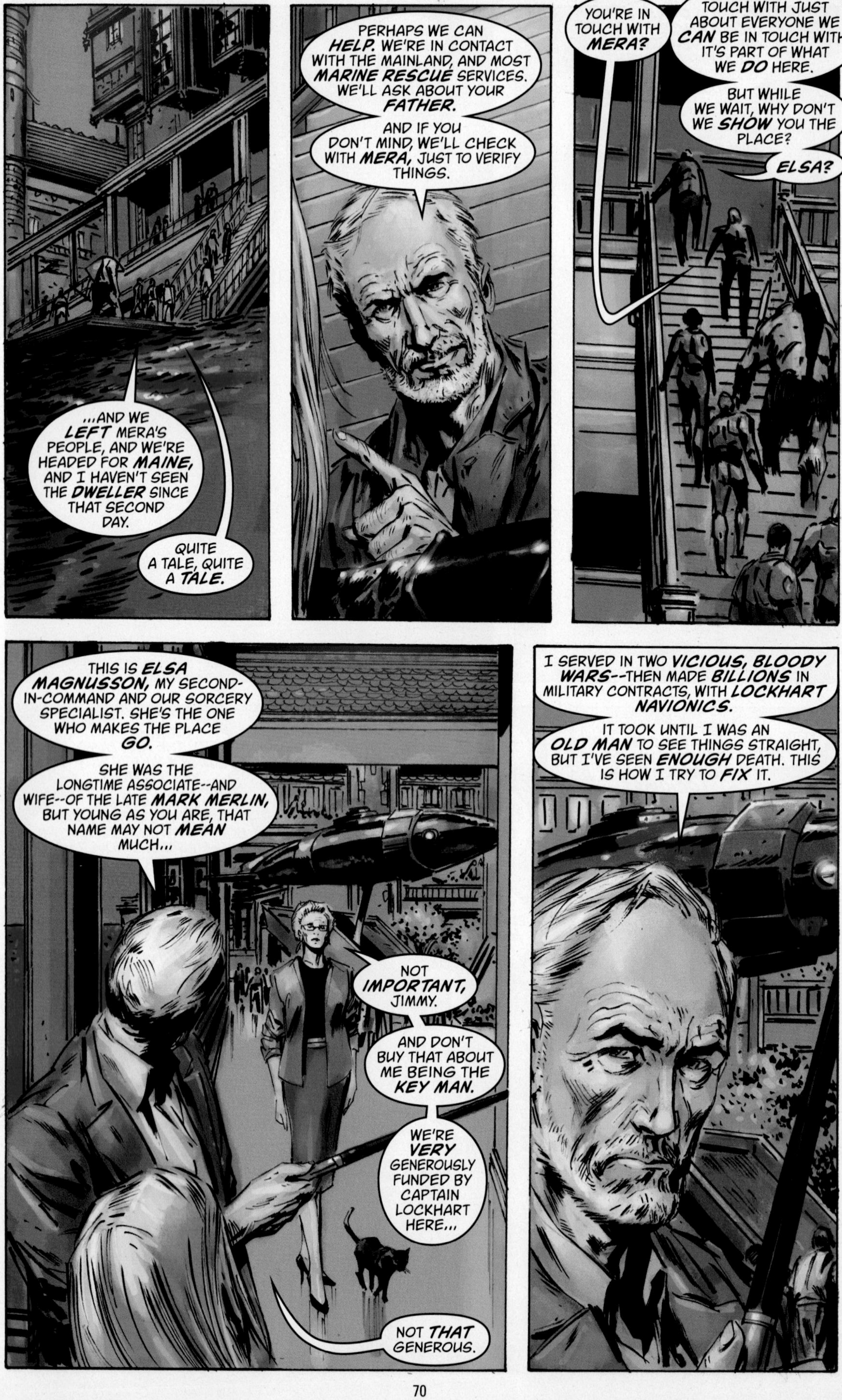
...AND WE LEFT MERA'S PEOPLE, AND WE'RE HEADED FOR MAINE, AND I HAVEN'T SEEN THE DWELLER SINCE THAT SECOND DAY.
QUITE A TALE, QUITE A TALE.
PERHAPS WE CAN HELP. WE'RE IN CONTACT WITH THE MAINLAND, AND MOST MARINE RESCUE SERVICES. WE'LL ASK ABOUT YOUR FATHER.
AND IF YOU DON'T MIND, WE'LL CHECK WITH MERA, JUST TO VERIFY THINGS.
YOU'RE IN TOUCH WITH MERA?
WE'RE IN TOUCH WITH JUST ABOUT EVERYONE WE CAN BE IN TOUCH WITH. IT'S PART OF WHAT WE DO HERE.
BUT WHILE WE WAIT, WHY DON'T WE SHOW YOU THE PLACE?
ELSA?
THIS IS ELSA MAGNUSSON, MY SECOND-IN-COMMAND AND OUR SORCERY SPECIALIST. SHE'S THE ONE WHO MAKES THE PLACE GO.
SHE WAS THE LONGTIME ASSOCIATE--AND WIFE--OF THE LATE MARK MERLIN, BUT YOUNG AS YOU ARE, THAT NAME MAY NOT MEAN MUCH...
NOT IMPORTANT, JIMMY.
AND DON'T BUY THAT ABOUT ME BEING THE KEY MAN.
WE'RE VERY GENEROUSLY FUNDED BY CAPTAIN LOCKHART HERE...
NOT THAT GENEROUS.
I SERVED IN TWO VICIOUS, BLOODY WARS--THEN MADE BILLIONS IN MILITARY CONTRACTS, WITH LOCKHART NAVIONICS.
IT TOOK UNTIL I WAS AN OLD MAN TO SEE THINGS STRAIGHT, BUT I'VE SEEN ENOUGH DEATH. THIS IS HOW I TRY TO FIX IT.

WINDWARD HOME IS A *CROSS-SPECIALIZATION THINK TANK*, ANSWERABLE TO NO GOVERNMENT, NO NATION. WE STAY *STRICTLY* IN INTERNATIONAL WATERS.

WE'VE BROUGHT TOGETHER *SCIENTISTS, PHILOSOPHERS, MYSTICS*-- THINKERS OF *ALL KINDS*, FROM THE HUMAN WORLD AND BEYOND.

WE TRY TO BROKER *NONVIOLENT SOLUTIONS* TO WORLD PROBLEMS, TRY TO GET PEOPLE TO LOOK AT THINGS IN A *DIFFERENT WAY.*

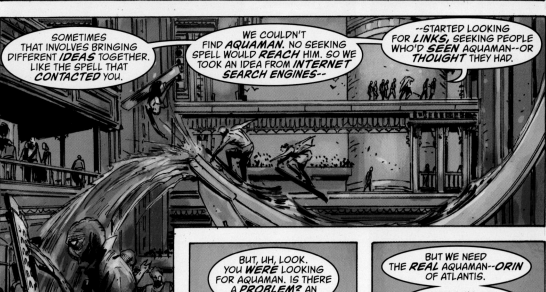

SOMETIMES THAT INVOLVES BRINGING DIFFERENT *IDEAS* TOGETHER. LIKE THE SPELL THAT *CONTACTED* YOU.

WE COULDN'T FIND *AQUAMAN*. NO SEEKING SPELL WOULD *REACH* HIM. SO WE TOOK AN IDEA FROM *INTERNET SEARCH ENGINES*--

--STARTED LOOKING FOR *LINKS*, SEEKING PEOPLE WHO'D *SEEN* AQUAMAN--OR *THOUGHT* THEY HAD.

AND PEOPLE DOWN THERE LOOK AT *ME*, AND THEY THINK "AQUAMAN," AND YOUR SPELL-THING NARROWS THE *SEARCH*...

PRETTY *SHARP.*

BUT, UH, LOOK. YOU *WERE* LOOKING FOR AQUAMAN. IS THERE A *PROBLEM?* AN EMERGENCY?

BECAUSE I CAN'T STAY OUT OF WATER ALL THAT *LONG*, AND--

NO, THERE'S NO *CRISIS.*

BUT WE NEED THE *REAL* AQUAMAN--*ORIN* OF ATLANTIS.

MAYBE WE CAN JUST *SHOW* YOU. WHAT WE HAVE--IT'S IN OUR *UNDERSEA CHAMBERS* ANYWAY. AND MAYBE YOU *CAN* HELP, SOMEHOW.

DANE CAN TAKE YOU.

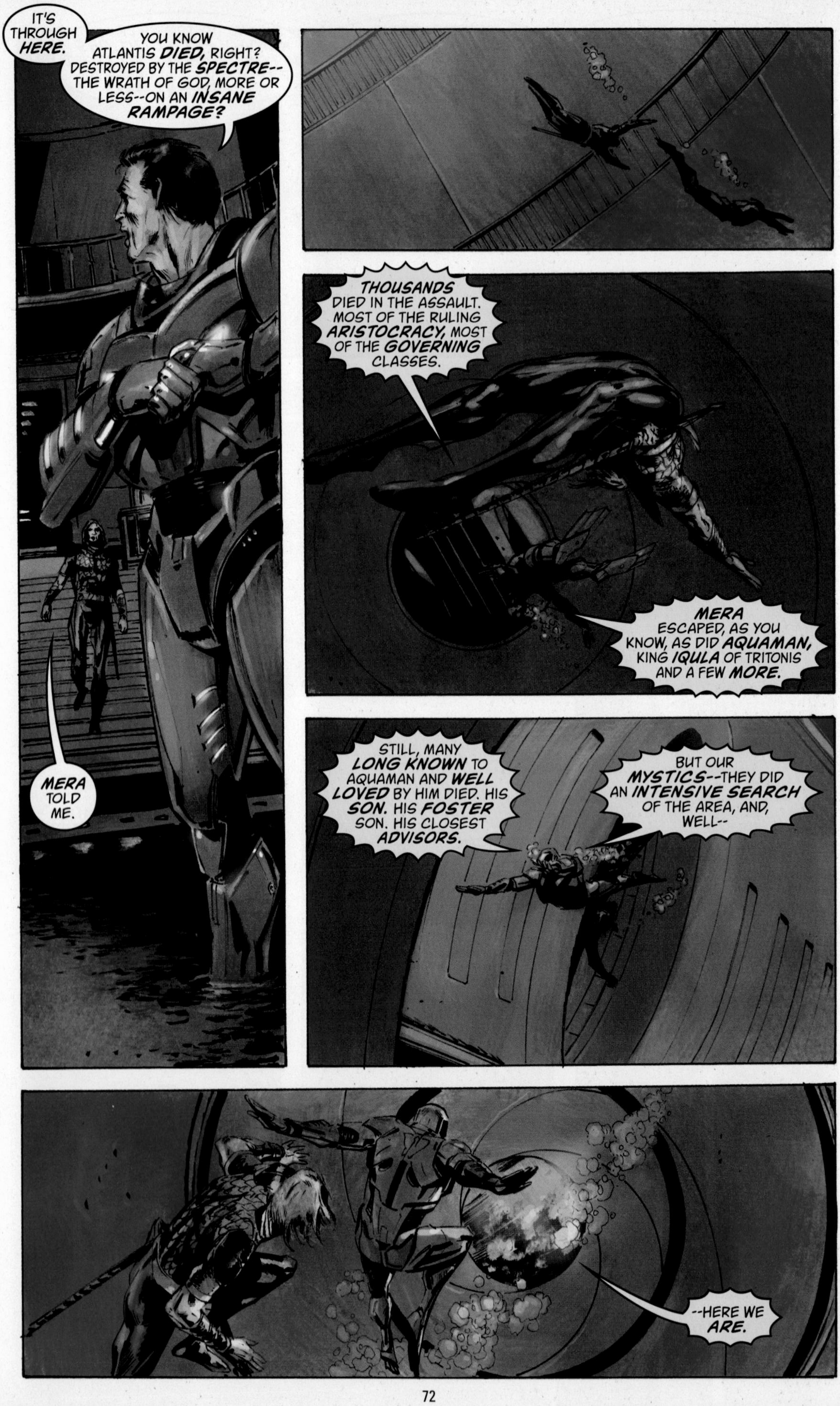
IT'S THROUGH HERE.
YOU KNOW ATLANTIS DIED, RIGHT? DESTROYED BY THE SPECTRE--THE WRATH OF GOD, MORE OR LESS--ON AN INSANE RAMPAGE?
MERA TOLD ME.
THOUSANDS DIED IN THE ASSAULT. MOST OF THE RULING ARISTOCRACY, MOST OF THE GOVERNING CLASSES.
MERA ESCAPED, AS YOU KNOW, AS DID AQUAMAN, KING IQULA OF TRITONIS AND A FEW MORE.
STILL, MANY LONG KNOWN TO AQUAMAN AND WELL LOVED BY HIM DIED. HIS SON. HIS FOSTER SON. HIS CLOSEST ADVISORS.
BUT OUR MYSTICS--THEY DID AN INTENSIVE SEARCH OF THE AREA, AND, WELL--
--HERE WE ARE.

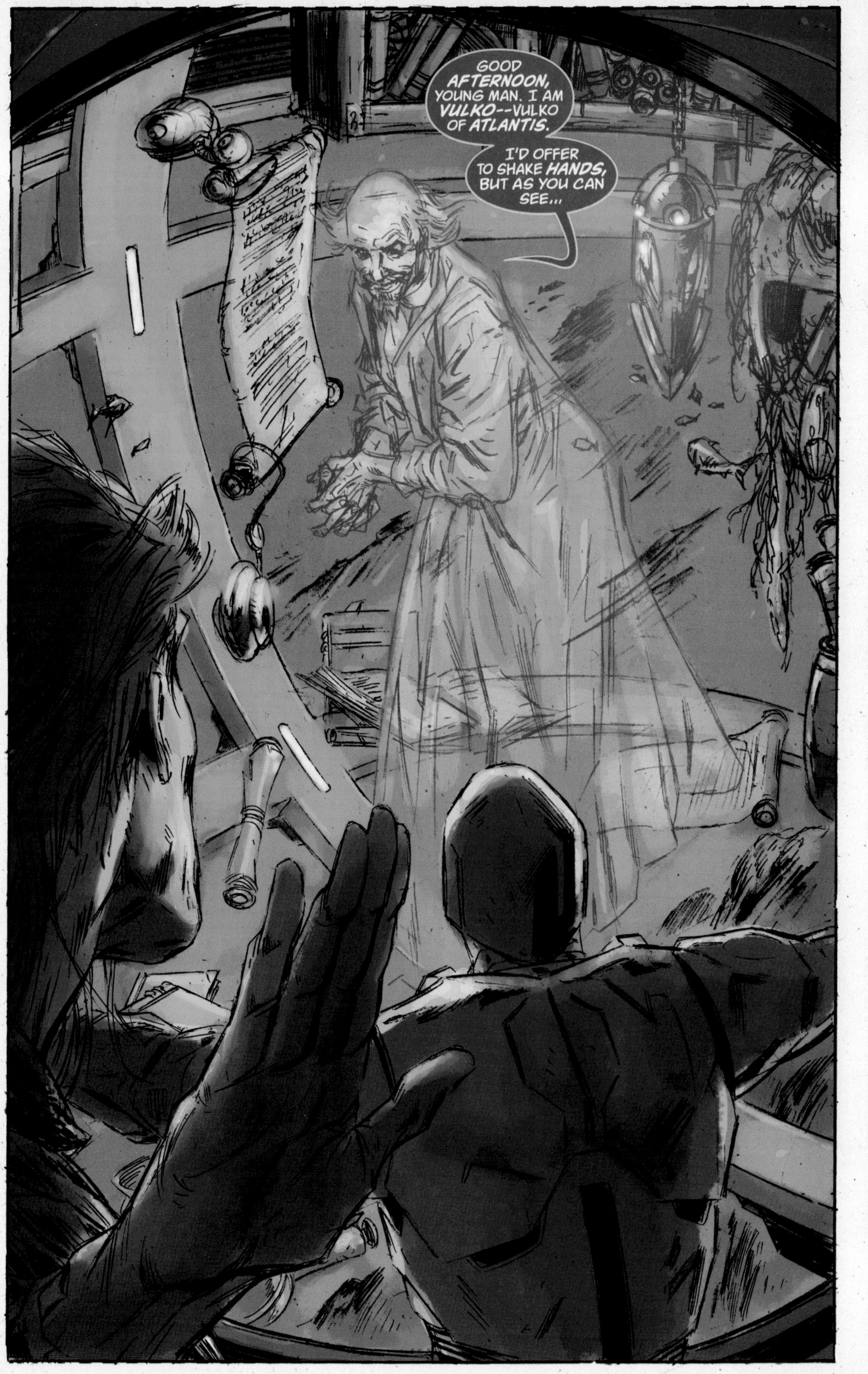
GOOD AFTERNOON, YOUNG MAN. I AM VULKO--VULKO OF ATLANTIS.
I'D OFFER TO SHAKE HANDS, BUT AS YOU CAN SEE...

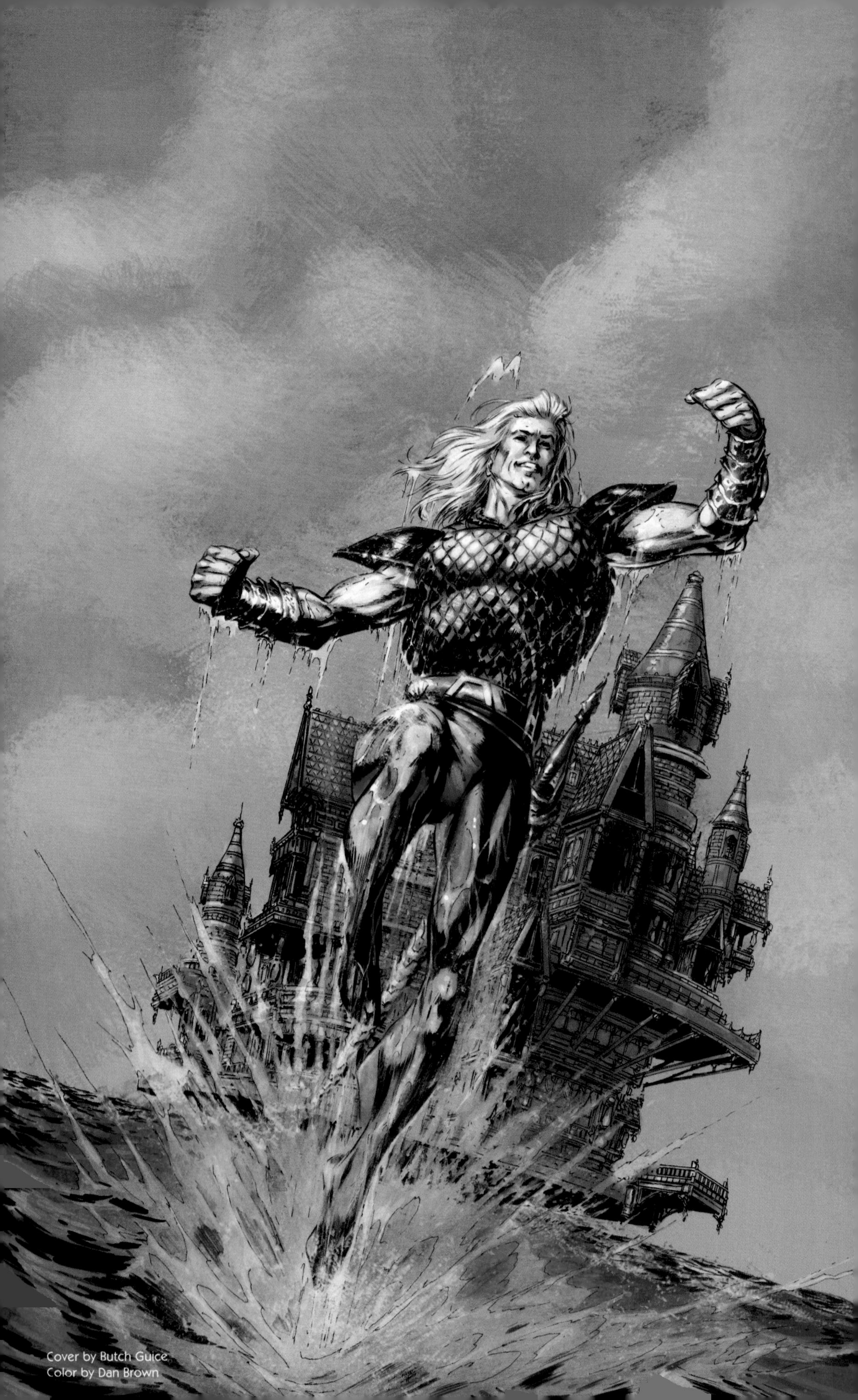

Cover by Butch Guice
Color by Dan Brown

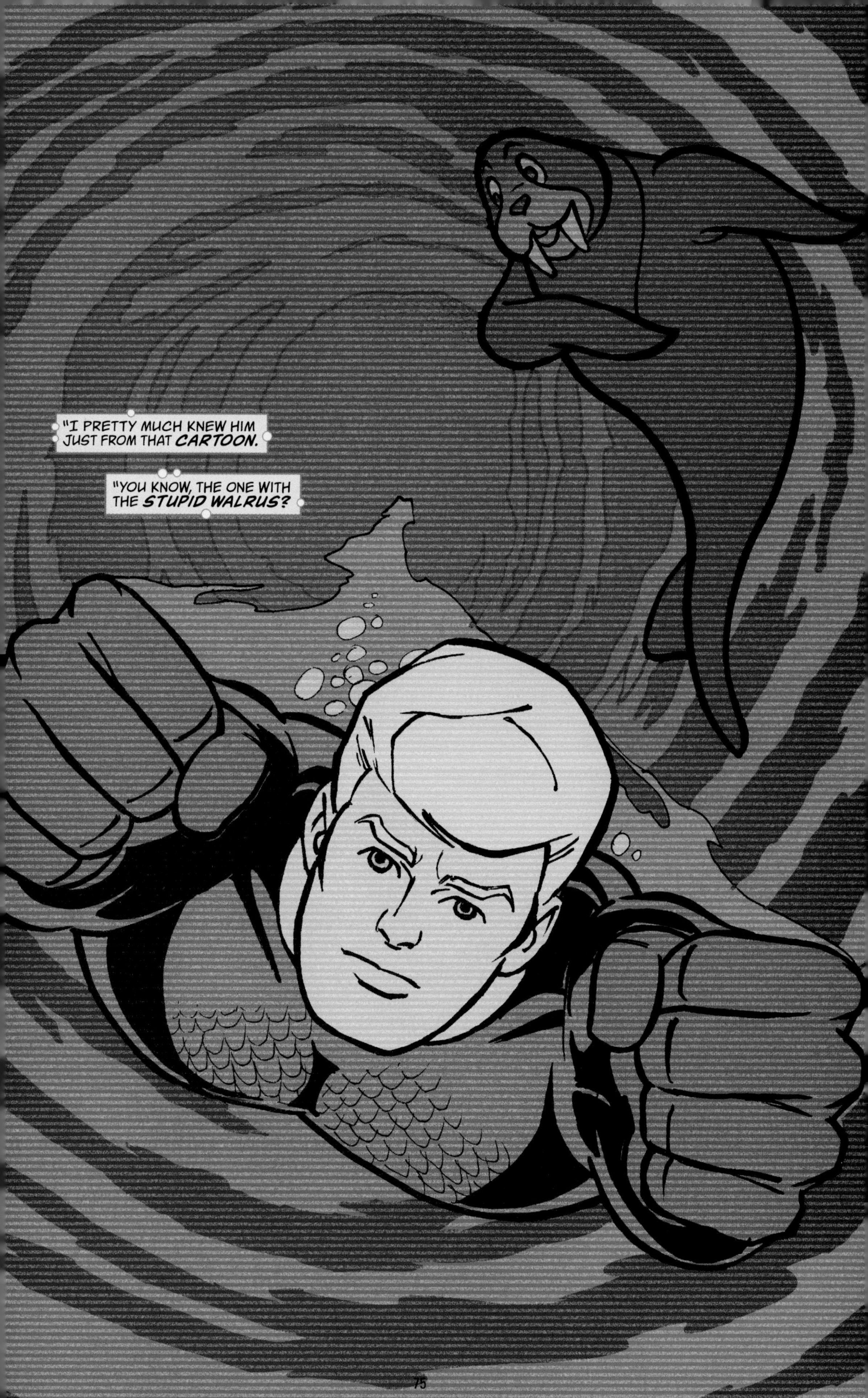
"I PRETTY MUCH KNEW HIM JUST FROM THAT CARTOON.
"YOU KNOW, THE ONE WITH THE STUPID WALRUS?

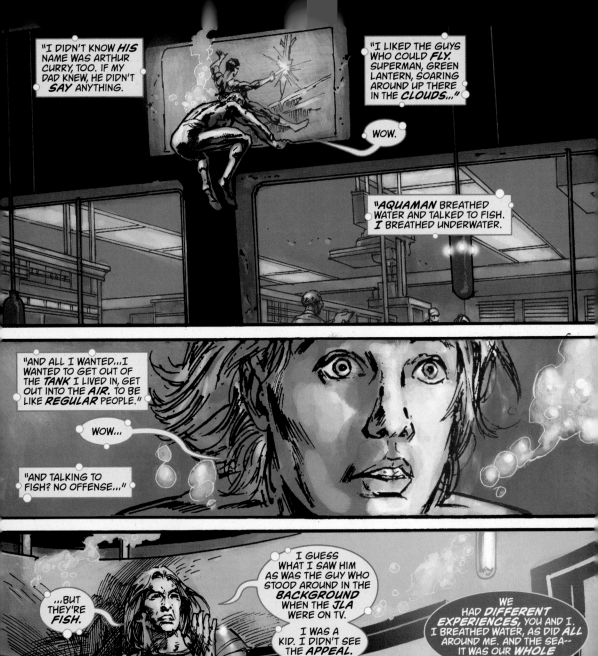

"I DIDN'T KNOW *HIS* NAME WAS ARTHUR CURRY, TOO. IF MY DAD KNEW, HE DIDN'T *SAY* ANYTHING."

"I LIKED THE GUYS WHO COULD *FLY.* SUPERMAN, GREEN LANTERN, SOARING AROUND UP THERE IN THE *CLOUDS*..."

WOW.

"*AQUAMAN* BREATHED WATER AND TALKED TO FISH. *I* BREATHED UNDERWATER."

"AND ALL I WANTED...I WANTED TO GET OUT OF THE *TANK* I LIVED IN, GET OUT INTO THE *AIR.* TO BE LIKE *REGULAR* PEOPLE."

WOW...

"AND TALKING TO FISH? NO OFFENSE..."

...BUT THEY'RE *FISH.*

I GUESS WHAT I SAW HIM AS WAS THE GUY WHO STOOD AROUND IN THE *BACKGROUND* WHEN THE *JLA* WERE ON TV.

I WAS A KID. I DIDN'T SEE THE *APPEAL.*

WE HAD *DIFFERENT EXPERIENCES*, YOU AND I. I BREATHED WATER, AS DID *ALL* AROUND ME. AND THE SEA-- IT WAS OUR *WHOLE WORLD.*

ARTHUR--*MY* AQUAMAN--WAS TO ME A *MONARCH*, A HERO, AN EXPLORER, AN *IMPETUOUS* MAN OF ACTION, A MAN OF *IDEALS.*

AND, I AM PROUD TO SAY...

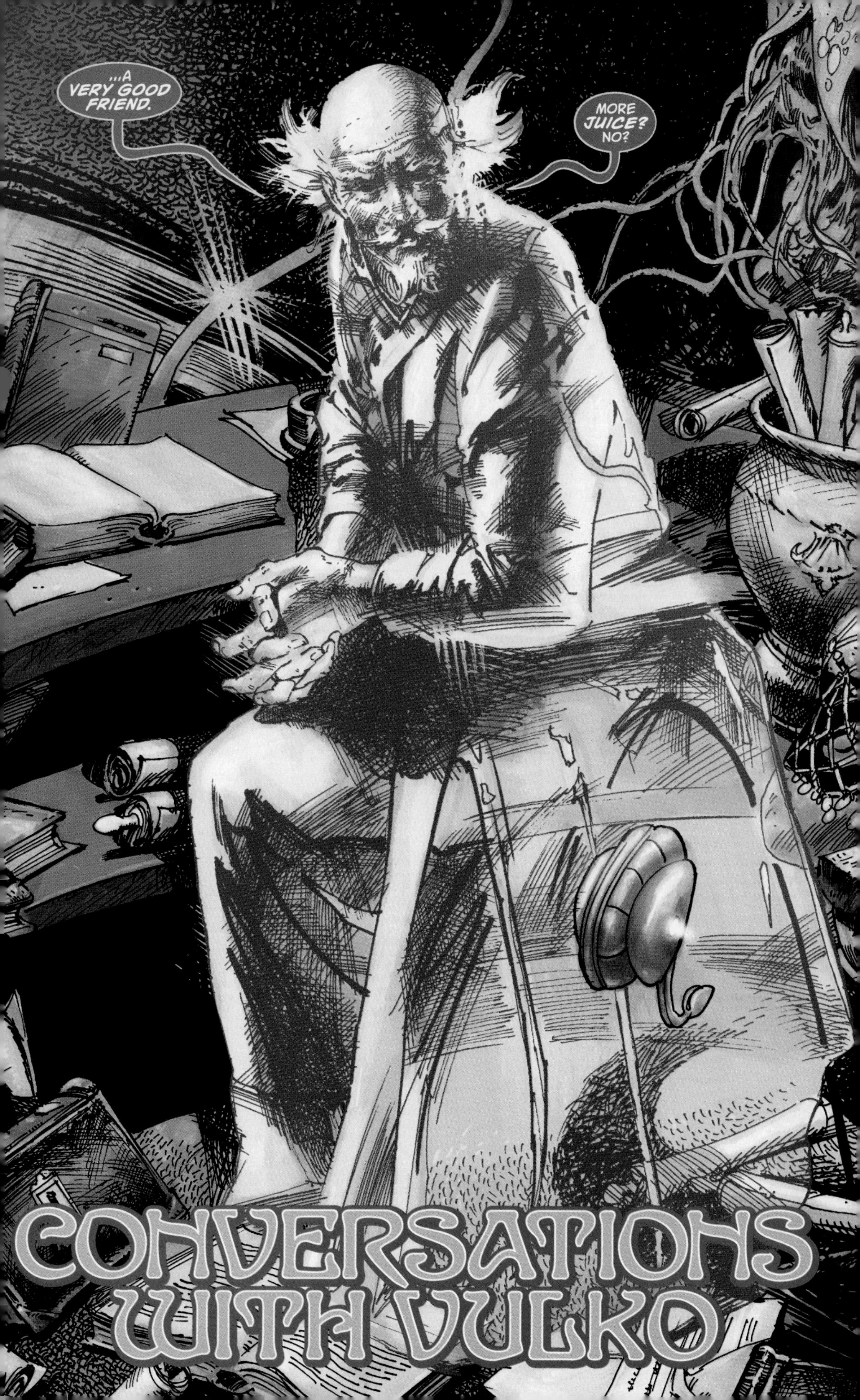
...A VERY GOOD FRIEND.
MORE JUICE? NO?
CONVERSATIONS WITH VULKO

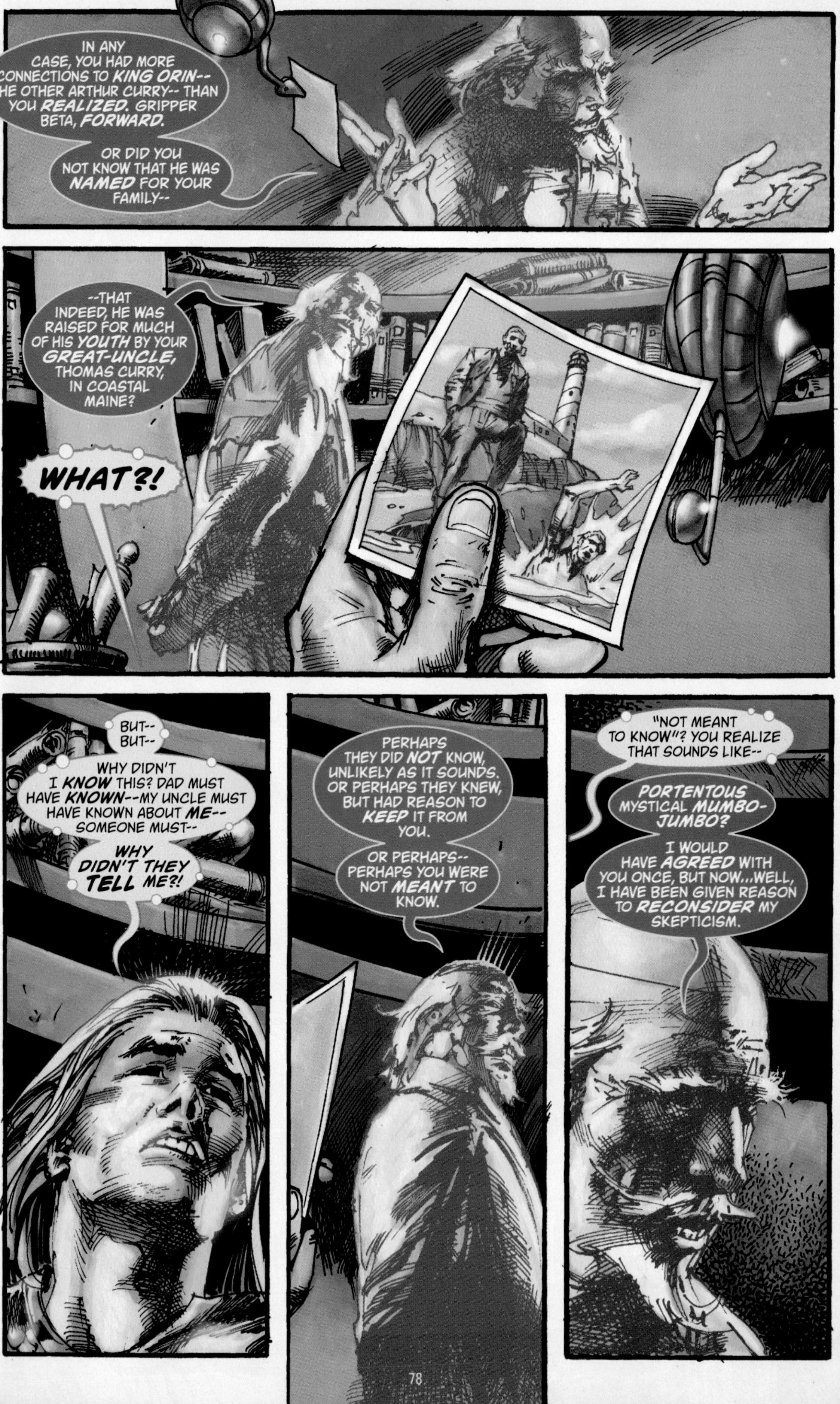
IN ANY CASE, YOU HAD MORE CONNECTIONS TO KING ORIN-- THE OTHER ARTHUR CURRY-- THAN YOU REALIZED. GRIPPER BETA, FORWARD.
OR DID YOU NOT KNOW THAT HE WAS NAMED FOR YOUR FAMILY--
--THAT INDEED, HE WAS RAISED FOR MUCH OF HIS YOUTH BY YOUR GREAT-UNCLE, THOMAS CURRY, IN COASTAL MAINE?
WHAT?!
BUT-- BUT--
WHY DIDN'T I KNOW THIS? DAD MUST HAVE KNOWN--MY UNCLE MUST HAVE KNOWN ABOUT ME-- SOMEONE MUST--
WHY DIDN'T THEY TELL ME?!
PERHAPS THEY DID NOT KNOW, UNLIKELY AS IT SOUNDS. OR PERHAPS THEY KNEW, BUT HAD REASON TO KEEP IT FROM YOU.
OR PERHAPS-- PERHAPS YOU WERE NOT MEANT TO KNOW.
"NOT MEANT TO KNOW"? YOU REALIZE THAT SOUNDS LIKE--
PORTENTOUS MYSTICAL MUMBO-JUMBO?
I WOULD HAVE AGREED WITH YOU ONCE, BUT NOW...WELL, I HAVE BEEN GIVEN REASON TO RECONSIDER MY SKEPTICISM.

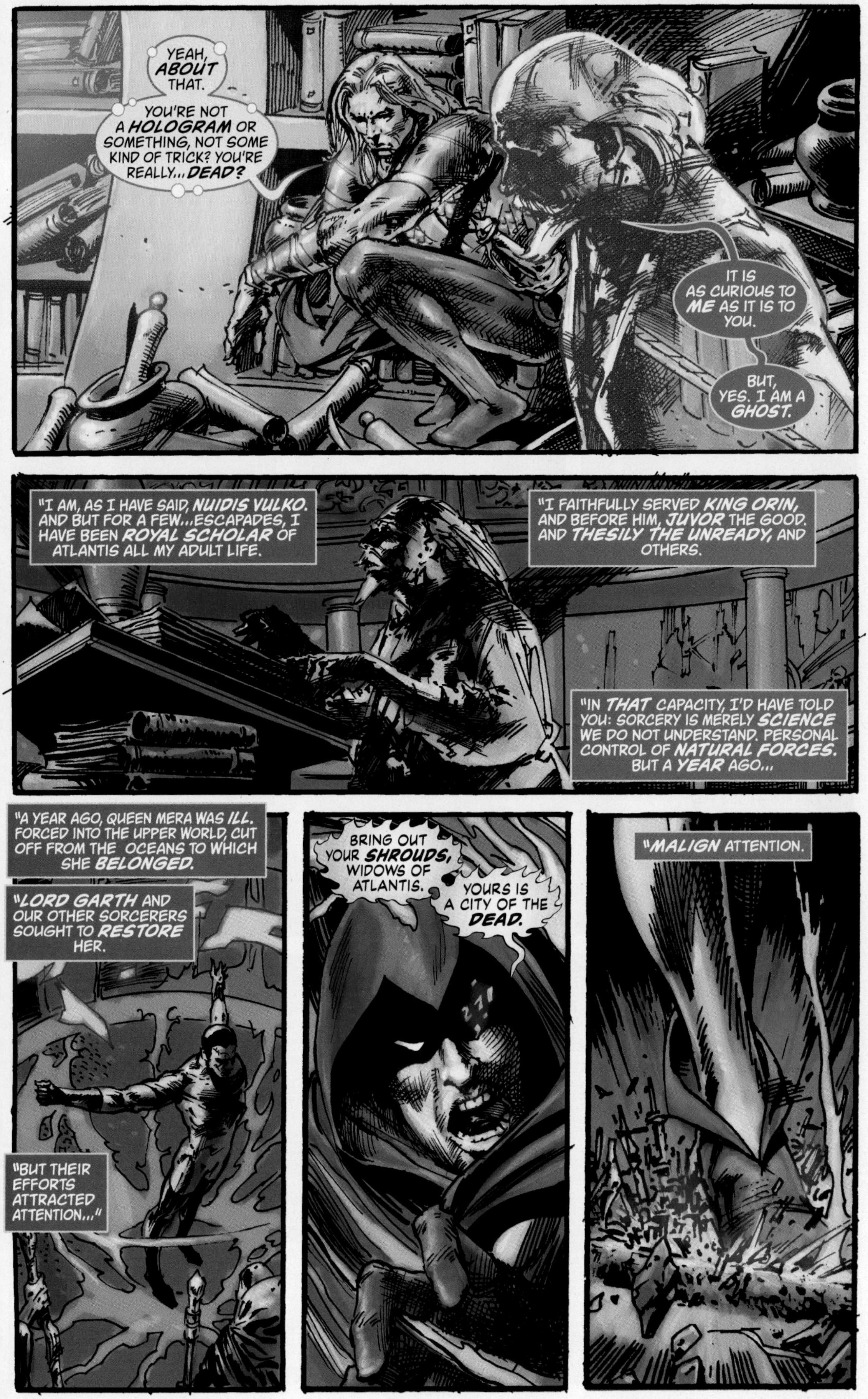

YEAH, ABOUT THAT.
YOU'RE NOT A HOLOGRAM OR SOMETHING, NOT SOME KIND OF TRICK? YOU'RE REALLY... DEAD?
IT IS AS CURIOUS TO ME AS IT IS TO YOU.
BUT, YES. I AM A GHOST.
"I AM, AS I HAVE SAID, NUIDIS VULKO. AND BUT FOR A FEW... ESCAPADES, I HAVE BEEN ROYAL SCHOLAR OF ATLANTIS ALL MY ADULT LIFE.
"I FAITHFULLY SERVED KING ORIN, AND BEFORE HIM, JUVOR THE GOOD. AND THESILY THE UNREADY, AND OTHERS.
"IN THAT CAPACITY, I'D HAVE TOLD YOU: SORCERY IS MERELY SCIENCE WE DO NOT UNDERSTAND. PERSONAL CONTROL OF NATURAL FORCES. BUT A YEAR AGO...
"A YEAR AGO, QUEEN MERA WAS ILL. FORCED INTO THE UPPER WORLD, CUT OFF FROM THE OCEANS TO WHICH SHE BELONGED.
"LORD GARTH AND OUR OTHER SORCERERS SOUGHT TO RESTORE HER.
"BUT THEIR EFFORTS ATTRACTED ATTENTION..."
BRING OUT YOUR SHROUDS, WIDOWS OF ATLANTIS.
YOURS IS A CITY OF THE DEAD.
"MALIGN ATTENTION.

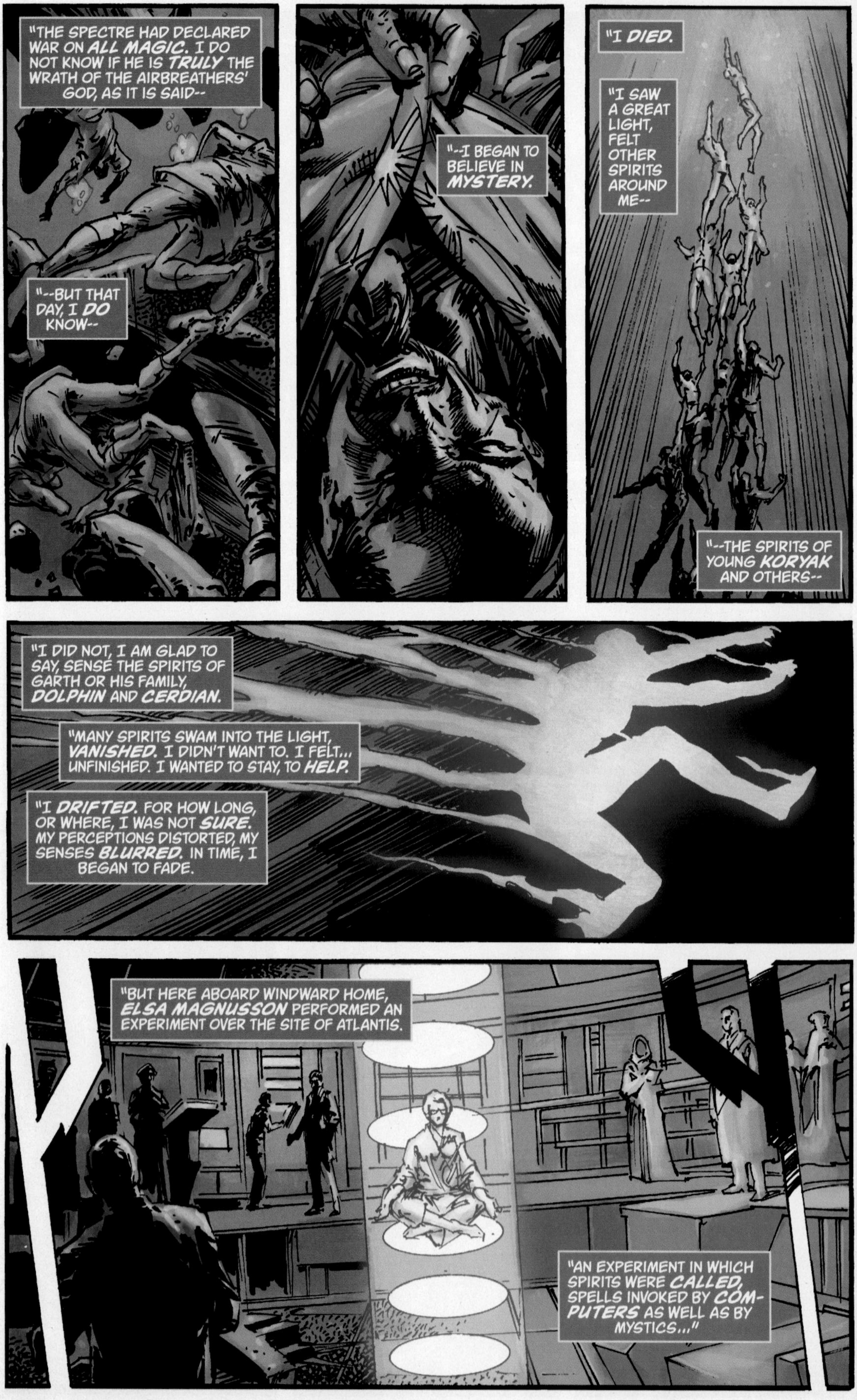
"THE SPECTRE HAD DECLARED WAR ON ALL MAGIC. I DO NOT KNOW IF HE IS TRULY THE WRATH OF THE AIRBREATHERS' GOD, AS IT IS SAID--
"--BUT THAT DAY, I DO KNOW--
"--I BEGAN TO BELIEVE IN MYSTERY.
"I DIED.
"I SAW A GREAT LIGHT, FELT OTHER SPIRITS AROUND ME--
"--THE SPIRITS OF YOUNG KORYAK AND OTHERS--
"I DID NOT, I AM GLAD TO SAY, SENSE THE SPIRITS OF GARTH OR HIS FAMILY, DOLPHIN AND CERDIAN.
"MANY SPIRITS SWAM INTO THE LIGHT, VANISHED. I DIDN'T WANT TO. I FELT... UNFINISHED. I WANTED TO STAY, TO HELP.
"I DRIFTED. FOR HOW LONG, OR WHERE, I WAS NOT SURE. MY PERCEPTIONS DISTORTED, MY SENSES BLURRED. IN TIME, I BEGAN TO FADE.
"BUT HERE ABOARD WINDWARD HOME, ELSA MAGNUSSON PERFORMED AN EXPERIMENT OVER THE SITE OF ATLANTIS.
"AN EXPERIMENT IN WHICH SPIRITS WERE CALLED, SPELLS INVOKED BY COMPUTERS AS WELL AS BY MYSTICS..."

...AND HERE I *AM*, JUST AS YOU SEE ME BEFORE YOU. I READ, I THINK, I MAKE BRIEF *ASTRAL JOURNEYS*.

IT'S ALL BEEN QUITE *FASCINATING*, REALLY.

AND YOU SAY YOU'RE HERE TO *HELP*.

TO HELP *HOW*? *WHO*?

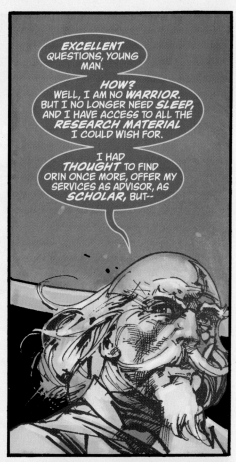

EXCELLENT QUESTIONS, YOUNG MAN.

HOW? WELL, I AM NO *WARRIOR*. BUT I NO LONGER NEED *SLEEP*, AND I HAVE ACCESS TO ALL THE *RESEARCH MATERIAL* I COULD WISH FOR.

I HAD *THOUGHT* TO FIND ORIN ONCE MORE, OFFER MY SERVICES AS ADVISOR, AS *SCHOLAR*, BUT--

BUT YOU MYSTICALLY *GOOGLED* HIM AND GOT ME.

THE DWELLER IN THE DEPTHS SAYS I *AM* AQUAMAN. THAT I'M GOING TO DO *GREAT THINGS*, BE A *BIG HERO*.

IS THAT *IT*, THEN? *SO LONG*, OLD AQUAMAN, SAY HEY TO THE *NEW* AQUAMAN, LET'S GET A *MOVE* ON?

I...*HOPE* NOT. KING ORIN... I HOPE HE IS NOT LOST TO US *FOREVER*.

BUT THERE, I THINK, I *CAN* PERHAPS HELP YOU.

YOU HAVE *TOLD* ME OF THE PROPHECIES THIS DWELLER MADE.

GO. REST. *EAT*. LET ME CONSULT MY TEXTS.

I WILL SEE WHAT I CAN *DISCOVER*.

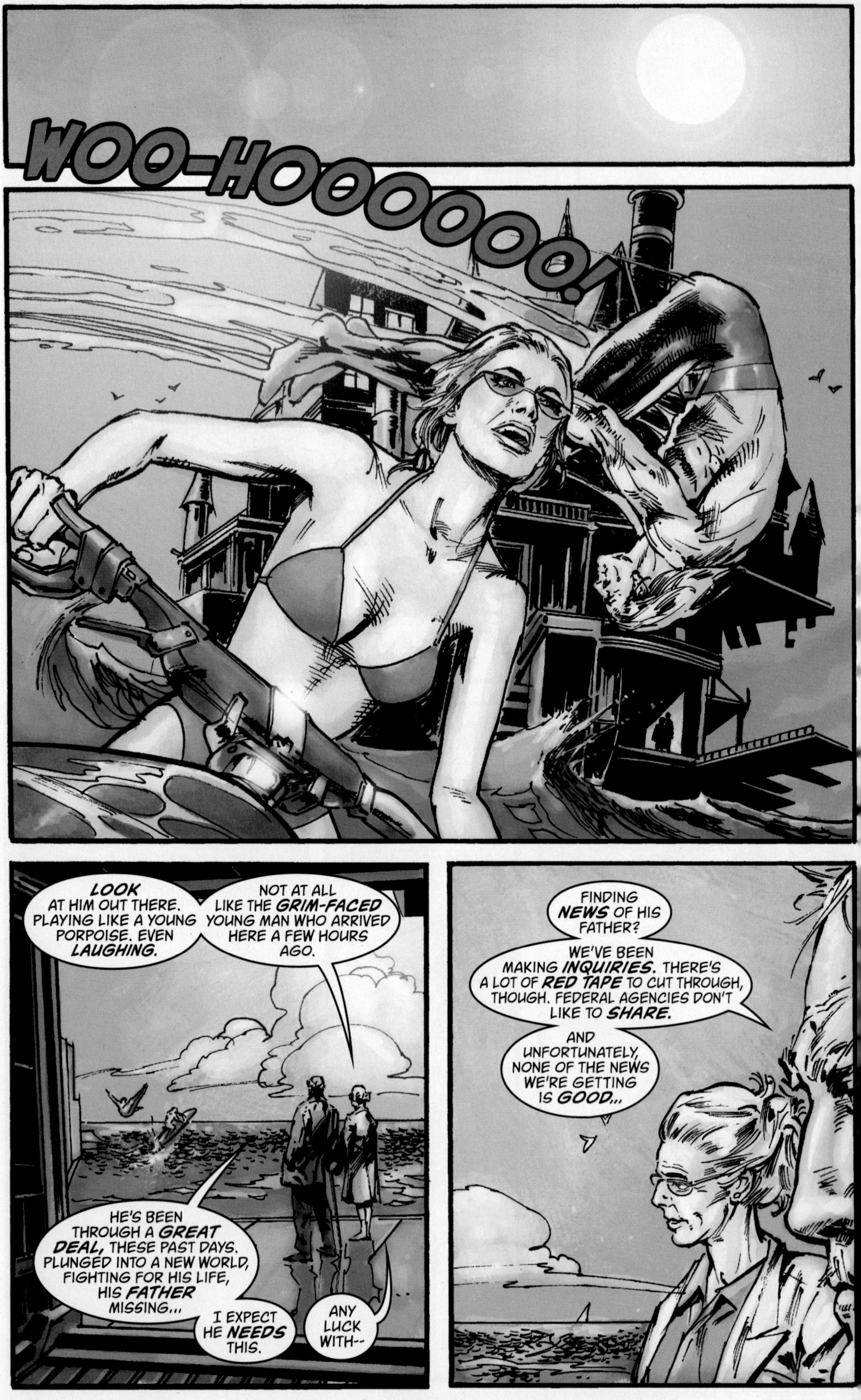
WOO-HOOOOOOO!
LOOK AT HIM OUT THERE. PLAYING LIKE A YOUNG PORPOISE. EVEN LAUGHING.
NOT AT ALL LIKE THE GRIM-FACED YOUNG MAN WHO ARRIVED HERE A FEW HOURS AGO.
HE'S BEEN THROUGH A GREAT DEAL, THESE PAST DAYS. PLUNGED INTO A NEW WORLD, FIGHTING FOR HIS LIFE, HIS FATHER MISSING...
I EXPECT HE NEEDS THIS.
ANY LUCK WITH--
FINDING NEWS OF HIS FATHER?
WE'VE BEEN MAKING INQUIRIES. THERE'S A LOT OF RED TAPE TO CUT THROUGH, THOUGH. FEDERAL AGENCIES DON'T LIKE TO SHARE.
AND UNFORTUNATELY, NONE OF THE NEWS WE'RE GETTING IS GOOD...

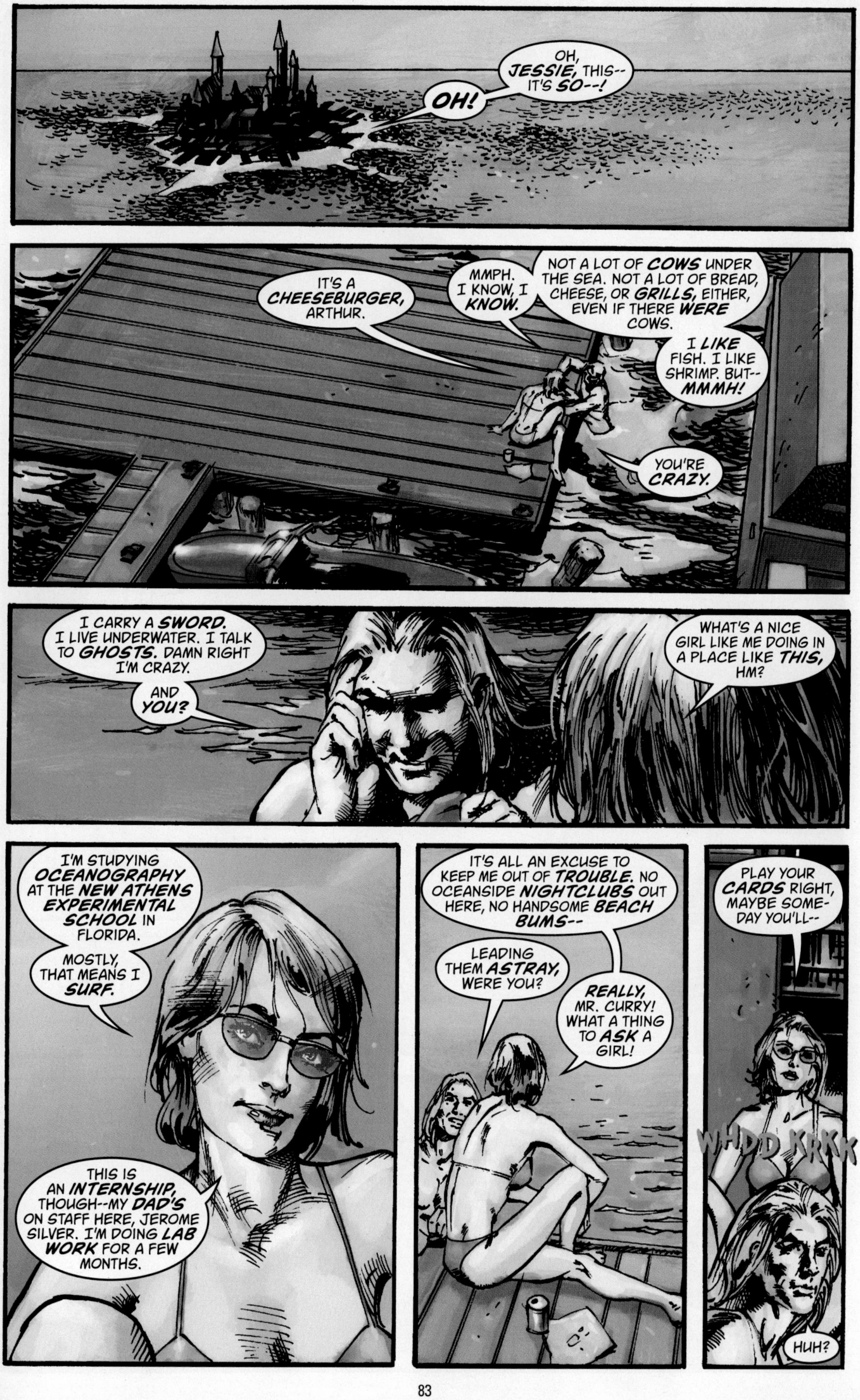

OH, JESSIE, THIS-- IT'S SO--!
OH!
IT'S A CHEESEBURGER, ARTHUR.
MMPH. I KNOW, I KNOW.
NOT A LOT OF COWS UNDER THE SEA. NOT A LOT OF BREAD, CHEESE, OR GRILLS, EITHER, EVEN IF THERE WERE COWS.
I LIKE FISH. I LIKE SHRIMP. BUT-- MMMH!
YOU'RE CRAZY.
I CARRY A SWORD. I LIVE UNDERWATER. I TALK TO GHOSTS. DAMN RIGHT I'M CRAZY.
AND YOU?
WHAT'S A NICE GIRL LIKE ME DOING IN A PLACE LIKE THIS, HM?
I'M STUDYING OCEANOGRAPHY AT THE NEW ATHENS EXPERIMENTAL SCHOOL IN FLORIDA.
MOSTLY, THAT MEANS I SURF.
THIS IS AN INTERNSHIP, THOUGH--MY DAD'S ON STAFF HERE, JEROME SILVER. I'M DOING LAB WORK FOR A FEW MONTHS.
IT'S ALL AN EXCUSE TO KEEP ME OUT OF TROUBLE. NO OCEANSIDE NIGHTCLUBS OUT HERE, NO HANDSOME BEACH BUMS--
LEADING THEM ASTRAY, WERE YOU?
REALLY, MR. CURRY! WHAT A THING TO ASK A GIRL!
PLAY YOUR CARDS RIGHT, MAYBE SOME-DAY YOU'LL--
WHDD KRKK
HUH?

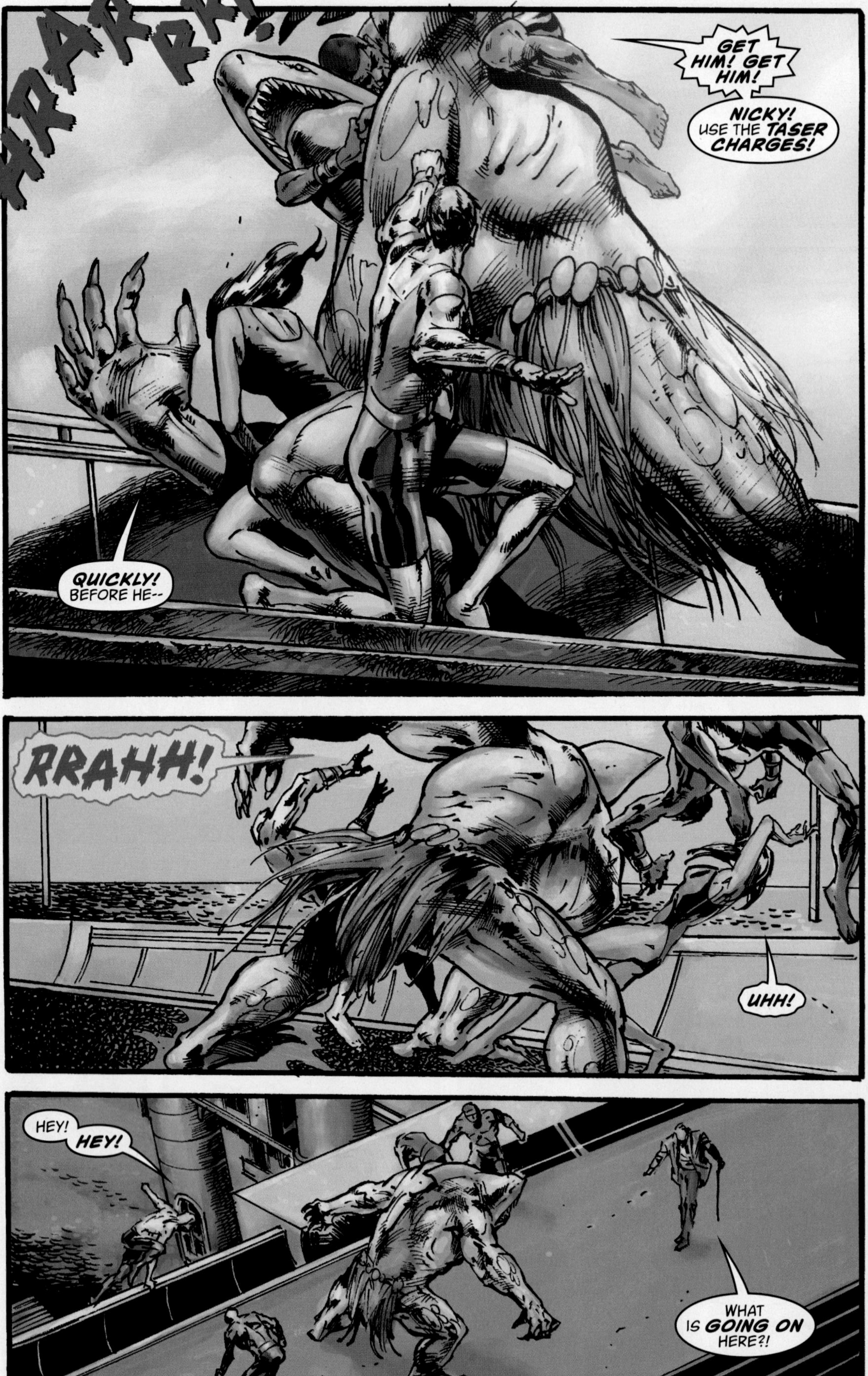
HRARRRR!
GET HIM! GET HIM!
NICKY! USE THE TASER CHARGES!
QUICKLY! BEFORE HE--
RRAHH!
UHH!
HEY! HEY!
WHAT IS GOING ON HERE?!

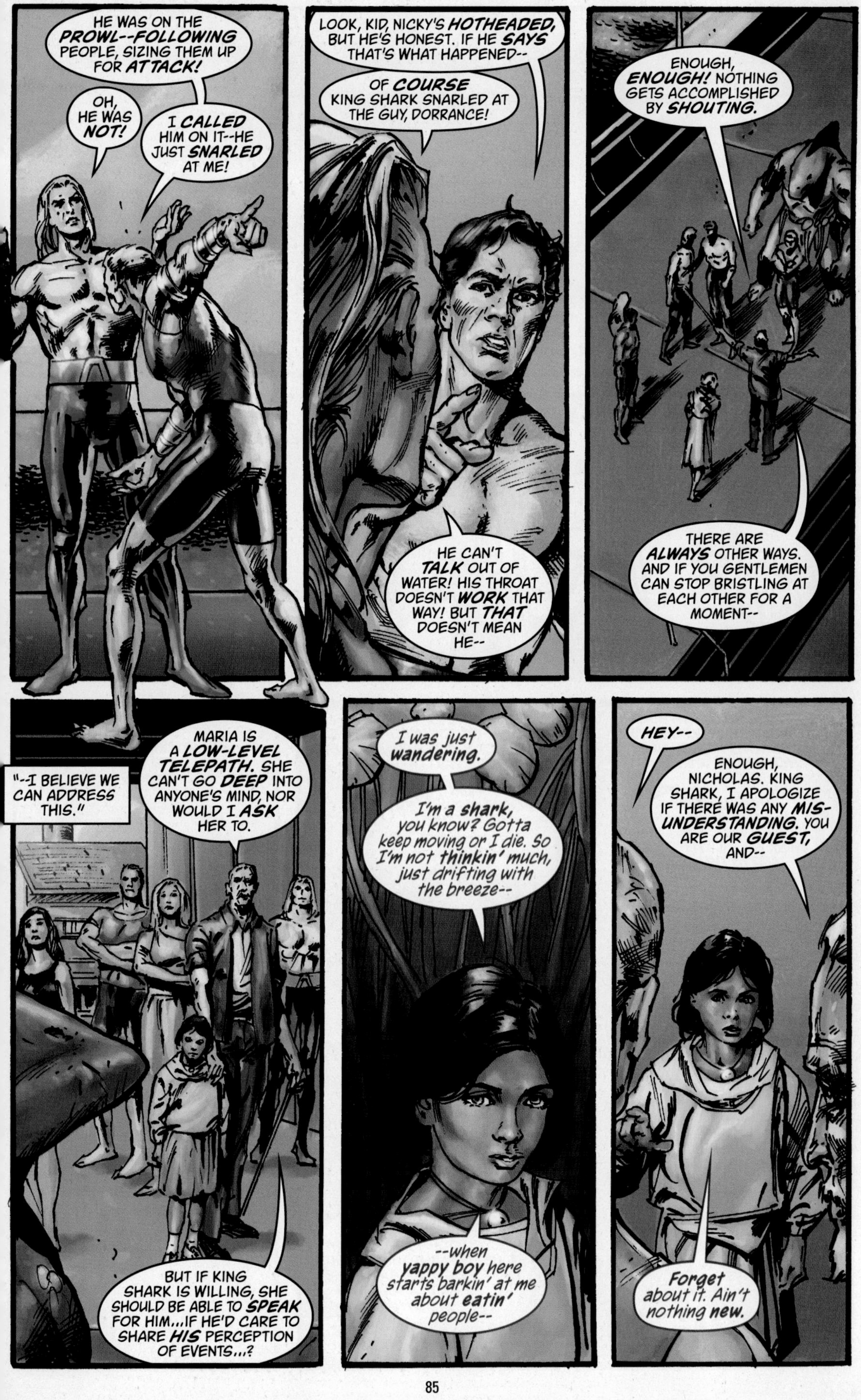
HE WAS ON THE PROWL--FOLLOWING PEOPLE, SIZING THEM UP FOR ATTACK!
OH, HE WAS NOT!
I CALLED HIM ON IT--HE JUST SNARLED AT ME!
LOOK, KID, NICKY'S HOTHEADED, BUT HE'S HONEST. IF HE SAYS THAT'S WHAT HAPPENED--
OF COURSE KING SHARK SNARLED AT THE GUY, DORRANCE!
HE CAN'T TALK OUT OF WATER! HIS THROAT DOESN'T WORK THAT WAY! BUT THAT DOESN'T MEAN HE--
ENOUGH, ENOUGH! NOTHING GETS ACCOMPLISHED BY SHOUTING.
THERE ARE ALWAYS OTHER WAYS. AND IF YOU GENTLEMEN CAN STOP BRISTLING AT EACH OTHER FOR A MOMENT--
"--I BELIEVE WE CAN ADDRESS THIS."
MARIA IS A LOW-LEVEL TELEPATH. SHE CAN'T GO DEEP INTO ANYONE'S MIND, NOR WOULD I ASK HER TO.
BUT IF KING SHARK IS WILLING, SHE SHOULD BE ABLE TO SPEAK FOR HIM...IF HE'D CARE TO SHARE HIS PERCEPTION OF EVENTS...?
I was just wandering.
I'm a shark, you know? Gotta keep moving or I die. So I'm not thinkin' much, just drifting with the breeze--
--when yappy boy here starts barkin' at me about eatin' people--
HEY--
ENOUGH, NICHOLAS. KING SHARK, I APOLOGIZE IF THERE WAS ANY MISUNDERSTANDING. YOU ARE OUR GUEST, AND--
Forget about it. Ain't nothing new.

Place is boring anyway-- --and don't **kid** yourself, yappy boy, you're **not** that tasty-looking.

Do what you gotta **do**, Arthur.

I'll wait **below.**

APOLOGIZING TO HIM! IT'S NOT **RIGHT**--

HE IS OUR **GUEST,** SIGOURNEY.

HE'S A **KILLER!** A **WANTED CRIMINAL!**

THEN CHASE HIM WHEN HE IS **ELSE- WHERE.**

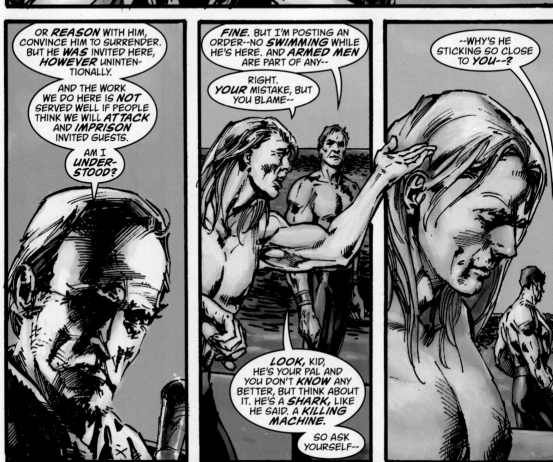

OR **REASON** WITH HIM, CONVINCE HIM TO SURRENDER. BUT HE **WAS** INVITED HERE, **HOWEVER** UNINTENTIONALLY.

AND THE WORK WE DO HERE IS **NOT** SERVED WELL IF PEOPLE THINK WE WILL **ATTACK** AND **IMPRISON** INVITED GUESTS.

AM I **UNDER- STOOD?**

FINE. BUT I'M POSTING AN ORDER--NO **SWIMMING** WHILE HE'S HERE. AND **ARMED MEN** ARE PART OF ANY--

RIGHT. **YOUR** MISTAKE, BUT YOU BLAME--

LOOK, KID, HE'S YOUR PAL AND YOU DON'T **KNOW** ANY BETTER, BUT THINK ABOUT IT. HE'S A **SHARK,** LIKE HE SAID. A **KILLING MACHINE.**

SO ASK YOURSELF--

--WHY'S HE STICKING SO CLOSE TO **YOU**--?

86

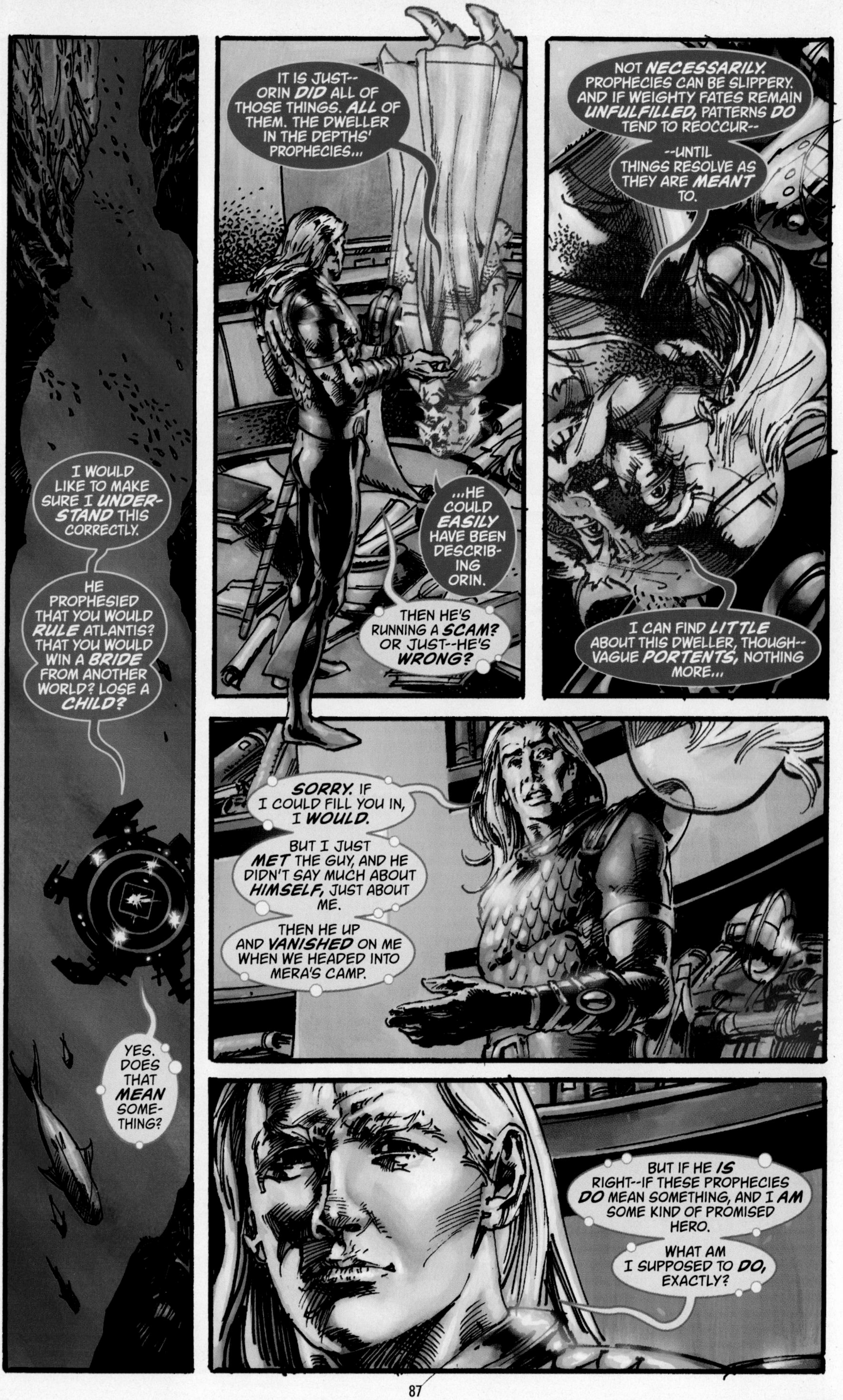
I WOULD LIKE TO MAKE SURE I UNDERSTAND THIS CORRECTLY.
HE PROPHESIED THAT YOU WOULD RULE ATLANTIS? THAT YOU WOULD WIN A BRIDE FROM ANOTHER WORLD? LOSE A CHILD?
YES. DOES THAT MEAN SOMETHING?
IT IS JUST-- ORIN DID ALL OF THOSE THINGS. ALL OF THEM. THE DWELLER IN THE DEPTHS' PROPHECIES...
...HE COULD EASILY HAVE BEEN DESCRIBING ORIN.
THEN HE'S RUNNING A SCAM? OR JUST--HE'S WRONG?
NOT NECESSARILY. PROPHECIES CAN BE SLIPPERY. AND IF WEIGHTY FATES REMAIN UNFULFILLED, PATTERNS DO TEND TO REOCCUR--
--UNTIL THINGS RESOLVE AS THEY ARE MEANT TO.
I CAN FIND LITTLE ABOUT THIS DWELLER, THOUGH-- VAGUE PORTENTS, NOTHING MORE...
SORRY. IF I COULD FILL YOU IN, I WOULD.
BUT I JUST MET THE GUY, AND HE DIDN'T SAY MUCH ABOUT HIMSELF, JUST ABOUT ME.
THEN HE UP AND VANISHED ON ME WHEN WE HEADED INTO MERA'S CAMP.
BUT IF HE IS RIGHT--IF THESE PROPHECIES DO MEAN SOMETHING, AND I AM SOME KIND OF PROMISED HERO.
WHAT AM I SUPPOSED TO DO, EXACTLY?

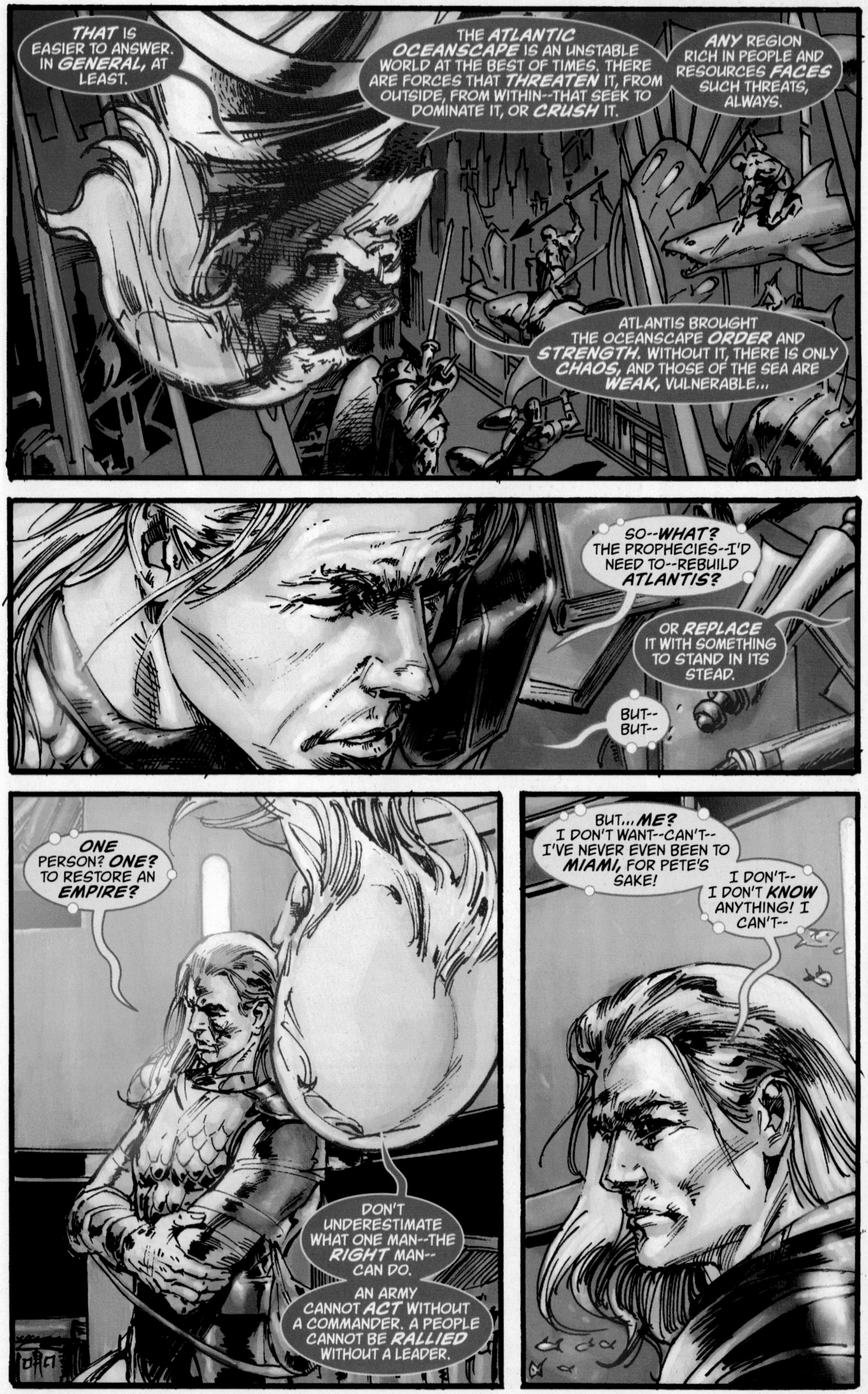
THAT IS EASIER TO ANSWER. IN GENERAL, AT LEAST.
THE ATLANTIC OCEANSCAPE IS AN UNSTABLE WORLD AT THE BEST OF TIMES. THERE ARE FORCES THAT THREATEN IT, FROM OUTSIDE, FROM WITHIN--THAT SEEK TO DOMINATE IT, OR CRUSH IT.
ANY REGION RICH IN PEOPLE AND RESOURCES FACES SUCH THREATS, ALWAYS.
ATLANTIS BROUGHT THE OCEANSCAPE ORDER AND STRENGTH. WITHOUT IT, THERE IS ONLY CHAOS, AND THOSE OF THE SEA ARE WEAK, VULNERABLE...
SO--WHAT? THE PROPHECIES--I'D NEED TO--REBUILD ATLANTIS?
OR REPLACE IT WITH SOMETHING TO STAND IN ITS STEAD.
BUT-- BUT--
ONE PERSON? ONE? TO RESTORE AN EMPIRE?
DON'T UNDERESTIMATE WHAT ONE MAN--THE RIGHT MAN--CAN DO.
AN ARMY CANNOT ACT WITHOUT A COMMANDER. A PEOPLE CANNOT BE RALLIED WITHOUT A LEADER.
BUT... ME? I DON'T WANT--CAN'T--I'VE NEVER EVEN BEEN TO MIAMI, FOR PETE'S SAKE!
I DON'T-- I DON'T KNOW ANYTHING! I CAN'T--

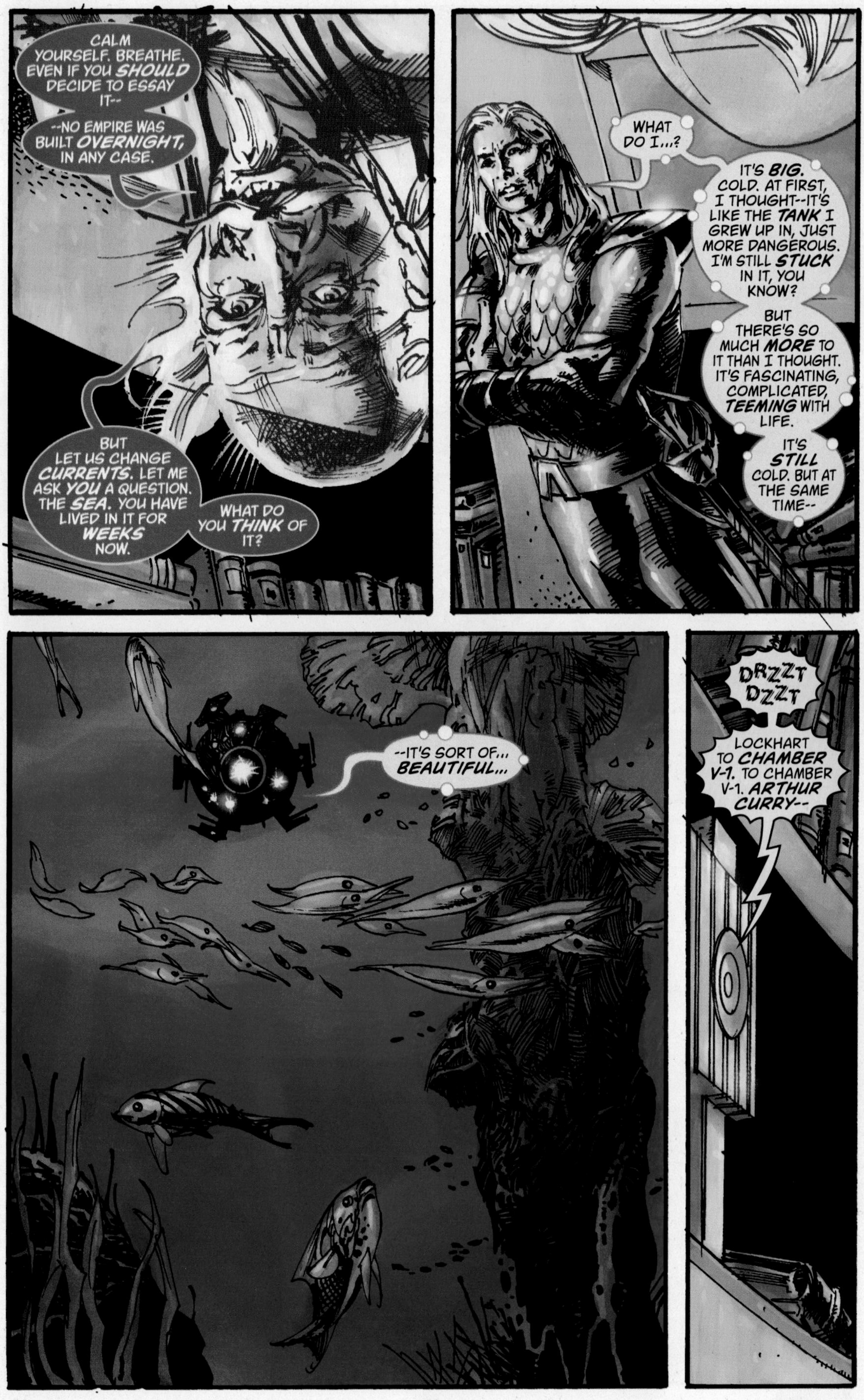

CALM YOURSELF. BREATHE. EVEN IF YOU SHOULD DECIDE TO ESSAY IT--
--NO EMPIRE WAS BUILT OVERNIGHT, IN ANY CASE.
BUT LET US CHANGE CURRENTS. LET ME ASK YOU A QUESTION. THE SEA. YOU HAVE LIVED IN IT FOR WEEKS NOW.
WHAT DO YOU THINK OF IT?
WHAT DO I...?
IT'S BIG. COLD. AT FIRST, I THOUGHT--IT'S LIKE THE TANK I GREW UP IN, JUST MORE DANGEROUS. I'M STILL STUCK IN IT, YOU KNOW?
BUT THERE'S SO MUCH MORE TO IT THAN I THOUGHT. IT'S FASCINATING, COMPLICATED, TEEMING WITH LIFE.
IT'S STILL COLD. BUT AT THE SAME TIME--
--IT'S SORT OF... BEAUTIFUL...
DRZZT DZZT
LOCKHART TO CHAMBER V-1. TO CHAMBER V-1. ARTHUR CURRY--

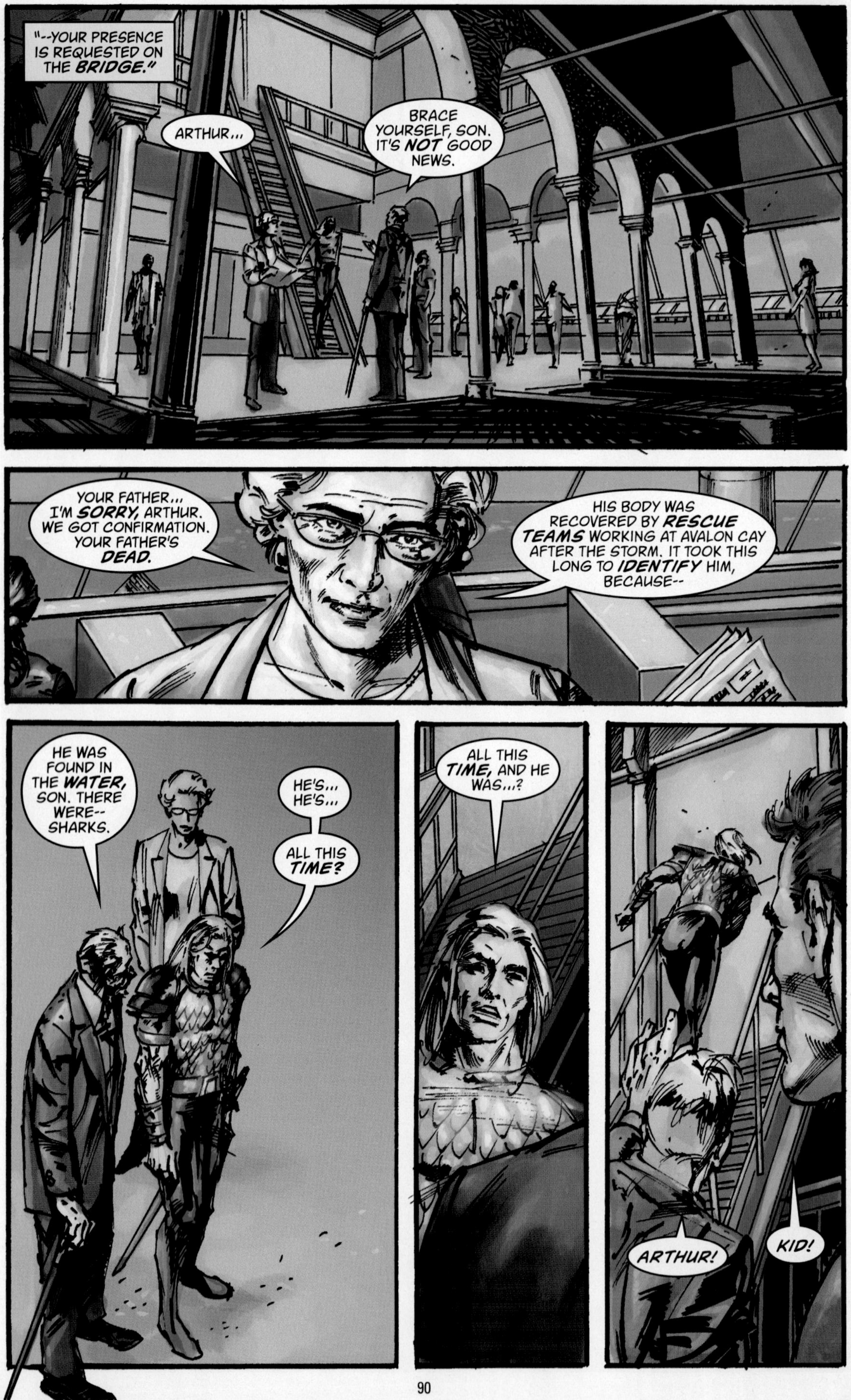
"--YOUR PRESENCE IS REQUESTED ON THE BRIDGE."
ARTHUR...
BRACE YOURSELF, SON. IT'S NOT GOOD NEWS.
YOUR FATHER... I'M SORRY, ARTHUR. WE GOT CONFIRMATION. YOUR FATHER'S DEAD.
HIS BODY WAS RECOVERED BY RESCUE TEAMS WORKING AT AVALON CAY AFTER THE STORM. IT TOOK THIS LONG TO IDENTIFY HIM, BECAUSE--
HE WAS FOUND IN THE WATER, SON. THERE WERE-- SHARKS.
HE'S... HE'S...
ALL THIS TIME?
ALL THIS TIME, AND HE WAS...?
ARTHUR!
KID!

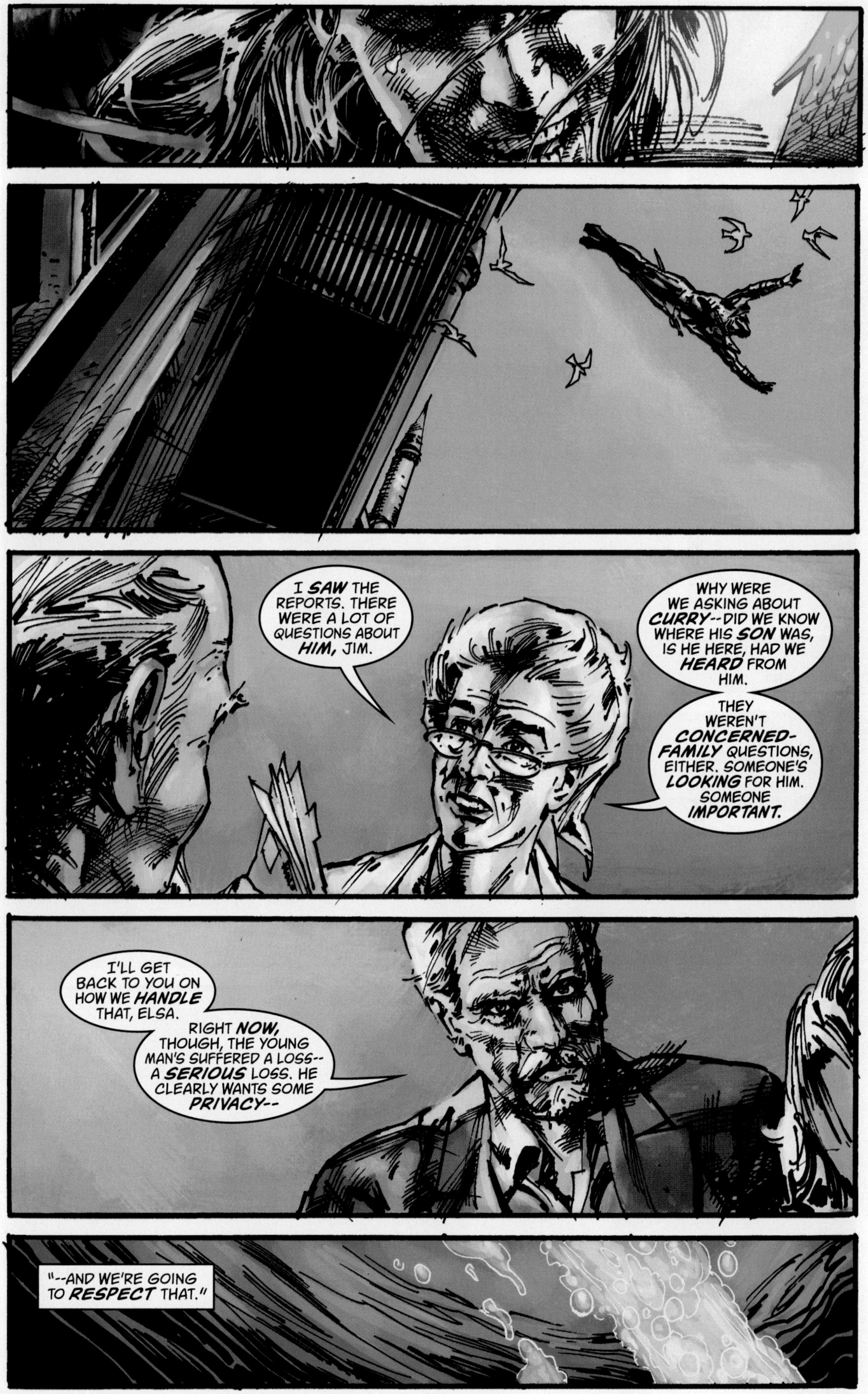
I SAW THE REPORTS. THERE WERE A LOT OF QUESTIONS ABOUT HIM, JIM.
WHY WERE WE ASKING ABOUT CURRY--DID WE KNOW WHERE HIS SON WAS, IS HE HERE, HAD WE HEARD FROM HIM.
THEY WEREN'T CONCERNED-FAMILY QUESTIONS, EITHER. SOMEONE'S LOOKING FOR HIM. SOMEONE IMPORTANT.
I'LL GET BACK TO YOU ON HOW WE HANDLE THAT, ELSA.
RIGHT NOW, THOUGH, THE YOUNG MAN'S SUFFERED A LOSS--A SERIOUS LOSS. HE CLEARLY WANTS SOME PRIVACY--
"--AND WE'RE GOING TO RESPECT THAT."

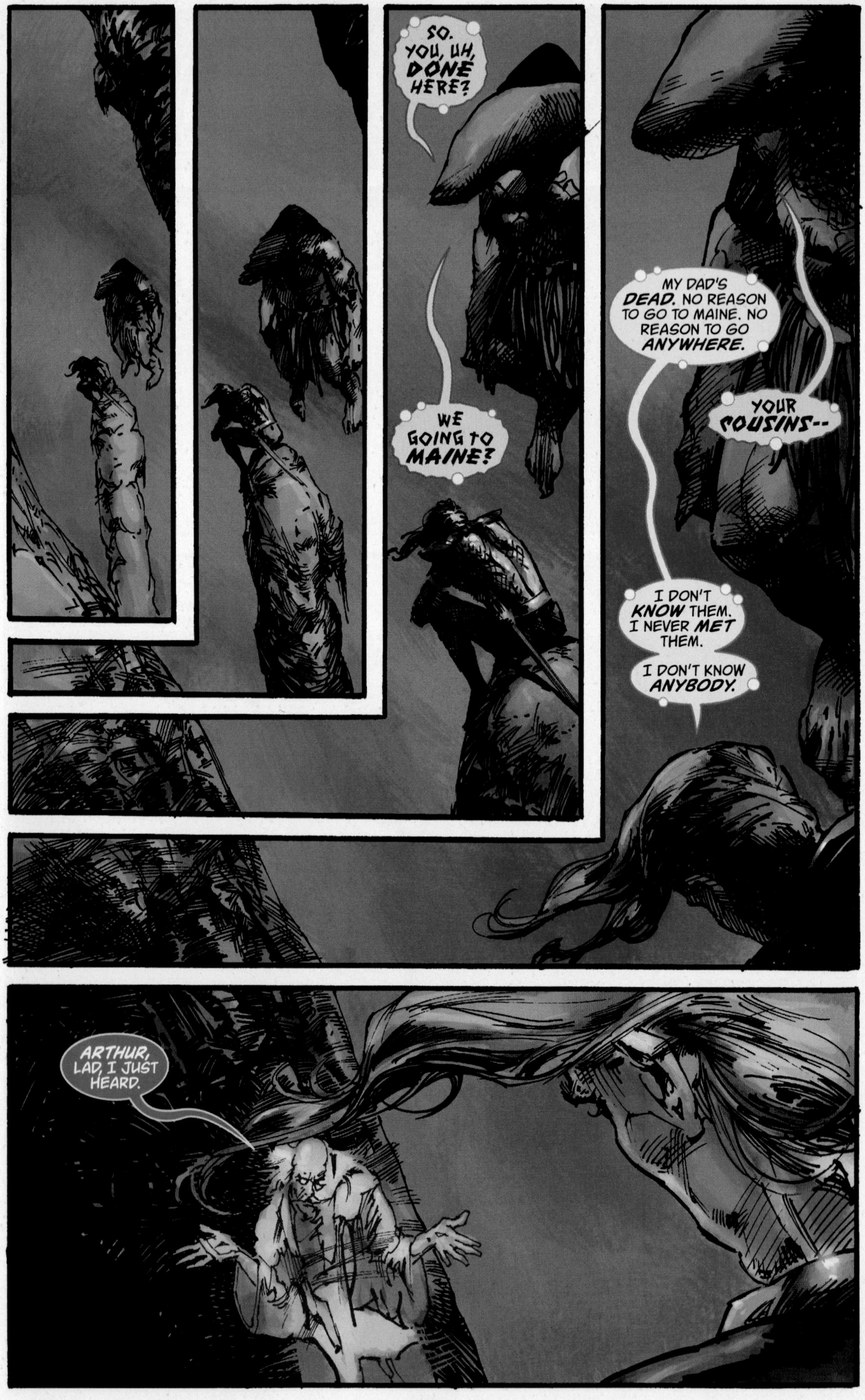

SO. YOU, UH, DONE HERE?
WE GOING TO MAINE?
YOUR COUSINS--
MY DAD'S DEAD. NO REASON TO GO TO MAINE. NO REASON TO GO ANYWHERE.
I DON'T KNOW THEM. I NEVER MET THEM.
I DON'T KNOW ANYBODY.
ARTHUR, LAD, I JUST HEARD.

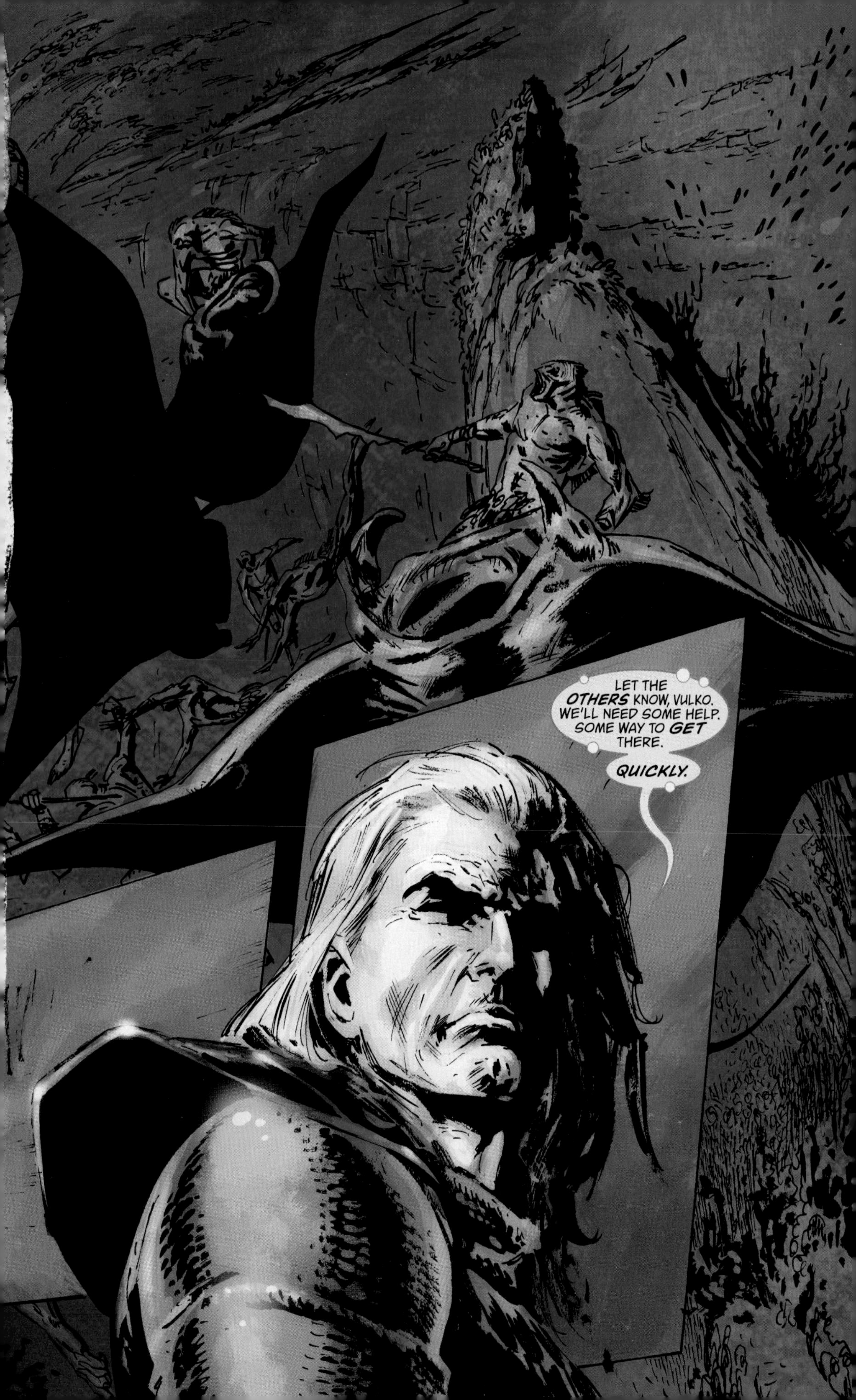
LET THE OTHERS KNOW, VULKO. WE'LL NEED SOME HELP. SOME WAY TO GET THERE.
QUICKLY.

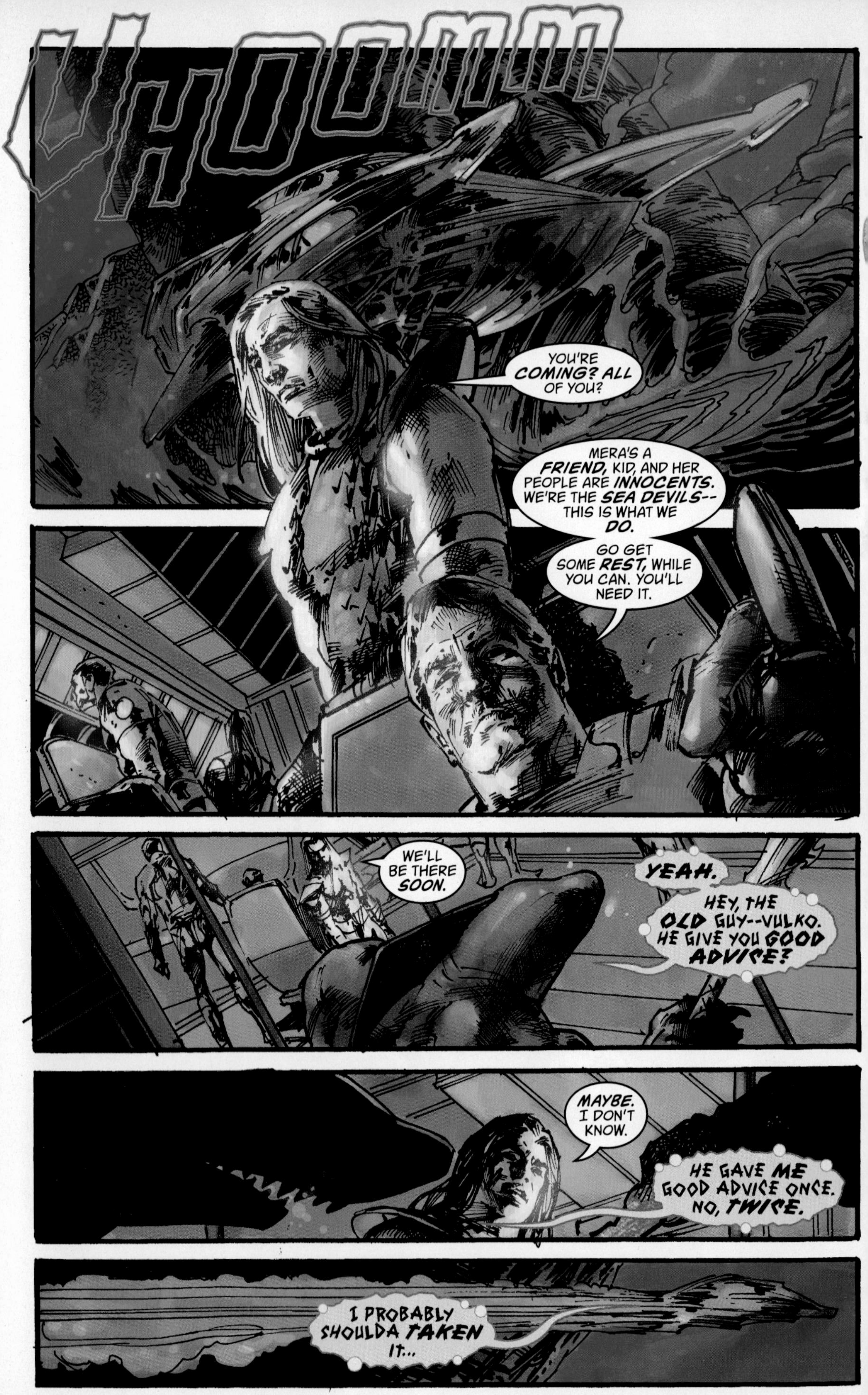
VHOOMM
YOU'RE COMING? ALL OF YOU?
MERA'S A FRIEND, KID, AND HER PEOPLE ARE INNOCENTS. WE'RE THE SEA DEVILS-- THIS IS WHAT WE DO.
GO GET SOME REST, WHILE YOU CAN. YOU'LL NEED IT.
WE'LL BE THERE SOON.
YEAH.
HEY, THE OLD GUY--VULKO. HE GIVE YOU GOOD ADVICE?
MAYBE. I DON'T KNOW.
HE GAVE ME GOOD ADVICE ONCE. NO, TWICE.
I PROBABLY SHOULDA TAKEN IT...

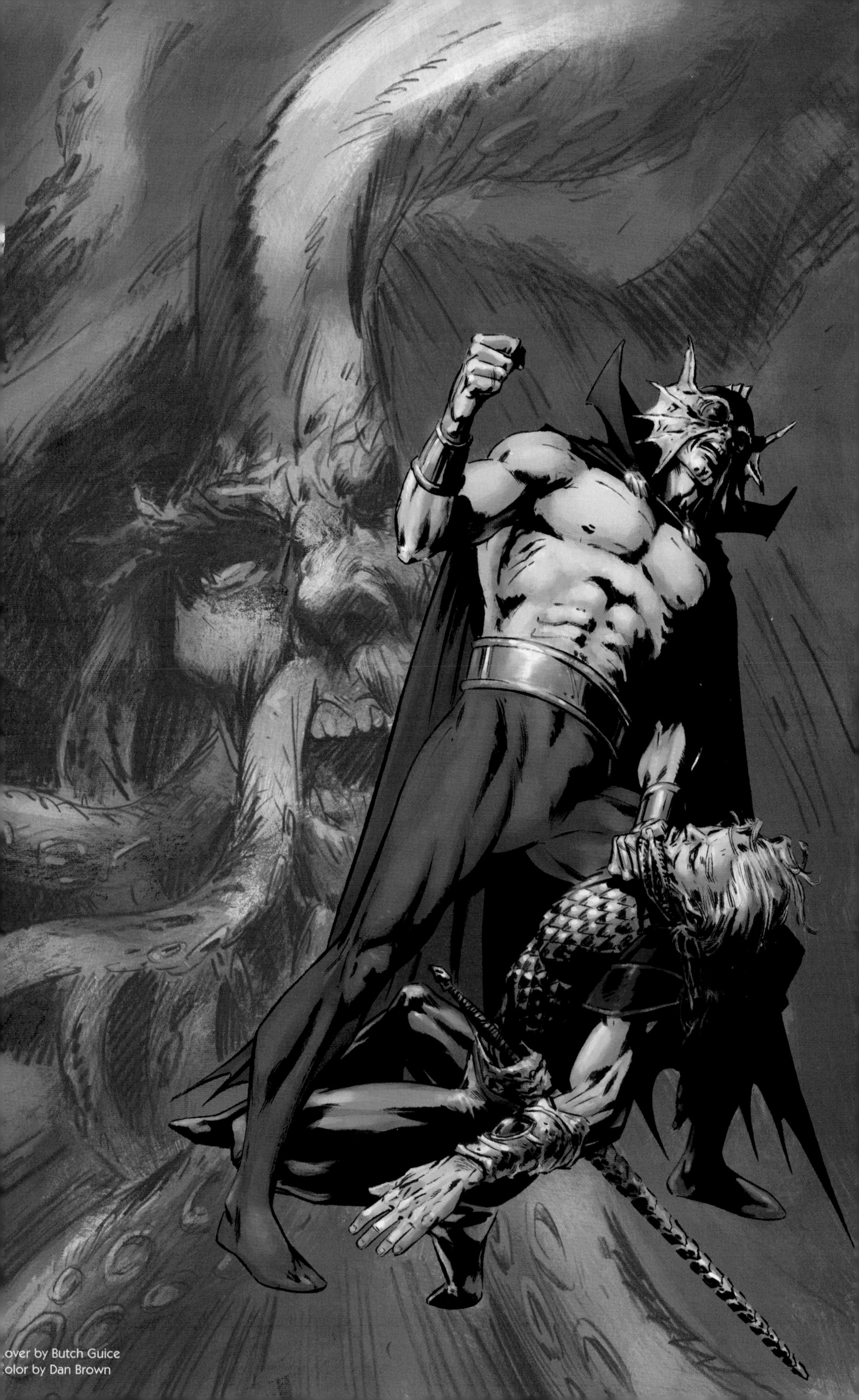

over by Butch Guice
olor by Dan Brown

PACHECO
MERINO

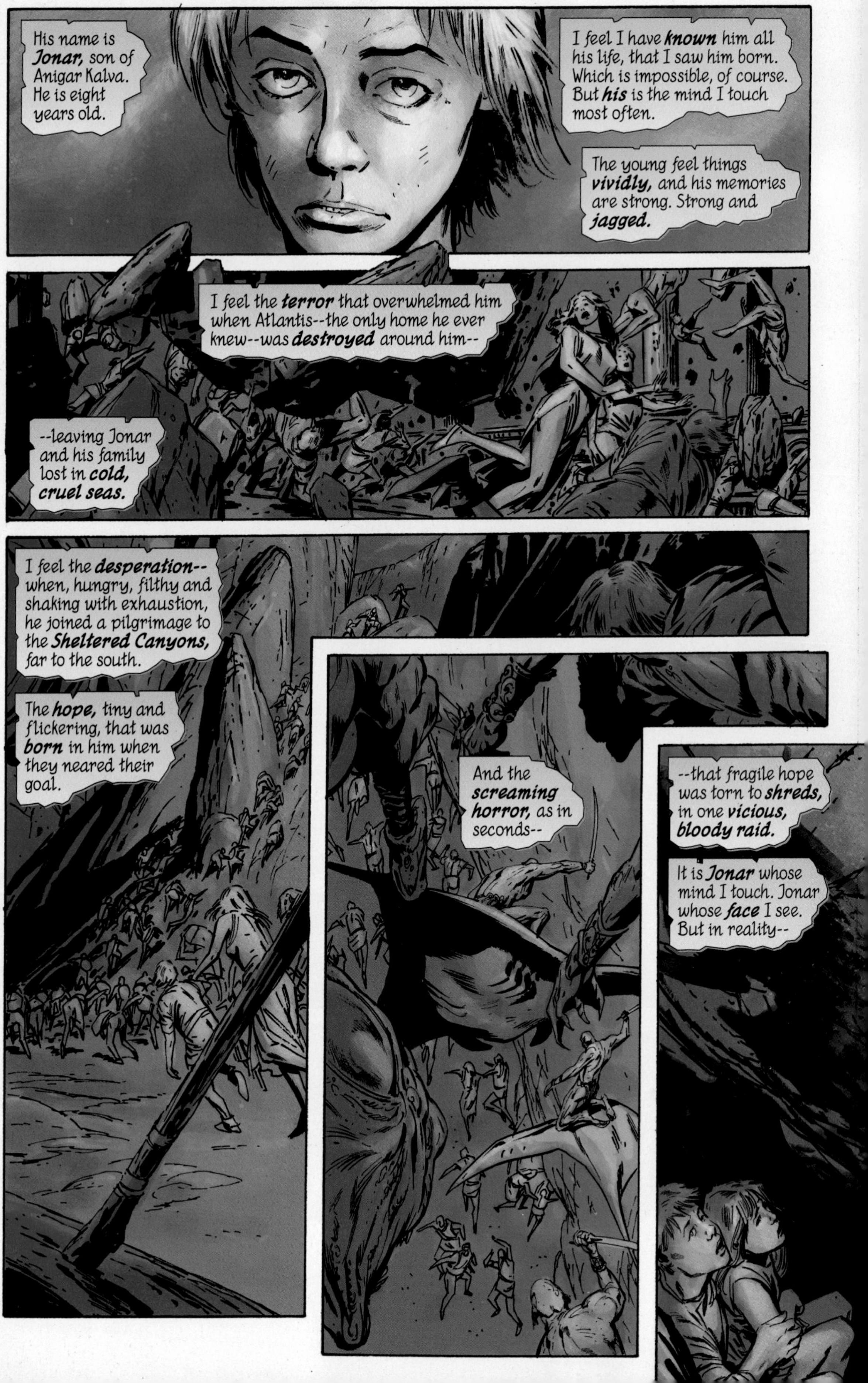
His name is Jonar, son of Anigar Kalva. He is eight years old.
I feel I have known him all his life, that I saw him born. Which is impossible, of course. But his is the mind I touch most often.
The young feel things vividly, and his memories are strong. Strong and jagged.
I feel the terror that overwhelmed him when Atlantis--the only home he ever knew--was destroyed around him--
--leaving Jonar and his family lost in cold, cruel seas.
I feel the desperation--when, hungry, filthy and shaking with exhaustion, he joined a pilgrimage to the Sheltered Canyons, far to the south.
The hope, tiny and flickering, that was born in him when they neared their goal.
And the screaming horror, as in seconds--
--that fragile hope was torn to shreds, in one vicious, bloody raid.
It is Jonar whose mind I touch. Jonar whose face I see. But in reality--

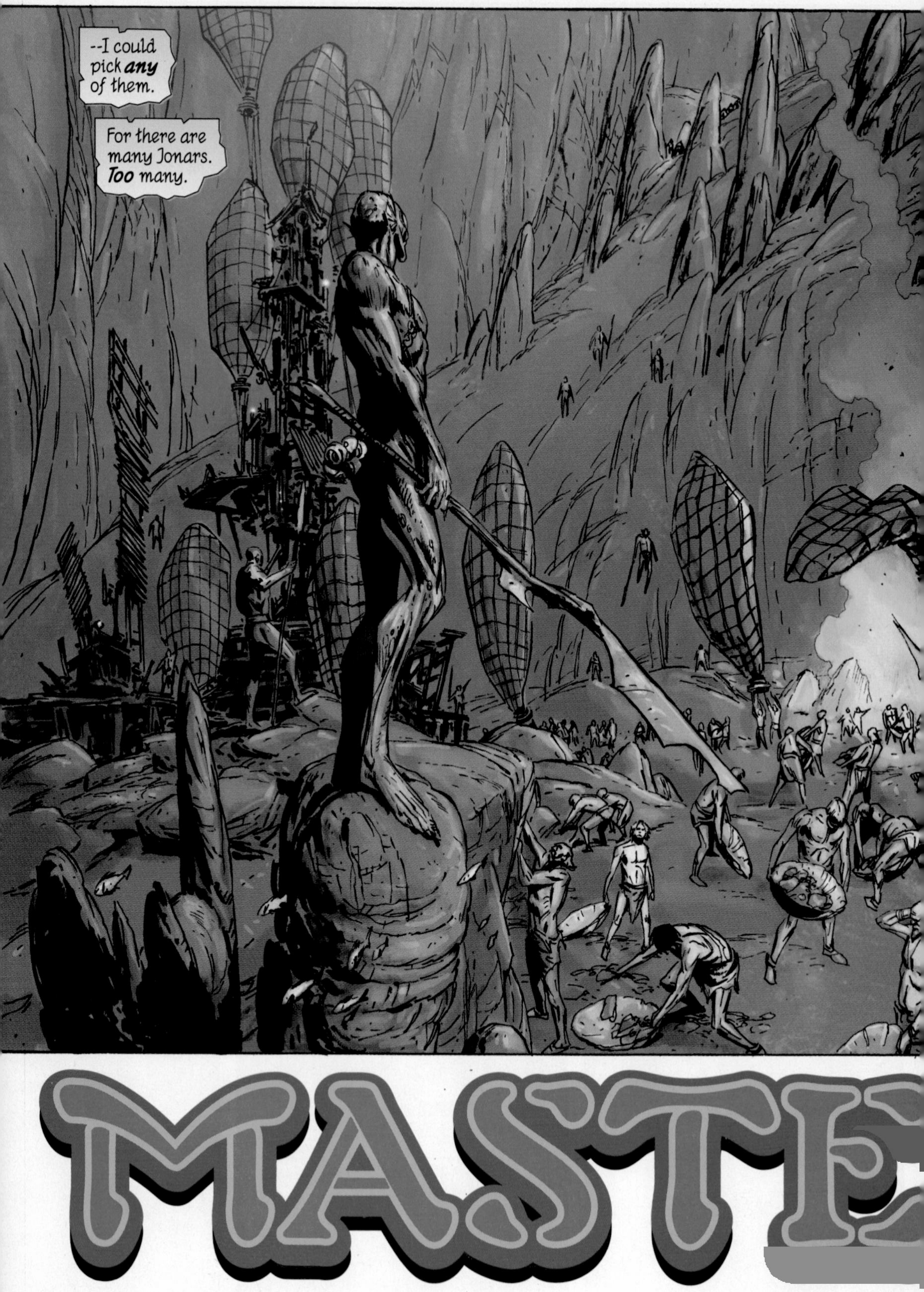
--I could pick **any** of them.
For there are many Jonars. **Too** many.
MASTE

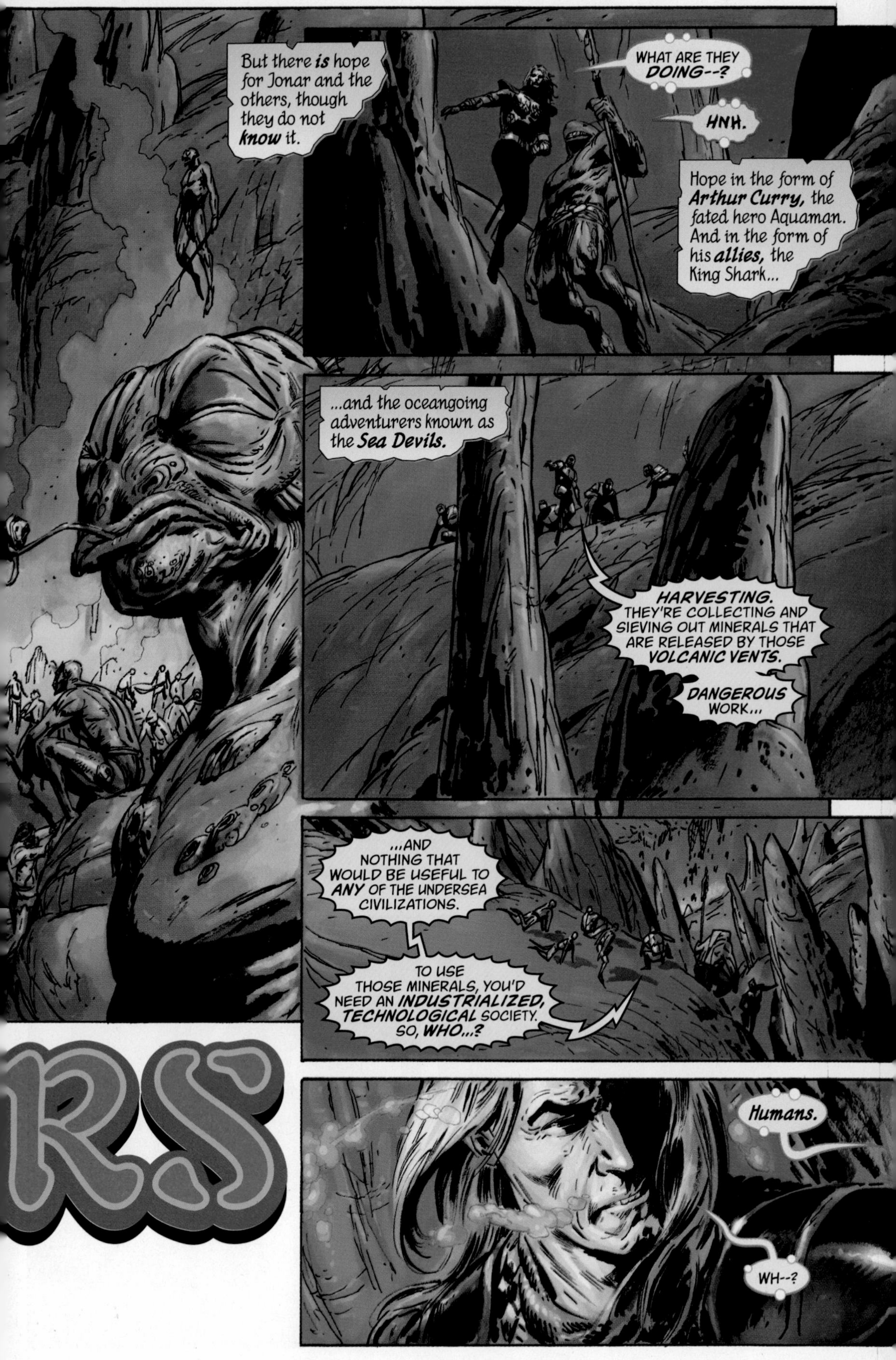

But there *is* hope for Jonar and the others, though they do not *know* it.
WHAT ARE THEY *DOING--?*
HNH.
Hope in the form of *Arthur Curry,* the fated hero Aquaman. And in the form of his *allies,* the King Shark...
...and the oceangoing adventurers known as the *Sea Devils.*
HARVESTING. THEY'RE COLLECTING AND SIEVING OUT MINERALS THAT ARE RELEASED BY THOSE *VOLCANIC VENTS.*
DANGEROUS WORK...
...AND NOTHING THAT WOULD BE USEFUL TO *ANY* OF THE UNDERSEA CIVILIZATIONS.
TO USE THOSE MINERALS, YOU'D NEED AN *INDUSTRIALIZED, TECHNOLOGICAL* SOCIETY. SO, *WHO...?*
Humans.
WH--?
RS

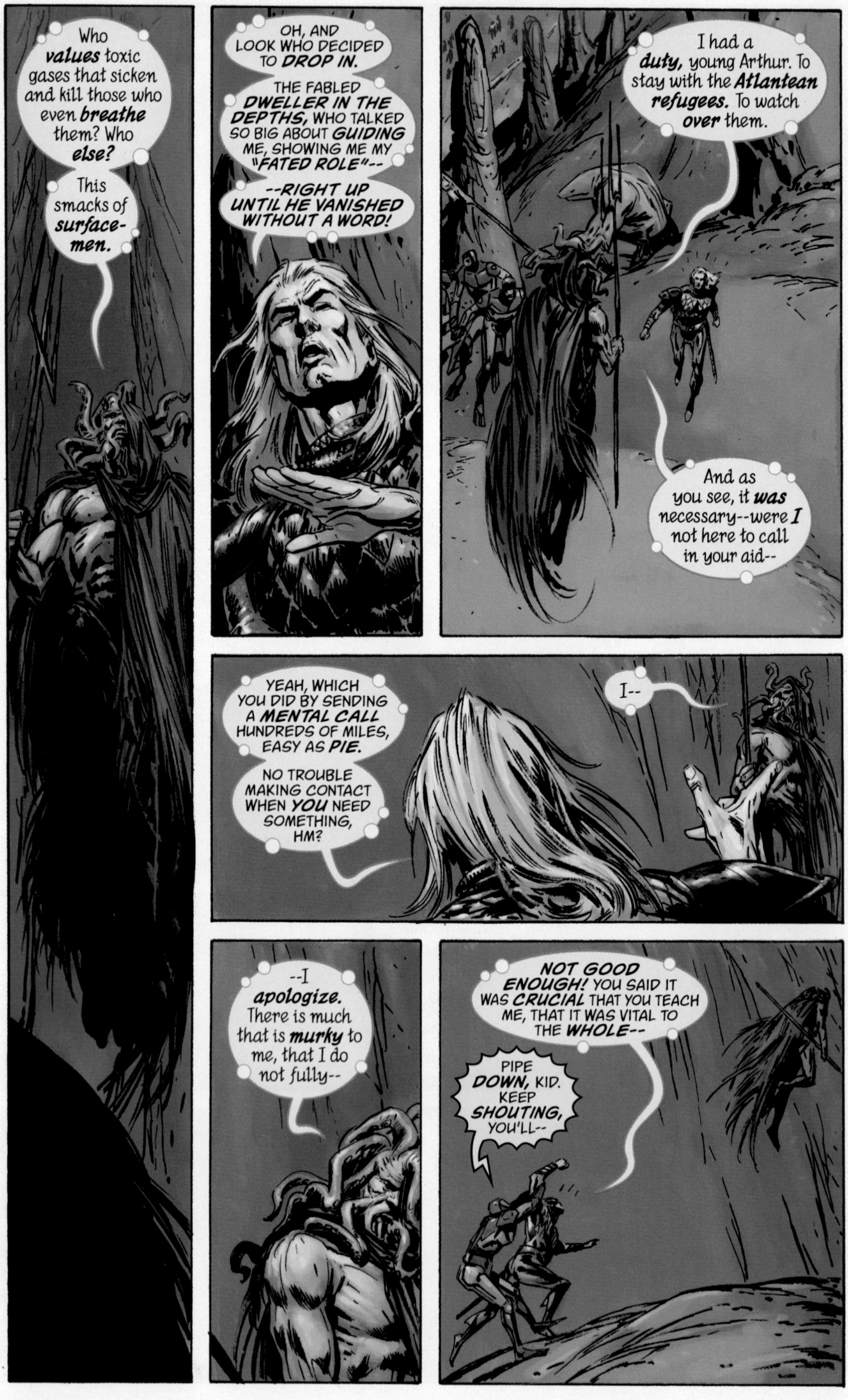
Who values toxic gases that sicken and kill those who even breathe them? Who else?
This smacks of surface-men.
OH, AND LOOK WHO DECIDED TO DROP IN.
THE FABLED DWELLER IN THE DEPTHS, WHO TALKED SO BIG ABOUT GUIDING ME, SHOWING ME MY "FATED ROLE"--
--RIGHT UP UNTIL HE VANISHED WITHOUT A WORD!
I had a duty, young Arthur. To stay with the Atlantean refugees. To watch over them.
And as you see, it was necessary--were I not here to call in your aid--
YEAH, WHICH YOU DID BY SENDING A MENTAL CALL HUNDREDS OF MILES, EASY AS PIE.
NO TROUBLE MAKING CONTACT WHEN YOU NEED SOMETHING, HM?
I--
--I apologize. There is much that is murky to me, that I do not fully--
NOT GOOD ENOUGH! YOU SAID IT WAS CRUCIAL THAT YOU TEACH ME, THAT IT WAS VITAL TO THE WHOLE--
PIPE DOWN, KID. KEEP SHOUTING, YOU'LL--

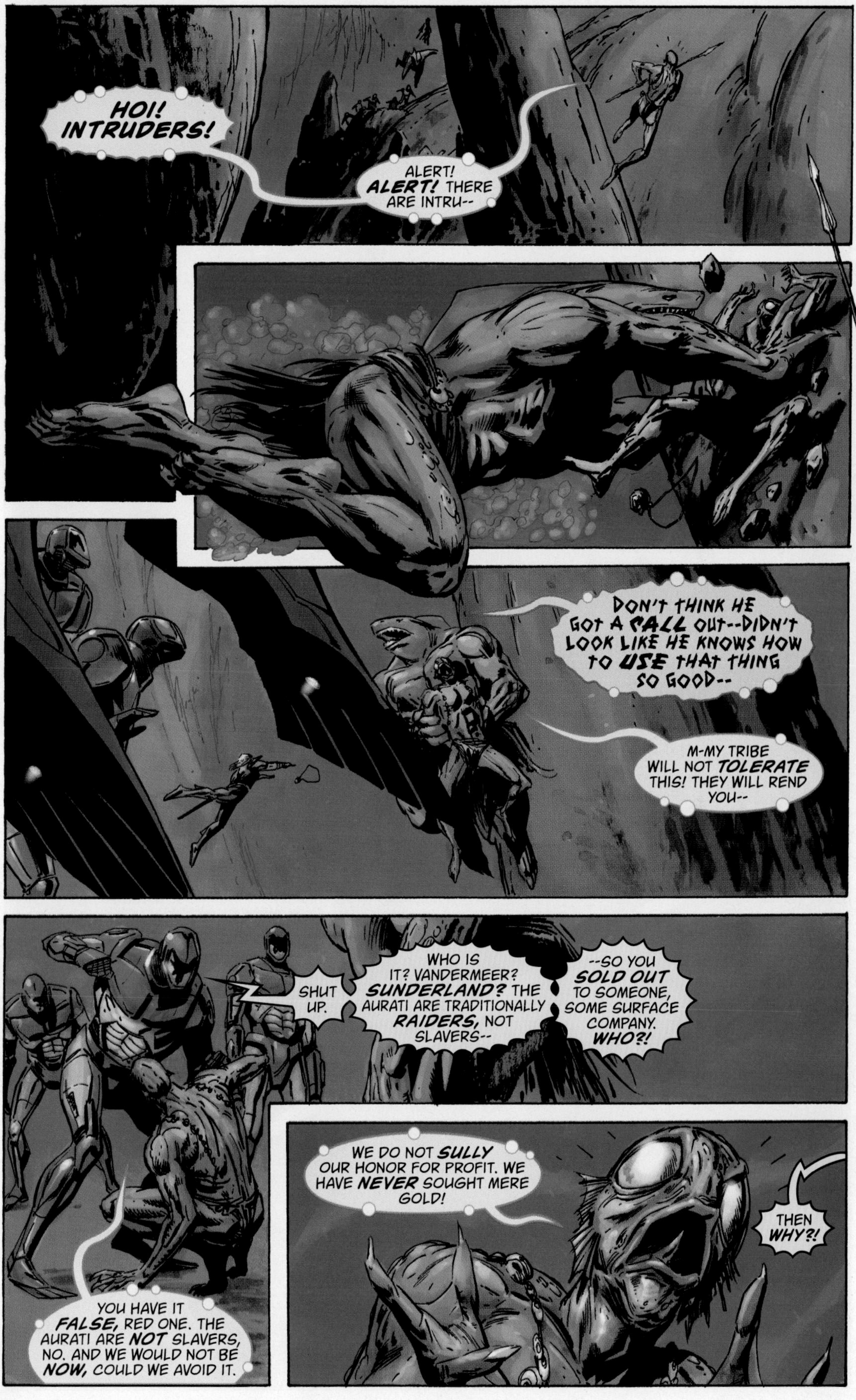
HOI! INTRUDERS!
ALERT! ALERT! THERE ARE INTRU--
DON'T THINK HE GOT A CALL OUT--DIDN'T LOOK LIKE HE KNOWS HOW TO USE THAT THING SO GOOD--
M-MY TRIBE WILL NOT TOLERATE THIS! THEY WILL REND YOU--
SHUT UP.
WHO IS IT? VANDERMEER? SUNDERLAND? THE AURATI ARE TRADITIONALLY RAIDERS, NOT SLAVERS--
--SO YOU SOLD OUT TO SOMEONE, SOME SURFACE COMPANY. WHO?!
YOU HAVE IT FALSE, RED ONE. THE AURATI ARE NOT SLAVERS, NO. AND WE WOULD NOT BE NOW, COULD WE AVOID IT.
WE DO NOT SULLY OUR HONOR FOR PROFIT. WE HAVE NEVER SOUGHT MERE GOLD!
THEN WHY?!

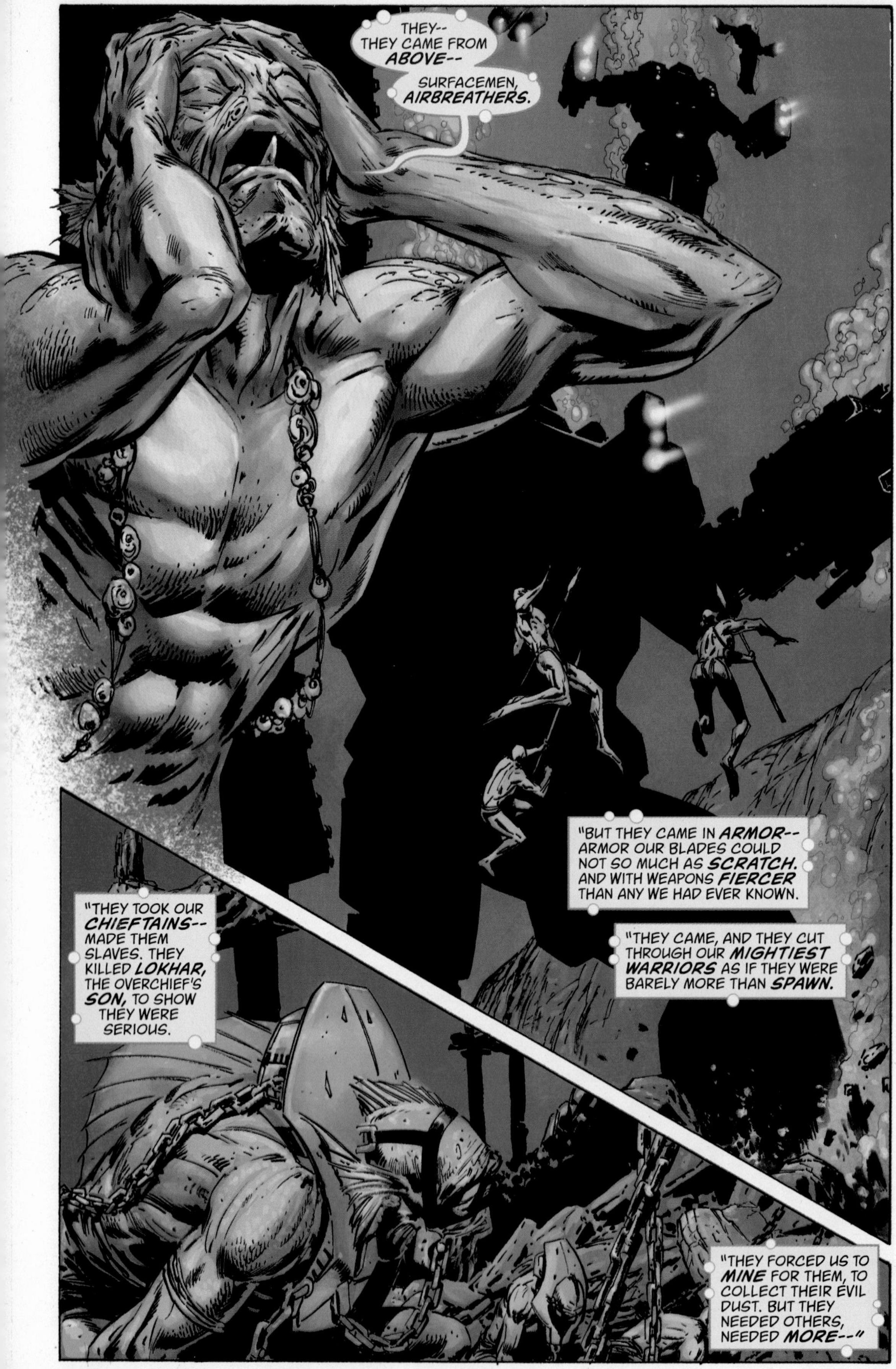
THEY-- THEY CAME FROM ABOVE--
SURFACEMEN, AIRBREATHERS.
"BUT THEY CAME IN ARMOR-- ARMOR OUR BLADES COULD NOT SO MUCH AS SCRATCH. AND WITH WEAPONS FIERCER THAN ANY WE HAD EVER KNOWN.
"THEY CAME, AND THEY CUT THROUGH OUR MIGHTIEST WARRIORS AS IF THEY WERE BARELY MORE THAN SPAWN.
"THEY TOOK OUR CHIEFTAINS-- MADE THEM SLAVES. THEY KILLED LOKHAR, THE OVERCHIEF'S SON, TO SHOW THEY WERE SERIOUS.
"THEY FORCED US TO MINE FOR THEM, TO COLLECT THEIR EVIL DUST. BUT THEY NEEDED OTHERS, NEEDED MORE--"

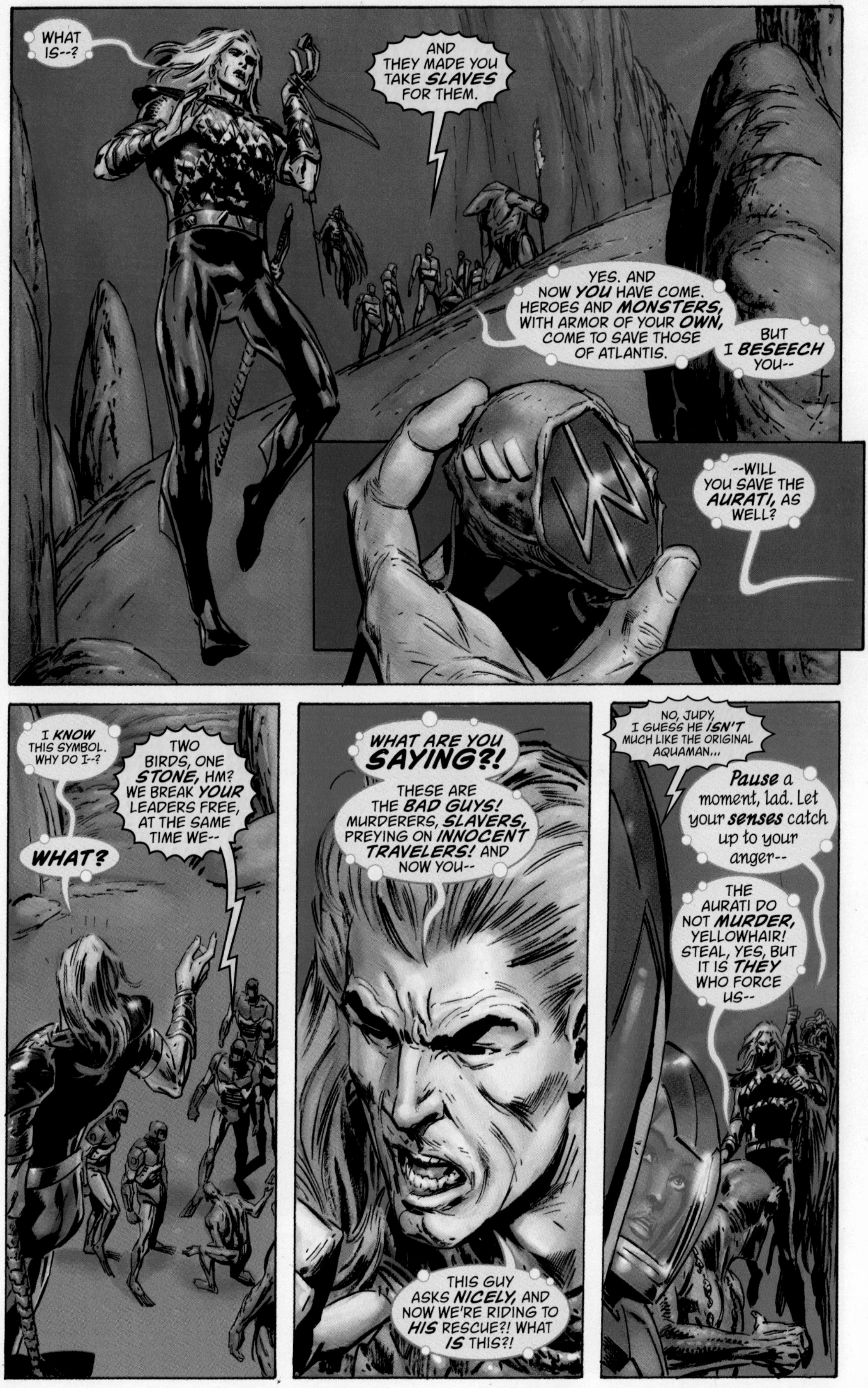
WHAT IS--?
AND THEY MADE YOU TAKE SLAVES FOR THEM.
YES. AND NOW YOU HAVE COME. HEROES AND MONSTERS, WITH ARMOR OF YOUR OWN, COME TO SAVE THOSE OF ATLANTIS.
BUT I BESEECH YOU--
--WILL YOU SAVE THE AURATI, AS WELL?
I KNOW THIS SYMBOL. WHY DO I--?
TWO BIRDS, ONE STONE, HM? WE BREAK YOUR LEADERS FREE, AT THE SAME TIME WE--
WHAT?
WHAT ARE YOU SAYING?!
THESE ARE THE BAD GUYS! MURDERERS, SLAVERS, PREYING ON INNOCENT TRAVELERS! AND NOW YOU--
THIS GUY ASKS NICELY, AND NOW WE'RE RIDING TO HIS RESCUE?! WHAT IS THIS?!
NO, JUDY, I GUESS HE ISN'T MUCH LIKE THE ORIGINAL AQUAMAN...
Pause a moment, lad. Let your senses catch up to your anger--
THE AURATI DO NOT MURDER, YELLOWHAIR! STEAL, YES, BUT IT IS THEY WHO FORCE US--

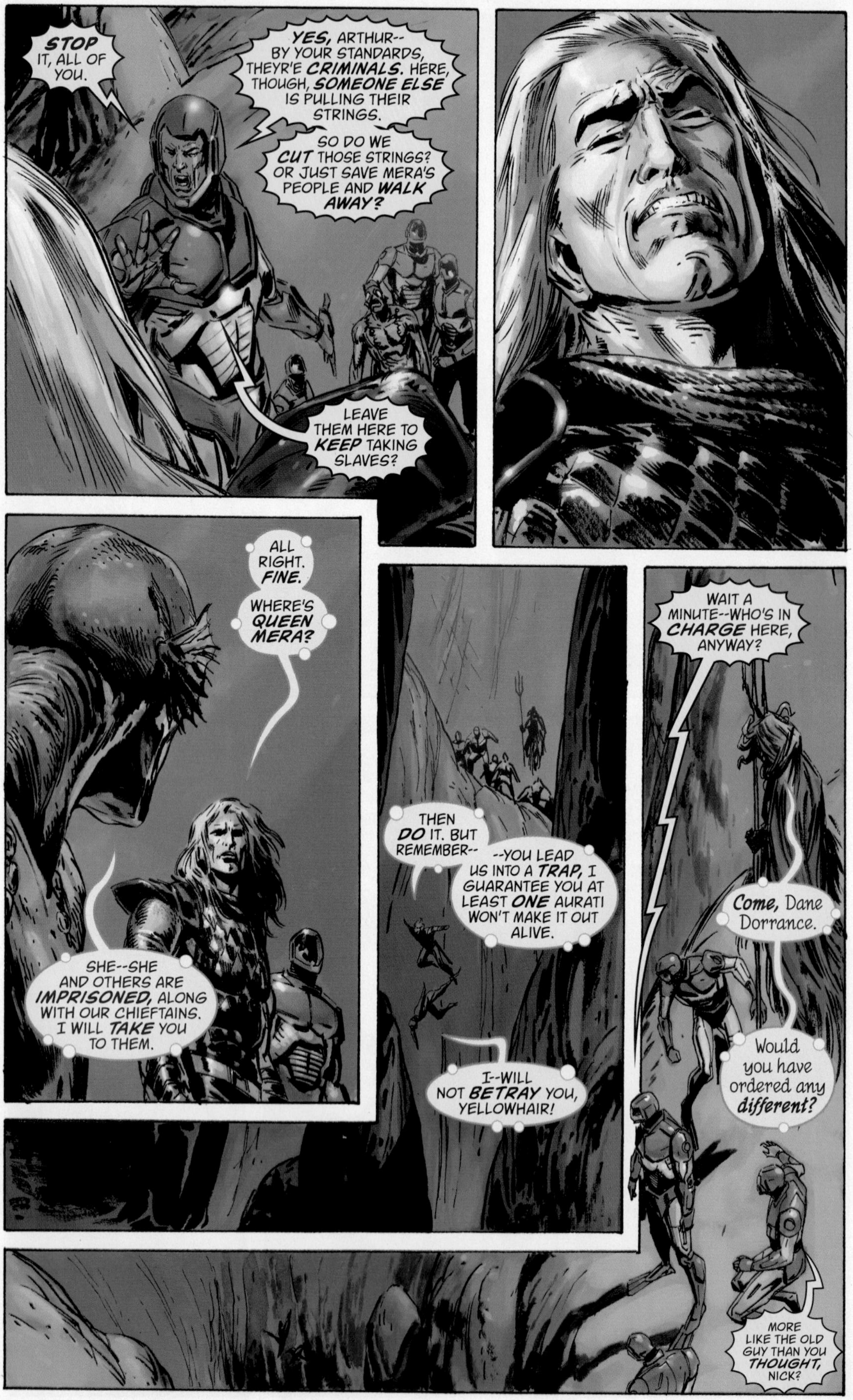
STOP IT, ALL OF YOU.
YES, ARTHUR-- BY YOUR STANDARDS, THEY'RE CRIMINALS. HERE, THOUGH, SOMEONE ELSE IS PULLING THEIR STRINGS.
SO DO WE CUT THOSE STRINGS? OR JUST SAVE MERA'S PEOPLE AND WALK AWAY?
LEAVE THEM HERE TO KEEP TAKING SLAVES?
ALL RIGHT. FINE.
WHERE'S QUEEN MERA?
SHE--SHE AND OTHERS ARE IMPRISONED, ALONG WITH OUR CHIEFTAINS. I WILL TAKE YOU TO THEM.
THEN DO IT. BUT REMEMBER--
--YOU LEAD US INTO A TRAP, I GUARANTEE YOU AT LEAST ONE AURATI WON'T MAKE IT OUT ALIVE.
I--WILL NOT BETRAY YOU, YELLOWHAIR!
WAIT A MINUTE--WHO'S IN CHARGE HERE, ANYWAY?
Come, Dane Dorrance.
Would you have ordered any different?
MORE LIKE THE OLD GUY THAN YOU THOUGHT, NICK?

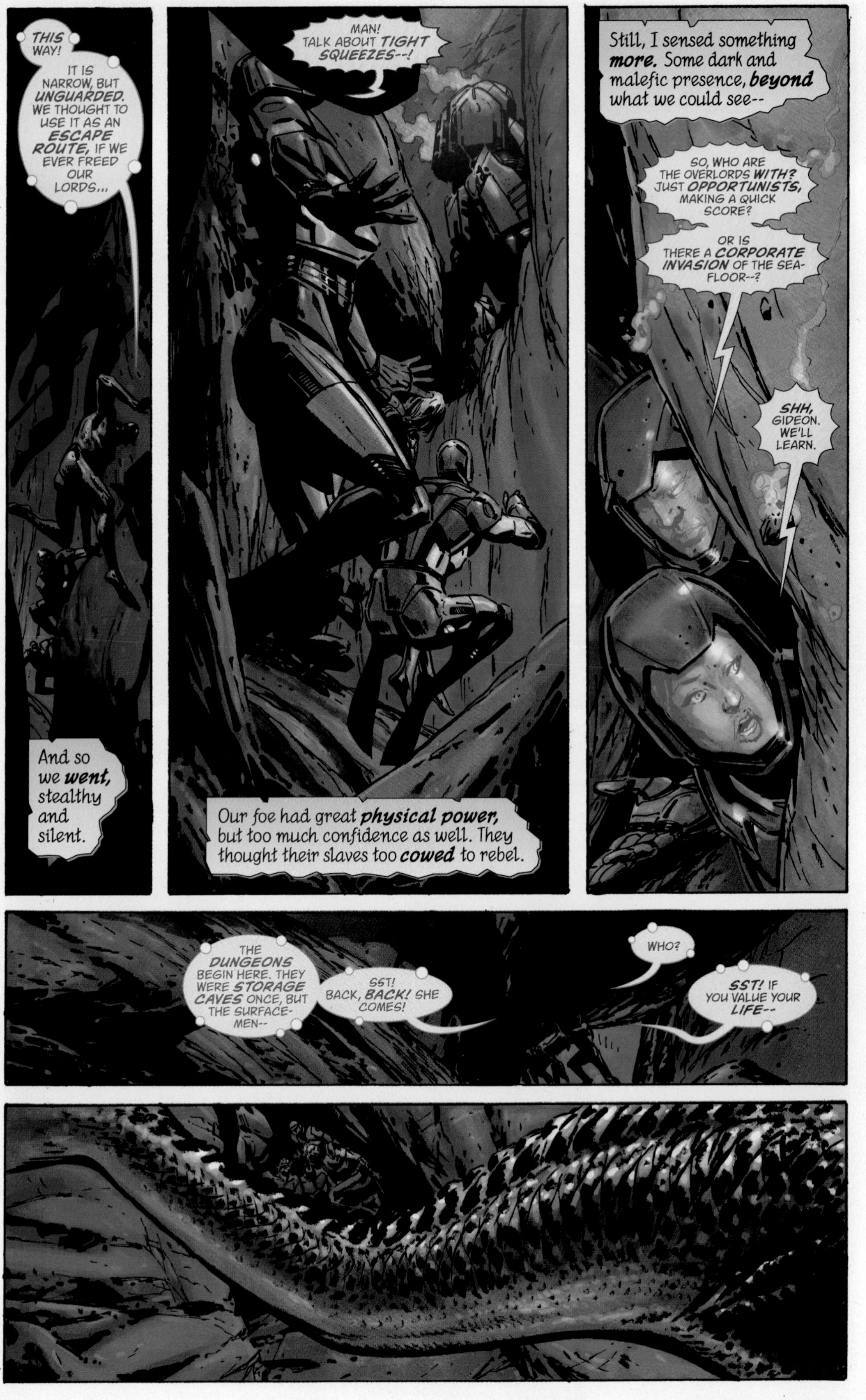

THIS WAY!
IT IS NARROW, BUT UNGUARDED. WE THOUGHT TO USE IT AS AN ESCAPE ROUTE, IF WE EVER FREED OUR LORDS...
And so we went, stealthy and silent.
MAN! TALK ABOUT TIGHT SQUEEZES--!
Our foe had great physical power, but too much confidence as well. They thought their slaves too cowed to rebel.
Still, I sensed something more. Some dark and malefic presence, beyond what we could see--
SO, WHO ARE THE OVERLORDS WITH? JUST OPPORTUNISTS, MAKING A QUICK SCORE?
OR IS THERE A CORPORATE INVASION OF THE SEA-FLOOR--?
SHH, GIDEON. WE'LL LEARN.
THE DUNGEONS BEGIN HERE. THEY WERE STORAGE CAVES ONCE, BUT THE SURFACE-MEN--
SST! BACK, BACK! SHE COMES!
WHO?
SST! IF YOU VALUE YOUR LIFE--

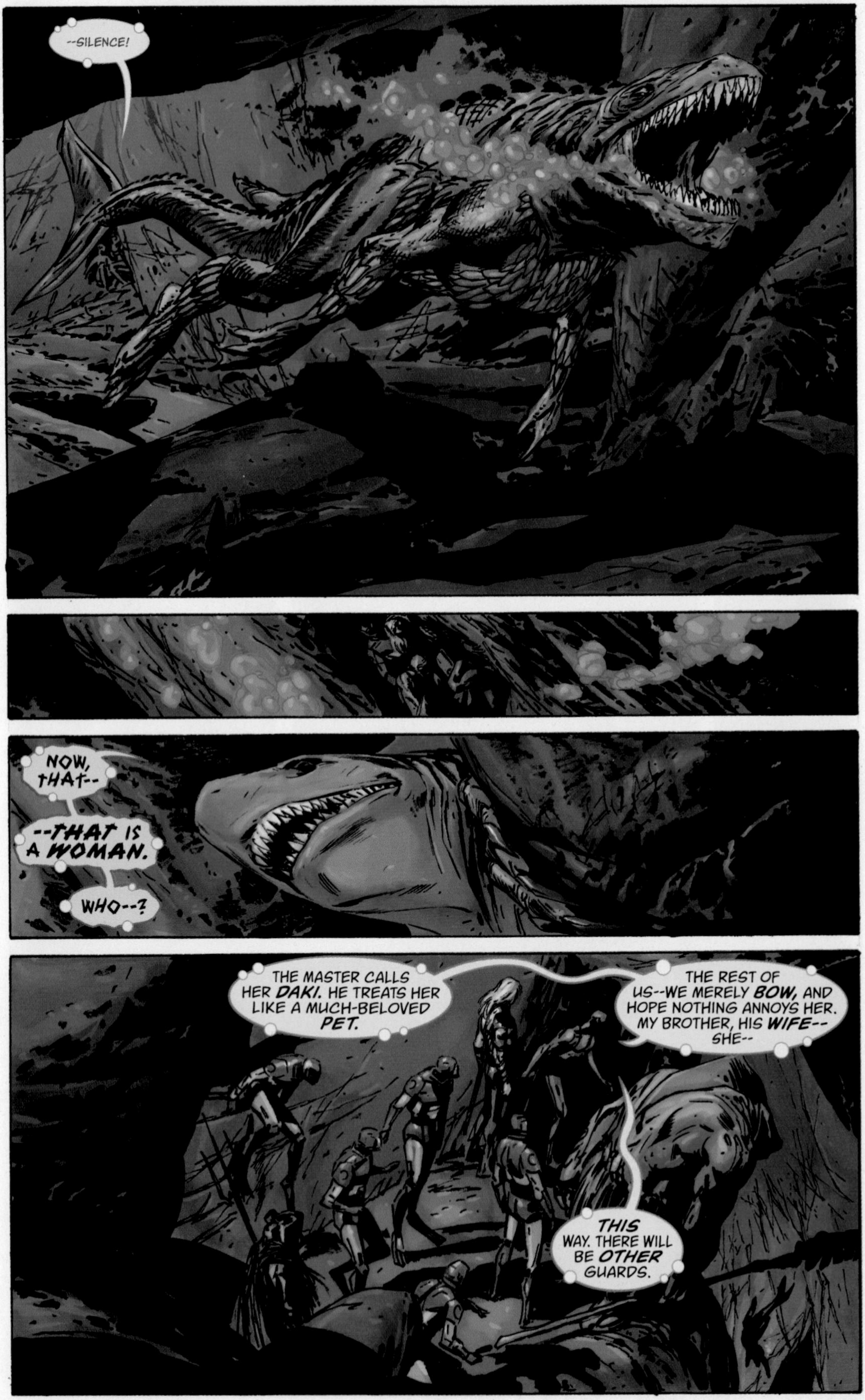
--SILENCE!
NOW, THAT--
--THAT IS A WOMAN.
WHO--?
THE MASTER CALLS HER DAKI. HE TREATS HER LIKE A MUCH-BELOVED PET.
THE REST OF US--WE MERELY BOW, AND HOPE NOTHING ANNOYS HER. MY BROTHER, HIS WIFE-- SHE--
THIS WAY. THERE WILL BE OTHER GUARDS.

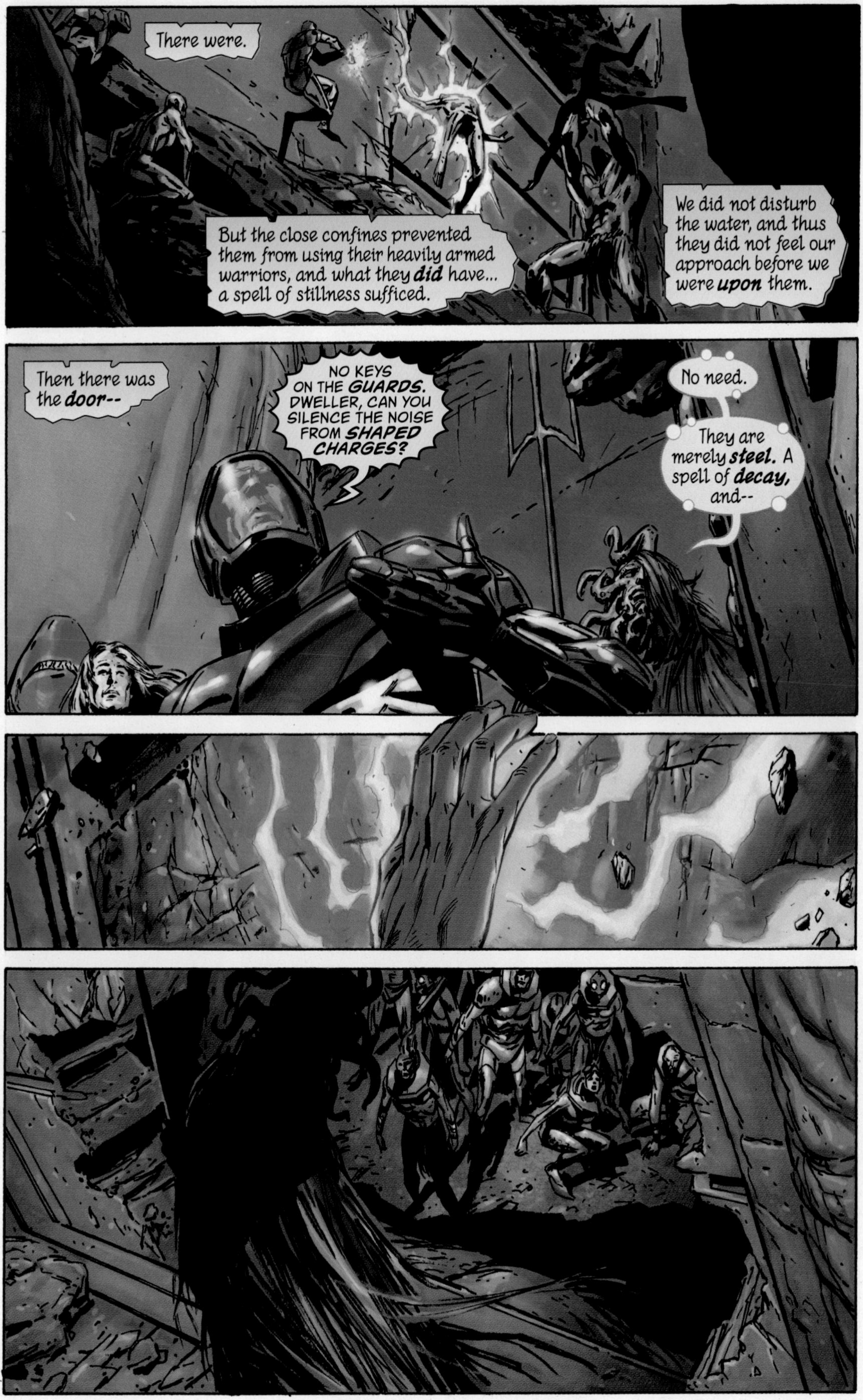
There were.
But the close confines prevented them from using their heavily armed warriors, and what they *did* have... a spell of stillness sufficed.
We did not disturb the water, and thus they did not feel our approach before we were *upon* them.
Then there was the *door--*
NO KEYS ON THE *GUARDS.* DWELLER, CAN YOU SILENCE THE NOISE FROM *SHAPED CHARGES?*
No need.
They are merely *steel.* A spell of *decay,* and--

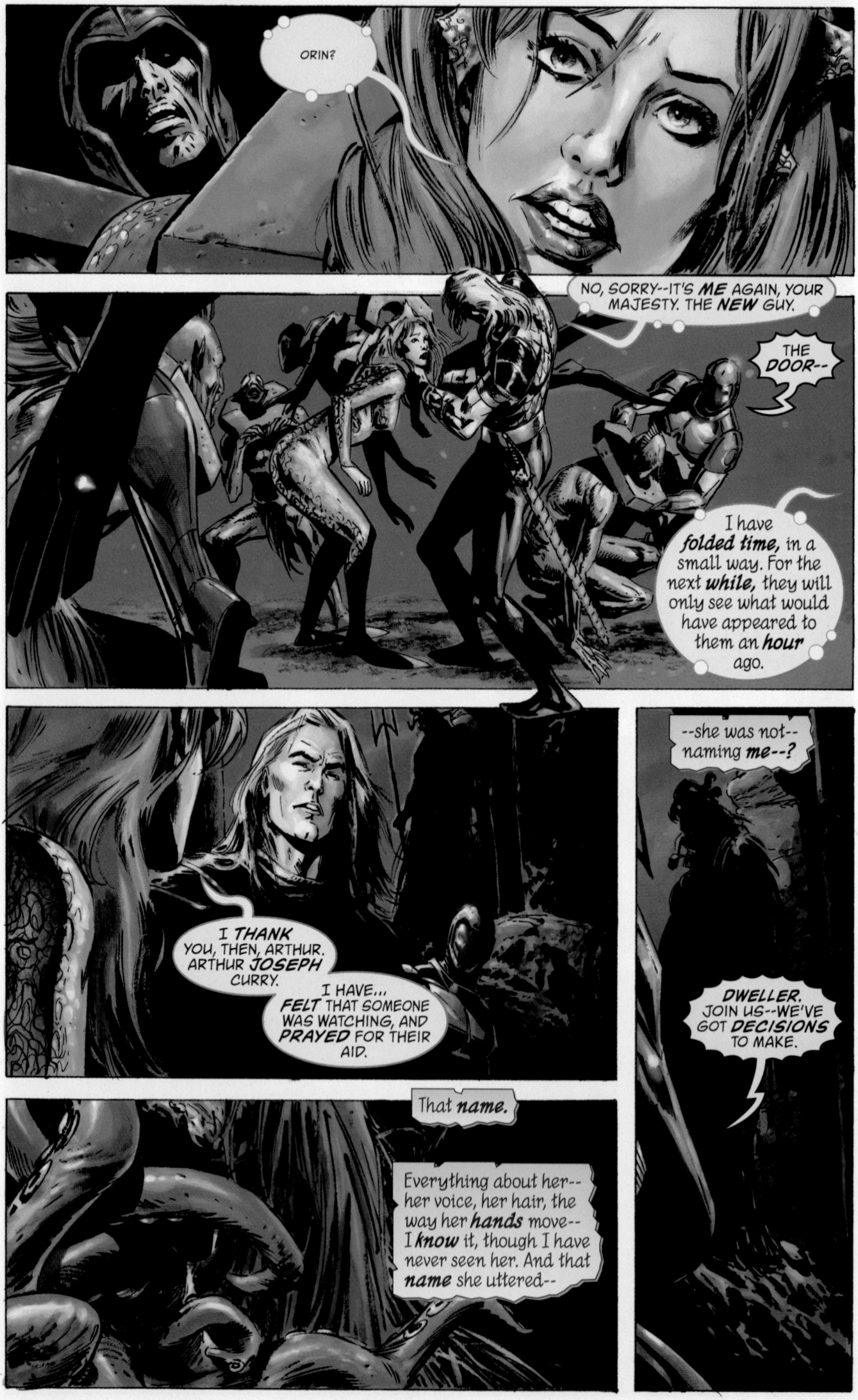
ORIN?
NO, SORRY--IT'S ME AGAIN, YOUR MAJESTY. THE NEW GUY.
THE DOOR--
I have folded time, in a small way. For the next while, they will only see what would have appeared to them an hour ago.
I THANK YOU, THEN, ARTHUR. ARTHUR JOSEPH CURRY.
I HAVE... FELT THAT SOMEONE WAS WATCHING, AND PRAYED FOR THEIR AID.
--she was not--naming me--?
DWELLER. JOIN US--WE'VE GOT DECISIONS TO MAKE.
That name.
Everything about her--her voice, her hair, the way her hands move--I know it, though I have never seen her. And that name she uttered--

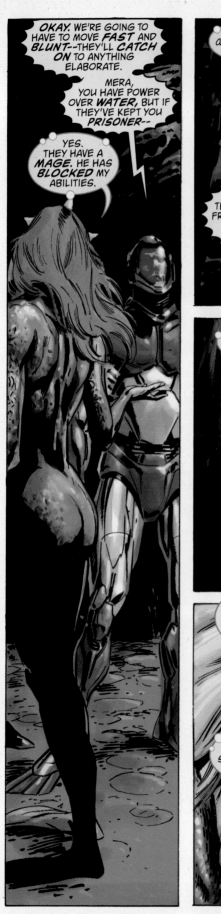

OKAY. WE'RE GOING TO HAVE TO MOVE *FAST* AND *BLUNT*--THEY'LL *CATCH ON* TO ANYTHING ELABORATE.

MERA, YOU HAVE POWER OVER *WATER*, BUT IF THEY'VE KEPT YOU *PRISONER*--

YES. THEY HAVE A *MAGE.* HE HAS *BLOCKED* MY ABILITIES.

I...sense him. His skills are *minor*, fragile. I will *deal* with him when the time comes.

GOOD, THEN. WE'LL GET THE WORD TO THE *OTHERS* THAT YOU'RE FREE. BOTH *ATLANTEANS* AND *AURATI* WILL RISE UP, AND WE'LL ATTACK--

--TAKE OUT THEIR *COMMANDERS* BEFORE THEY KNOW WHAT'S--

LET THE *AURATI* FIGHT THEIR *OWN* BATTLES. WE CAN *SLIP AWAY*, RISK THE LIVES OF *NO MORE* ATLANTEAN WOMEN AND CHILDREN.

ATSIUL--

WHOA, *WHOA.*

I KNOW WHERE YOU'RE *COMING* FROM, ATSIUL, BUT WE ALREADY *DANCED* THIS DANCE, AND THERE'S NO *TIME.*

SETTLE SCORES *AFTER-WARD*, IF YOU WANT. BUT RIGHT NOW, WE'RE HELPING *EVERYONE.*

OH? YOU GIVE ATLANTEANS *ORDERS* NOW, YELLOWHAIR? HAVE YOU ADOPTED THE *RANK* TO GO WITH THE COLORS YOU WEAR?

LOOK, FRIEND, I SAVED YOUR *LIFE*--

AND PROMPTLY *ABANDONED* US--

WANT TO GET DUMPED ON YOUR CAN *AGAIN*, YOU LITTLE--

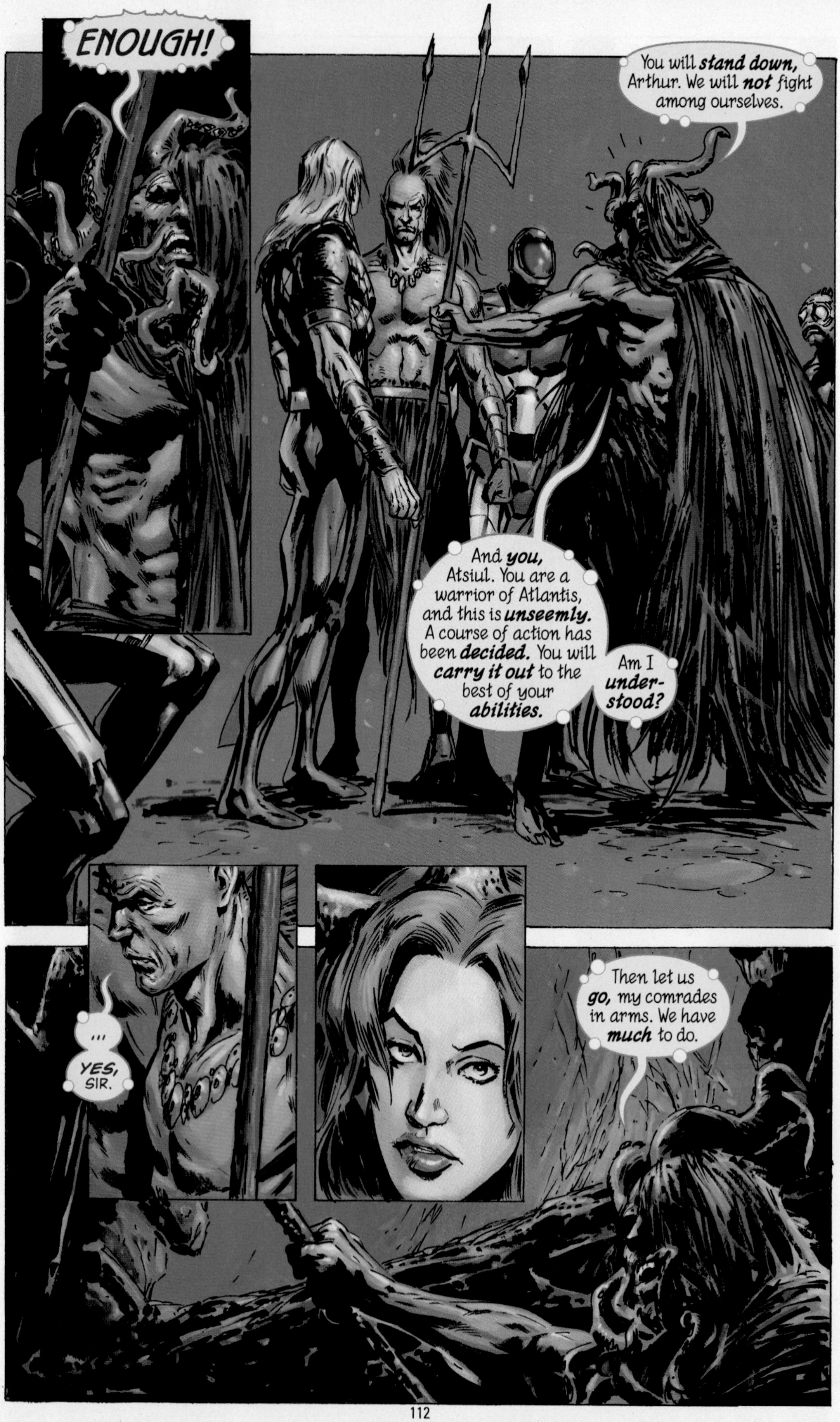
ENOUGH!
You will stand down, Arthur. We will not fight among ourselves.
And you, Atsiul. You are a warrior of Atlantis, and this is unseemly. A course of action has been decided. You will carry it out to the best of your abilities.
Am I under-stood?
... YES, SIR.
Then let us go, my comrades in arms. We have much to do.

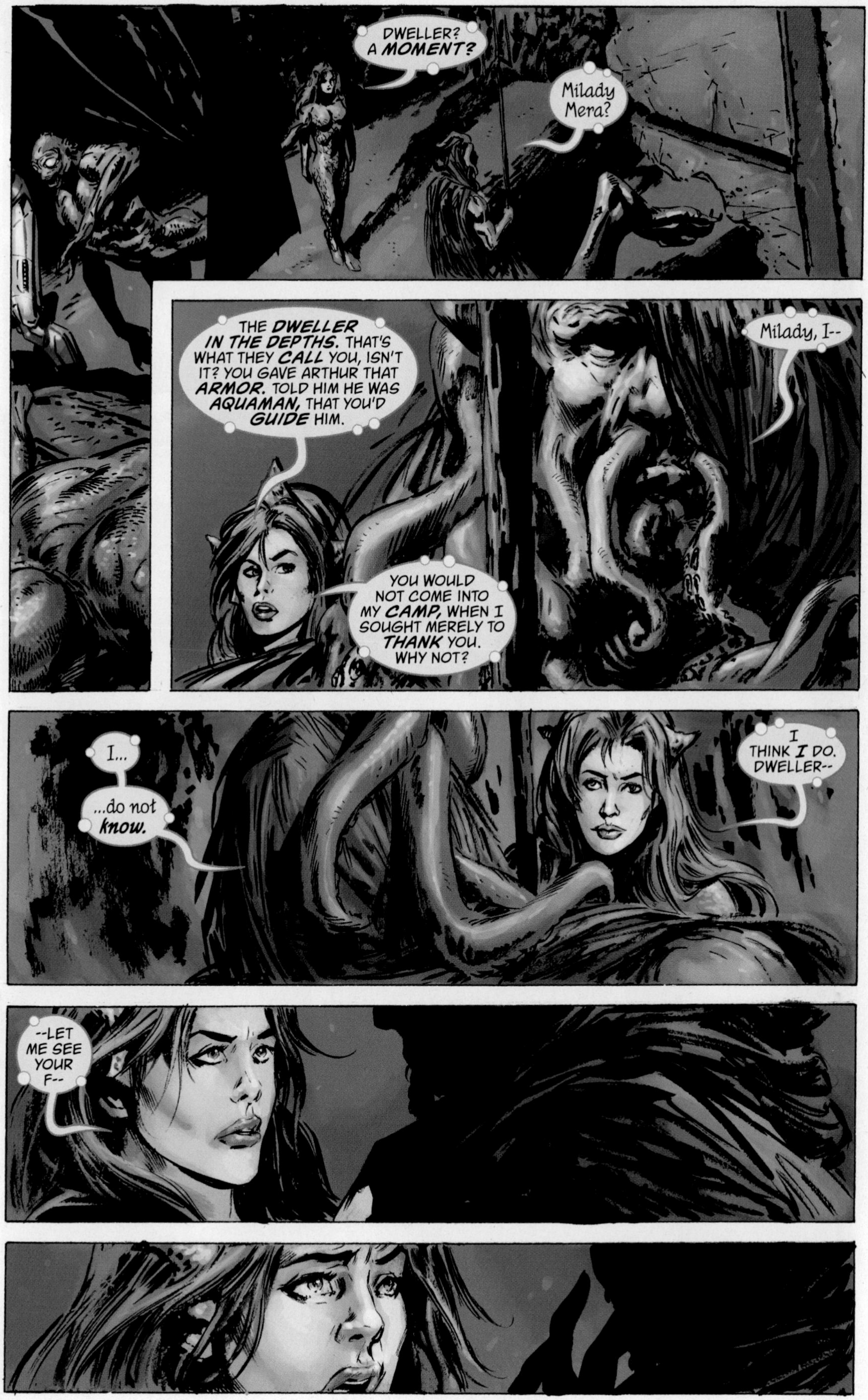
DWELLER? A MOMENT?
Milady Mera?
THE DWELLER IN THE DEPTHS. THAT'S WHAT THEY CALL YOU, ISN'T IT? YOU GAVE ARTHUR THAT ARMOR. TOLD HIM HE WAS AQUAMAN, THAT YOU'D GUIDE HIM.
Milady, I--
YOU WOULD NOT COME INTO MY CAMP, WHEN I SOUGHT MERELY TO THANK YOU. WHY NOT?
I...
...do not know.
I THINK I DO. DWELLER--
--LET ME SEE YOUR F--

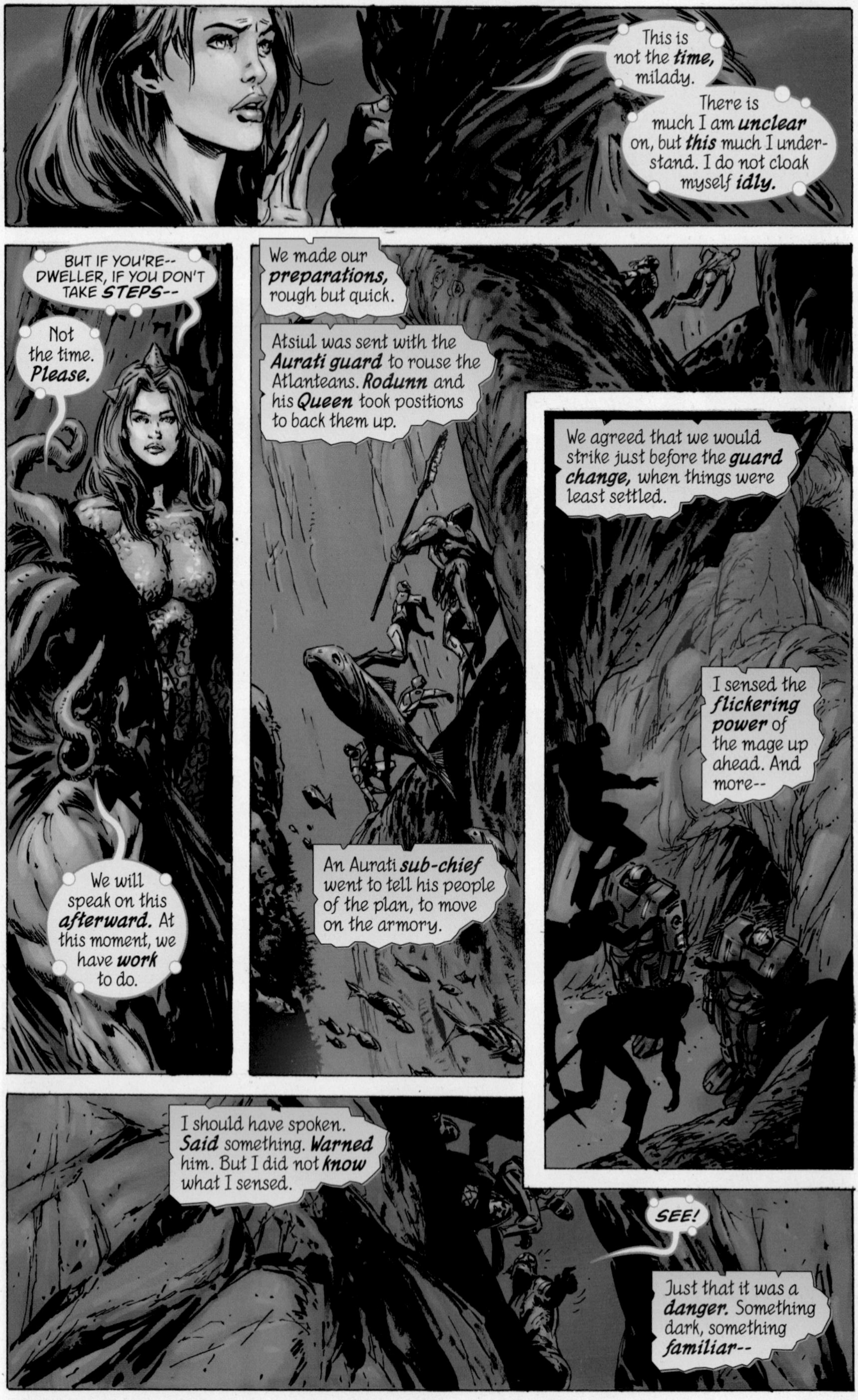
This is not the time, milady.
There is much I am unclear on, but this much I understand. I do not cloak myself idly.
BUT IF YOU'RE-- DWELLER, IF YOU DON'T TAKE STEPS--
Not the time. Please.
We will speak on this afterward. At this moment, we have work to do.
We made our preparations, rough but quick.
Atsiul was sent with the Aurati guard to rouse the Atlanteans. Rodunn and his Queen took positions to back them up.
An Aurati sub-chief went to tell his people of the plan, to move on the armory.
We agreed that we would strike just before the guard change, when things were least settled.
I sensed the flickering power of the mage up ahead. And more--
I should have spoken. Said something. Warned him. But I did not know what I sensed.
SEE!
Just that it was a danger. Something dark, something familiar--

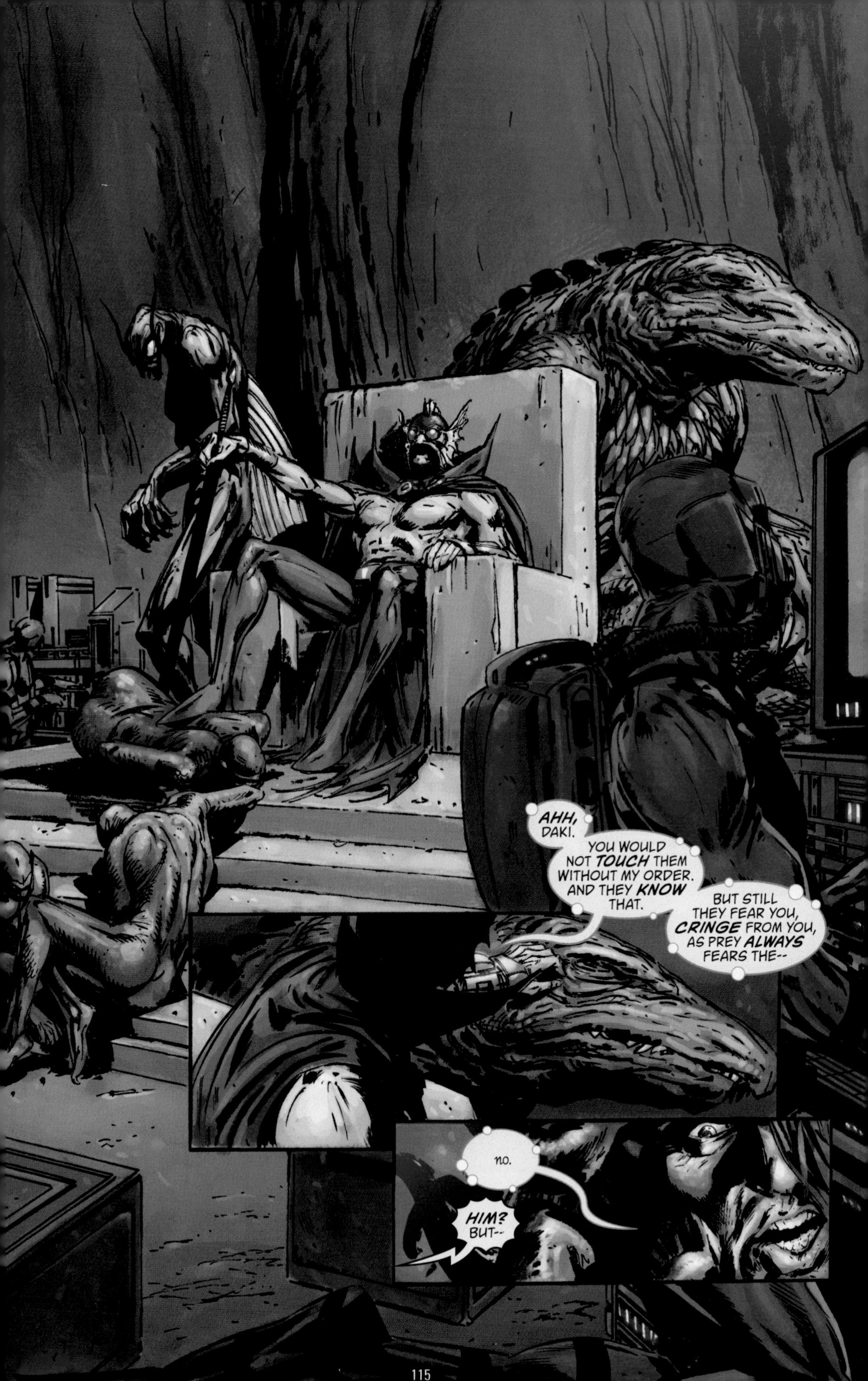
AHH, DAKI.
YOU WOULD NOT TOUCH THEM WITHOUT MY ORDER. AND THEY KNOW THAT.
BUT STILL THEY FEAR YOU, CRINGE FROM YOU, AS PREY ALWAYS FEARS THE--
no.
HIM? BUT--

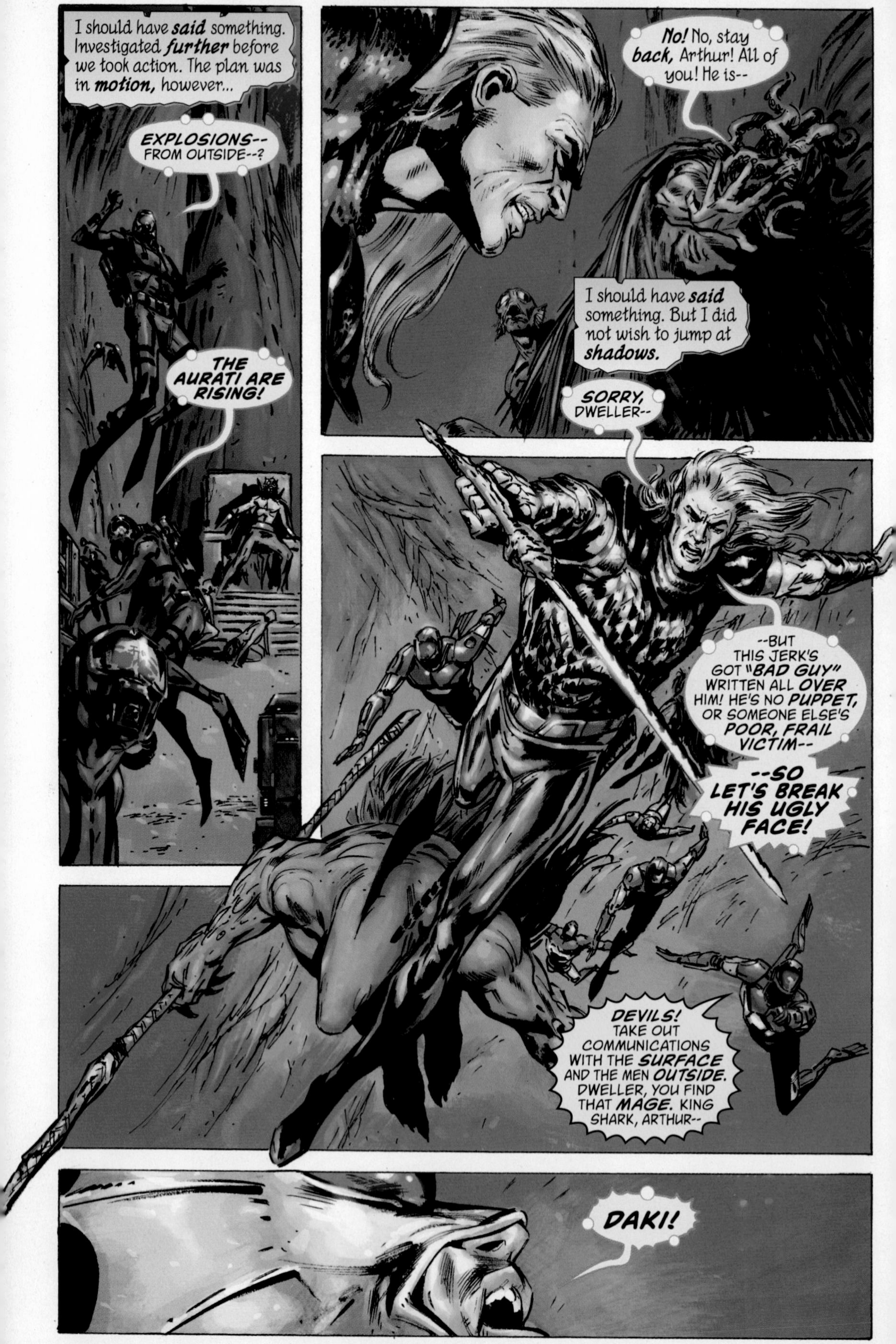

I should have said something. Investigated further before we took action. The plan was in motion, however...
EXPLOSIONS-- FROM OUTSIDE--?
THE AURATI ARE RISING!
No! No, stay back, Arthur! All of you! He is--
I should have said something. But I did not wish to jump at shadows.
SORRY, DWELLER--
--BUT THIS JERK'S GOT "BAD GUY" WRITTEN ALL OVER HIM! HE'S NO PUPPET, OR SOMEONE ELSE'S POOR, FRAIL VICTIM--
--SO LET'S BREAK HIS UGLY FACE!
DEVILS! TAKE OUT COMMUNICATIONS WITH THE SURFACE AND THE MEN OUTSIDE. DWELLER, YOU FIND THAT MAGE. KING SHARK, ARTHUR--
DAKI!

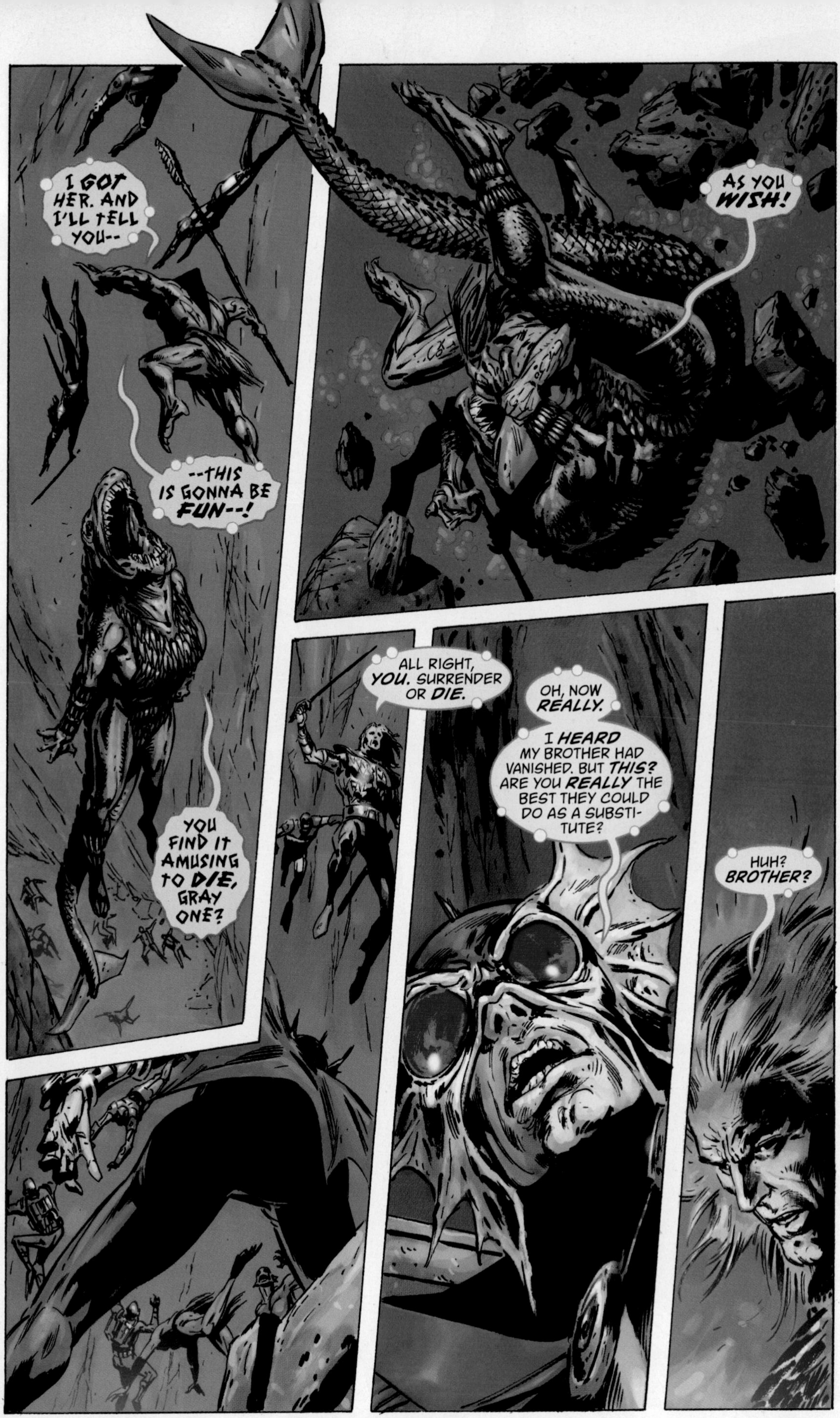
I GOT HER. AND I'LL TELL YOU--
AS YOU WISH!
--THIS IS GONNA BE FUN--!
YOU FIND IT AMUSING TO DIE, GRAY ONE?
ALL RIGHT, YOU. SURRENDER OR DIE.
OH, NOW REALLY.
I HEARD MY BROTHER HAD VANISHED. BUT THIS? ARE YOU REALLY THE BEST THEY COULD DO AS A SUBSTITUTE?
HUH? BROTHER?

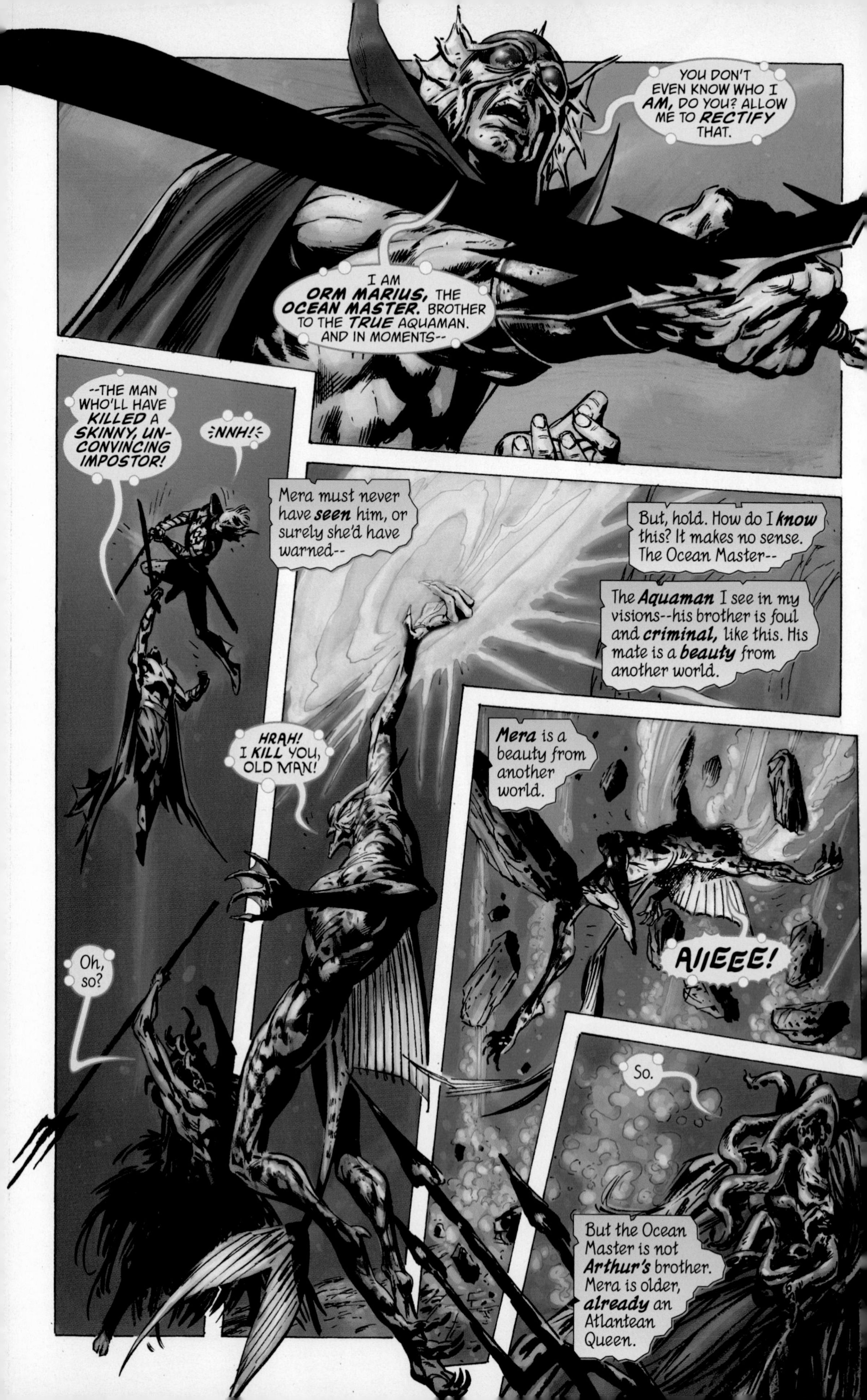
YOU DON'T EVEN KNOW WHO I AM, DO YOU? ALLOW ME TO RECTIFY THAT.
I AM ORM MARIUS, THE OCEAN MASTER. BROTHER TO THE TRUE AQUAMAN. AND IN MOMENTS--
--THE MAN WHO'LL HAVE KILLED A SKINNY, UNCONVINCING IMPOSTOR!
NNH!
Mera must never have seen him, or surely she'd have warned--
But, hold. How do I know this? It makes no sense. The Ocean Master--
The Aquaman I see in my visions--his brother is foul and criminal, like this. His mate is a beauty from another world.
HRAH! I KILL YOU, OLD MAN!
Oh, so?
Mera is a beauty from another world.
AIIEEE!
So.
But the Ocean Master is not Arthur's brother. Mera is older, already an Atlantean Queen.

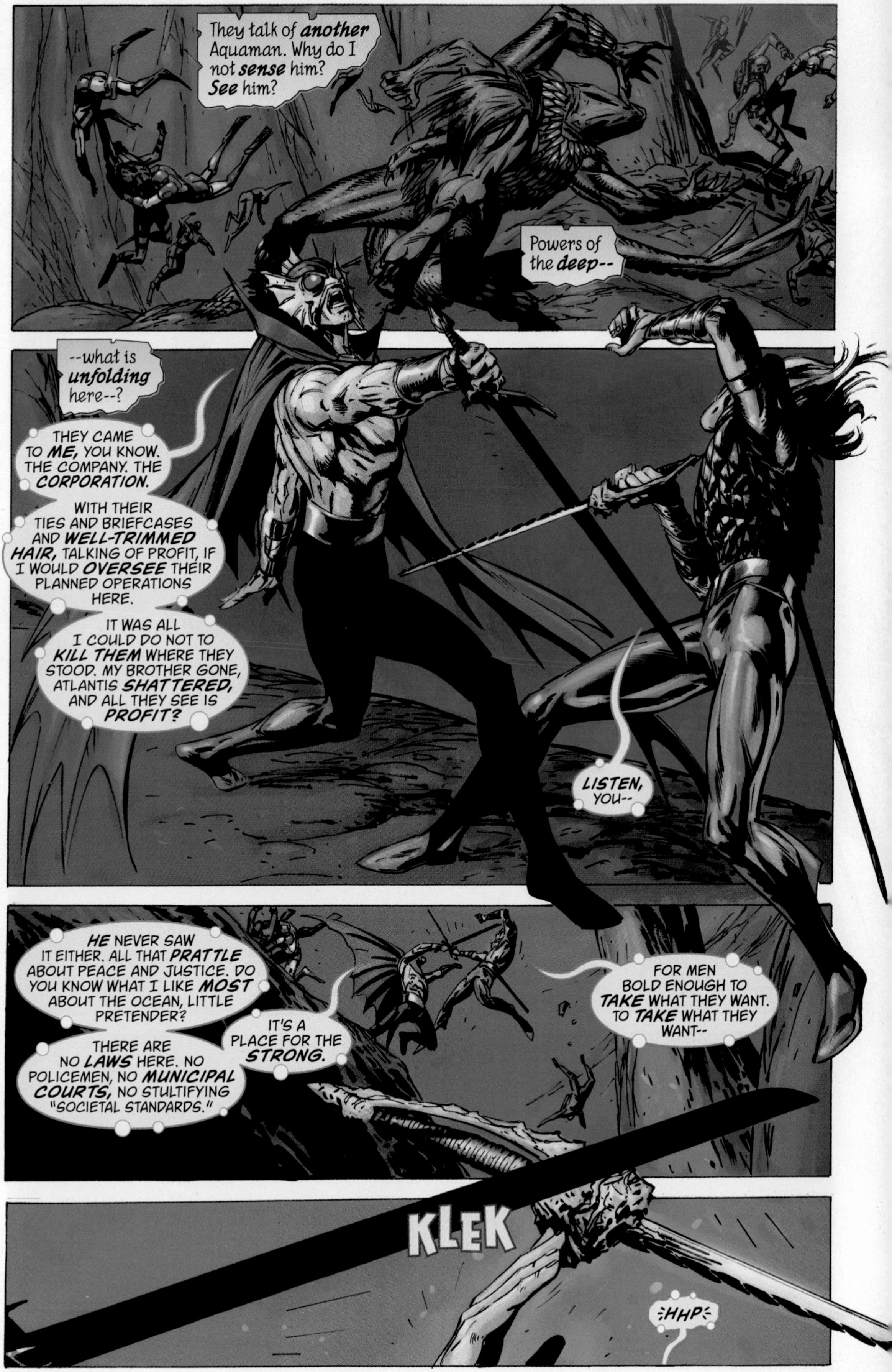

They talk of another Aquaman. Why do I not sense him? See him?
Powers of the deep--
--what is unfolding here--?
THEY CAME TO ME, YOU KNOW. THE COMPANY. THE CORPORATION.
WITH THEIR TIES AND BRIEFCASES AND WELL-TRIMMED HAIR, TALKING OF PROFIT, IF I WOULD OVERSEE THEIR PLANNED OPERATIONS HERE.
IT WAS ALL I COULD DO NOT TO KILL THEM WHERE THEY STOOD. MY BROTHER GONE, ATLANTIS SHATTERED, AND ALL THEY SEE IS PROFIT?
LISTEN, YOU--
HE NEVER SAW IT EITHER. ALL THAT PRATTLE ABOUT PEACE AND JUSTICE. DO YOU KNOW WHAT I LIKE MOST ABOUT THE OCEAN, LITTLE PRETENDER?
THERE ARE NO LAWS HERE. NO POLICEMEN, NO MUNICIPAL COURTS, NO STULTIFYING "SOCIETAL STANDARDS."
IT'S A PLACE FOR THE STRONG.
FOR MEN BOLD ENOUGH TO TAKE WHAT THEY WANT. TO TAKE WHAT THEY WANT--
KLEK
HHP

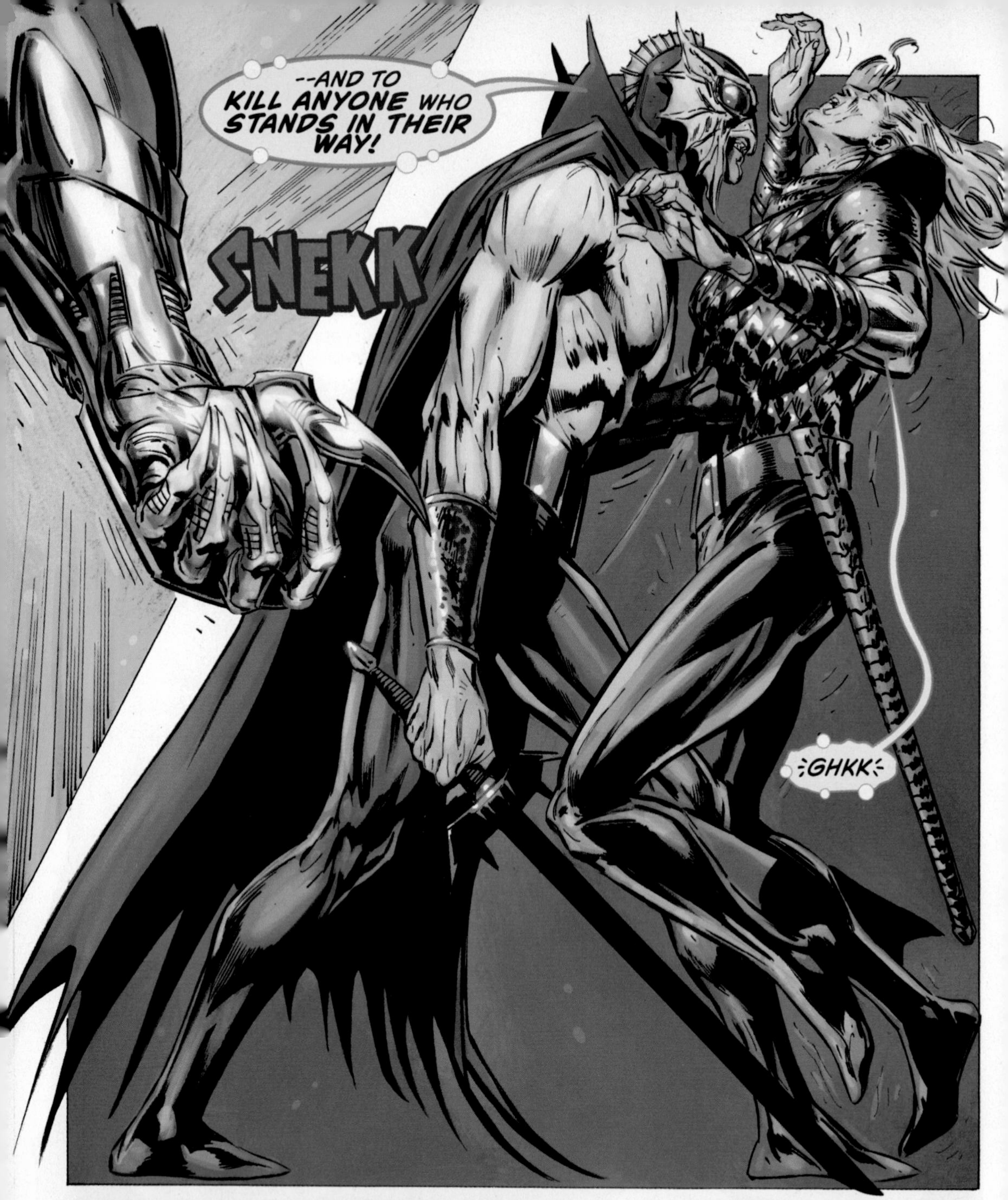
--AND TO KILL ANYONE WHO STANDS IN THEIR WAY!
SNEKK
GHKK

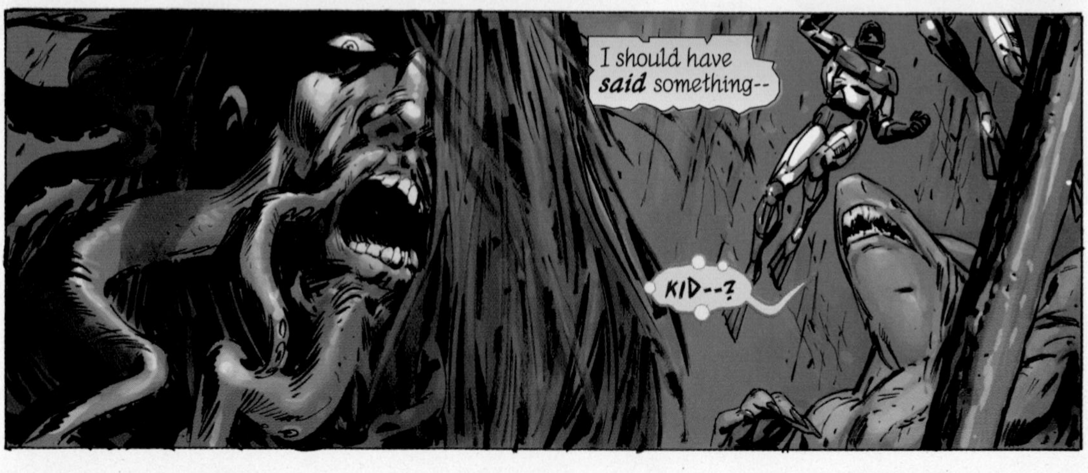
I should have *said* something--
KID--?

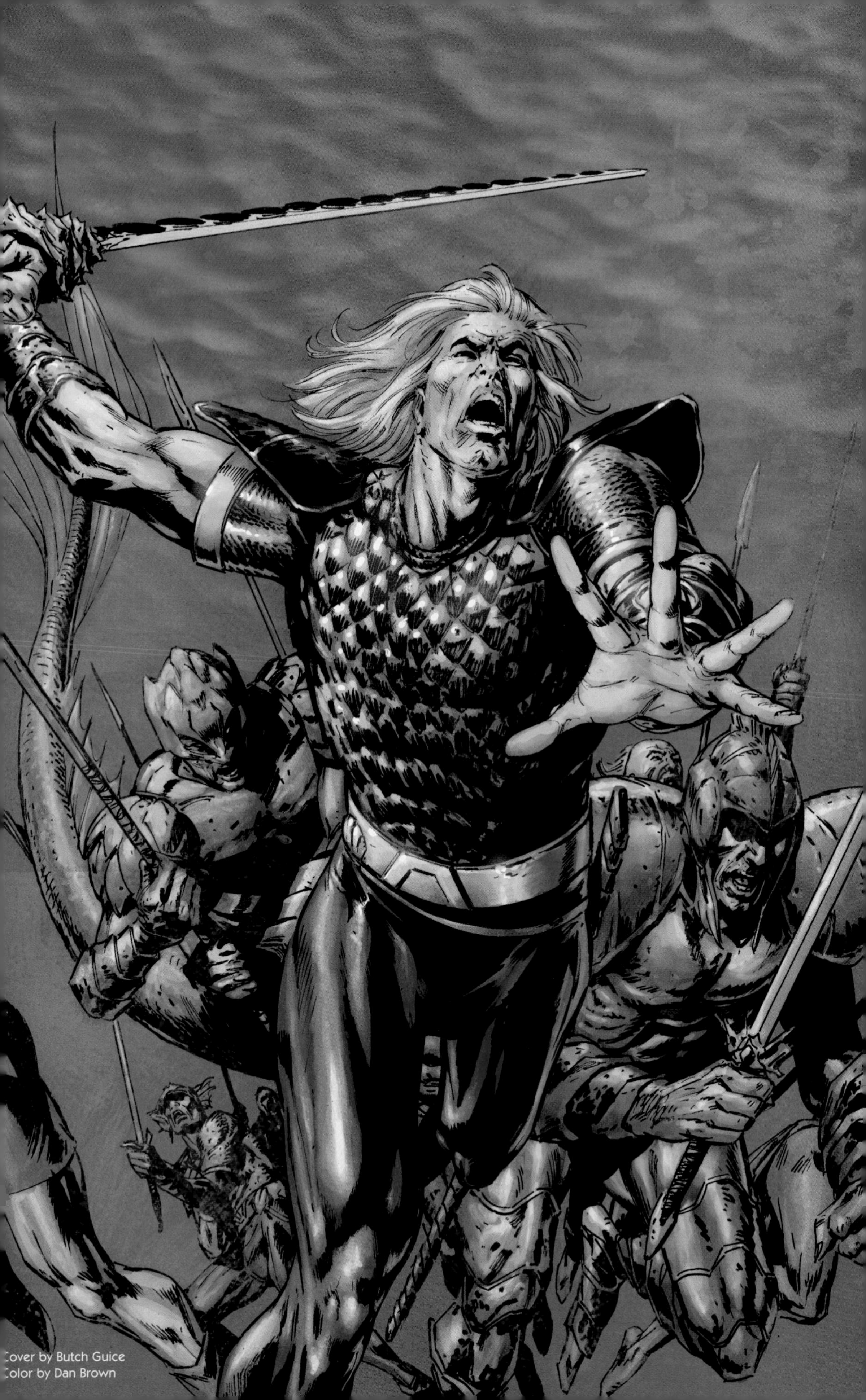

Cover by Butch Guice
Color by Dan Brown

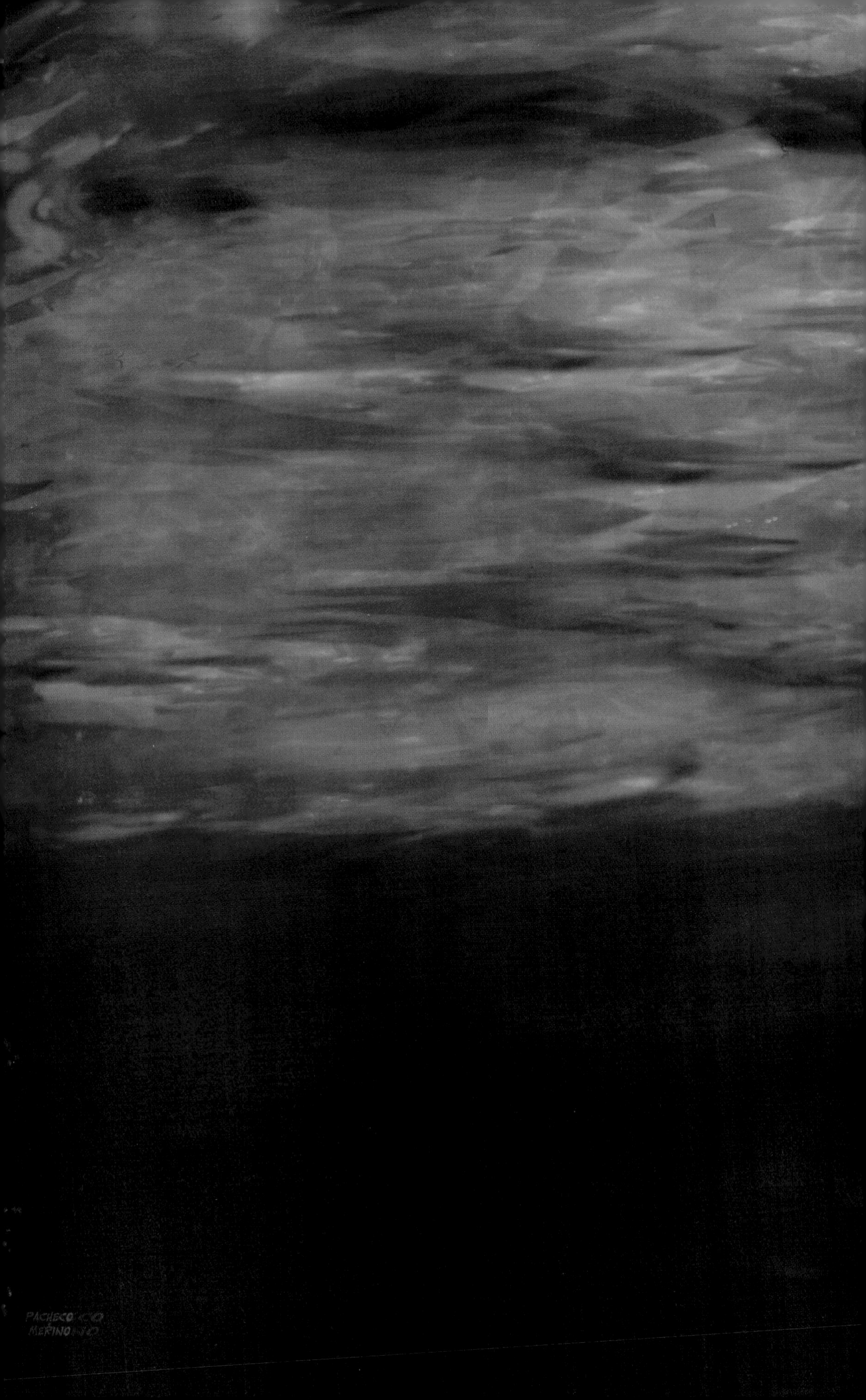
PACHECO
MERINO

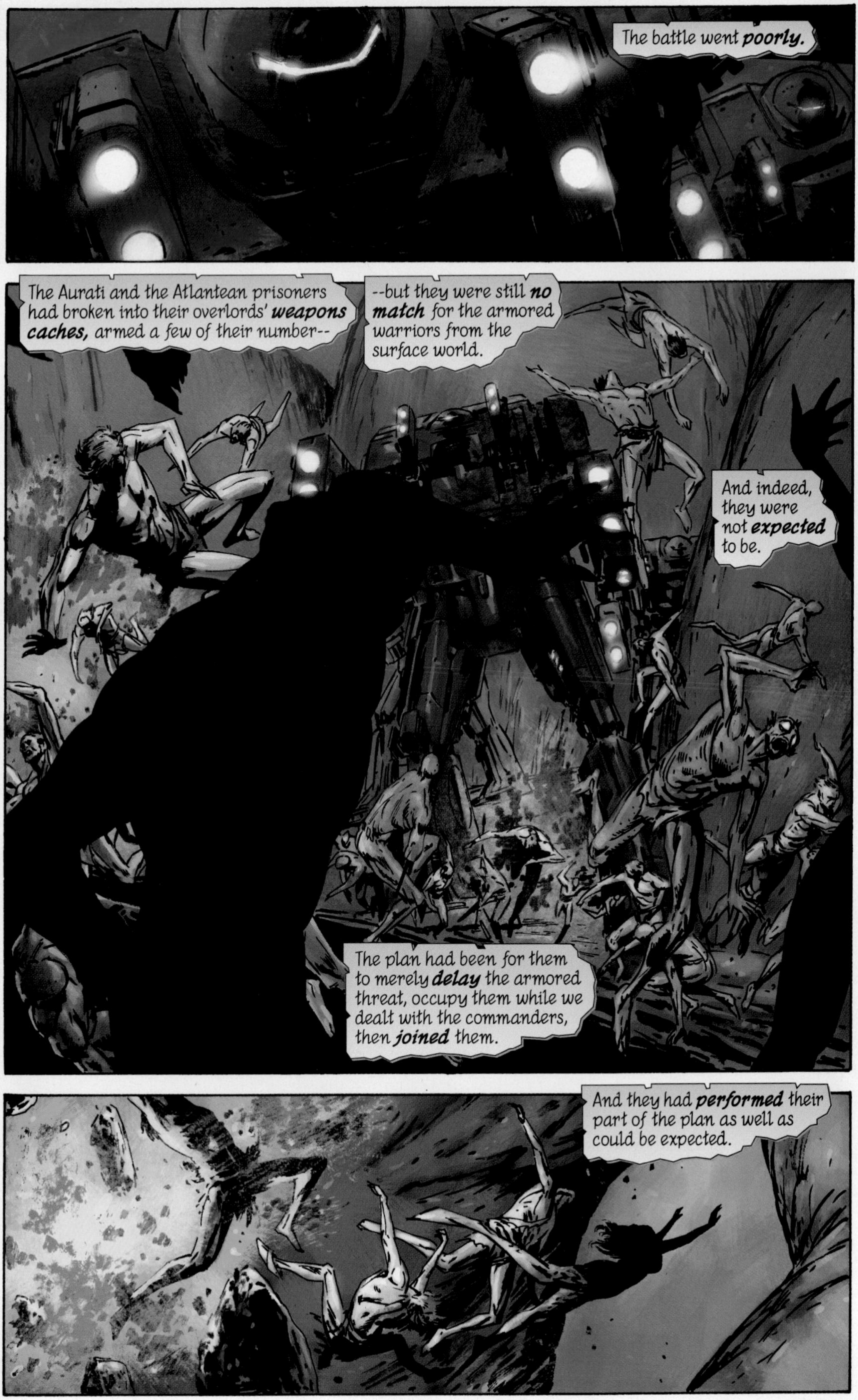
The battle went **poorly.**
The Aurati and the Atlantean prisoners had broken into their overlords' **weapons caches,** armed a few of their number--
--but they were still **no match** for the armored warriors from the surface world.
And indeed, they were not **expected** to be.
The plan had been for them to merely **delay** the armored threat, occupy them while we dealt with the commanders, then **joined** them.
And they had **performed** their part of the plan as well as could be expected.

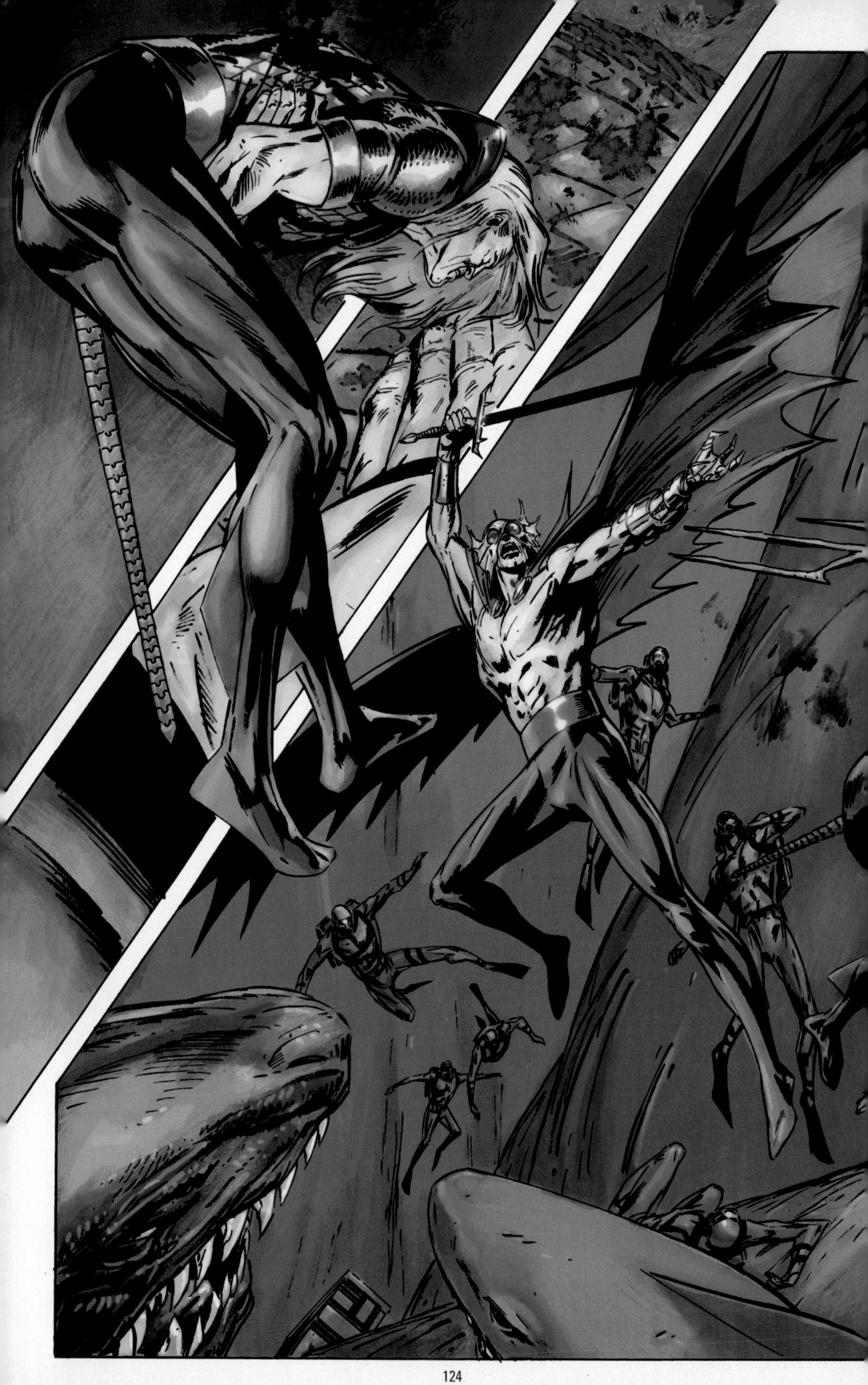

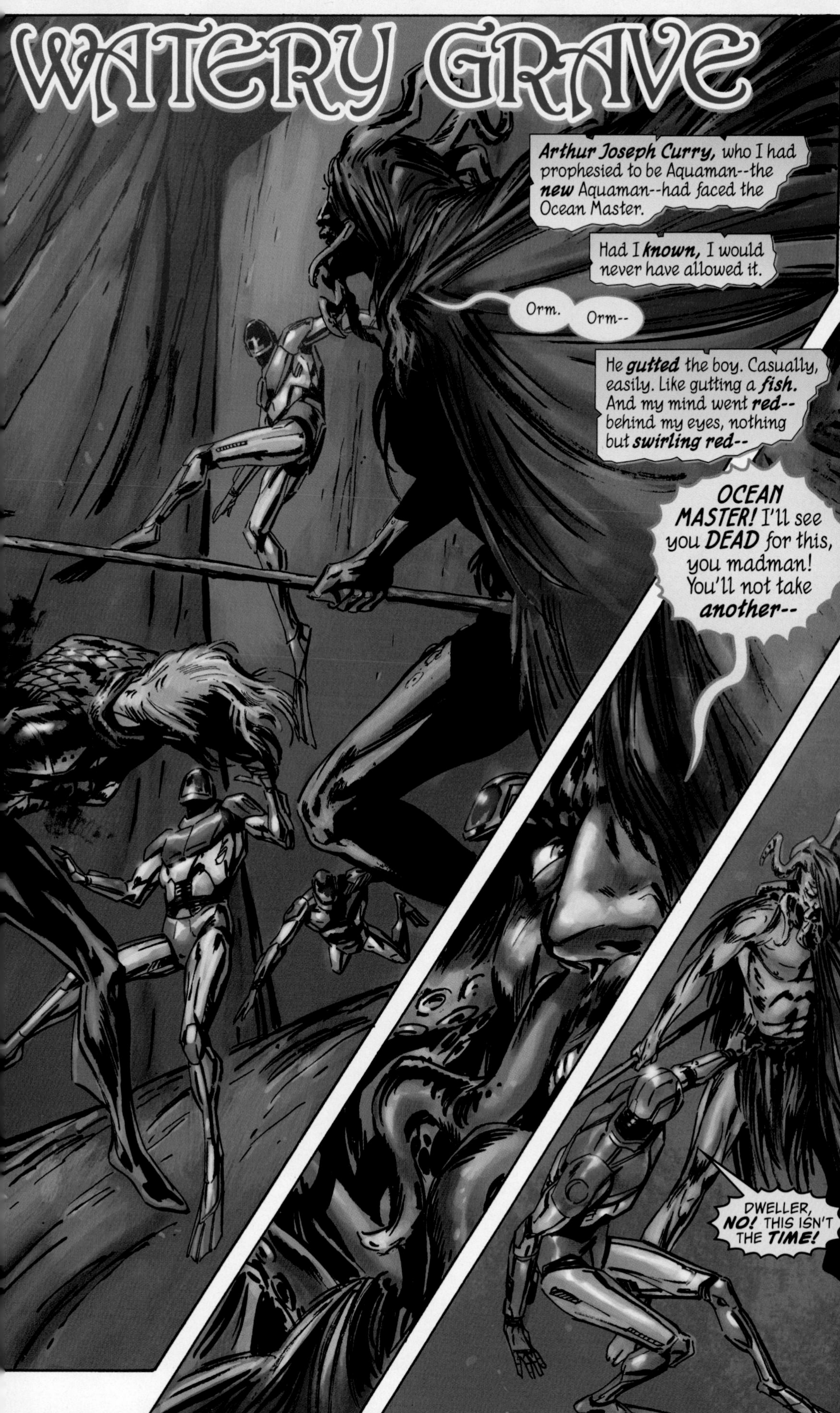
WATERY GRAVE
Arthur Joseph Curry, who I had prophesied to be Aquaman--the new Aquaman--had faced the Ocean Master.
Had I known, I would never have allowed it.
Orm.
Orm--
He gutted the boy. Casually, easily. Like gutting a fish. And my mind went red--behind my eyes, nothing but swirling red--
OCEAN MASTER! I'll see you DEAD for this, you madman! You'll not take another--
DWELLER, NO! THIS ISN'T THE TIME!

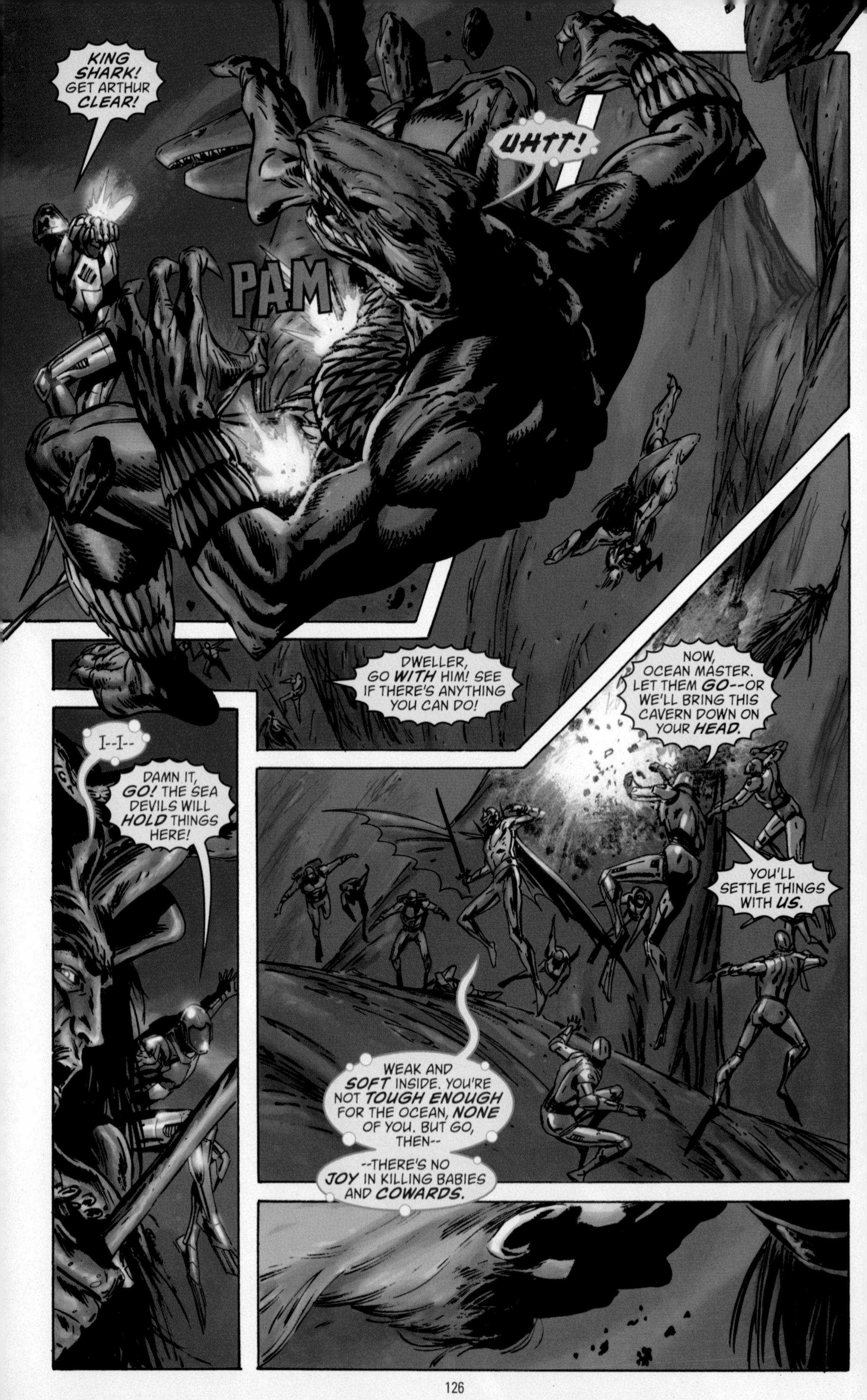
KING SHARK! GET ARTHUR CLEAR!
UHTT!
PAM
DWELLER, GO WITH HIM! SEE IF THERE'S ANYTHING YOU CAN DO!
NOW, OCEAN MASTER. LET THEM GO--OR WE'LL BRING THIS CAVERN DOWN ON YOUR HEAD.
I--I--
DAMN IT, GO! THE SEA DEVILS WILL HOLD THINGS HERE!
YOU'LL SETTLE THINGS WITH US.
WEAK AND SOFT INSIDE. YOU'RE NOT TOUGH ENOUGH FOR THE OCEAN, NONE OF YOU. BUT GO, THEN--
--THERE'S NO JOY IN KILLING BABIES AND COWARDS.

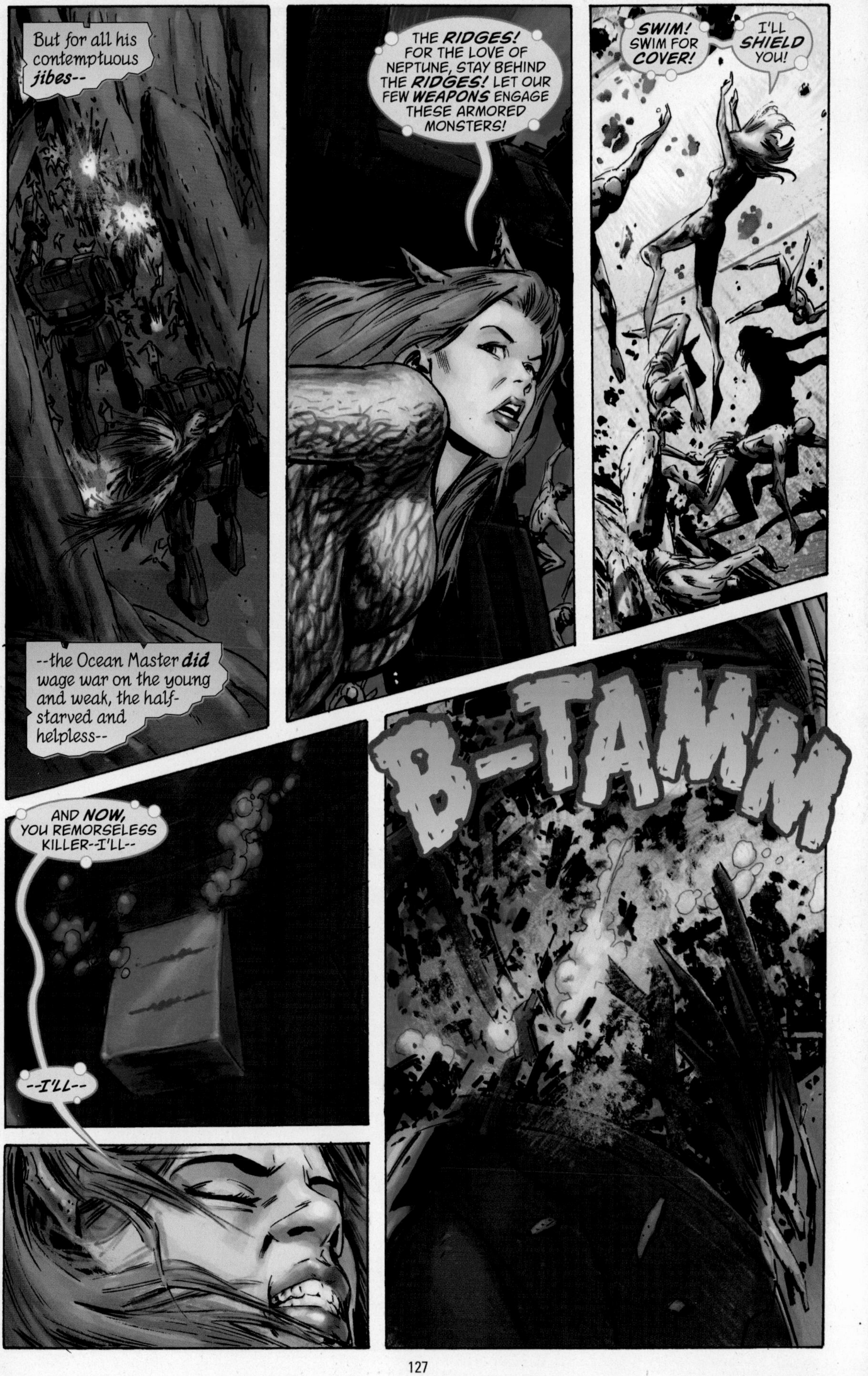
But for all his contemptuous jibes--
THE RIDGES! FOR THE LOVE OF NEPTUNE, STAY BEHIND THE RIDGES! LET OUR FEW WEAPONS ENGAGE THESE ARMORED MONSTERS!
SWIM! SWIM FOR COVER!
I'LL SHIELD YOU!
--the Ocean Master did wage war on the young and weak, the half-starved and helpless--
B-TAMM
AND NOW, YOU REMORSELESS KILLER--I'LL--
--I'LL--

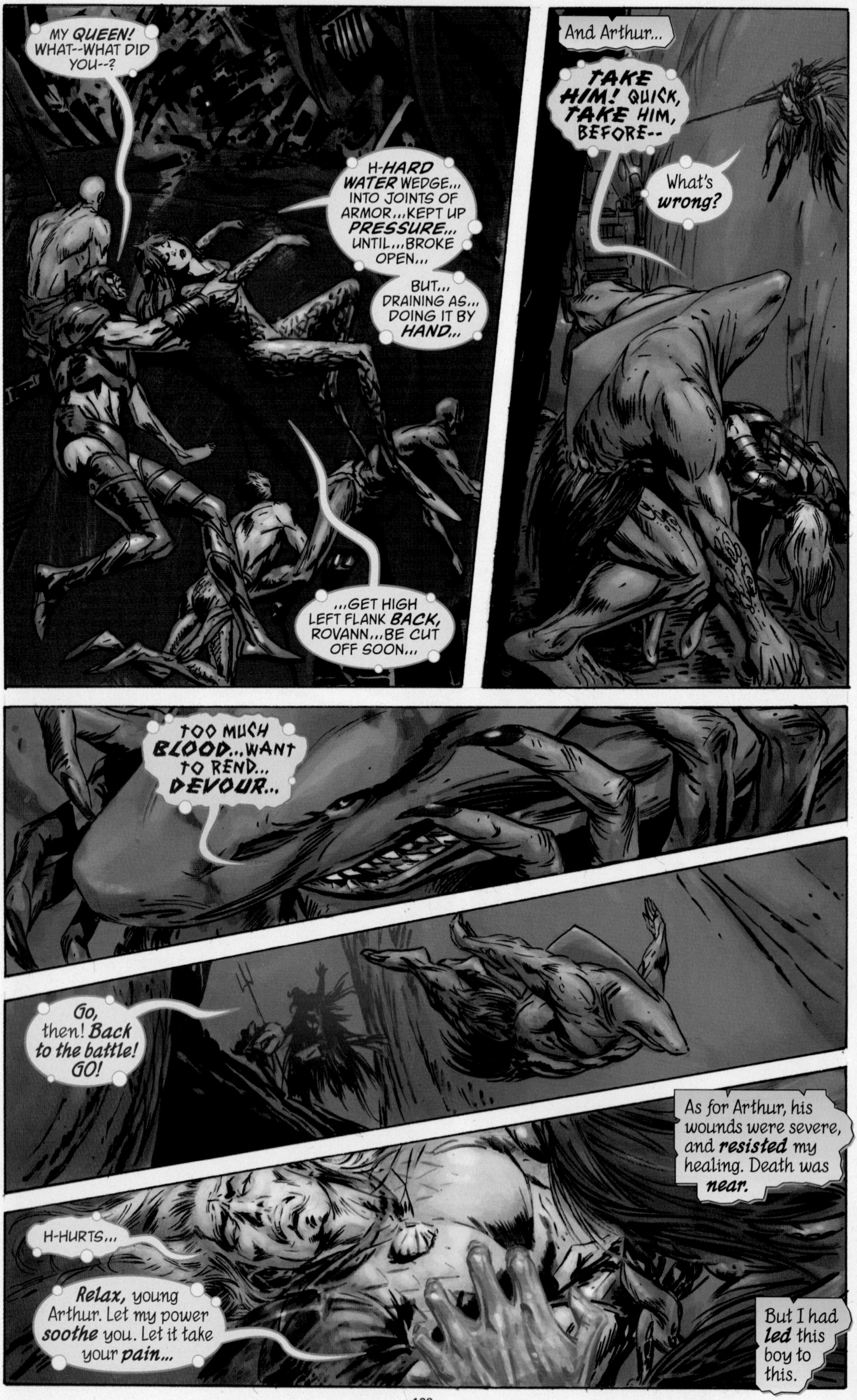
MY QUEEN! WHAT--WHAT DID YOU--?
H-HARD WATER WEDGE... INTO JOINTS OF ARMOR... KEPT UP PRESSURE... UNTIL... BROKE OPEN...
BUT... DRAINING AS... DOING IT BY HAND...
...GET HIGH LEFT FLANK BACK, ROVANN... BE CUT OFF SOON...
And Arthur...
TAKE HIM! QUICK, TAKE HIM, BEFORE--
What's wrong?
TOO MUCH BLOOD... WANT TO REND... DEVOUR...
Go, then! Back to the battle! GO!
As for Arthur, his wounds were severe, and resisted my healing. Death was near.
H-HURTS...
Relax, young Arthur. Let my power soothe you. Let it take your pain...
But I had led this boy to this.

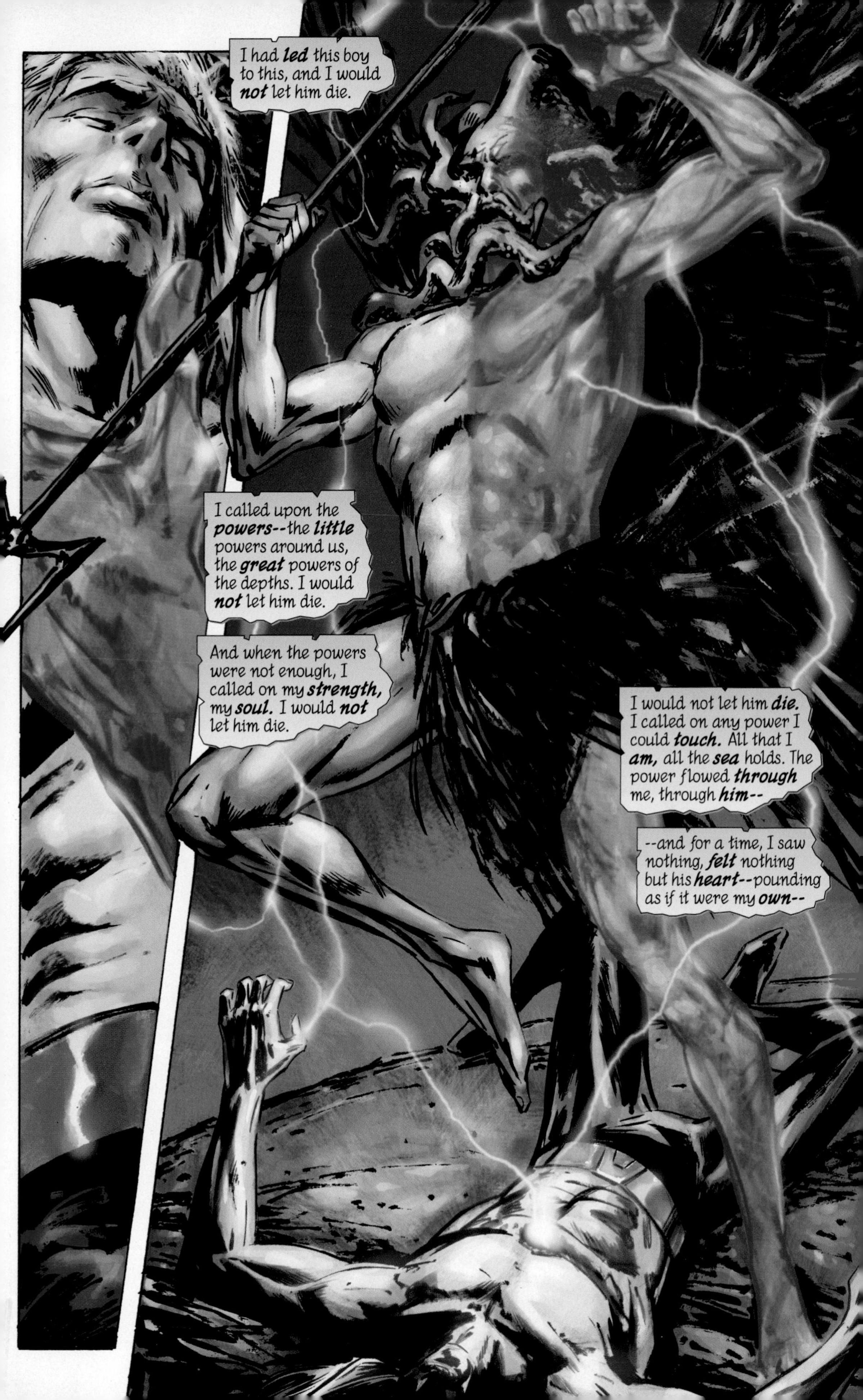

I had **led** this boy to this, and I would **not** let him die.
I called upon the **powers**--the **little** powers around us, the **great** powers of the depths. I would **not** let him die.
And when the powers were not enough, I called on my **strength,** my **soul.** I would **not** let him die.
I would not let him **die.** I called on any power I could **touch.** All that I **am,** all the **sea** holds. The power flowed **through** me, through **him**--
--and for a time, I saw nothing, **felt** nothing but his **heart**--pounding as if it were my **own**--

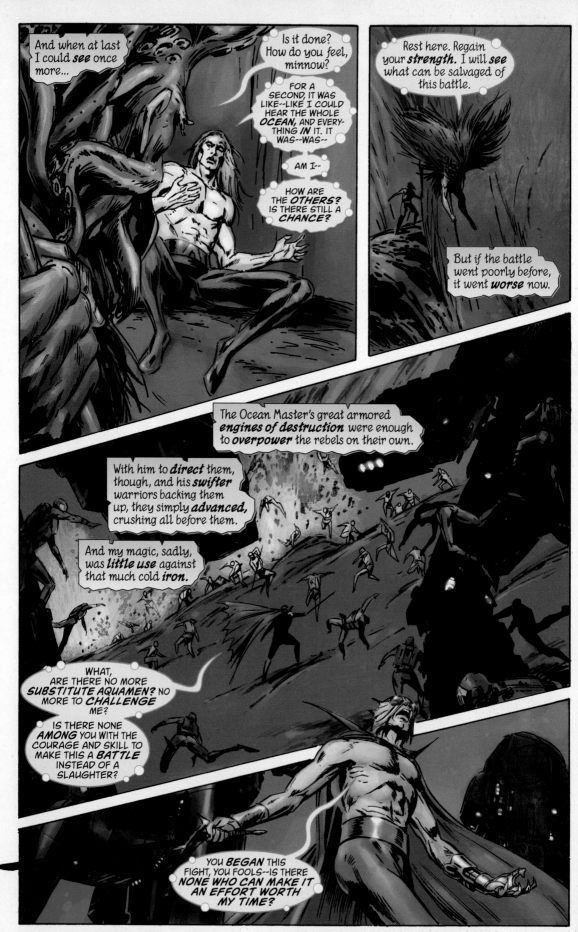

And when at last I could *see* once more...

Is it done? How do you *feel*, minnow?

FOR A SECOND, IT WAS LIKE--LIKE I COULD HEAR THE WHOLE *OCEAN*, AND EVERY-THING *IN* IT. IT WAS--WAS--

AM I--

HOW ARE THE *OTHERS*? IS THERE STILL A *CHANCE*?

Rest here. Regain your *strength*. I will *see* what can be salvaged of this battle.

But if the battle went poorly before, it went *worse* now.

The Ocean Master's great armored *engines of destruction* were enough to *overpower* the rebels on their own.

With him to *direct* them, though, and his *swifter* warriors backing them up, they simply *advanced*, crushing all before them.

And my magic, sadly, was *little use* against that much cold *iron*.

WHAT, ARE THERE NO MORE *SUBSTITUTE AQUAMEN?* NO MORE TO *CHALLENGE* ME?

IS THERE NONE *AMONG* YOU WITH THE COURAGE AND SKILL TO MAKE THIS A *BATTLE* INSTEAD OF A SLAUGHTER?

YOU *BEGAN* THIS FIGHT, YOU FOOLS--IS THERE *NONE WHO CAN MAKE IT AN EFFORT WORTH MY TIME?*

130

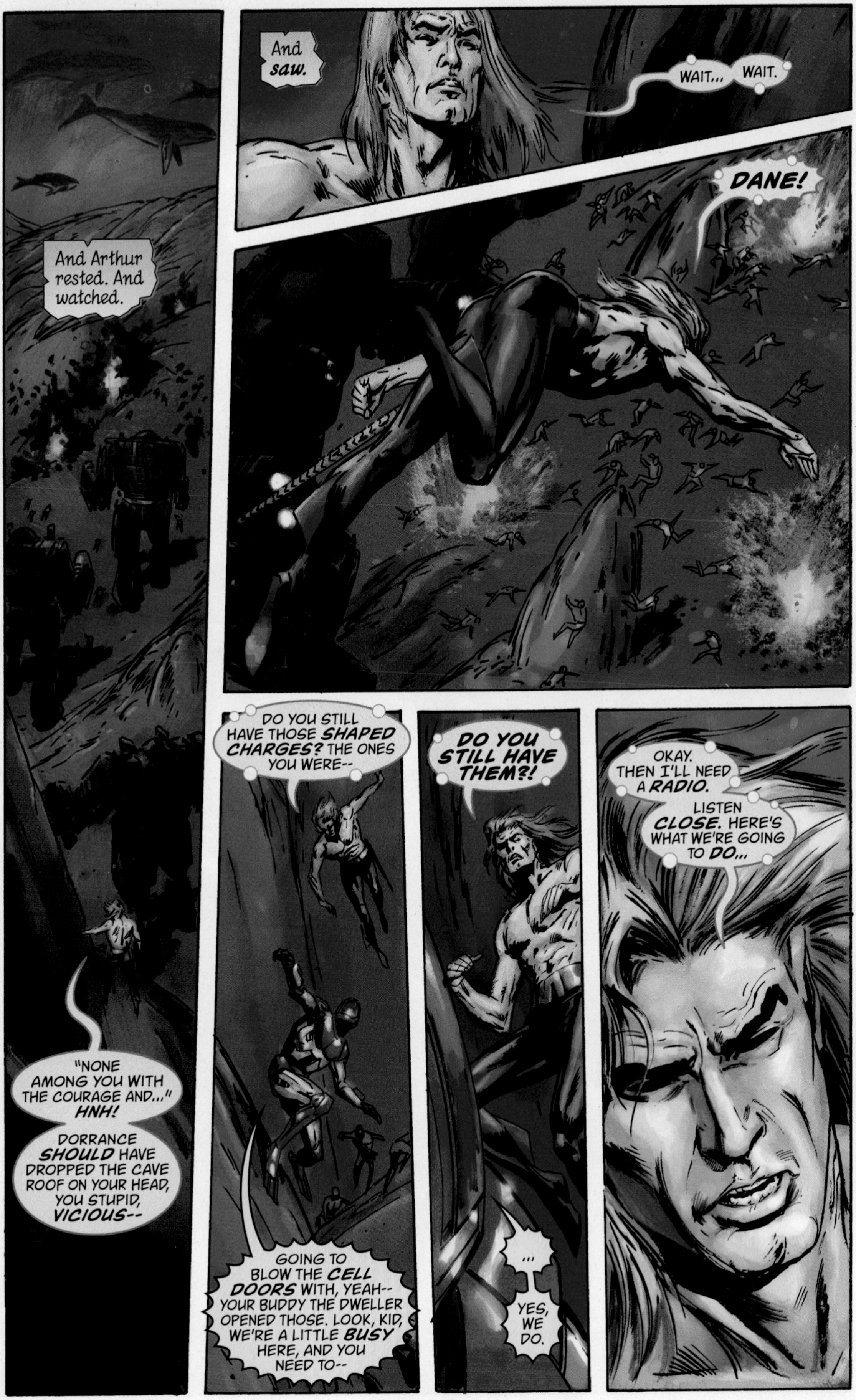

And Arthur rested. And watched.
And saw.
WAIT... WAIT.
DANE!
"NONE AMONG YOU WITH THE COURAGE AND..." HNH!
DORRANCE SHOULD HAVE DROPPED THE CAVE ROOF ON YOUR HEAD, YOU STUPID, VICIOUS--
DO YOU STILL HAVE THOSE SHAPED CHARGES? THE ONES YOU WERE--
GOING TO BLOW THE CELL DOORS WITH, YEAH-- YOUR BUDDY THE DWELLER OPENED THOSE. LOOK, KID, WE'RE A LITTLE BUSY HERE, AND YOU NEED TO--
DO YOU STILL HAVE THEM?!
...
YES, WE DO.
OKAY. THEN I'LL NEED A RADIO.
LISTEN CLOSE. HERE'S WHAT WE'RE GOING TO DO...

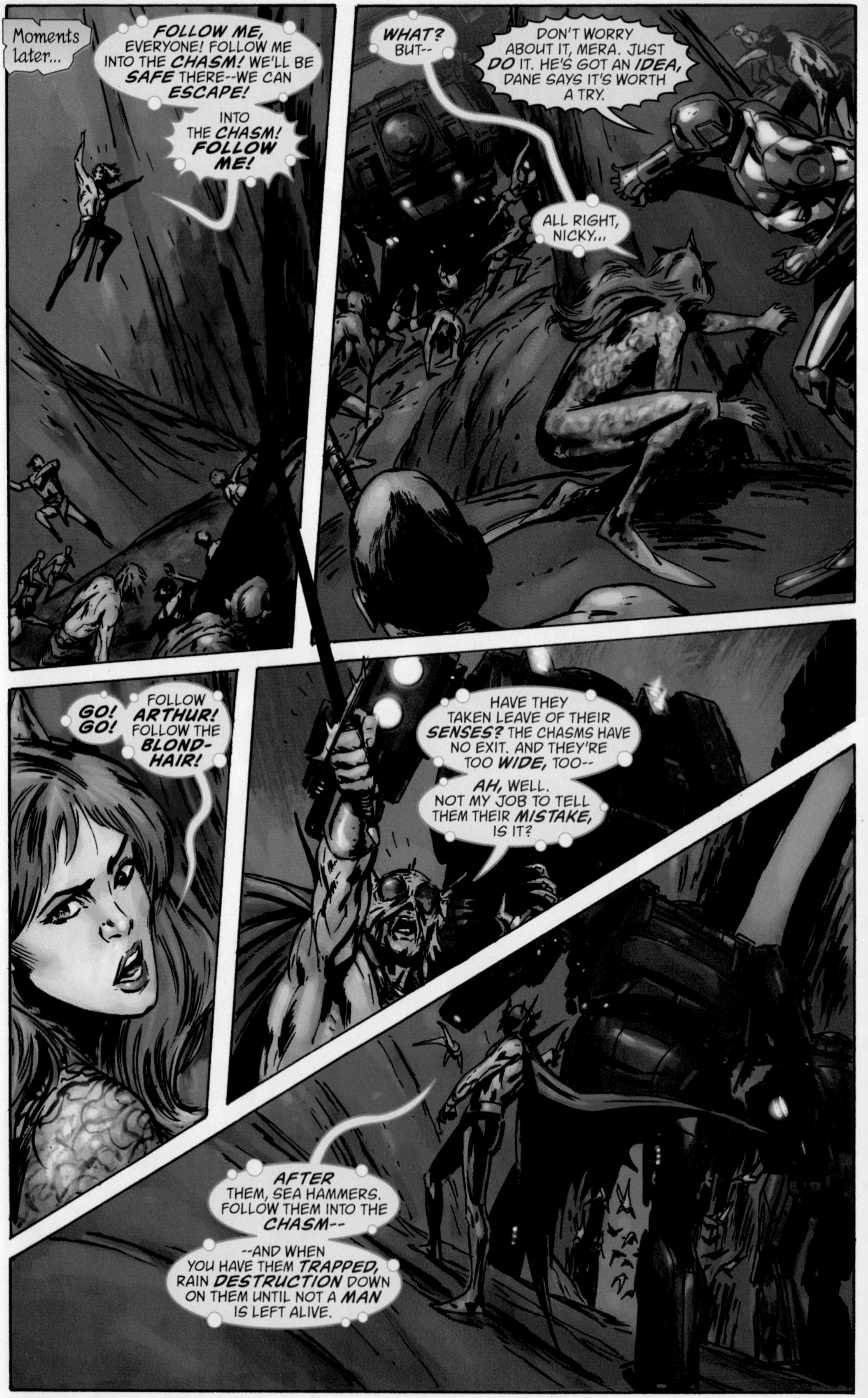

Moments later...
FOLLOW ME, EVERYONE! FOLLOW ME INTO THE CHASM! WE'LL BE SAFE THERE--WE CAN ESCAPE!
INTO THE CHASM! FOLLOW ME!
WHAT? BUT--
DON'T WORRY ABOUT IT, MERA. JUST DO IT. HE'S GOT AN IDEA, DANE SAYS IT'S WORTH A TRY.
ALL RIGHT, NICKY...
GO! GO!
FOLLOW ARTHUR! FOLLOW THE BLOND-HAIR!
HAVE THEY TAKEN LEAVE OF THEIR SENSES? THE CHASMS HAVE NO EXIT. AND THEY'RE TOO WIDE, TOO--
AH, WELL. NOT MY JOB TO TELL THEM THEIR MISTAKE, IS IT?
AFTER THEM, SEA HAMMERS. FOLLOW THEM INTO THE CHASM--
--AND WHEN YOU HAVE THEM TRAPPED, RAIN DESTRUCTION DOWN ON THEM UNTIL NOT A MAN IS LEFT ALIVE.

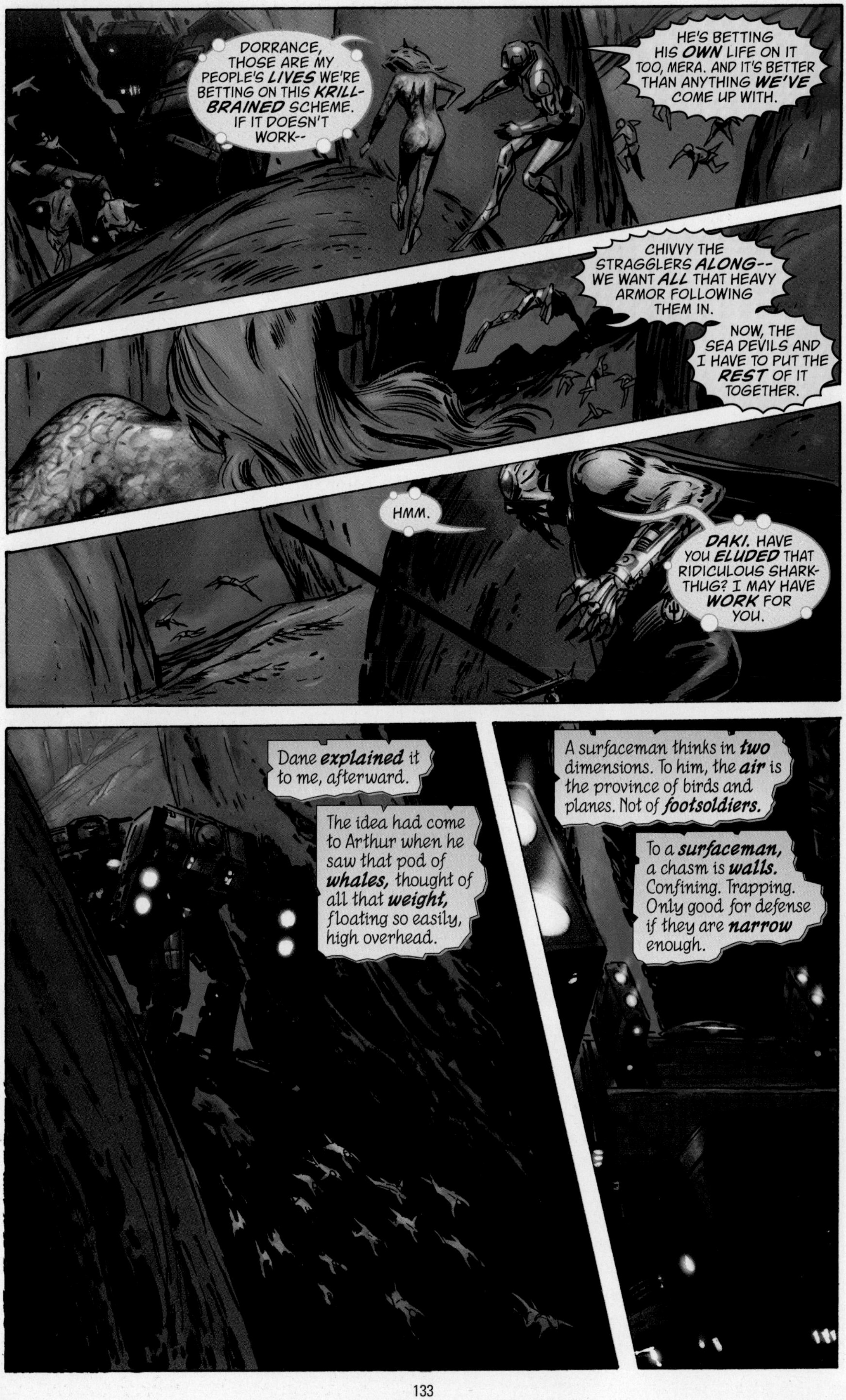
DORRANCE, THOSE ARE MY PEOPLE'S LIVES WE'RE BETTING ON THIS KRILL-BRAINED SCHEME. IF IT DOESN'T WORK--
HE'S BETTING HIS OWN LIFE ON IT TOO, MERA. AND IT'S BETTER THAN ANYTHING WE'VE COME UP WITH.
CHIVVY THE STRAGGLERS ALONG--WE WANT ALL THAT HEAVY ARMOR FOLLOWING THEM IN.
NOW, THE SEA DEVILS AND I HAVE TO PUT THE REST OF IT TOGETHER.
HMM.
DAKI. HAVE YOU ELUDED THAT RIDICULOUS SHARK-THUG? I MAY HAVE WORK FOR YOU.
Dane explained it to me, afterward.
The idea had come to Arthur when he saw that pod of whales, thought of all that weight, floating so easily, high overhead.
A surfaceman thinks in two dimensions. To him, the air is the province of birds and planes. Not of footsoldiers.
To a surfaceman, a chasm is walls. Confining. Trapping. Only good for defense if they are narrow enough.

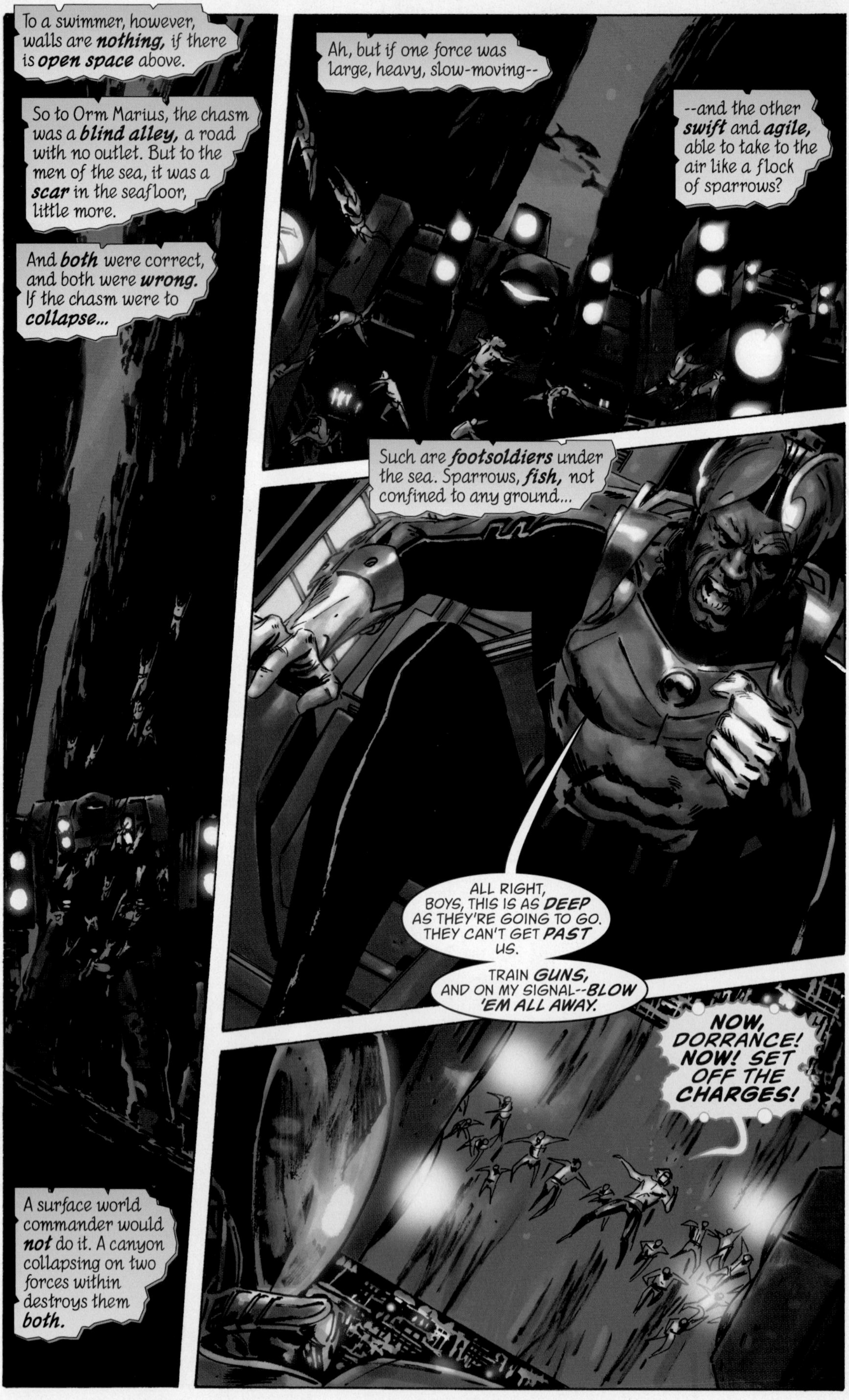
To a swimmer, however, walls are **nothing,** if there is **open space** above.
So to Orm Marius, the chasm was a **blind alley,** a road with no outlet. But to the men of the sea, it was a **scar** in the seafloor, little more.
And **both** were correct, and both were **wrong.** If the chasm were to **collapse...**
Ah, but if one force was large, heavy, slow-moving--
--and the other **swift** and **agile,** able to take to the air like a flock of sparrows?
Such are **footsoldiers** under the sea. Sparrows, **fish,** not confined to any ground...
ALL RIGHT, BOYS, THIS IS AS **DEEP** AS THEY'RE GOING TO GO. THEY CAN'T GET **PAST** US.
TRAIN **GUNS,** AND ON MY SIGNAL--**BLOW 'EM ALL AWAY.**
A surface world commander would **not** do it. A canyon collapsing on two forces within destroys them **both.**
NOW, DORRANCE! NOW! SET OFF THE CHARGES!

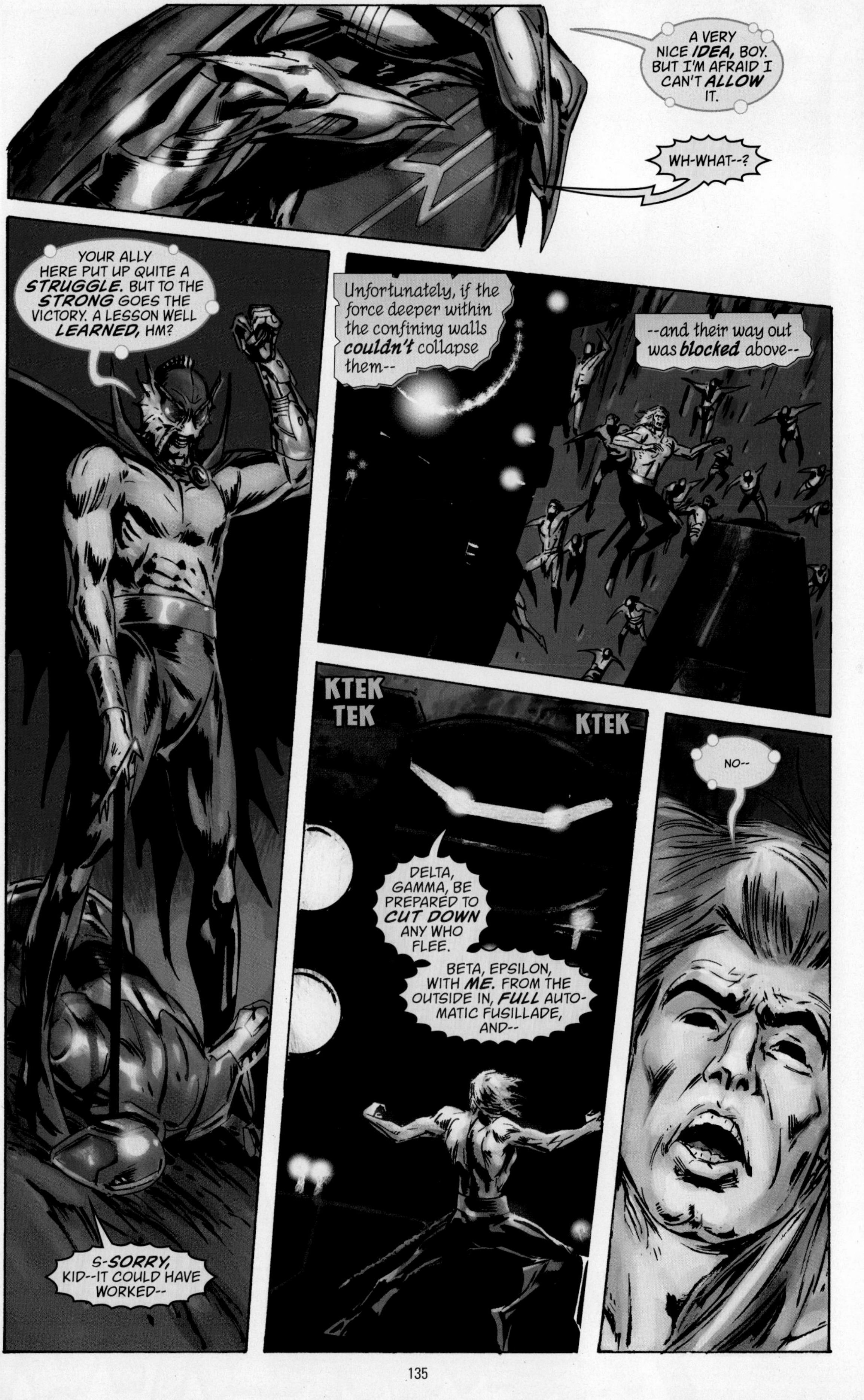
A VERY NICE IDEA, BOY. BUT I'M AFRAID I CAN'T ALLOW IT.
WH-WHAT--?
YOUR ALLY HERE PUT UP QUITE A STRUGGLE. BUT TO THE STRONG GOES THE VICTORY. A LESSON WELL LEARNED, HM?
S-SORRY, KID--IT COULD HAVE WORKED--
Unfortunately, if the force deeper within the confining walls couldn't collapse them--
--and their way out was blocked above--
KTEK TEK
KTEK
DELTA, GAMMA, BE PREPARED TO CUT DOWN ANY WHO FLEE.
BETA, EPSILON, WITH ME. FROM THE OUTSIDE IN, FULL AUTO-MATIC FUSILLADE, AND--
NO--

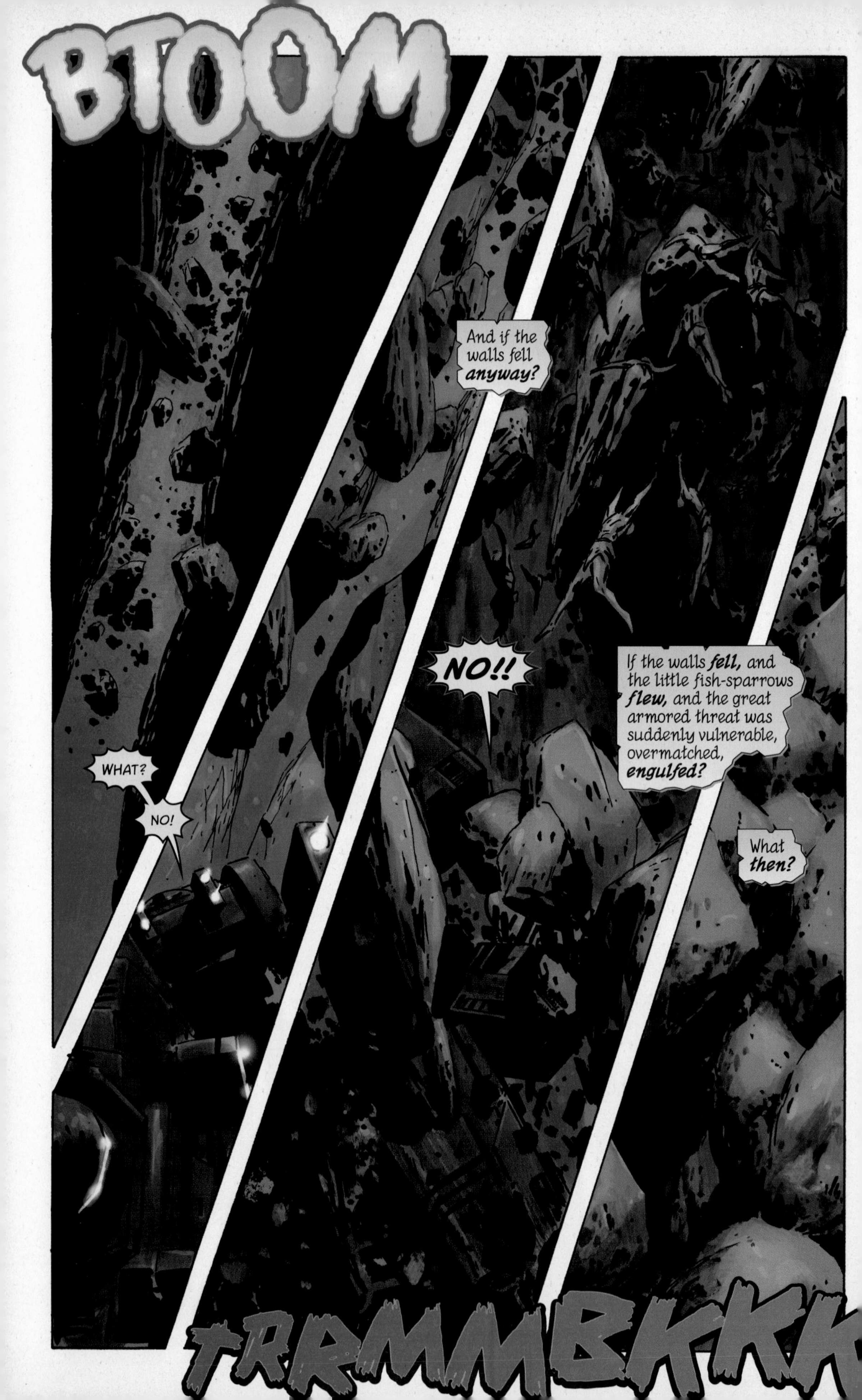
BTOOM
WHAT?
NO!
And if the walls fell anyway?
NO!!
If the walls fell, and the little fish-sparrows flew, and the great armored threat was suddenly vulnerable, overmatched, engulfed?
What then?
TRRMMBKKK

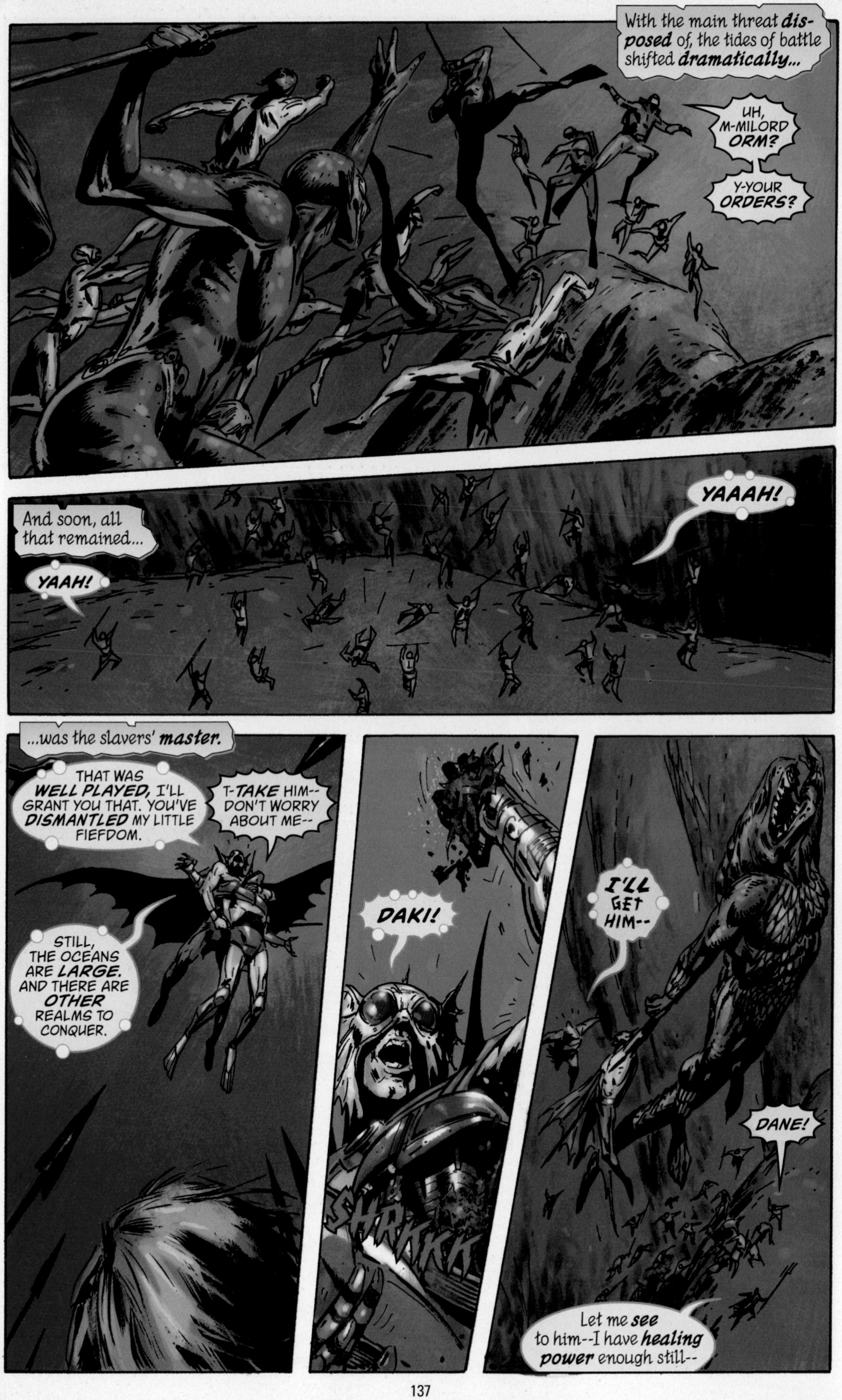
With the main threat disposed of, the tides of battle shifted dramatically...
UH, M-MILORD ORM?
Y-YOUR ORDERS?
And soon, all that remained...
YAAAH!
YAAH!
...was the slavers' master.
THAT WAS WELL PLAYED, I'LL GRANT YOU THAT. YOU'VE DISMANTLED MY LITTLE FIEFDOM.
T-TAKE HIM-- DON'T WORRY ABOUT ME--
STILL, THE OCEANS ARE LARGE. AND THERE ARE OTHER REALMS TO CONQUER.
DAKI!
SHRKKK
I'LL GET HIM--
DANE!
Let me see to him--I have healing power enough still--

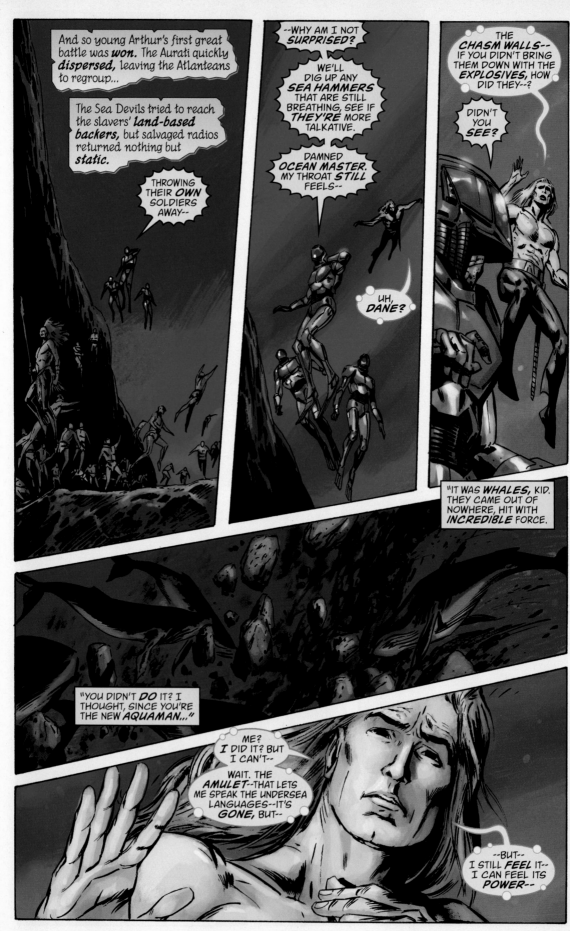

And so young Arthur's first great battle was **won.** The Aurati quickly **dispersed,** leaving the Atlanteans to regroup...

The Sea Devils tried to reach the slavers' **land-based backers,** but salvaged radios returned nothing but **static.**

THROWING THEIR **OWN** SOLDIERS AWAY--

--WHY AM I NOT **SURPRISED?**

WE'LL DIG UP ANY **SEA HAMMERS** THAT ARE STILL **BREATHING,** SEE IF **THEY'RE** MORE TALKATIVE.

DAMNED **OCEAN MASTER.** MY THROAT **STILL** FEELS--

UH, **DANE?**

THE **CHASM WALLS**-- IF YOU DIDN'T BRING THEM DOWN WITH THE **EXPLOSIVES,** HOW DID THEY--?

DIDN'T YOU **SEE?**

"IT WAS **WHALES,** KID. THEY CAME OUT OF NOWHERE, HIT WITH **INCREDIBLE** FORCE.

"YOU DIDN'T **DO** IT? I THOUGHT, SINCE YOU'RE THE NEW **AQUAMAN...**"

ME? **I** DID IT? BUT I CAN'T-- WAIT. THE **AMULET**--THAT LETS ME SPEAK THE UNDERSEA LANGUAGES--IT'S **GONE,** BUT--

--BUT-- I STILL **FEEL** IT-- I CAN FEEL ITS **POWER**--

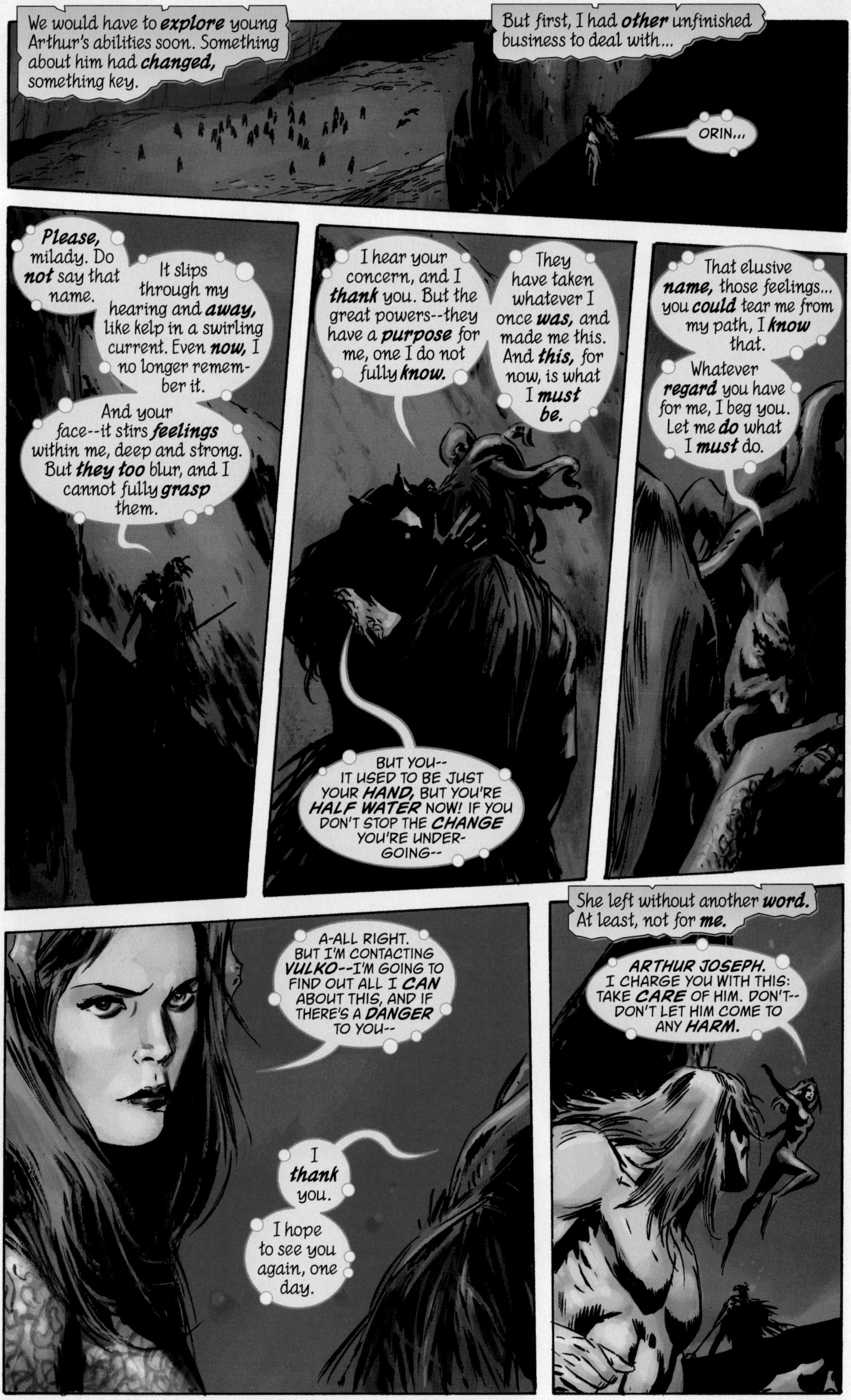
We would have to explore young Arthur's abilities soon. Something about him had changed, something key.
But first, I had other unfinished business to deal with...
ORIN...
Please, milady. Do not say that name.
It slips through my hearing and away, like kelp in a swirling current. Even now, I no longer remember it.
And your face--it stirs feelings within me, deep and strong. But they too blur, and I cannot fully grasp them.
I hear your concern, and I thank you. But the great powers--they have a purpose for me, one I do not fully know.
They have taken whatever I once was, and made me this. And this, for now, is what I must be.
BUT YOU-- IT USED TO BE JUST YOUR HAND, BUT YOU'RE HALF WATER NOW! IF YOU DON'T STOP THE CHANGE YOU'RE UNDER-GOING--
That elusive name, those feelings... you could tear me from my path, I know that.
Whatever regard you have for me, I beg you. Let me do what I must do.
A-ALL RIGHT. BUT I'M CONTACTING VULKO--I'M GOING TO FIND OUT ALL I CAN ABOUT THIS, AND IF THERE'S A DANGER TO YOU--
I thank you.
I hope to see you again, one day.
She left without another word. At least, not for me.
ARTHUR JOSEPH. I CHARGE YOU WITH THIS: TAKE CARE OF HIM. DON'T-- DON'T LET HIM COME TO ANY HARM.

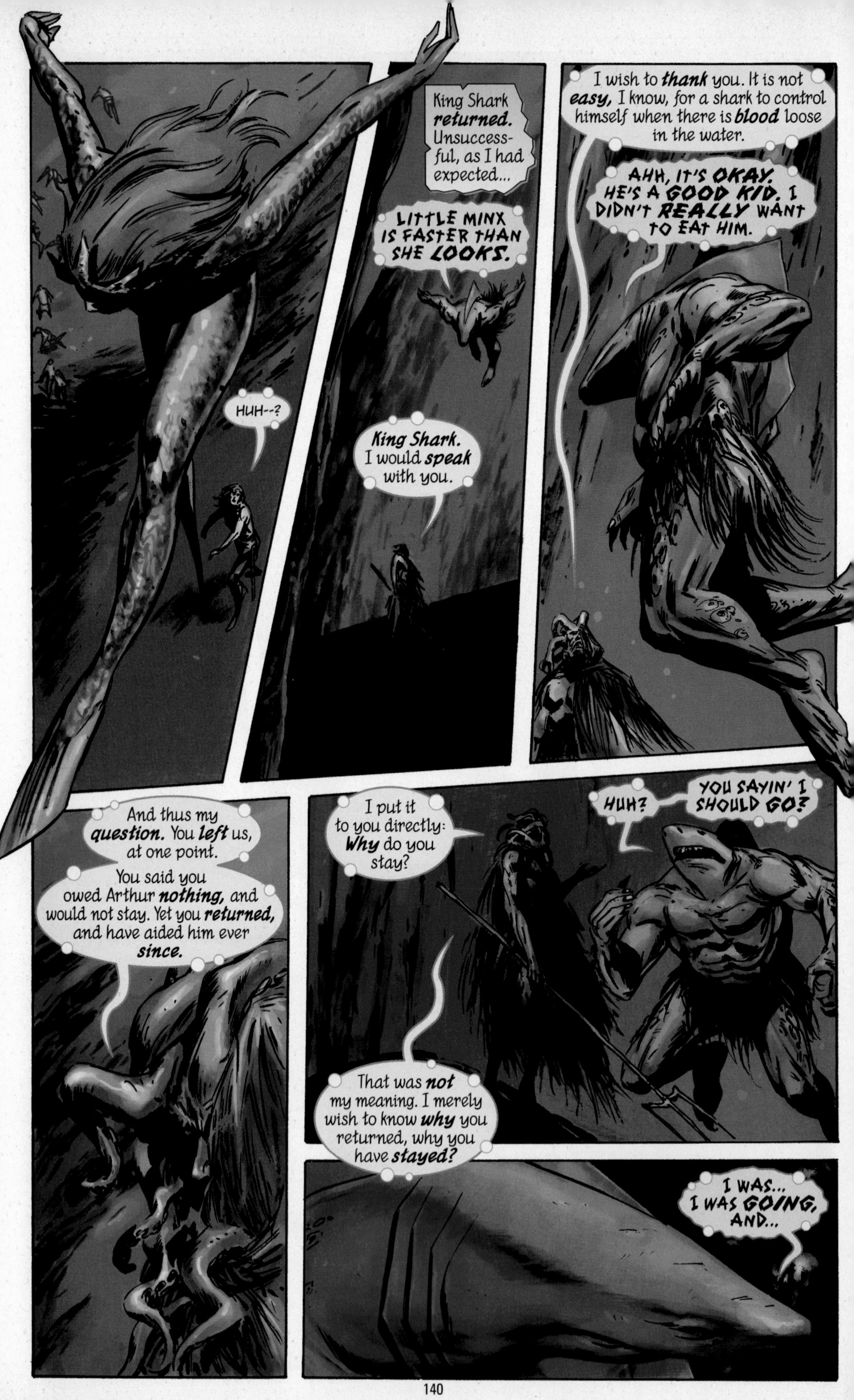
HUH--?
King Shark returned. Unsuccessful, as I had expected...
LITTLE MINX IS FASTER THAN SHE LOOKS.
King Shark. I would speak with you.
I wish to thank you. It is not easy, I know, for a shark to control himself when there is blood loose in the water.
AHH, IT'S OKAY. HE'S A GOOD KID. I DIDN'T REALLY WANT TO EAT HIM.
And thus my question. You left us, at one point.
You said you owed Arthur nothing, and would not stay. Yet you returned, and have aided him ever since.
I put it to you directly: Why do you stay?
HUH?
YOU SAYIN' I SHOULD GO?
That was not my meaning. I merely wish to know why you returned, why you have stayed?
I WAS... I WAS GOING, AND...

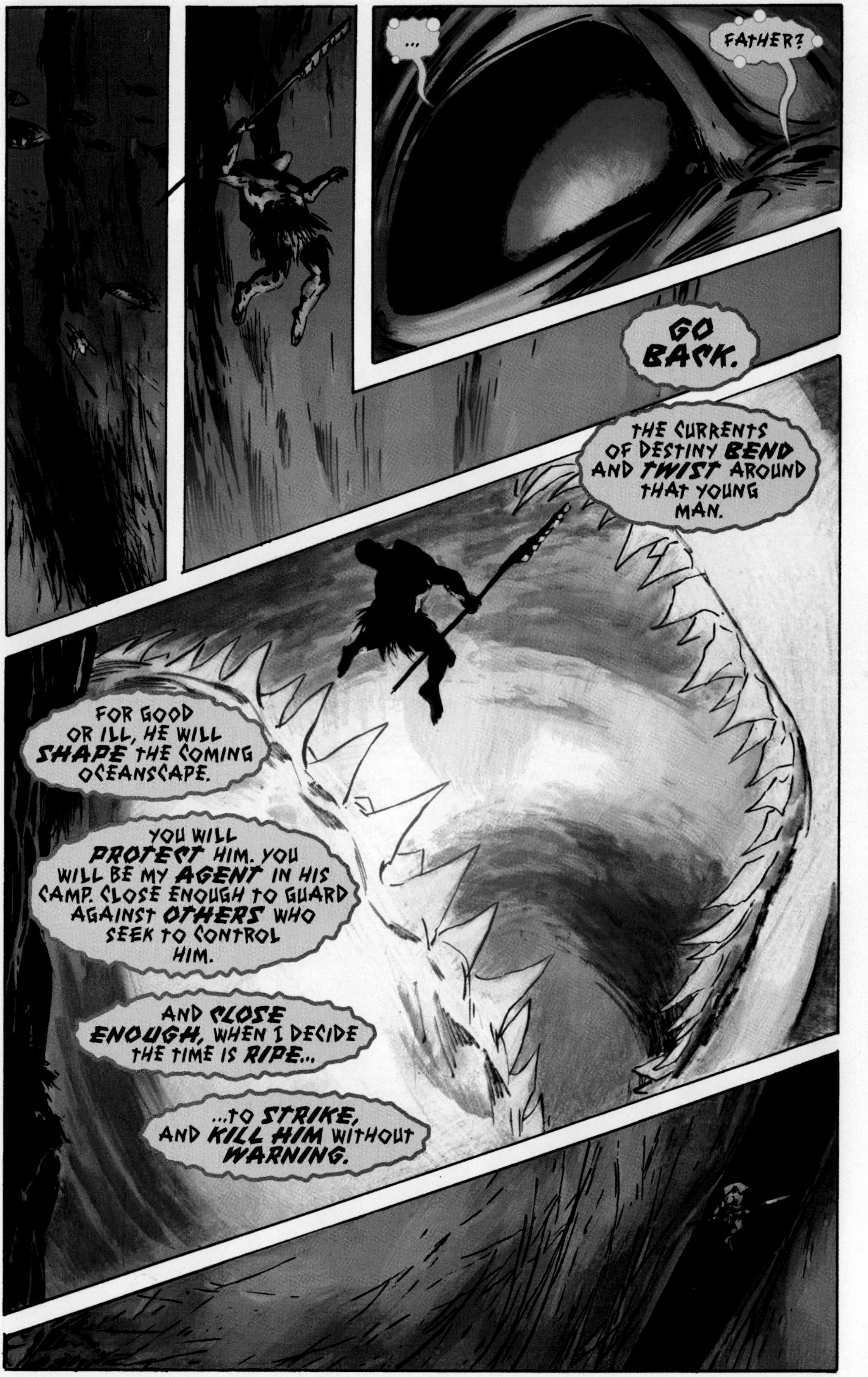
...
FATHER?
GO BACK.
THE CURRENTS OF DESTINY BEND AND TWIST AROUND THAT YOUNG MAN.
FOR GOOD OR ILL, HE WILL SHAPE THE COMING OCEANSCAPE.
YOU WILL PROTECT HIM. YOU WILL BE MY AGENT IN HIS CAMP. CLOSE ENOUGH TO GUARD AGAINST OTHERS WHO SEEK TO CONTROL HIM.
AND CLOSE ENOUGH, WHEN I DECIDE THE TIME IS RIPE...
...TO STRIKE, AND KILL HIM WITHOUT WARNING.

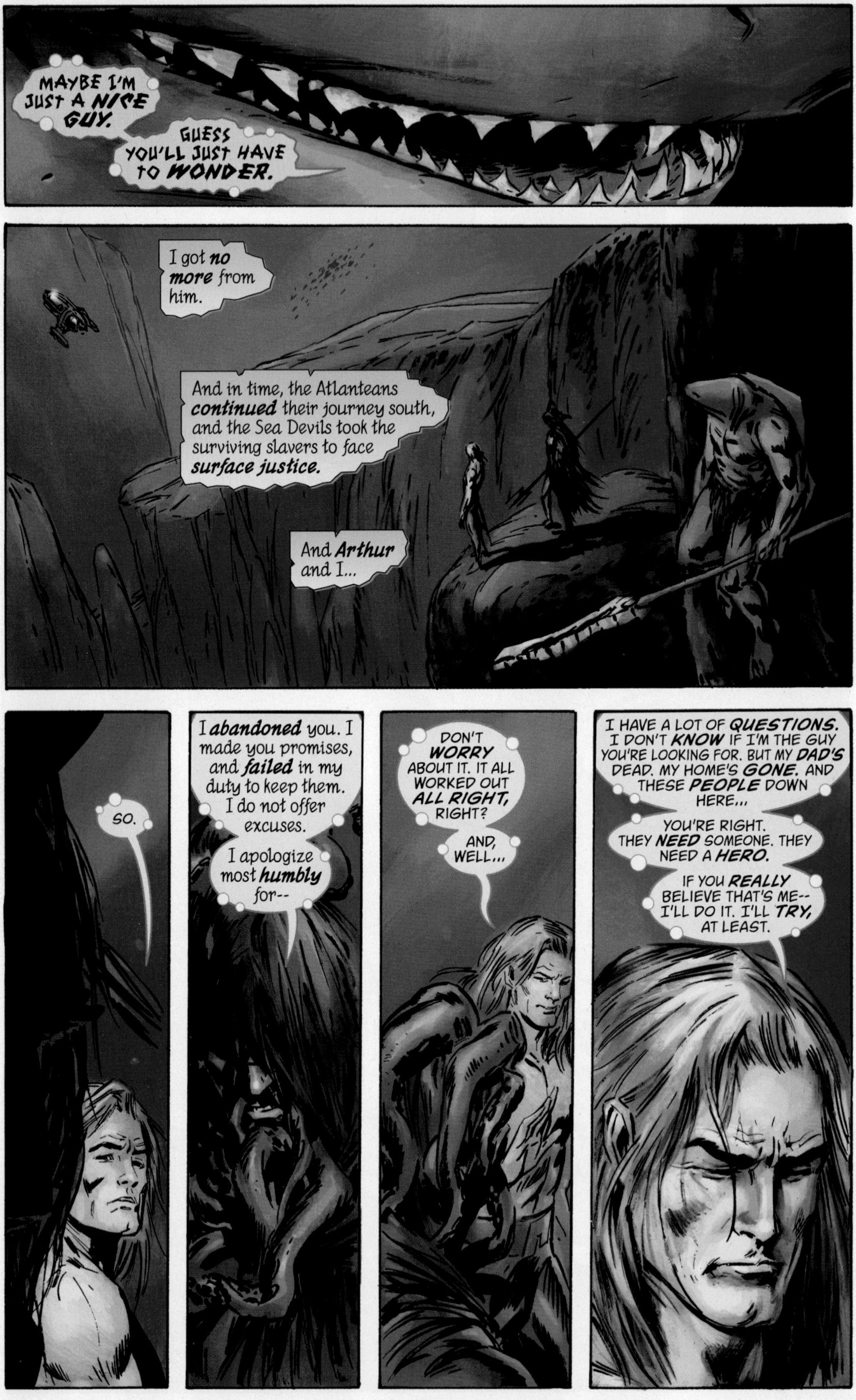

MAYBE I'M JUST A NICE GUY.
GUESS YOU'LL JUST HAVE TO WONDER.
I got no more from him.
And in time, the Atlanteans continued their journey south, and the Sea Devils took the surviving slavers to face surface justice.
And Arthur and I...
SO.
I abandoned you. I made you promises, and failed in my duty to keep them. I do not offer excuses.
I apologize most humbly for--
DON'T WORRY ABOUT IT. IT ALL WORKED OUT ALL RIGHT, RIGHT?
AND, WELL...
I HAVE A LOT OF QUESTIONS. I DON'T KNOW IF I'M THE GUY YOU'RE LOOKING FOR. BUT MY DAD'S DEAD. MY HOME'S GONE. AND THESE PEOPLE DOWN HERE...
YOU'RE RIGHT. THEY NEED SOMEONE. THEY NEED A HERO.
IF YOU REALLY BELIEVE THAT'S ME-- I'LL DO IT. I'LL TRY, AT LEAST.

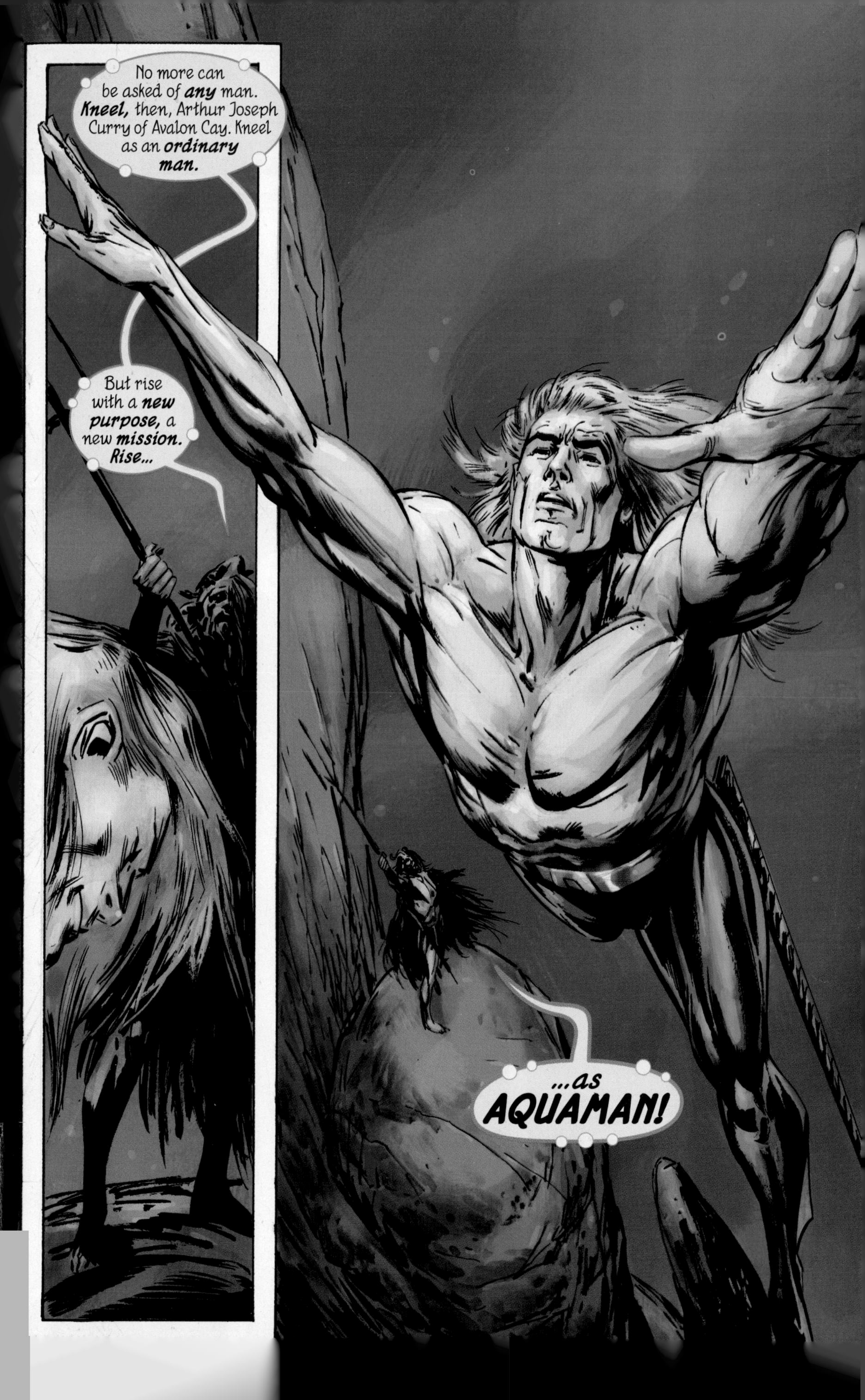
No more can be asked of **any** man. **Kneel,** then, Arthur Joseph Curry of Avalon Cay. Kneel as an **ordinary man.**
But rise with a **new purpose,** a new **mission. Rise...**
...as AQUAMAN!

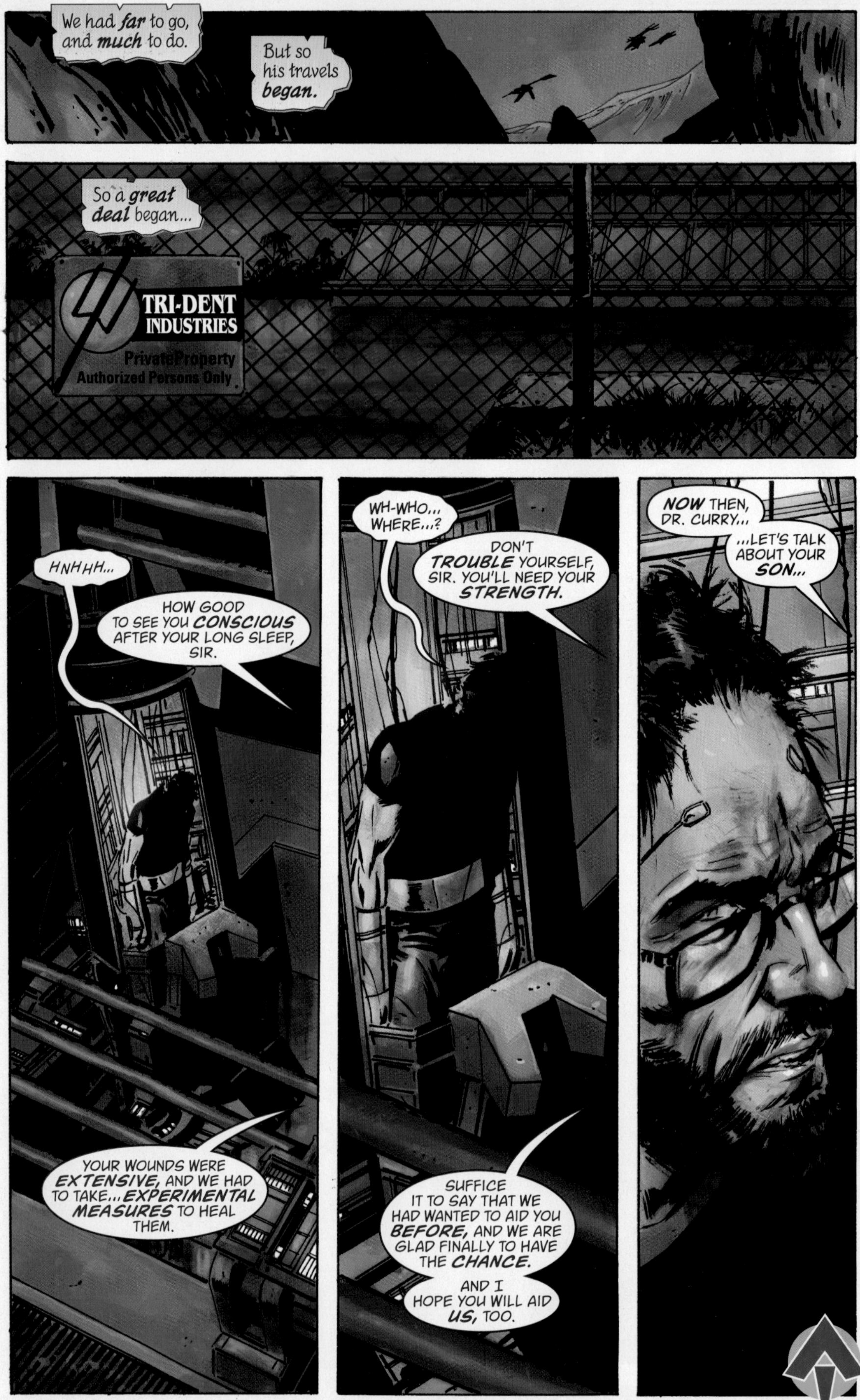

We had far to go, and much to do.
But so his travels began.
So a great deal began...
TRI-DENT INDUSTRIES
Private Property
Authorized Persons Only
HNHHH...
HOW GOOD TO SEE YOU CONSCIOUS AFTER YOUR LONG SLEEP, SIR.
YOUR WOUNDS WERE EXTENSIVE, AND WE HAD TO TAKE...EXPERIMENTAL MEASURES TO HEAL THEM.
WH-WHO... WHERE...?
DON'T TROUBLE YOURSELF, SIR. YOU'LL NEED YOUR STRENGTH.
SUFFICE IT TO SAY THAT WE HAD WANTED TO AID YOU BEFORE, AND WE ARE GLAD FINALLY TO HAVE THE CHANCE.
AND I HOPE YOU WILL AID US, TOO.
NOW THEN, DR. CURRY...
...LET'S TALK ABOUT YOUR SON...

AFTERLIFT

CHIP ZDARSKY WRITER

JASON LOO ARTIST

PARIS ALLEYNE COLORIST

ADITYA BIDIKAR LETTERER

ALLISON O'TOOLE EDITOR

DARK HORSE BOOKS

DARK HORSE TEAM

PRESIDENT AND PUBLISHER **MIKE RICHARDSON**
EDITOR **DANIEL CHABON**
ASSISTANT EDITOR **CHUCK HOWITT**
DESIGNER **BRENNAN THOME**
DIGITAL ART TECHNICIAN **JASON RICKERD**

Neil Hankerson Executive Vice President • Tom Weddle Chief Financial Officer • Randy Stradley Vice President of Publishing • Nick McWhorter Chief Business Development Officer • Dale LaFountain Chief Information Officer • Matt Parkinson Vice President of Marketing • Vanessa Todd-Holmes Vice President of Production and Scheduling • Mark Bernardi Vice President of Book Trade and Digital Sales • Ken Lizzi General Counsel • Dave Marshall Editor in Chief • Davey Estrada Editorial Director • Chris Warner Senior Books Editor • Cary Grazzini Director of Specialty Projects • Lia Ribacchi Art Director • Matt Dryer Director of Digital Art and Prepress • Michael Gombos Senior Director of Licensed Publications • Kari Yadro Director of Custom Programs • Kari Torson Director of International Licensing • Sean Brice Director of Trade Sales

Published by Dark Horse Books / A division of Dark Horse Comics LLC / 10956 SE Main Street / Milwaukie, OR 97222

First edition: February 2021 / Trade paperback ISBN: 978-1-50672-440-9

10 9 8 7 6 5 4 3 2 1
Printed in China

Comic Shop Locator Service: comicshoplocator.com

This volume collects *Afterlift* #1–#5.

Library of Congress Cataloging-in-Publication Data

Names: Zdarsky, Chip, writer. | Loo, Jason, artist. | Alleyne, Paris,
   colourist. | Bidikar, Aditya, letterer.
Title: Afterlift / Chip Zdarsky, writer ; Jason Loo, artist ; Paris
   Alleyne, colorist ; Aditya Bidikar,letterer.
Description: First edition. | Milwaukie, OR : Dark Horse Comics, 2021. |
   "Collects the ComiXology original series Afterlift in a print format" |
   Summary: "Ride-share driver Janice Chen has enough to deal with, from
   annoying passengers to overbearing parents. But when she picks up a pair
   of mysterious passengers who are pursued by otherworldly forces, Janice
   realizes that her already-terrible day might be headed straight to
   hell."-- Provided by publisher.
Identifiers: LCCN 2020033086 | ISBN 9781506724409 (trade paperback)
Subjects: LCSH: Comic books, strips, etc.
Classification: LCC PN6728.A3496 Z33 2021 | DDC 741.5/973--dc23
LC record available at https://lccn.loc.gov/2020033086

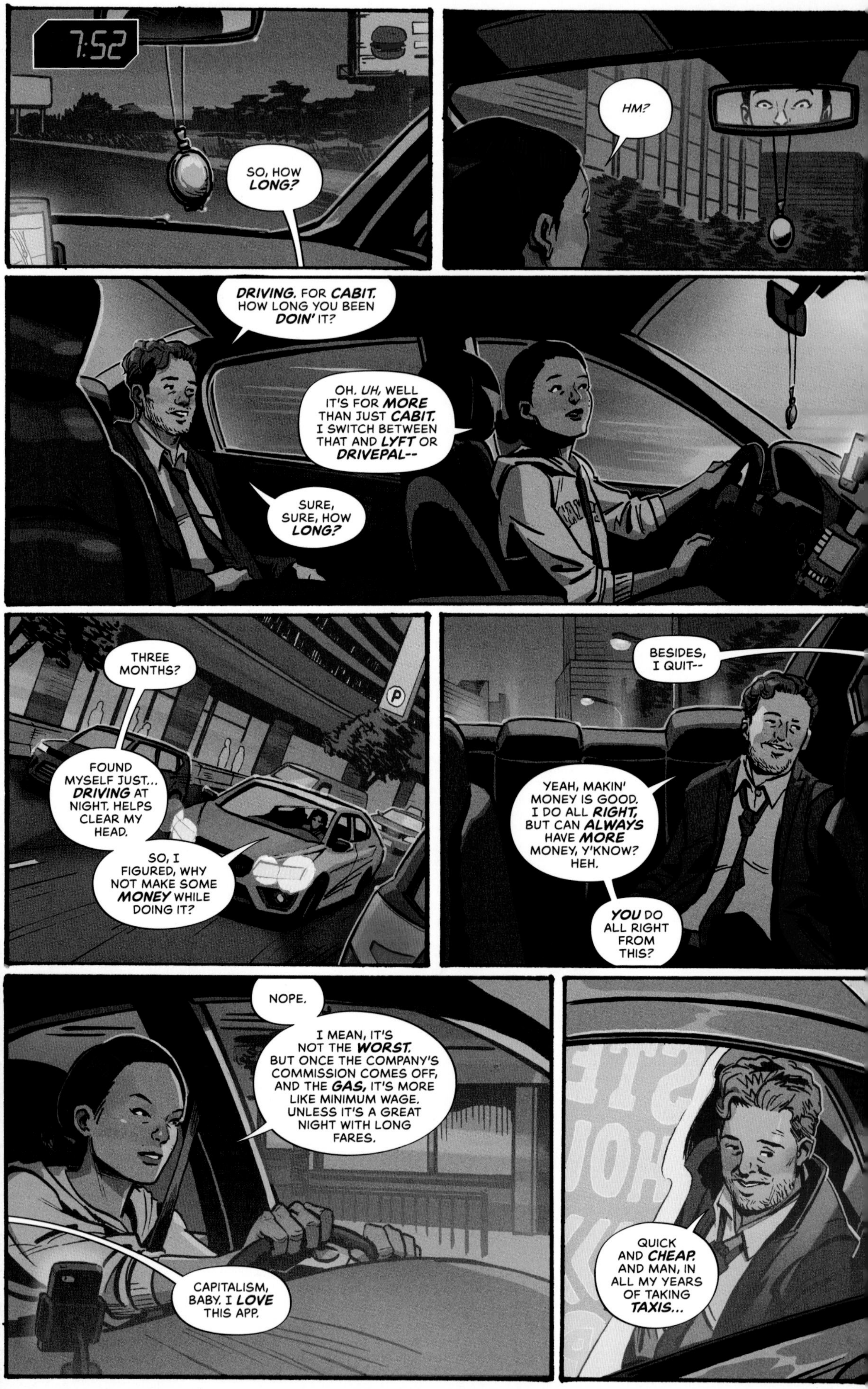
7:52
SO, HOW LONG?
HM?
DRIVING. FOR CABIT. HOW LONG YOU BEEN DOIN' IT?
OH. UH, WELL IT'S FOR MORE THAN JUST CABIT. I SWITCH BETWEEN THAT AND LYFT OR DRIVEPAL--
SURE, SURE, HOW LONG?
THREE MONTHS?
FOUND MYSELF JUST... DRIVING AT NIGHT. HELPS CLEAR MY HEAD.
SO, I FIGURED, WHY NOT MAKE SOME MONEY WHILE DOING IT?
BESIDES, I QUIT--
YEAH, MAKIN' MONEY IS GOOD. I DO ALL RIGHT, BUT CAN ALWAYS HAVE MORE MONEY, Y'KNOW? HEH.
YOU DO ALL RIGHT FROM THIS?
NOPE.
I MEAN, IT'S NOT THE WORST. BUT ONCE THE COMPANY'S COMMISSION COMES OFF, AND THE GAS, IT'S MORE LIKE MINIMUM WAGE. UNLESS IT'S A GREAT NIGHT WITH LONG FARES.
CAPITALISM, BABY. I LOVE THIS APP.
QUICK AND CHEAP. AND MAN, IN ALL MY YEARS OF TAKING TAXIS...

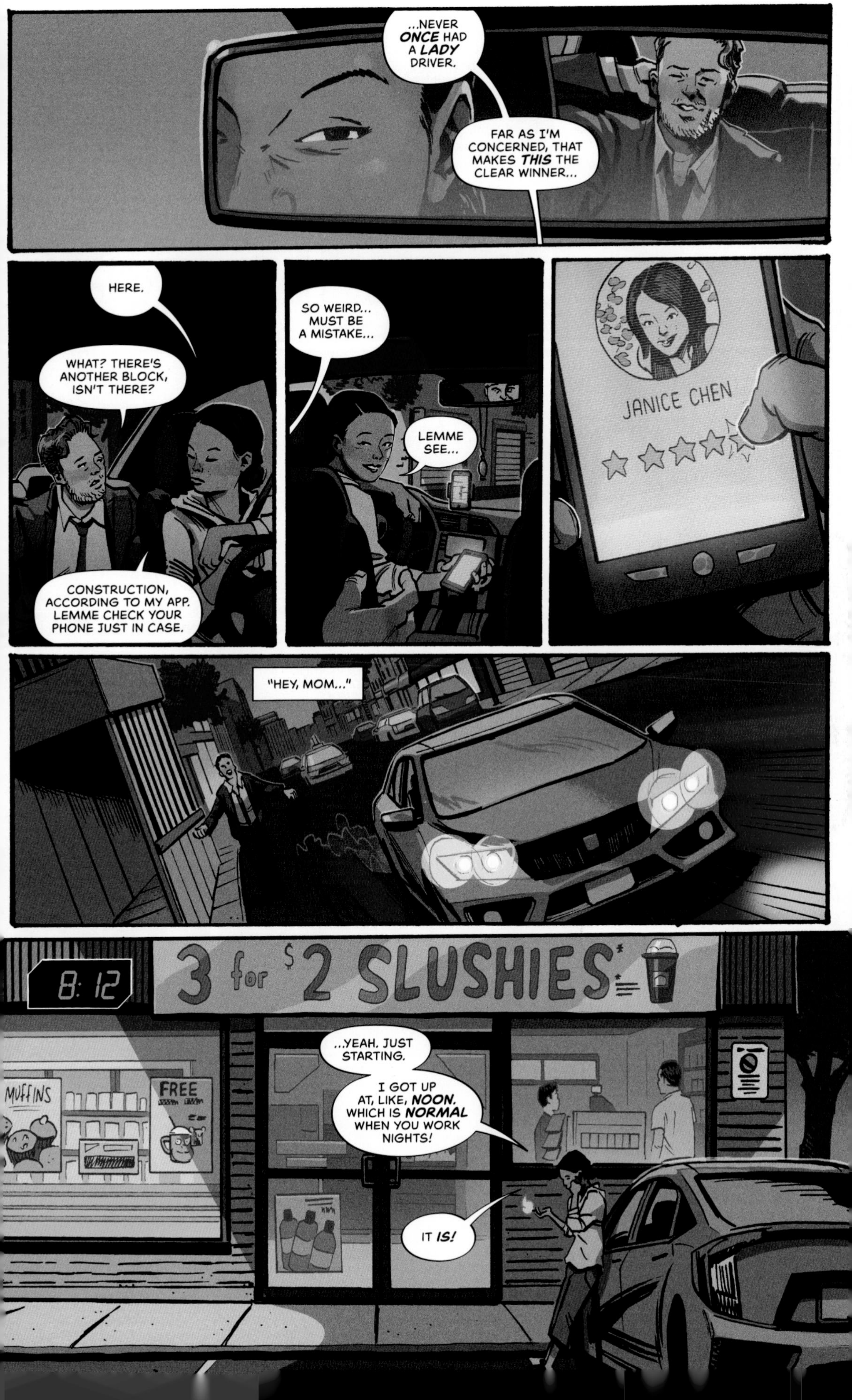
...NEVER ONCE HAD A LADY DRIVER.
FAR AS I'M CONCERNED, THAT MAKES THIS THE CLEAR WINNER...
HERE.
WHAT? THERE'S ANOTHER BLOCK, ISN'T THERE?
CONSTRUCTION, ACCORDING TO MY APP. LEMME CHECK YOUR PHONE JUST IN CASE.
SO WEIRD... MUST BE A MISTAKE...
LEMME SEE...
JANICE CHEN
"HEY, MOM..."
8:12
3 for $2 SLUSHIES*
MUFFINS
FREE
...YEAH. JUST STARTING.
I GOT UP AT, LIKE, NOON, WHICH IS NORMAL WHEN YOU WORK NIGHTS!
IT IS!

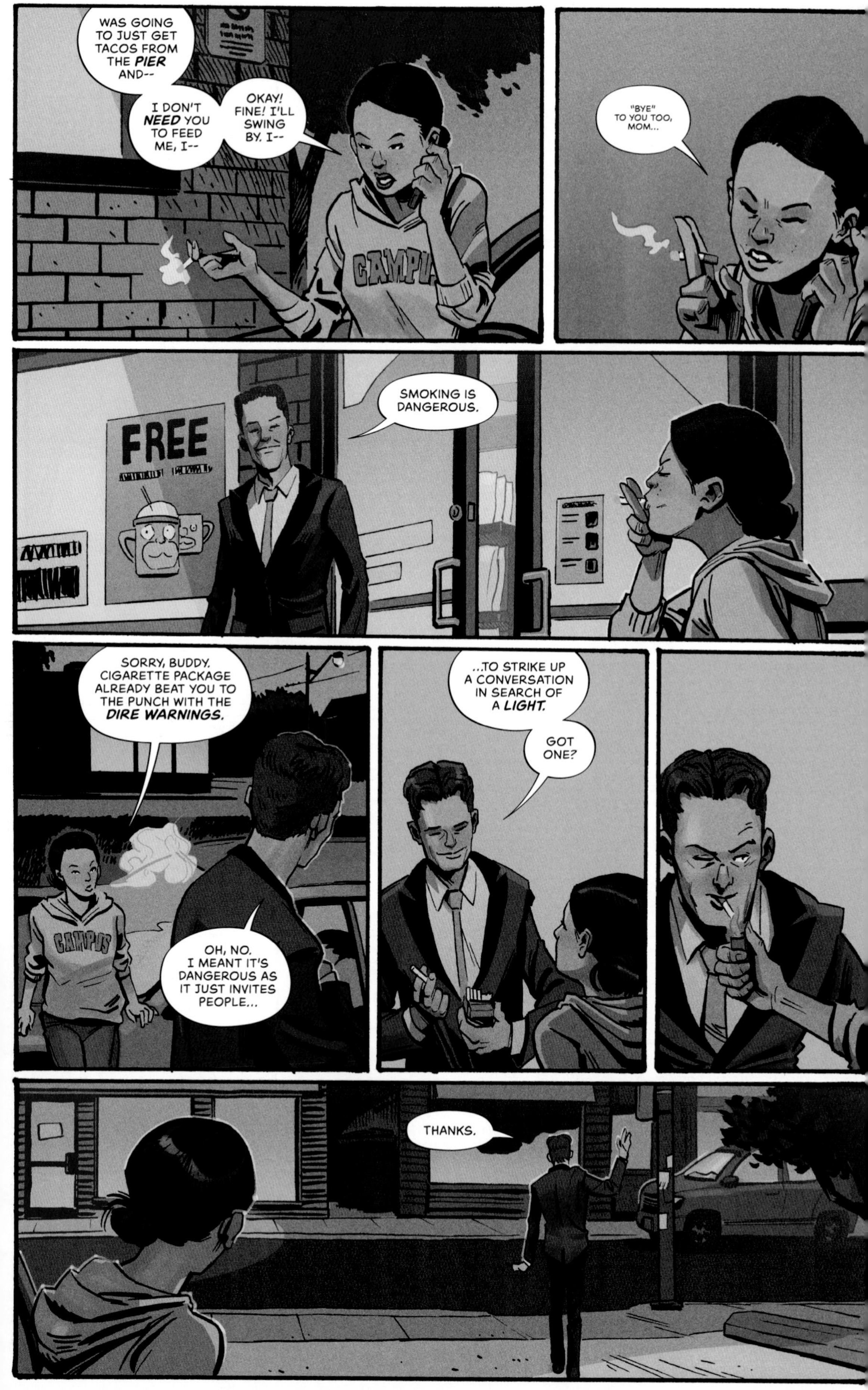
WAS GOING TO JUST GET TACOS FROM THE *PIER* AND--
I DON'T *NEED* YOU TO FEED ME, I--
OKAY! FINE! I'LL SWING BY. I--
"BYE" TO YOU TOO, MOM...
FREE
SMOKING IS DANGEROUS.
SORRY, BUDDY. CIGARETTE PACKAGE ALREADY BEAT YOU TO THE PUNCH WITH THE *DIRE WARNINGS.*
CAMPUS
OH, NO. I MEANT IT'S DANGEROUS AS IT JUST INVITES PEOPLE...
...TO STRIKE UP A CONVERSATION IN SEARCH OF A *LIGHT.*
GOT ONE?
THANKS.

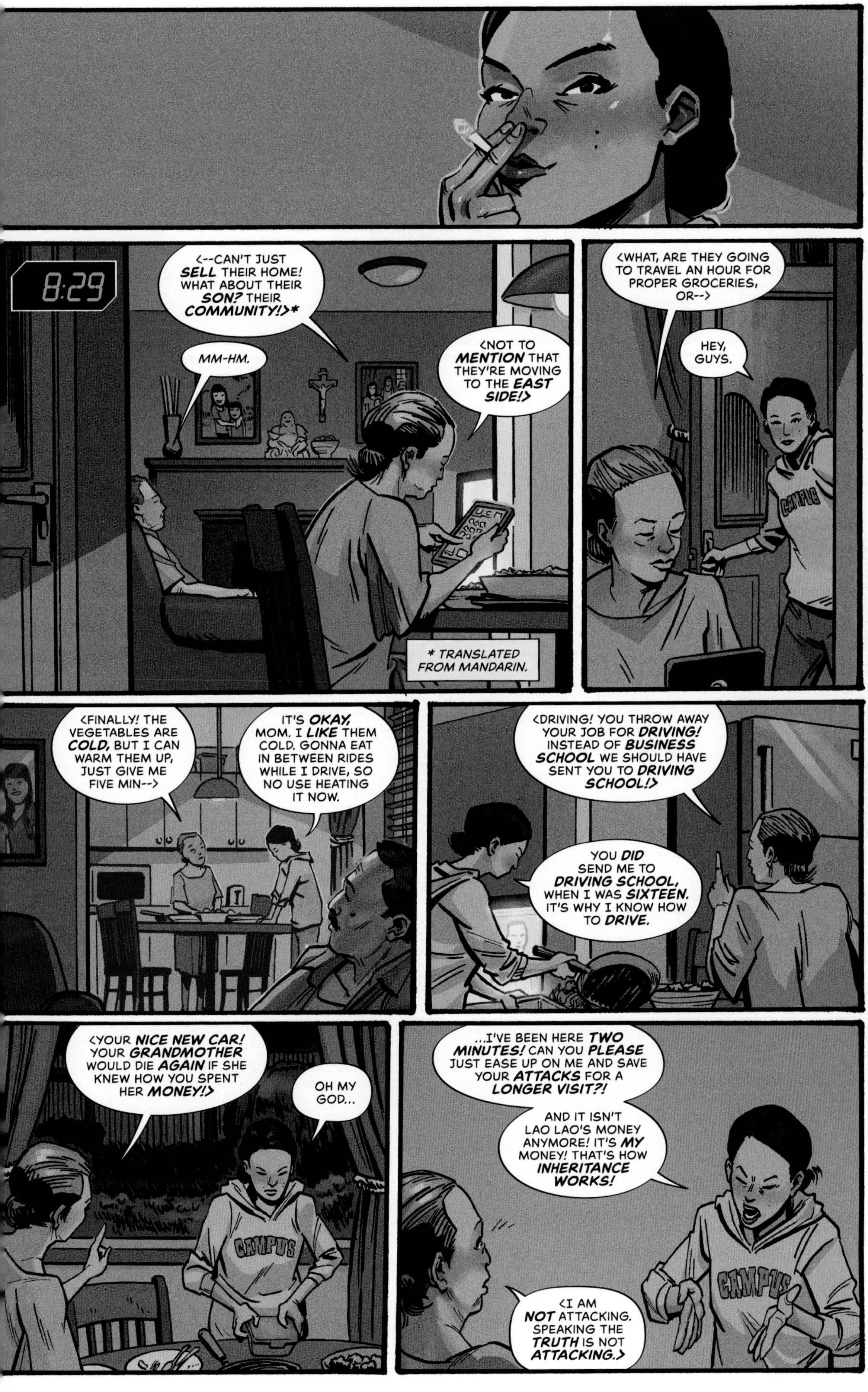
8:29
<--CAN'T JUST SELL THEIR HOME! WHAT ABOUT THEIR SON? THEIR COMMUNITY!>*
MM-HM.
<NOT TO MENTION THAT THEY'RE MOVING TO THE EAST SIDE!>
* TRANSLATED FROM MANDARIN.
<WHAT, ARE THEY GOING TO TRAVEL AN HOUR FOR PROPER GROCERIES, OR-->
HEY, GUYS.
<FINALLY! THE VEGETABLES ARE COLD, BUT I CAN WARM THEM UP, JUST GIVE ME FIVE MIN-->
IT'S OKAY, MOM. I LIKE THEM COLD. GONNA EAT IN BETWEEN RIDES WHILE I DRIVE, SO NO USE HEATING IT NOW.
<DRIVING! YOU THROW AWAY YOUR JOB FOR DRIVING! INSTEAD OF BUSINESS SCHOOL WE SHOULD HAVE SENT YOU TO DRIVING SCHOOL!>
YOU DID SEND ME TO DRIVING SCHOOL, WHEN I WAS SIXTEEN. IT'S WHY I KNOW HOW TO DRIVE.
<YOUR NICE NEW CAR! YOUR GRANDMOTHER WOULD DIE AGAIN IF SHE KNEW HOW YOU SPENT HER MONEY!>
OH MY GOD...
...I'VE BEEN HERE TWO MINUTES! CAN YOU PLEASE JUST EASE UP ON ME AND SAVE YOUR ATTACKS FOR A LONGER VISIT?!
AND IT ISN'T LAO LAO'S MONEY ANYMORE! IT'S MY MONEY! THAT'S HOW INHERITANCE WORKS!
<I AM NOT ATTACKING. SPEAKING THE TRUTH IS NOT ATTACKING.>

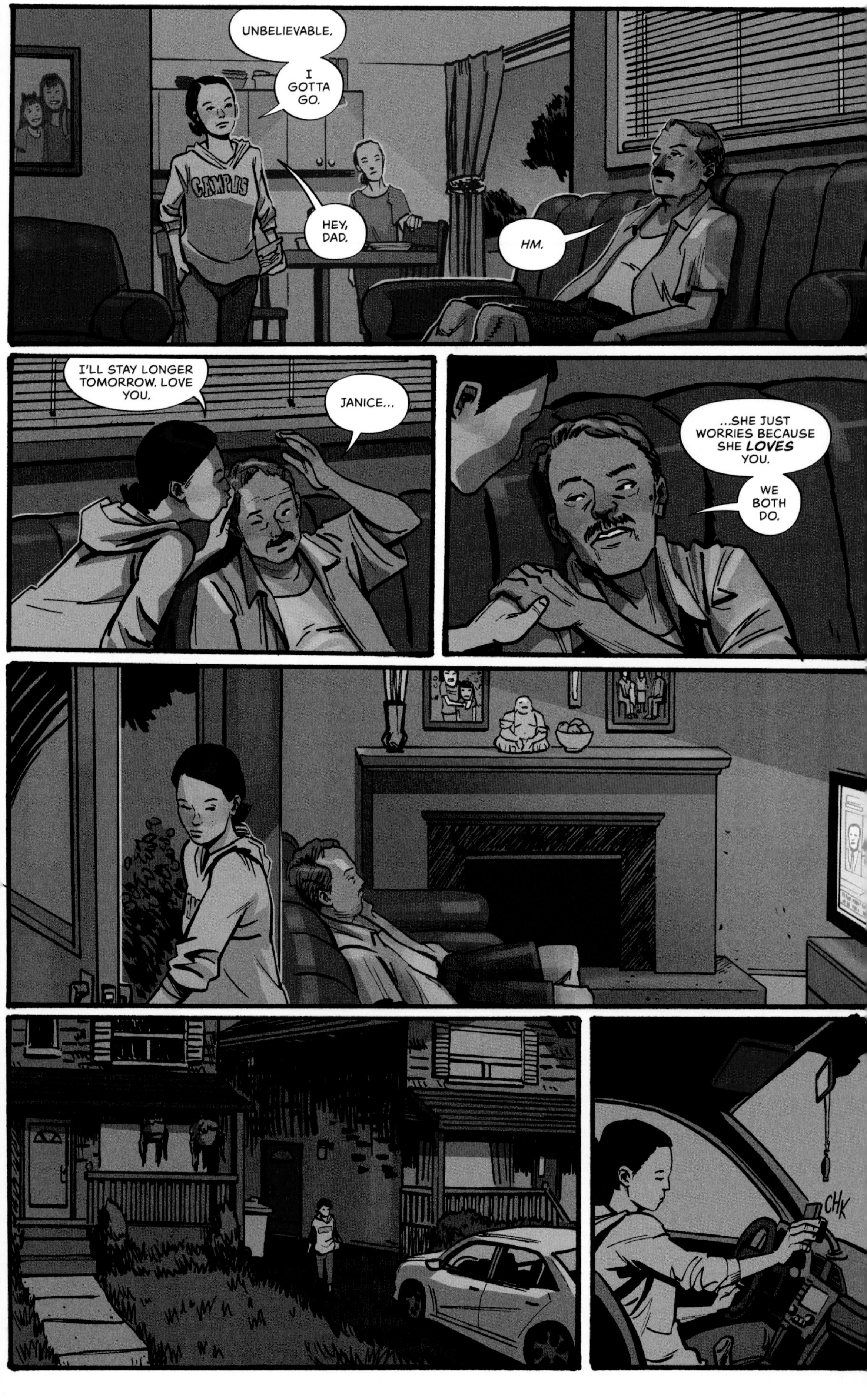
UNBELIEVABLE.
I GOTTA GO.
HEY, DAD.
HM.
I'LL STAY LONGER TOMORROW. LOVE YOU.
JANICE...
...SHE JUST WORRIES BECAUSE SHE **LOVES** YOU.
WE BOTH DO.
CHK

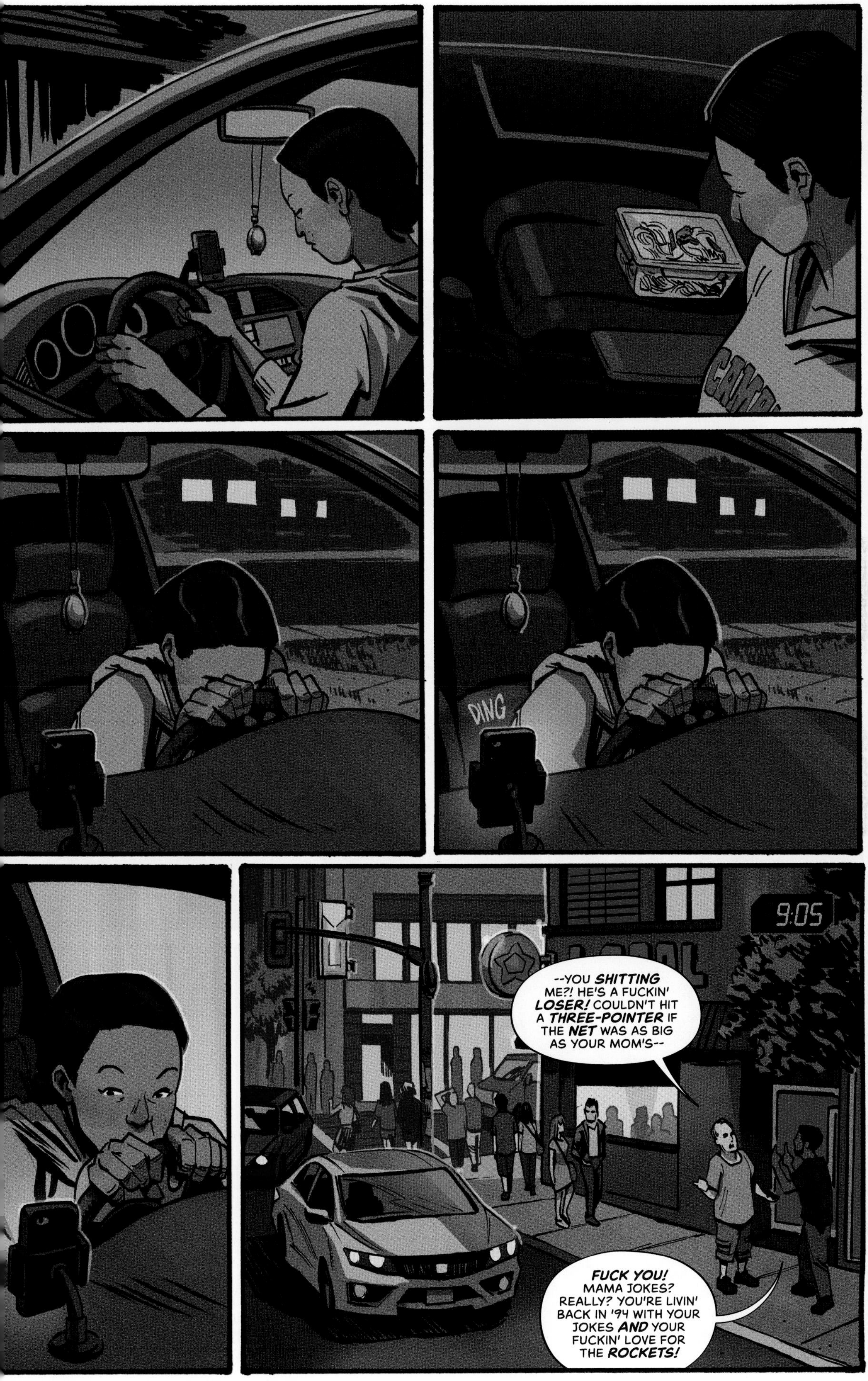
DING
9:05
--YOU SHITTING ME?! HE'S A FUCKIN' LOSER! COULDN'T HIT A THREE-POINTER IF THE NET WAS AS BIG AS YOUR MOM'S--
FUCK YOU! MAMA JOKES? REALLY? YOU'RE LIVIN' BACK IN '94 WITH YOUR JOKES AND YOUR FUCKIN' LOVE FOR THE ROCKETS!

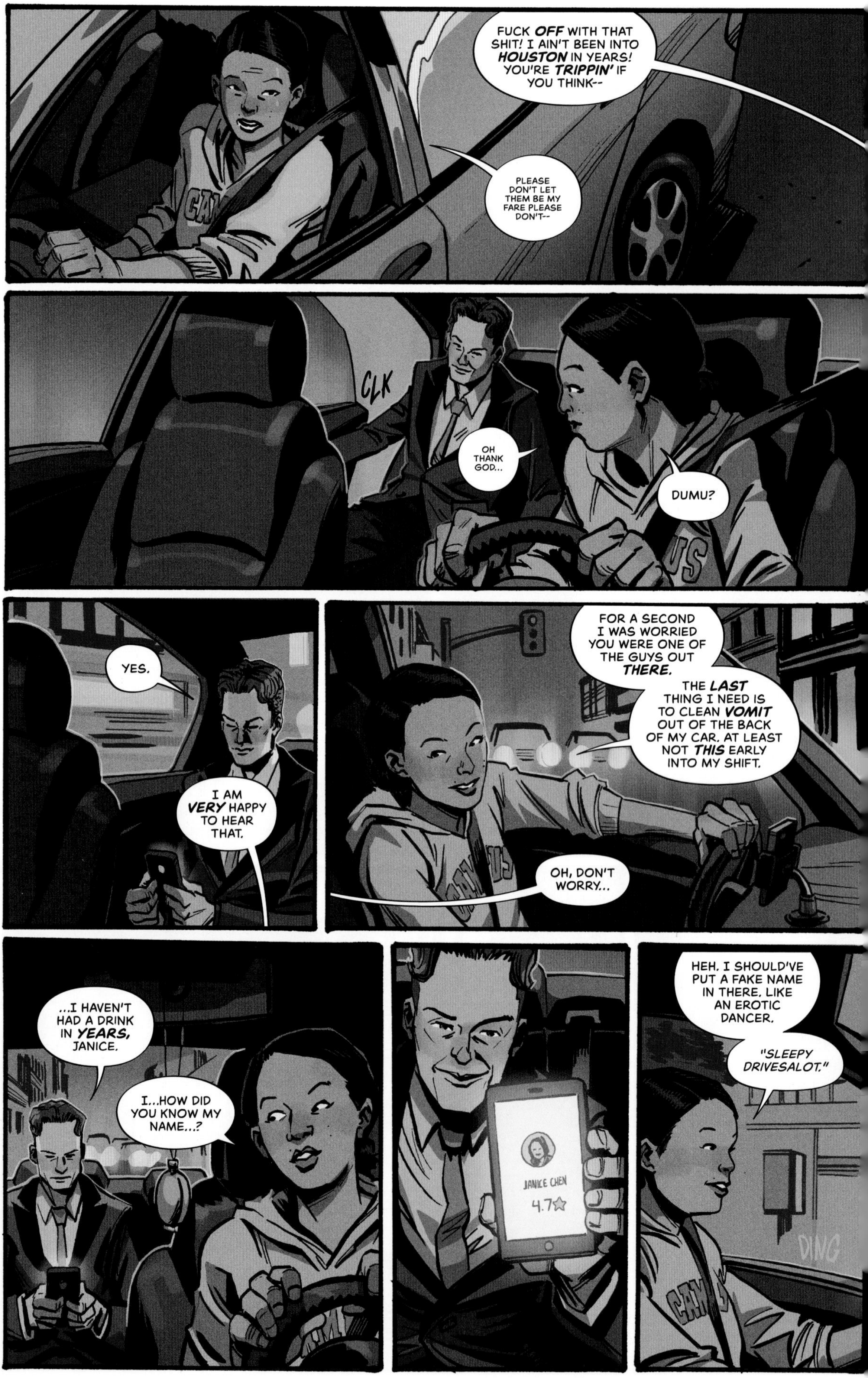
FUCK OFF WITH THAT SHIT! I AIN'T BEEN INTO HOUSTON IN YEARS! YOU'RE TRIPPIN' IF YOU THINK--
PLEASE DON'T LET THEM BE MY FARE PLEASE DON'T--
CLK
OH THANK GOD...
DUMU?
YES.
I AM VERY HAPPY TO HEAR THAT.
FOR A SECOND I WAS WORRIED YOU WERE ONE OF THE GUYS OUT THERE.
THE LAST THING I NEED IS TO CLEAN VOMIT OUT OF THE BACK OF MY CAR. AT LEAST NOT THIS EARLY INTO MY SHIFT.
OH, DON'T WORRY...
...I HAVEN'T HAD A DRINK IN YEARS, JANICE.
I...HOW DID YOU KNOW MY NAME...?
JANICE CHEN
4.7
HEH. I SHOULD'VE PUT A FAKE NAME IN THERE, LIKE AN EROTIC DANCER.
"SLEEPY DRIVESALOT."
DING

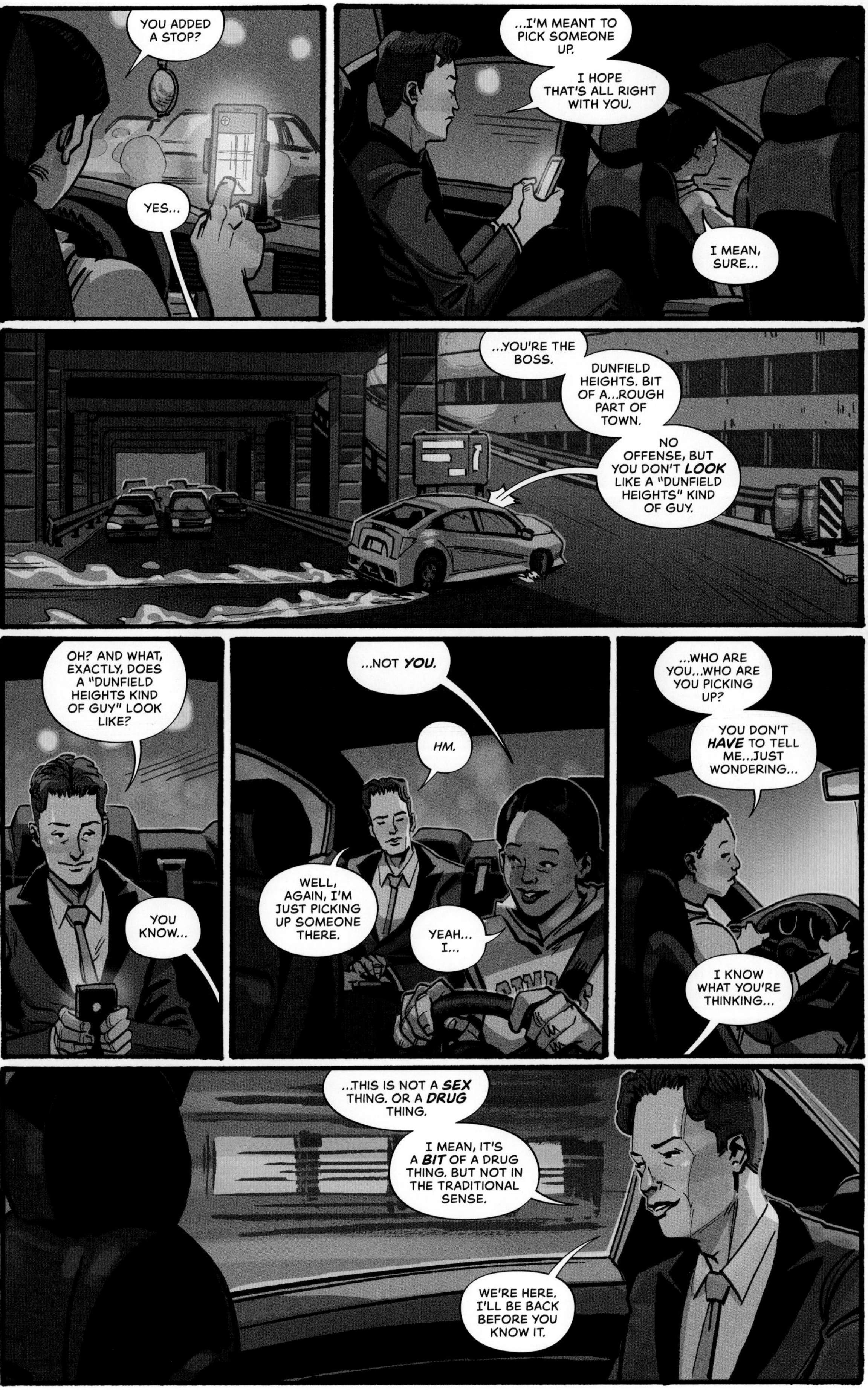
YOU ADDED A STOP?
YES...
...I'M MEANT TO PICK SOMEONE UP.
I HOPE THAT'S ALL RIGHT WITH YOU.
I MEAN, SURE...
...YOU'RE THE BOSS.
DUNFIELD HEIGHTS. BIT OF A...ROUGH PART OF TOWN.
NO OFFENSE, BUT YOU DON'T LOOK LIKE A "DUNFIELD HEIGHTS" KIND OF GUY.
OH? AND WHAT, EXACTLY, DOES A "DUNFIELD HEIGHTS KIND OF GUY" LOOK LIKE?
YOU KNOW...
...NOT YOU.
HM.
WELL, AGAIN, I'M JUST PICKING UP SOMEONE THERE.
YEAH... I...
...WHO ARE YOU...WHO ARE YOU PICKING UP?
YOU DON'T HAVE TO TELL ME...JUST WONDERING...
I KNOW WHAT YOU'RE THINKING...
...THIS IS NOT A SEX THING. OR A DRUG THING.
I MEAN, IT'S A BIT OF A DRUG THING. BUT NOT IN THE TRADITIONAL SENSE.
WE'RE HERE. I'LL BE BACK BEFORE YOU KNOW IT.

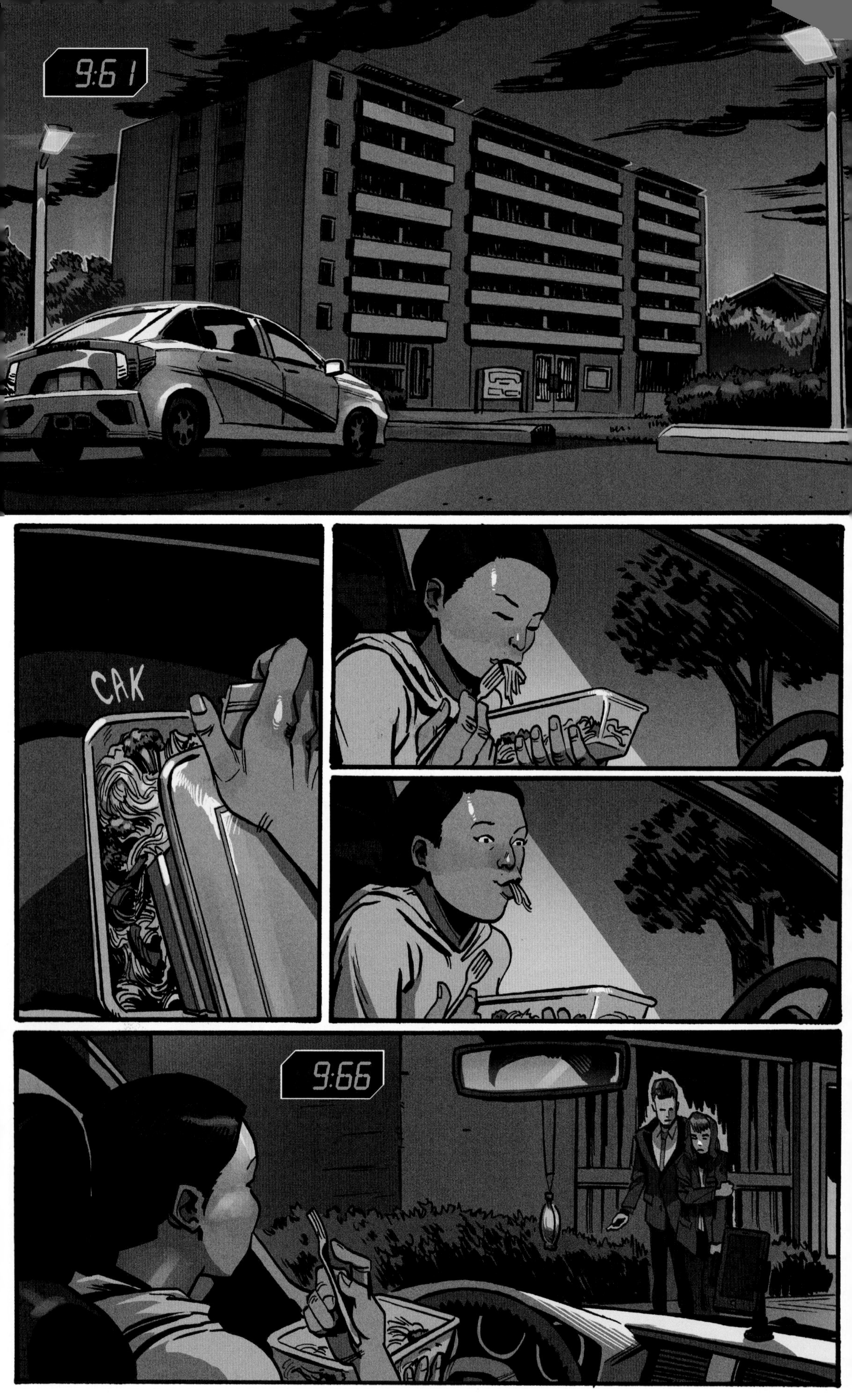
9:61
CAK
9:66

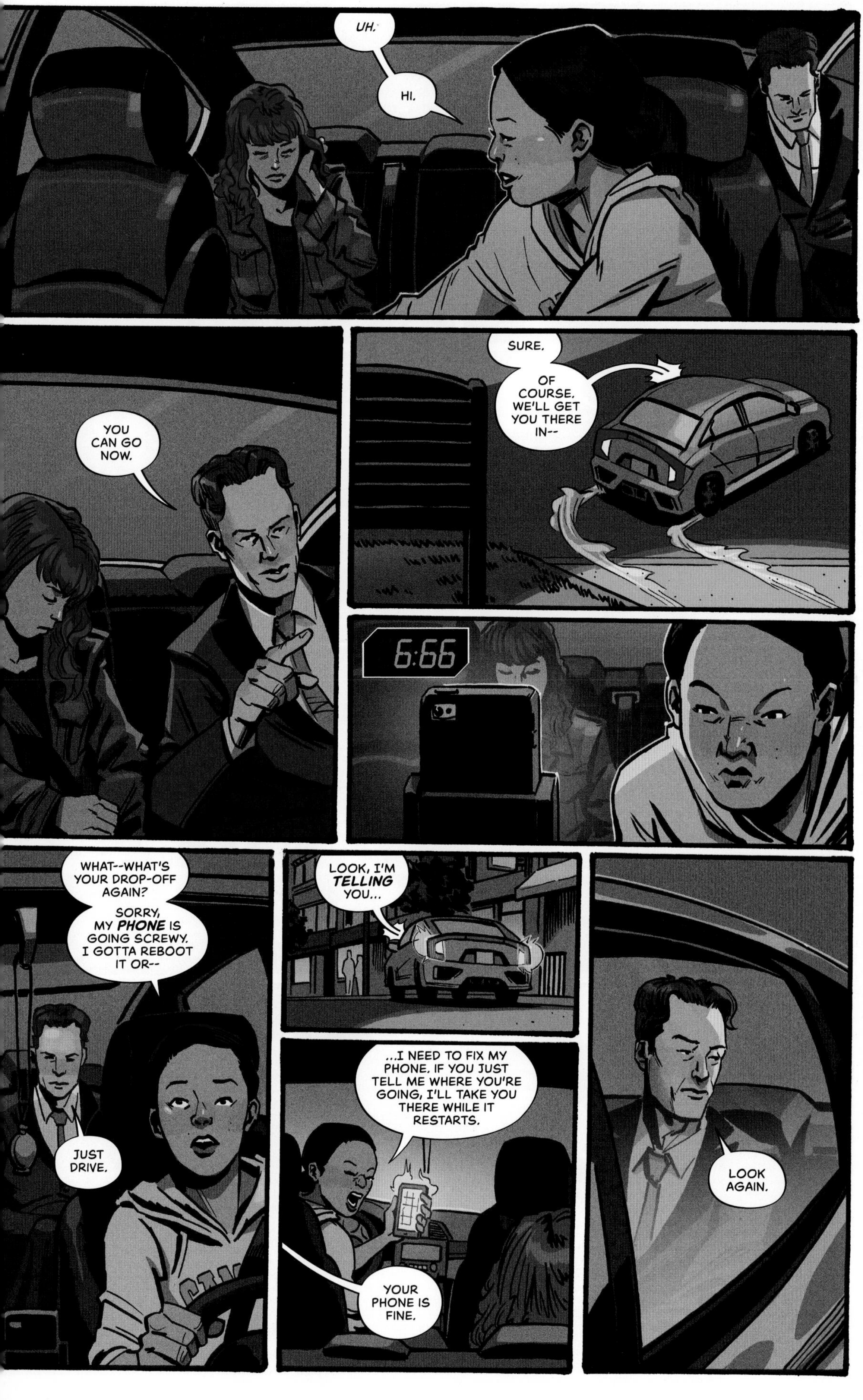
UH.
HI.
YOU CAN GO NOW.
SURE.
OF COURSE. WE'LL GET YOU THERE IN--
6:66
WHAT--WHAT'S YOUR DROP-OFF AGAIN?
SORRY, MY ***PHONE*** IS GOING SCREWY. I GOTTA REBOOT IT OR--
JUST DRIVE.
LOOK, I'M ***TELLING*** YOU...
...I NEED TO FIX MY PHONE. IF YOU JUST TELL ME WHERE YOU'RE GOING, I'LL TAKE YOU THERE WHILE IT RESTARTS.
YOUR PHONE IS FINE.
LOOK AGAIN.

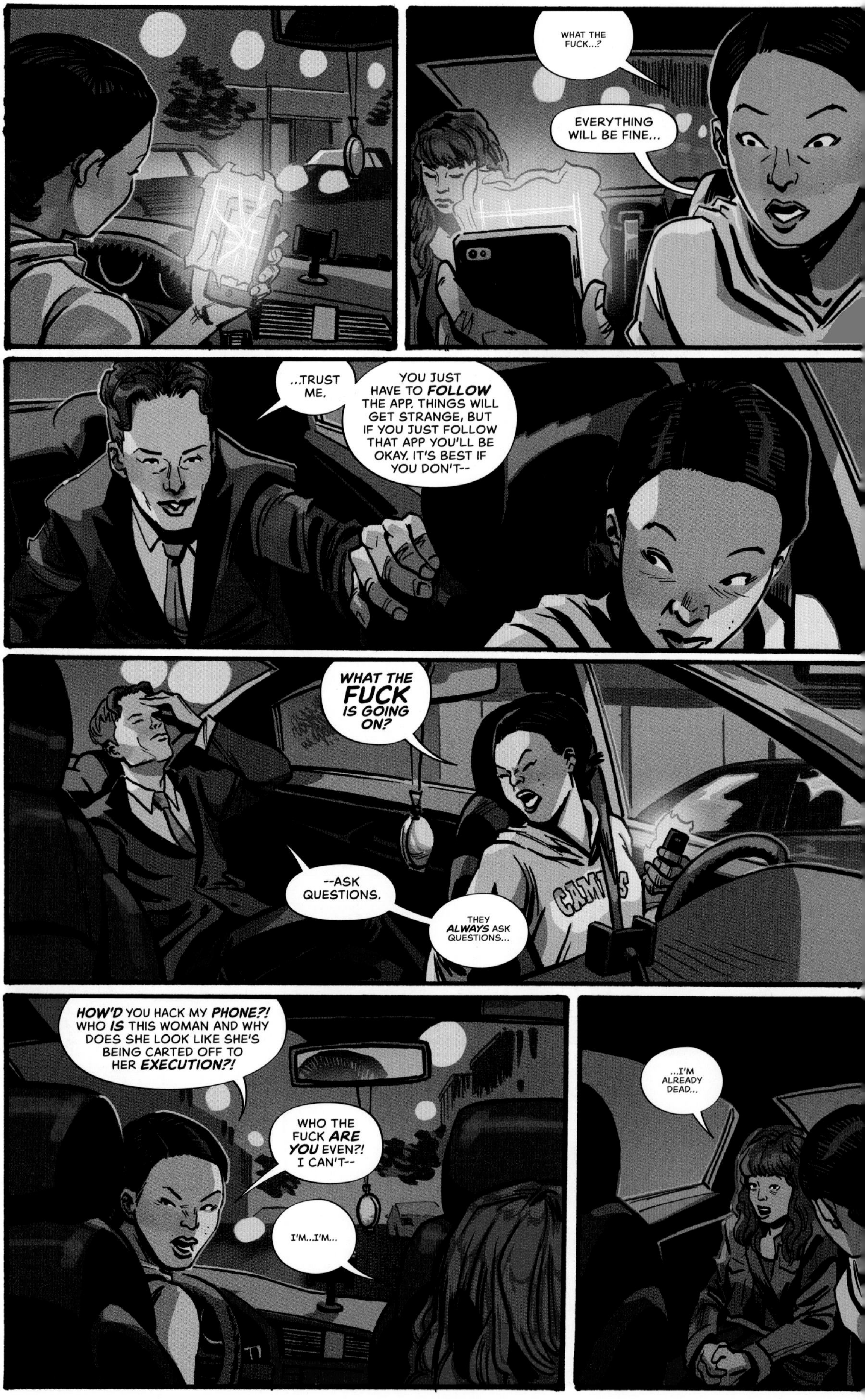
WHAT THE FUCK...?
EVERYTHING WILL BE FINE...
...TRUST ME.
YOU JUST HAVE TO FOLLOW THE APP. THINGS WILL GET STRANGE, BUT IF YOU JUST FOLLOW THAT APP YOU'LL BE OKAY. IT'S BEST IF YOU DON'T--
WHAT THE FUCK IS GOING ON?
--ASK QUESTIONS.
THEY ALWAYS ASK QUESTIONS...
HOW'D YOU HACK MY PHONE?! WHO IS THIS WOMAN AND WHY DOES SHE LOOK LIKE SHE'S BEING CARTED OFF TO HER EXECUTION?!
WHO THE FUCK ARE YOU EVEN?! I CAN'T--
I'M...I'M...
...I'M ALREADY DEAD...

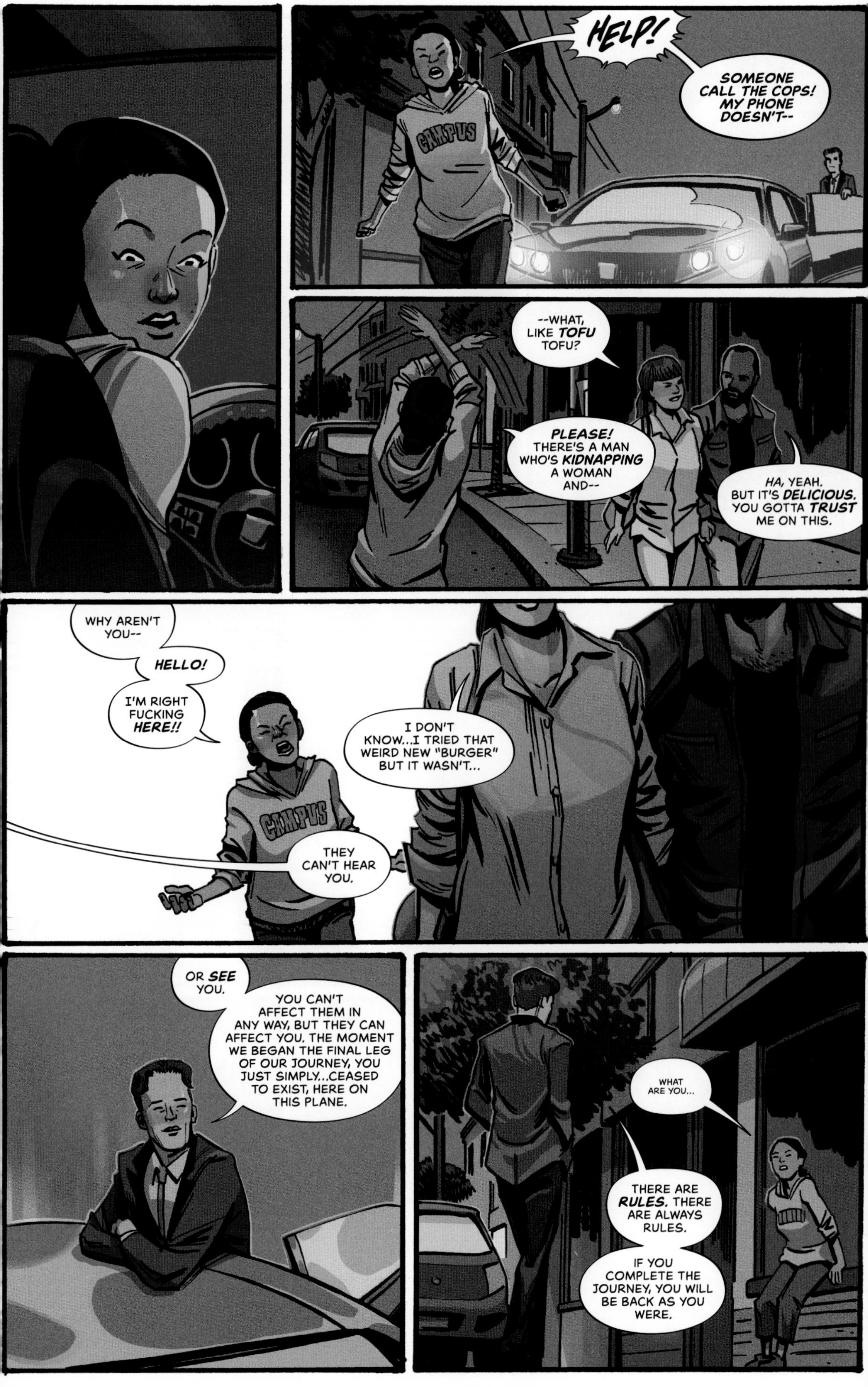

HELP!
SOMEONE CALL THE COPS! MY PHONE DOESN'T--
--WHAT, LIKE TOFU TOFU?
PLEASE! THERE'S A MAN WHO'S KIDNAPPING A WOMAN AND--
HA, YEAH. BUT IT'S DELICIOUS. YOU GOTTA TRUST ME ON THIS.
WHY AREN'T YOU--
HELLO!
I'M RIGHT FUCKING HERE!!
I DON'T KNOW...I TRIED THAT WEIRD NEW "BURGER" BUT IT WASN'T...
THEY CAN'T HEAR YOU.
OR SEE YOU.
YOU CAN'T AFFECT THEM IN ANY WAY, BUT THEY CAN AFFECT YOU. THE MOMENT WE BEGAN THE FINAL LEG OF OUR JOURNEY, YOU JUST SIMPLY...CEASED TO EXIST, HERE ON THIS PLANE.
WHAT ARE YOU...
THERE ARE RULES. THERE ARE ALWAYS RULES.
IF YOU COMPLETE THE JOURNEY, YOU WILL BE BACK AS YOU WERE.

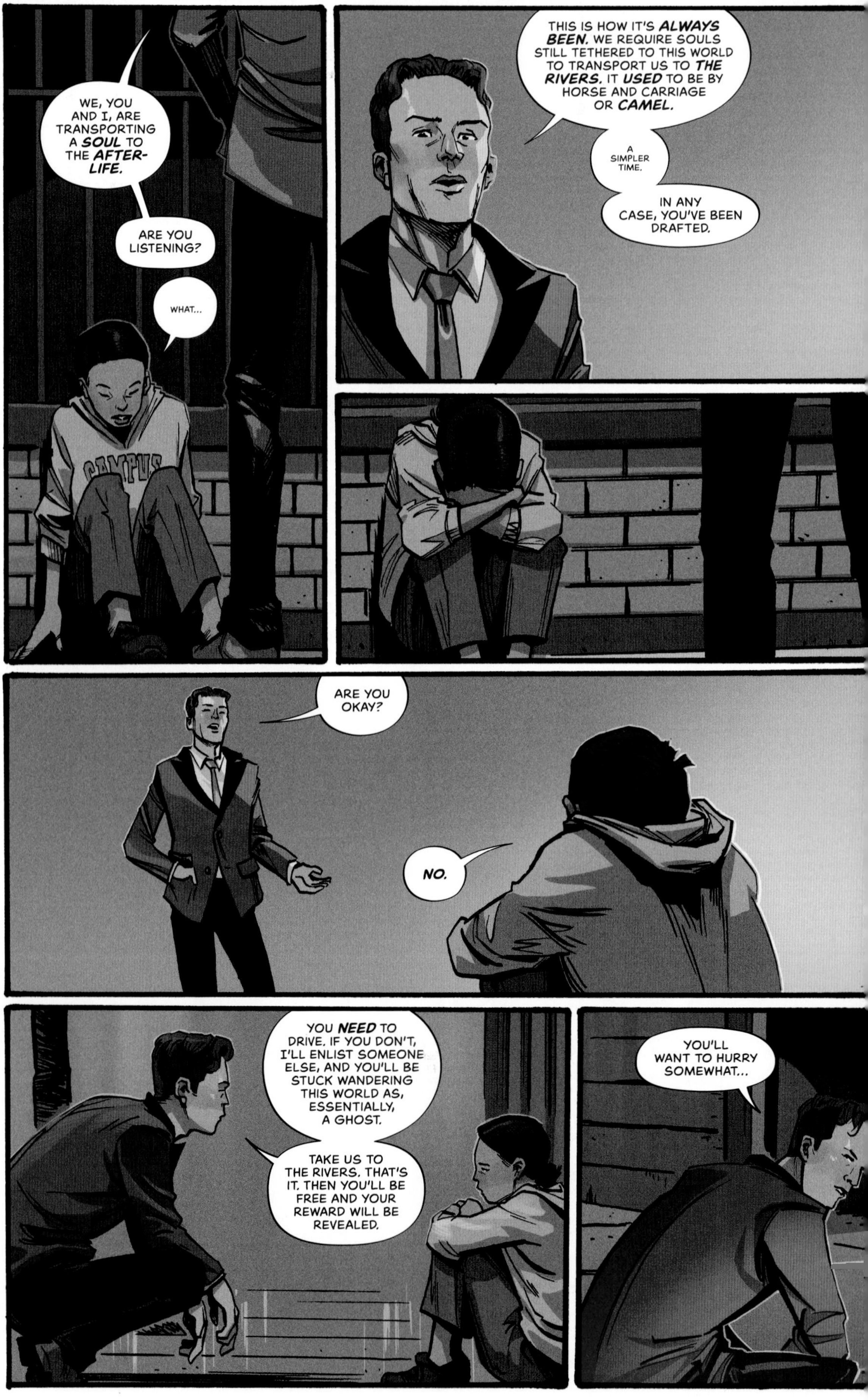
WE, YOU AND I, ARE TRANSPORTING A SOUL TO THE AFTER-LIFE.
ARE YOU LISTENING?
WHAT...
CAMPUS
THIS IS HOW IT'S ALWAYS BEEN. WE REQUIRE SOULS STILL TETHERED TO THIS WORLD TO TRANSPORT US TO THE RIVERS. IT USED TO BE BY HORSE AND CARRIAGE OR CAMEL.
A SIMPLER TIME.
IN ANY CASE, YOU'VE BEEN DRAFTED.
ARE YOU OKAY?
NO.
YOU NEED TO DRIVE. IF YOU DON'T, I'LL ENLIST SOMEONE ELSE, AND YOU'LL BE STUCK WANDERING THIS WORLD AS, ESSENTIALLY, A GHOST.
TAKE US TO THE RIVERS. THAT'S IT. THEN YOU'LL BE FREE AND YOUR REWARD WILL BE REVEALED.
YOU'LL WANT TO HURRY SOMEWHAT...

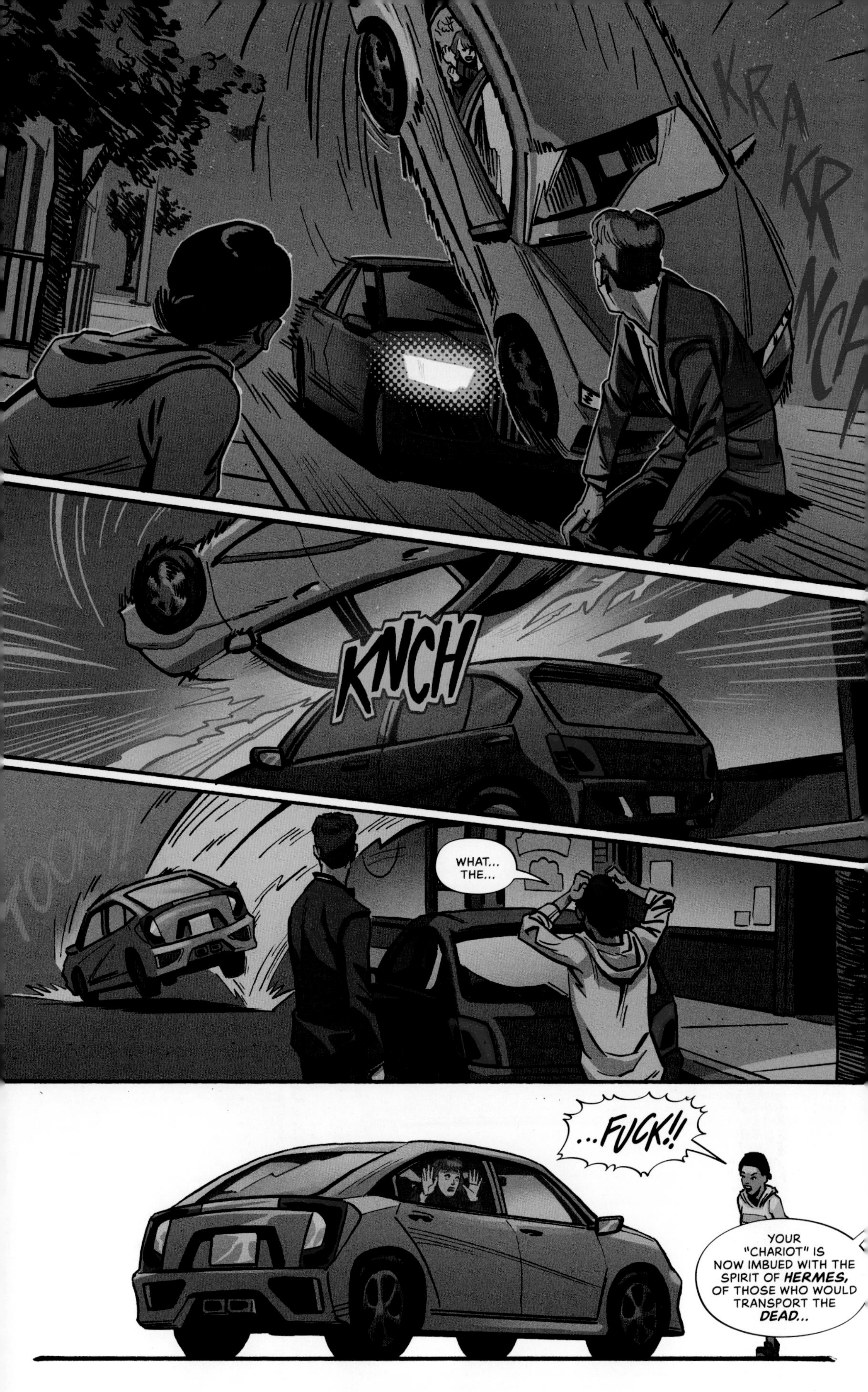
KRAKRANCH
KNCH
TOOM!
WHAT... THE...
...FUCK!!
YOUR "CHARIOT" IS NOW IMBUED WITH THE SPIRIT OF HERMES, OF THOSE WHO WOULD TRANSPORT THE DEAD...

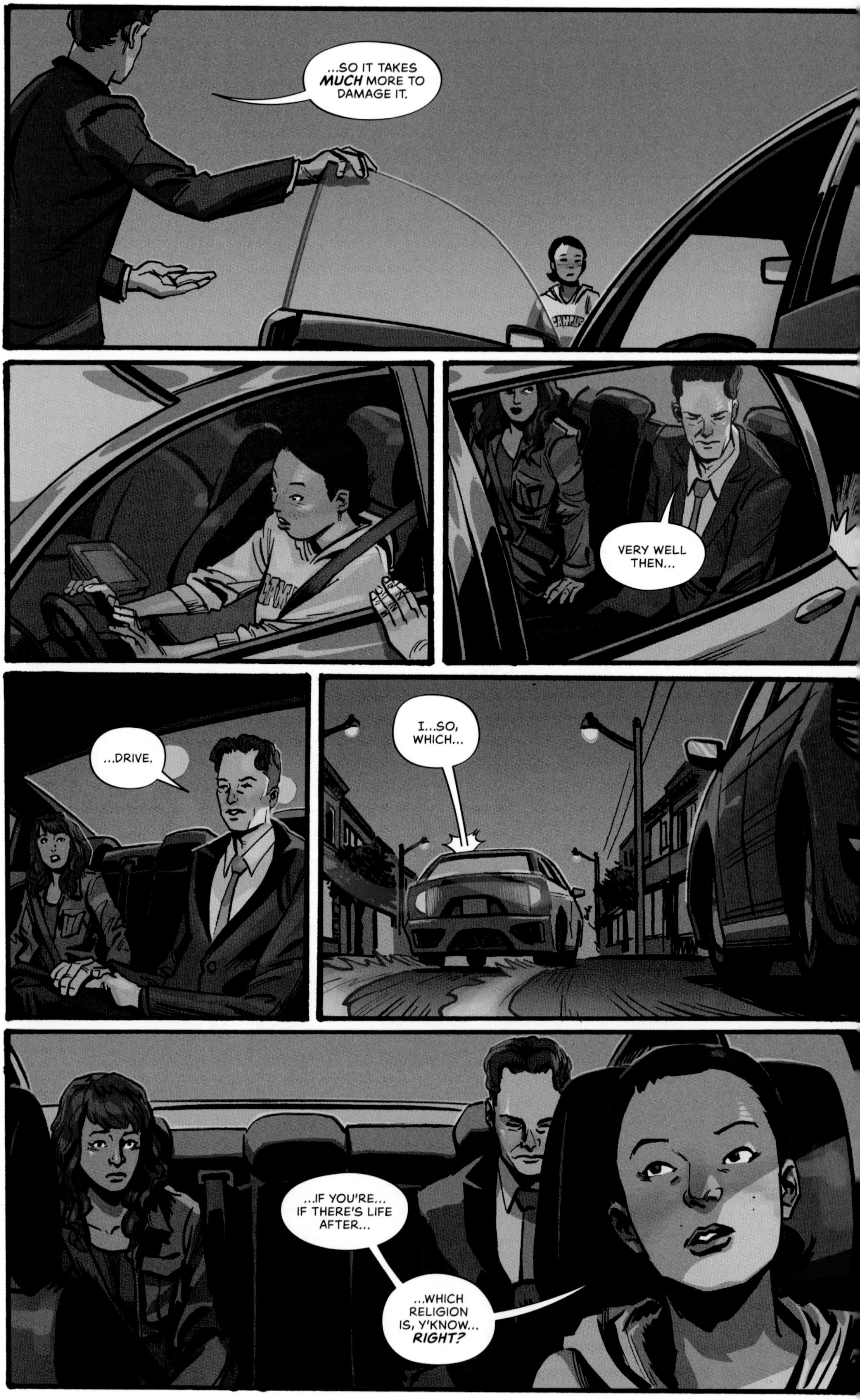
...SO IT TAKES MUCH MORE TO DAMAGE IT.
VERY WELL THEN...
...DRIVE.
I...SO, WHICH...
...IF YOU'RE... IF THERE'S LIFE AFTER...
...WHICH RELIGION IS, Y'KNOW... RIGHT?

ALL OF THEM. *NONE* OF THEM.

LIFE BEYOND THIS IS A *COLLISION* OF IDEAS AND PLACES, FORMED FROM THE UNCONSCIOUS OF THE *LIVING* AND THE DESIRES OF *CREATORS* FAR REMOVED FROM US ALL.

YOUR HEAVEN IS DIFFERENT FROM THE HEAVEN OF A CHILD IN THE FARTHEST CORNER OF THE GLOBE, AND YET THEY'RE THE *SAME.*

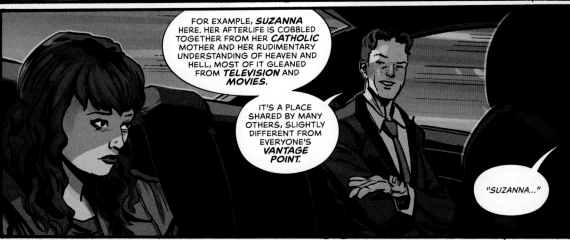

FOR EXAMPLE, *SUZANNA* HERE. HER AFTERLIFE IS COBBLED TOGETHER FROM HER *CATHOLIC* MOTHER AND HER RUDIMENTARY UNDERSTANDING OF HEAVEN AND HELL, MOST OF IT GLEANED FROM *TELEVISION* AND *MOVIES.*

IT'S A PLACE SHARED BY MANY OTHERS, SLIGHTLY DIFFERENT FROM EVERYONE'S *VANTAGE POINT.*

"SUZANNA..."

...THAT'S... THAT'S A NICE NAME.

ARE YOU...ARE YOU REALLY DEAD?

I...I THINK SO, YES. I DON'T REALLY REMEMBER WHAT...

AN OVERDOSE.

OR, MORE ACCURATELY, AN *ERRONEOUS DOSE.* HEROIN LACED WITH *CARFENTANIL.*

I...OH. I DIDN'T...

IT'S ALL OVER NOW, DEAR.

I'M... I'M SORRY, SUZANNA.

I'VE BEEN FREAKING THE FUCK *OUT* AND *YOU'VE* JUST--

IT'S OKAY...

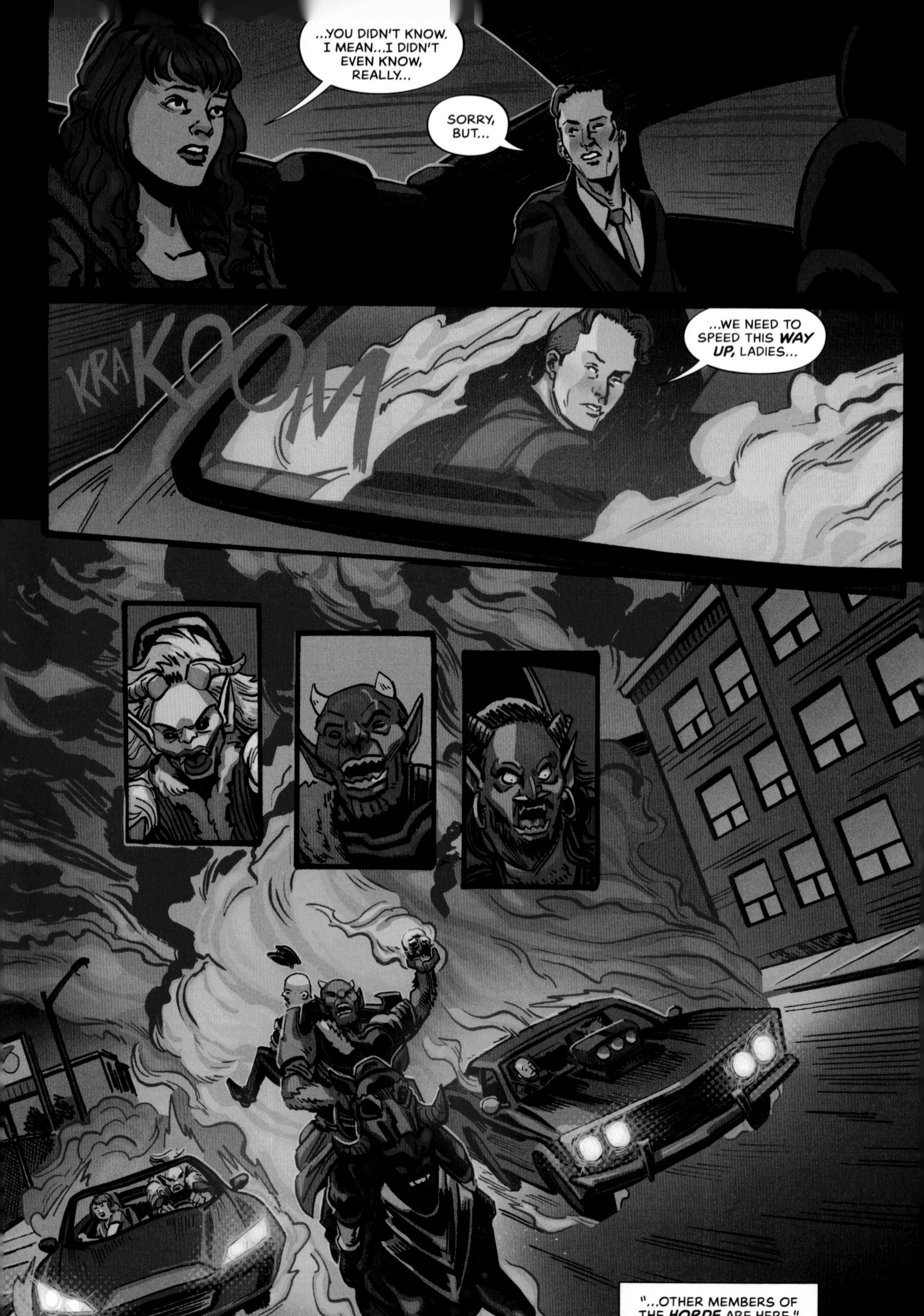

...YOU DIDN'T KNOW. I MEAN...I DIDN'T EVEN KNOW, REALLY...
SORRY, BUT...
KRAKOOM
...WE NEED TO SPEED THIS **WAY UP,** LADIES...
"...OTHER MEMBERS OF THE **HORDE** ARE HERE."

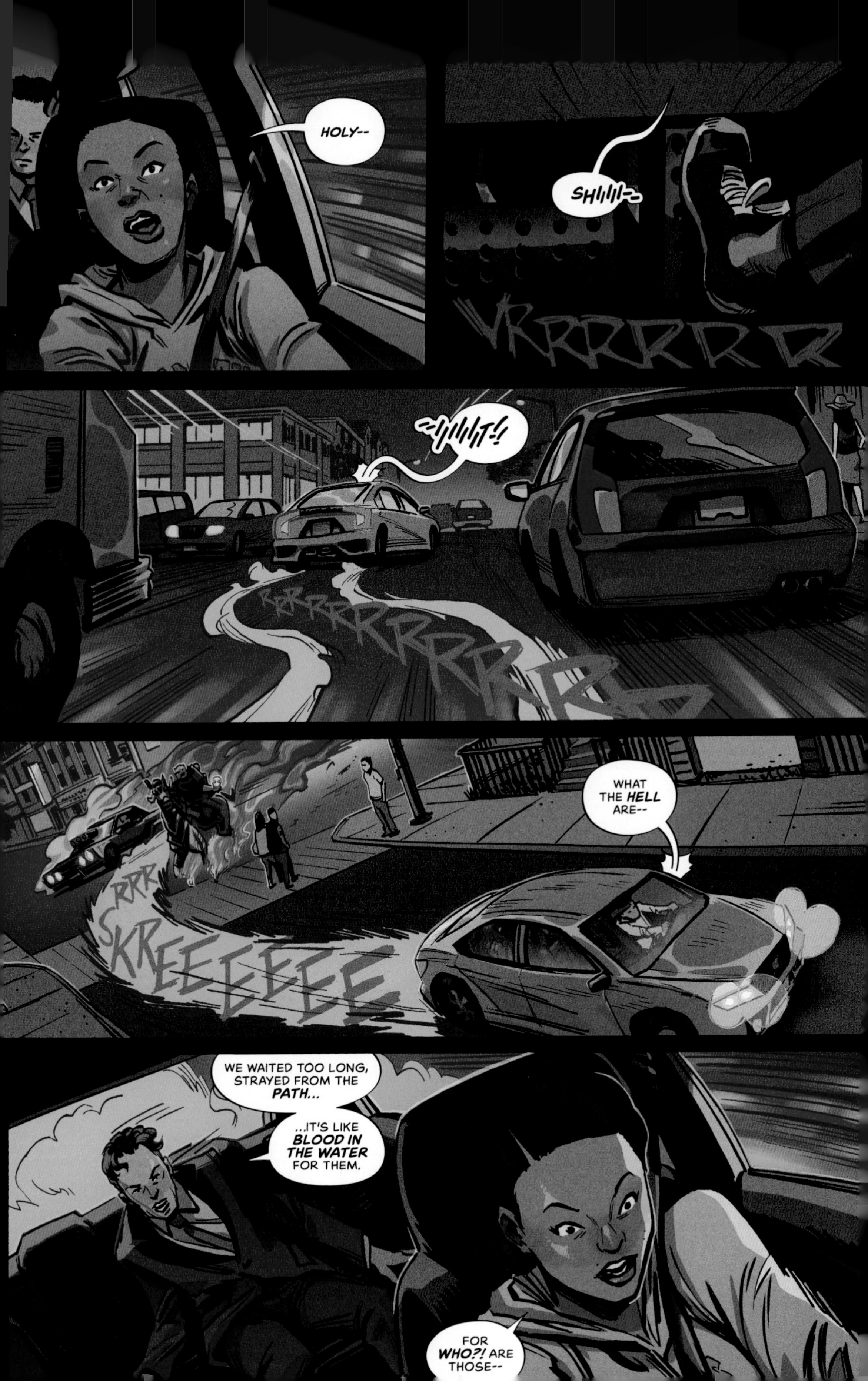
HOLY--
SHHHH--
VRRRRRRR
--HHHHIT--!!
RRRRRRRRRR
WHAT THE **HELL** ARE--
RRR
SKREEEEEE
WE WAITED TOO LONG, STRAYED FROM THE **PATH**...
...IT'S LIKE **BLOOD IN THE WATER** FOR THEM.
FOR **WHO?!** ARE THOSE--

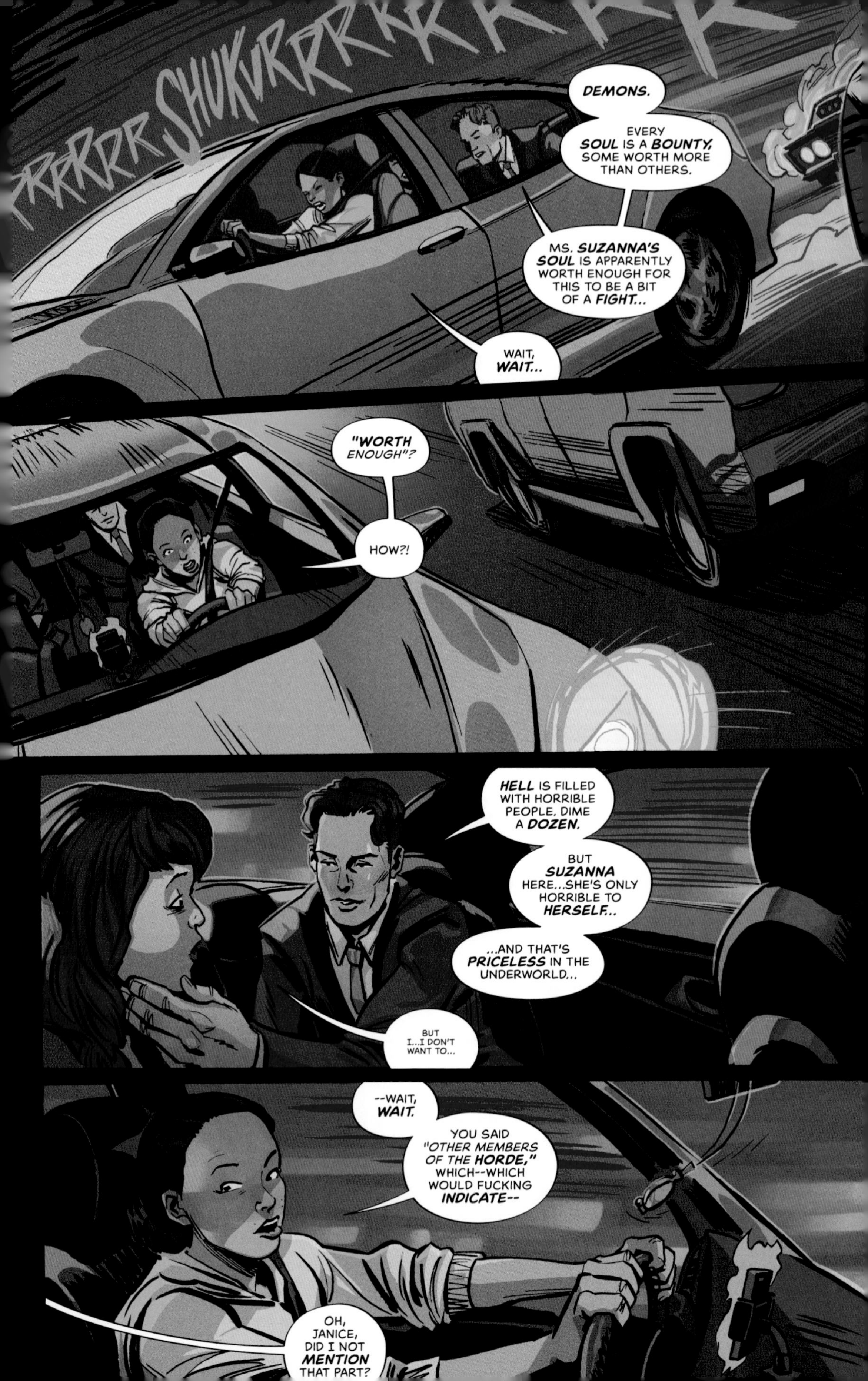

RRRRRR SHUKVRRRRRKKKK
DEMONS.
EVERY SOUL IS A BOUNTY, SOME WORTH MORE THAN OTHERS.
MS. SUZANNA'S SOUL IS APPARENTLY WORTH ENOUGH FOR THIS TO BE A BIT OF A FIGHT...
WAIT, WAIT...
"WORTH ENOUGH"?
HOW?!
HELL IS FILLED WITH HORRIBLE PEOPLE, DIME A DOZEN.
BUT SUZANNA HERE...SHE'S ONLY HORRIBLE TO HERSELF...
...AND THAT'S PRICELESS IN THE UNDERWORLD...
BUT I...I DON'T WANT TO...
--WAIT, WAIT.
YOU SAID "OTHER MEMBERS OF THE HORDE," WHICH--WHICH WOULD FUCKING INDICATE--
OH, JANICE, DID I NOT MENTION THAT PART?

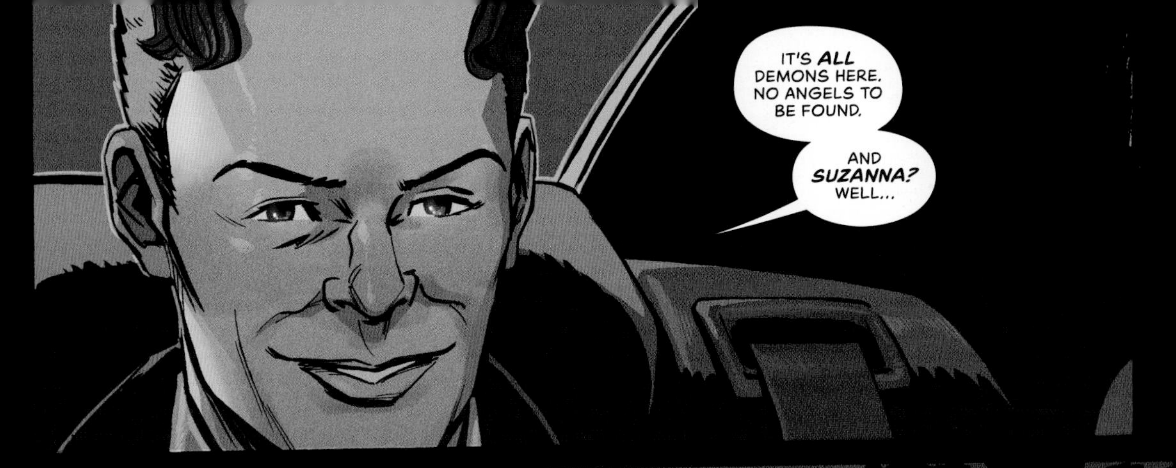
IT'S ALL DEMONS HERE. NO ANGELS TO BE FOUND.
AND SUZANNA? WELL...

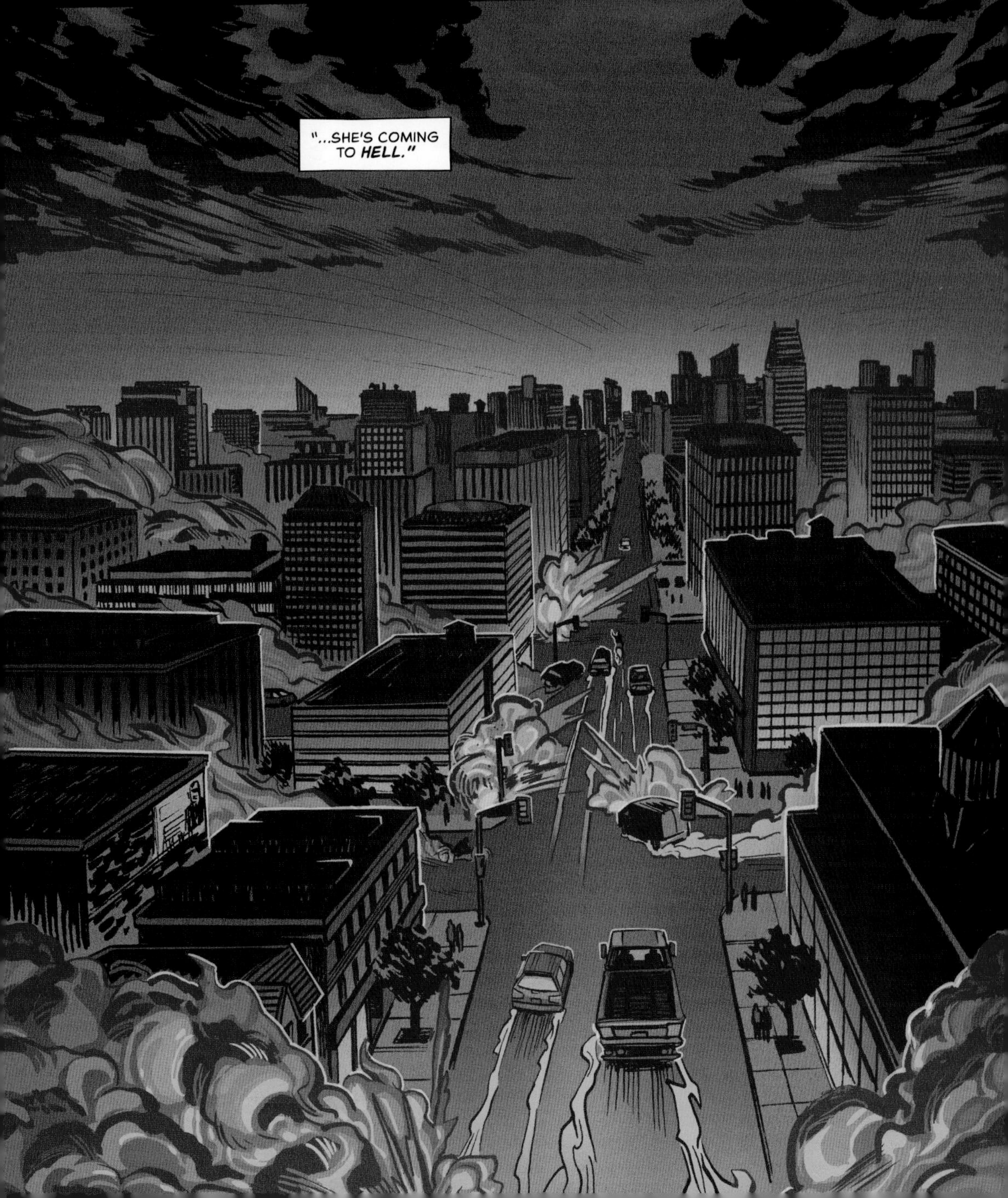
"...SHE'S COMING TO HELL."

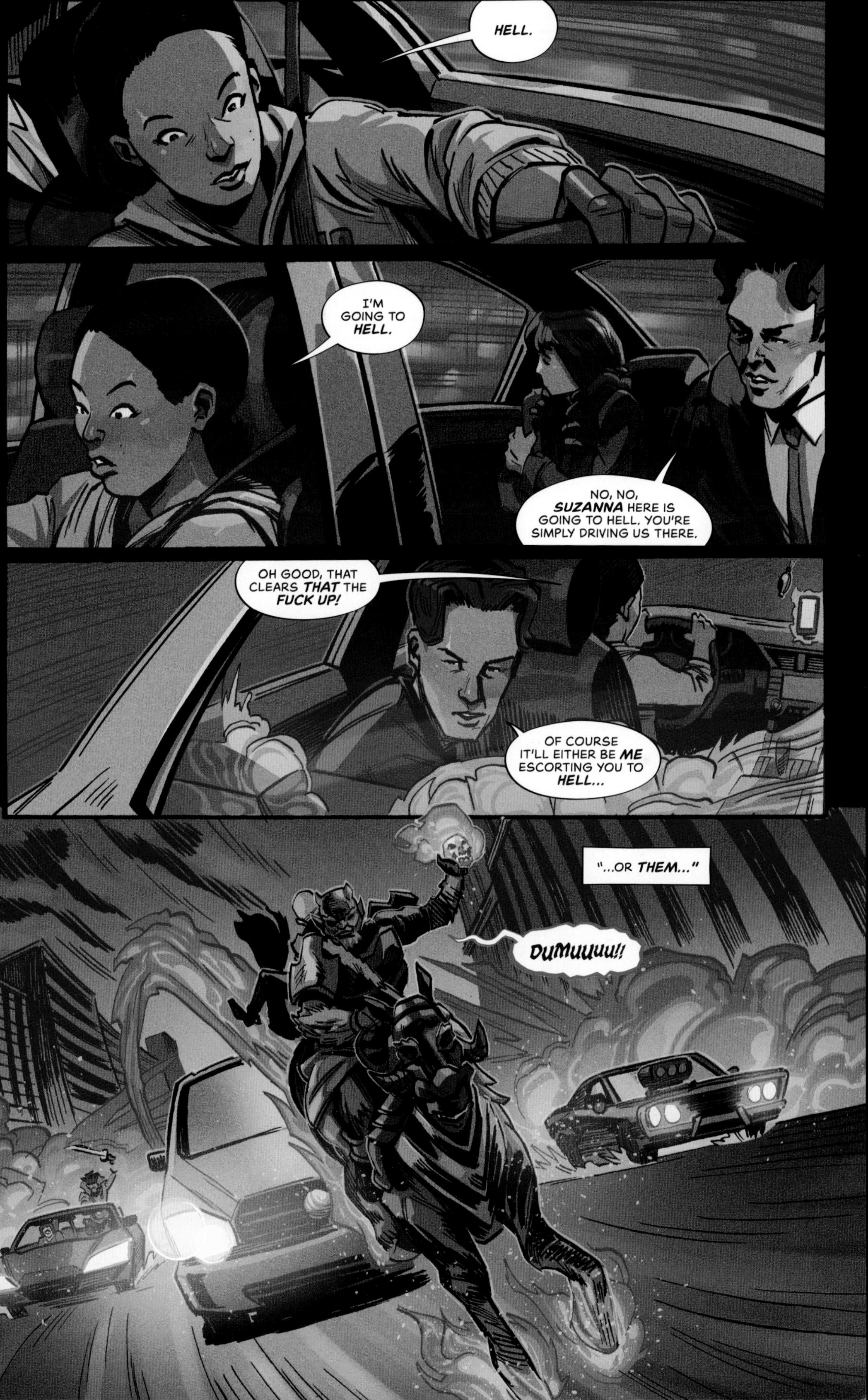
HELL.
I'M GOING TO HELL.
NO, NO, SUZANNA HERE IS GOING TO HELL. YOU'RE SIMPLY DRIVING US THERE.
OH GOOD, THAT CLEARS THAT THE FUCK UP!
OF COURSE IT'LL EITHER BE ME ESCORTING YOU TO HELL...
"...OR THEM..."
DUMUUUU!!

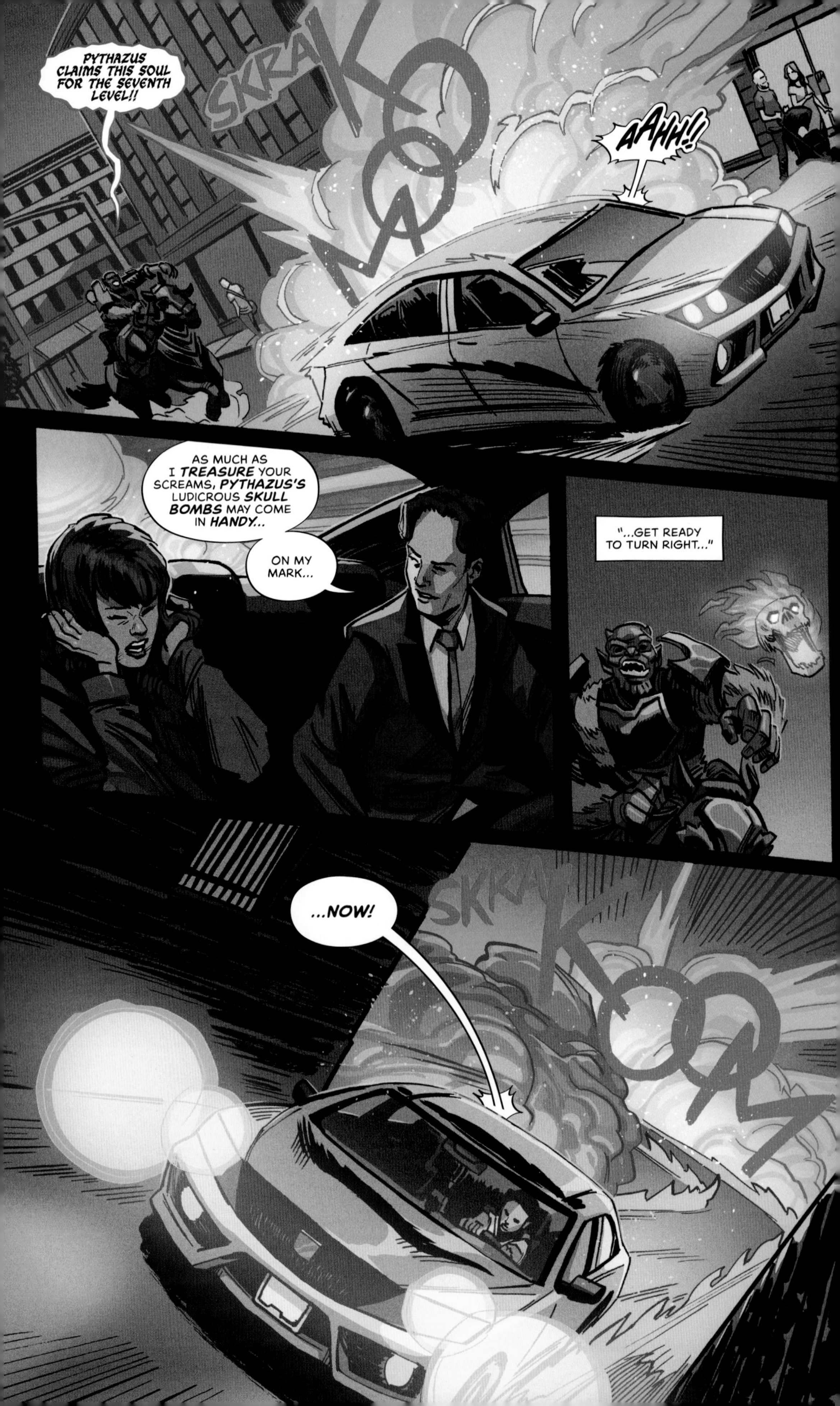
PYTHAZUS CLAIMS THIS SOUL FOR THE SEVENTH LEVEL!!
SKRAKOOM
AAHH!!
AS MUCH AS I TREASURE YOUR SCREAMS, PYTHAZUS'S LUDICROUS SKULL BOMBS MAY COME IN HANDY...
ON MY MARK...
"...GET READY TO TURN RIGHT..."
...NOW!
SKRAKOOM

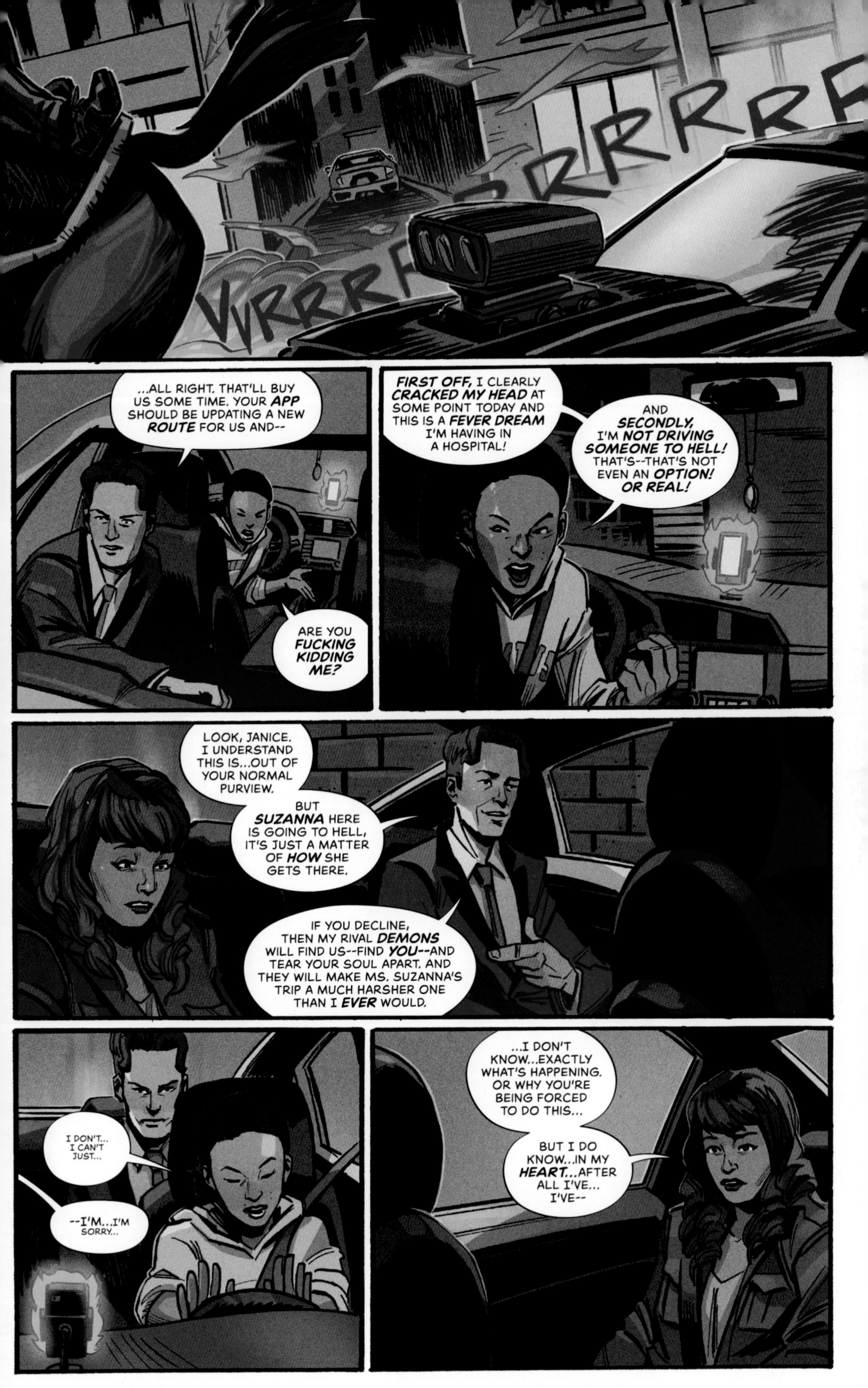
VVRRRRRRRRRRRRRR
...ALL RIGHT. THAT'LL BUY US SOME TIME. YOUR APP SHOULD BE UPDATING A NEW ROUTE FOR US AND--
ARE YOU FUCKING KIDDING ME?
FIRST OFF, I CLEARLY CRACKED MY HEAD AT SOME POINT TODAY AND THIS IS A FEVER DREAM I'M HAVING IN A HOSPITAL!
AND SECONDLY, I'M NOT DRIVING SOMEONE TO HELL! THAT'S--THAT'S NOT EVEN AN OPTION! OR REAL!
LOOK, JANICE. I UNDERSTAND THIS IS...OUT OF YOUR NORMAL PURVIEW.
BUT SUZANNA HERE IS GOING TO HELL, IT'S JUST A MATTER OF HOW SHE GETS THERE.
IF YOU DECLINE, THEN MY RIVAL DEMONS WILL FIND US--FIND YOU--AND TEAR YOUR SOUL APART. AND THEY WILL MAKE MS. SUZANNA'S TRIP A MUCH HARSHER ONE THAN I EVER WOULD.
I DON'T... I CAN'T JUST...
--I'M...I'M SORRY...
...I DON'T KNOW...EXACTLY WHAT'S HAPPENING. OR WHY YOU'RE BEING FORCED TO DO THIS...
BUT I DO KNOW...IN MY HEART...AFTER ALL I'VE... I'VE--

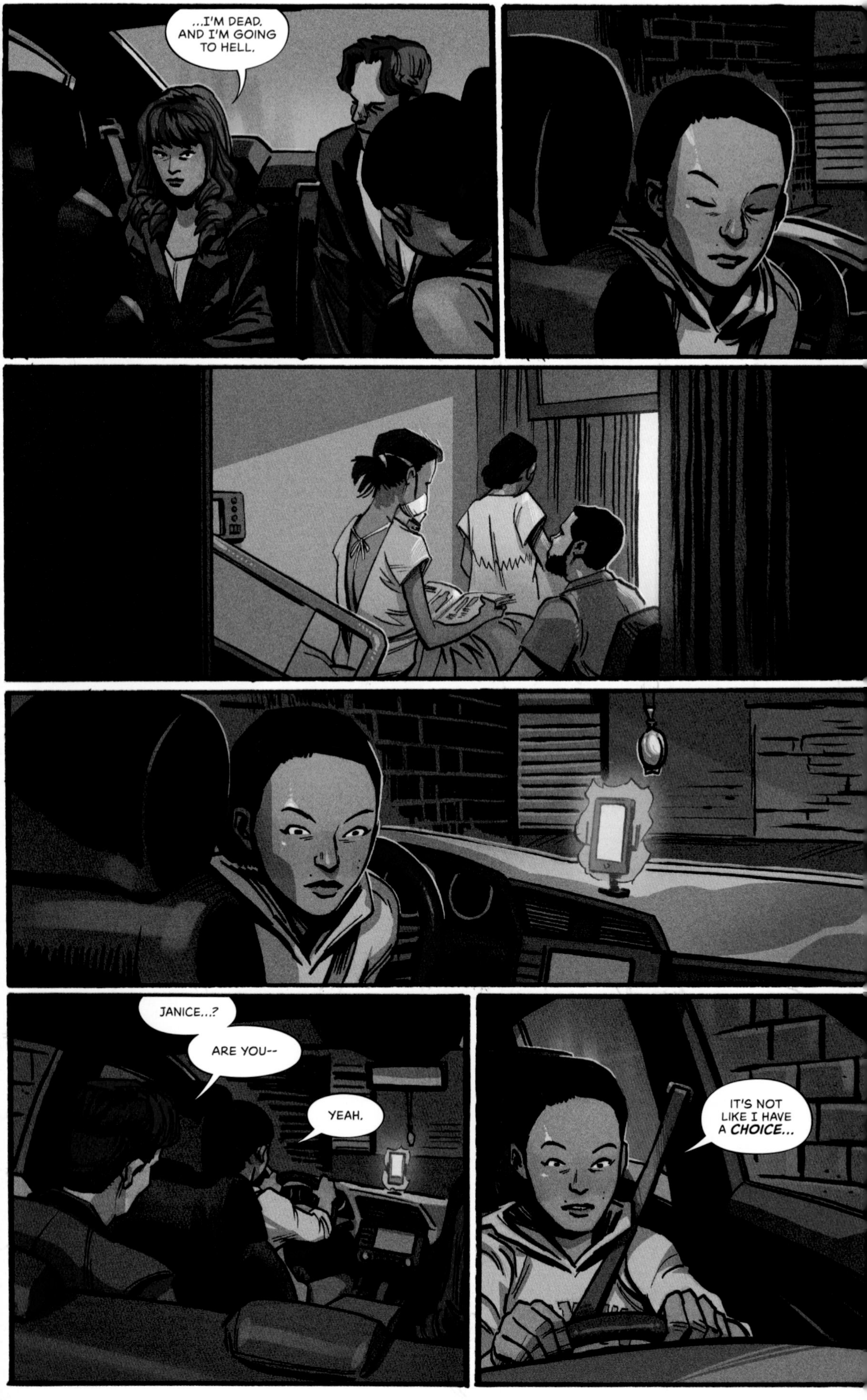
...I'M DEAD. AND I'M GOING TO HELL.
JANICE...?
ARE YOU--
YEAH.
IT'S NOT LIKE I HAVE A ***CHOICE...***

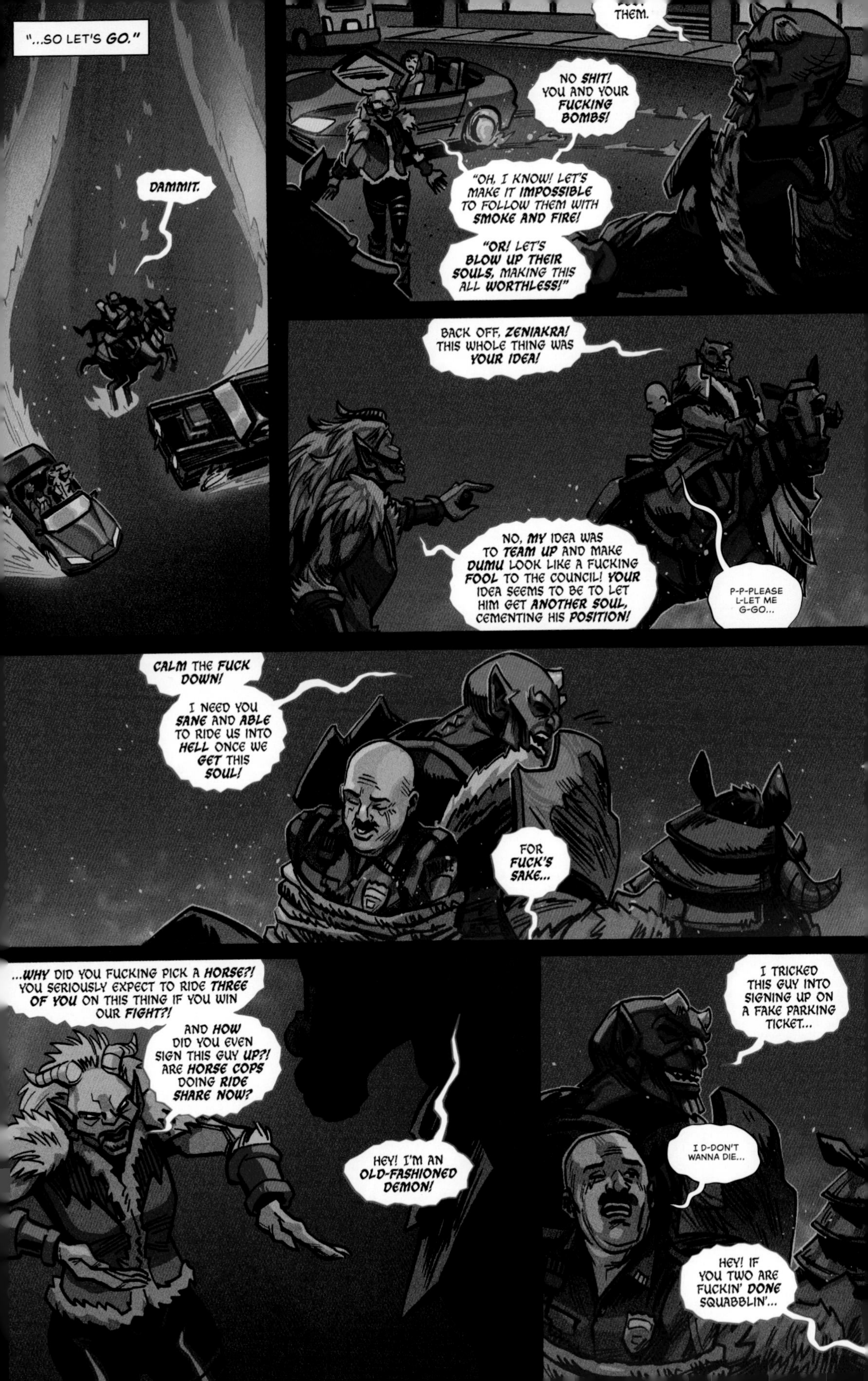
"...SO LET'S GO."
DAMMIT.
THEM.
NO SHIT! YOU AND YOUR FUCKING BOMBS!
"OH, I KNOW! LET'S MAKE IT IMPOSSIBLE TO FOLLOW THEM WITH SMOKE AND FIRE!
"OR! LET'S BLOW UP THEIR SOULS, MAKING THIS ALL WORTHLESS!"
BACK OFF, ZENIAKRA! THIS WHOLE THING WAS YOUR IDEA!
NO, MY IDEA WAS TO TEAM UP AND MAKE DUMU LOOK LIKE A FUCKING FOOL TO THE COUNCIL! YOUR IDEA SEEMS TO BE TO LET HIM GET ANOTHER SOUL, CEMENTING HIS POSITION!
P-P-PLEASE L-LET ME G-GO...
CALM THE FUCK DOWN!
I NEED YOU SANE AND ABLE TO RIDE US INTO HELL ONCE WE GET THIS SOUL!
FOR FUCK'S SAKE...
...WHY DID YOU FUCKING PICK A HORSE?! YOU SERIOUSLY EXPECT TO RIDE THREE OF YOU ON THIS THING IF YOU WIN OUR FIGHT?!
AND HOW DID YOU EVEN SIGN THIS GUY UP?! ARE HORSE COPS DOING RIDE SHARE NOW?
HEY! I'M AN OLD-FASHIONED DEMON!
I TRICKED THIS GUY INTO SIGNING UP ON A FAKE PARKING TICKET...
I D-DON'T WANNA DIE...
HEY! IF YOU TWO ARE FUCKIN' DONE SQUABBLIN'...

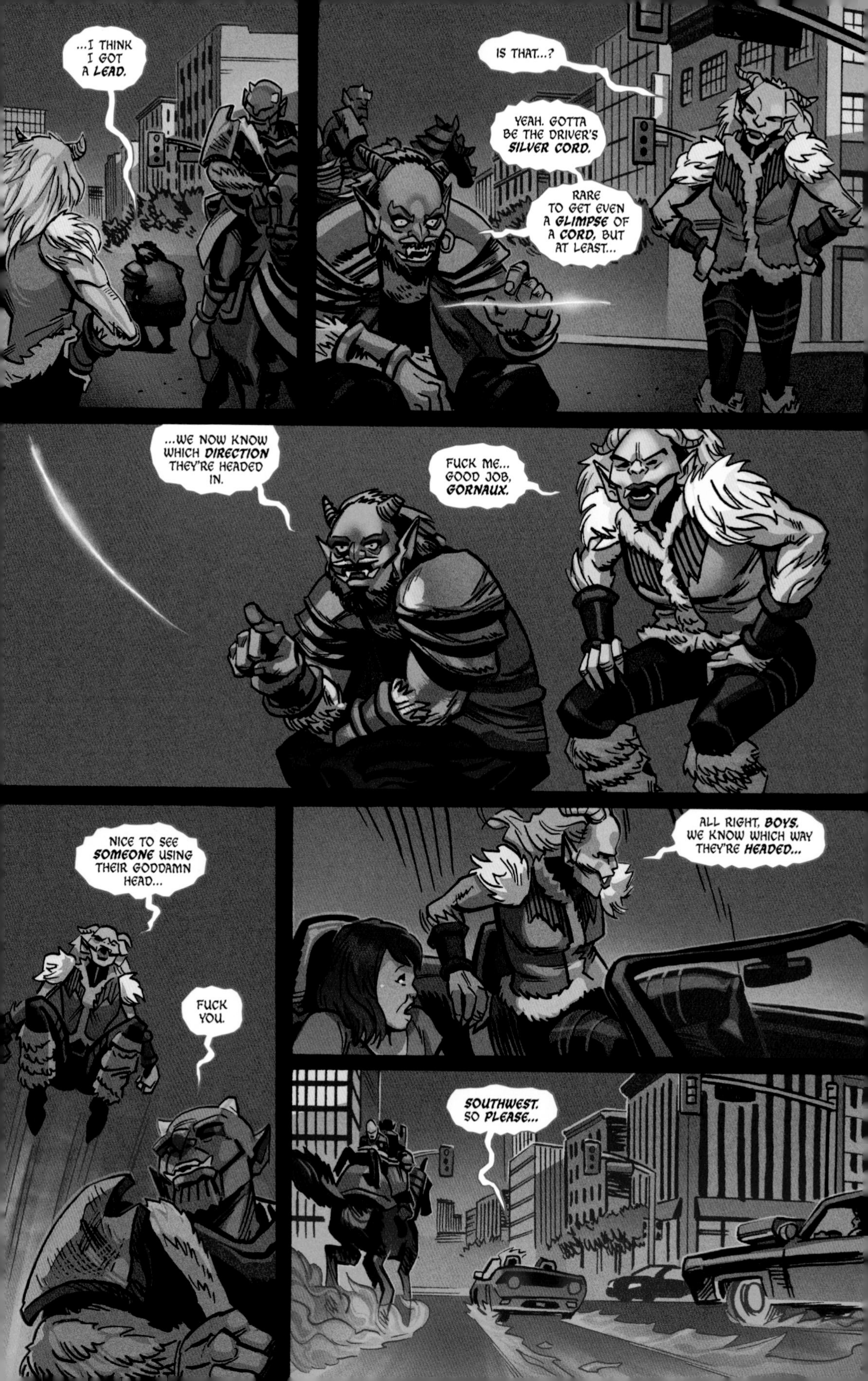
...I THINK I GOT A LEAD.
IS THAT...?
YEAH. GOTTA BE THE DRIVER'S SILVER CORD.
RARE TO GET EVEN A GLIMPSE OF A CORD, BUT AT LEAST...
...WE NOW KNOW WHICH DIRECTION THEY'RE HEADED IN.
FUCK ME... GOOD JOB, GORNAUX.
NICE TO SEE SOMEONE USING THEIR GODDAMN HEAD...
FUCK YOU.
ALL RIGHT, BOYS. WE KNOW WHICH WAY THEY'RE HEADED...
SOUTHWEST. SO PLEASE...

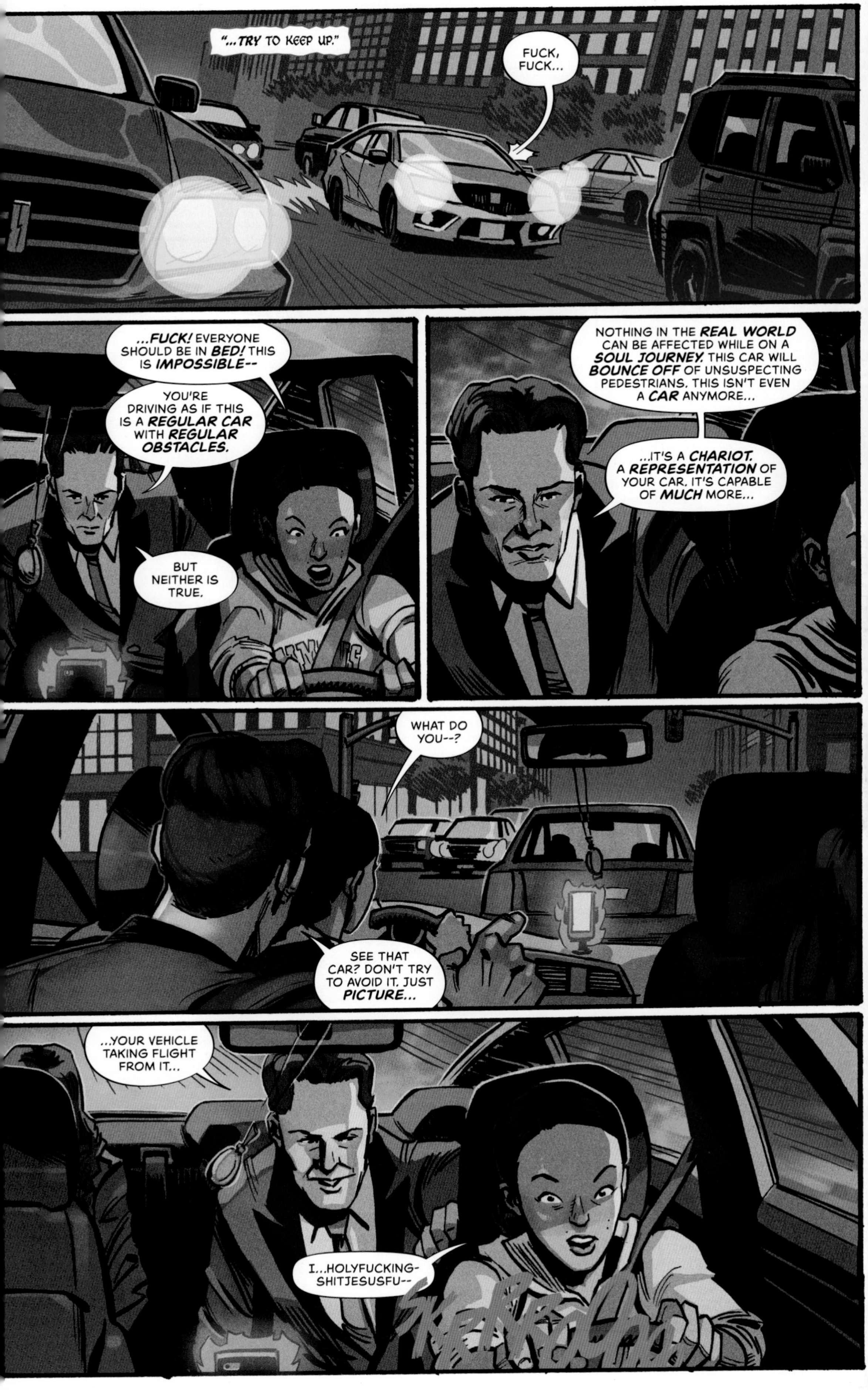
"...TRY TO KEEP UP."
FUCK, FUCK...
...FUCK! EVERYONE SHOULD BE IN BED! THIS IS IMPOSSIBLE--
YOU'RE DRIVING AS IF THIS IS A REGULAR CAR WITH REGULAR OBSTACLES.
BUT NEITHER IS TRUE.
NOTHING IN THE REAL WORLD CAN BE AFFECTED WHILE ON A SOUL JOURNEY. THIS CAR WILL BOUNCE OFF OF UNSUSPECTING PEDESTRIANS. THIS ISN'T EVEN A CAR ANYMORE...
...IT'S A CHARIOT. A REPRESENTATION OF YOUR CAR. IT'S CAPABLE OF MUCH MORE...
WHAT DO YOU--?
SEE THAT CAR? DON'T TRY TO AVOID IT. JUST PICTURE...
...YOUR VEHICLE TAKING FLIGHT FROM IT...
I...HOLYFUCKING-SHITJESUSFU--

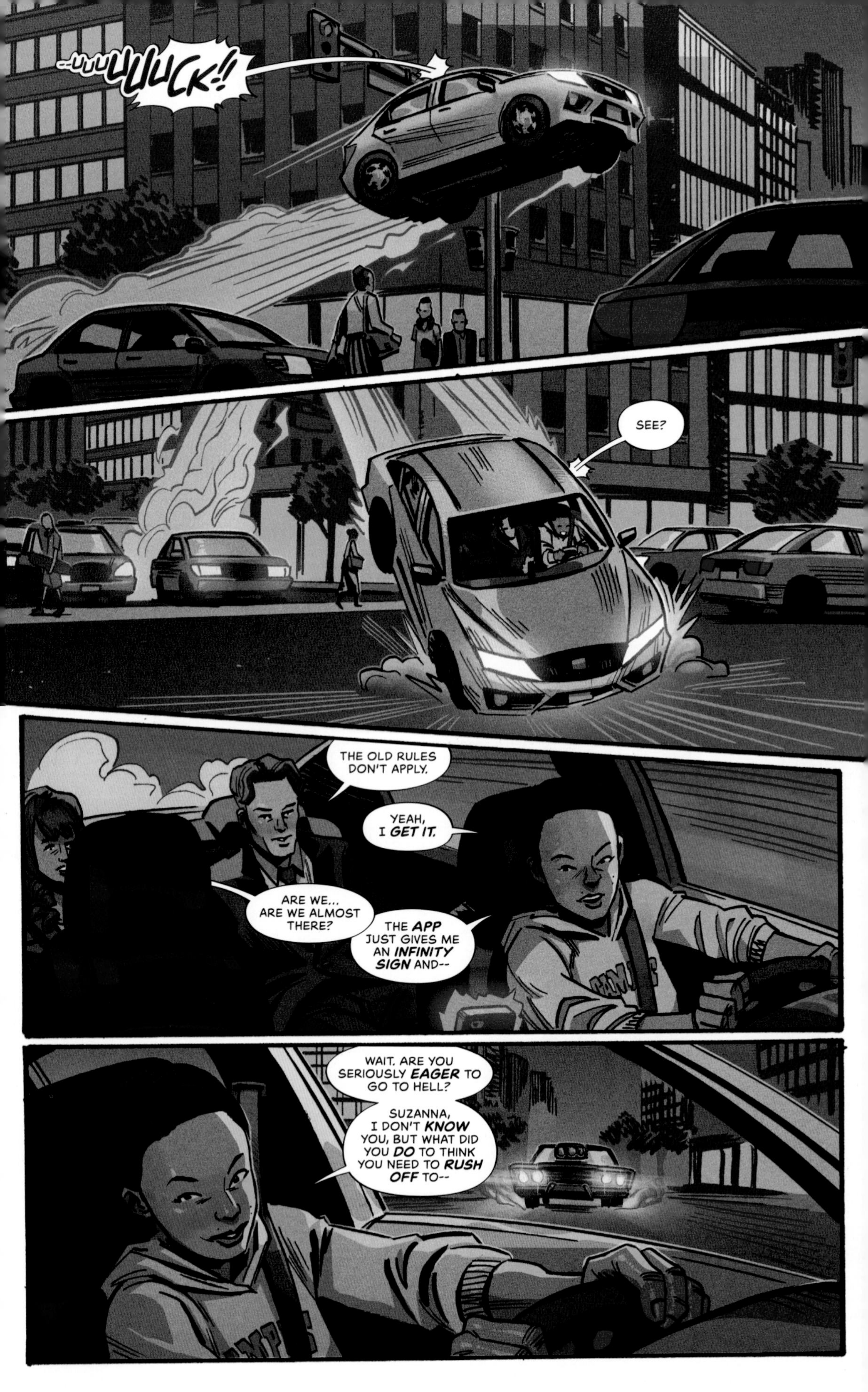
--UUUUUUCK!!
SEE?
THE OLD RULES DON'T APPLY.
YEAH, I GET IT.
ARE WE... ARE WE ALMOST THERE?
THE APP JUST GIVES ME AN INFINITY SIGN AND--
WAIT. ARE YOU SERIOUSLY EAGER TO GO TO HELL?
SUZANNA, I DON'T KNOW YOU, BUT WHAT DID YOU DO TO THINK YOU NEED TO RUSH OFF TO--

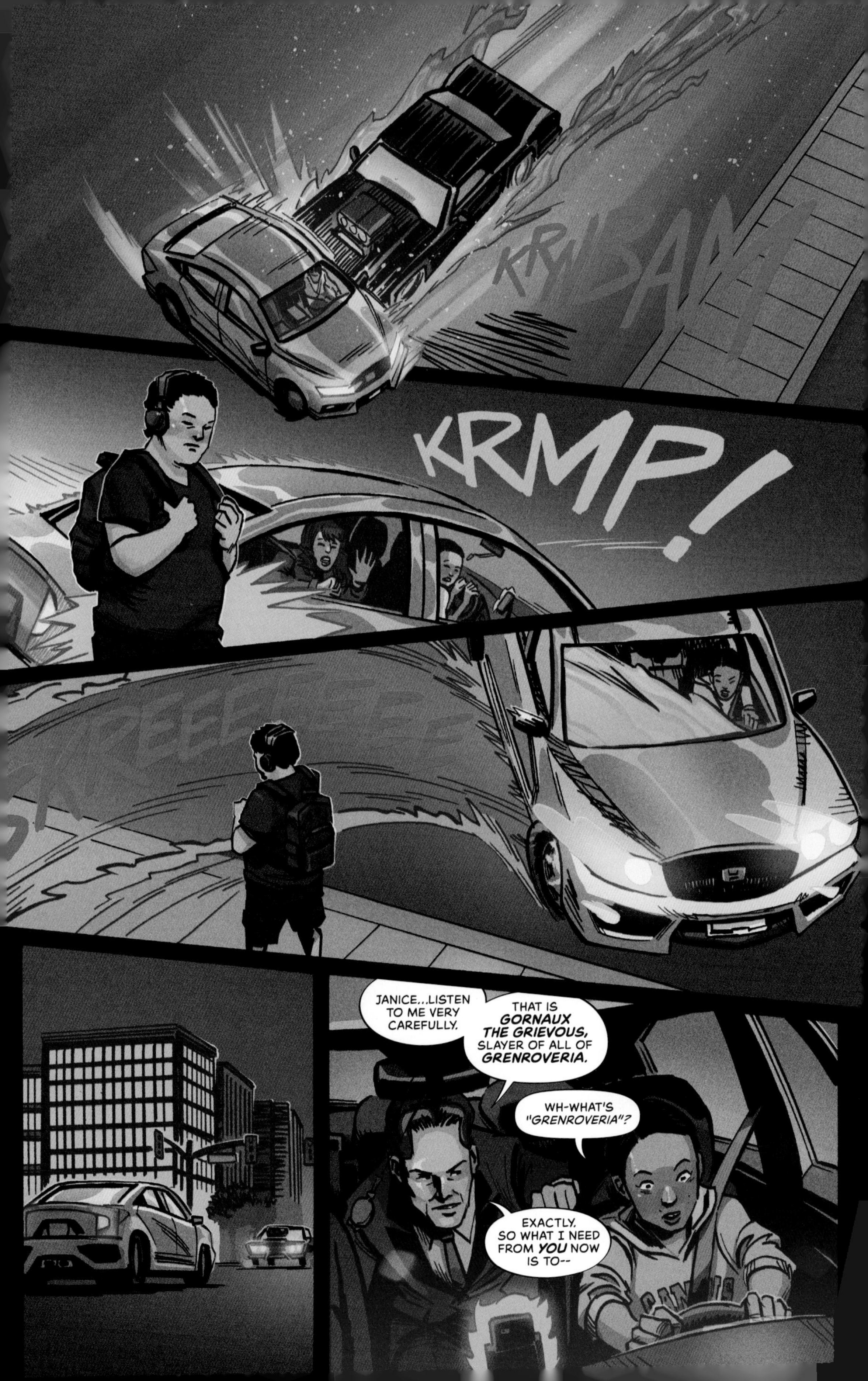
KRMP!
JANICE...LISTEN TO ME VERY CAREFULLY.
THAT IS GORNAUX THE GRIEVOUS, SLAYER OF ALL OF GRENROVERIA.
WH-WHAT'S "GRENROVERIA"?
EXACTLY. SO WHAT I NEED FROM YOU NOW IS TO--

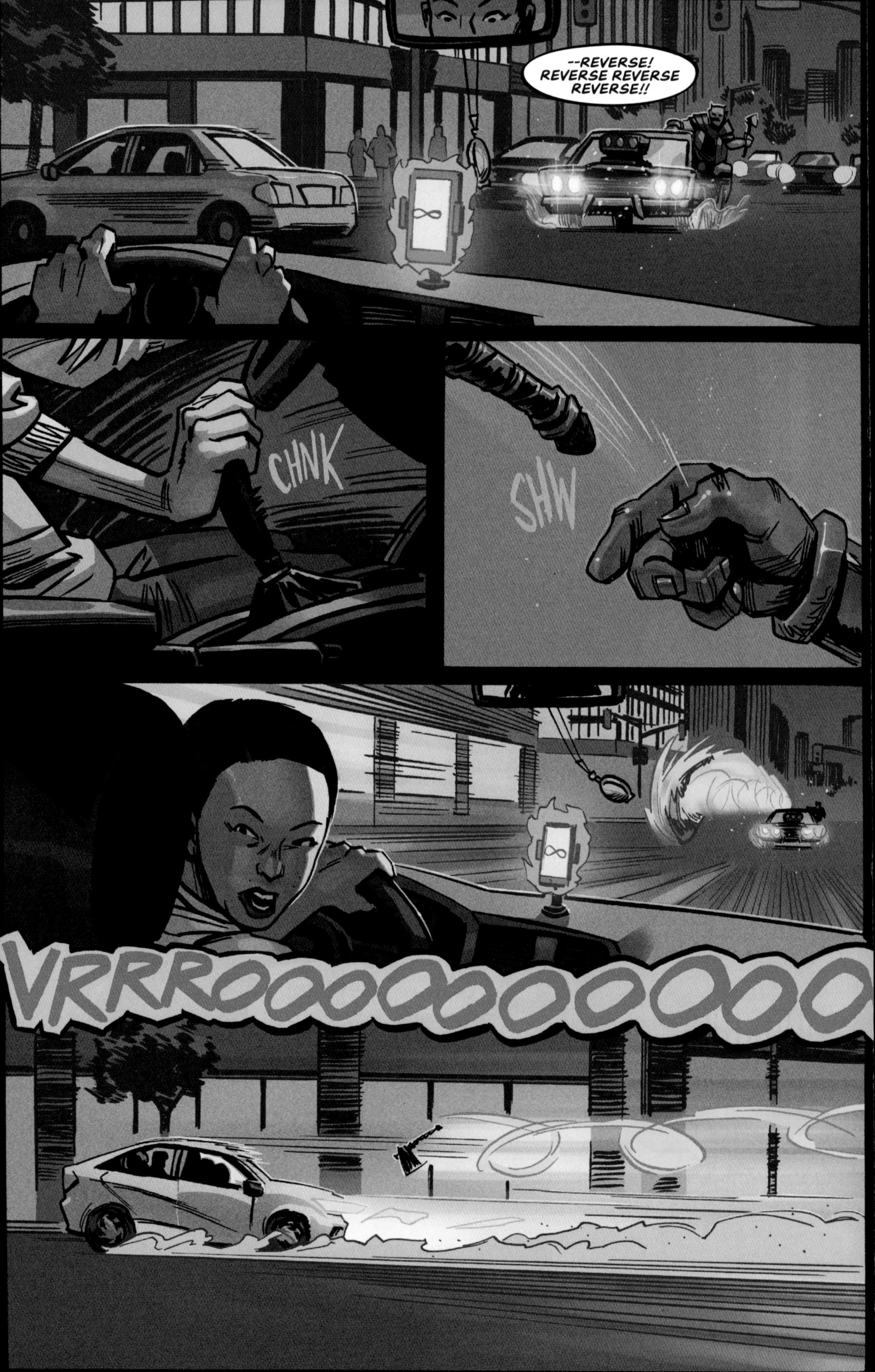
--REVERSE! REVERSE REVERSE REVERSE!!
CHNK
SHW
VRRROOOOOOOOOOO

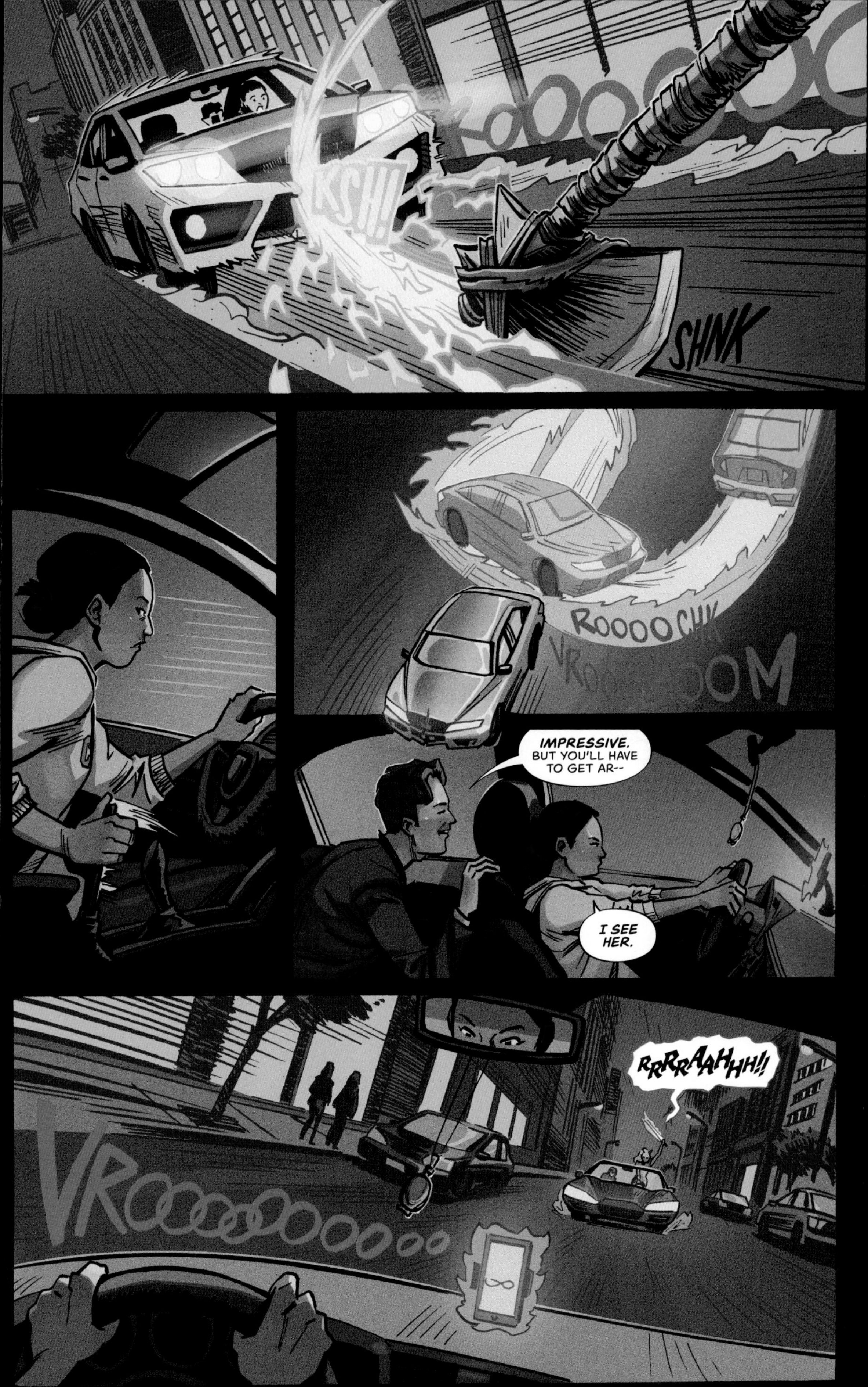
KSH!
SHINK
ROOOOCHK
VROOOOOM
IMPRESSIVE. BUT YOU'LL HAVE TO GET AR--
I SEE HER.
RRRRAAHHH!!
VROOOOOOOOOoo

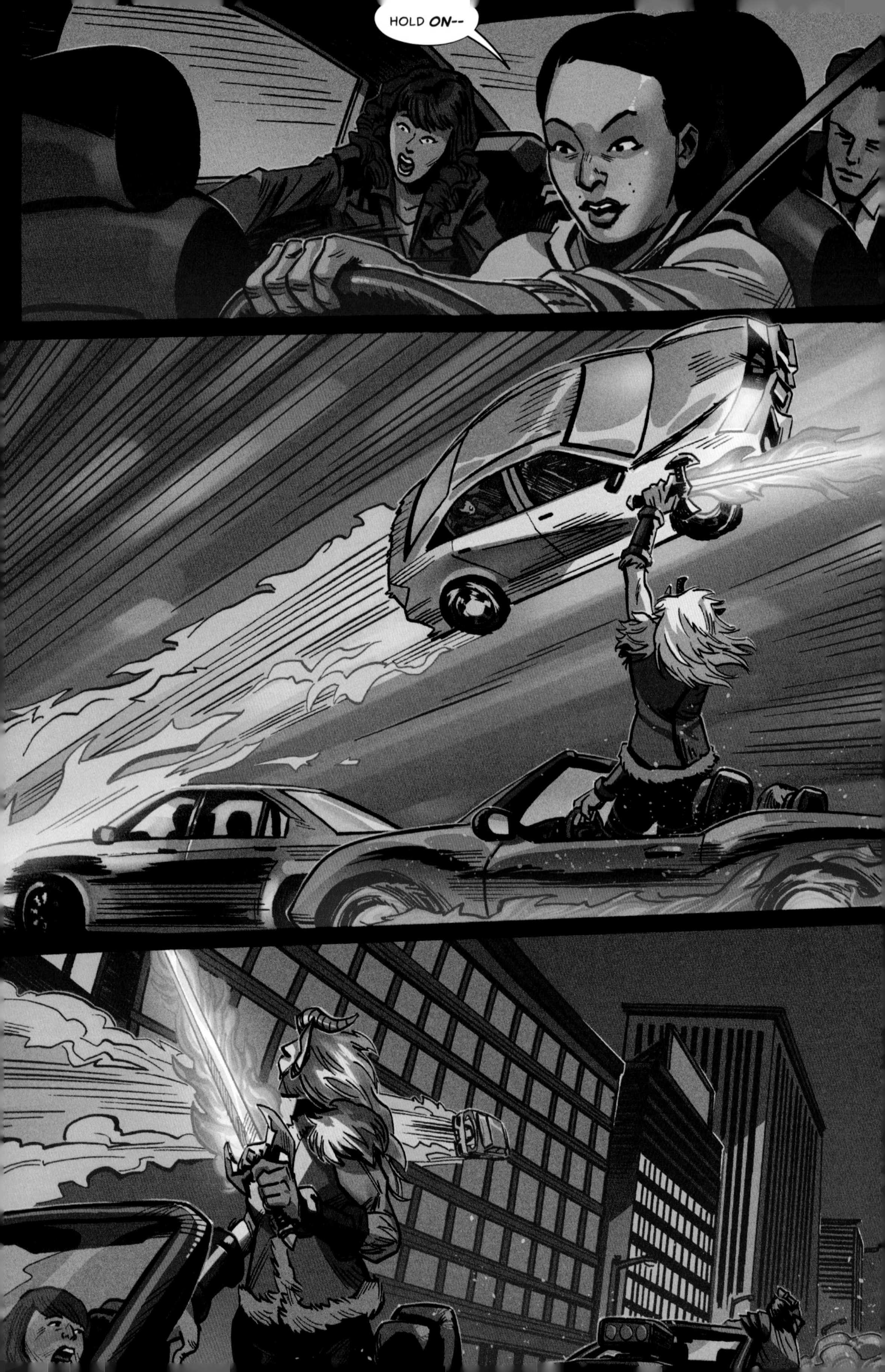
HOLD ON--

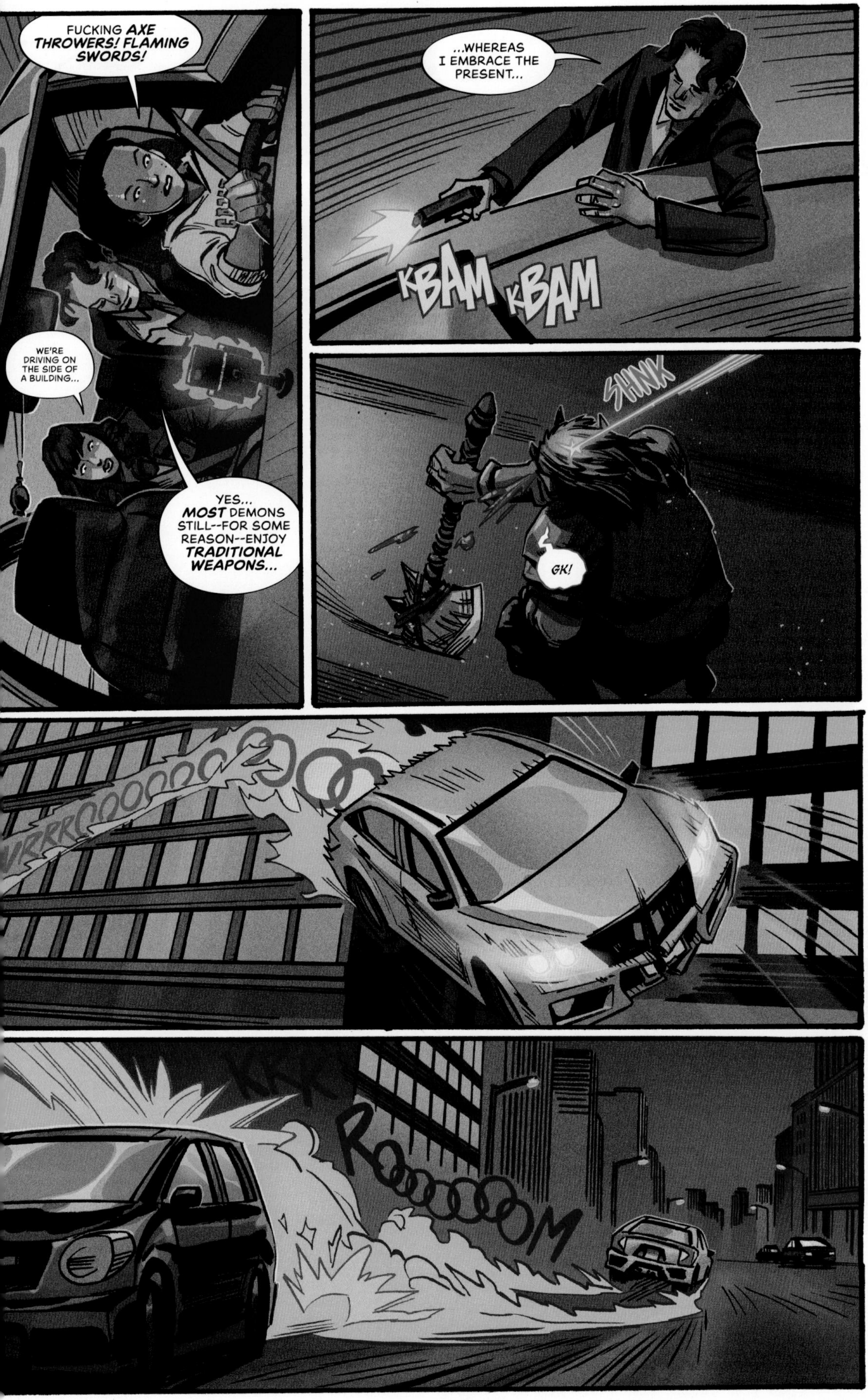

FUCKING AXE THROWERS! FLAMING SWORDS!
WE'RE DRIVING ON THE SIDE OF A BUILDING...
YES... MOST DEMONS STILL--FOR SOME REASON--ENJOY TRADITIONAL WEAPONS...
...WHEREAS I EMBRACE THE PRESENT...
KBAM KBAM
SHNK
GK!
VRRRROOOOOOOOOM
ROOOOOOOM

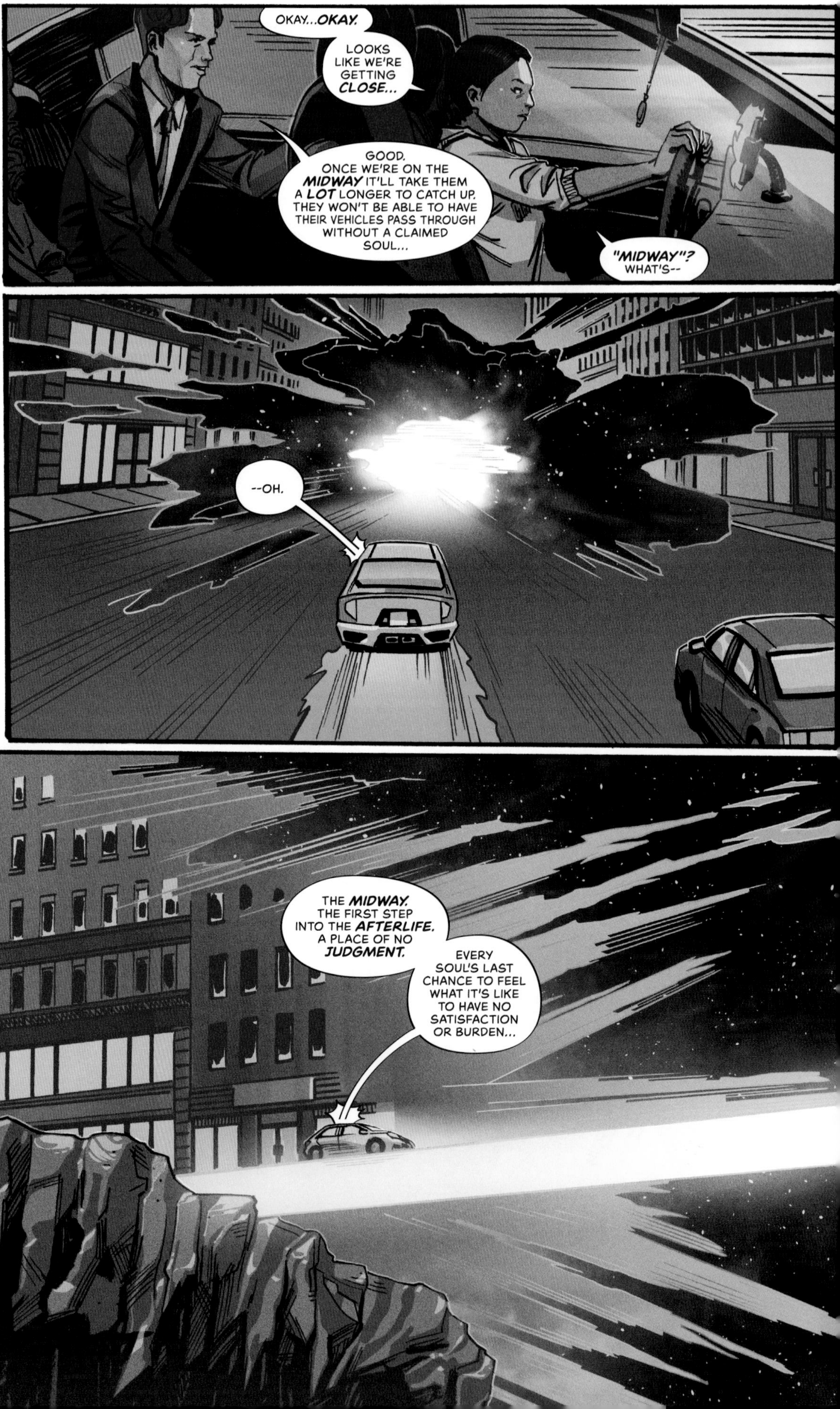

OKAY...OKAY.
LOOKS LIKE WE'RE GETTING CLOSE...
GOOD. ONCE WE'RE ON THE MIDWAY IT'LL TAKE THEM A LOT LONGER TO CATCH UP. THEY WON'T BE ABLE TO HAVE THEIR VEHICLES PASS THROUGH WITHOUT A CLAIMED SOUL...
"MIDWAY"? WHAT'S--
--OH.
THE MIDWAY. THE FIRST STEP INTO THE AFTERLIFE. A PLACE OF NO JUDGMENT.
EVERY SOUL'S LAST CHANCE TO FEEL WHAT IT'S LIKE TO HAVE NO SATISFACTION OR BURDEN...

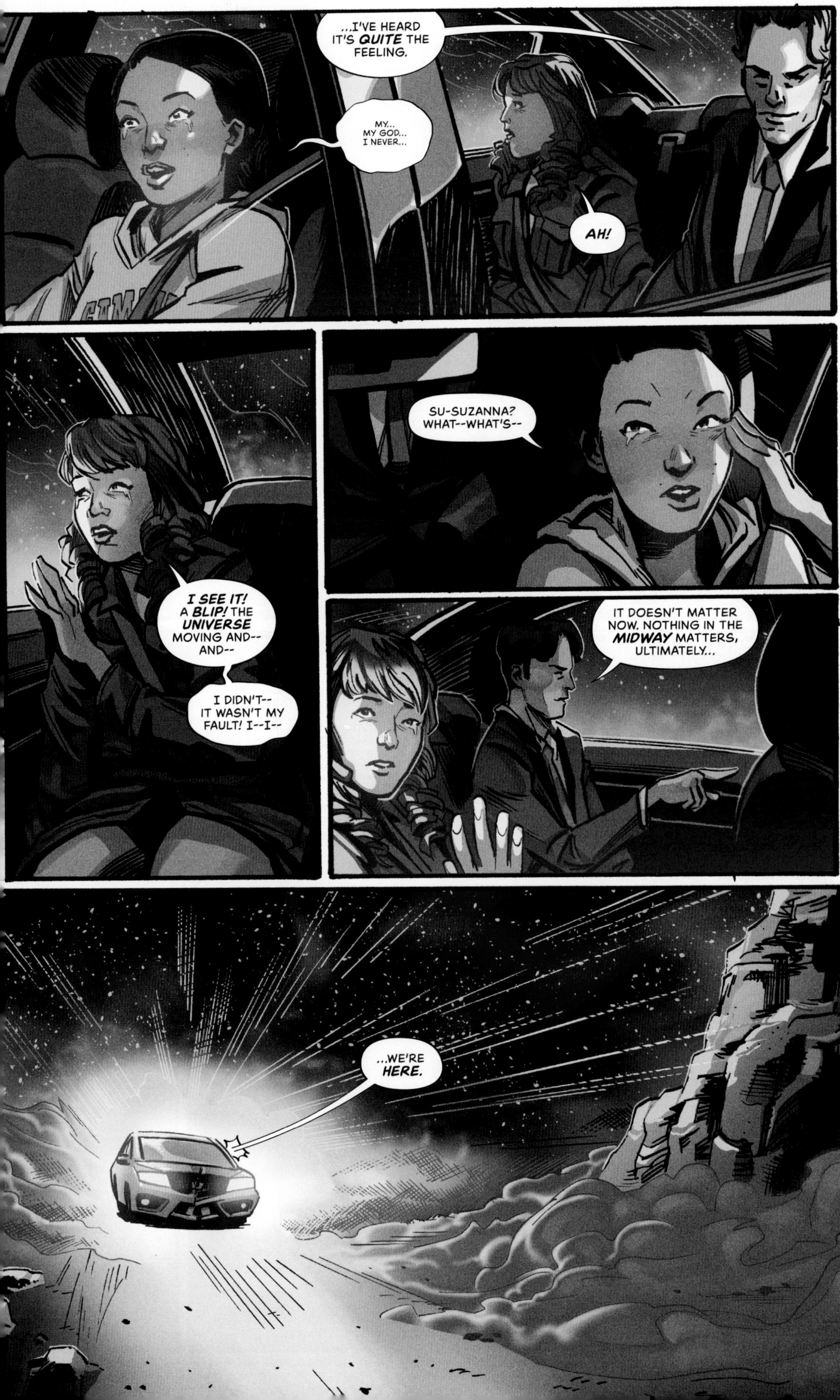
...I'VE HEARD IT'S QUITE THE FEELING.
MY... MY GOD... I NEVER...
AH!
I SEE IT! A BLIP! THE UNIVERSE MOVING AND--AND--
I DIDN'T-- IT WASN'T MY FAULT! I--I--
SU-SUZANNA? WHAT--WHAT'S--
IT DOESN'T MATTER NOW. NOTHING IN THE MIDWAY MATTERS, ULTIMATELY...
...WE'RE HERE.

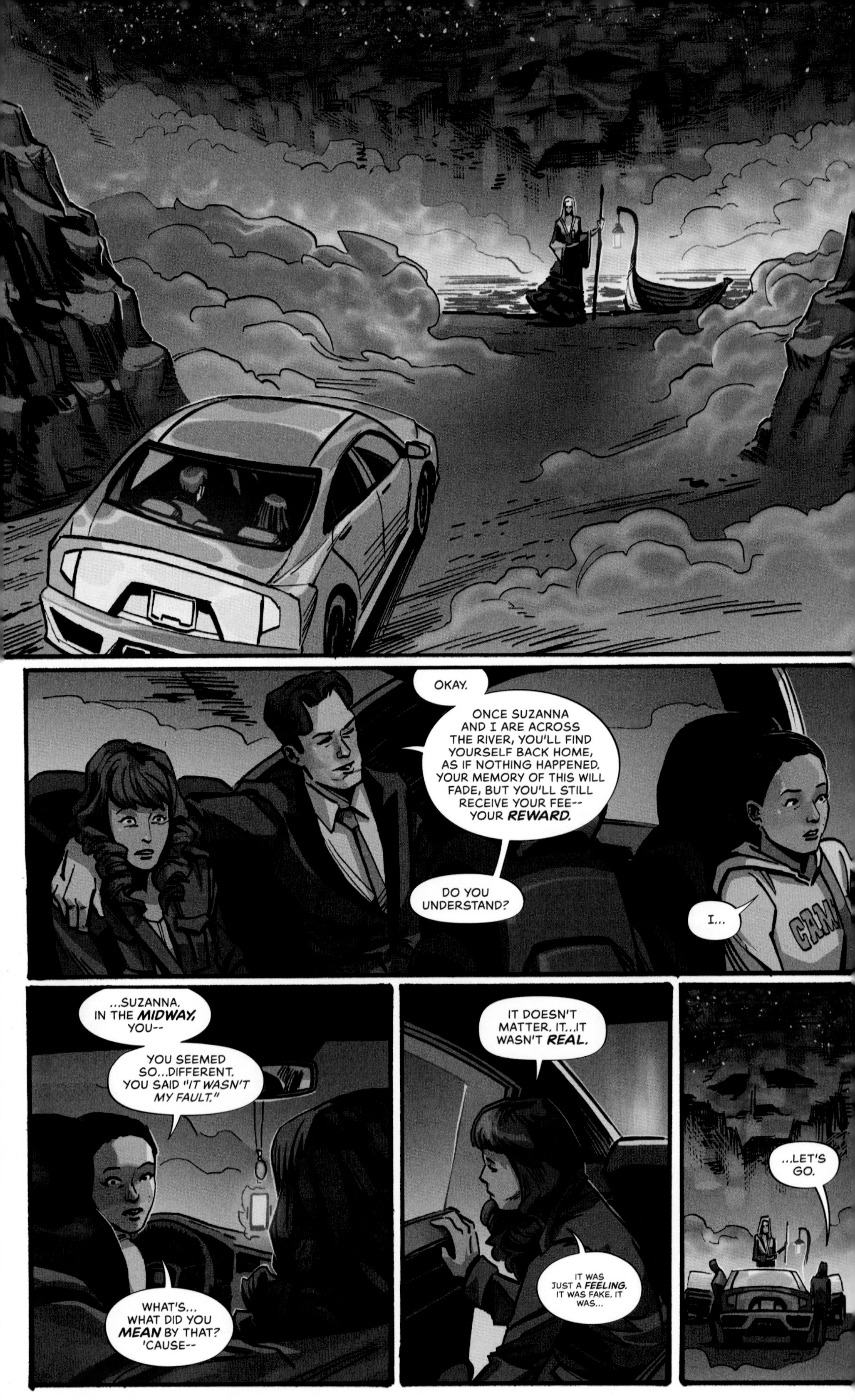
OKAY.
ONCE SUZANNA AND I ARE ACROSS THE RIVER, YOU'LL FIND YOURSELF BACK HOME, AS IF NOTHING HAPPENED. YOUR MEMORY OF THIS WILL FADE, BUT YOU'LL STILL RECEIVE YOUR FEE-- YOUR *REWARD.*
DO YOU UNDERSTAND?
I...
...SUZANNA, IN THE *MIDWAY,* YOU--
YOU SEEMED SO...DIFFERENT. YOU SAID *"IT WASN'T MY FAULT."*
WHAT'S... WHAT DID YOU *MEAN* BY THAT? 'CAUSE--
IT DOESN'T MATTER. IT...IT WASN'T *REAL.*
IT WAS JUST A *FEELING.* IT WAS FAKE. IT WAS...
...LET'S GO.

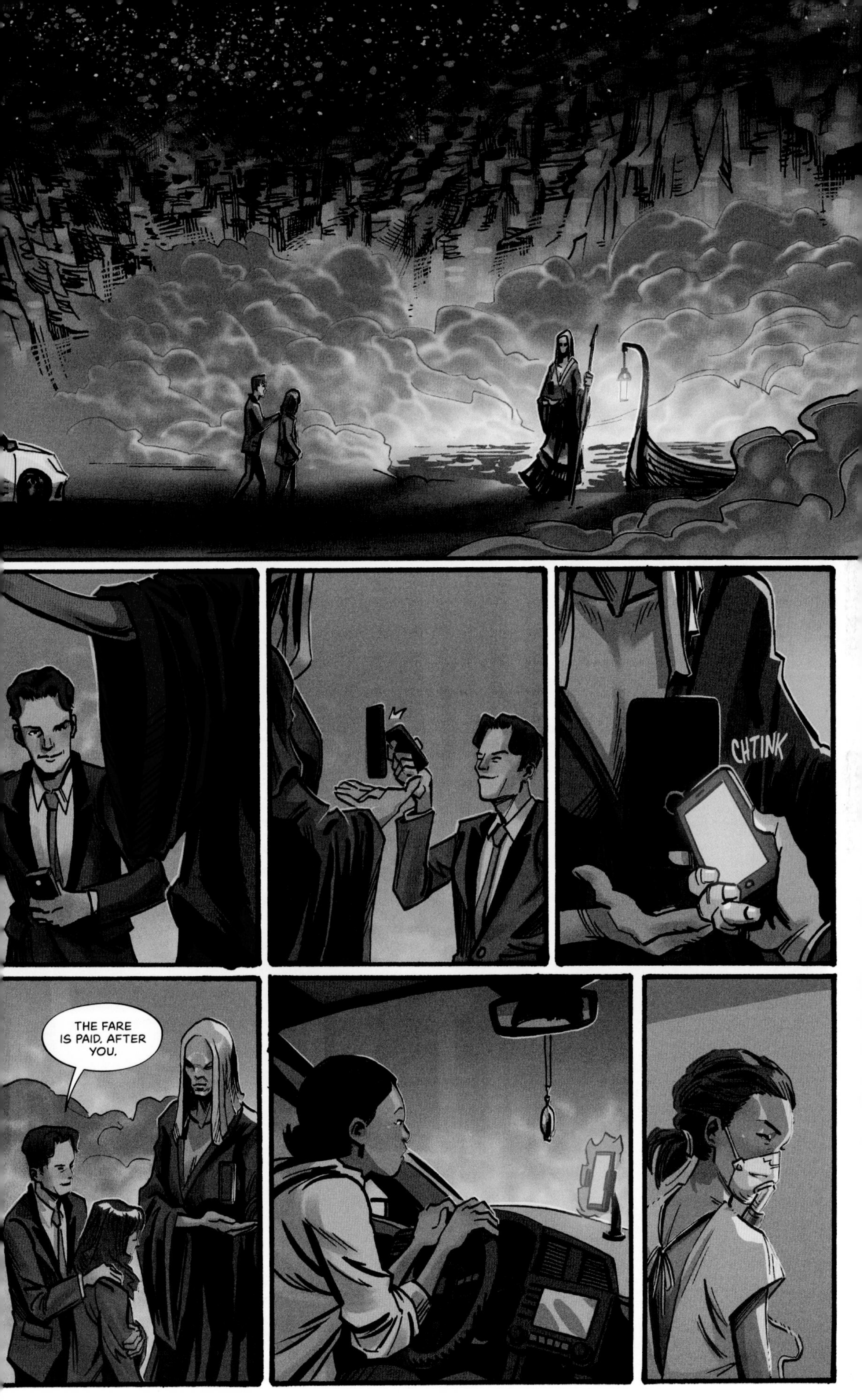
CHTINK
THE FARE IS PAID. AFTER YOU.

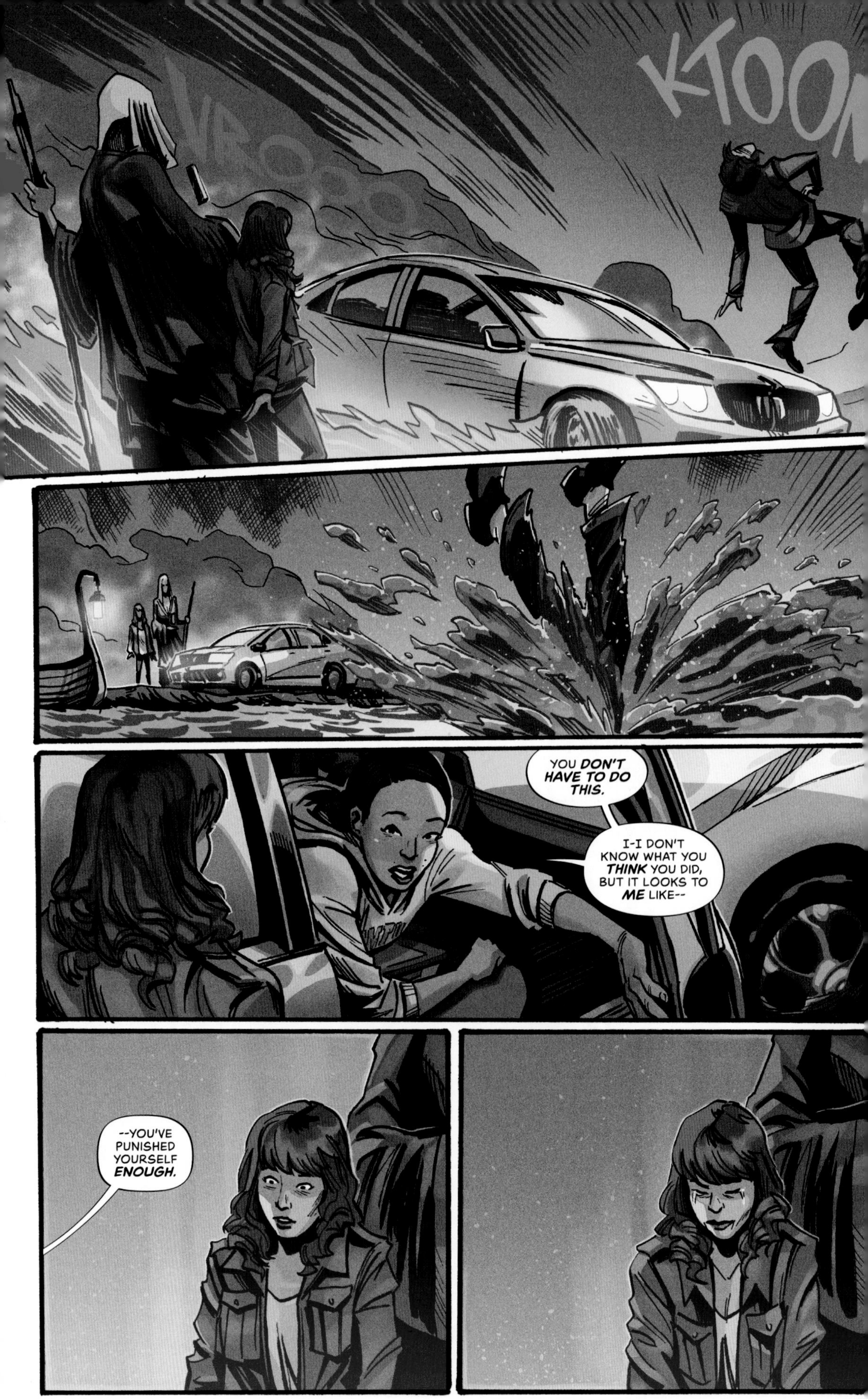
VROOOOOO
KTOOM
YOU DON'T HAVE TO DO THIS.
I-I DON'T KNOW WHAT YOU THINK YOU DID, BUT IT LOOKS TO ME LIKE--
--YOU'VE PUNISHED YOURSELF ENOUGH.

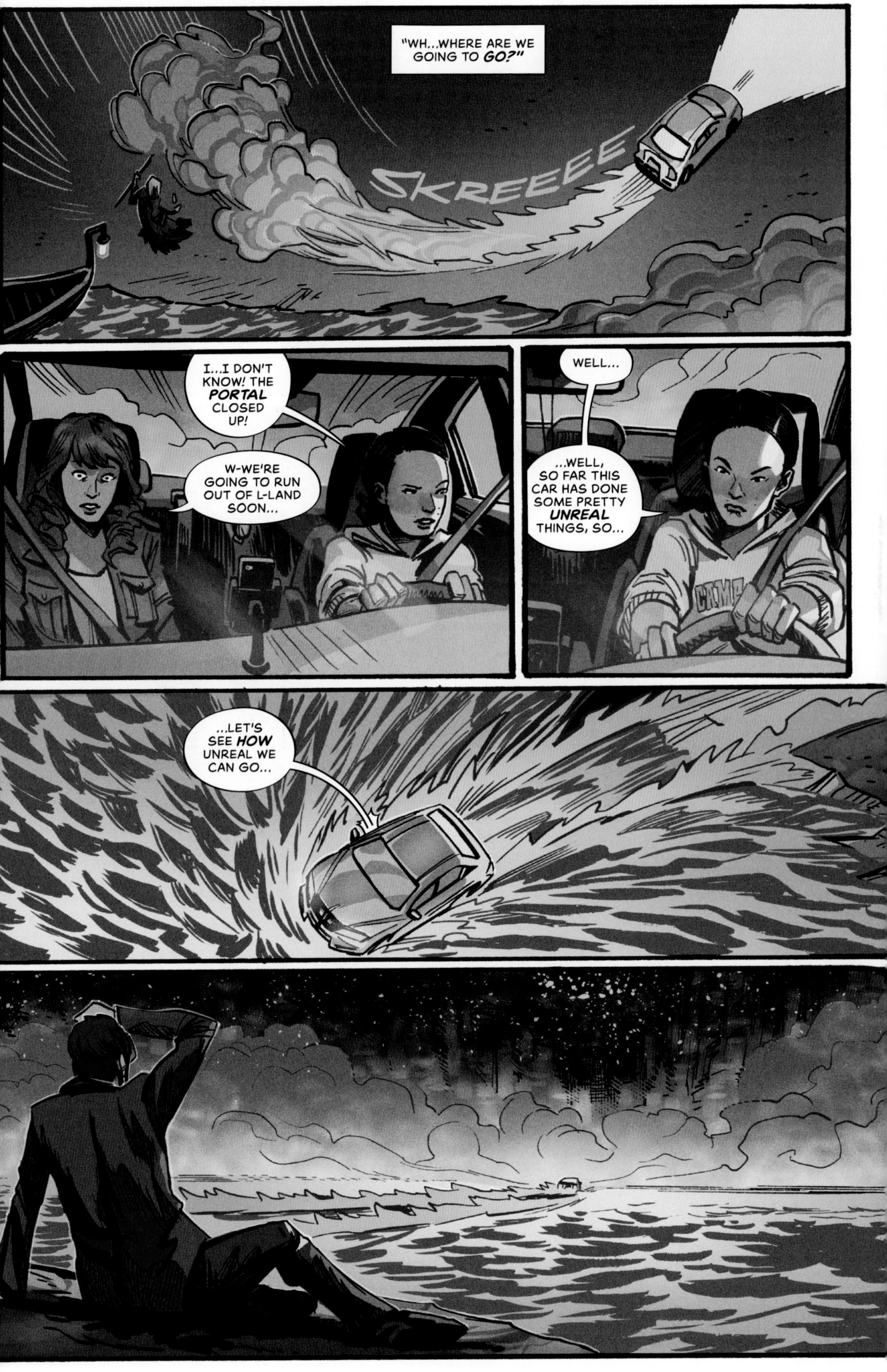
"WH...WHERE ARE WE GOING TO GO?"
SKREEEEE
I...I DON'T KNOW! THE PORTAL CLOSED UP!
W-WE'RE GOING TO RUN OUT OF L-LAND SOON...
WELL...
...WELL, SO FAR THIS CAR HAS DONE SOME PRETTY UNREAL THINGS, SO...
...LET'S SEE HOW UNREAL WE CAN GO...

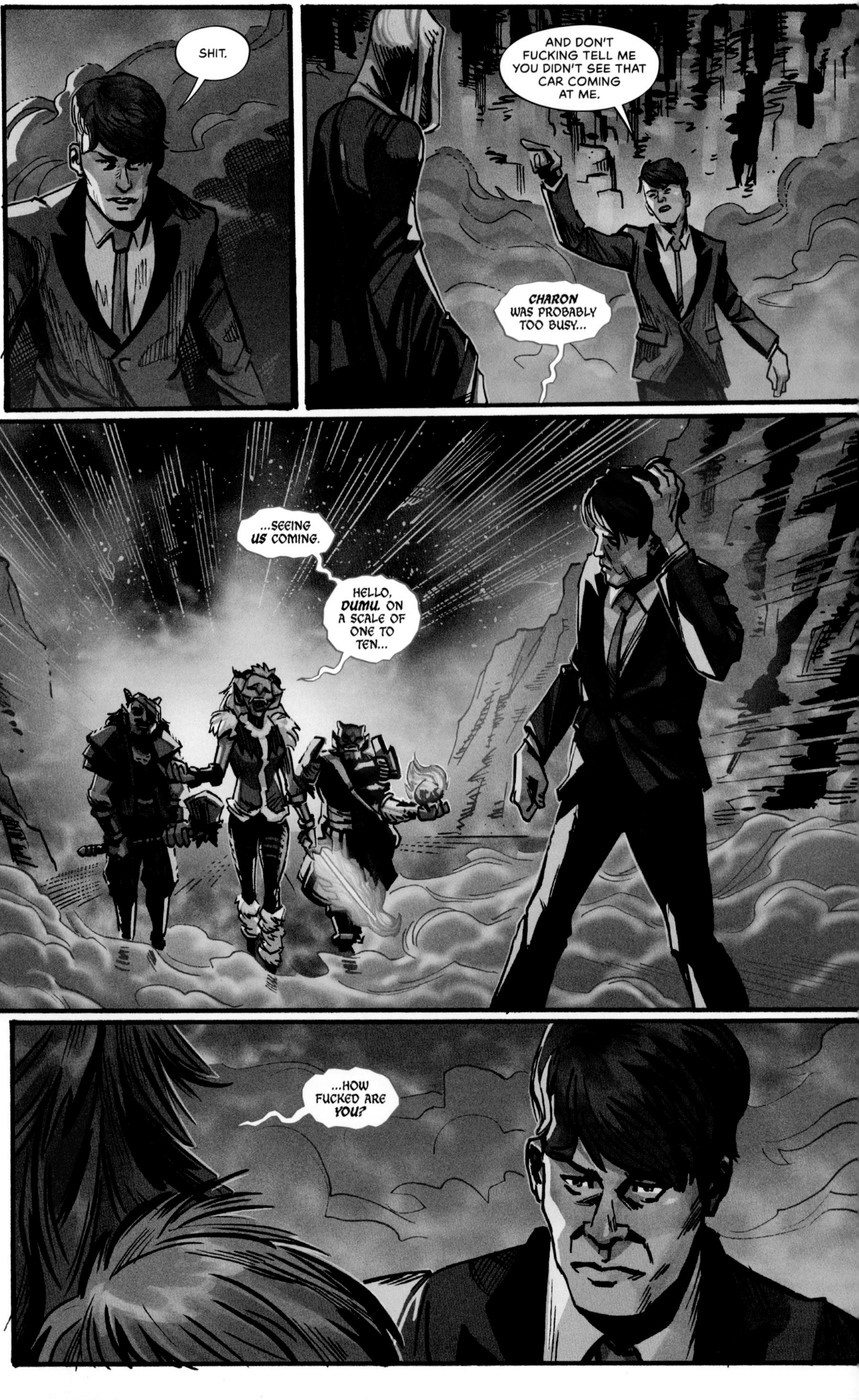
SHIT.
AND DON'T FUCKING TELL ME YOU DIDN'T SEE THAT CAR COMING AT ME.
CHARON WAS PROBABLY TOO BUSY...
...SEEING US COMING.
HELLO, DUMU. ON A SCALE OF ONE TO TEN...
...HOW FUCKED ARE YOU?

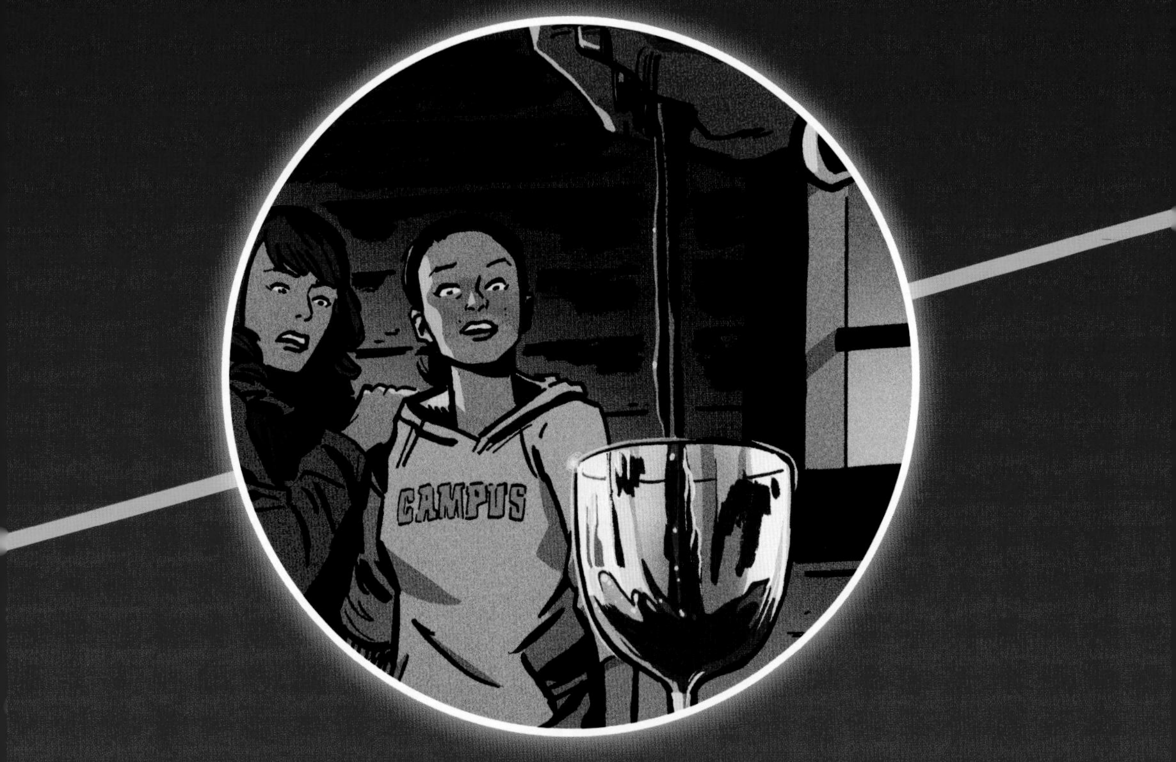
CAMPUS

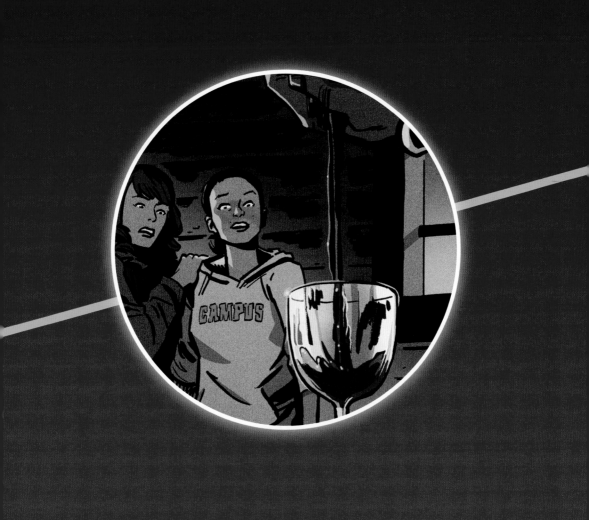

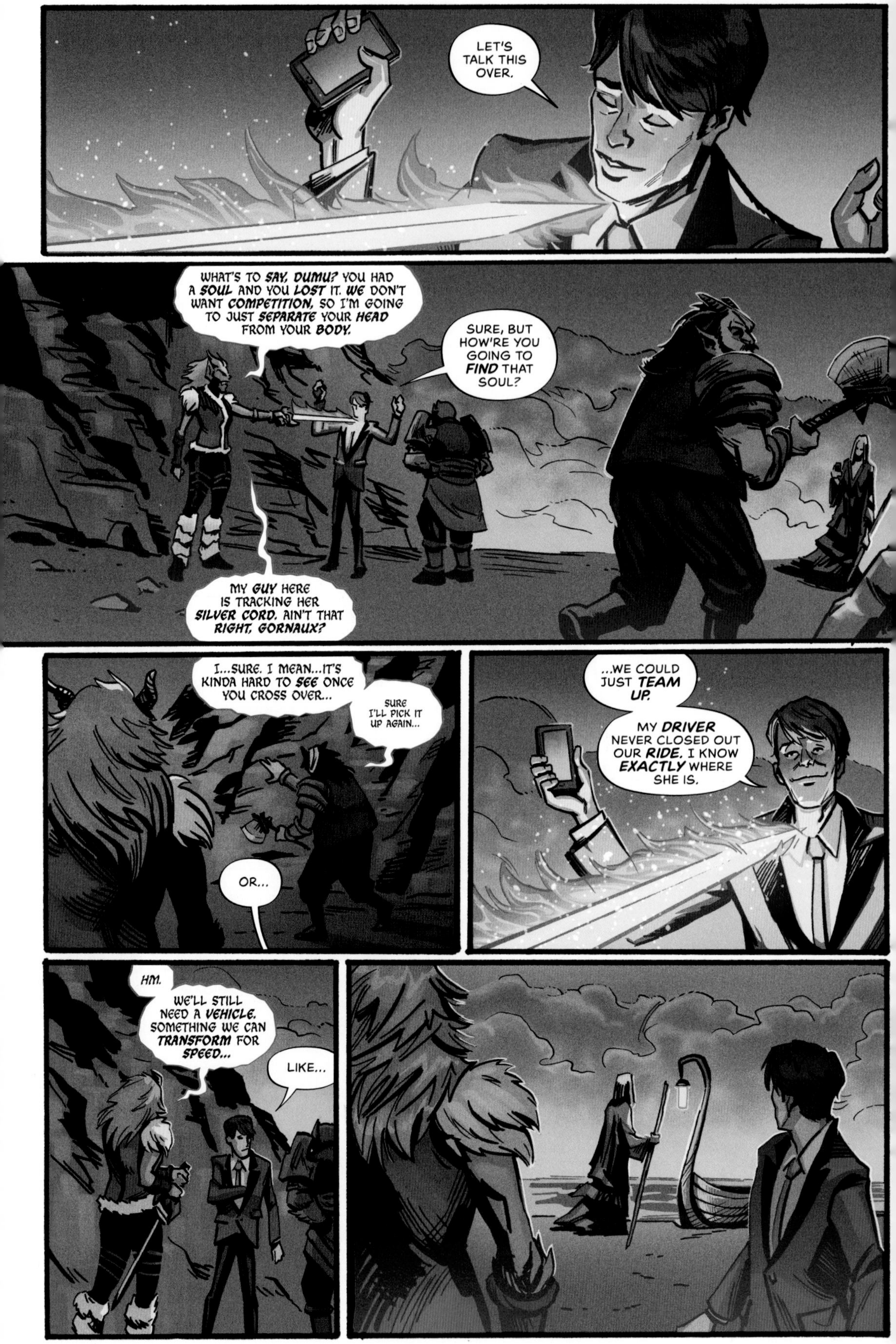
LET'S TALK THIS OVER.
WHAT'S TO SAY, DUMU? YOU HAD A SOUL AND YOU LOST IT. WE DON'T WANT COMPETITION, SO I'M GOING TO JUST SEPARATE YOUR HEAD FROM YOUR BODY.
SURE, BUT HOW'RE YOU GOING TO FIND THAT SOUL?
MY GUY HERE IS TRACKING HER SILVER CORD. AIN'T THAT RIGHT, GORNAUX?
I...SURE. I MEAN...IT'S KINDA HARD TO SEE ONCE YOU CROSS OVER...
SURE I'LL PICK IT UP AGAIN...
OR...
...WE COULD JUST TEAM UP.
MY DRIVER NEVER CLOSED OUT OUR RIDE. I KNOW EXACTLY WHERE SHE IS.
HM.
WE'LL STILL NEED A VEHICLE. SOMETHING WE CAN TRANSFORM FOR SPEED...
LIKE...

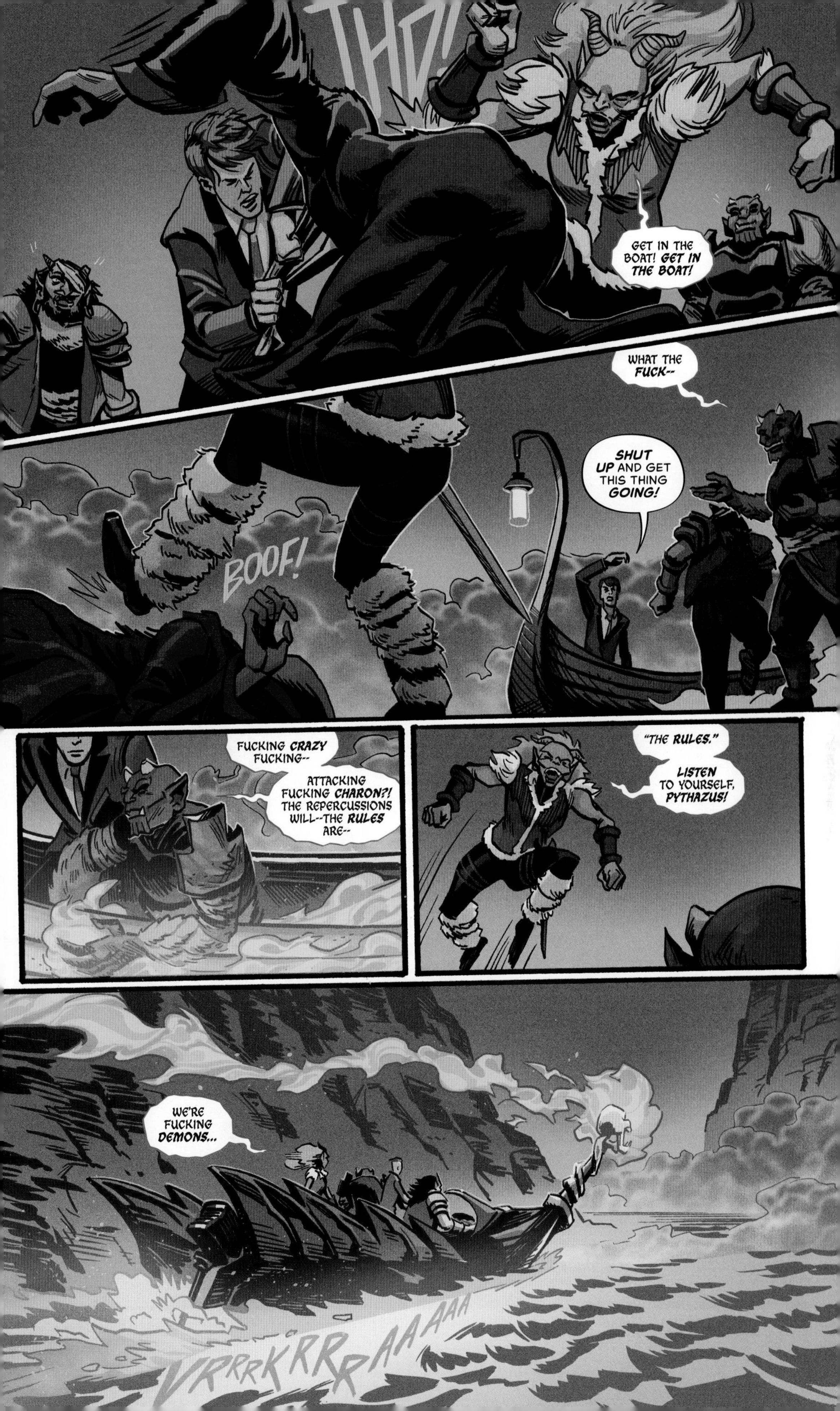
THD!
GET IN THE BOAT! GET IN THE BOAT!
WHAT THE FUCK--
SHUT UP AND GET THIS THING GOING!
BOOF!
FUCKING CRAZY FUCKING--
ATTACKING FUCKING CHARON?! THE REPERCUSSIONS WILL--THE RULES ARE--
"THE RULES."
LISTEN TO YOURSELF, PYTHAZUS!
WE'RE FUCKING DEMONS...
VRRRKRRRRAAAAAA

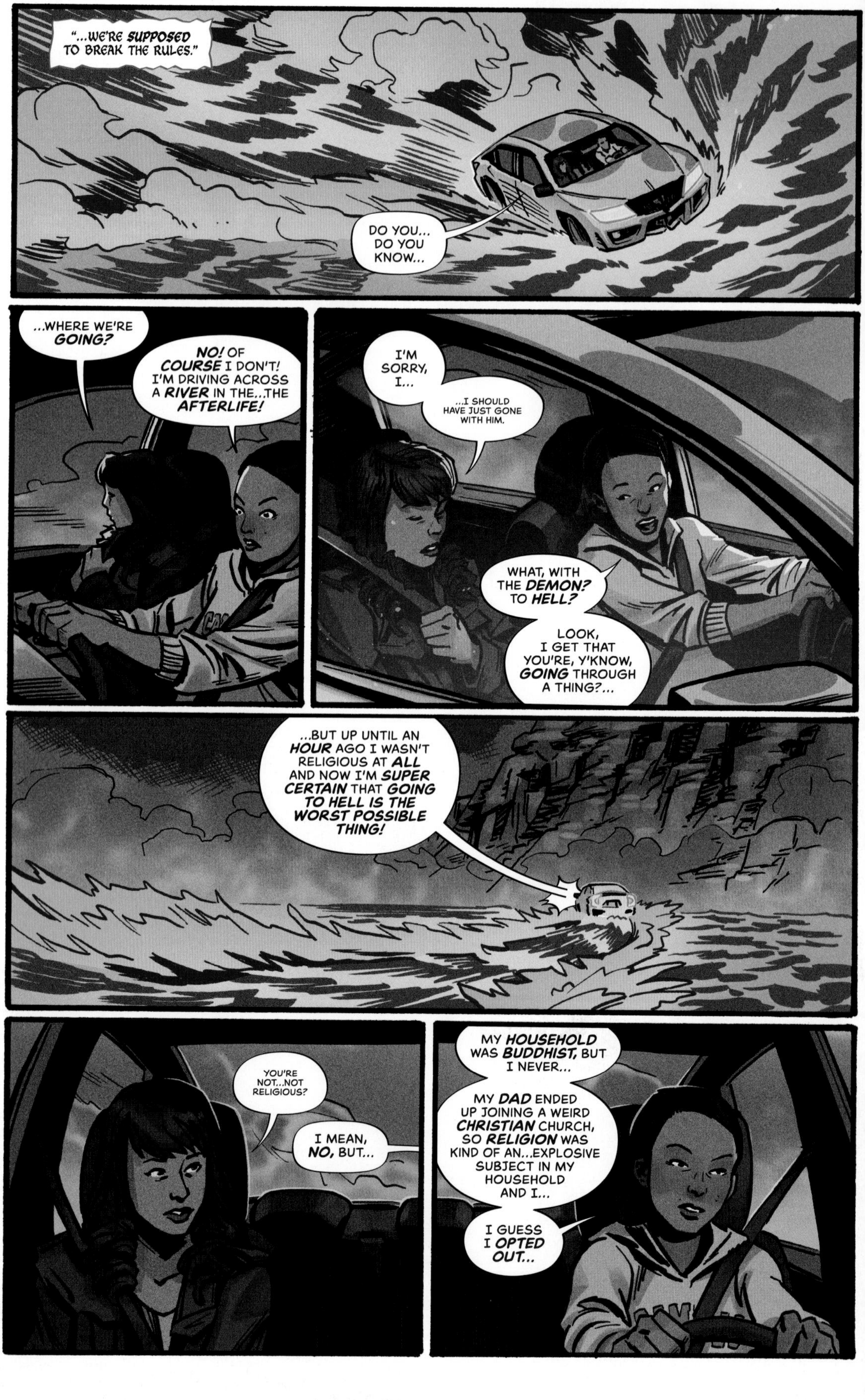
"...WE'RE SUPPOSED TO BREAK THE RULES."
DO YOU... DO YOU KNOW...
...WHERE WE'RE GOING?
NO! OF COURSE I DON'T! I'M DRIVING ACROSS A RIVER IN THE...THE AFTERLIFE!
I'M SORRY, I...
...I SHOULD HAVE JUST GONE WITH HIM.
WHAT, WITH THE DEMON? TO HELL?
LOOK, I GET THAT YOU'RE, Y'KNOW, GOING THROUGH A THING?...
...BUT UP UNTIL AN HOUR AGO I WASN'T RELIGIOUS AT ALL AND NOW I'M SUPER CERTAIN THAT GOING TO HELL IS THE WORST POSSIBLE THING!
YOU'RE NOT...NOT RELIGIOUS?
I MEAN, NO, BUT...
MY HOUSEHOLD WAS BUDDHIST, BUT I NEVER...
MY DAD ENDED UP JOINING A WEIRD CHRISTIAN CHURCH, SO RELIGION WAS KIND OF AN...EXPLOSIVE SUBJECT IN MY HOUSEHOLD AND I...
I GUESS I OPTED OUT...

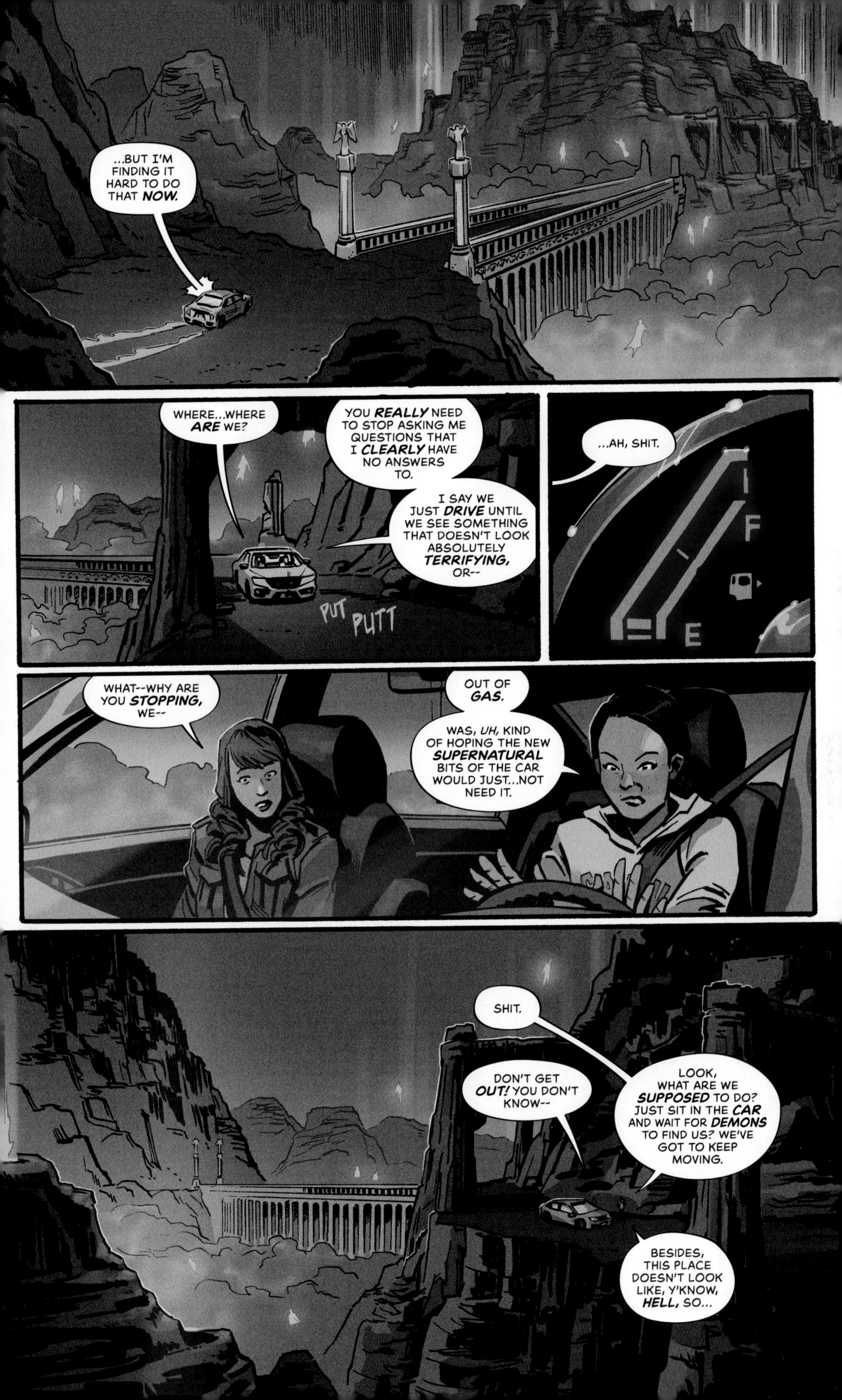
...BUT I'M FINDING IT HARD TO DO THAT NOW.
WHERE...WHERE ARE WE?
YOU REALLY NEED TO STOP ASKING ME QUESTIONS THAT I CLEARLY HAVE NO ANSWERS TO.
I SAY WE JUST DRIVE UNTIL WE SEE SOMETHING THAT DOESN'T LOOK ABSOLUTELY TERRIFYING, OR--
PUT PUTT
...AH, SHIT.
F
E
WHAT--WHY ARE YOU STOPPING, WE--
OUT OF GAS.
WAS, UH, KIND OF HOPING THE NEW SUPERNATURAL BITS OF THE CAR WOULD JUST...NOT NEED IT.
SHIT.
DON'T GET OUT! YOU DON'T KNOW--
LOOK, WHAT ARE WE SUPPOSED TO DO? JUST SIT IN THE CAR AND WAIT FOR DEMONS TO FIND US? WE'VE GOT TO KEEP MOVING.
BESIDES, THIS PLACE DOESN'T LOOK LIKE, Y'KNOW, HELL, SO...

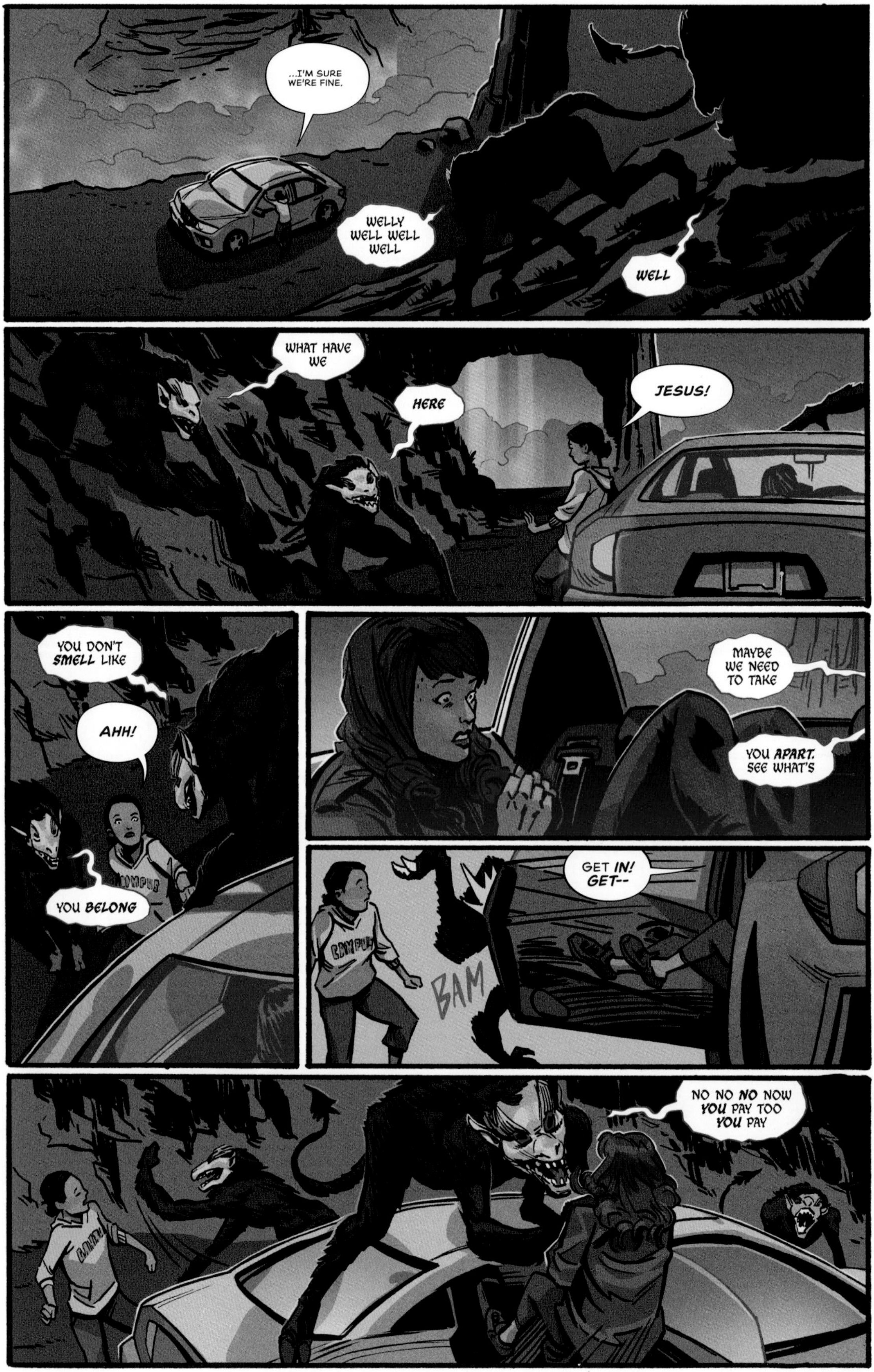
...I'M SURE WE'RE FINE.
WELLY WELL WELL WELL
WELL
WHAT HAVE WE
HERE
JESUS!
YOU DON'T SMELL LIKE
AHH!
YOU BELONG
MAYBE WE NEED TO TAKE
YOU APART. SEE WHAT'S
GET IN! GET--
BAM
NO NO NO NOW YOU PAY TOO YOU PAY

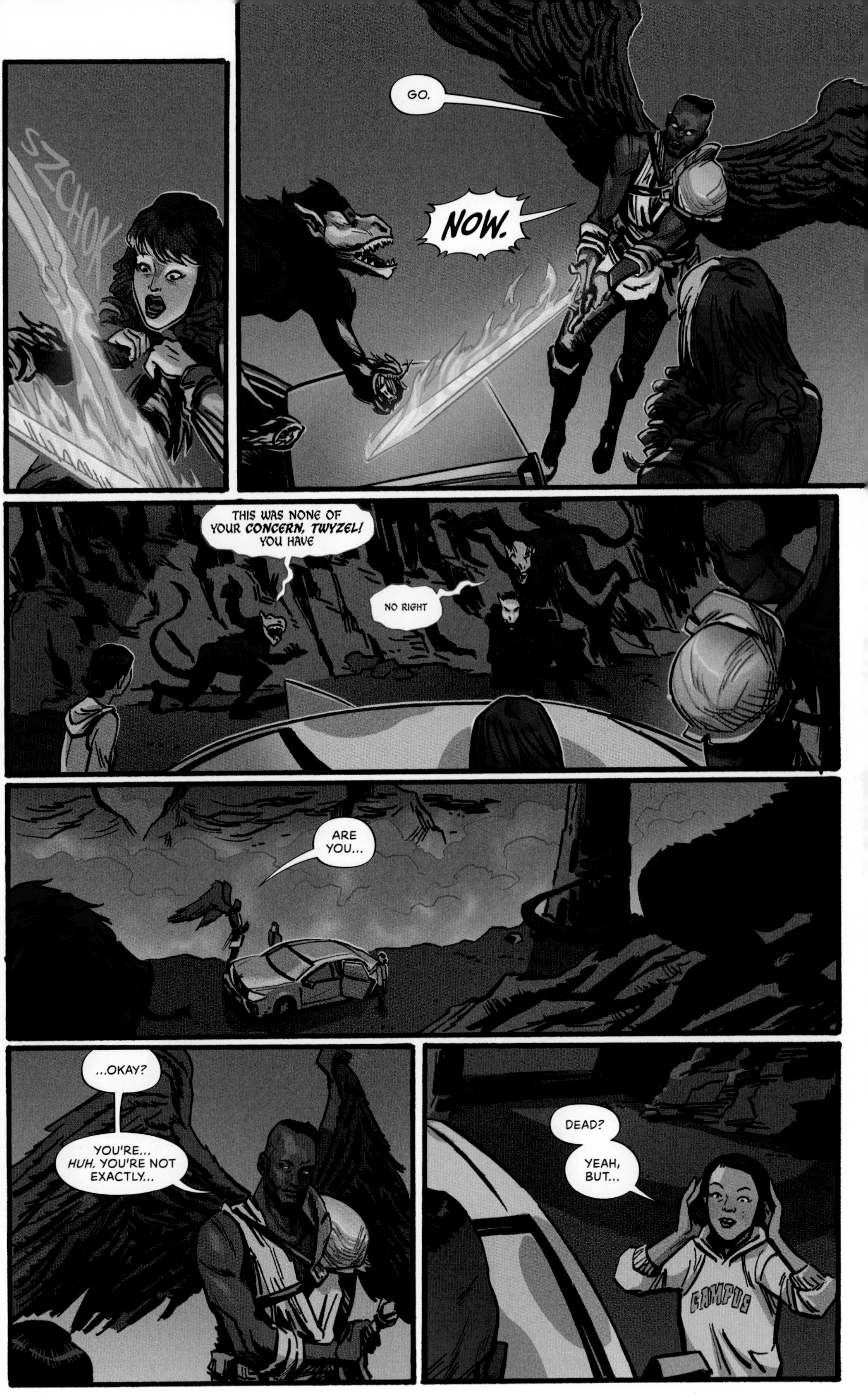

SZCHOK
GO.
NOW.
THIS WAS NONE OF YOUR CONCERN, TWYZEL! YOU HAVE
NO RIGHT
ARE YOU...
...OKAY?
YOU'RE... HUH. YOU'RE NOT EXACTLY...
DEAD?
YEAH, BUT...
CAMPUS

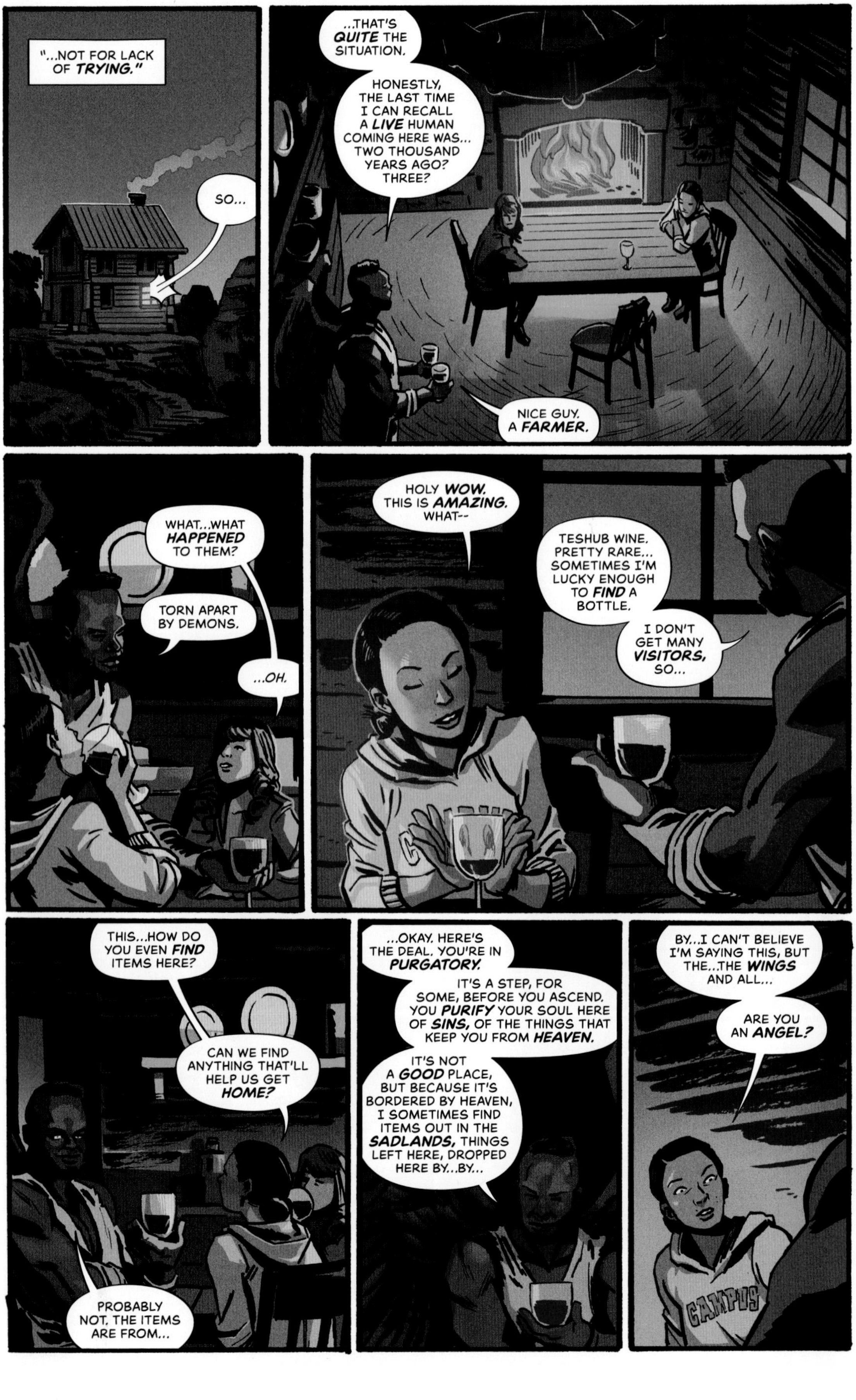

"...NOT FOR LACK OF TRYING."
SO...
...THAT'S QUITE THE SITUATION.
HONESTLY, THE LAST TIME I CAN RECALL A LIVE HUMAN COMING HERE WAS... TWO THOUSAND YEARS AGO? THREE?
NICE GUY. A FARMER.
WHAT...WHAT HAPPENED TO THEM?
TORN APART BY DEMONS.
...OH.
HOLY WOW. THIS IS AMAZING. WHAT--
TESHUB WINE. PRETTY RARE... SOMETIMES I'M LUCKY ENOUGH TO FIND A BOTTLE.
I DON'T GET MANY VISITORS, SO...
THIS...HOW DO YOU EVEN FIND ITEMS HERE?
CAN WE FIND ANYTHING THAT'LL HELP US GET HOME?
PROBABLY NOT. THE ITEMS ARE FROM...
...OKAY. HERE'S THE DEAL. YOU'RE IN PURGATORY.
IT'S A STEP, FOR SOME, BEFORE YOU ASCEND. YOU PURIFY YOUR SOUL HERE OF SINS, OF THE THINGS THAT KEEP YOU FROM HEAVEN.
IT'S NOT A GOOD PLACE, BUT BECAUSE IT'S BORDERED BY HEAVEN, I SOMETIMES FIND ITEMS OUT IN THE SADLANDS, THINGS LEFT HERE, DROPPED HERE BY...BY...
BY...I CAN'T BELIEVE I'M SAYING THIS, BUT THE...THE WINGS AND ALL...
ARE YOU AN ANGEL?
CAMPUS

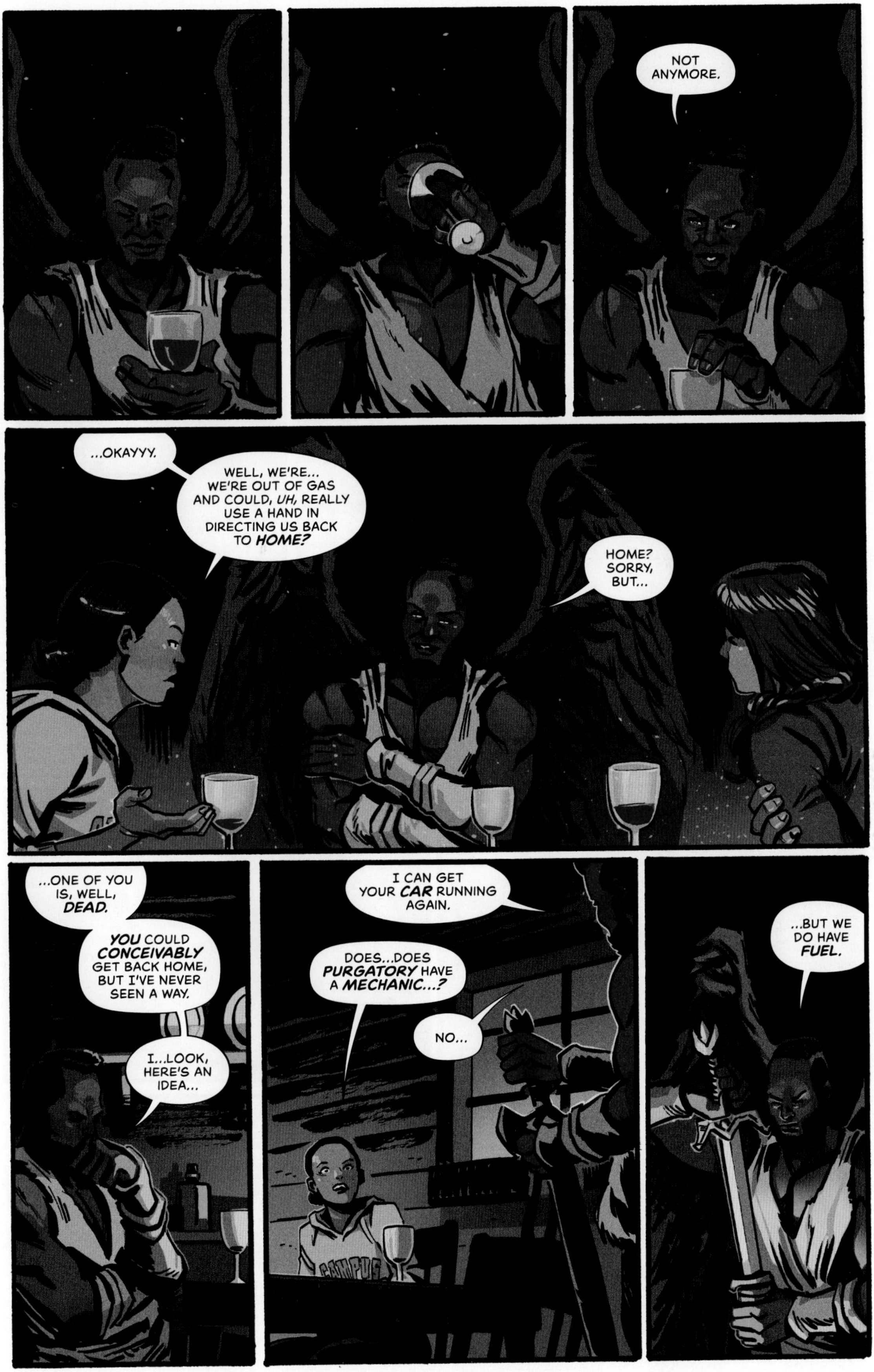
NOT ANYMORE.
...OKAYYY.
WELL, WE'RE... WE'RE OUT OF GAS AND COULD, *UH,* REALLY USE A HAND IN DIRECTING US BACK TO ***HOME?***
HOME? SORRY, BUT...
...ONE OF YOU IS, WELL, ***DEAD.***
YOU COULD ***CONCEIVABLY*** GET BACK HOME, BUT I'VE NEVER SEEN A WAY.
I...LOOK, HERE'S AN IDEA...
I CAN GET YOUR ***CAR*** RUNNING AGAIN.
DOES...DOES ***PURGATORY*** HAVE A ***MECHANIC...?***
NO...
...BUT WE DO HAVE ***FUEL.***

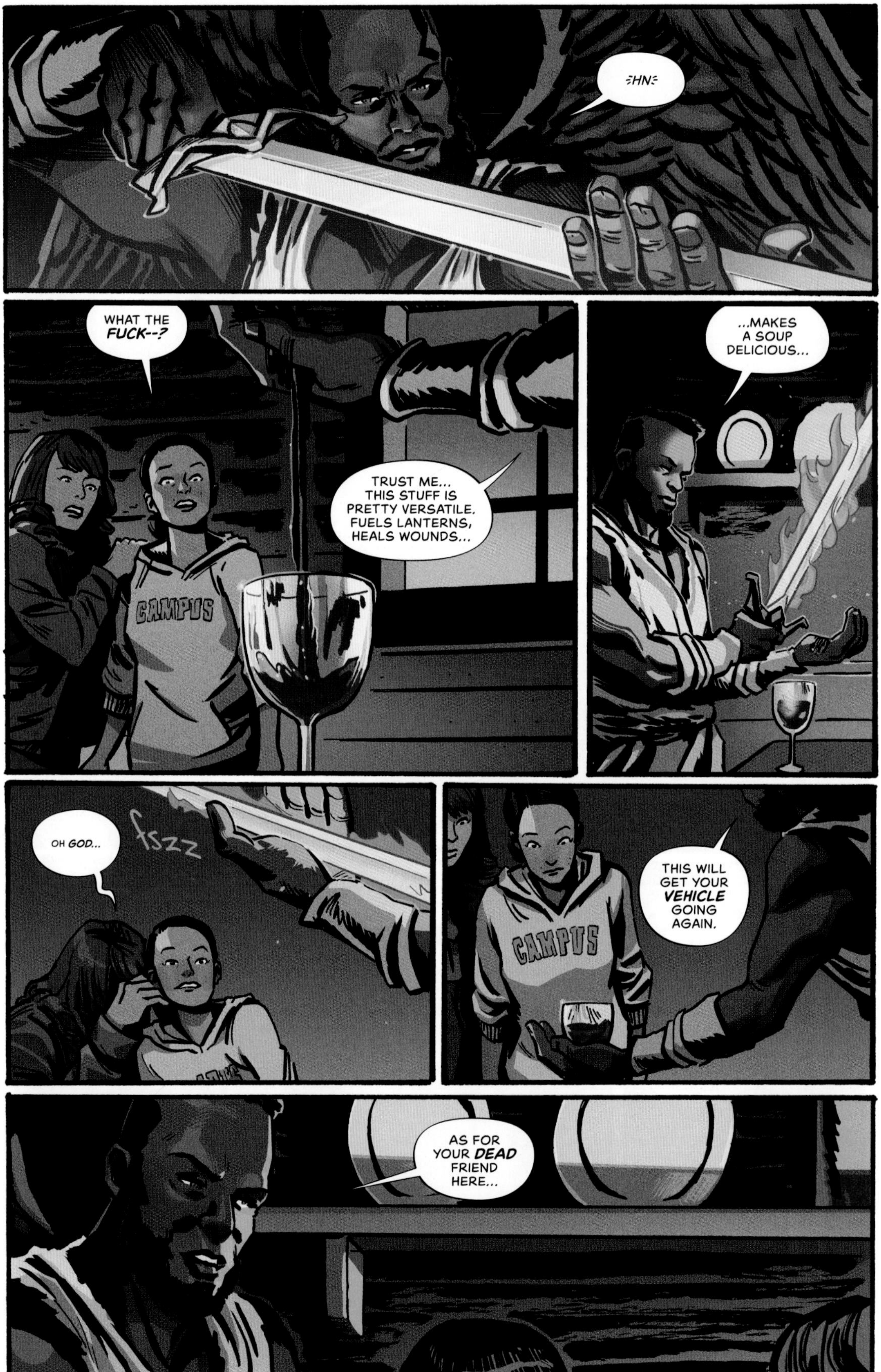
HN
WHAT THE FUCK--?
TRUST ME... THIS STUFF IS PRETTY VERSATILE. FUELS LANTERNS, HEALS WOUNDS...
...MAKES A SOUP DELICIOUS...
CAMPUS
OH GOD...
fszz
THIS WILL GET YOUR VEHICLE GOING AGAIN.
CAMPUS
AS FOR YOUR DEAD FRIEND HERE...

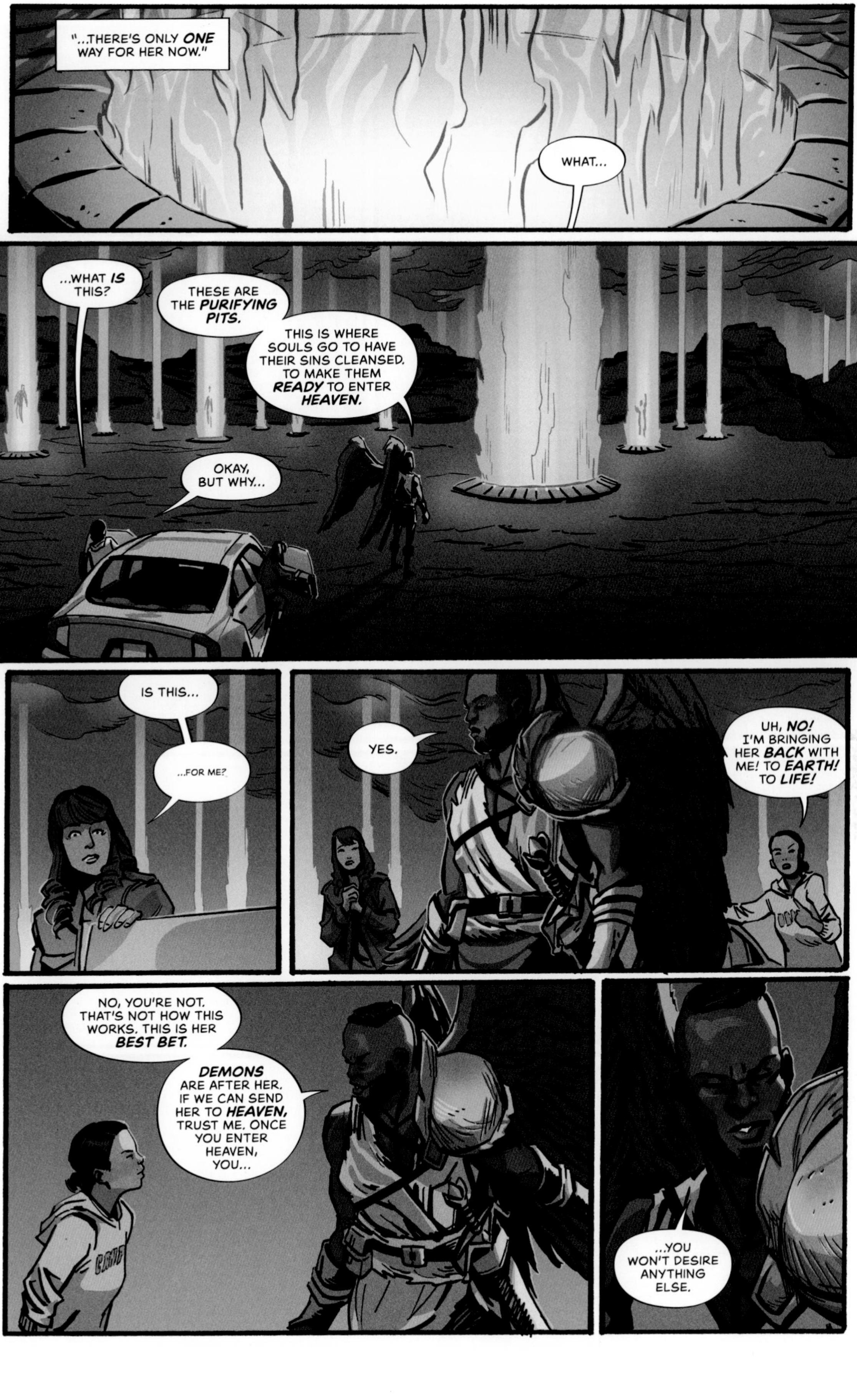
"...THERE'S ONLY ONE WAY FOR HER NOW."
WHAT...
...WHAT IS THIS?
THESE ARE THE PURIFYING PITS.
THIS IS WHERE SOULS GO TO HAVE THEIR SINS CLEANSED, TO MAKE THEM READY TO ENTER HEAVEN.
OKAY, BUT WHY...
IS THIS...
...FOR ME?
YES.
UH, NO! I'M BRINGING HER BACK WITH ME! TO EARTH! TO LIFE!
NO, YOU'RE NOT. THAT'S NOT HOW THIS WORKS. THIS IS HER BEST BET.
DEMONS ARE AFTER HER. IF WE CAN SEND HER TO HEAVEN, TRUST ME. ONCE YOU ENTER HEAVEN, YOU...
...YOU WON'T DESIRE ANYTHING ELSE.

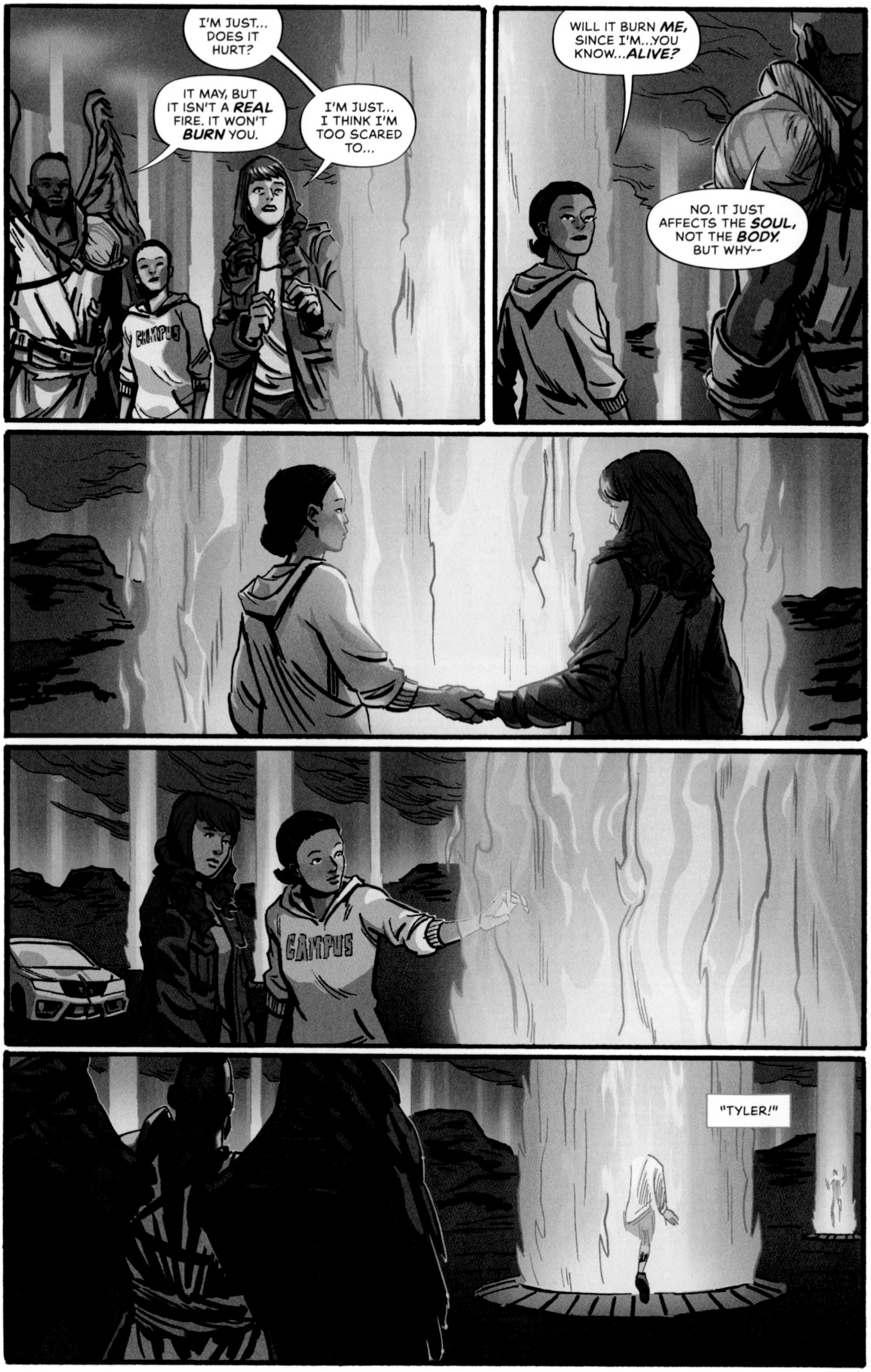
I'M JUST... DOES IT HURT?
IT MAY, BUT IT ISN'T A REAL FIRE. IT WON'T BURN YOU.
I'M JUST... I THINK I'M TOO SCARED TO...
CAMPUS
WILL IT BURN ME, SINCE I'M...YOU KNOW...ALIVE?
NO. IT JUST AFFECTS THE SOUL, NOT THE BODY. BUT WHY--
CAMPUS
"TYLER!"

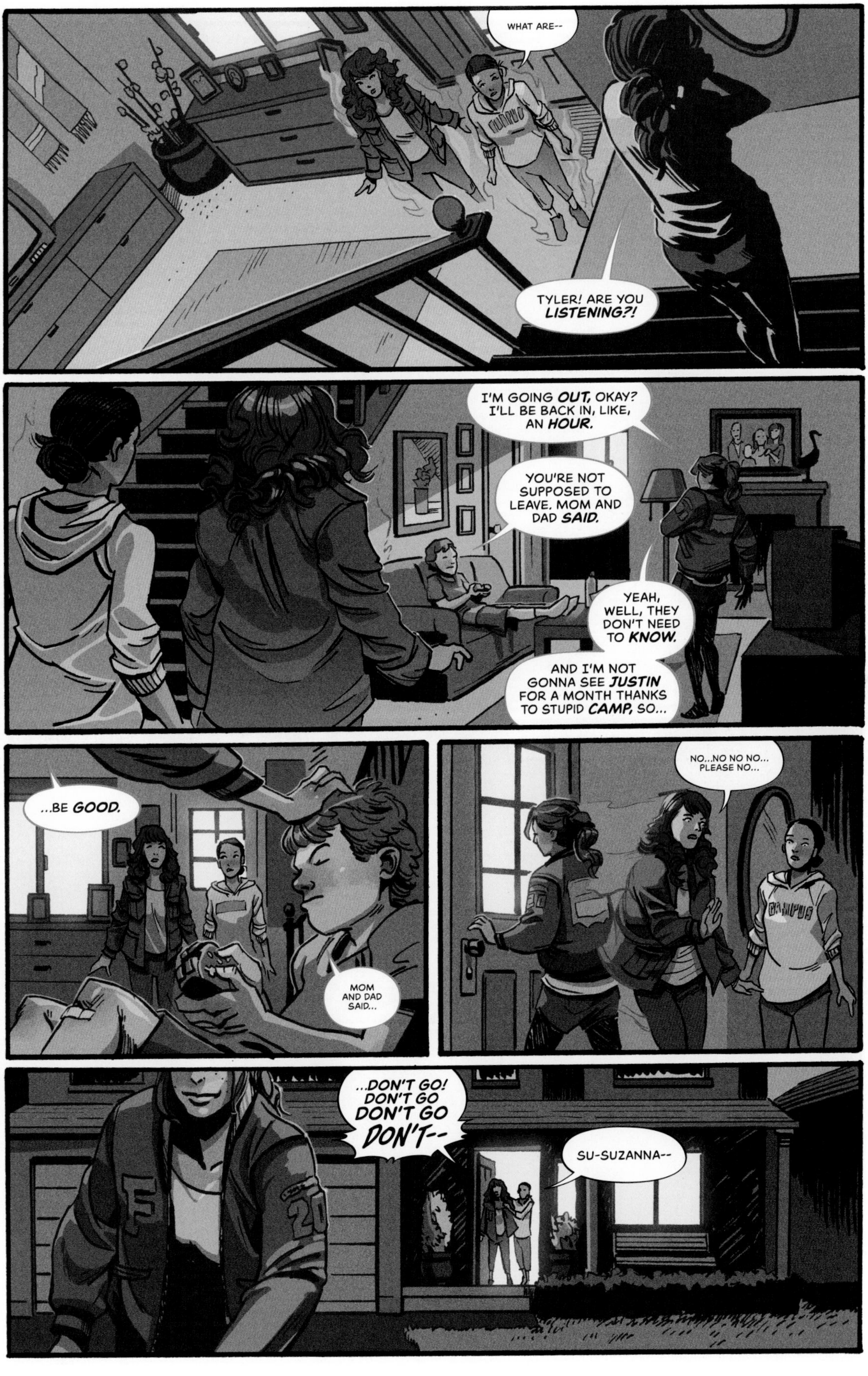
WHAT ARE--
TYLER! ARE YOU LISTENING?!
I'M GOING OUT, OKAY? I'LL BE BACK IN, LIKE, AN HOUR.
YOU'RE NOT SUPPOSED TO LEAVE. MOM AND DAD SAID.
YEAH, WELL, THEY DON'T NEED TO KNOW.
AND I'M NOT GONNA SEE JUSTIN FOR A MONTH THANKS TO STUPID CAMP, SO...
...BE GOOD.
MOM AND DAD SAID...
NO...NO NO NO... PLEASE NO...
...DON'T GO! DON'T GO DON'T GO DON'T--
SU-SUZANNA--

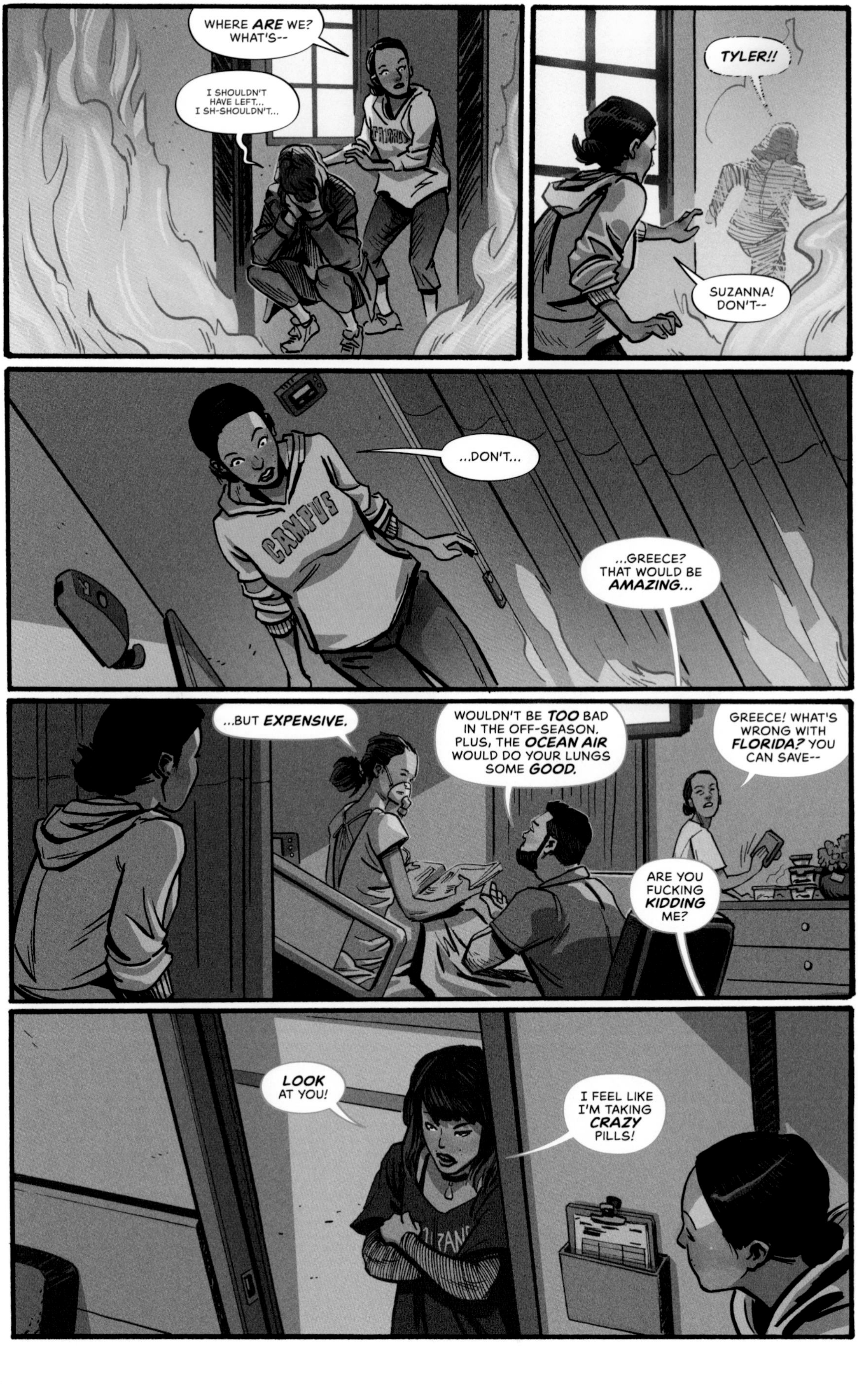
WHERE ARE WE? WHAT'S--
I SHOULDN'T HAVE LEFT... I SH-SHOULDN'T...
TYLER!!
SUZANNA! DON'T--
...DON'T...
...GREECE? THAT WOULD BE AMAZING...
...BUT EXPENSIVE.
WOULDN'T BE TOO BAD IN THE OFF-SEASON. PLUS, THE OCEAN AIR WOULD DO YOUR LUNGS SOME GOOD.
GREECE! WHAT'S WRONG WITH FLORIDA? YOU CAN SAVE--
ARE YOU FUCKING KIDDING ME?
LOOK AT YOU!
I FEEL LIKE I'M TAKING CRAZY PILLS!

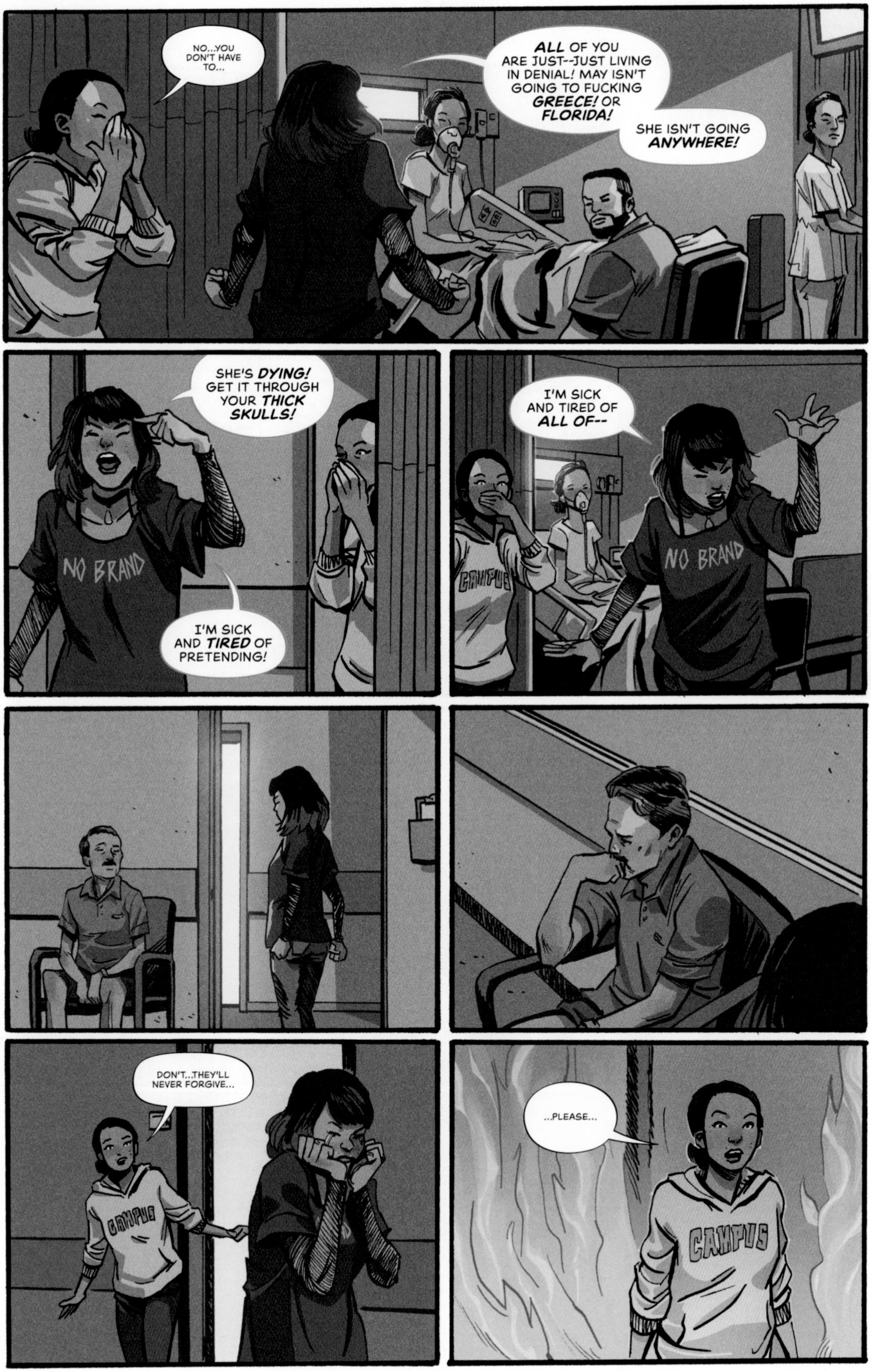
NO...YOU DON'T HAVE TO...
ALL OF YOU ARE JUST--JUST LIVING IN DENIAL! MAY ISN'T GOING TO FUCKING GREECE! OR FLORIDA!
SHE ISN'T GOING ANYWHERE!
SHE'S DYING! GET IT THROUGH YOUR THICK SKULLS!
I'M SICK AND TIRED OF PRETENDING!
NO BRAND
I'M SICK AND TIRED OF ALL OF--
CAMPUS
NO BRAND
DON'T...THEY'LL NEVER FORGIVE...
CAMPUS
...PLEASE...
CAMPUS

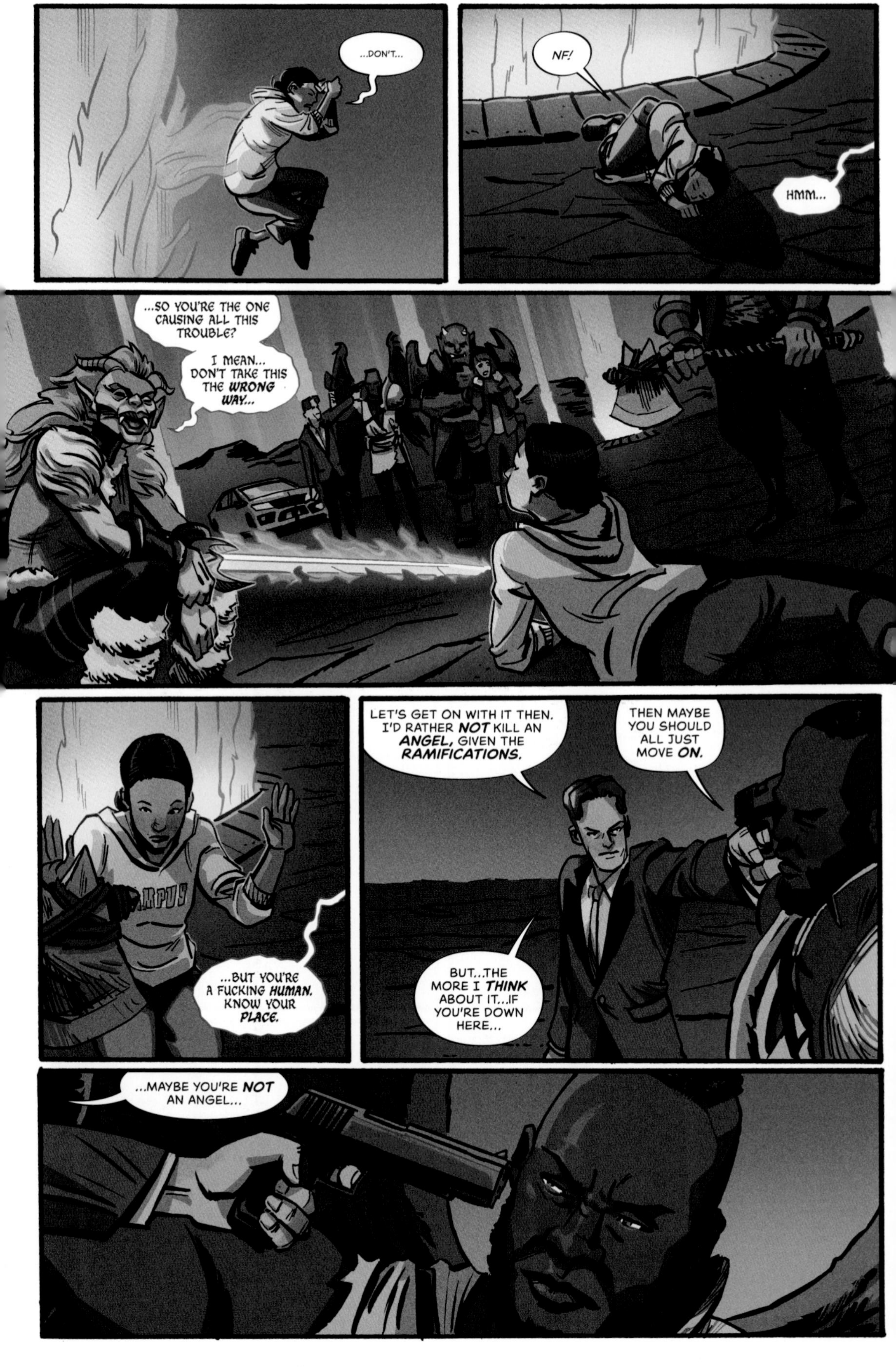
...DON'T...
NF!
HMM...
...SO YOU'RE THE ONE CAUSING ALL THIS TROUBLE?
I MEAN... DON'T TAKE THIS THE WRONG WAY...
...BUT YOU'RE A FUCKING HUMAN. KNOW YOUR PLACE.
LET'S GET ON WITH IT THEN. I'D RATHER NOT KILL AN ANGEL, GIVEN THE RAMIFICATIONS.
THEN MAYBE YOU SHOULD ALL JUST MOVE ON.
BUT...THE MORE I THINK ABOUT IT...IF YOU'RE DOWN HERE...
...MAYBE YOU'RE NOT AN ANGEL...

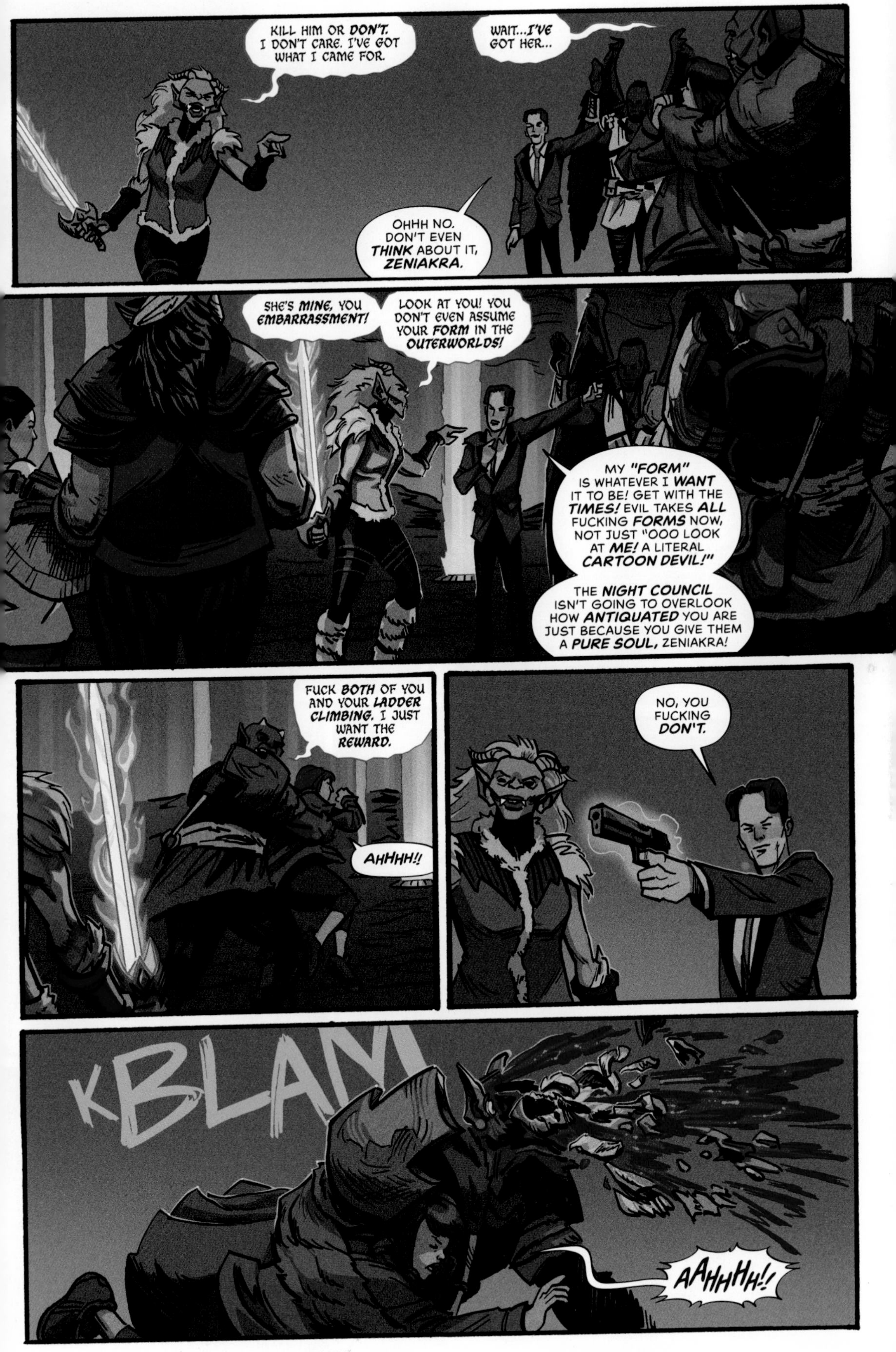
KILL HIM OR DON'T. I DON'T CARE. I'VE GOT WHAT I CAME FOR.
WAIT...I'VE GOT HER...
OHHH NO. DON'T EVEN THINK ABOUT IT, ZENIAKRA.
SHE'S MINE, YOU EMBARRASSMENT!
LOOK AT YOU! YOU DON'T EVEN ASSUME YOUR FORM IN THE OUTERWORLDS!
MY "FORM" IS WHATEVER I WANT IT TO BE! GET WITH THE TIMES! EVIL TAKES ALL FUCKING FORMS NOW, NOT JUST "OOO LOOK AT ME! A LITERAL CARTOON DEVIL!"
THE NIGHT COUNCIL ISN'T GOING TO OVERLOOK HOW ANTIQUATED YOU ARE JUST BECAUSE YOU GIVE THEM A PURE SOUL, ZENIAKRA!
FUCK BOTH OF YOU AND YOUR LADDER CLIMBING. I JUST WANT THE REWARD.
AHHHH!!
NO, YOU FUCKING DON'T.
KBLAM
AAHHHH!!

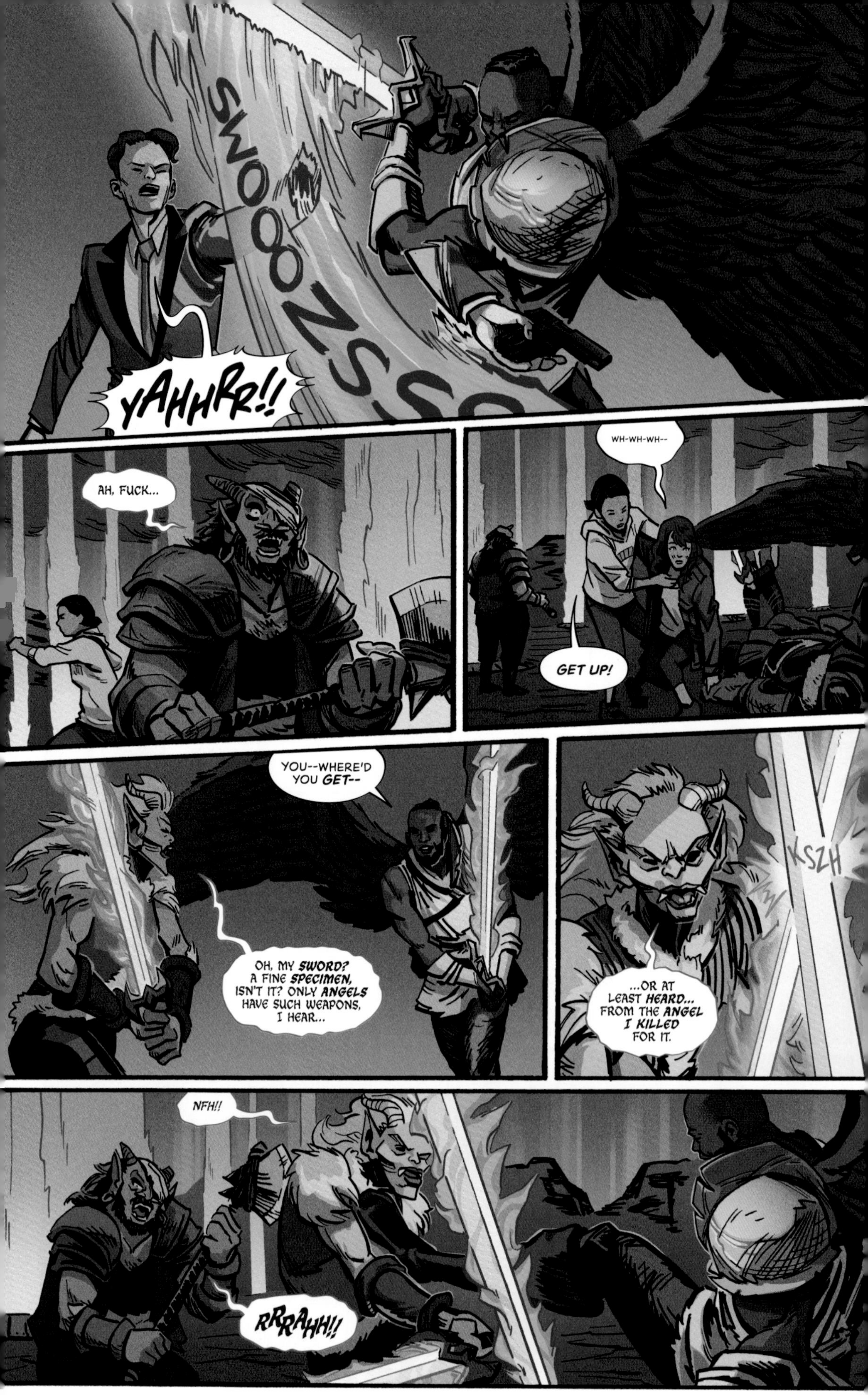
SWOOOSSSH
YAHHRR!!
AH, FUCK...
WH-WH-WH--
GET UP!
YOU--WHERE'D YOU GET--
OH, MY SWORD? A FINE SPECIMEN, ISN'T IT? ONLY ANGELS HAVE SUCH WEAPONS, I HEAR...
KSZH
...OR AT LEAST HEARD... FROM THE ANGEL I KILLED FOR IT.
NFH!!
RRRAHH!!

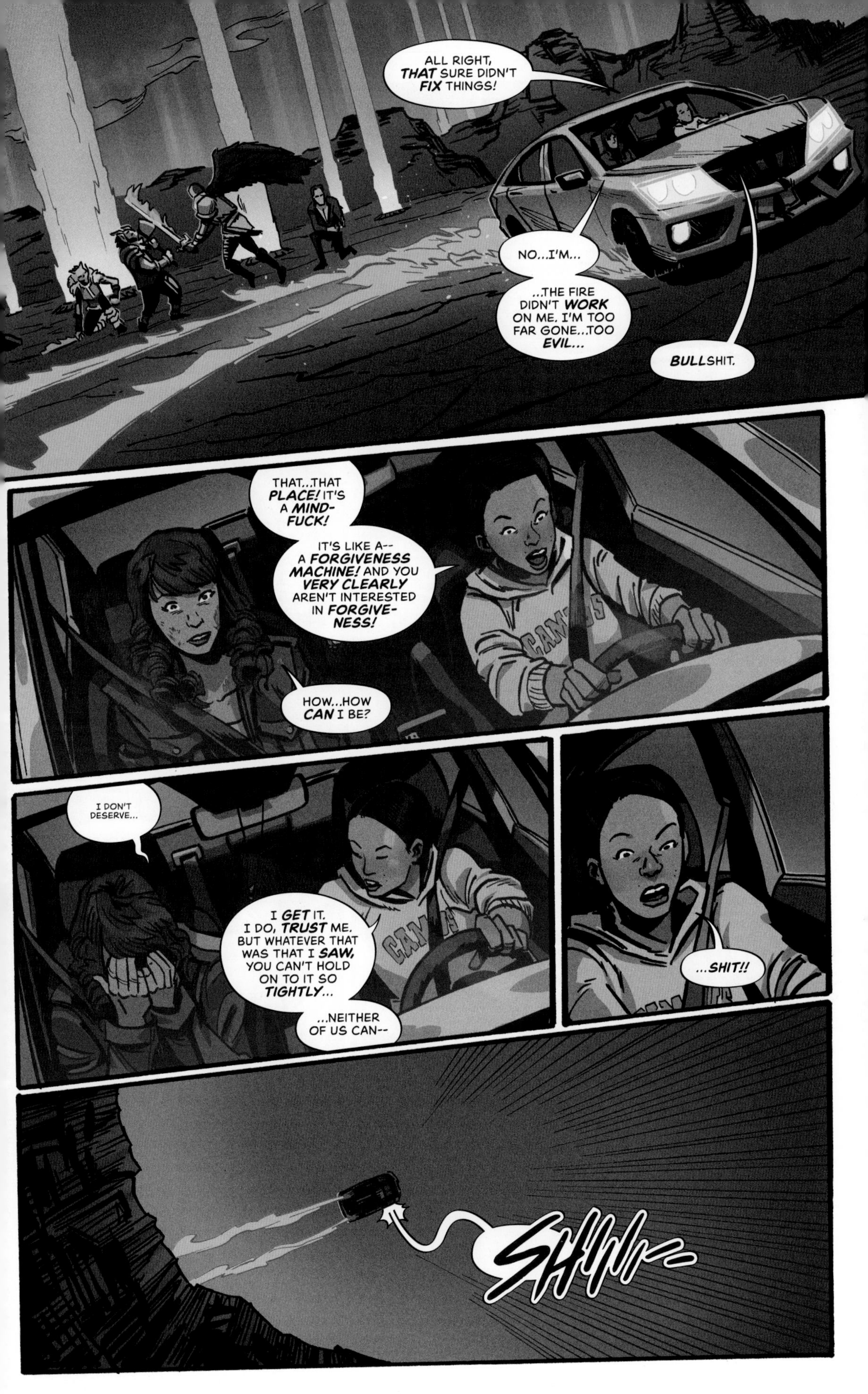

ALL RIGHT, THAT SURE DIDN'T FIX THINGS!
NO...I'M...
...THE FIRE DIDN'T WORK ON ME. I'M TOO FAR GONE...TOO EVIL...
BULLSHIT.
THAT...THAT PLACE! IT'S A MIND-FUCK!
IT'S LIKE A-- A FORGIVENESS MACHINE! AND YOU VERY CLEARLY AREN'T INTERESTED IN FORGIVE-NESS!
HOW...HOW CAN I BE?
I DON'T DESERVE...
I GET IT. I DO, TRUST ME. BUT WHATEVER THAT WAS THAT I SAW, YOU CAN'T HOLD ON TO IT SO TIGHTLY...
...NEITHER OF US CAN--
...SHIT!!
SHHH

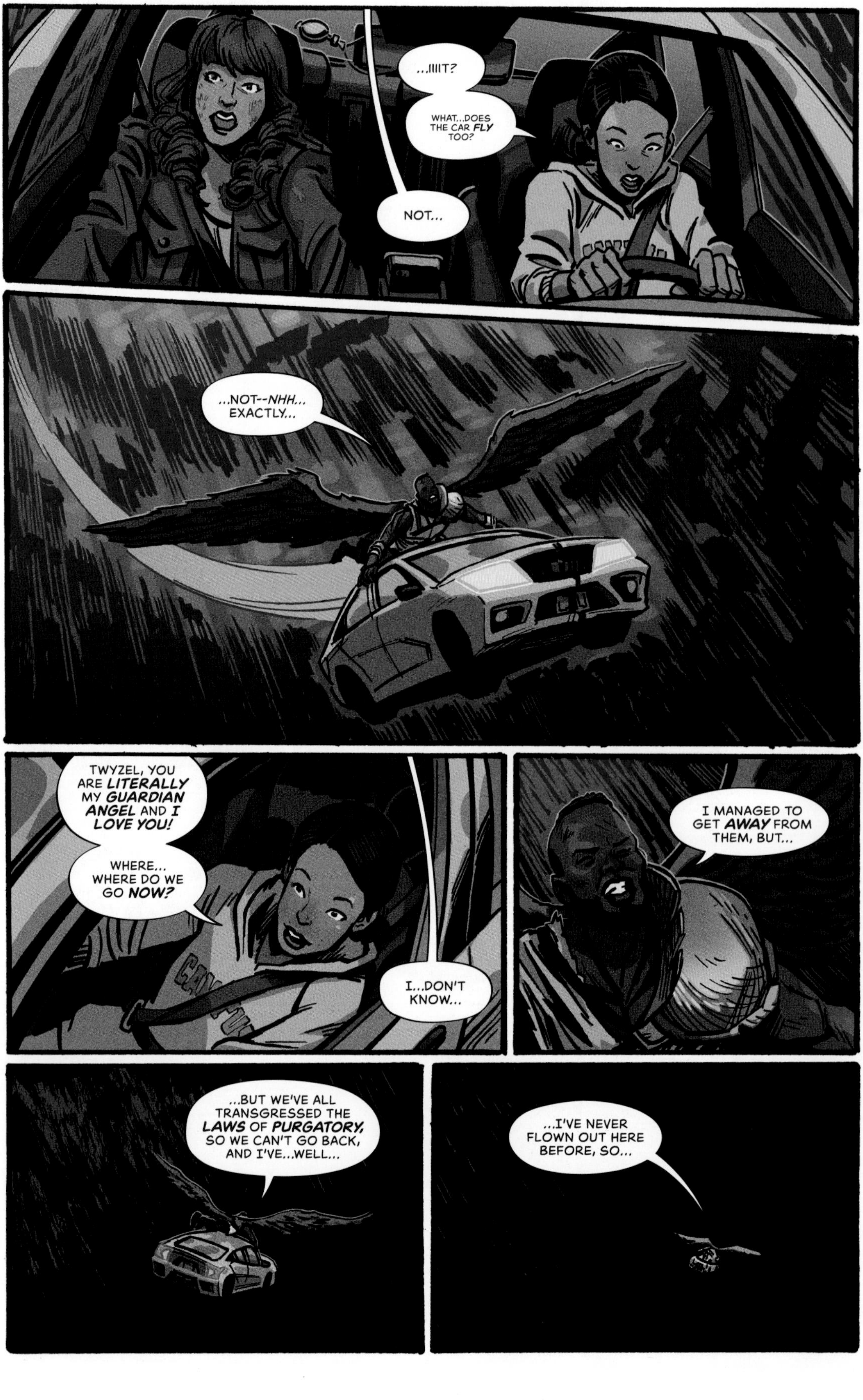
...IIIIT?
WHAT...DOES THE CAR FLY TOO?
NOT...
...NOT--NHH... EXACTLY...
TWYZEL, YOU ARE LITERALLY MY GUARDIAN ANGEL AND I LOVE YOU!
WHERE... WHERE DO WE GO NOW?
I...DON'T KNOW...
I MANAGED TO GET AWAY FROM THEM, BUT...
...BUT WE'VE ALL TRANSGRESSED THE LAWS OF PURGATORY, SO WE CAN'T GO BACK, AND I'VE...WELL...
...I'VE NEVER FLOWN OUT HERE BEFORE, SO...

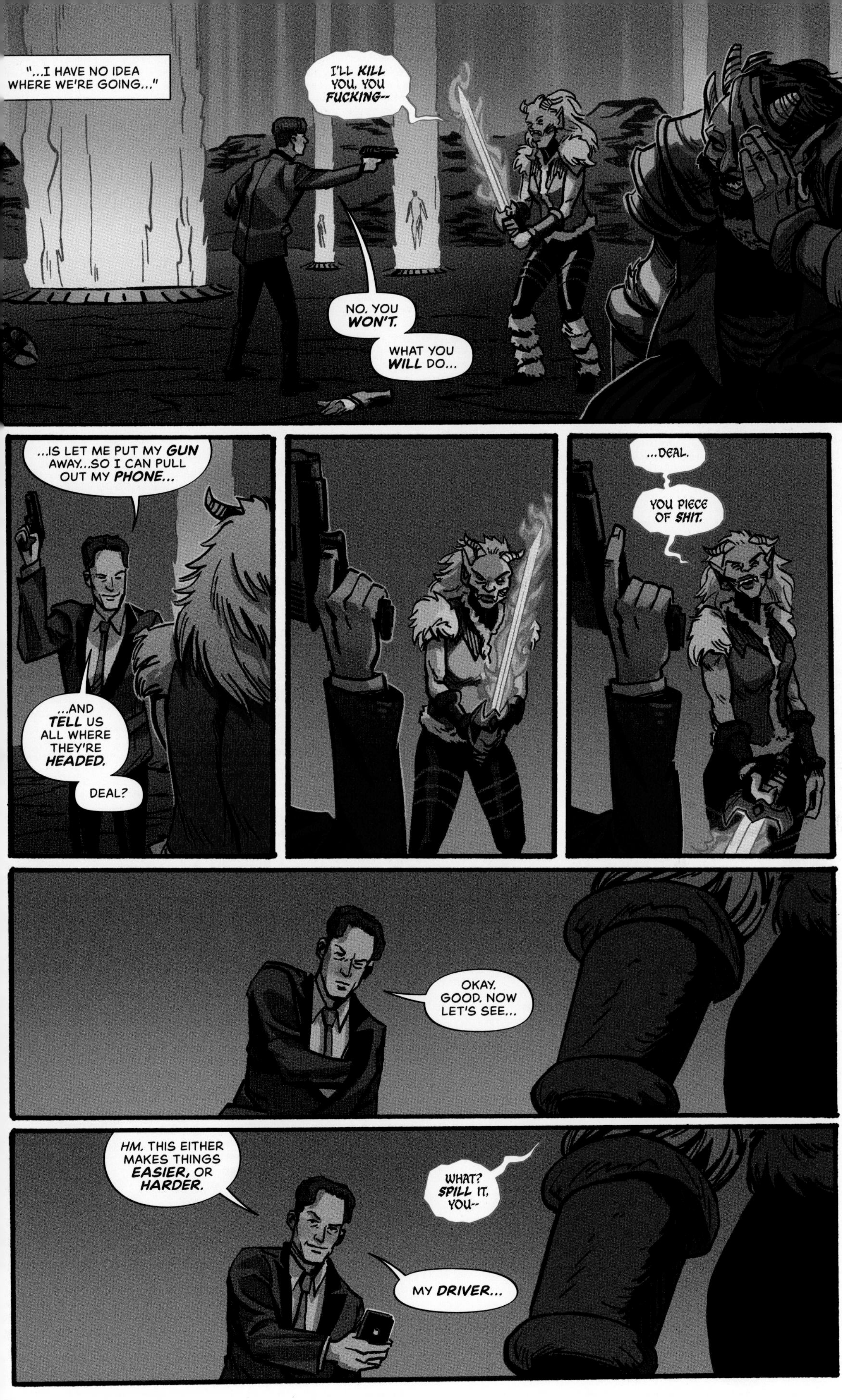
"...I HAVE NO IDEA WHERE WE'RE GOING..."
I'LL KILL YOU, YOU FUCKING--
NO, YOU WON'T.
WHAT YOU WILL DO...
...IS LET ME PUT MY GUN AWAY...SO I CAN PULL OUT MY PHONE...
...AND TELL US ALL WHERE THEY'RE HEADED.
DEAL?
...DEAL.
YOU PIECE OF SHIT.
OKAY. GOOD. NOW LET'S SEE...
HM. THIS EITHER MAKES THINGS EASIER, OR HARDER.
WHAT? SPILL IT, YOU--
MY DRIVER...

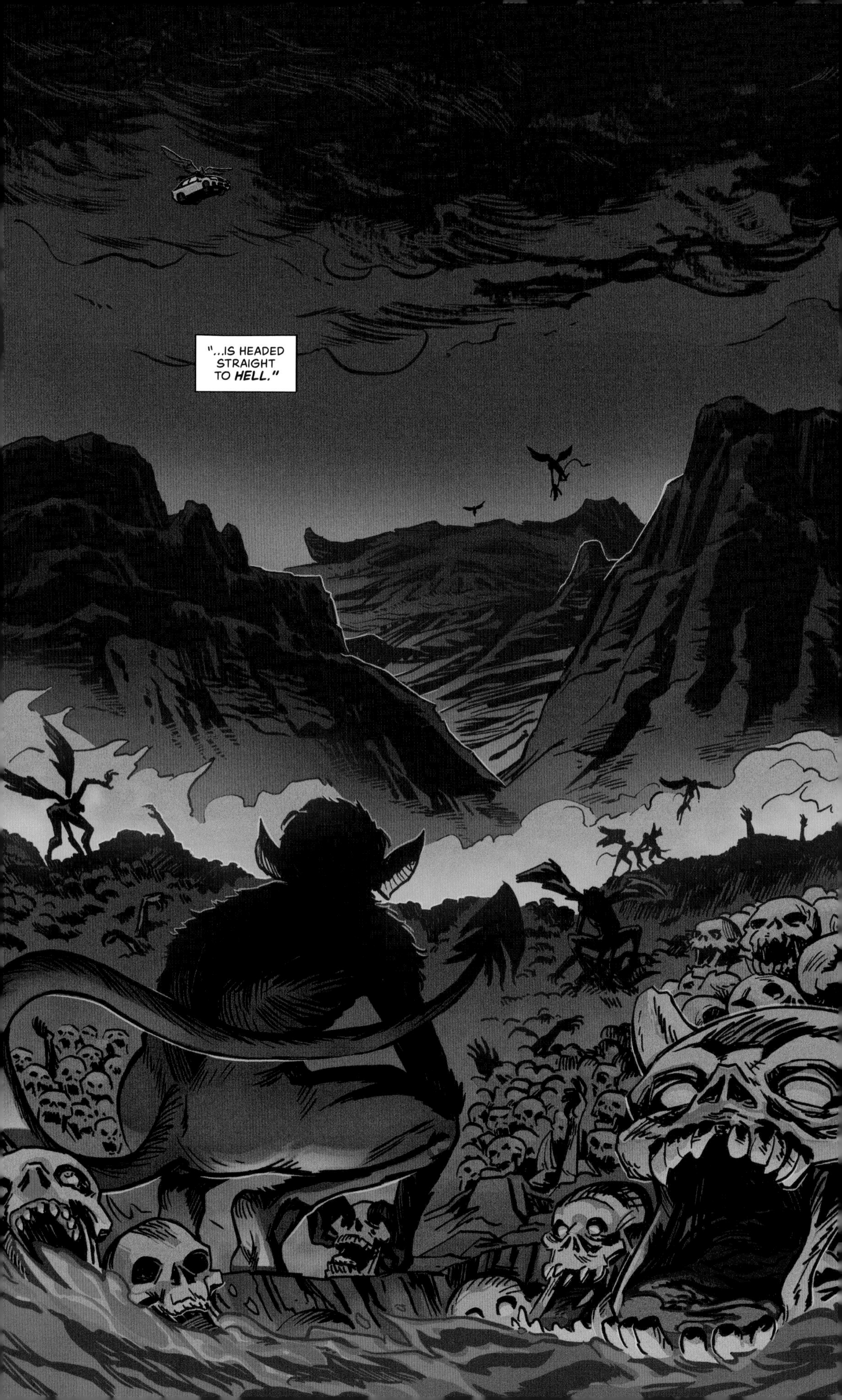
"...IS HEADED
STRAIGHT
TO *HELL.*"

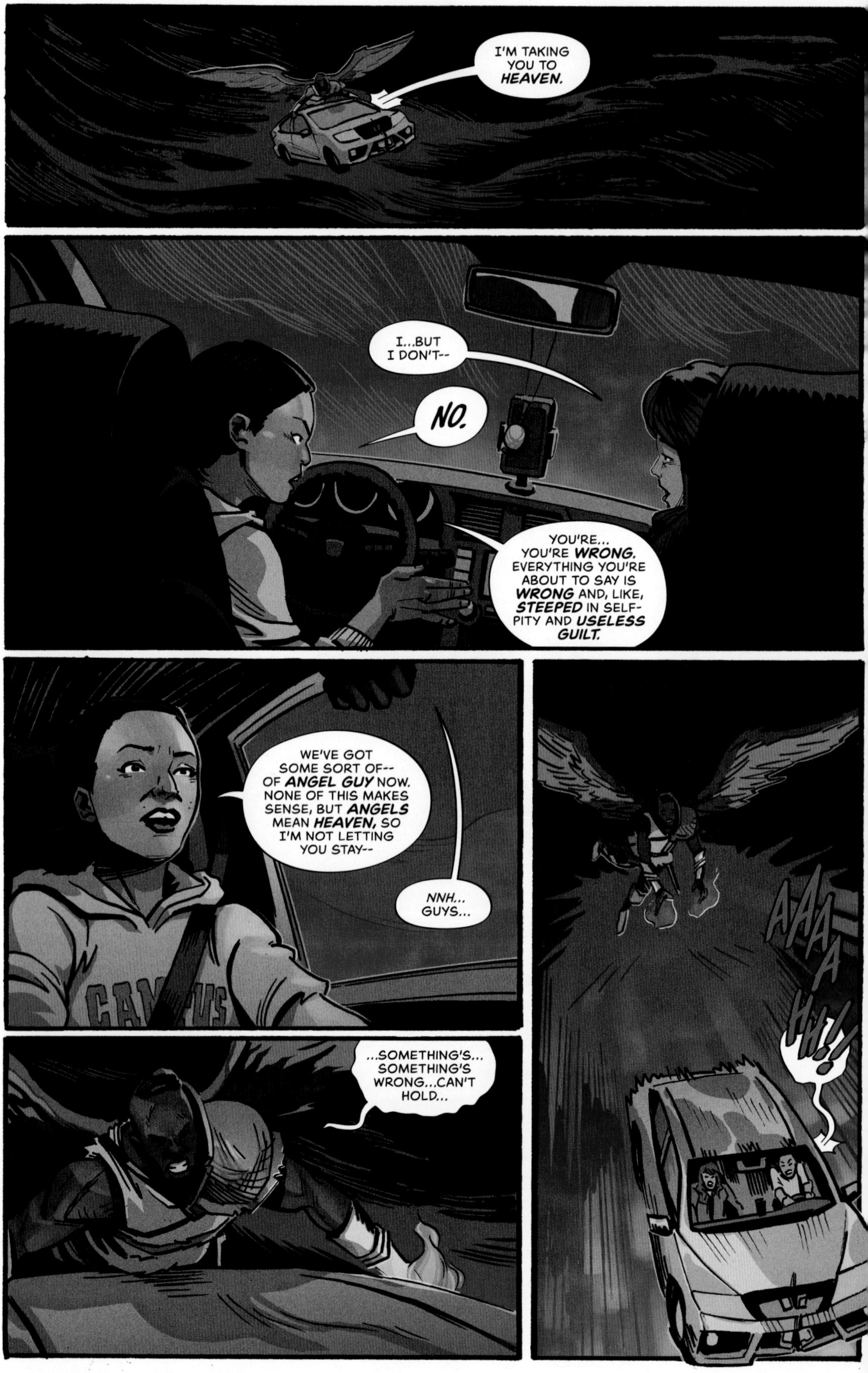
I'M TAKING YOU TO HEAVEN.
I...BUT I DON'T--
NO.
YOU'RE... YOU'RE WRONG. EVERYTHING YOU'RE ABOUT TO SAY IS WRONG AND, LIKE, STEEPED IN SELF-PITY AND USELESS GUILT.
WE'VE GOT SOME SORT OF-- OF ANGEL GUY NOW. NONE OF THIS MAKES SENSE, BUT ANGELS MEAN HEAVEN, SO I'M NOT LETTING YOU STAY--
NNH... GUYS...
...SOMETHING'S... SOMETHING'S WRONG...CAN'T HOLD...
AAAAAHH!!

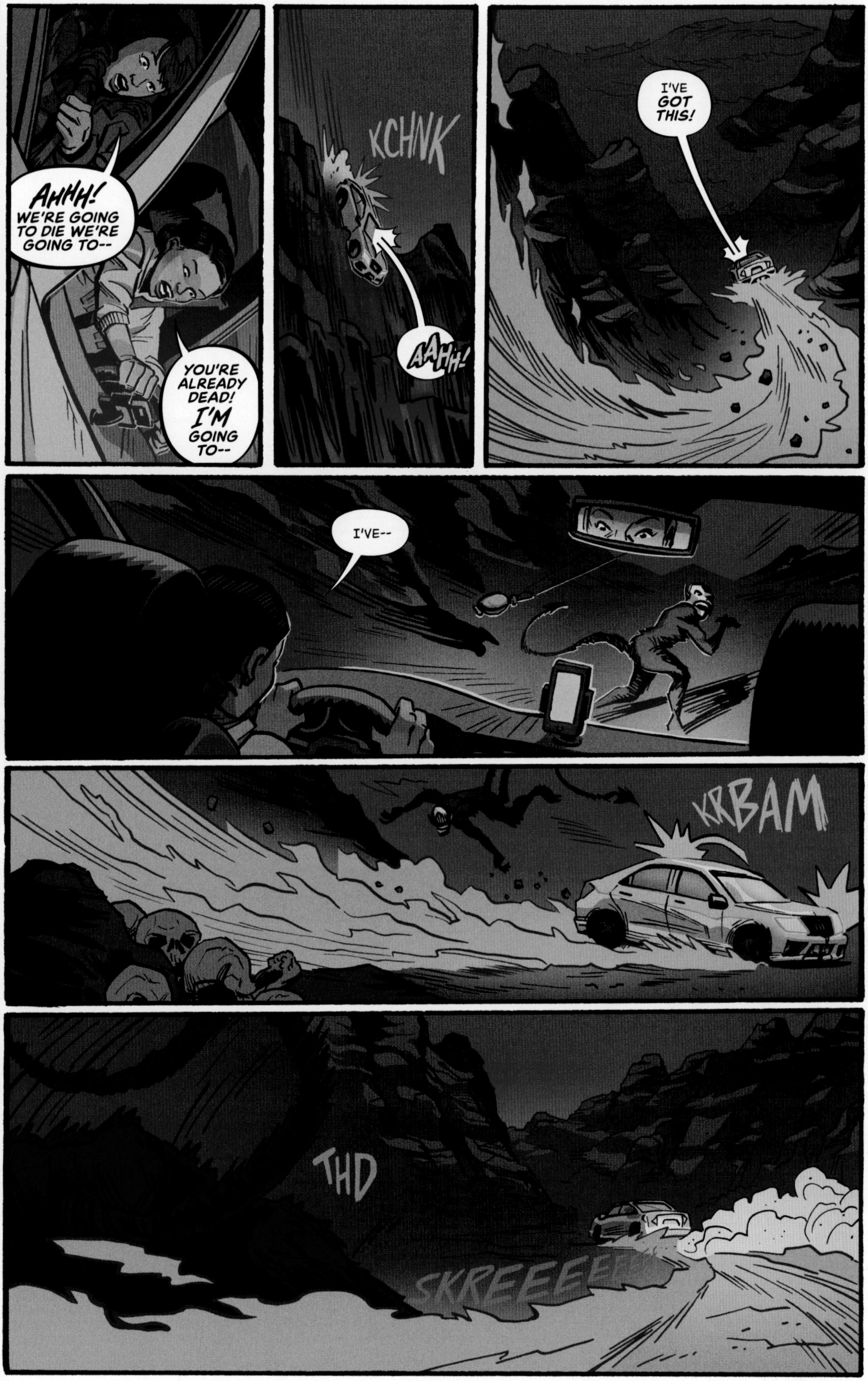
AHHH! WE'RE GOING TO DIE WE'RE GOING TO--
YOU'RE ALREADY DEAD! I'M GOING TO--
KCHNK
AAHH!
I'VE GOT THIS!
I'VE--
KRBAM
THD
SKREEEEE

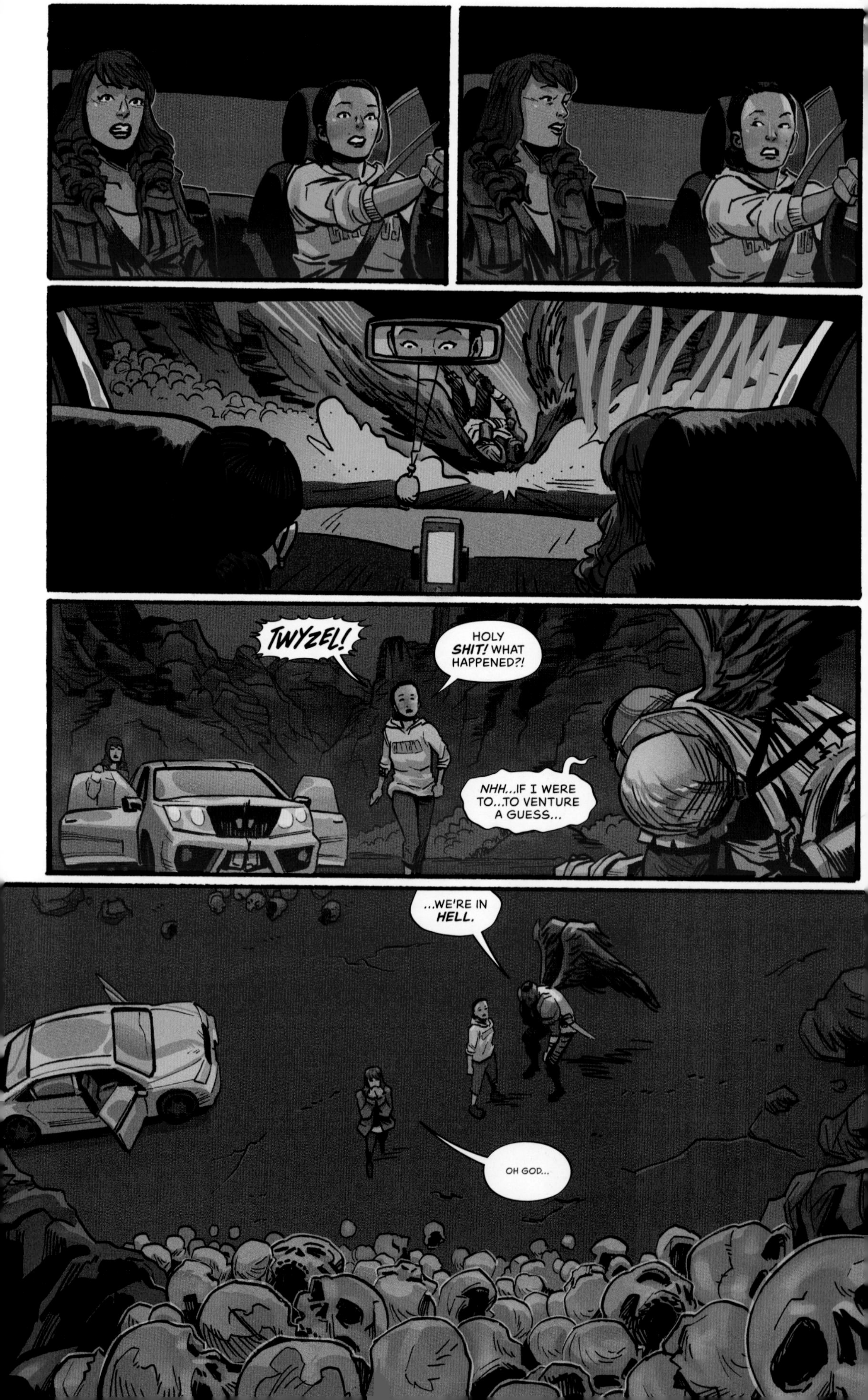

TWYZEL!
HOLY SHIT! WHAT HAPPENED?!
NHH...IF I WERE TO...TO VENTURE A GUESS...
...WE'RE IN HELL.
OH GOD...

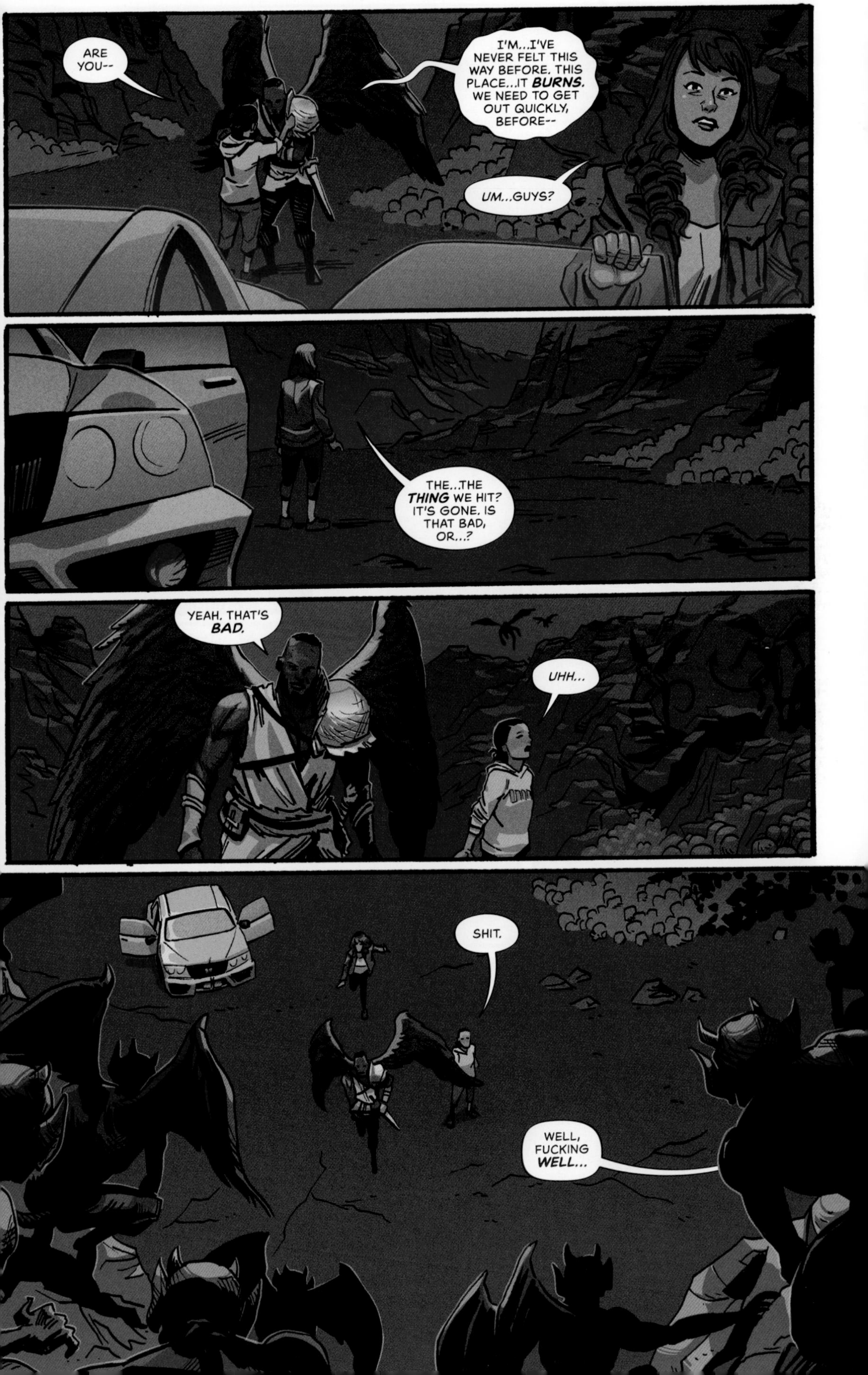
ARE YOU--
I'M...I'VE NEVER FELT THIS WAY BEFORE. THIS PLACE...IT BURNS. WE NEED TO GET OUT QUICKLY, BEFORE--
UM...GUYS?
THE...THE THING WE HIT? IT'S GONE. IS THAT BAD, OR...?
YEAH. THAT'S BAD.
UHH...
SHIT.
WELL, FUCKING WELL...

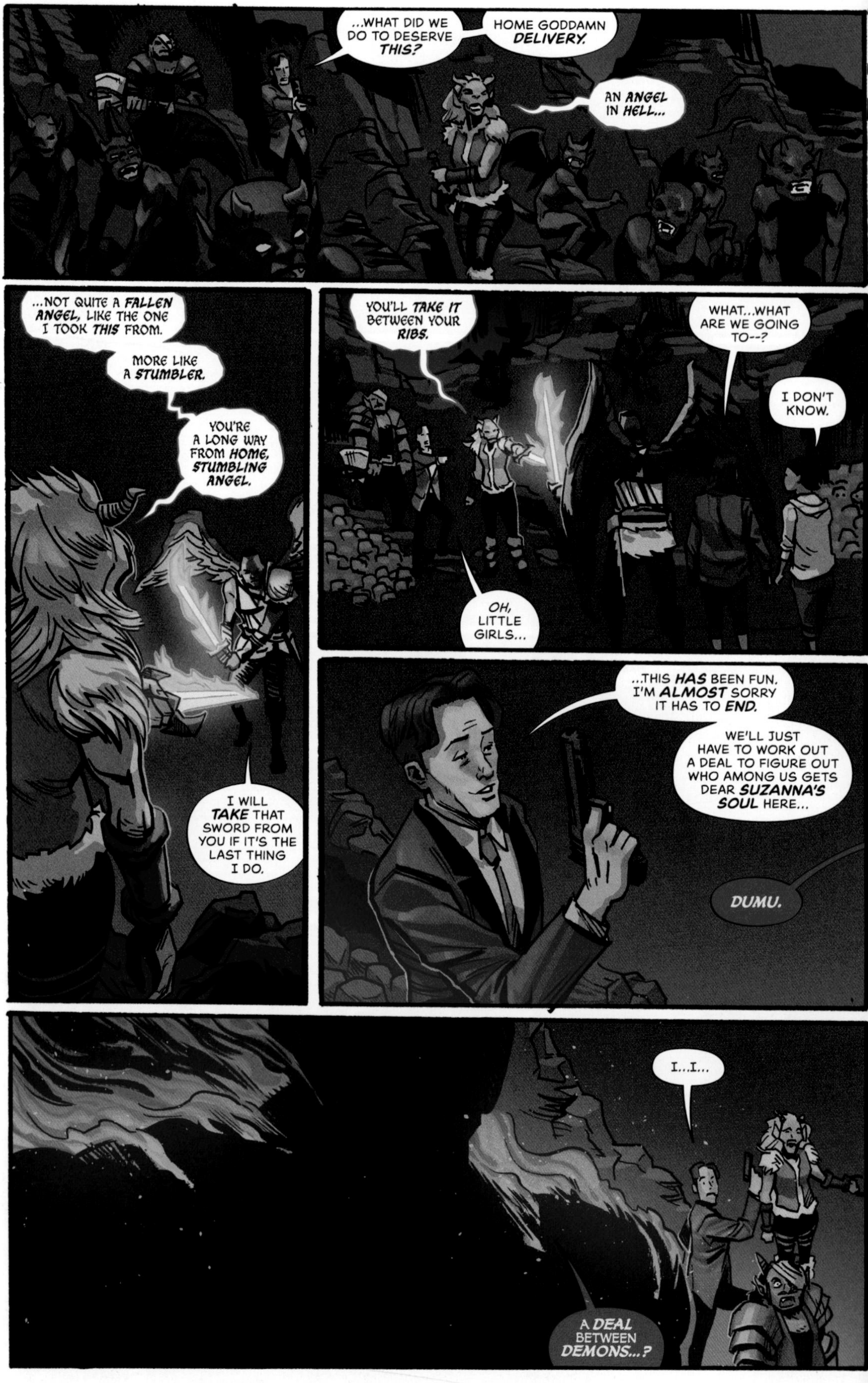
...WHAT DID WE DO TO DESERVE THIS?
HOME GODDAMN DELIVERY.
AN ANGEL IN HELL...
...NOT QUITE A FALLEN ANGEL, LIKE THE ONE I TOOK THIS FROM.
MORE LIKE A STUMBLER.
YOU'RE A LONG WAY FROM HOME, STUMBLING ANGEL.
I WILL TAKE THAT SWORD FROM YOU IF IT'S THE LAST THING I DO.
YOU'LL TAKE IT BETWEEN YOUR RIBS.
WHAT...WHAT ARE WE GOING TO--?
I DON'T KNOW.
OH, LITTLE GIRLS...
...THIS HAS BEEN FUN. I'M ALMOST SORRY IT HAS TO END.
WE'LL JUST HAVE TO WORK OUT A DEAL TO FIGURE OUT WHO AMONG US GETS DEAR SUZANNA'S SOUL HERE...
DUMU.
I...I...
A DEAL BETWEEN DEMONS...?

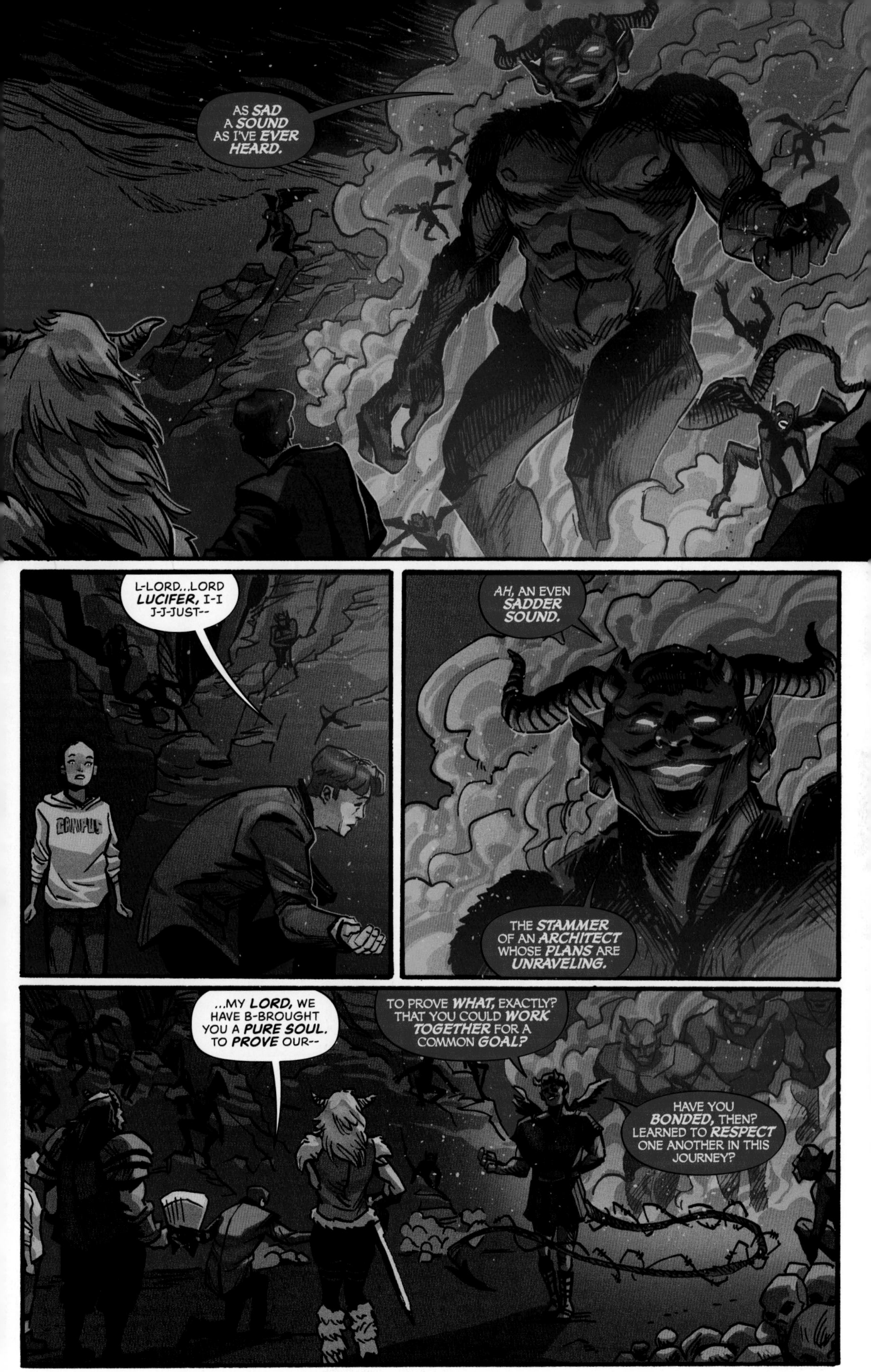
AS SAD A SOUND AS I'VE EVER HEARD.
L-LORD...LORD LUCIFER, I-I J-J-JUST--
AH, AN EVEN SADDER SOUND.
THE STAMMER OF AN ARCHITECT WHOSE PLANS ARE UNRAVELING.
...MY LORD, WE HAVE B-BROUGHT YOU A PURE SOUL. TO PROVE OUR--
TO PROVE WHAT, EXACTLY? THAT YOU COULD WORK TOGETHER FOR A COMMON GOAL?
HAVE YOU BONDED, THEN? LEARNED TO RESPECT ONE ANOTHER IN THIS JOURNEY?

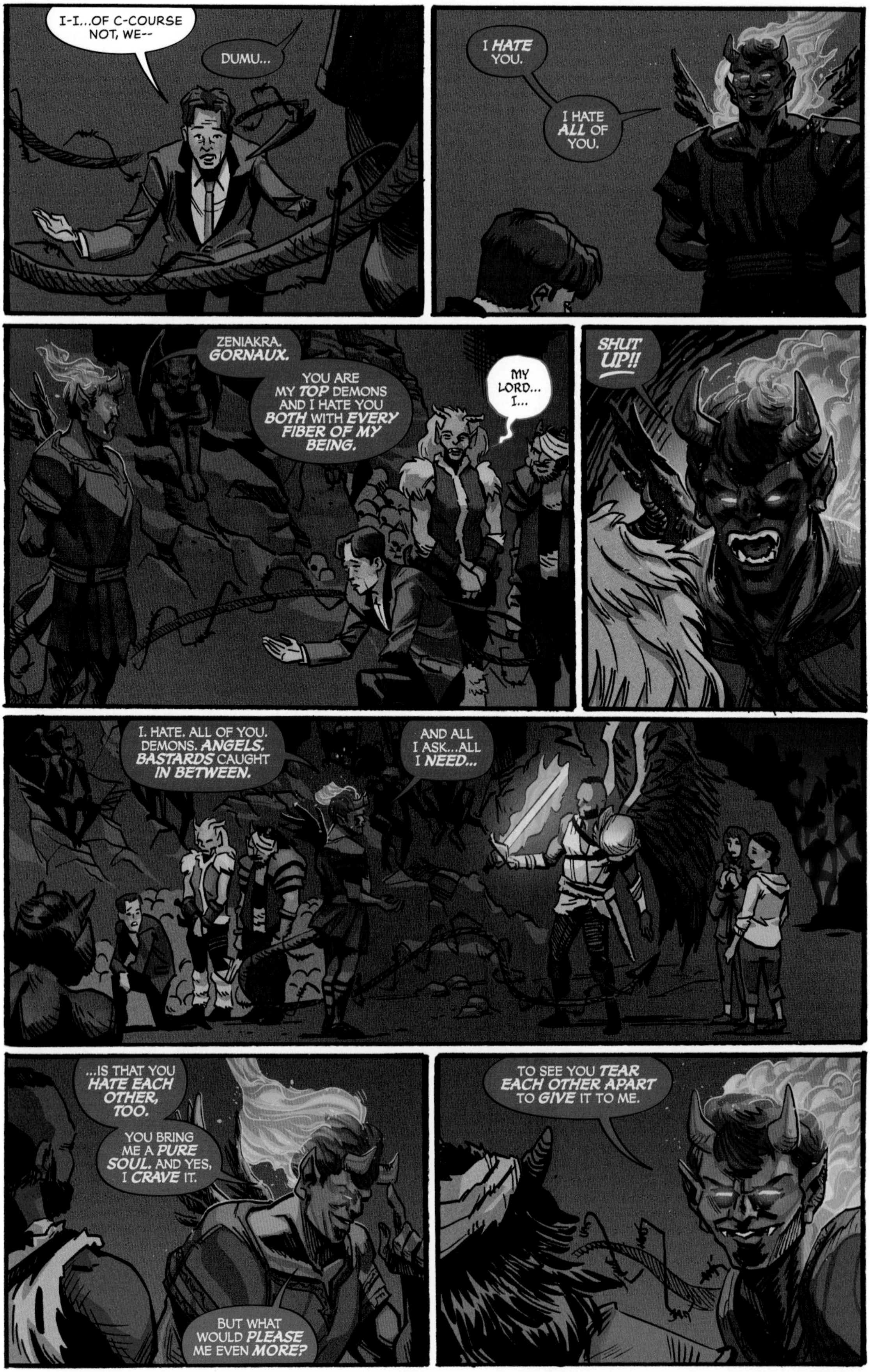

I-I...OF C-COURSE NOT, WE--
DUMU...
I HATE YOU.
I HATE ALL OF YOU.
ZENIAKRA. GORNAUX.
YOU ARE MY TOP DEMONS AND I HATE YOU BOTH WITH EVERY FIBER OF MY BEING.
MY LORD... I...
SHUT UP!!
I. HATE. ALL OF YOU. DEMONS. ANGELS. BASTARDS CAUGHT IN BETWEEN.
AND ALL I ASK...ALL I NEED...
...IS THAT YOU HATE EACH OTHER, TOO.
YOU BRING ME A PURE SOUL, AND YES, I CRAVE IT.
BUT WHAT WOULD PLEASE ME EVEN MORE?
TO SEE YOU TEAR EACH OTHER APART TO GIVE IT TO ME.

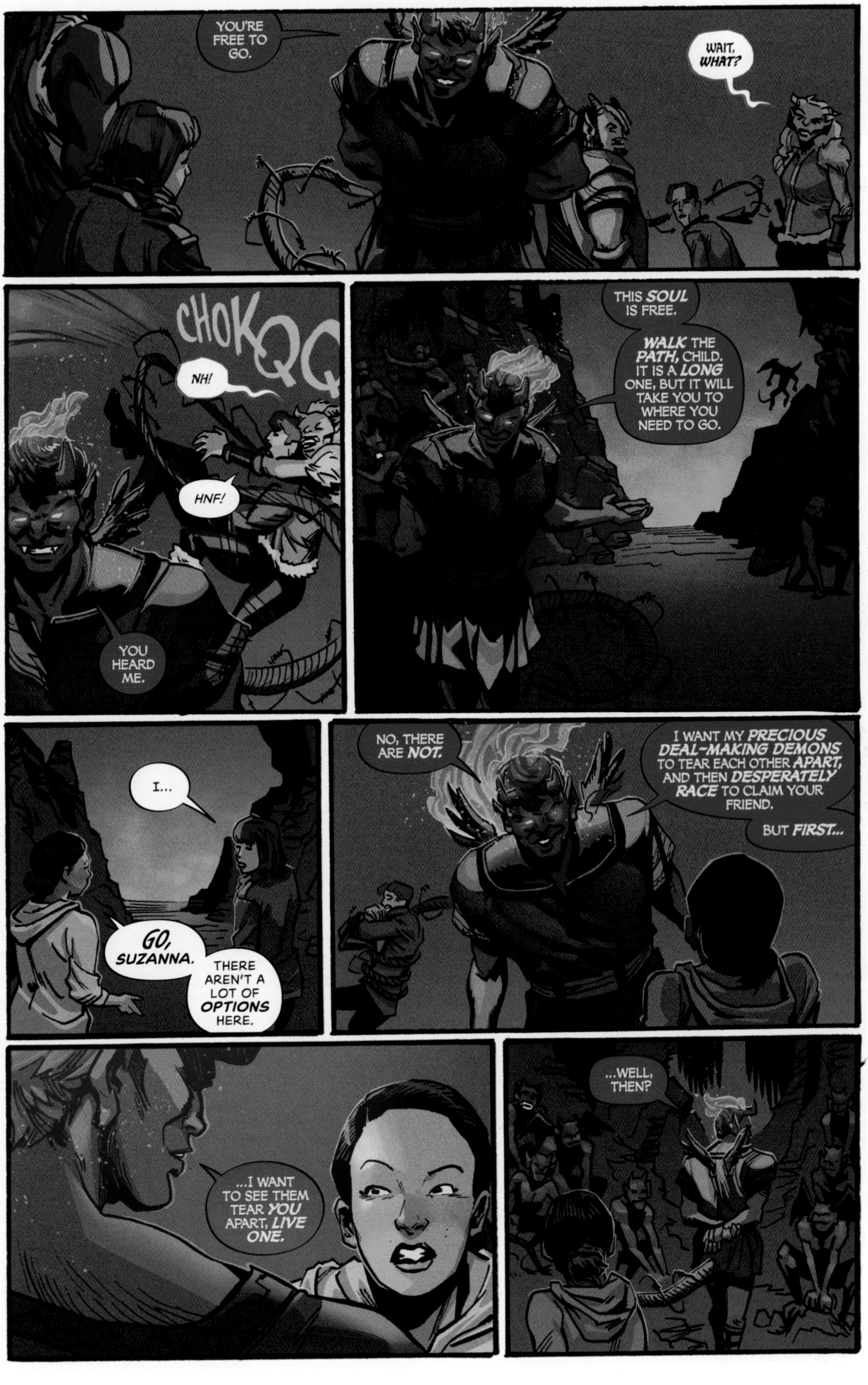
YOU'RE FREE TO GO.
WAIT, WHAT?
CHOKQQ
NH!
HNF!
YOU HEARD ME.
THIS SOUL IS FREE.
WALK THE PATH, CHILD. IT IS A LONG ONE, BUT IT WILL TAKE YOU TO WHERE YOU NEED TO GO.
I...
GO, SUZANNA.
THERE AREN'T A LOT OF OPTIONS HERE.
NO, THERE ARE NOT.
I WANT MY PRECIOUS DEAL-MAKING DEMONS TO TEAR EACH OTHER APART, AND THEN DESPERATELY RACE TO CLAIM YOUR FRIEND.
BUT FIRST...
...I WANT TO SEE THEM TEAR YOU APART, LIVE ONE.
...WELL, THEN?

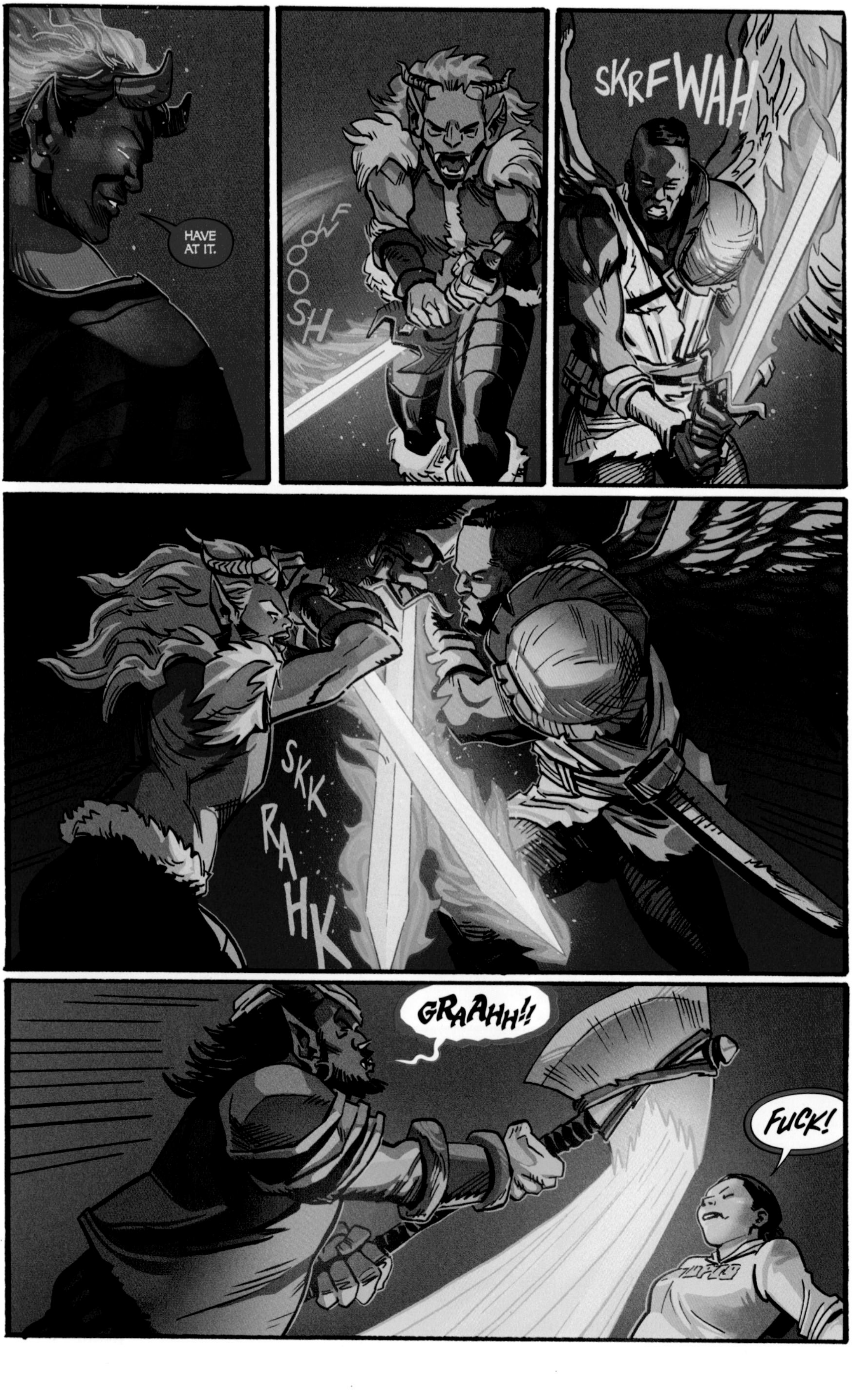
HAVE AT IT.
FOOOOSH
SKRFWAH
SKKRAHK
GRAAHH!!
FUCK!

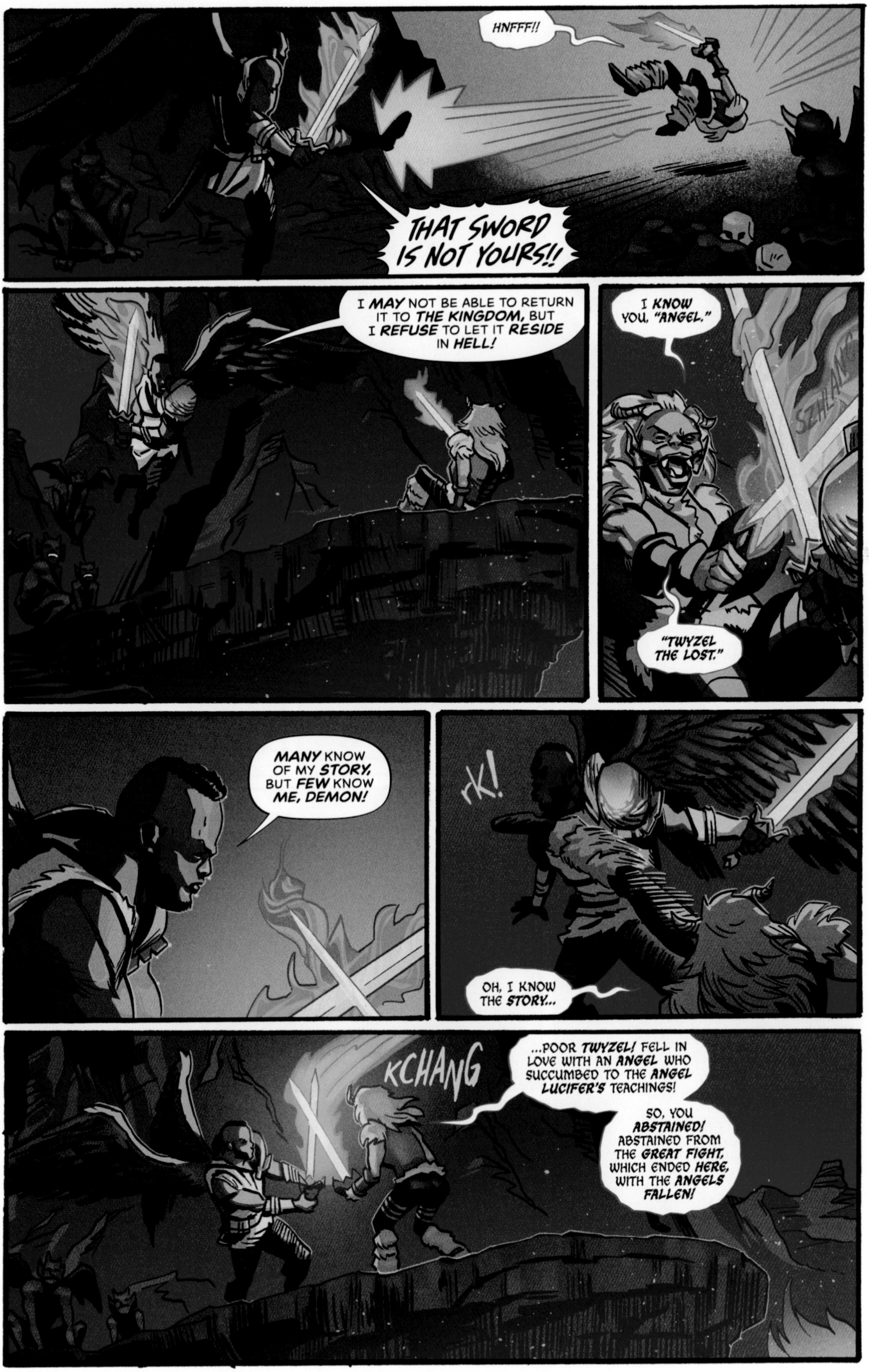
HNFFF!!
THAT SWORD IS NOT YOURS!!
I MAY NOT BE ABLE TO RETURN IT TO THE KINGDOM, BUT I REFUSE TO LET IT RESIDE IN HELL!
I KNOW YOU, "ANGEL."
SZHLANG
"TWYZEL THE LOST."
MANY KNOW OF MY STORY, BUT FEW KNOW ME, DEMON!
rK!
OH, I KNOW THE STORY...
KCHANG
...POOR TWYZEL! FELL IN LOVE WITH AN ANGEL WHO SUCCUMBED TO THE ANGEL LUCIFER'S TEACHINGS!
SO, YOU ABSTAINED! ABSTAINED FROM THE GREAT FIGHT, WHICH ENDED HERE, WITH THE ANGELS FALLEN!

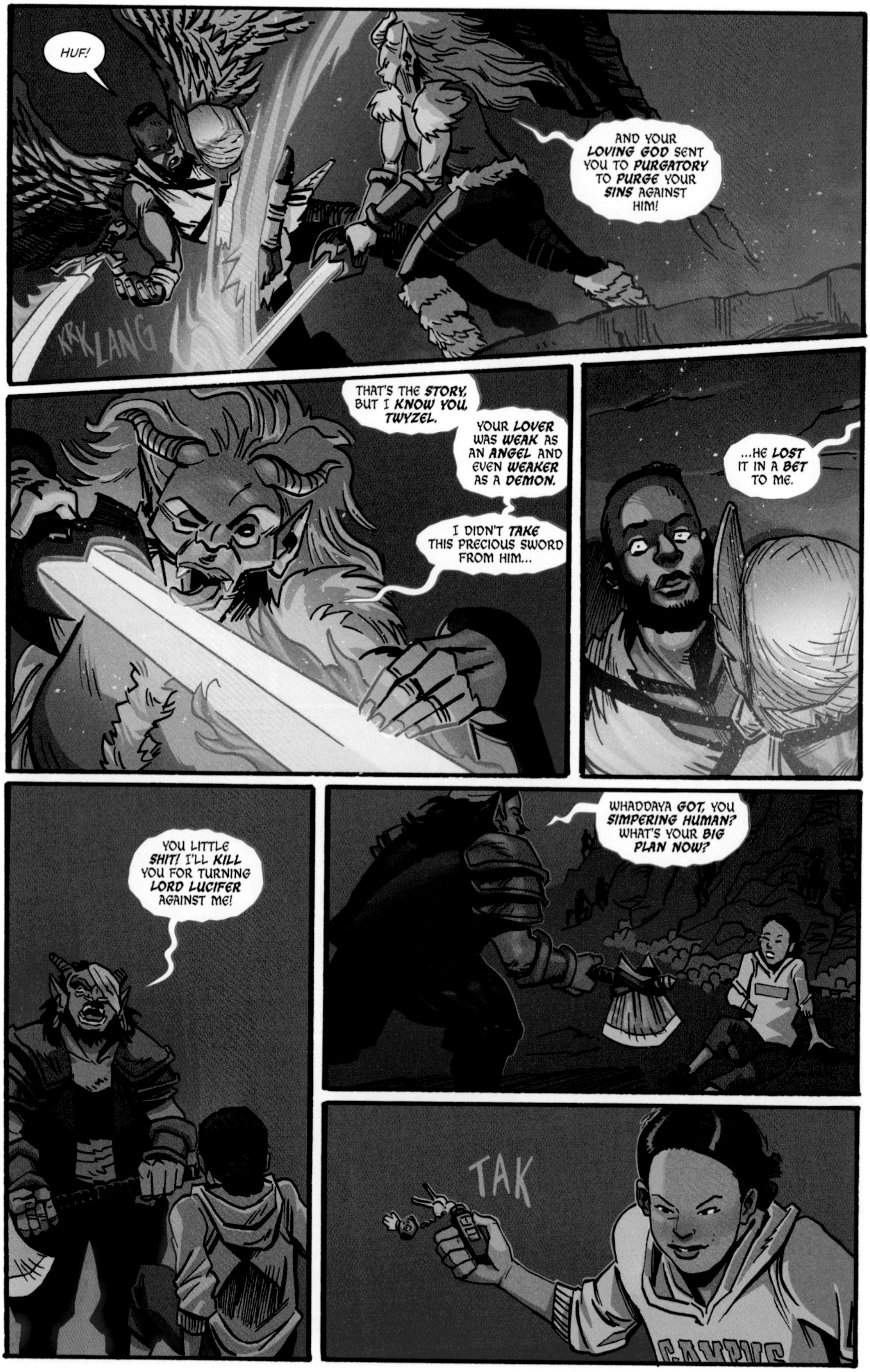
HUF!
AND YOUR LOVING GOD SENT YOU TO PURGATORY TO PURGE YOUR SINS AGAINST HIM!
KRKLANG
THAT'S THE STORY, BUT I KNOW YOU, TWYZEL.
YOUR LOVER WAS WEAK AS AN ANGEL AND EVEN WEAKER AS A DEMON.
I DIDN'T TAKE THIS PRECIOUS SWORD FROM HIM...
...HE LOST IT IN A BET TO ME.
YOU LITTLE SHIT! I'LL KILL YOU FOR TURNING LORD LUCIFER AGAINST ME!
WHADDAYA GOT, YOU SIMPERING HUMAN? WHAT'S YOUR BIG PLAN NOW?
TAK

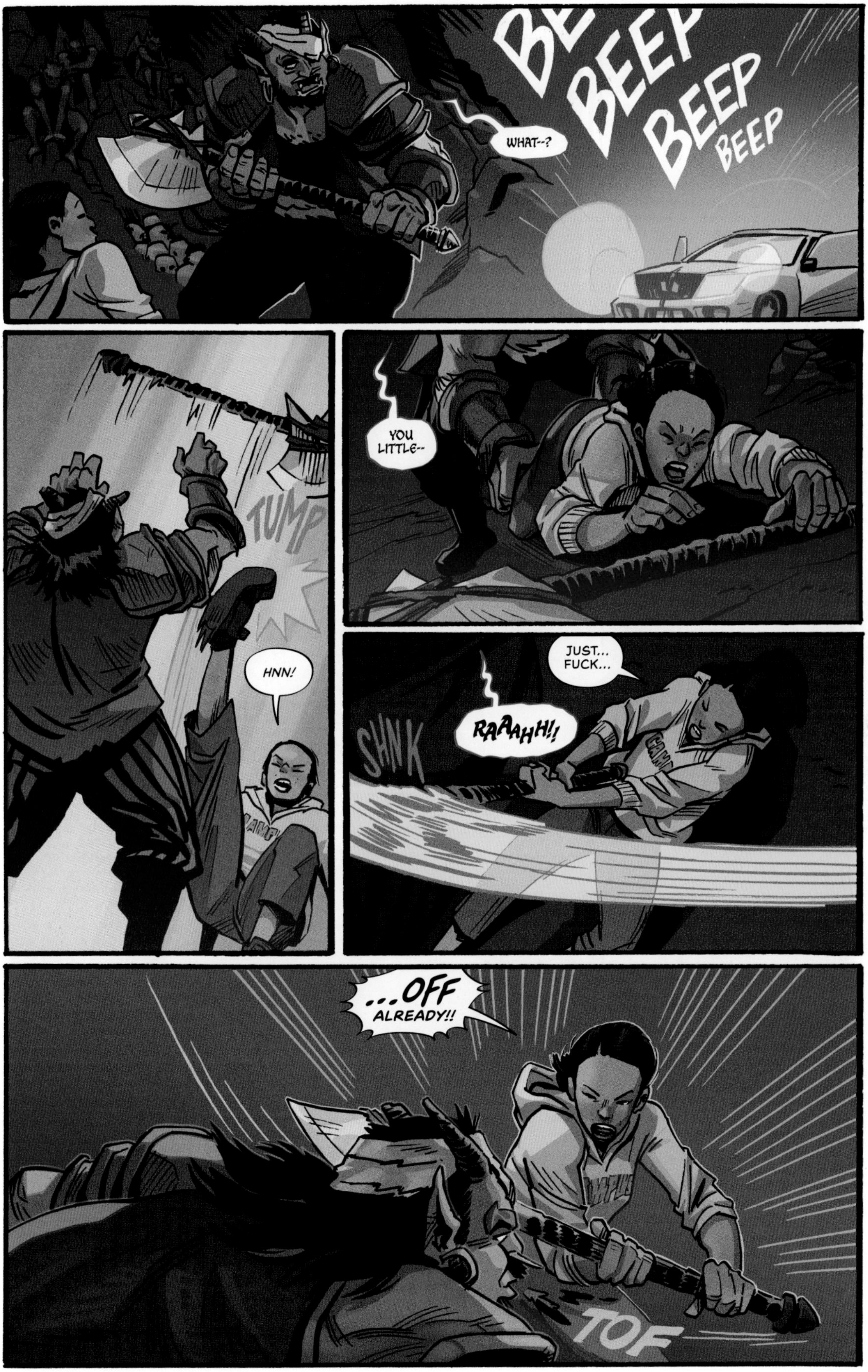
BEEP BEEP BEEP BEEP
WHAT--?
TUMP
HNN!
YOU LITTLE--
JUST... FUCK...
RAAAHH!!
SHNK
...OFF ALREADY!!
TOF

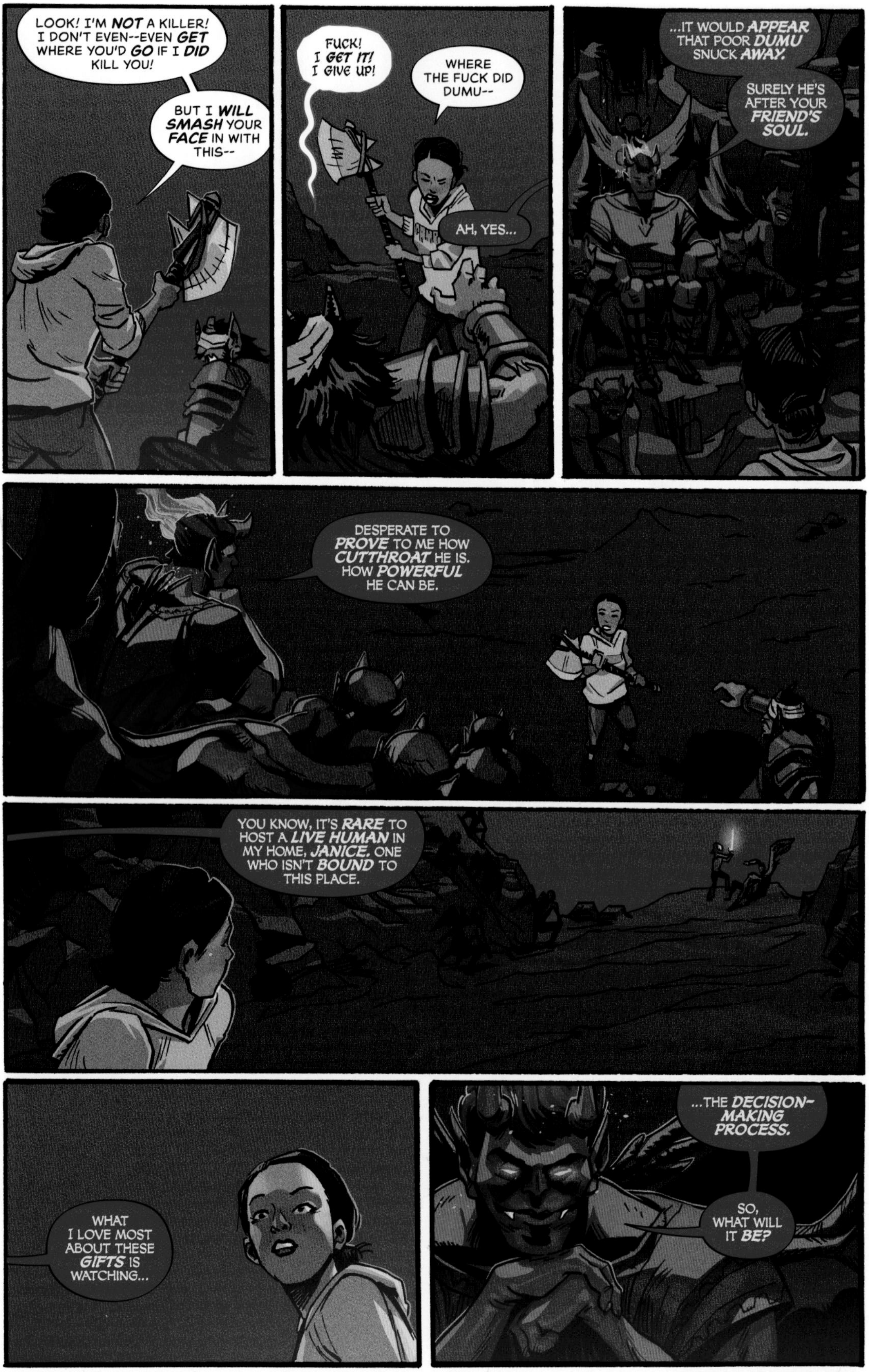
LOOK! I'M NOT A KILLER! I DON'T EVEN--EVEN GET WHERE YOU'D GO IF I DID KILL YOU!
BUT I WILL SMASH YOUR FACE IN WITH THIS--
FUCK! I GET IT! I GIVE UP!
WHERE THE FUCK DID DUMU--
AH, YES...
...IT WOULD APPEAR THAT POOR DUMU SNUCK AWAY.
SURELY HE'S AFTER YOUR FRIEND'S SOUL.
DESPERATE TO PROVE TO ME HOW CUTTHROAT HE IS. HOW POWERFUL HE CAN BE.
YOU KNOW, IT'S RARE TO HOST A LIVE HUMAN IN MY HOME, JANICE. ONE WHO ISN'T BOUND TO THIS PLACE.
WHAT I LOVE MOST ABOUT THESE GIFTS IS WATCHING...
...THE DECISION-MAKING PROCESS.
SO, WHAT WILL IT BE?

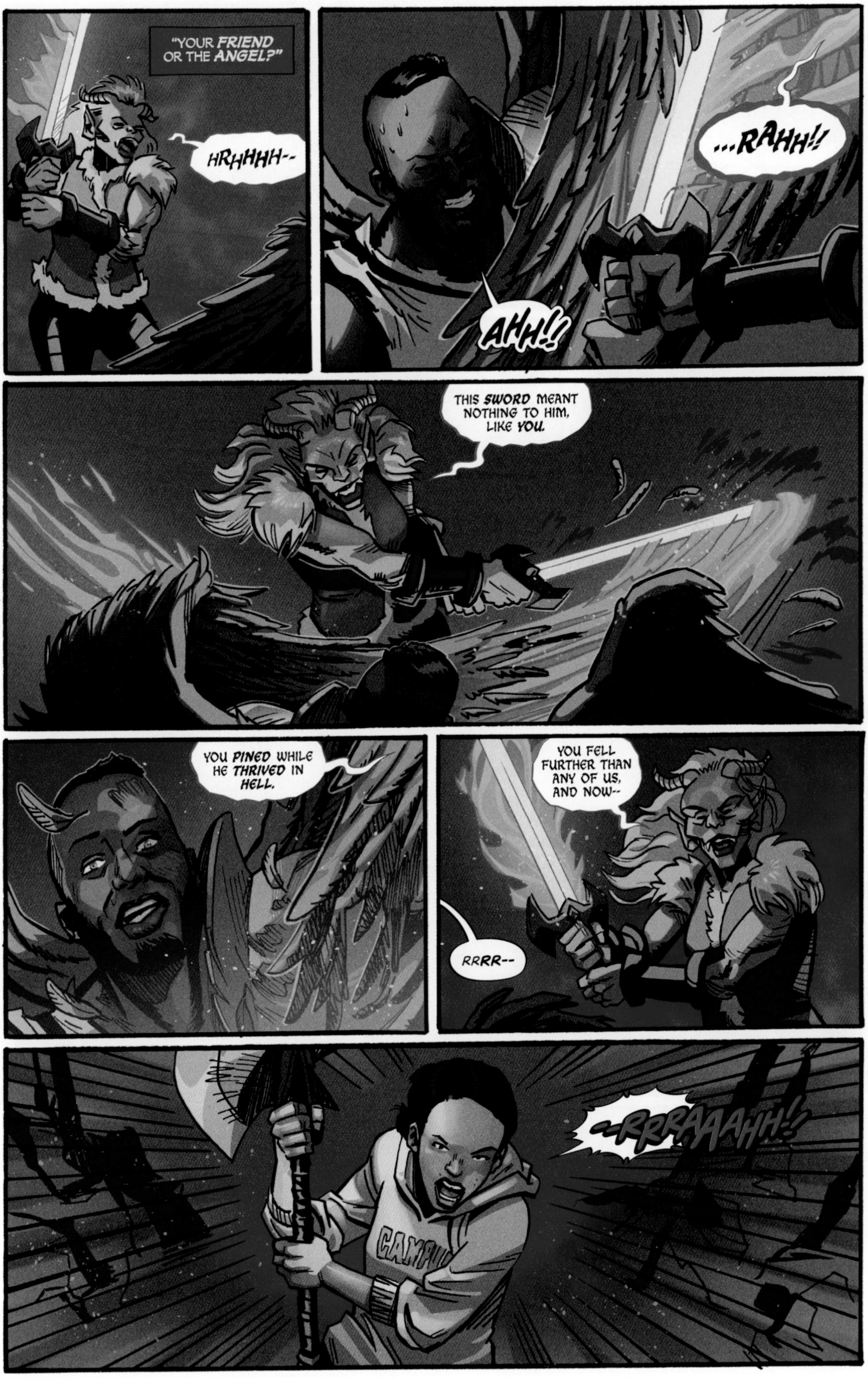
"YOUR FRIEND OR THE ANGEL?"
HRHHHH--
...RAHH!!
AHH!!
THIS SWORD MEANT NOTHING TO HIM, LIKE YOU.
YOU PINED WHILE HE THRIVED IN HELL.
YOU FELL FURTHER THAN ANY OF US, AND NOW--
RRRR--
--RRRAAAHH!!

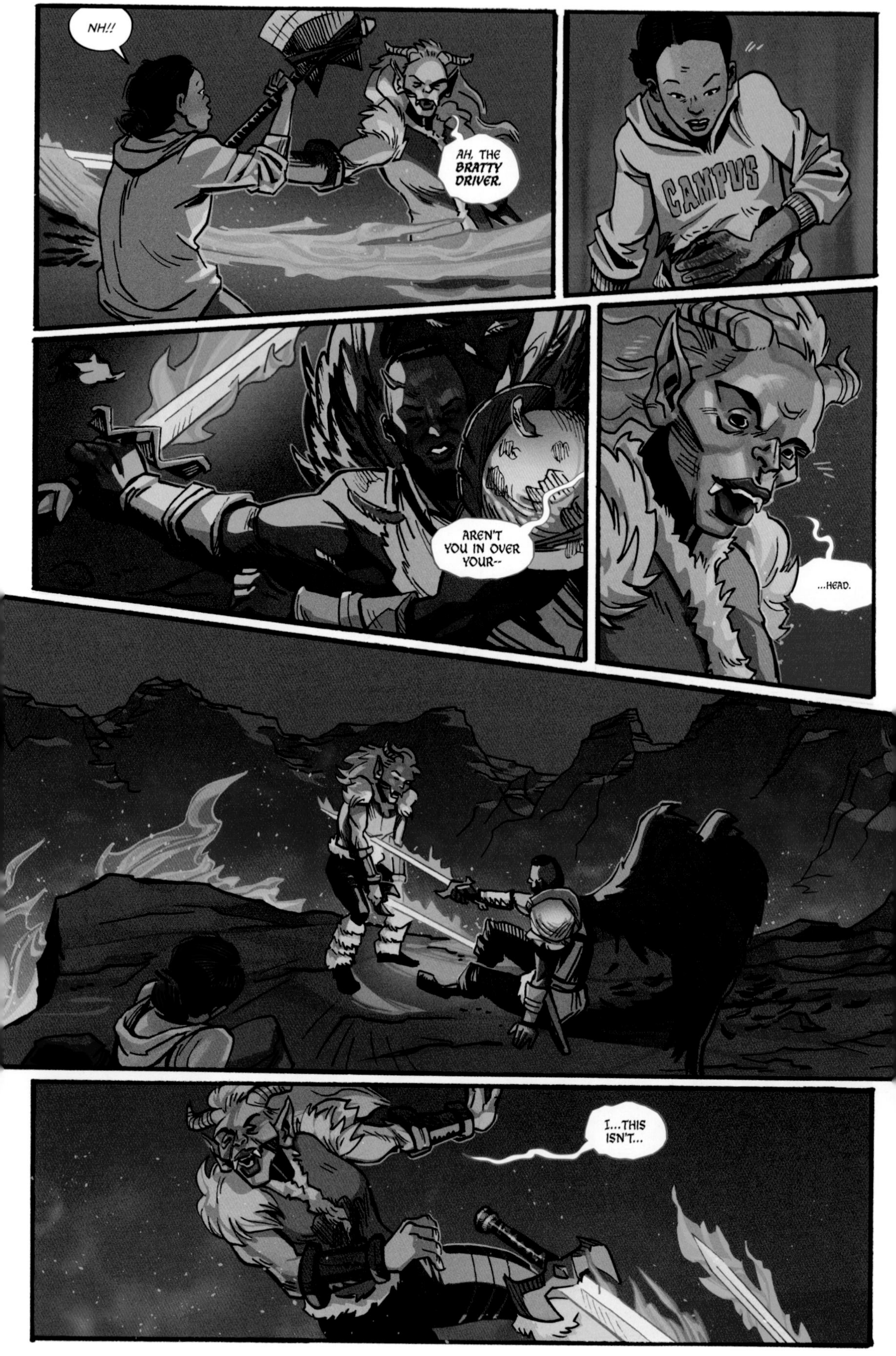
NH!!
AH, THE BRATTY DRIVER.
AREN'T YOU IN OVER YOUR--
...HEAD.
I...THIS ISN'T...

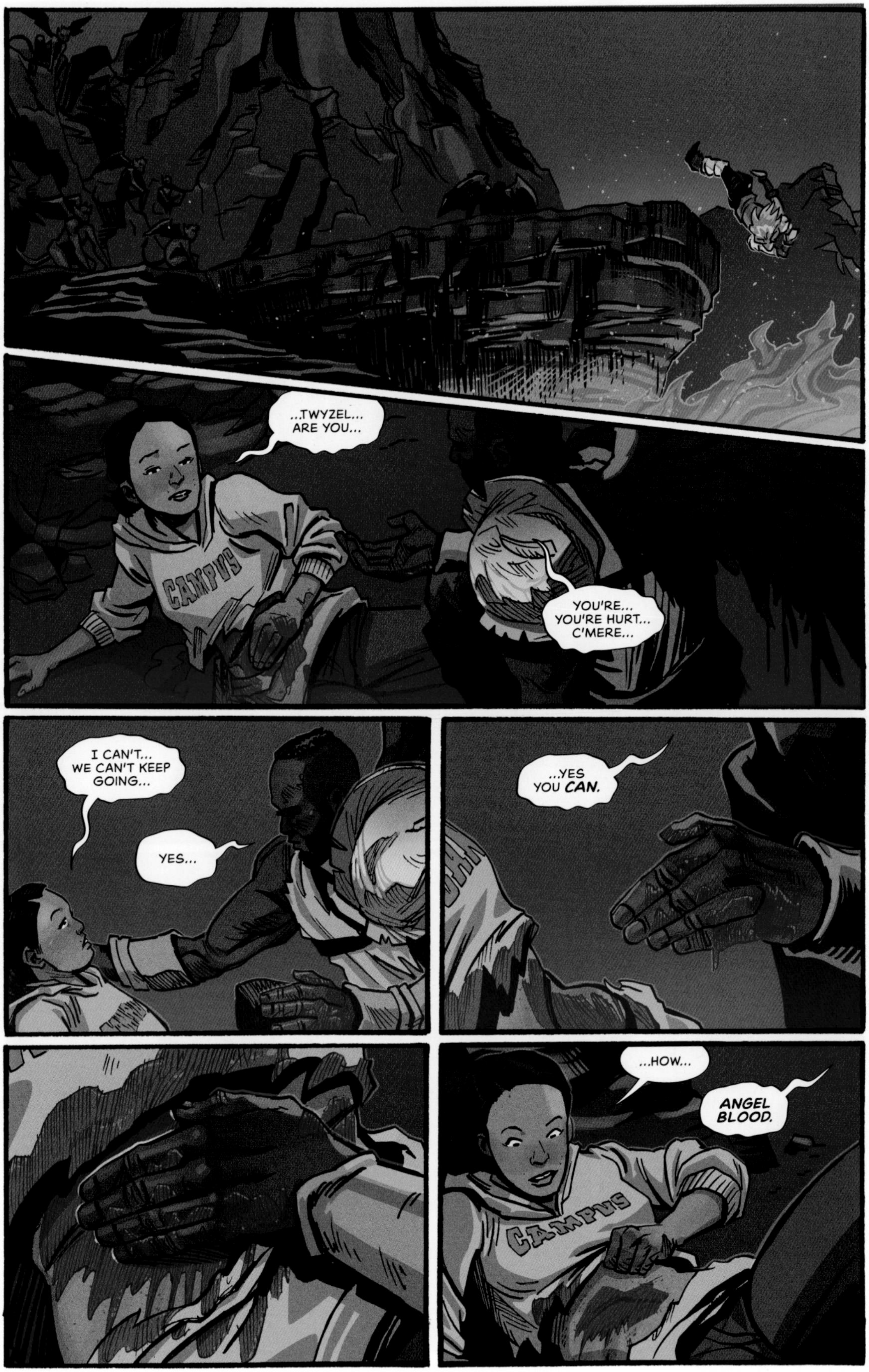
...TWYZEL... ARE YOU...
YOU'RE... YOU'RE HURT... C'MERE...
I CAN'T... WE CAN'T KEEP GOING...
YES...
...YES YOU CAN.
...HOW...
ANGEL BLOOD.

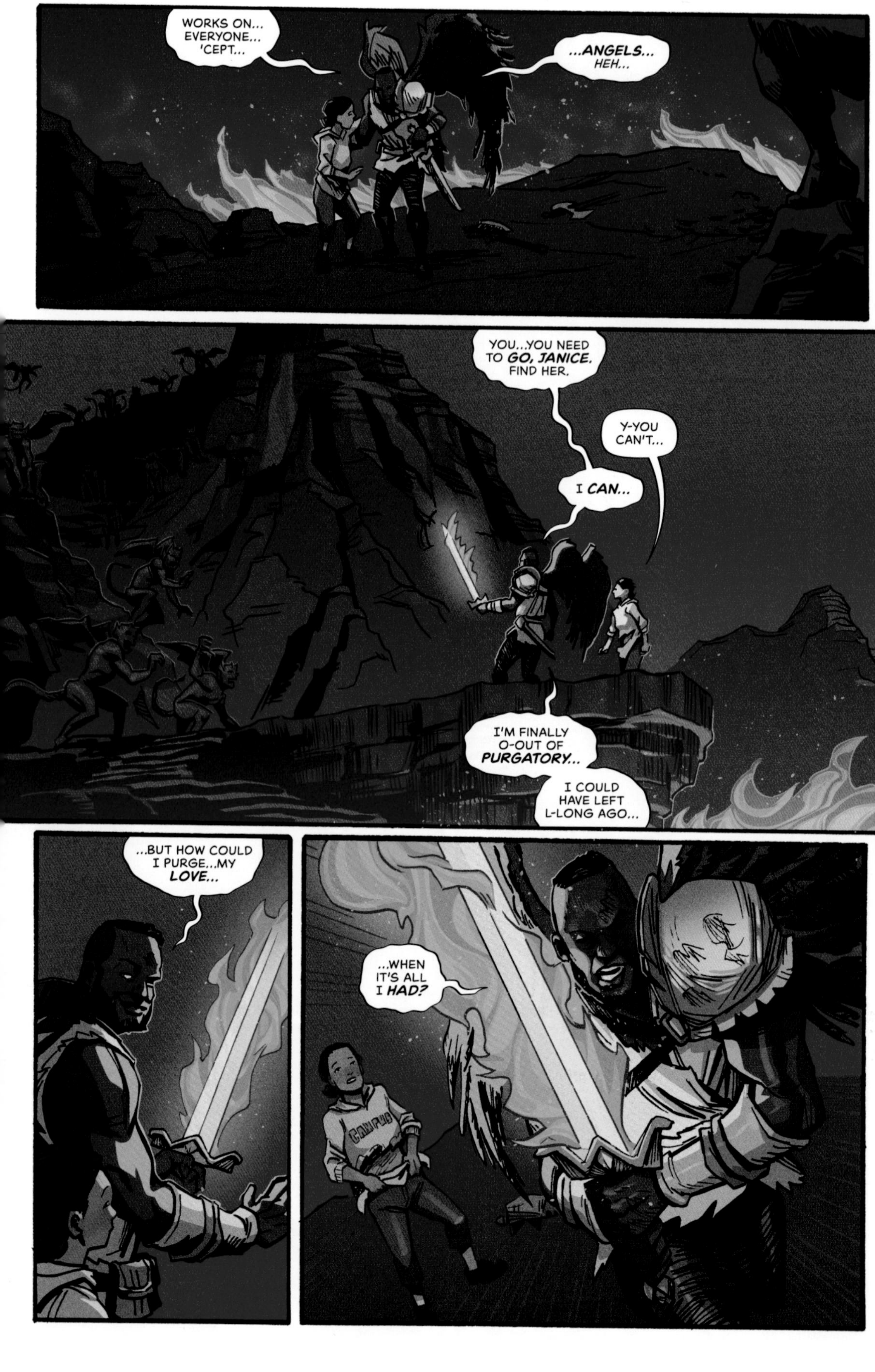

WORKS ON... EVERYONE... 'CEPT...
...ANGELS... HEH...
YOU...YOU NEED TO GO, JANICE. FIND HER.
Y-YOU CAN'T...
I CAN...
I'M FINALLY O-OUT OF PURGATORY...
I COULD HAVE LEFT L-LONG AGO...
...BUT HOW COULD I PURGE...MY LOVE...
...WHEN IT'S ALL I HAD?

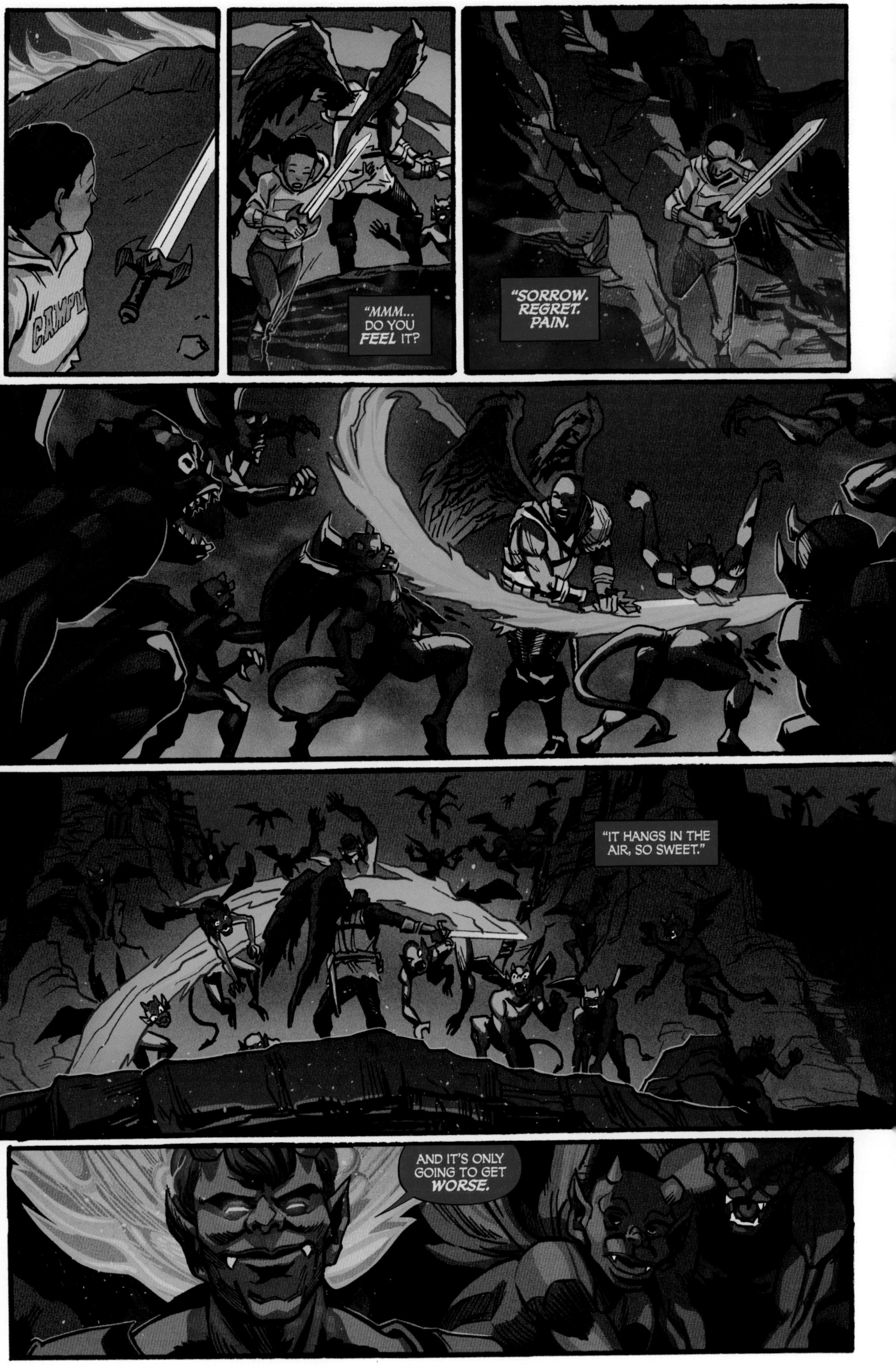

CAMPU
"MMM... DO YOU FEEL IT?
"SORROW. REGRET. PAIN.
"IT HANGS IN THE AIR, SO SWEET."
AND IT'S ONLY GOING TO GET WORSE.

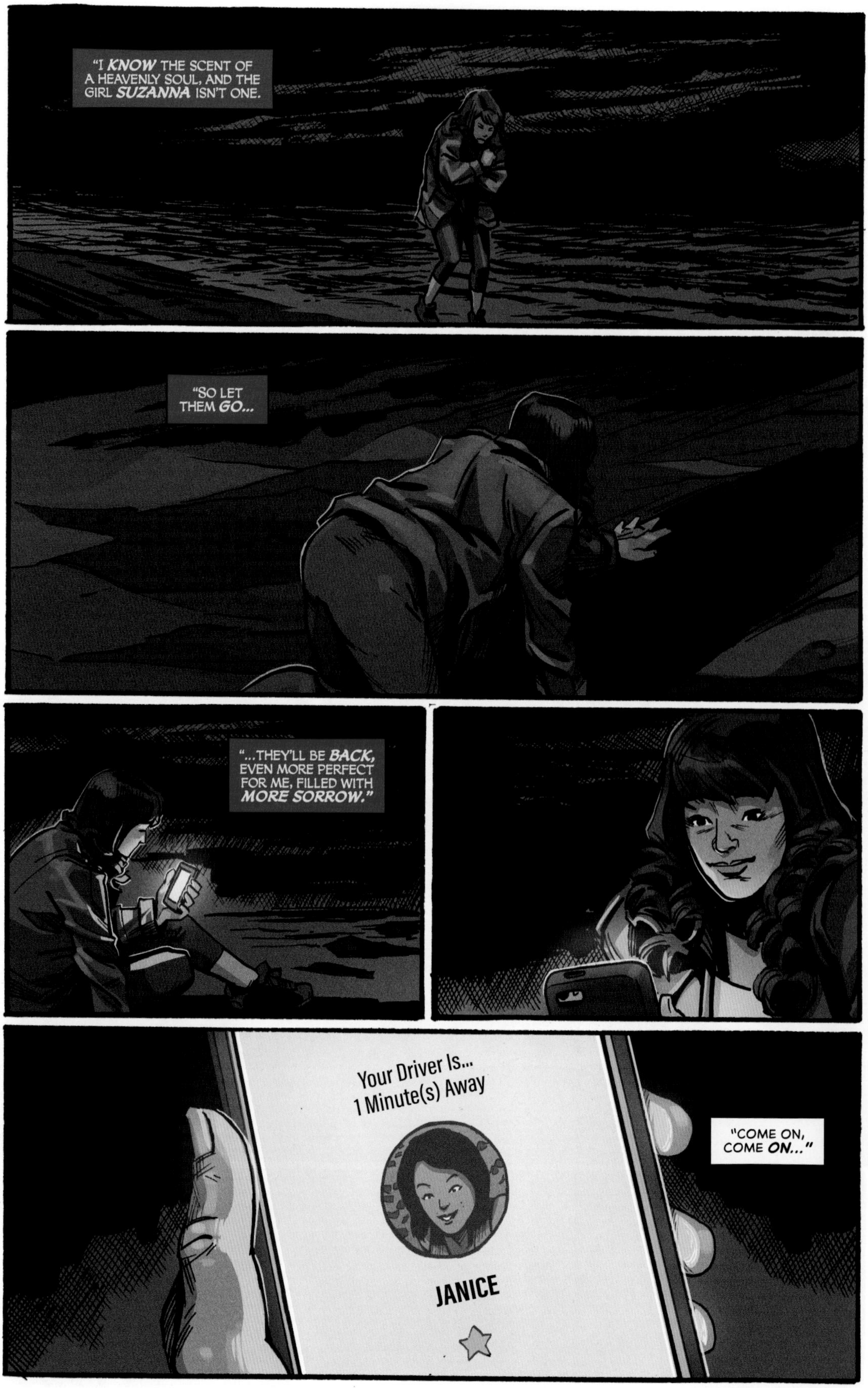
"I KNOW THE SCENT OF A HEAVENLY SOUL, AND THE GIRL SUZANNA ISN'T ONE.
"SO LET THEM GO...
"...THEY'LL BE BACK, EVEN MORE PERFECT FOR ME, FILLED WITH MORE SORROW."
Your Driver Is... 1 Minute(s) Away
JANICE
"COME ON, COME ON..."

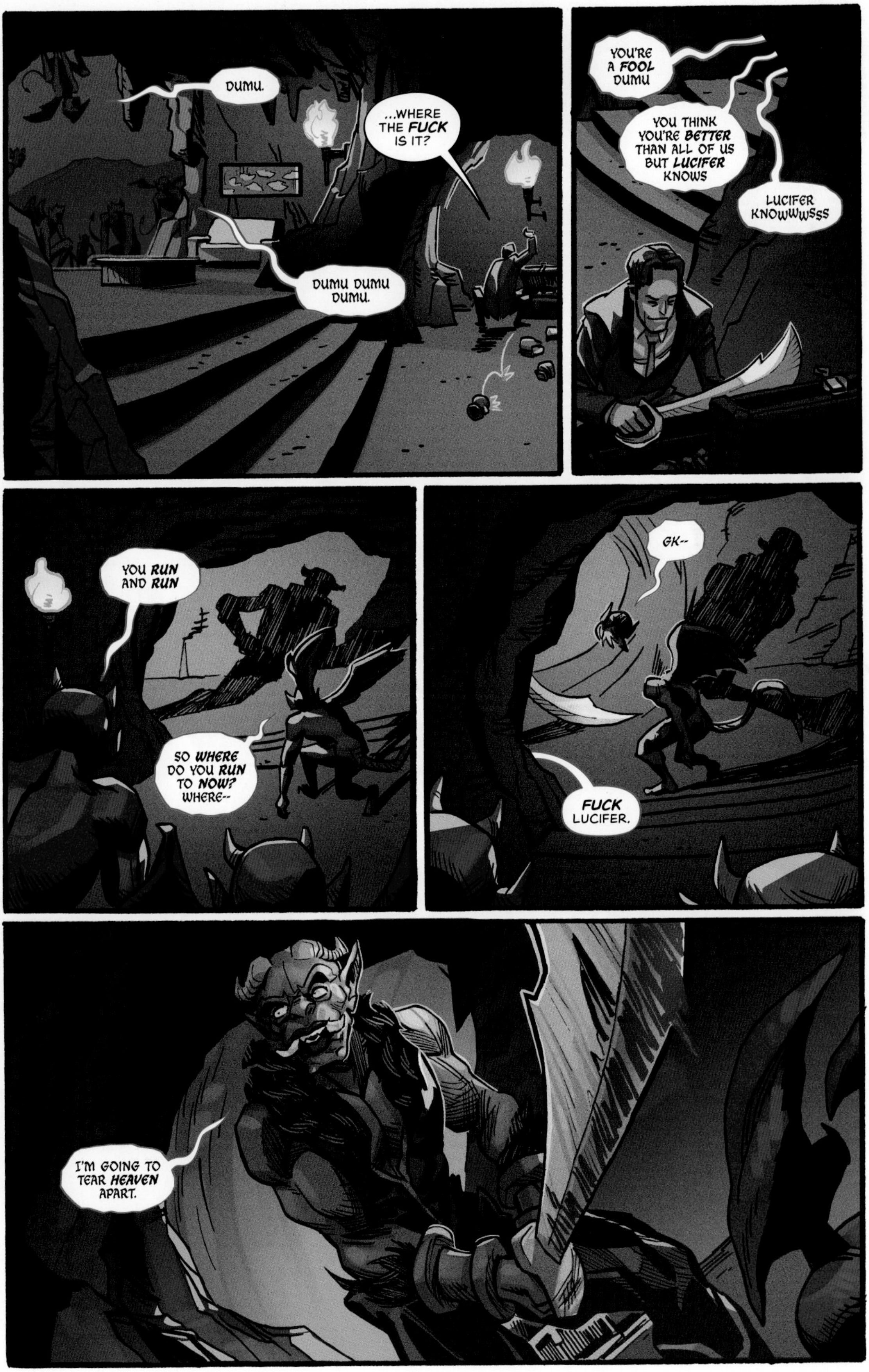
DUMU.
...WHERE THE FUCK IS IT?
DUMU DUMU DUMU.
YOU'RE A FOOL DUMU
YOU THINK YOU'RE BETTER THAN ALL OF US BUT LUCIFER KNOWS
LUCIFER KNOWWWSSS
YOU RUN AND RUN
SO WHERE DO YOU RUN TO NOW? WHERE--
GK--
FUCK LUCIFER.
I'M GOING TO TEAR HEAVEN APART.

"IS THIS...
THE END OF
THE ROAD?"

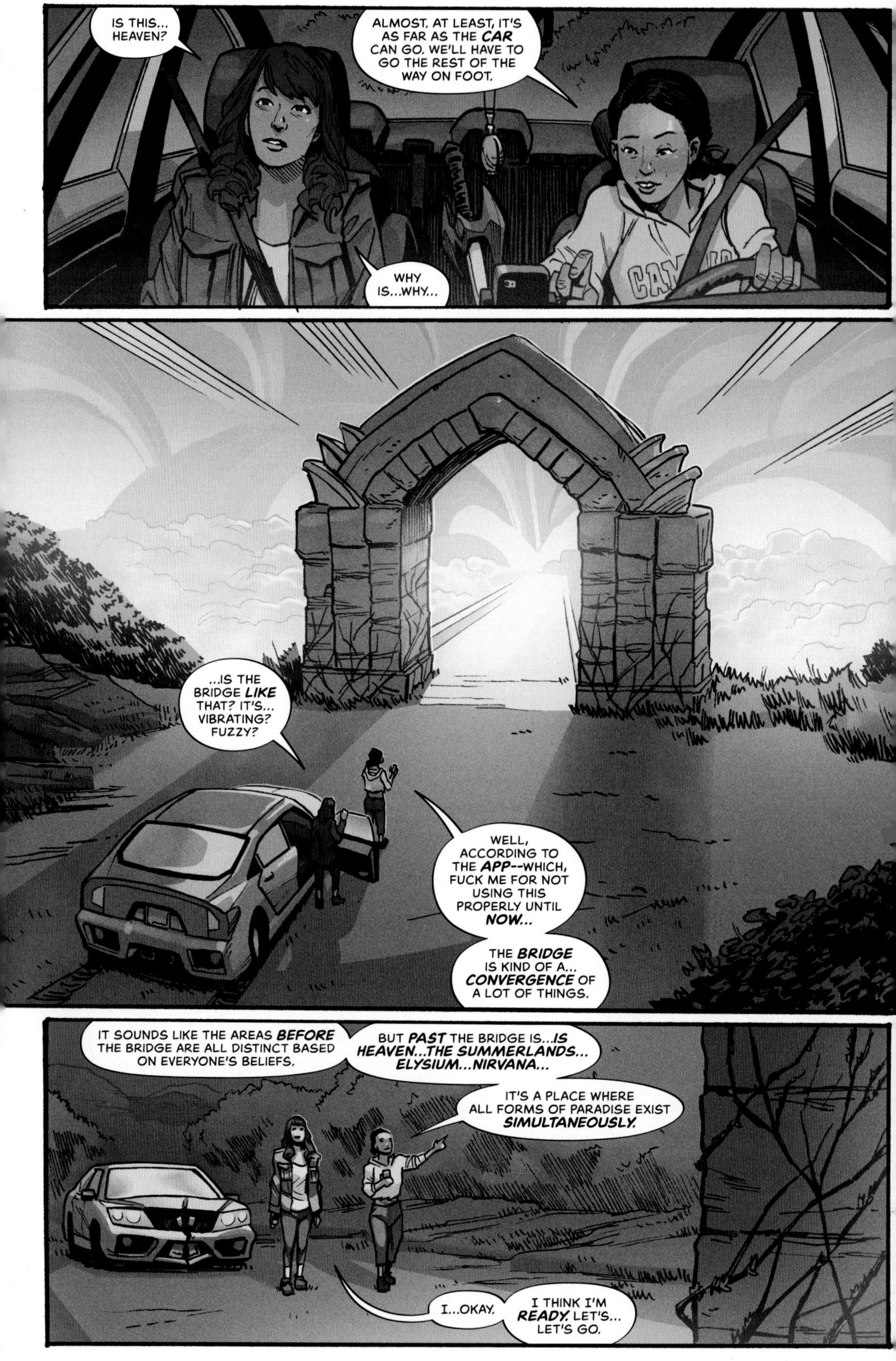
IS THIS... HEAVEN?
ALMOST. AT LEAST, IT'S AS FAR AS THE *CAR* CAN GO. WE'LL HAVE TO GO THE REST OF THE WAY ON FOOT.
WHY IS...WHY...
...IS THE BRIDGE *LIKE* THAT? IT'S... VIBRATING? FUZZY?
WELL, ACCORDING TO THE *APP*--WHICH, FUCK ME FOR NOT USING THIS PROPERLY UNTIL *NOW*...
THE *BRIDGE* IS KIND OF A... *CONVERGENCE* OF A LOT OF THINGS.
IT SOUNDS LIKE THE AREAS *BEFORE* THE BRIDGE ARE ALL DISTINCT BASED ON EVERYONE'S BELIEFS.
BUT *PAST* THE BRIDGE IS...*IS HEAVEN...THE SUMMERLANDS... ELYSIUM...NIRVANA...*
IT'S A PLACE WHERE ALL FORMS OF PARADISE EXIST *SIMULTANEOUSLY.*
I...OKAY.
I THINK I'M *READY.* LET'S... LET'S GO.

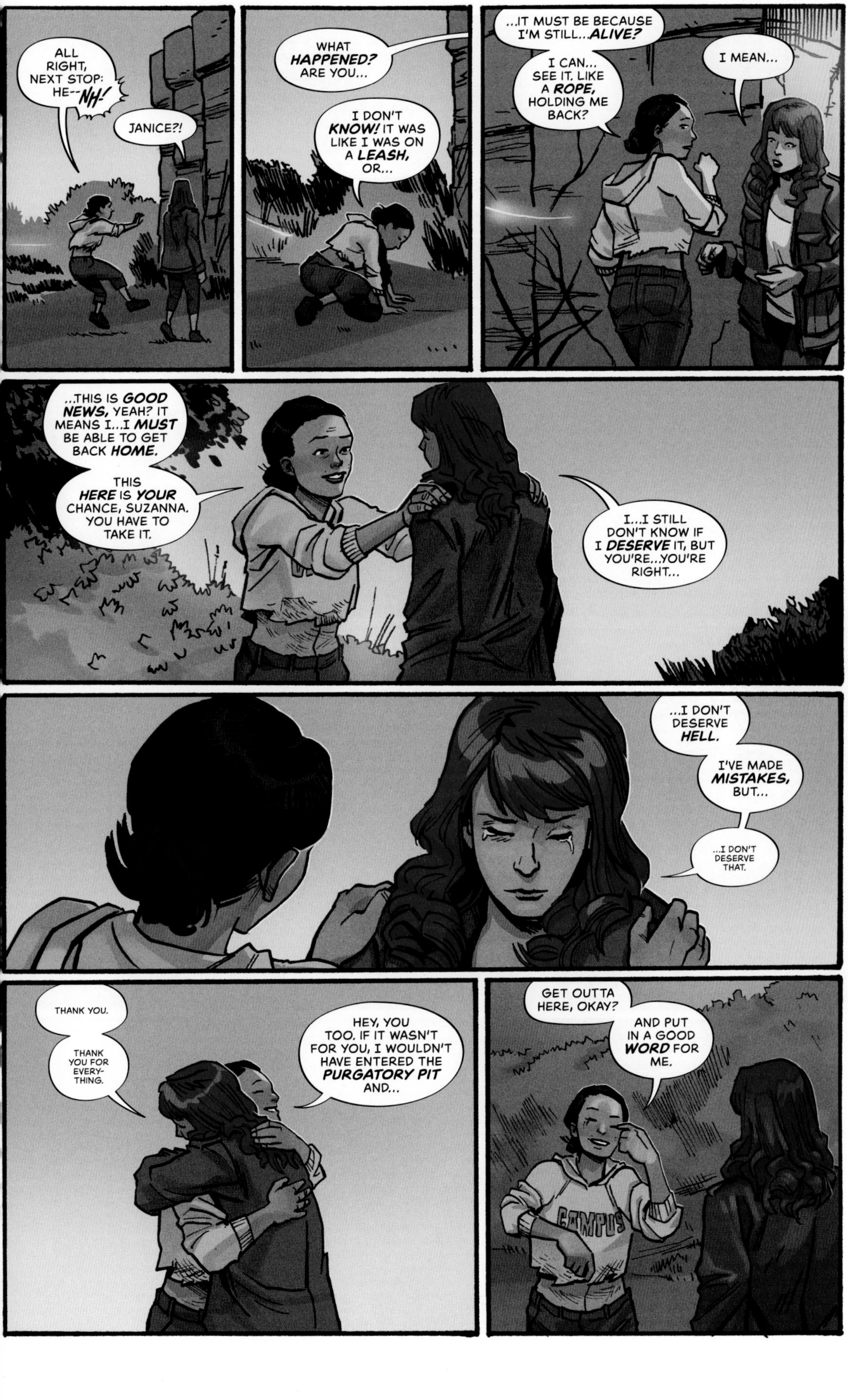

ALL RIGHT, NEXT STOP: HE--NH!
JANICE?!
WHAT HAPPENED? ARE YOU...
I DON'T KNOW! IT WAS LIKE I WAS ON A LEASH, OR...
...IT MUST BE BECAUSE I'M STILL...ALIVE?
I CAN... SEE IT. LIKE A ROPE, HOLDING ME BACK?
I MEAN...
...THIS IS GOOD NEWS, YEAH? IT MEANS I...I MUST BE ABLE TO GET BACK HOME.
THIS HERE IS YOUR CHANCE, SUZANNA. YOU HAVE TO TAKE IT.
I...I STILL DON'T KNOW IF I DESERVE IT, BUT YOU'RE...YOU'RE RIGHT...
...I DON'T DESERVE HELL.
I'VE MADE MISTAKES, BUT...
...I DON'T DESERVE THAT.
THANK YOU.
THANK YOU FOR EVERY-THING.
HEY, YOU TOO. IF IT WASN'T FOR YOU, I WOULDN'T HAVE ENTERED THE PURGATORY PIT AND...
GET OUTTA HERE, OKAY?
AND PUT IN A GOOD WORD FOR ME.
CAMPUS

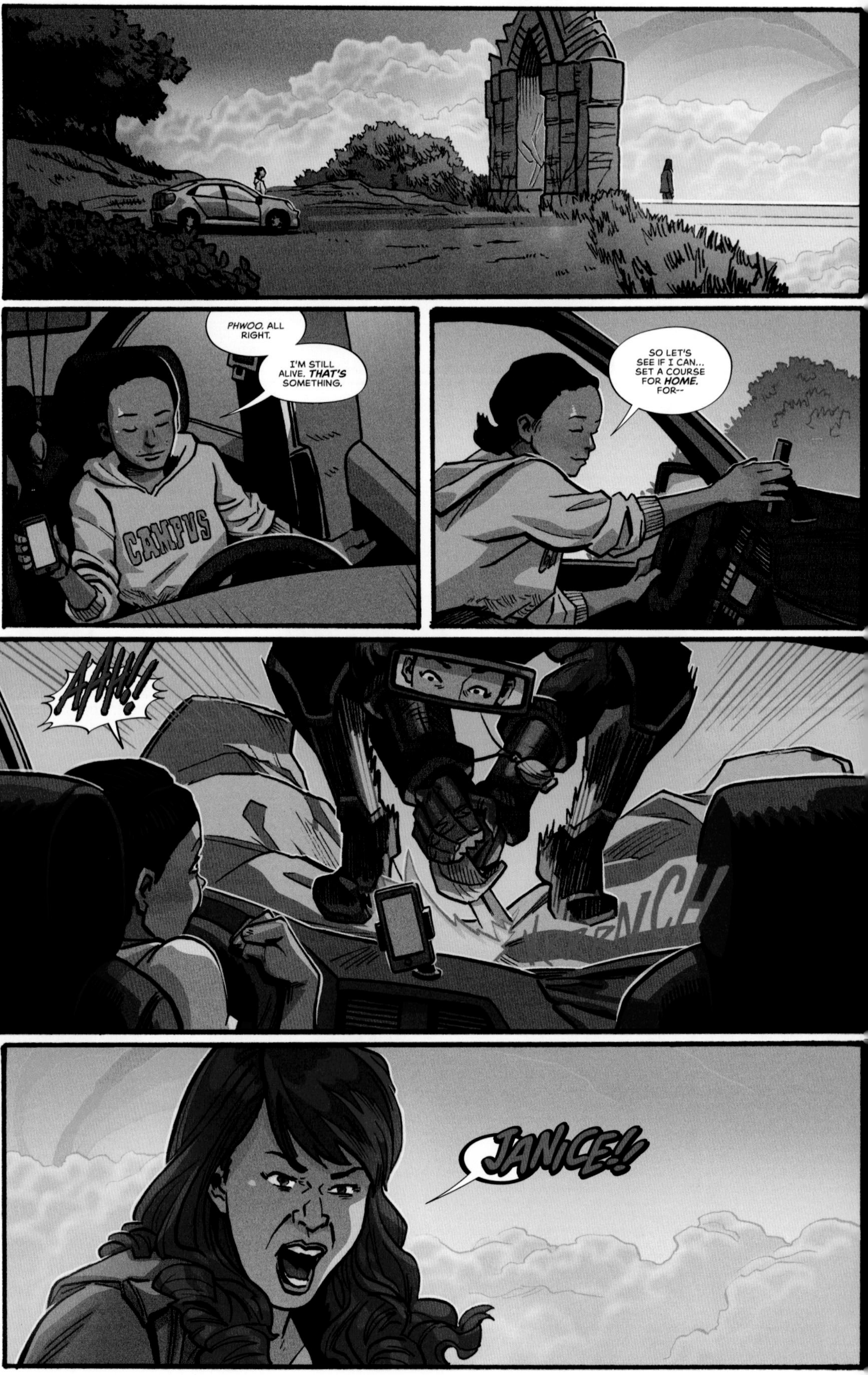
PHWOO. ALL RIGHT.
I'M STILL ALIVE. ***THAT'S*** SOMETHING.
CAMPUS
SO LET'S SEE IF I CAN... SET A COURSE FOR ***HOME.*** FOR--
AAH!!
JANICE!!

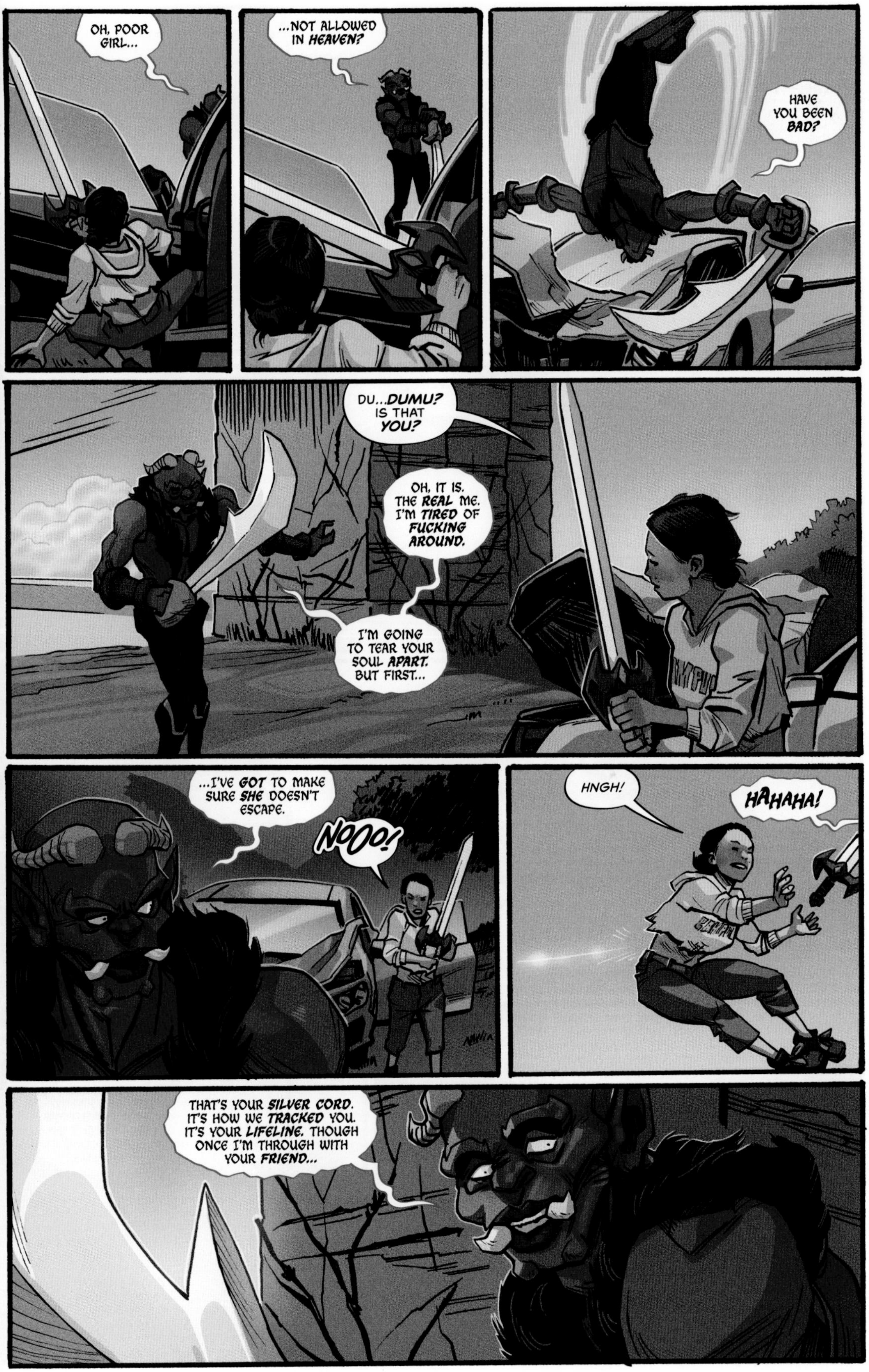

OH, POOR GIRL...
...NOT ALLOWED IN HEAVEN?
HAVE YOU BEEN BAD?
DU...DUMU? IS THAT YOU?
OH, IT IS. THE REAL ME. I'M TIRED OF FUCKING AROUND.
I'M GOING TO TEAR YOUR SOUL APART. BUT FIRST...
...I'VE GOT TO MAKE SURE SHE DOESN'T ESCAPE.
NOOO!
HNGH!
HAHAHA!
THAT'S YOUR SILVER CORD. IT'S HOW WE TRACKED YOU. IT'S YOUR LIFELINE. THOUGH ONCE I'M THROUGH WITH YOUR FRIEND...

...IT WON'T BE FOR *LONG.*

HAHAHA!!

NHH! *SUZANNA!!*

NO NO NO NO

HAHAHA!

OH, SO *CLOSE!* BUT STILL...

...SO FAR!

AHHH!!

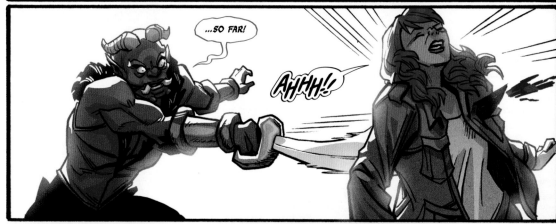

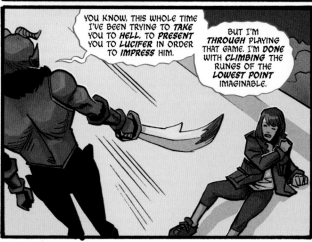

YOU KNOW, THIS WHOLE TIME I'VE BEEN TRYING TO *TAKE* YOU TO *HELL.* TO *PRESENT* YOU TO *LUCIFER* IN ORDER TO *IMPRESS* HIM.

BUT I'M *THROUGH* PLAYING THAT GAME. I'M *DONE* WITH *CLIMBING* THE RUNGS OF THE *LOWEST POINT* IMAGINABLE.

NO. *DUMU* EXISTS FOR *DUMU* NOW. AND WHAT DOES *DUMU* WANT?

HE WANTS TO *CUT* YOU TO *RIBBONS* BEFORE THE *HORDES OF HELL* COME GET YOU.

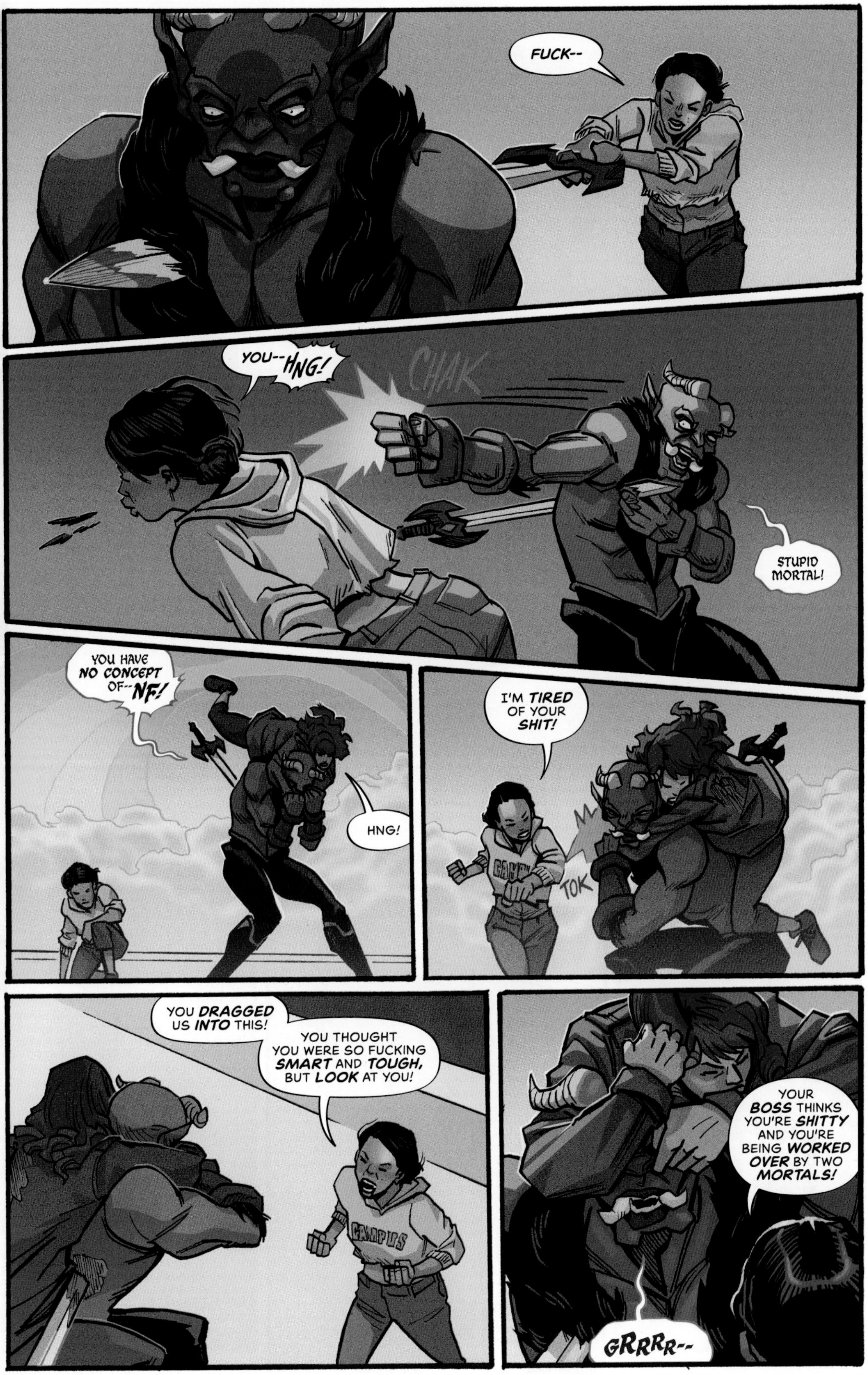
FUCK--
YOU--HNG!
CHAK
STUPID MORTAL!
YOU HAVE NO CONCEPT OF--NF!
HNG!
I'M TIRED OF YOUR SHIT!
TOK
YOU DRAGGED US INTO THIS!
YOU THOUGHT YOU WERE SO FUCKING SMART AND TOUGH, BUT LOOK AT YOU!
YOUR BOSS THINKS YOU'RE SHITTY AND YOU'RE BEING WORKED OVER BY TWO MORTALS!
GRRRR--

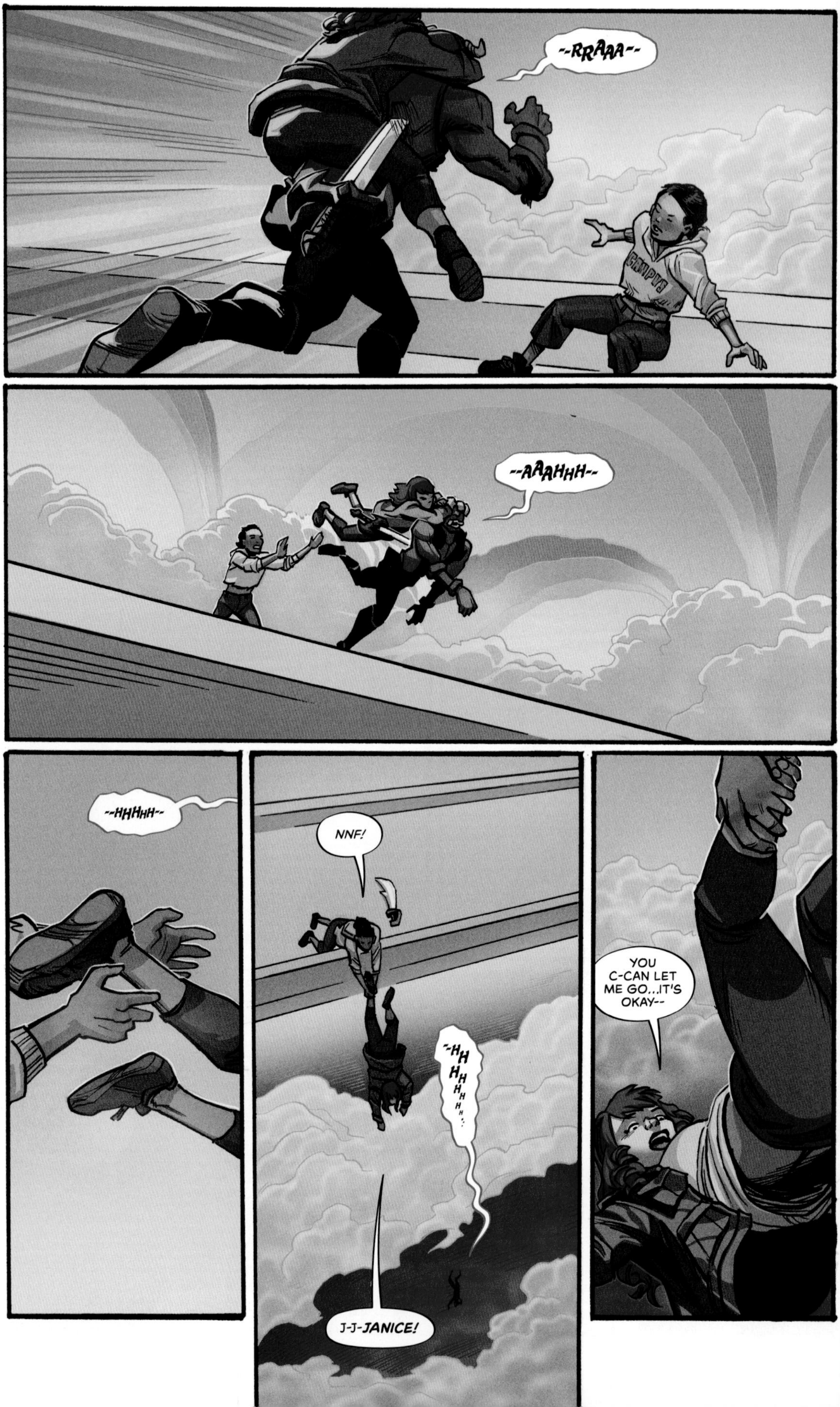
--RRAAA--
--AAAHHH--
--HHHHH--
NNF!
--HHHHHH...
J-J-JANICE!
YOU C-CAN LET ME GO...IT'S OKAY--

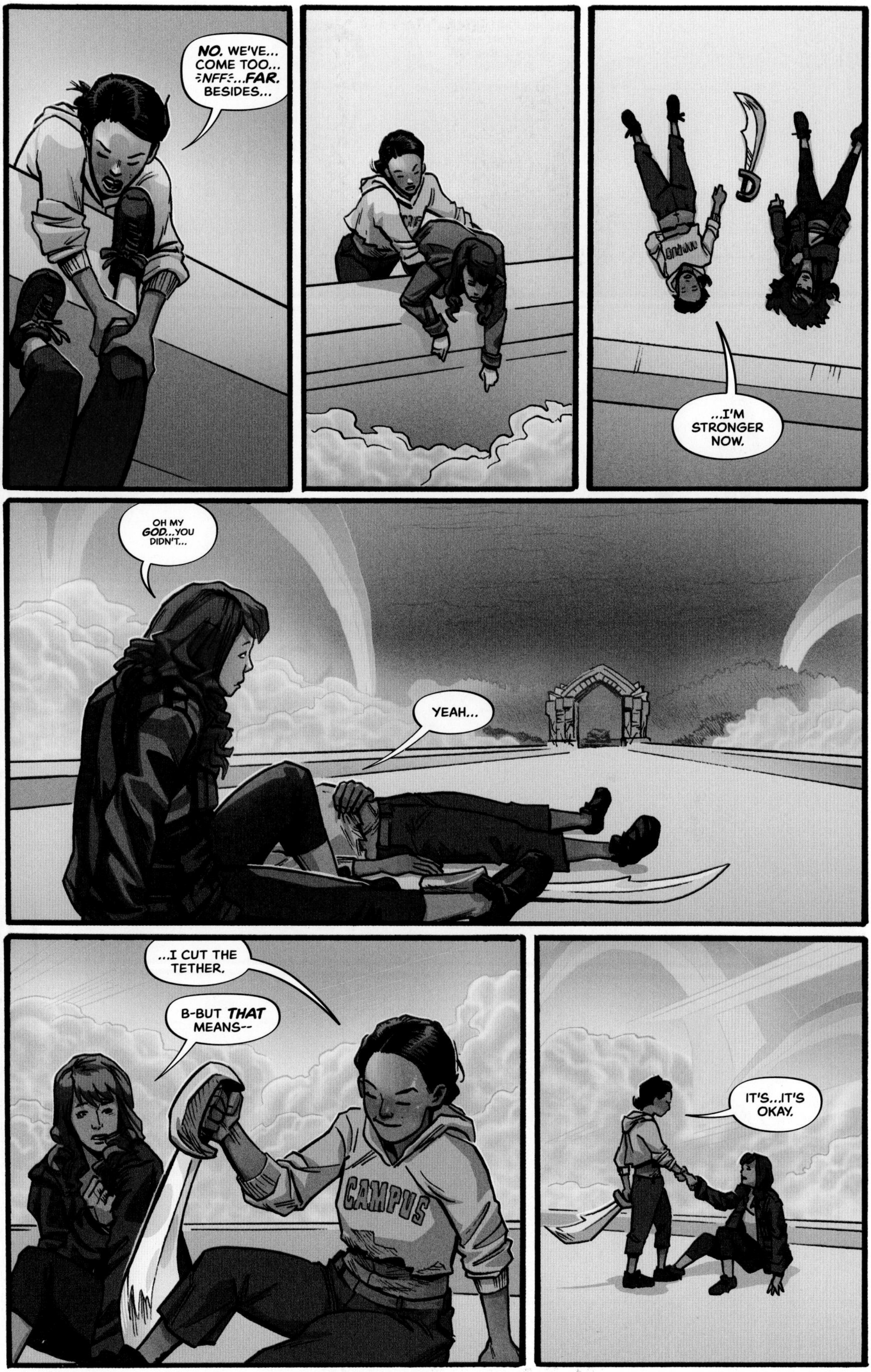
NO. WE'VE... COME TOO... NFF... FAR. BESIDES...
...I'M STRONGER NOW.
OH MY GOD...YOU DIDN'T...
YEAH...
...I CUT THE TETHER.
B-BUT THAT MEANS--
CAMPUS
IT'S...IT'S OKAY.

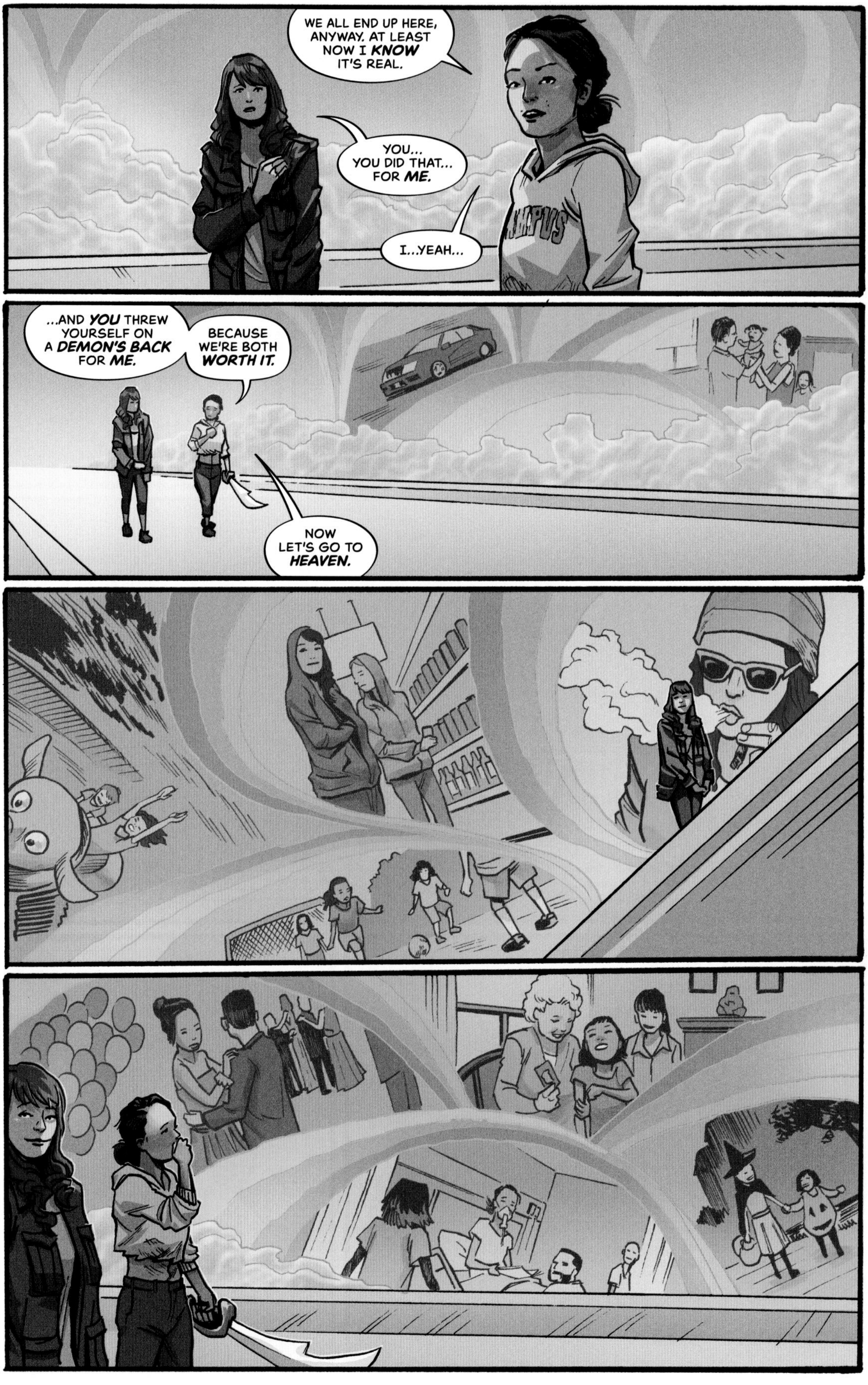
WE ALL END UP HERE, ANYWAY. AT LEAST NOW I **KNOW** IT'S REAL.
YOU... YOU DID THAT... FOR **ME.**
I...YEAH...
...AND **YOU** THREW YOURSELF ON A **DEMON'S BACK** FOR **ME.**
BECAUSE WE'RE BOTH **WORTH IT.**
NOW LET'S GO TO **HEAVEN.**

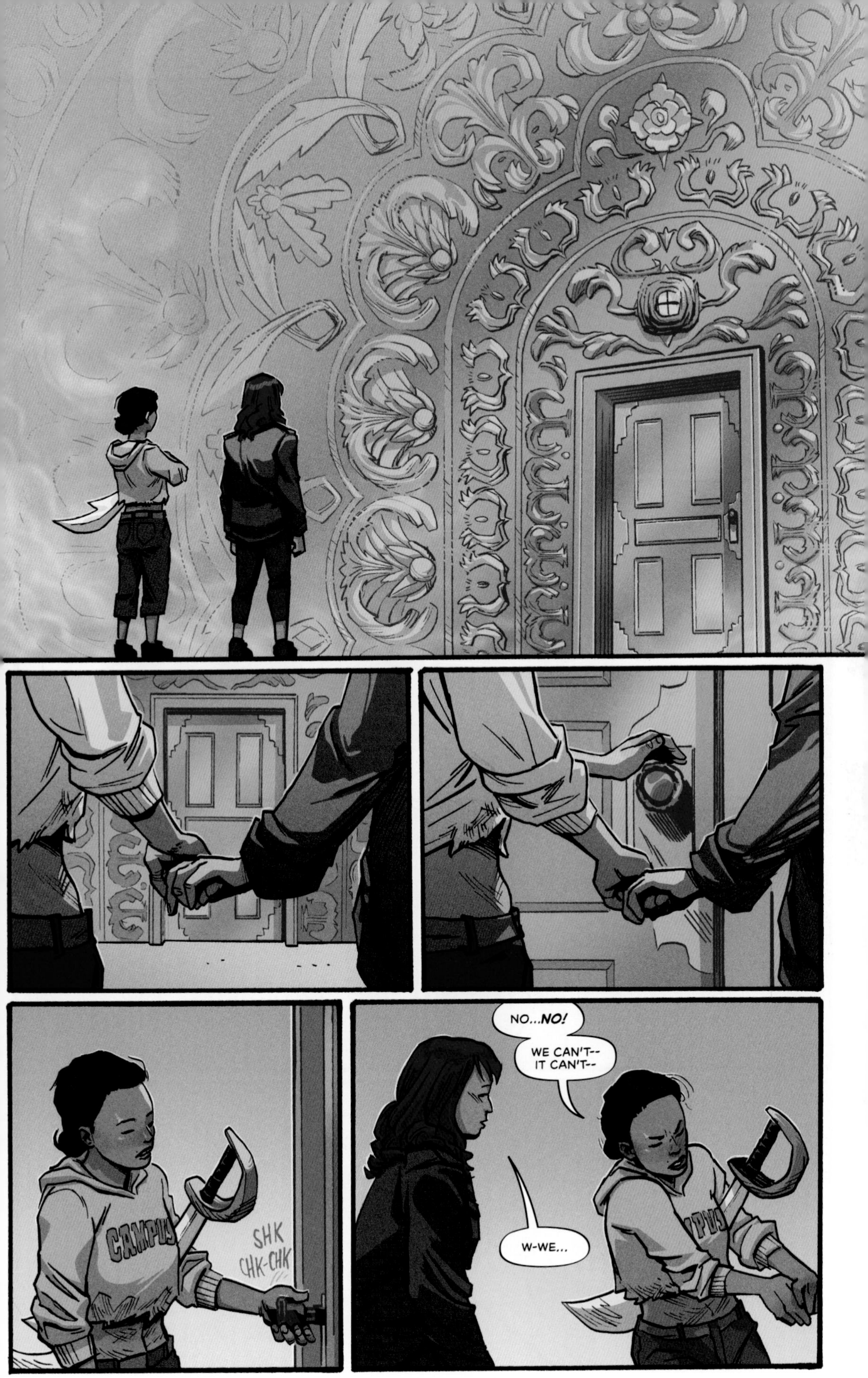
SHK
CHK-CHK
NO...NO!
WE CAN'T--
IT CAN'T--
W-WE...

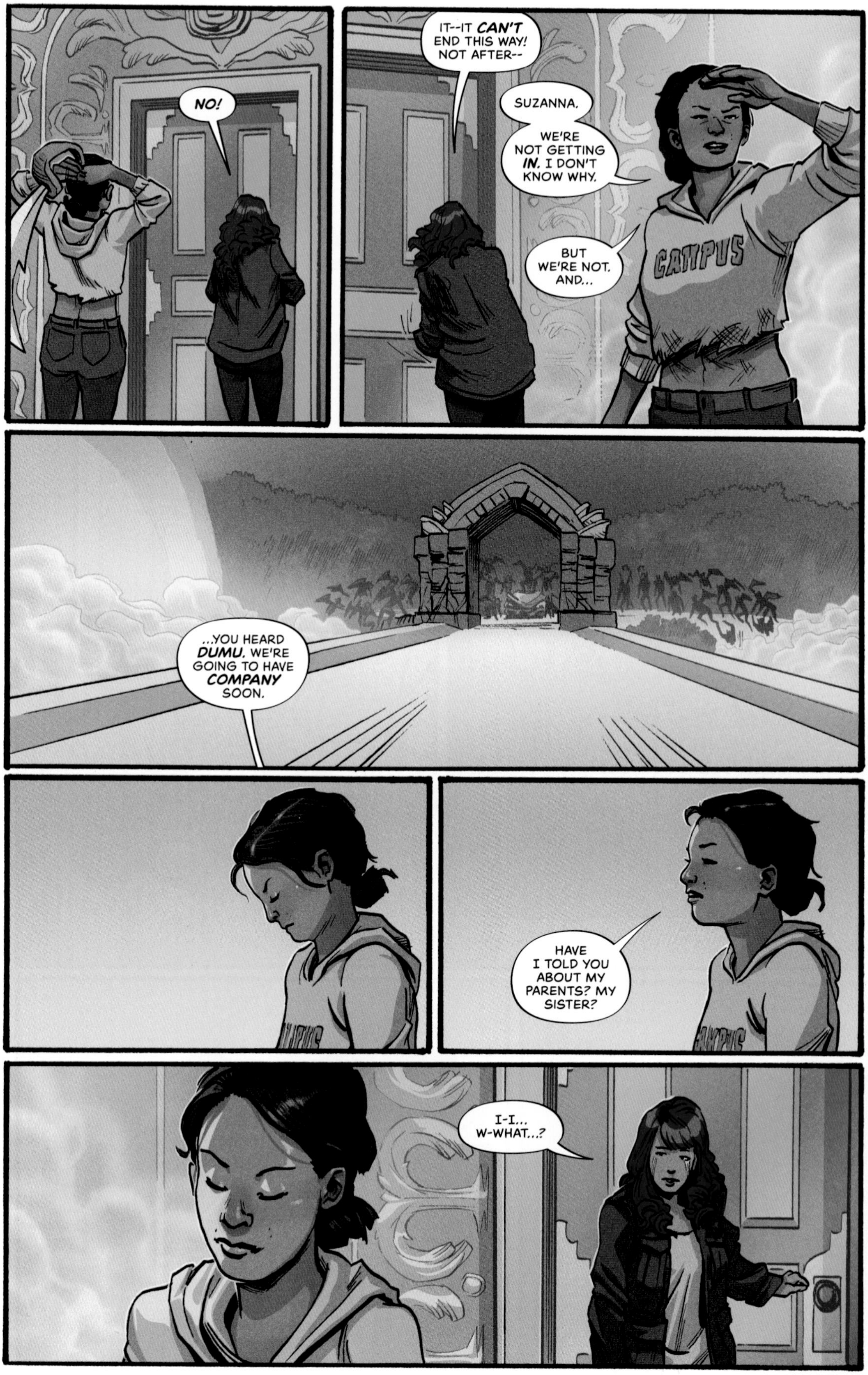
NO!
IT--IT CAN'T END THIS WAY! NOT AFTER--
SUZANNA.
WE'RE NOT GETTING IN. I DON'T KNOW WHY.
BUT WE'RE NOT. AND...
...YOU HEARD DUMU. WE'RE GOING TO HAVE COMPANY SOON.
HAVE I TOLD YOU ABOUT MY PARENTS? MY SISTER?
I-I... W-WHAT...?

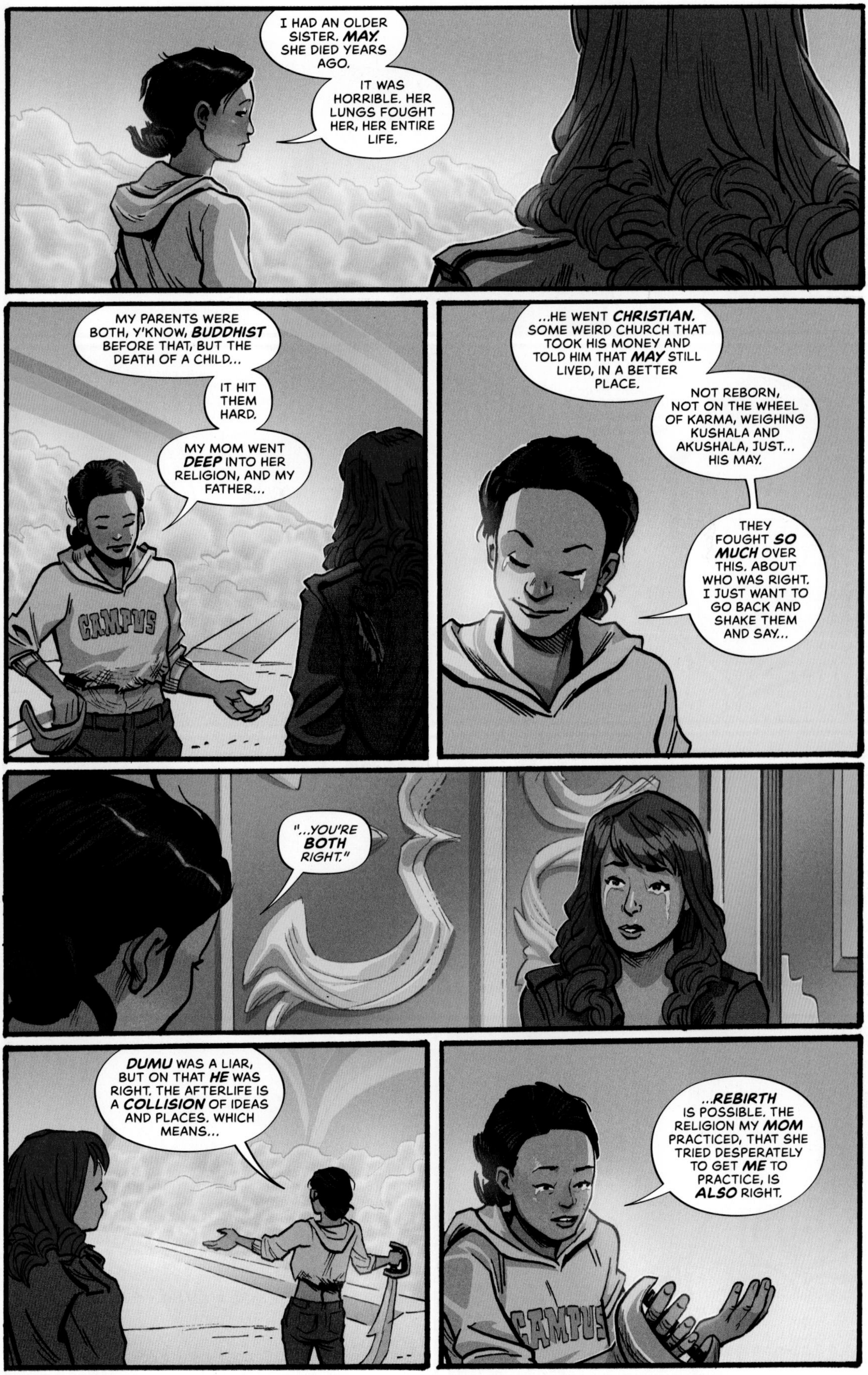
I HAD AN OLDER SISTER. MAY. SHE DIED YEARS AGO.
IT WAS HORRIBLE. HER LUNGS FOUGHT HER, HER ENTIRE LIFE.
MY PARENTS WERE BOTH, Y'KNOW, BUDDHIST BEFORE THAT, BUT THE DEATH OF A CHILD...
IT HIT THEM HARD.
MY MOM WENT DEEP INTO HER RELIGION, AND MY FATHER...
CAMPUS
...HE WENT CHRISTIAN. SOME WEIRD CHURCH THAT TOOK HIS MONEY AND TOLD HIM THAT MAY STILL LIVED, IN A BETTER PLACE.
NOT REBORN, NOT ON THE WHEEL OF KARMA, WEIGHING KUSHALA AND AKUSHALA, JUST... HIS MAY.
THEY FOUGHT SO MUCH OVER THIS. ABOUT WHO WAS RIGHT. I JUST WANT TO GO BACK AND SHAKE THEM AND SAY...
"...YOU'RE BOTH RIGHT."
DUMU WAS A LIAR, BUT ON THAT HE WAS RIGHT. THE AFTERLIFE IS A COLLISION OF IDEAS AND PLACES. WHICH MEANS...
...REBIRTH IS POSSIBLE. THE RELIGION MY MOM PRACTICED, THAT SHE TRIED DESPERATELY TO GET ME TO PRACTICE, IS ALSO RIGHT.
CAMPUS

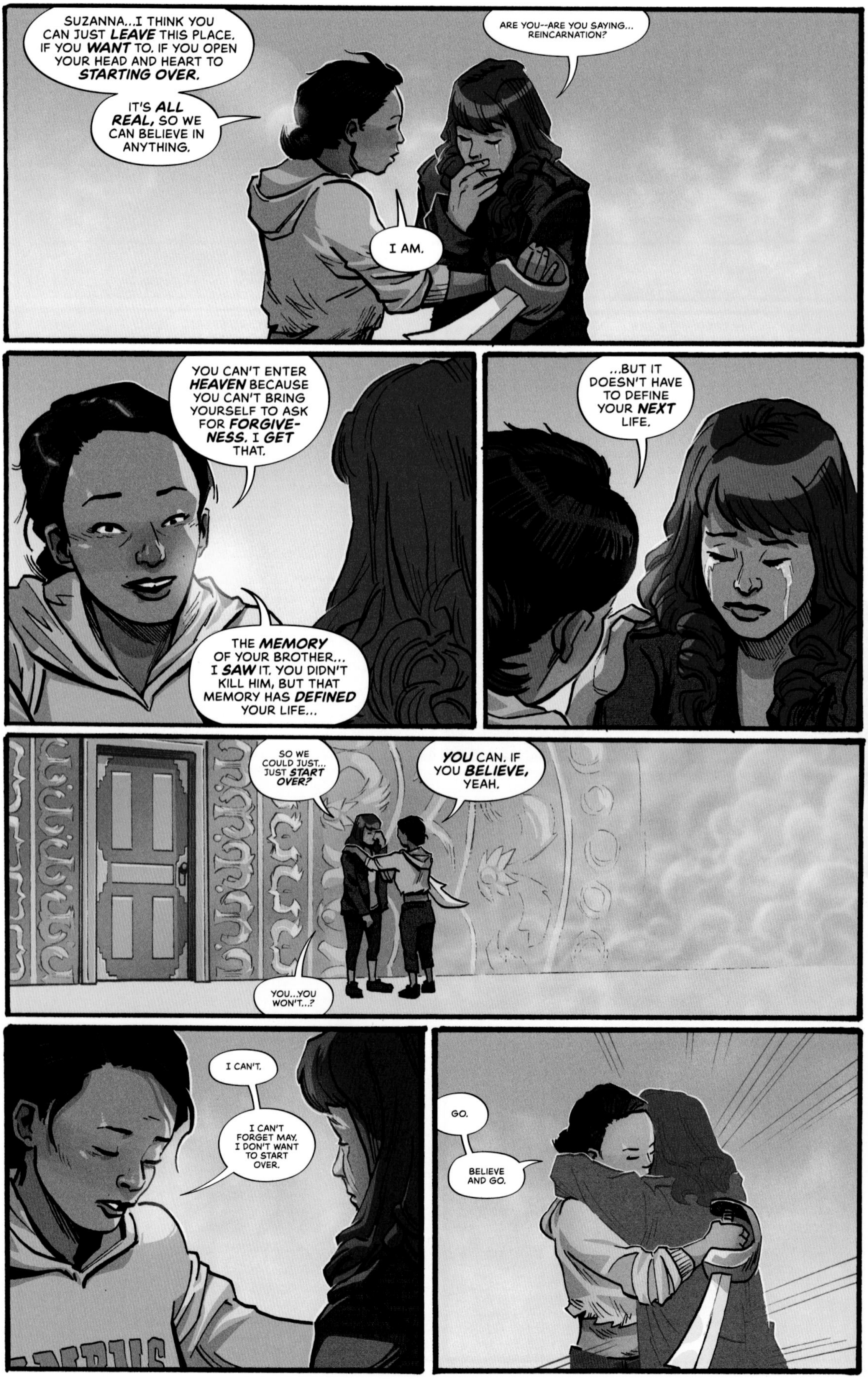

SUZANNA...I THINK YOU CAN JUST LEAVE THIS PLACE. IF YOU WANT TO. IF YOU OPEN YOUR HEAD AND HEART TO STARTING OVER.
IT'S ALL REAL, SO WE CAN BELIEVE IN ANYTHING.
ARE YOU--ARE YOU SAYING... REINCARNATION?
I AM.
YOU CAN'T ENTER HEAVEN BECAUSE YOU CAN'T BRING YOURSELF TO ASK FOR FORGIVE-NESS. I GET THAT.
THE MEMORY OF YOUR BROTHER... I SAW IT. YOU DIDN'T KILL HIM, BUT THAT MEMORY HAS DEFINED YOUR LIFE...
...BUT IT DOESN'T HAVE TO DEFINE YOUR NEXT LIFE.
SO WE COULD JUST... JUST START OVER?
YOU CAN. IF YOU BELIEVE, YEAH.
YOU...YOU WON'T...?
I CAN'T.
I CAN'T FORGET MAY. I DON'T WANT TO START OVER.
GO.
BELIEVE AND GO.

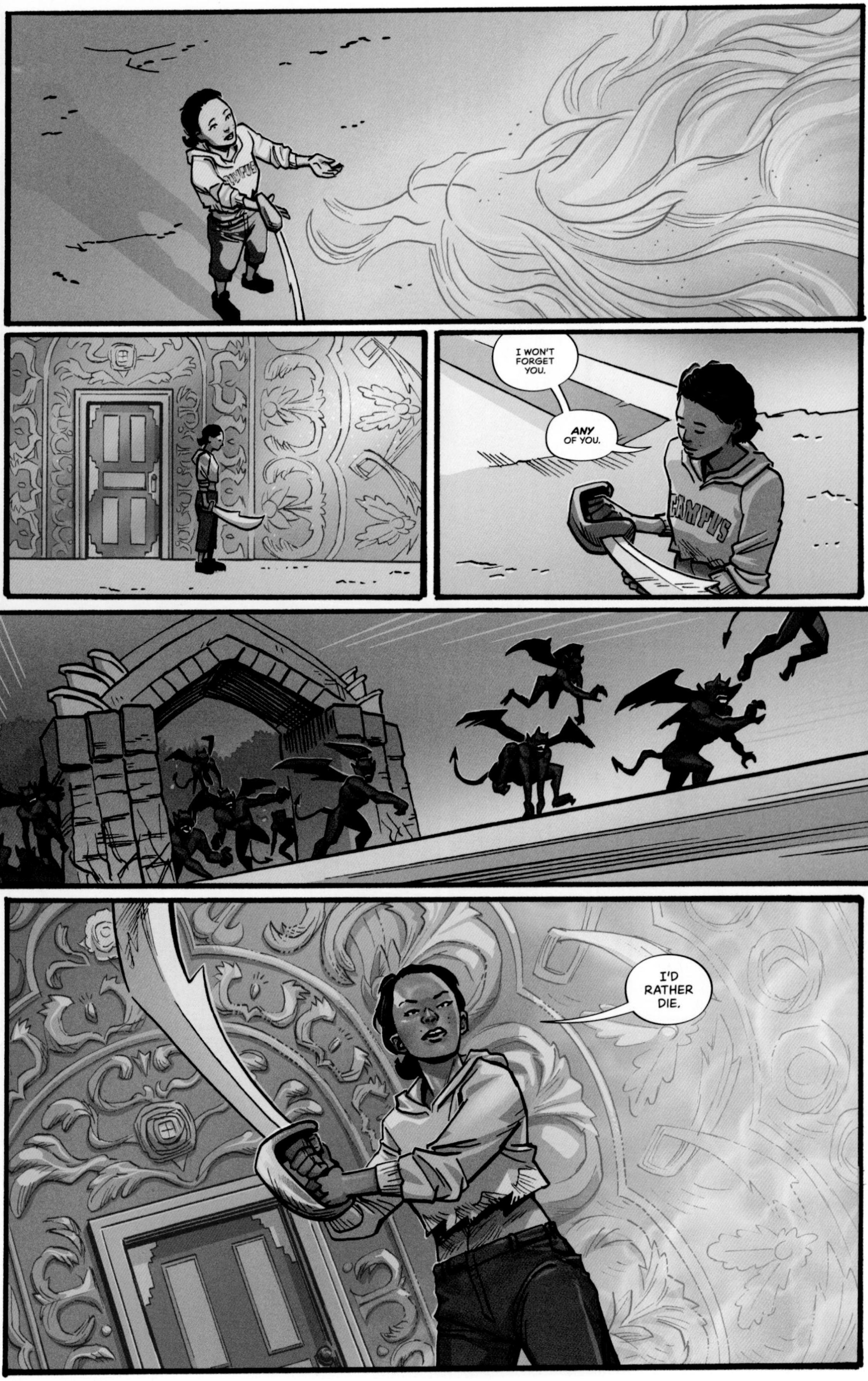
I WON'T FORGET YOU.
ANY OF YOU.
I'D RATHER DIE.

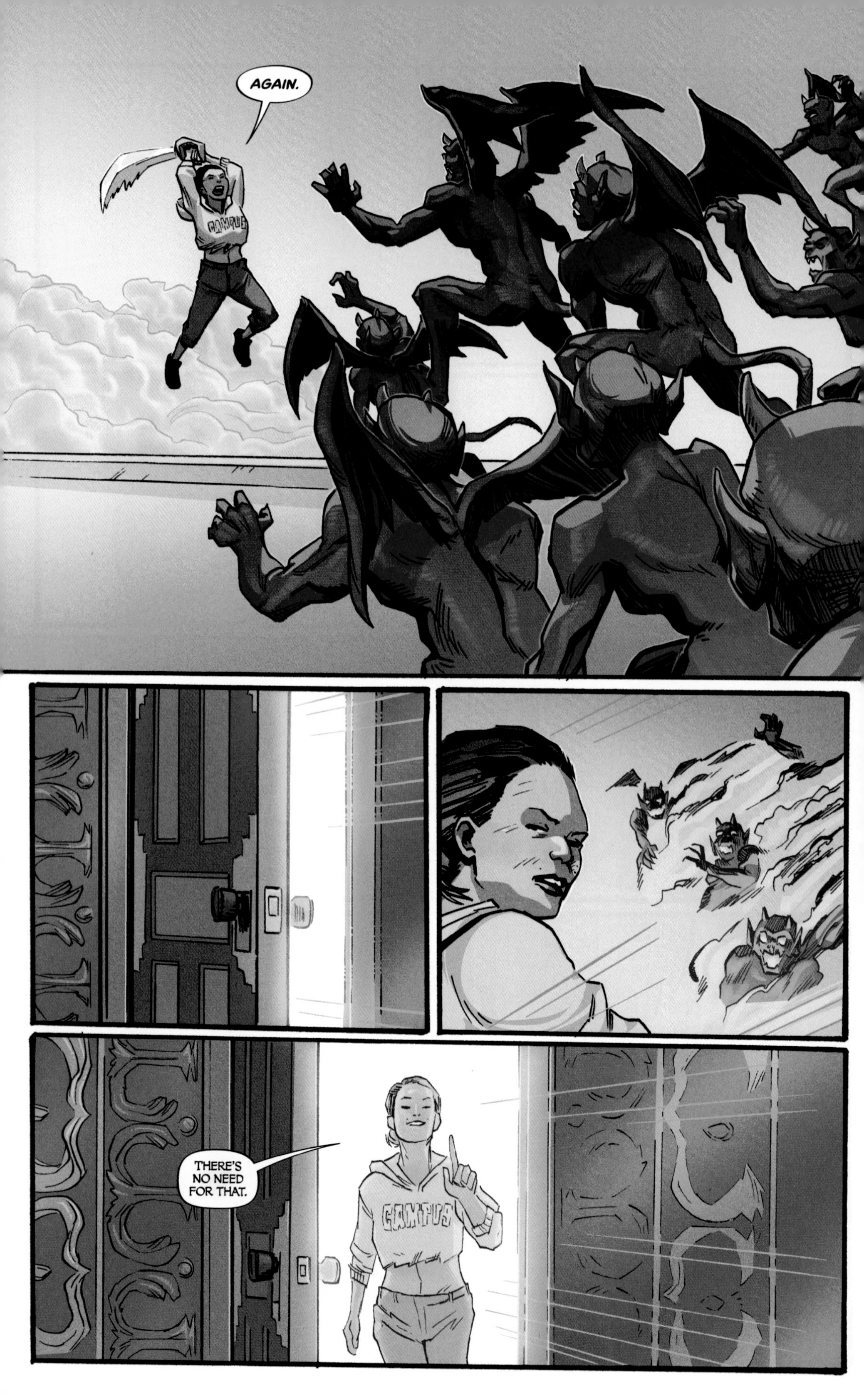
AGAIN.
CAMPUS
THERE'S NO NEED FOR THAT.
CAMPUS

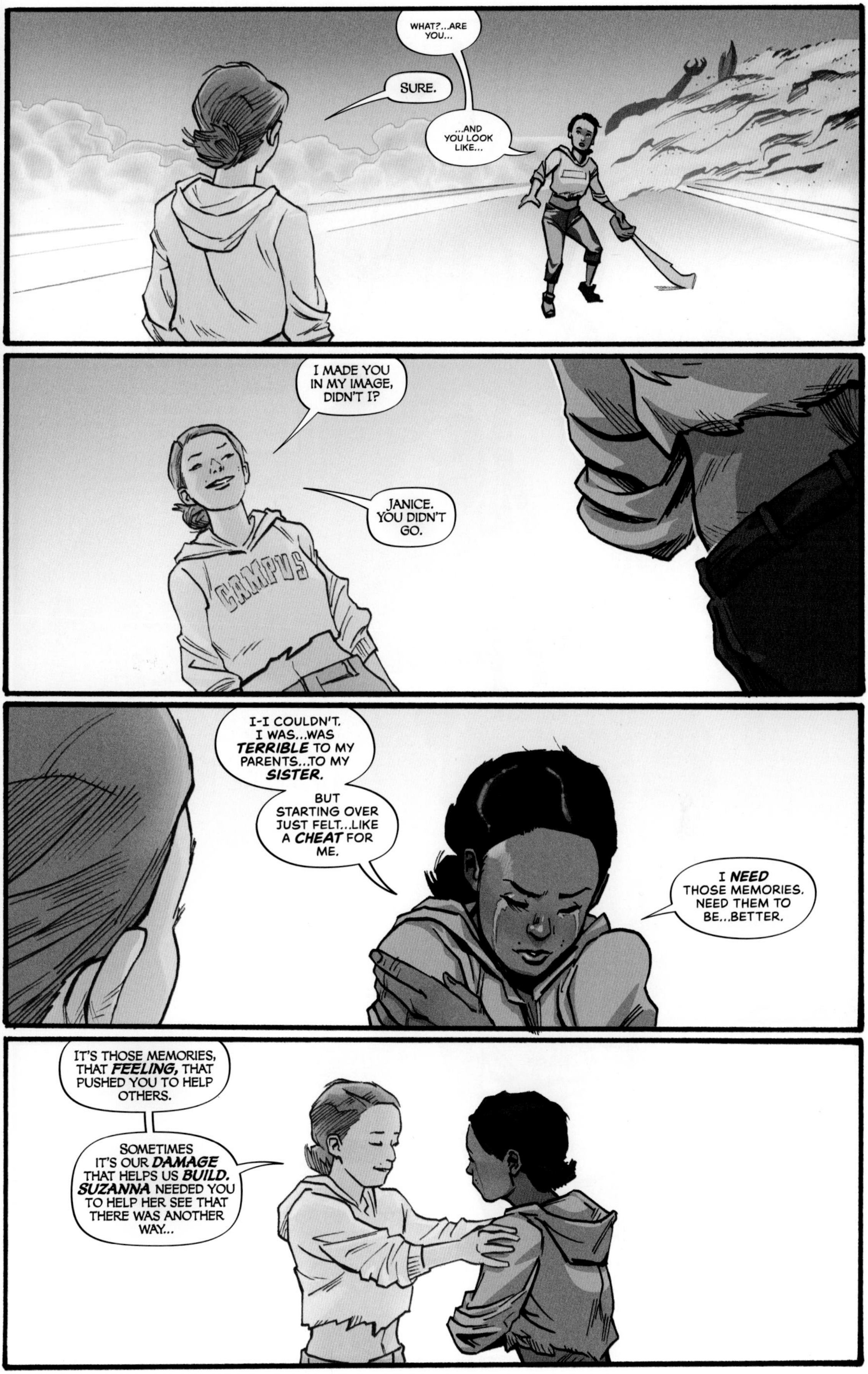
WHAT?...ARE YOU...
SURE.
...AND YOU LOOK LIKE...
I MADE YOU IN MY IMAGE, DIDN'T I?
JANICE. YOU DIDN'T GO.
I-I COULDN'T. I WAS...WAS TERRIBLE TO MY PARENTS...TO MY SISTER.
BUT STARTING OVER JUST FELT...LIKE A CHEAT FOR ME.
I NEED THOSE MEMORIES. NEED THEM TO BE...BETTER.
IT'S THOSE MEMORIES, THAT FEELING, THAT PUSHED YOU TO HELP OTHERS.
SOMETIMES IT'S OUR DAMAGE THAT HELPS US BUILD. SUZANNA NEEDED YOU TO HELP HER SEE THAT THERE WAS ANOTHER WAY...

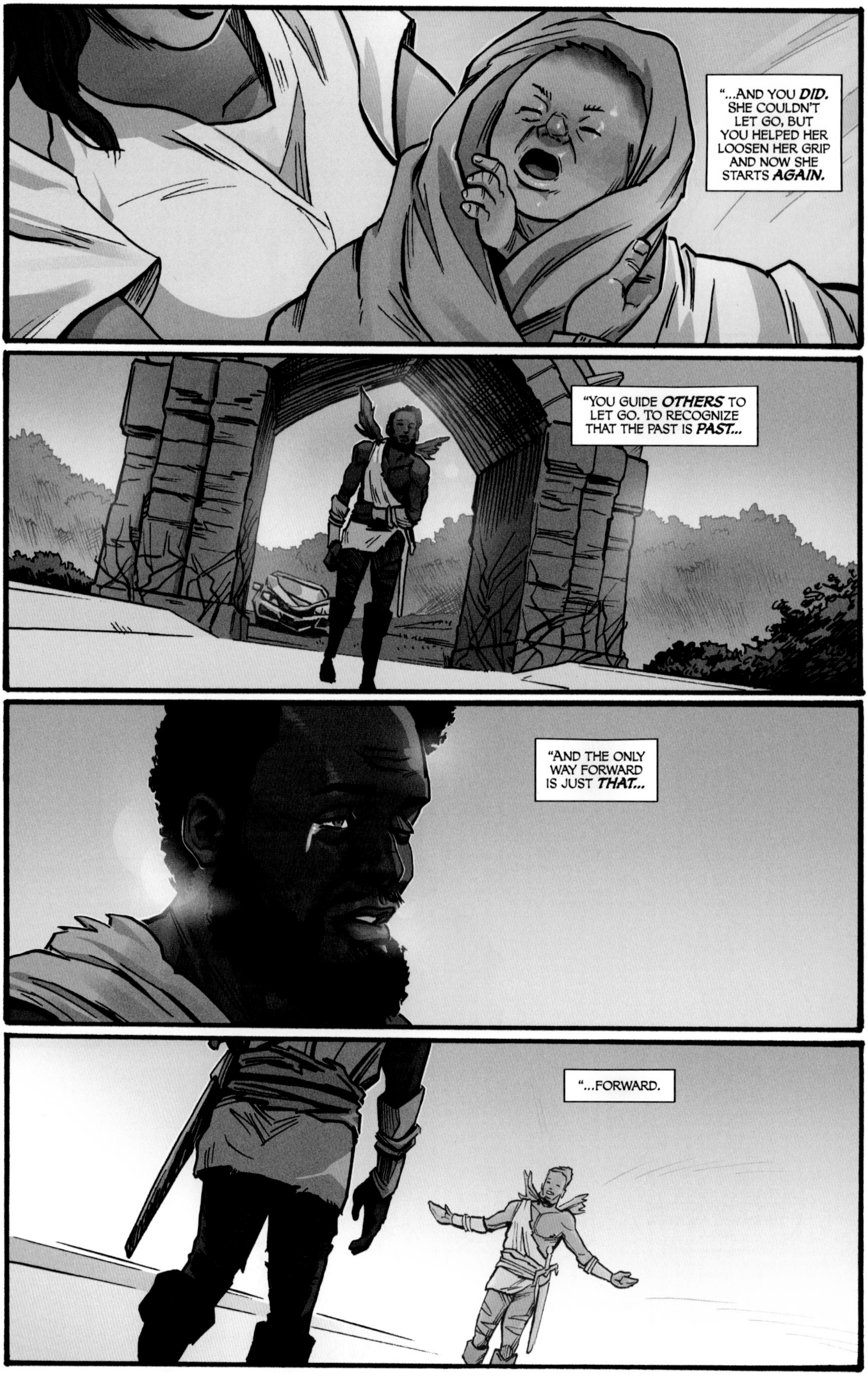
"...AND YOU DID. SHE COULDN'T LET GO, BUT YOU HELPED HER LOOSEN HER GRIP AND NOW SHE STARTS AGAIN.
"YOU GUIDE OTHERS TO LET GO. TO RECOGNIZE THAT THE PAST IS PAST...
"AND THE ONLY WAY FORWARD IS JUST THAT...
"...FORWARD.

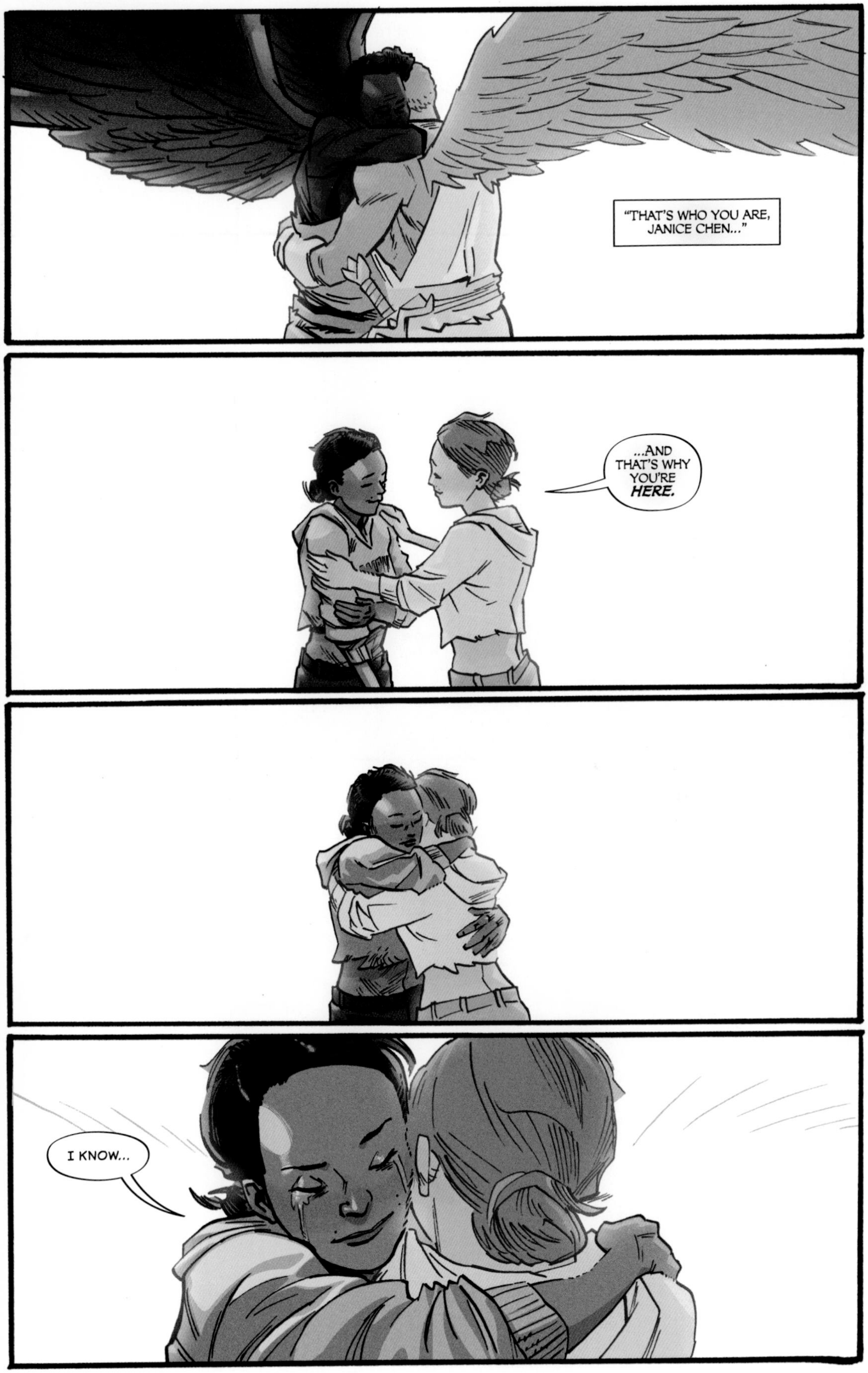
"THAT'S WHO YOU ARE, JANICE CHEN..."
...AND THAT'S WHY YOU'RE *HERE.*
I KNOW...

**"...I KNOW
THAT NOW."**

"HELLO...?"

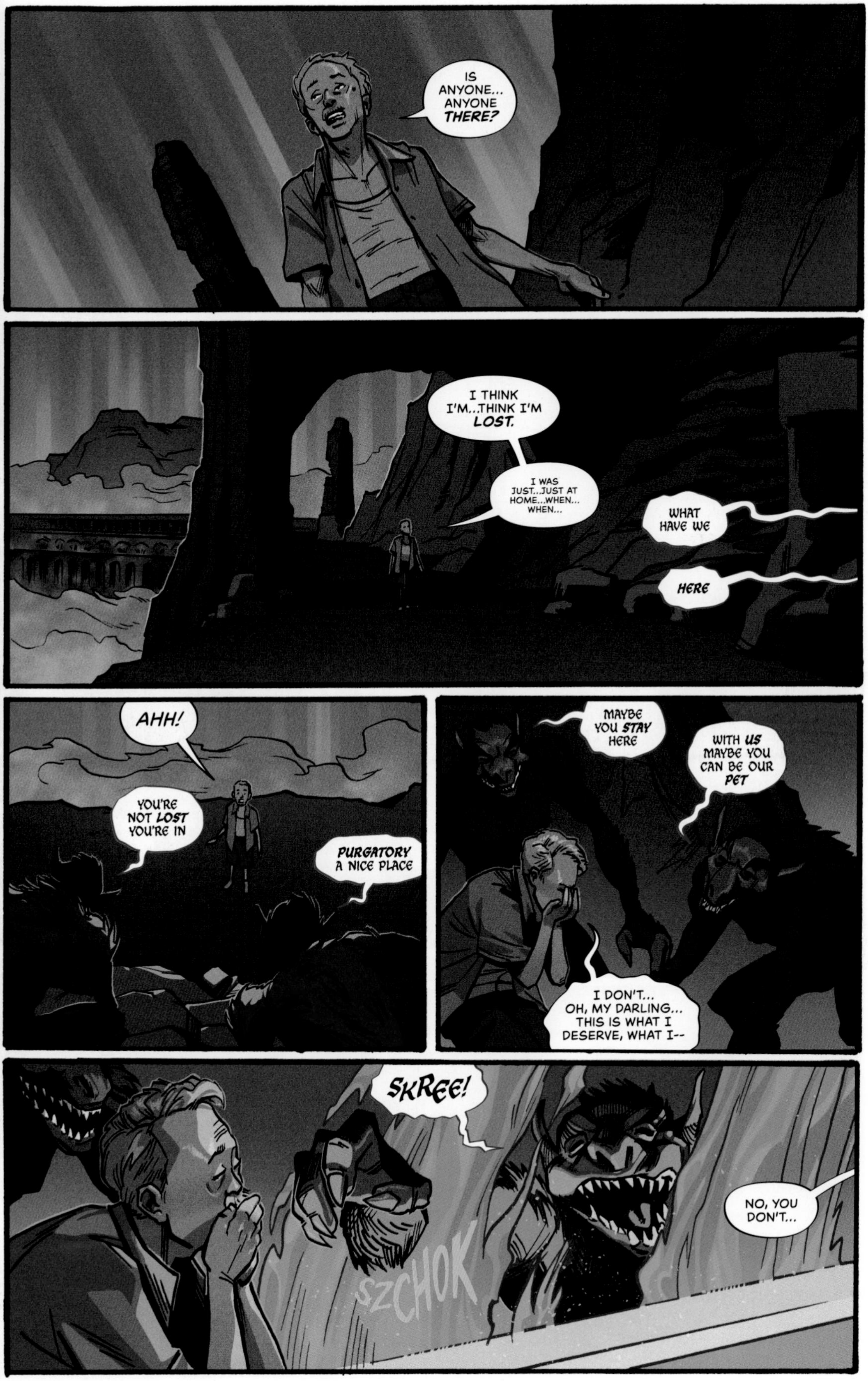

IS ANYONE... ANYONE THERE?
I THINK I'M...THINK I'M LOST.
I WAS JUST...JUST AT HOME...WHEN... WHEN...
WHAT HAVE WE
HERE
AHH!
YOU'RE NOT LOST YOU'RE IN
PURGATORY A NICE PLACE
MAYBE YOU STAY HERE
WITH US MAYBE YOU CAN BE OUR PET
I DON'T... OH, MY DARLING... THIS IS WHAT I DESERVE, WHAT I--
SKREE!
SZCHOK
NO, YOU DON'T...

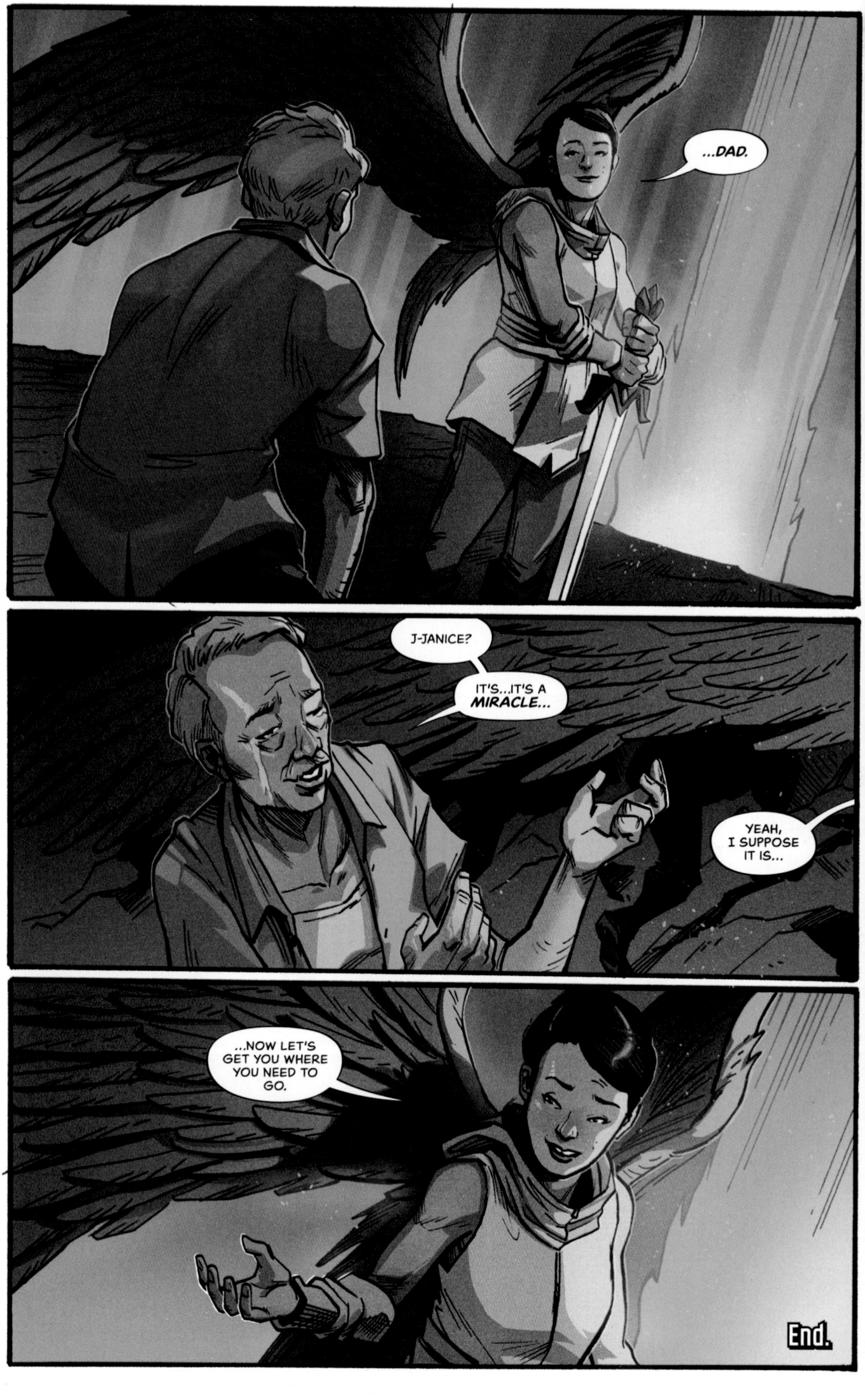
...DAD.
J-JANICE?
IT'S...IT'S A MIRACLE...
YEAH, I SUPPOSE IT IS...
...NOW LET'S GET YOU WHERE YOU NEED TO GO.
End.

CHIP ZDARSKY
JASON LOO
AFTERLIFT
PARIS ALLEYNE
ADITYA BIDIKAR
ALLISON O'TOOLE
COMIXOLOGY
ORIGINALS

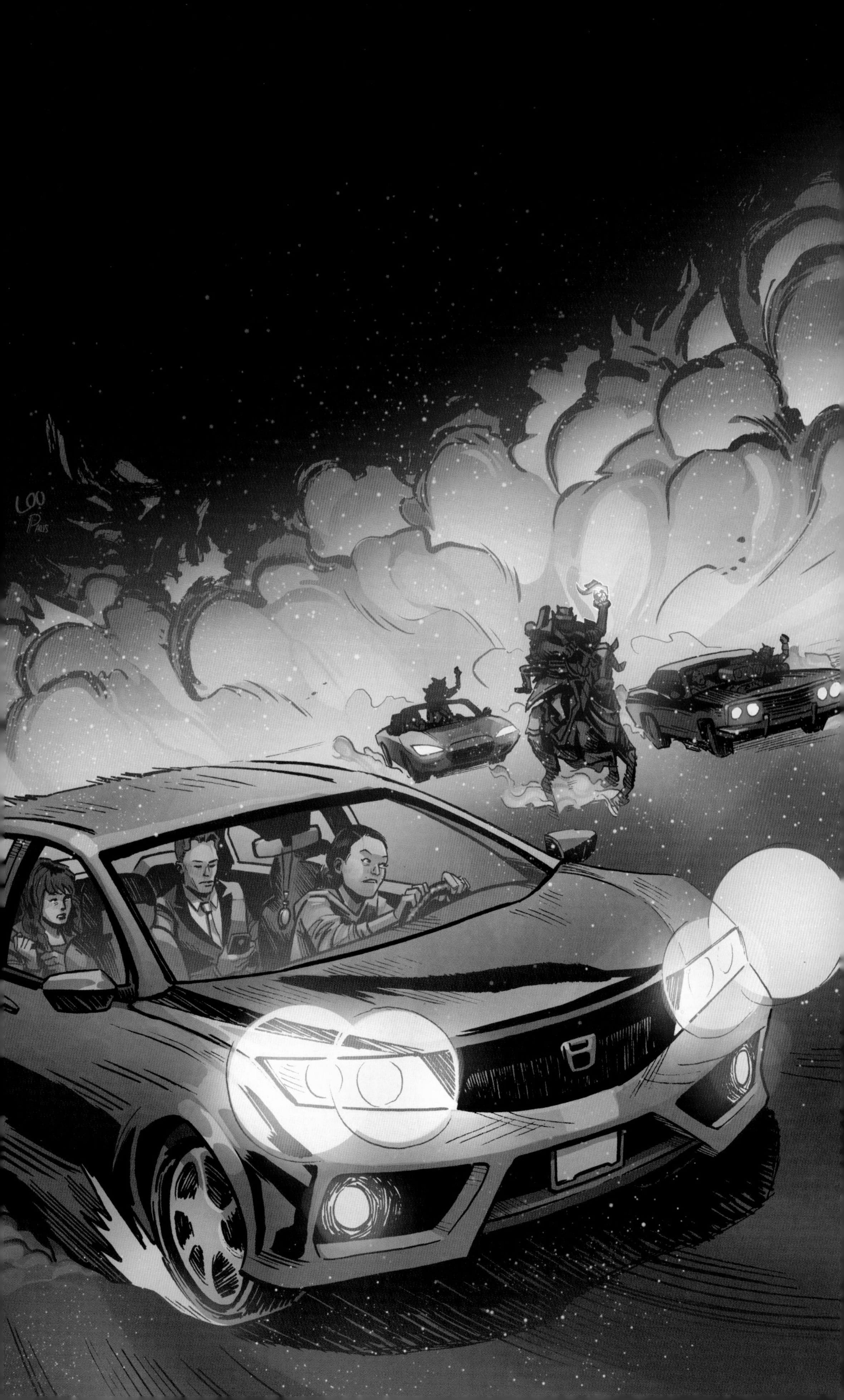

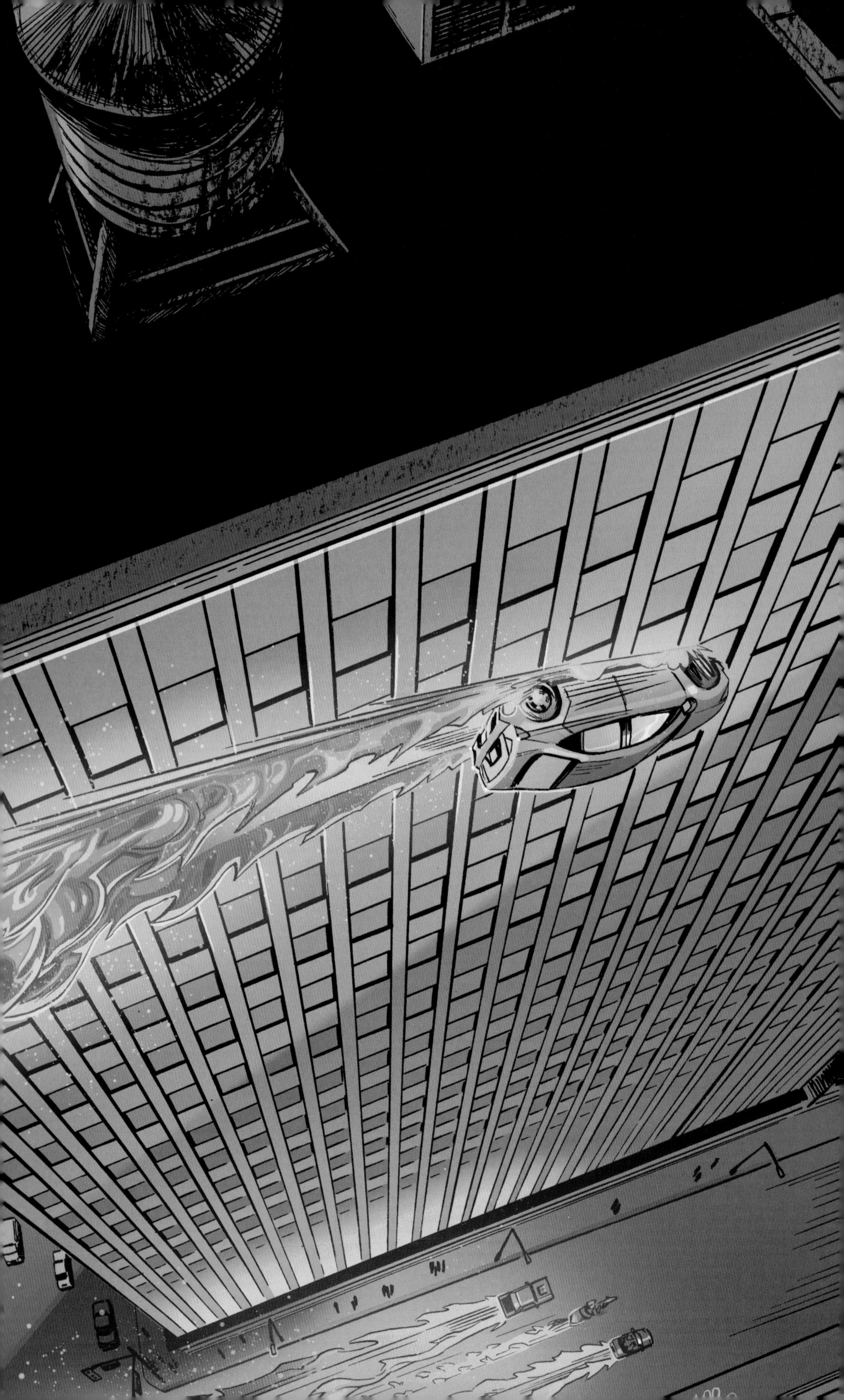

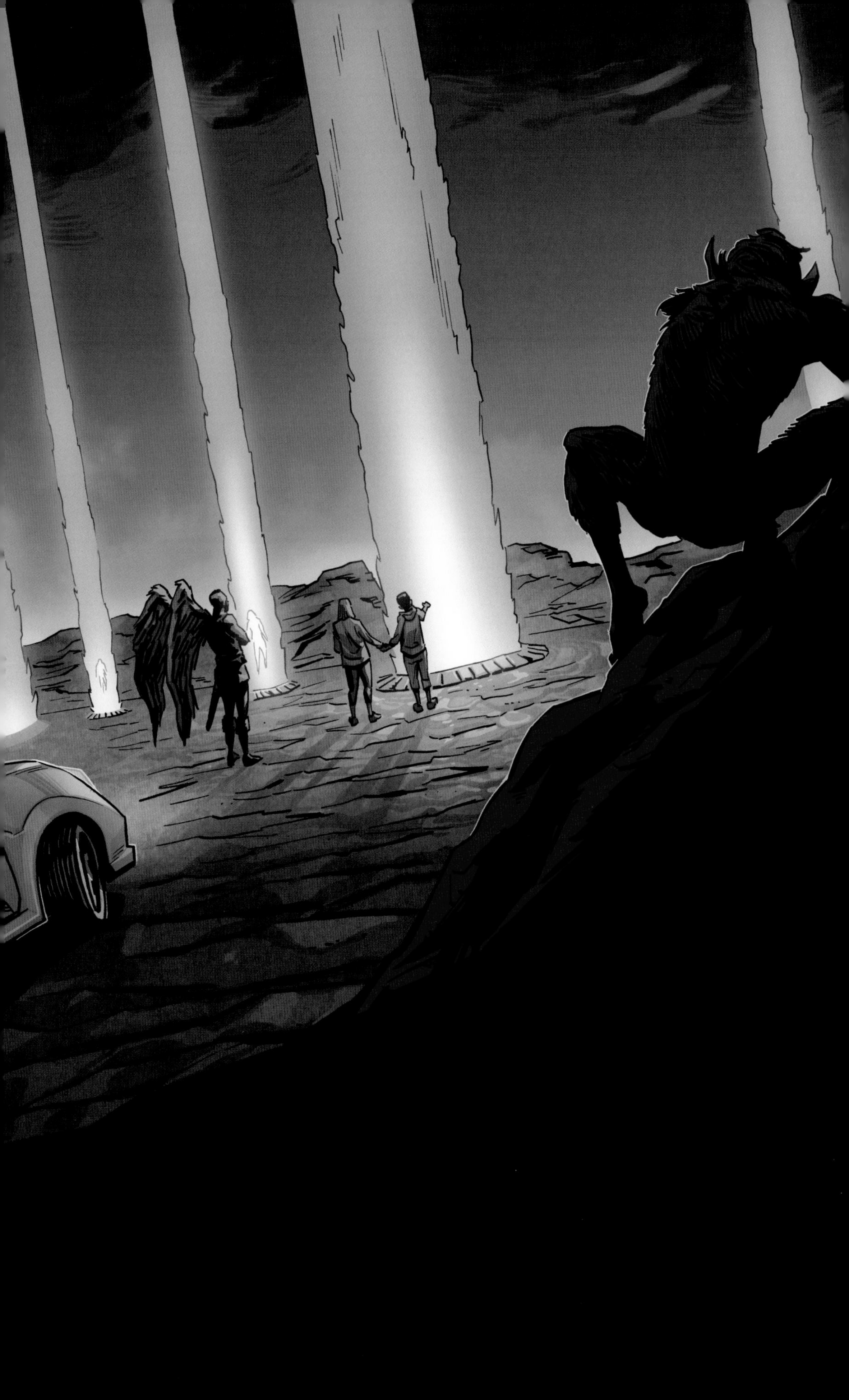

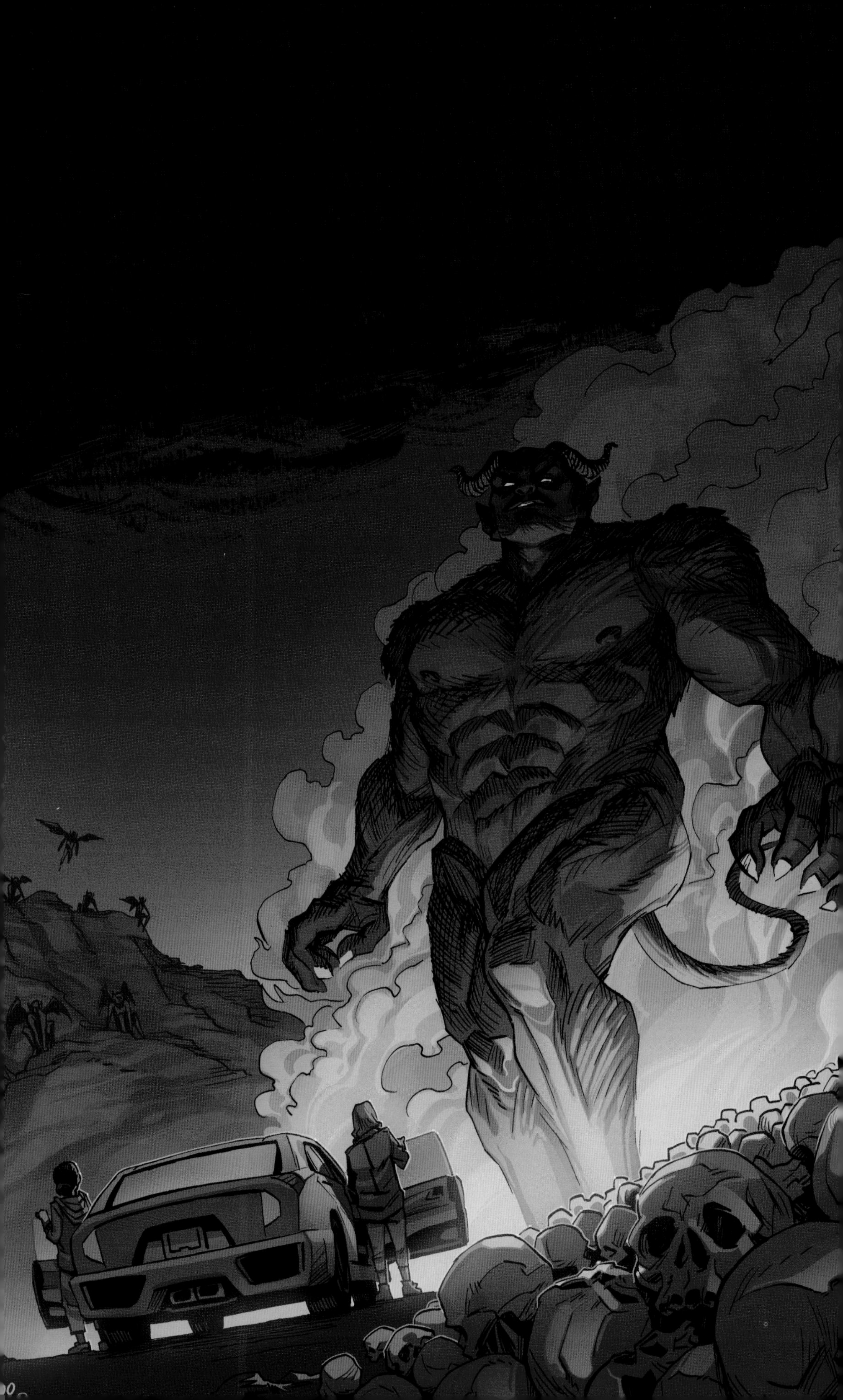

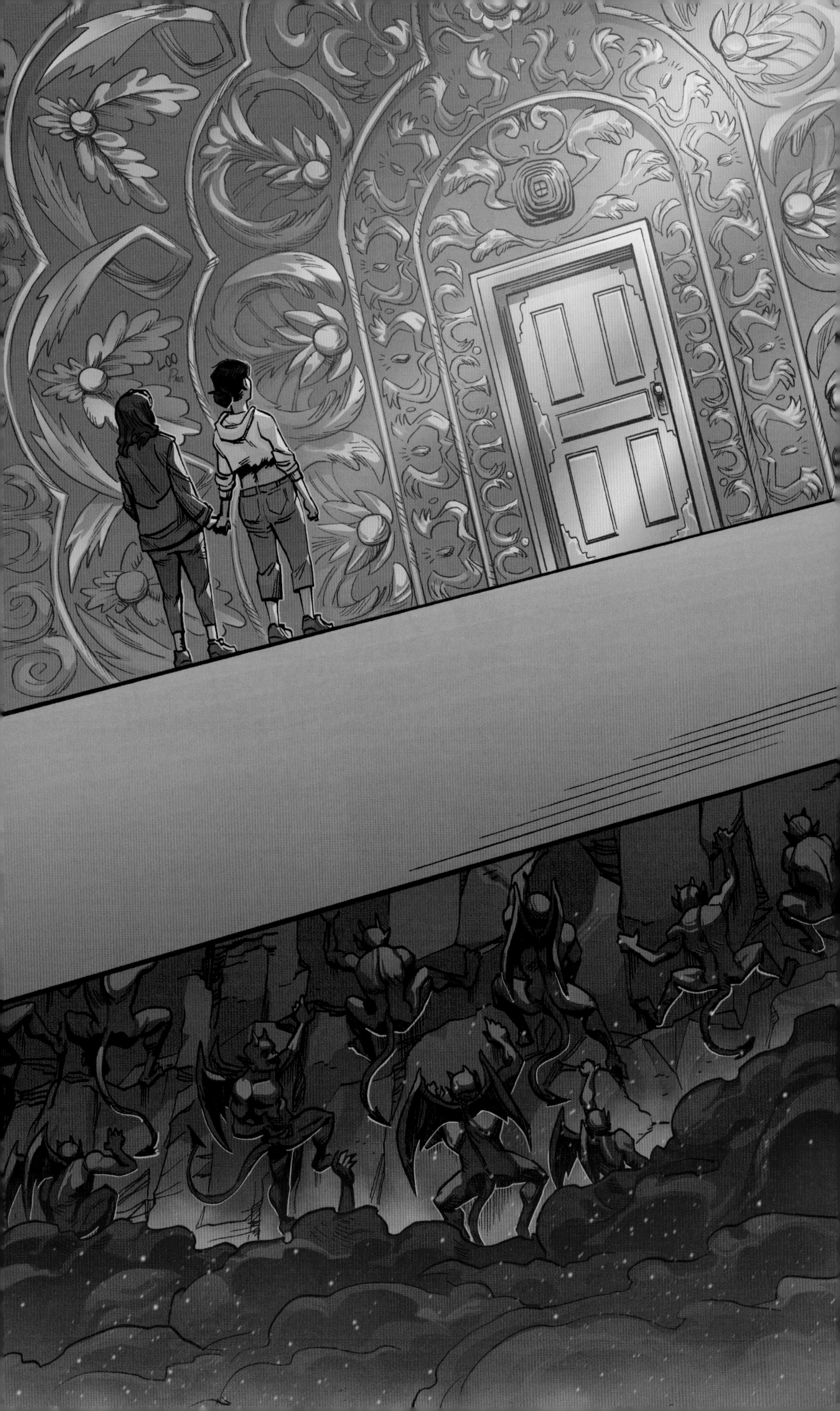
LOO

JASON LOO SKETCHBOOK

CHIP: I knew Jason was a great artist, but I had no idea just how great until the sketches started coming in and I got to see how he refines and improves constantly. In contrast, I am a lazy artist who never gets better because I want to go play video games now.

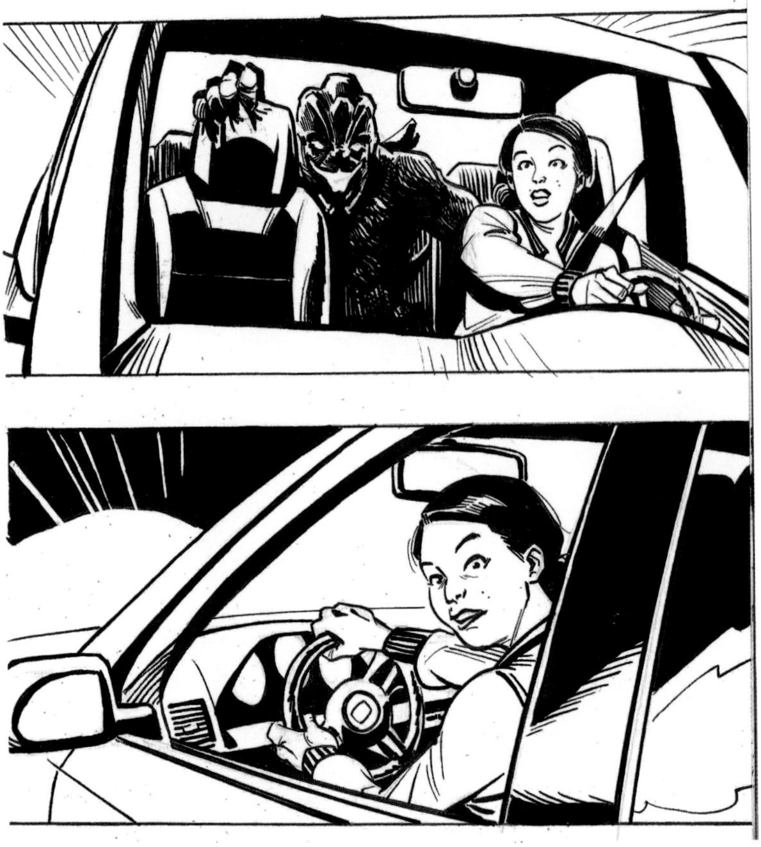

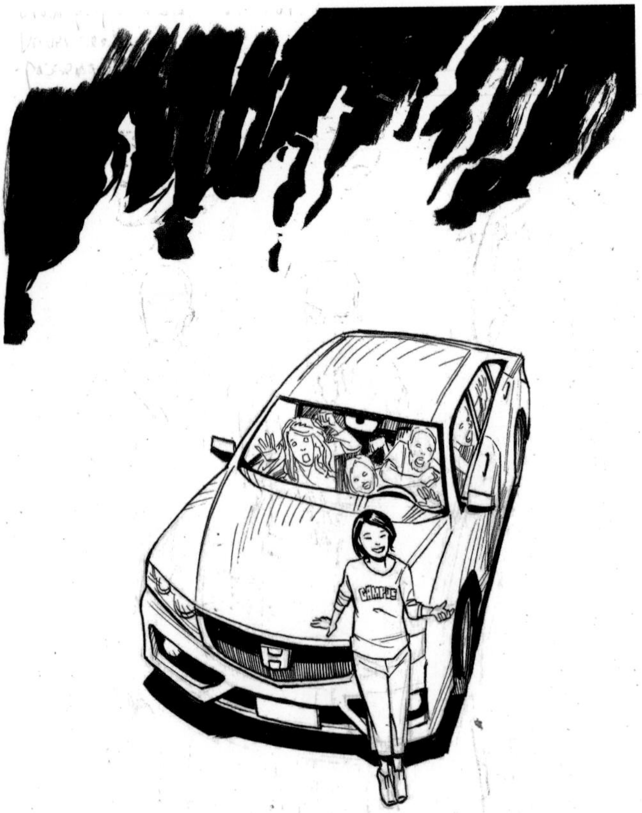

JASON: Chip gave me—at most—three sentences about the project, and I just ran with it before getting the first script. I was drawing a number of scenes that I'd think would happen in the comic, like demons and lost souls chasing the car. I wanted to capture more dynamic action shots that I normally wouldn't have drawn in my earlier comic works.

CHIP: See? Three sentences! I'm L-A-Z-Y.

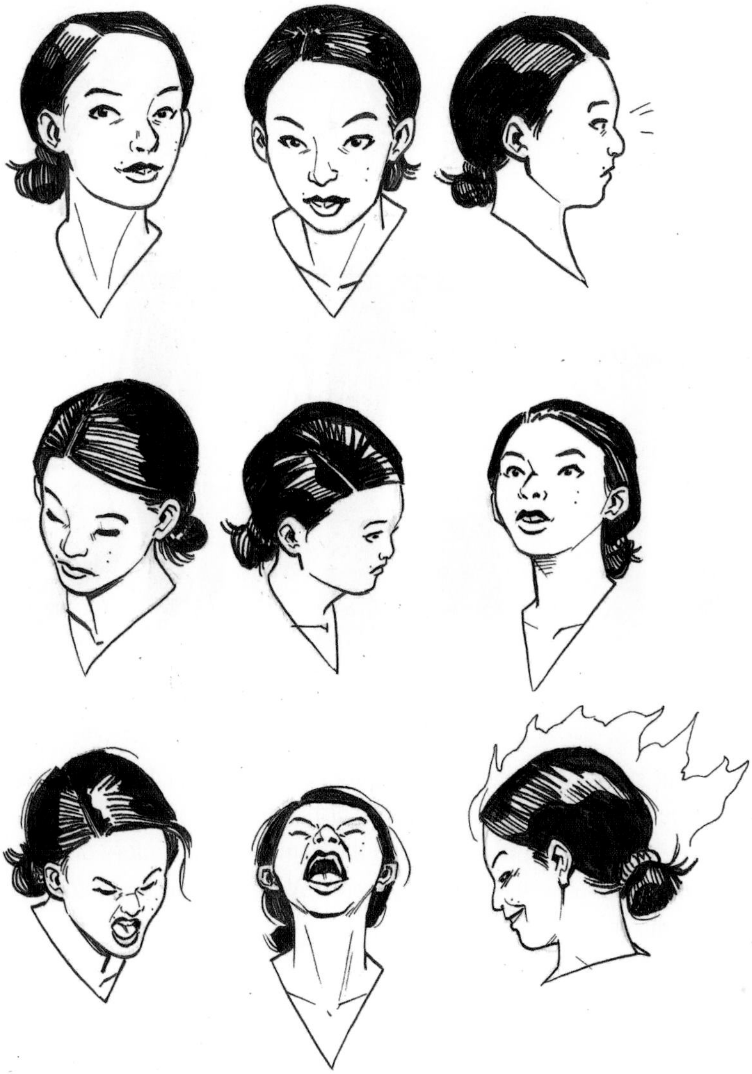

JASON: Besides working with Chip, I was also excited that the lead character was Asian, like in my last comic series. In that series, my mom was the inspiration behind one of the supporting characters. After hearing that, my cousin Justin joked one Christmas that I should draw his sister (also my cousin) Marsha in my next comic. She was going through chemo, so I thought, "Wouldn't it be awesome to draw her kicking butt?" I even drew her little birthmarks.

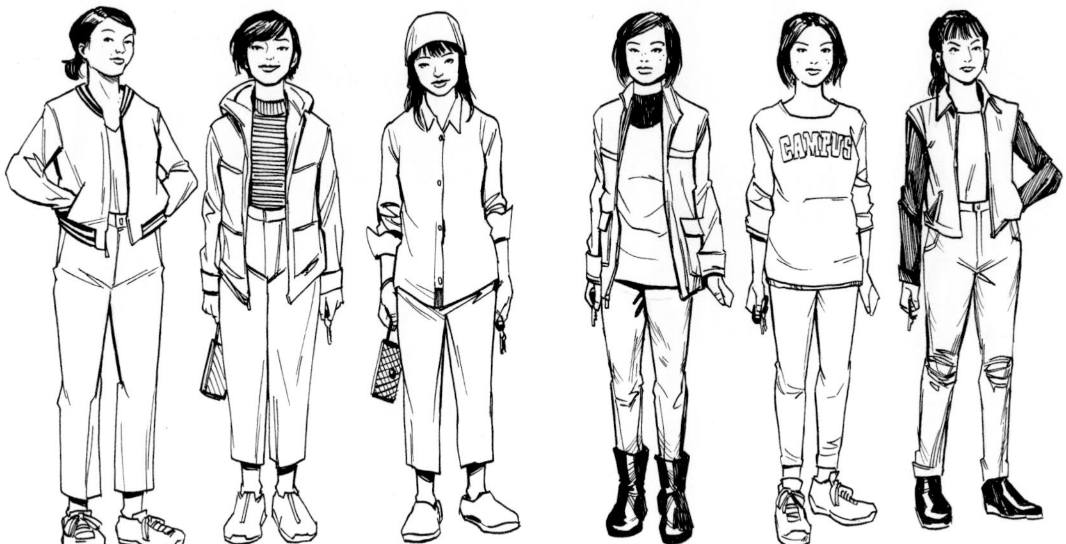
CAMPUS

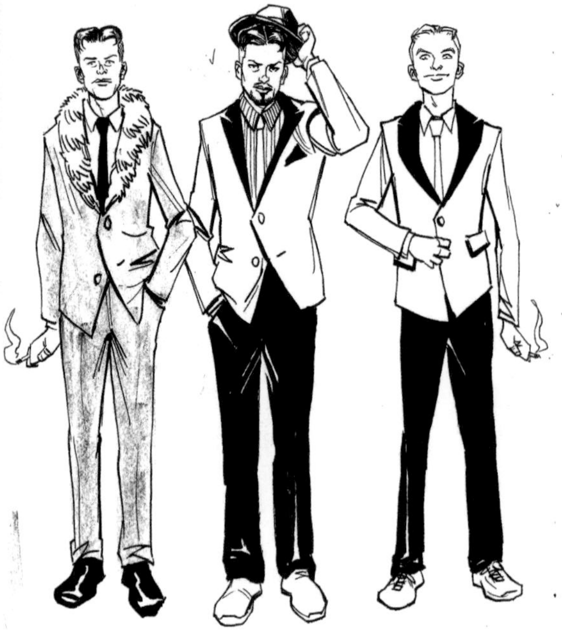

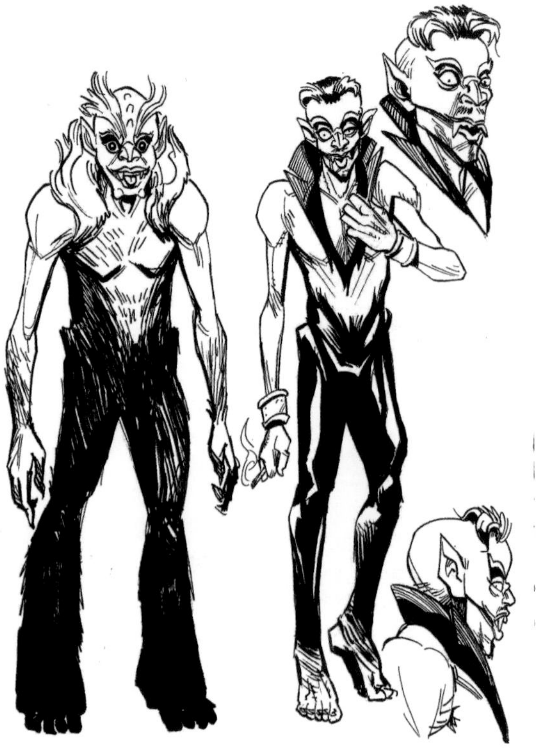

JASON: For Dumu, I Googled designer suits by Versace and Dolce & Gabbana and thought of how those designs would transform into his demon form. I drew him with bangs parted in the middle for all his concepts, to look like his horns. All the demon faces were inspired by Indonesian demon masks that my uncle had displayed in his house since I was little. I wanted the demons to look more distinct than the ones seen in Western media and European Christian paintings.

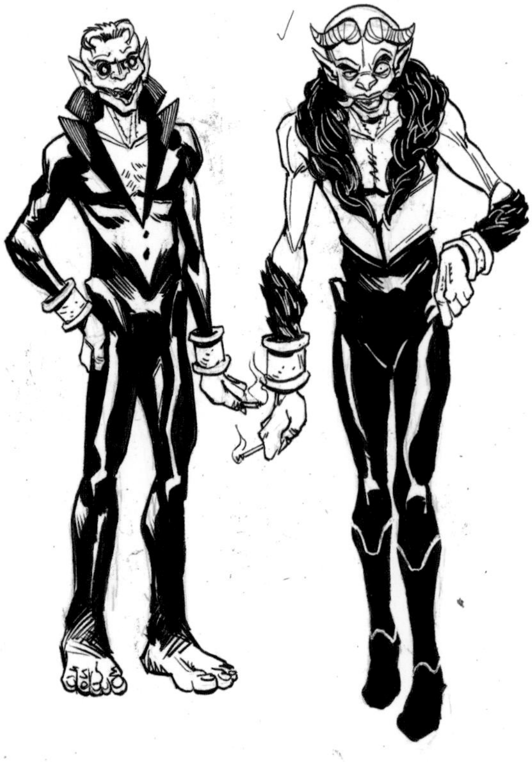

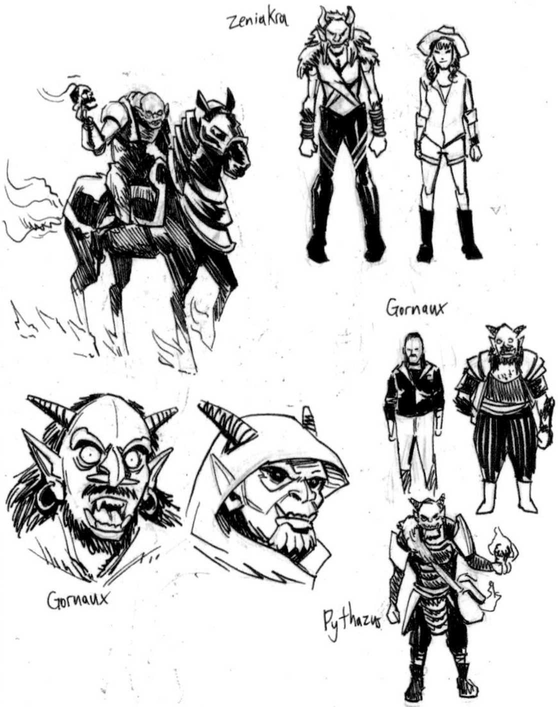
Zeniakra
Gornaux
Gornaux
Pythazus

CHIP: I made Jason draw a lot of cars, and for that I'll be eternally sorry. But, also, it turns out he's really good at it.

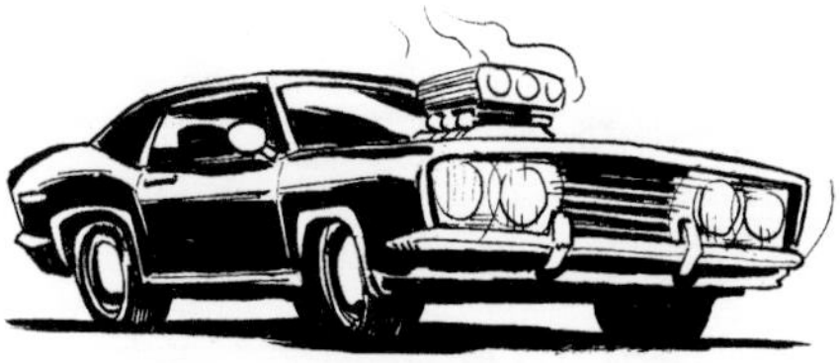

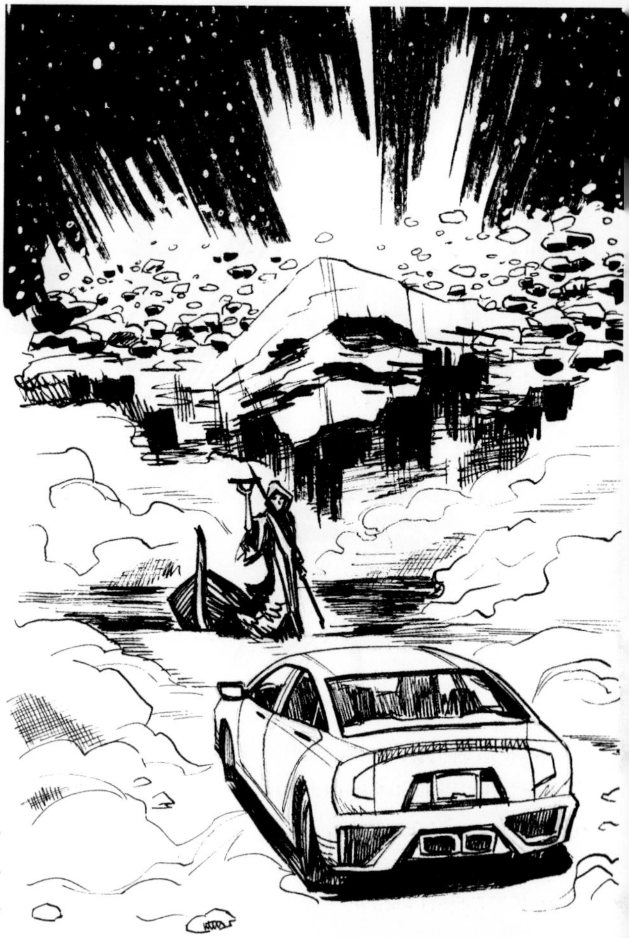

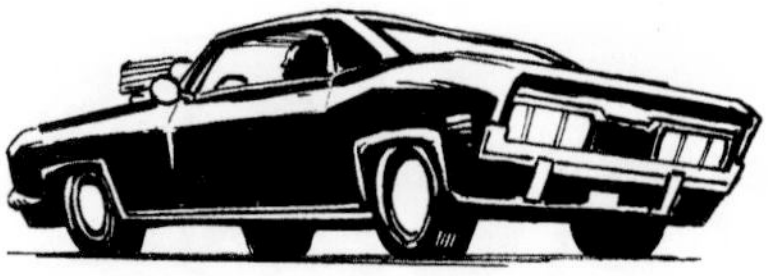

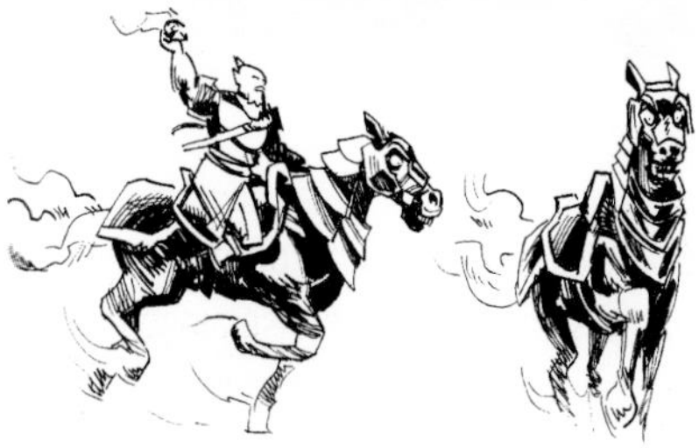

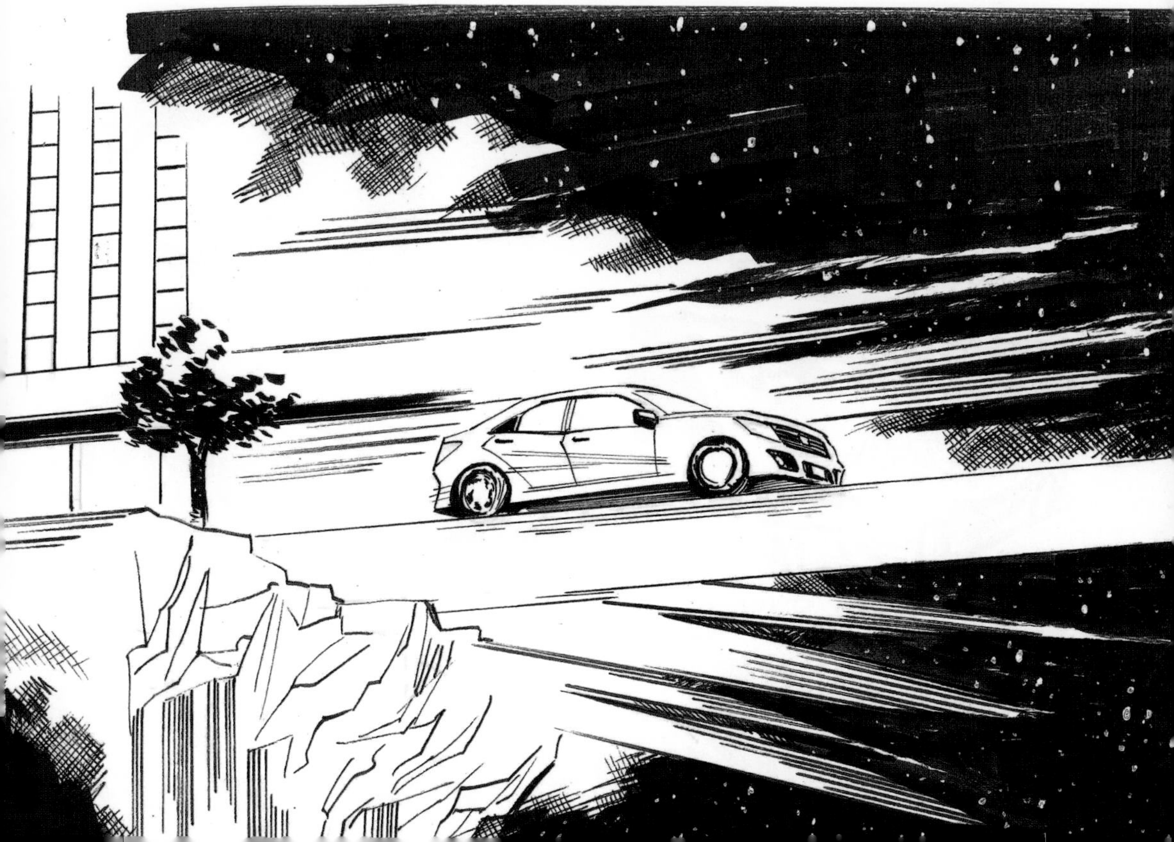

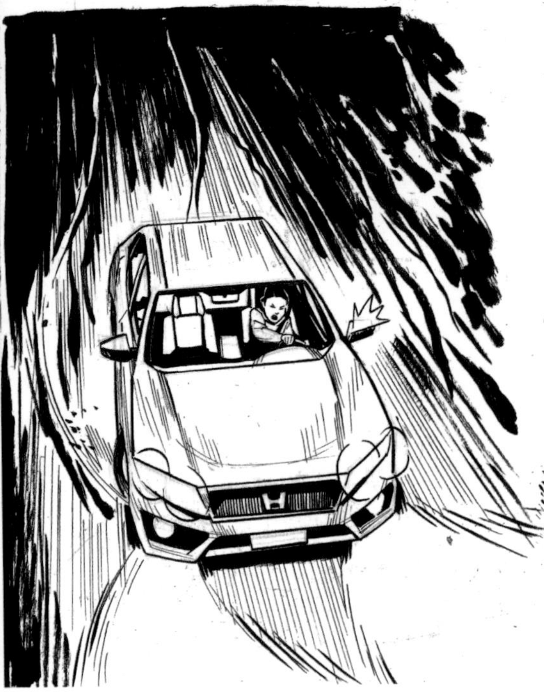

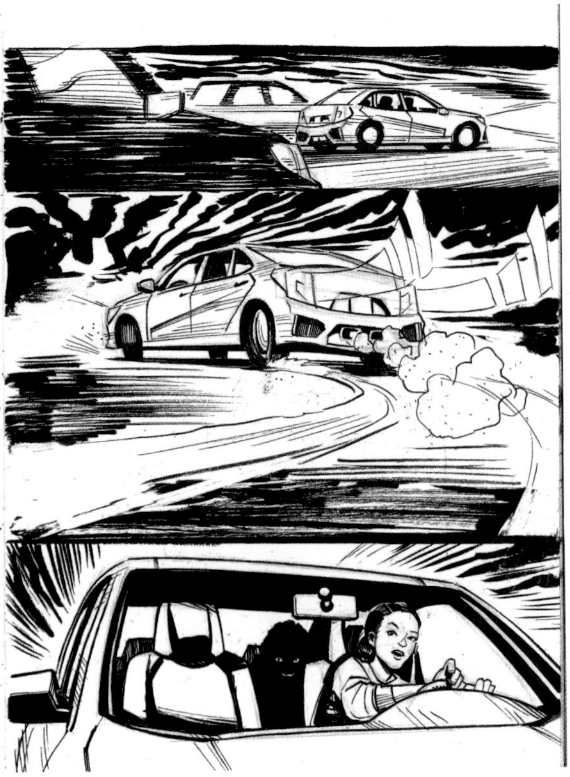

JASON: Drawing cars was one challenge. Drawing cars zipping through the afterlife was another.

CHIP: I SAID I WAS SORRY.

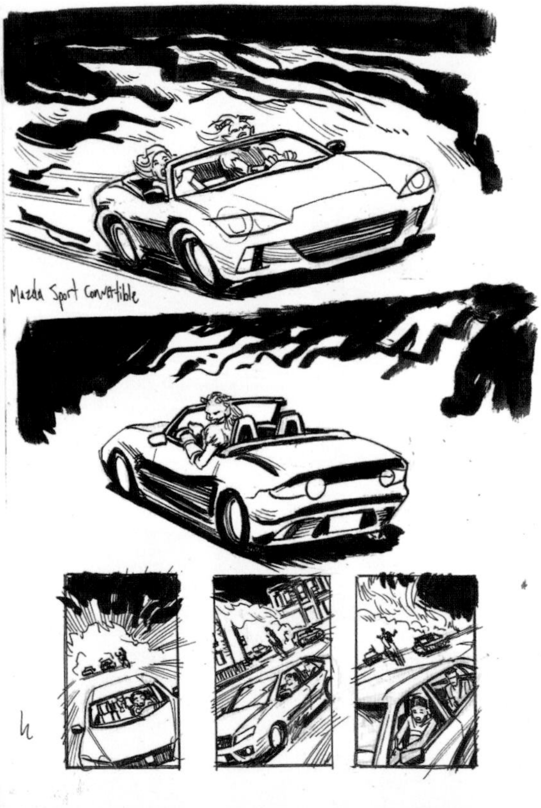
Mazda Sport Convertible

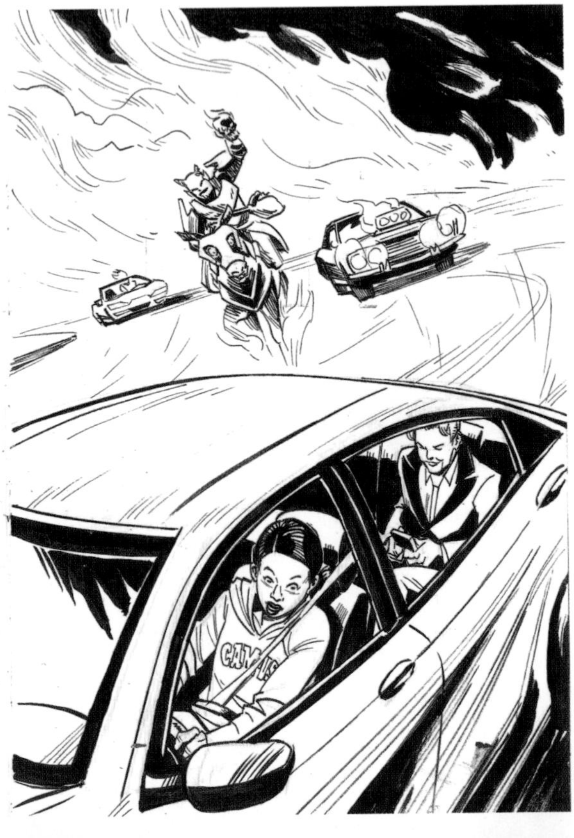

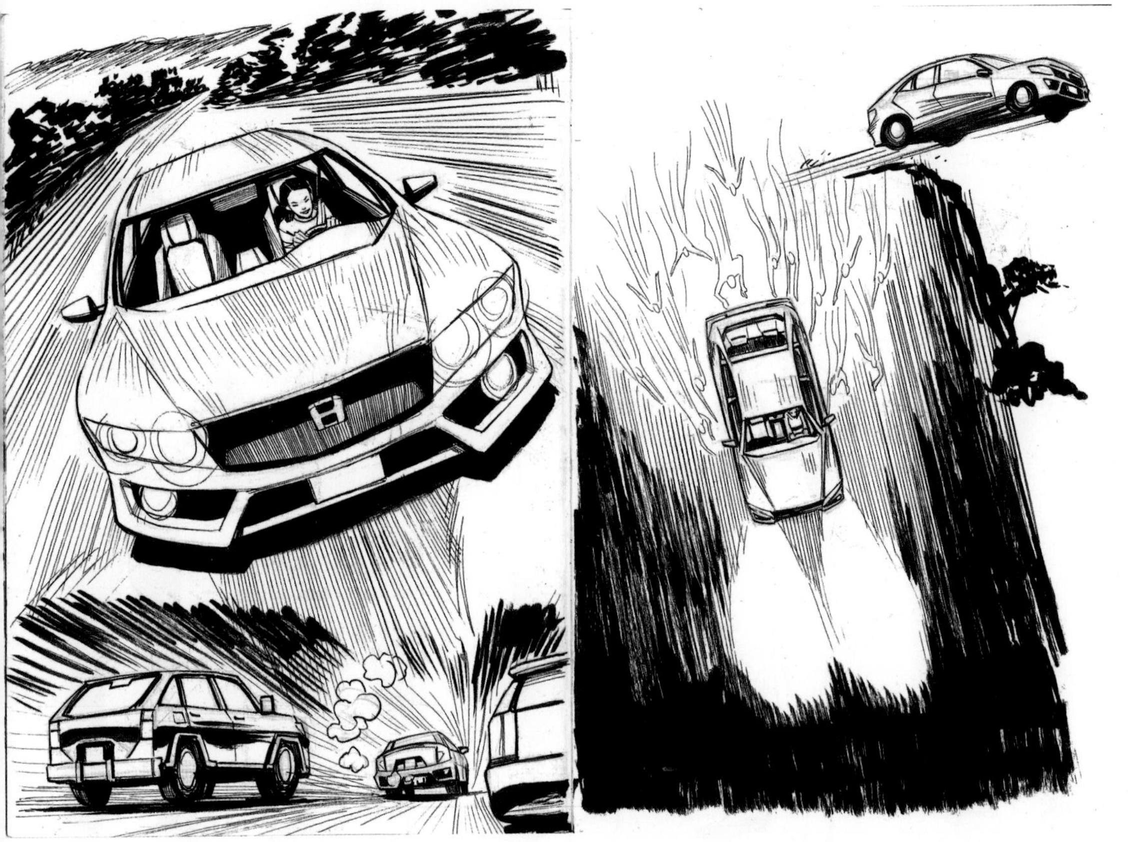

JASON: Chip warned me I was going to be drawing lots of cars in this series, so I practiced drawing them freehand for a month. I wouldn't consider myself a technical drawer, so I treated the cars like they were characters. I took notes from *Initial D* when drawing cars in motion. Look at those speed lines!

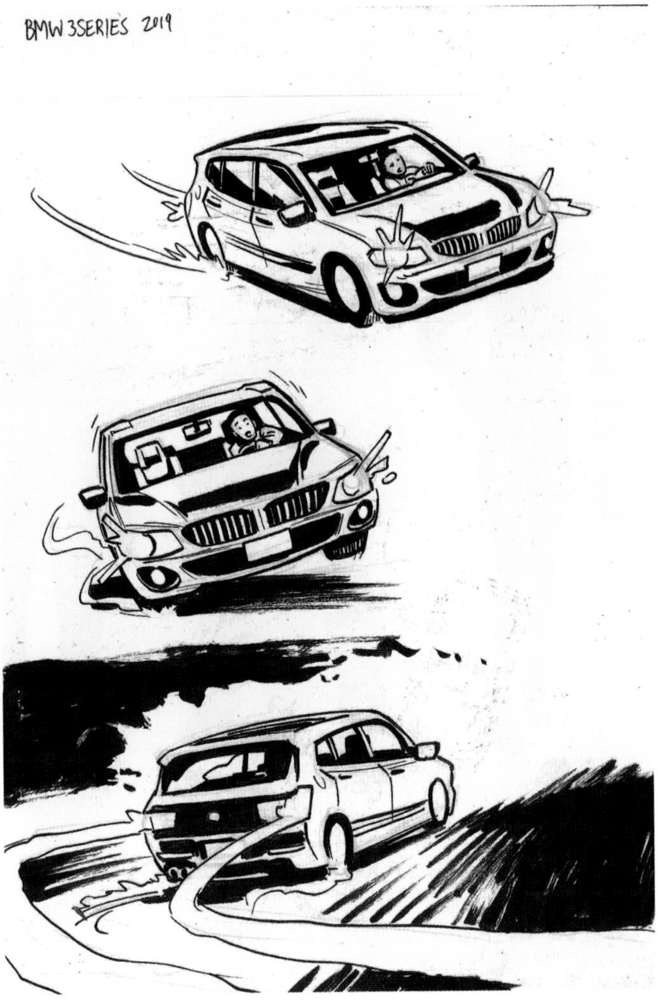
BMW 3SERIES 2019

COLOR SKETCHES

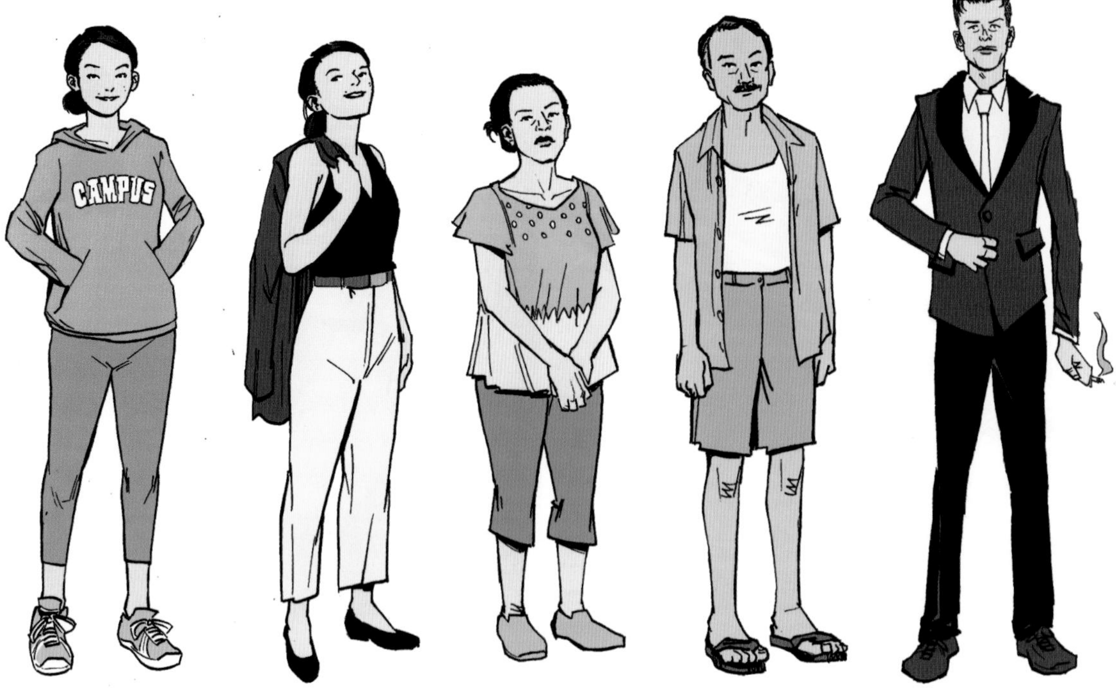
CAMPUS

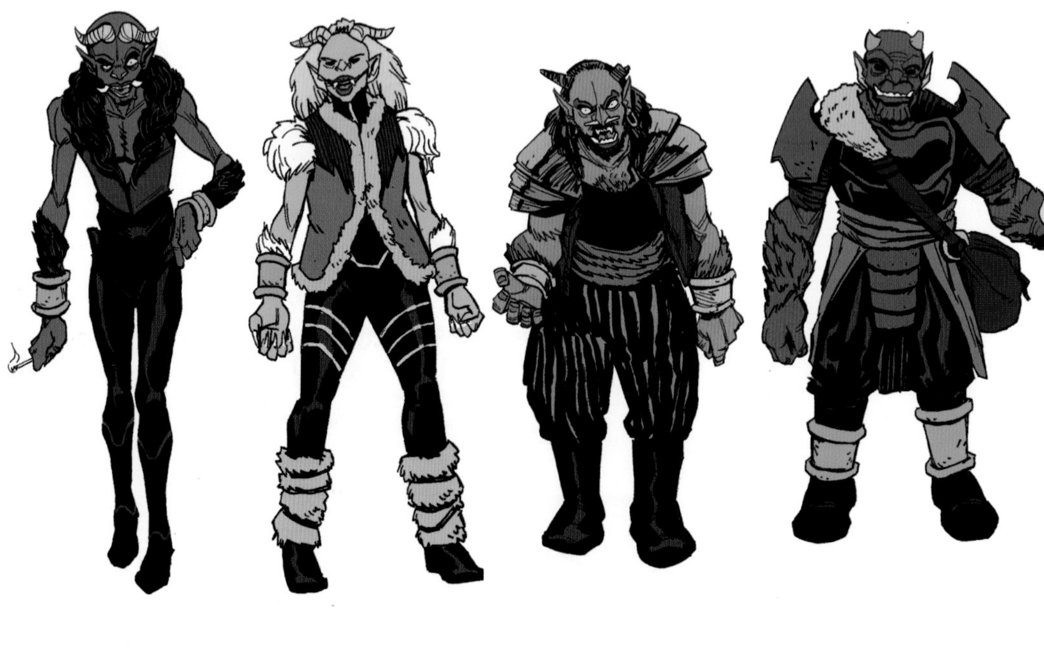

ANATOMY OF A PAGE

CHIP: KRNBAM!! KRMP! SKREEEE! EEEECH! This is my actual job. That's just wild. No, you can't have it! Get away! I have a knife! SLASH! SLASH!

PAGE NINE

9.1 BAM! GORNAUX T-BONES the CAR.

SFX: KRNBAM!!

9.2 the BACK HALF of the CAR hits an OBLIVIOUS PEDESTRIAN, which…

SFX: KRMP!

9.3 …sends it SPINNING past the PEDESTRIAN down the STREET….

SFX: SKREEEEE

9.4 …and to a STOP, now facing down the street back at GORNAUX, OP.

SFX: EEEECH!

9.5 In the CAR, JANICE is stunned. DUMU leans in, looking out the FRONT WINDSHIELD with CONCERN.

DUMU: Janice…listen to me very carefully.

DUMU: That is GORNAUX THE GRIEVOUS, slayer of all of GRENROVERIA.

JANICE: Wh-what's "Granroveria?"

DUMU: Exactly. So what I need from YOU now is to—

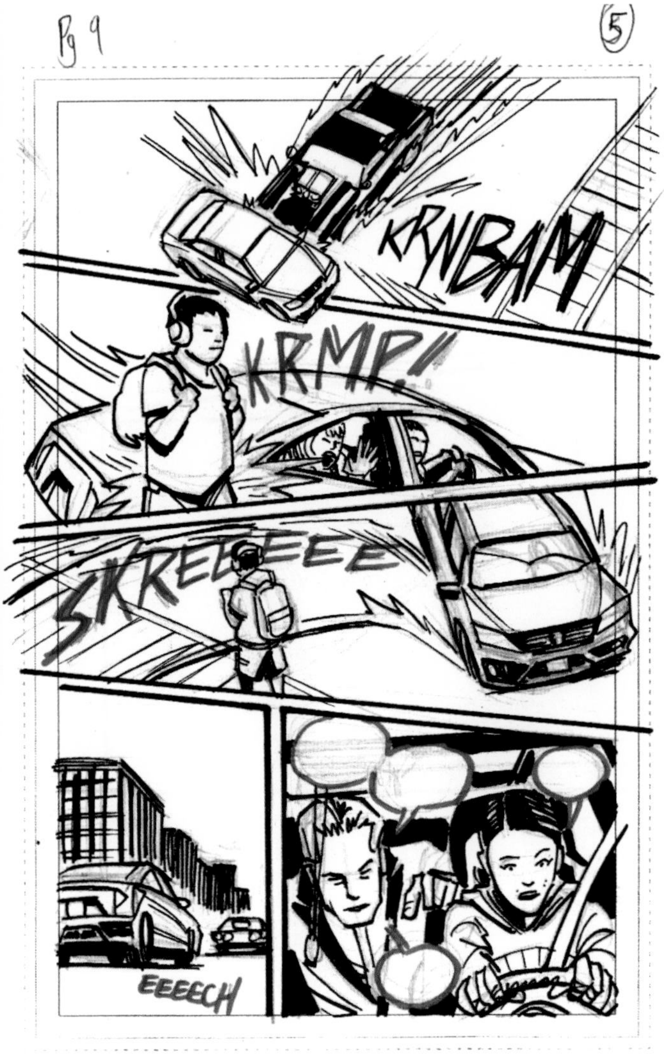

Pg 9
5
KRNBAM
KRMP!
EEEECH

JASON: Did I mention drawing cars was hard? This page was pretty fun to draw, though. I think I used my Transformers cars to figure out the motion and composition.

I like to draw my thumbnail layouts with a lot more readability. I learned this approach from comic artist Leonard Kirk. A lot of things can be solved with detailed layouts so that the penciling stage then becomes a tighter copy.

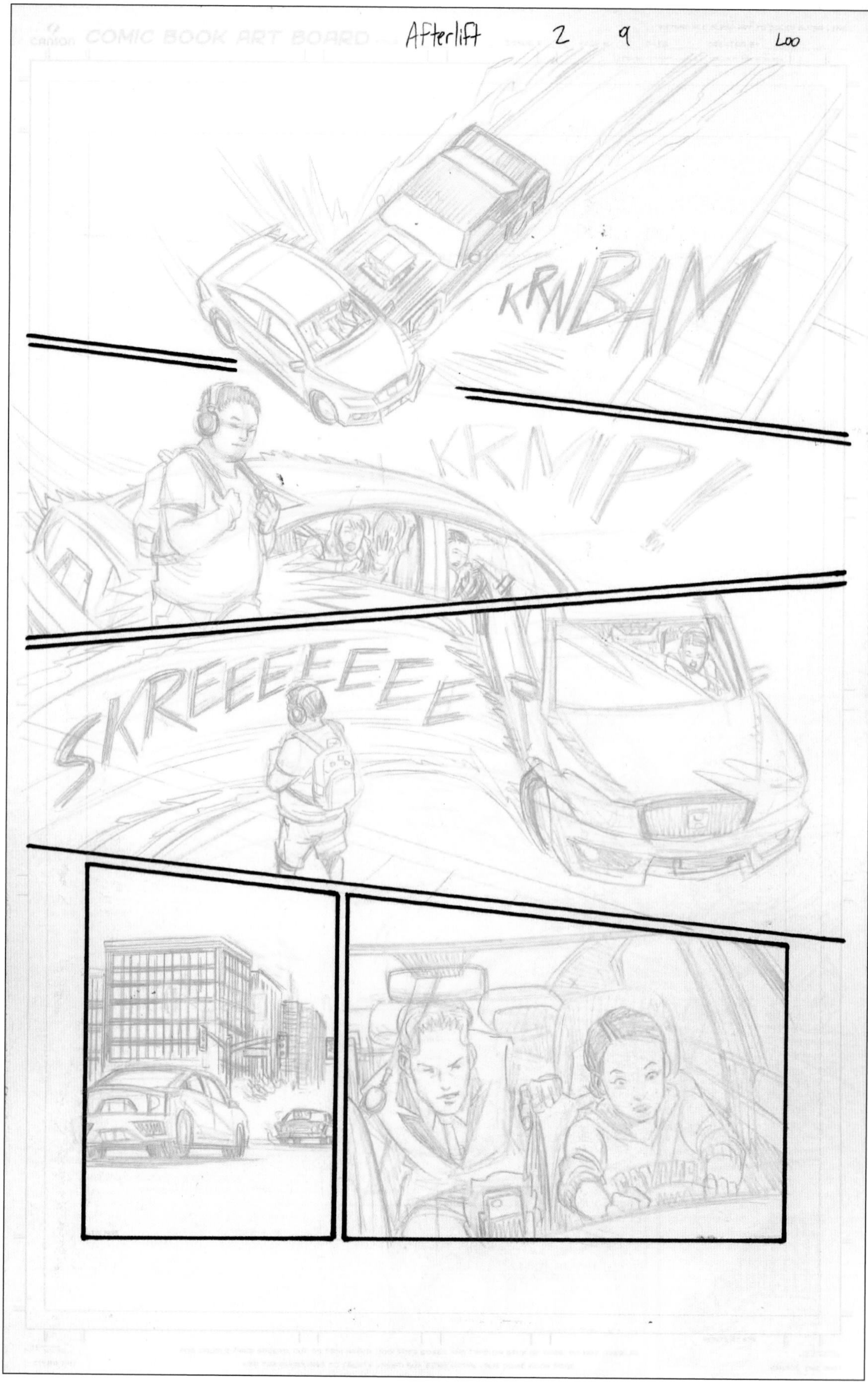
Afterlift 2 9
KRNBAM
KRMP!
SKREEEEEEEE

JASON: Pencils drawn with a Pilot Color Eno mechanical pen with non-photo blue lead.

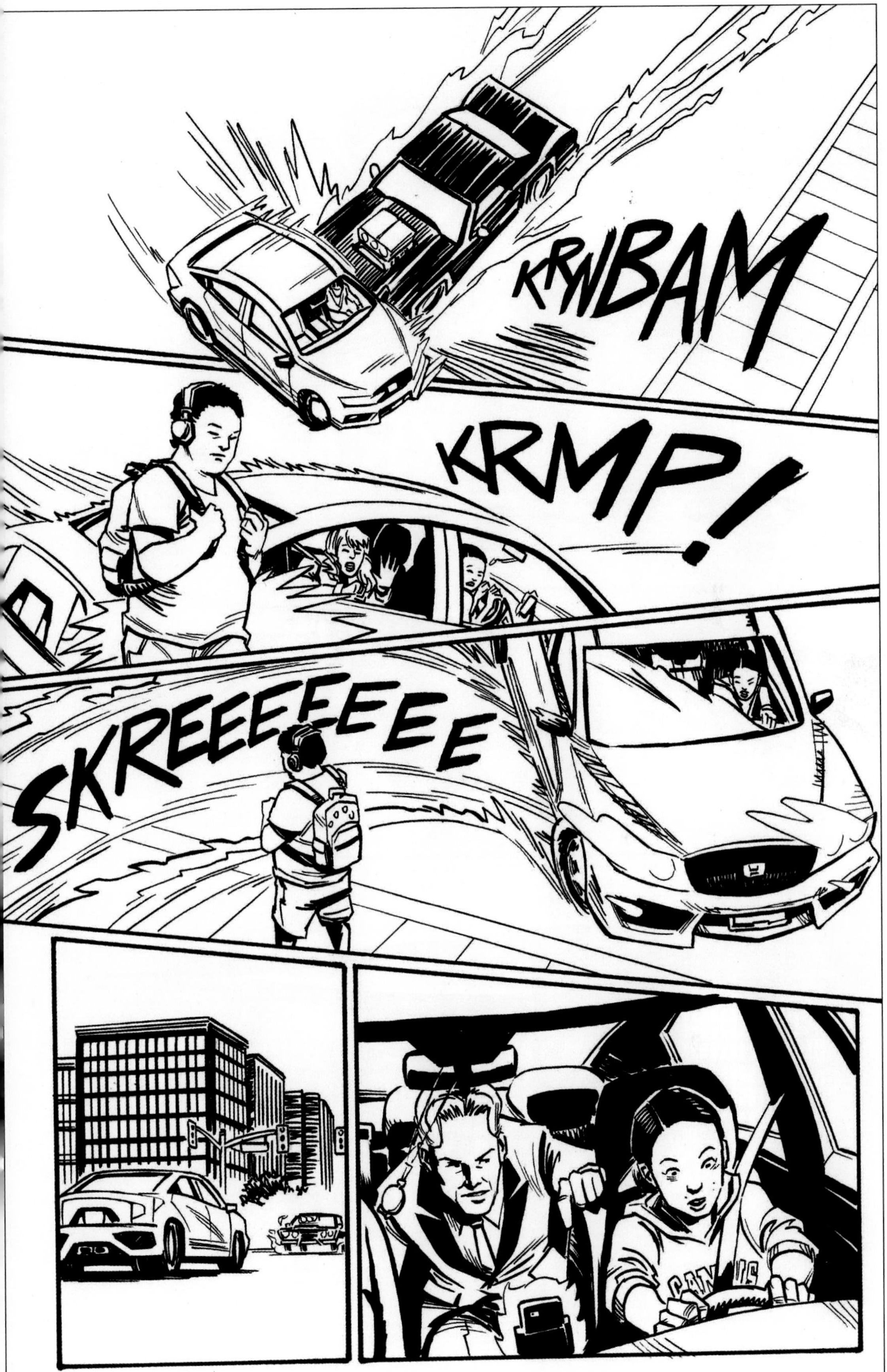
KRNBAM
KRMP!
SKREEEEEEEE

JASON: Inked with Pigma Micron pens and a Pentel brush marker

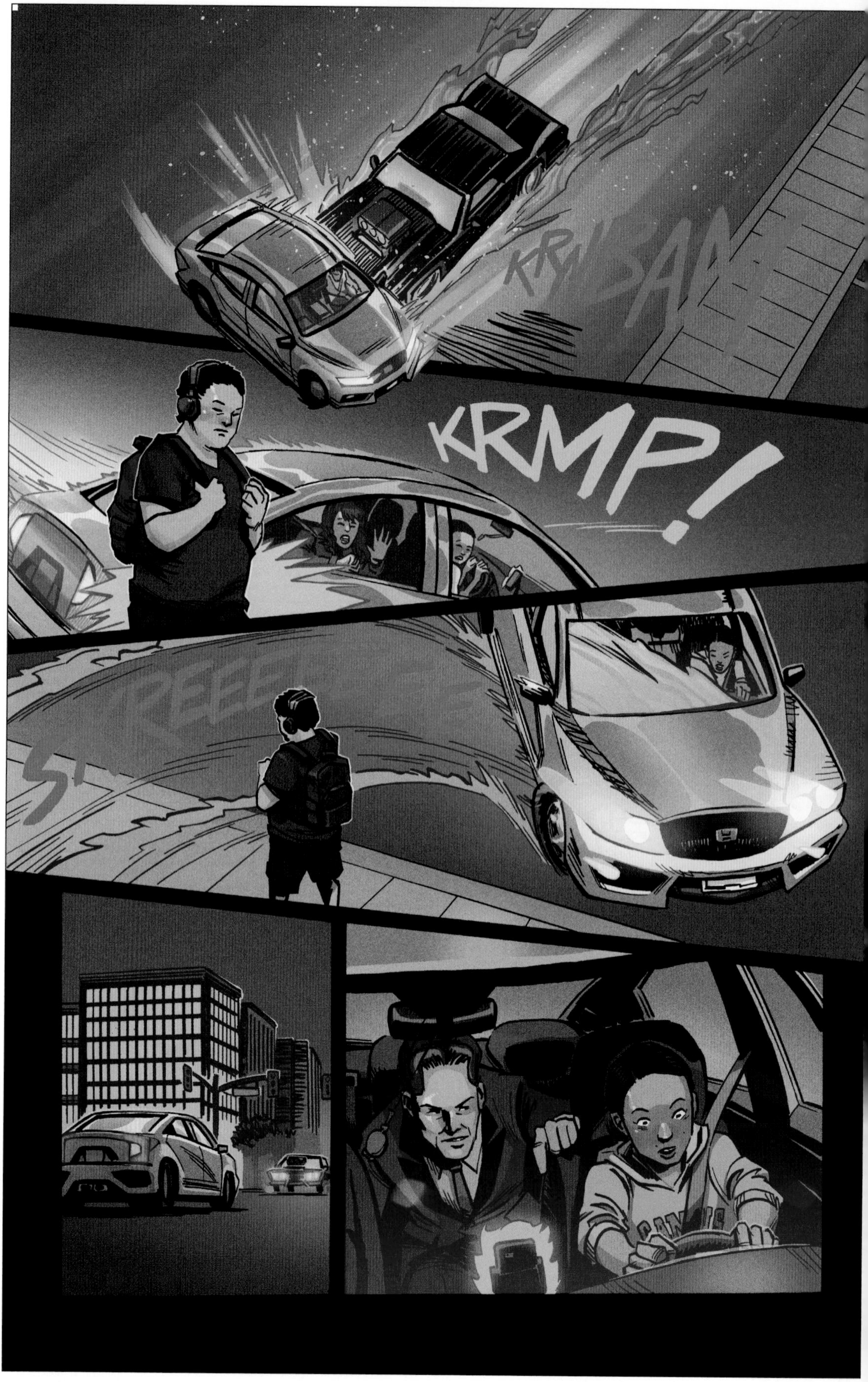
KRAM
KRMP!
SKREEE

JASON: Paris's colors knocking it out of the ballpark!

CHIP ZDARSKY

Chip Zdarsky is the award-winning illustrator and cocreator of *Sex Criminals* for Image Comics, and has written *Spider-Man: Life Story* and *Daredevil* for Marvel Comics, and *Jughead* for Archie Comics. He loves long walks in the park while listing his projects.

instagram/twitter: @zdarsky

JASON LOO

Jason Loo is a Toronto-based cartoonist best known for *The Pitiful Human-Lizard*, a comic-book series he wrote and drew, set in Toronto about a struggling Canadian superhero making the best out of his shortcomings. Loo was nominated for the 2018 Doug Wright Spotlight Award for his work on the book.

Other comic works by Jason include a short story for the *Toronto Comics* anthology and art for volume five of *Kill Shakespeare* for IDW Publishing.

instagram/twitter: @Rebel_Loo • jasonloo.pb.online

PARIS ALLEYNE

Paris is a comic-book artist and colorist from Toronto.

instagram: @parisalleyne

ADITYA BIDIKAR

Aditya Bidikar is a comics letterer based in India. His recent work includes *The White Trees*, *Little Bird*, *Bloodborne*, and *These Savage Shores*, among others.

twitter: @adityab • adityab.net

ALLISON O'TOOLE

Allison O'Toole is a freelance comics editor, and a lover of monsters and dogs. She has edited a number of anthologies, including Shuster Award–winning *Wayward Sisters*, and series including *The Pitiful Human-Lizard*, *Seeress*, and *Life, Death & Sorcery*.

twitter: @AllisonMOToole • allisonotoole.com

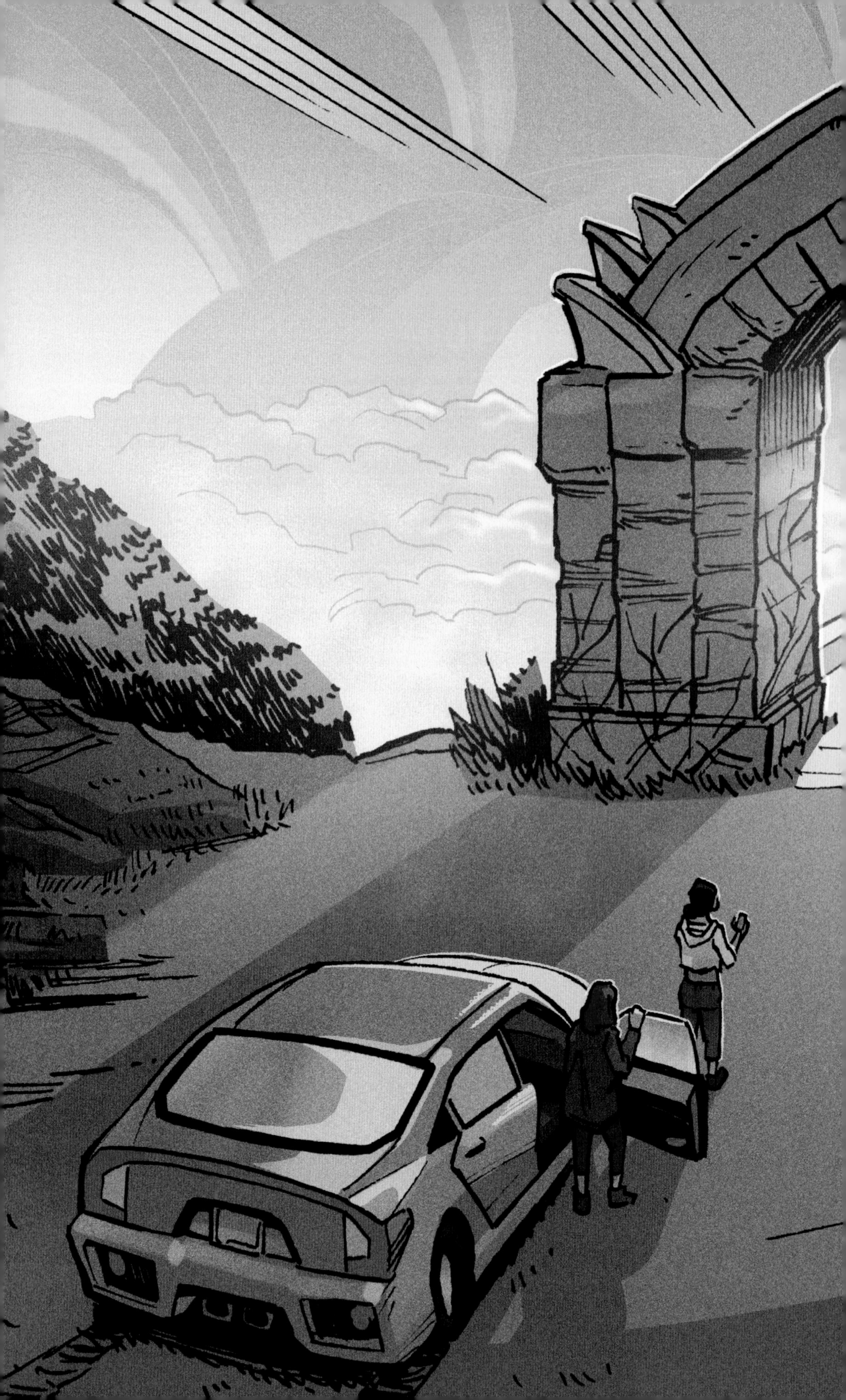

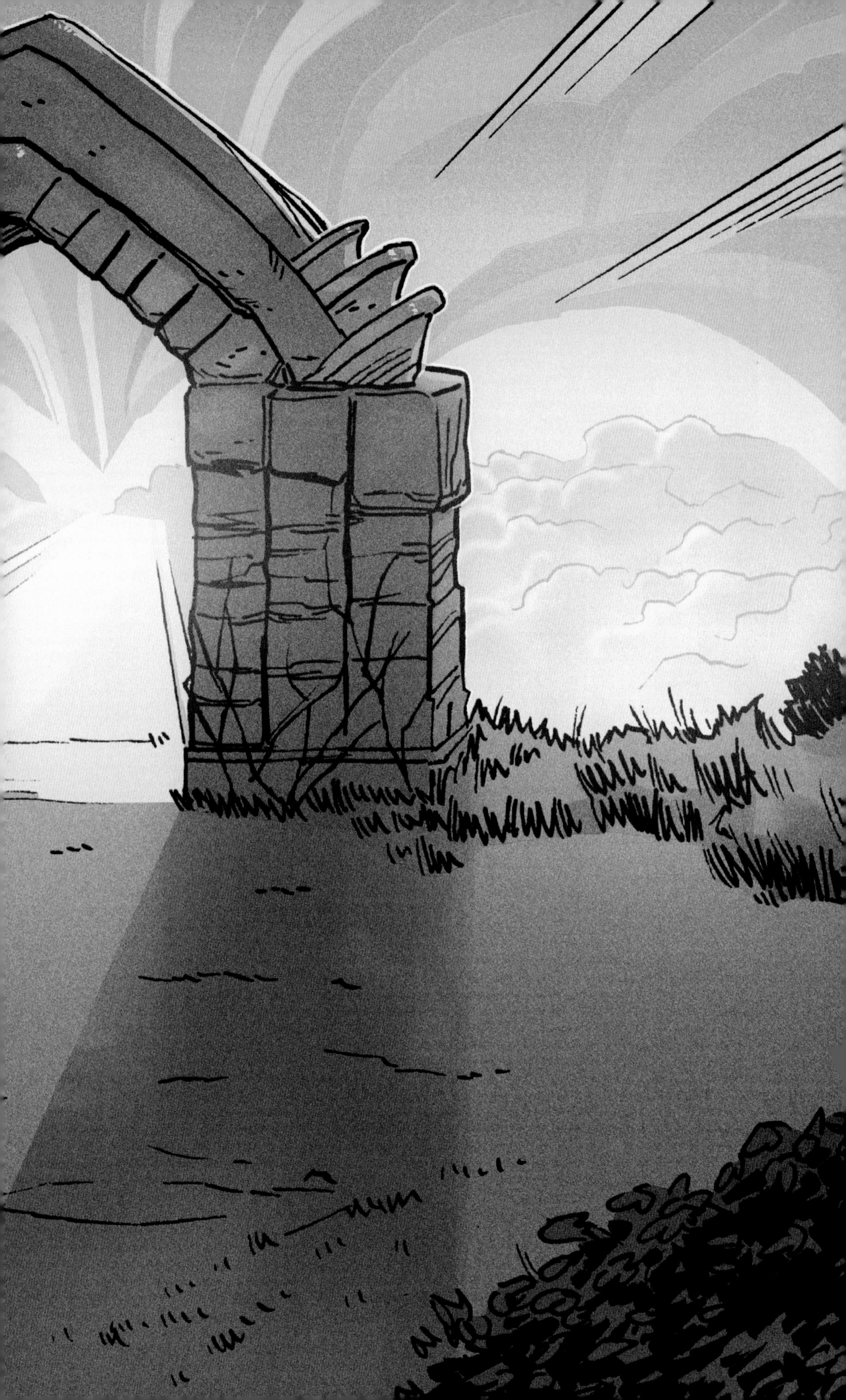

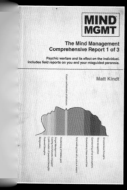

SABERTOOTH SWORDSMAN
Damon Gentry and Aaron Conley
Granted the form of the Sabertooth Swordsman by the Cloud God of Sasquatch Mountain, a simple farmer embarks on a treacherous journey to the Mastodon's fortress!

ISBN 978-1-61655-176-6 | $17.99

PIXU: THE MARK OF EVIL
Gabriel Bá, Becky Cloonan, Vasilis Lolos, and Fábio Moon
This gripping tale of urban horror follows the lives of five lonely strangers who discover a dark mark scrawled on the walls of their building. As the walls come alive, everyone is slowly driven mad, stripped of free will, leaving only confusion, chaos, and eventual death.

ISBN 978-1-61655-813-0 | $14.99

SACRIFICE
Sam Humphries, Dalton Rose, Bryan Lee O'Malley, and others
What happens when a troubled youth is plucked from modern society and sent on a psychedelic journey into the heart of the Aztec civilization—one of the greatest and most bloodthirsty times in human history?

ISBN 978-1-59582-985-6 | $19.99

DE:TALES
Fábio Moon and Gabriel Bá
Brimming with all the details of human life, Moon and Bá's charming stories move from the urban reality of their home in São Paulo to the magical realism of their Latin American background. Named by *Booklist* as one of the 10 Best Graphic Novels of 2010.

ISBN 978-1-59582-557-5 | $19.99

MIND MGMT OMNIBUS
Matt Kindt
This globe-spanning tale of espionage explores the adventures of a journalist investigating the mystery of a commercial flight where everyone aboard loses their memories. Each omnibus volume collects two volumes of the Eisner Award–winning series!

VOLUME 1: THE MANAGER AND THE FUTURIST
ISBN 978-1-50670-460-9 | $24.99

VOLUME 2: THE HOME MAKER AND THE MAGICIAN
ISBN 978-1-50670-461-6 | $24.99

VOLUME 3: THE ERASER AND THE IMMORTALS
ISBN 978-1-50670-462-3 | $24.99

THE ULTIMATE **MONSTER** COLLECTOR'S EDITIONS!

OVER-SIZED, HARDCOVER, GILT-EDGED COLLECTION'S OF DARK HORSE'S EARLIEST SERIES!

TERMINATOR
THE ORIGINAL COMICS SERIES
TEMPEST AND ONE SHOT

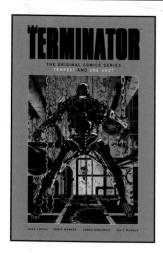

The Terminator: The Original Comics Series Tempest and One Shot

written by John Arcudi and James Robinson,
illustrated by Chris Warner and Matt Wagner

ISBN 978-1-50670-550-7

30TH ANNIVERSARY
ALIENS
THE ORIGINAL COMICS SERIES
MARK VERHEIDEN
MARK A. NELSON

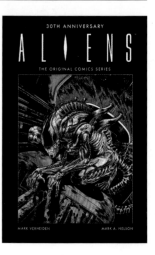

Aliens 30th Anniversary: The Original Comics Series

written by Mark Verheiden,
illustrated by Mark A. Nelson

ISBN 978-1-50670-078-6

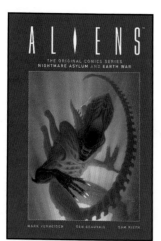

ALIENS
THE ORIGINAL COMICS SERIES
NIGHTMARE ASYLUM AND EARTH WAR

Aliens: The Original Comics Series Nightmare Asylum and Earth War

written by Mark Verheiden,
illustrated by Denis Beauvais and Sam Kieth

ISBN 978-1-50670-356-5

30TH ANNIVERSARY
PREDATOR
THE ORIGINAL COMICS SERIES
CONCRETE JUNGLE AND OTHER STORIES
MARK VERHEIDEN
CHRIS WARNER
RON RANDALL

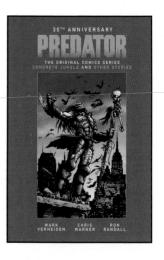

Predator: The Original Comics Series Concrete Jungle and Other Stories

written by Mark Verheiden,
illustrated by Chris Warner and Ron Randall

ISBN 978-1-50670-342-8

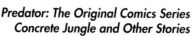

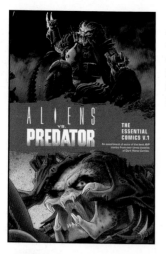

ALIENS
VS.
PREDATOR
THE ESSENTIAL COMICS V.1

Aliens vs Predator: The Essential Comics Volume 1

Written by Randy Stradley,
illustrated by Chris Warner, Phill Norwood,
Mike Manley, and Rick Leonardi

ISBN 978-1-50671-567-4

30TH ANNIVERSARY
ALIENS
VS.
PREDATOR
THE ORIGINAL COMICS SERIES

Aliens vs Predator: The Original Comics Series 30th Anniversary Edition

written by Randy Stradley,
illustrated by Chris Warner and Phill Norwood

ISBN 978-1-50671-568-1